HUNTERS AND GATHERERS IN THE MODERN WORLD

HUNTERS AND GATHERERS IN THE MODERN WORLD

Conflict, Resistance, and Self-Determination

Edited by
Peter P. Schweitzer, Megan Biesele
and Robert K. Hitchcock

Berghahn Books
NEW YORK • OXFORD

Published in 2000 by **Berghahn Books**
www.berghahnbooks.com

© 2000 Peter P. Schweitzer, Megan Biesele, and Robert K. Hitchcock

Library of Congress Cataloging-in-Publication Data

Hunters and gatherers in the modern world : conflict, resistance, and
  self-determination / edited by Peter P. Schweitzer, Megan Biesele, and
  Robert K. Hitchcock.
     p.   cm.
  Includes bibliographical references.
  ISBN 1-57181-101-X (alk. paper).
    1. Hunting and gathering societies—Political aspects. 2. Hunting
and gathering societies—Government policy. 3. Indigenous peoples—
Politics and government. 4. Culture conflict. 5. Ethnicity. 6. Government,
Resistance to. 7. Self-determination, National. 8. Conflict management.
I. Schweitzer, Peter P. II. Biesele, Megan. III. Hitchcock, Robert K.
GN388.H874 1999   98-44905
306.3'64—dc21   CIP

British Library Cataloguing in Publication Data

A catalogue record for this book is available from the British Library

Printed in the United States on acid-free paper

To the memories of

Linda J. Ellanna
1940–1997

and

Aleksandr I. Pika
1951–1995

CONTENTS

List of Illustrations   x

Preface   xi

Introduction *by Robert K. Hitchcock and Megan Biesele*   1

1. Silence and Other Misunderstandings: Russian   29
   Anthropology, Western Hunter-Gatherer Debates,
   and Siberian Peoples
   Peter P. Schweitzer

I. Warfare and Conflict Resolution

2. Visions of Conflict, Conflicts of Vision among   55
   Contemporary Dene Tha
   Jean-Guy A. Goulet

3. Warfare among the Hunters and Fishermen of   77
   Western Siberia
   Liudmila A. Chindina

4. Homicide and Aggression among the Agta of Eastern   94
   Luzon, the Philippines, 1910–1985
   Marcus B. Griffin

5. Conflict Management in a Modern Inuit Community   110
   Jean L. Briggs

6. Wars and Chiefs among the Samoyeds and Ugrians of   125
   Western Siberia
   Andrei V. Golovnev

7. Ritual Violence among the Peoples of Northeastern Siberia   150
   Elena P. Batianova

8. Patterns of War and Peace among Complex Hunter-   164
   Gatherers: The Case of the Northwest Coast of North America
   Leland Donald

II. Resistance, Identity, and the State

9. The Concept of an International Ethnoecological Refuge 183
   Olga Murashko

10. Aboriginal Responses to Mining in Australia: Economic 192
    Aspirations, Cultural Revival, and the Politics of
    Indigenous Protest
    David S. Trigger

11. Political Movement, Legal Reformation, and Transformation 206
    of Ainu Identity
    Takashi Irimoto

12. Tracking the "Wild Tungus" in Taimyr: Identity, Ecology, 223
    and Mobile Economies in Arctic Siberia
    David G. Anderson

13. Marginality with a Difference, or How the Huaorani 244
    Preserve Their Sharing Relations and Naturalize
    Outside Powers
    Laura Rival

III. Ecology, Demography, and Market Issues

14. "Interest in the Present" in the Nationwide Monetary 263
    Economy: The Case of Mbuti Hunters in Zaire
    Mitsuo Ichikawa

15. Dynamics of Adaptation to Market Economy among the 275
    Ayoréode of Northwest Paraguay
    Volker von Bremen

16. Can Hunter-Gatherers Live in Tropical Rain Forests? 287
    The Pleistocene Island Melanesian Evidence
    Matthew Spriggs

17. The Ju/'hoansi San under Two States: Impacts of the South 305
    West African Administration and the Government of the
    Republic of Namibia
    Megan Biesele and Robert K. Hitchcock

18. Russia's Northern Indigenous Peoples: Are They Dying Out? 327
    Dmitrii D. Bogoiavlenskii

IV. Gender and Representation

19. Gender Role Transformation among Australian Aborigines 343
    Robert Tonkinson

20. Names That Escape the State: Hai//om Naming Practices   361
    versus Domination and Isolation
    Thomas Widlok

21. Central African Government's and International NGOs'   380
    Perceptions of Baka Pygmy Development
    Barry S. Hewlett

22. The Role of Women in Mansi Society   391
    Elena G. Fedorova

23. Peacemaking Ideology in a Headhunting Society: *Hudhud,*   399
    Women's Epic of the Ifugao
    Maria V. Staniukovich

V. World-View and Religious Determination

24. Painting as Politics: Exposing Historical Processes in   413
    Hunter-Gatherer Rock Art
    Thomas A. Dowson

25. Gifts from the Immortal Ancestors: Cosmology and   427
    Ideology of Jahai Sharing
    Cornelia M. I. van der Sluys

26. Time in the Traditional World-View of the Kets: Materials   455
    on the Bear Cult
    Evgeniia A. Alekseenko

27. Lexicon as a Source for Understanding Sel'kup Knowledge   460
    of Religion
    Alexandra A. Kim

Notes on Contributors   475

Appendix: A Note on the Spelling of Siberian Ethnonyms   485

Index   487

LIST OF ILLUSTRATIONS

Figures

6.1 Centers of Military Expansion in Western Siberia in the   127
Sixteenth and Seventeenth Centuries

10.1 Century Mine, Showing Pipeline Route Options   194

17.1 Ju/'hoan Settlements in the Nyae Nyae Region, Namibia   309

20.1 Cross Naming, Ego Male   369

20.2 Cross Naming, Ego Female   369

24.1 Rock Painting of a Trance Dance from the Eastern Free   421
State Province, South Africa

24.2 Rock Painting of a Trance Dance from the Area in the   421
Southeastern Mountains Colonists Called "Nomansland"

Tables

I.1 Estimated Numbers of the World's Indigenous Peoples   5
Who Are or Were Hunter-Gatherers

I.2 Areas Controlled by Indigenous Peoples   17

3.1 Bone Identifications from the Samus' Sites   82

3.2 Osteological Data from the Kulai Sites   87

4.1 Non-Alcohol-Related Agta:Agta Homicides, Eastern Luzon   104

4.2 Alcohol-Related Homicides among the Casiguran Agta   106

17.1 Comparative Data on Living Standards of San in Namibia   312
Generally and Eastern Otjozondjupa Specifically

18.1 Population Dynamics of the Indigenous Northern Peoples   329
(of the former USSR; by population censuses)

18.2 Population Dynamics of the Indigenous Northern Peoples   330
in Native Regions

18.3 Life Expectancy (at birth; in years)   332

18.4 Infant Mortality (per 1,000 live births)   332

18.5 Deaths by Causes (percentage of total number of deaths)   333

18.6 Total Fertility Rate   336

18.7 Widowhood (1988–89; per 1,000 same-age group)   337

20.1 Hai//om "Great Names" and Corresponding Owambo   373
Clan Names

PREFACE

This book had its genesis at the Seventh International Conference of Hunting and Gathering Societies (CHAGS 7), which was hosted by the Institute of Ethnology and Anthropology of the Russian Academy of Sciences in Moscow, Russia, from 18–22 August 1993. The co-organizers of the conference were Dr. Victor Shnirelman of the Institute of Ethnology and Anthropology, Russian Academy of Sciences, and the late Dr. Linda J. Ellanna of the Department of Anthropology, University of Alaska Fairbanks. The conference convener was Dr. Valery Tishkov, Director of the Institute of Ethnology and Anthropology, Russian Academy of Sciences. Dr. Richard Lee of the Department of Anthropology, University of Toronto, was a co-chair of CHAGS 7.

Financial support for the conference was provided by the Division of Polar Programs of the U.S. National Science Foundation and the Wenner-Gren Foundation for Anthropological Research. The Institute of Ethnology and Anthropology, Russian Academy of Sciences, Moscow; the Department of Anthropology, University of Alaska Fairbanks, Alaska; and the Department of Anthropology, University of Toronto, Ontario, Canada, provided both logistical and financial support for the conference and the publication of the abstracts and sets of papers presented at CHAGS 7. In addition, we would like to thank the conference staff, Irina Babich of the Russian Academy of Sciences, and Tracie Cogdill of the University of Alaska Fairbanks.

The organizing committee for CHAGS 7 included Pierrette Désy, University of Quebec; Linda Ellanna and Peter Schweitzer, University of Alaska Fairbanks; Robert Hitchcock, University of Nebraska-Lincoln; Richard Lee, University of Toronto; Victor Shnirelman and Valery Tishkov, Institute of Ethnology and Anthropology, Moscow; Eric Alden Smith, University of Washington; and Polly Wiessner, Max Planck Institute for Human Ethology. Symposia co-chairs included Zoya P. Sokolova, the late Aleksandr Pika, Sofia Maretina, Victor Shnirelman, and Sergei Arutiunov of the Institute of Ethnology and Anthropology, Russian Academy of Sciences; Tim Ingold of the University of Manchester; and Robert Hitchcock, Eric Alden Smith, Pierrette Désy, and Polly Wiessner.

This volume could never have been produced without the invaluable assistance of Tracie Cogdill, Stacie McIntosh, and Jenny Newton of the Department of Anthropology, University of Alaska Fairbanks, and the financial assistance of the Wenner-Gren Foundation. Marion Berghahn, Jonathan Bowen, Shawn Kendrick, and Janine Treves of Berghahn Books have been unflagging supporters of our efforts throughout the editing and production of this volume. We wish to express our deepest appreciation to Berghahn Books, the Wenner-Gren Foundation, and the University of Alaska Fairbanks for making it possible for this book to be published.

INTRODUCTION

Robert K. Hitchcock and Megan Biesele

The world's hunting and gathering peoples have been the subject of intensive study and debate for well over a century. Today, at the beginning of the third millennium, those populations who have relied on wild plant and animal products for their livelihoods are actively engaged in interactions and debates with the governments of the states in which they live and with a variety of international organizations, both indigenous and nonindigenous. There is a worldwide movement among hunter-gatherers and other indigenous peoples aimed at promoting their basic civil, political, social, economic, and cultural rights (Anaya 1996; Barsh 1996; Durning 1992; Hitchcock 1994; Lee and Daly 1999; Maybury-Lewis 1997). The actions taken by hunter-gatherers and those who represent them and advocate on their behalf have served to place indigenous peoples' rights firmly on the international agenda.

Hunters and gatherers have been the subject of anthropological study and debate as long as the discipline of anthropology has been in existence. At the time European colonization began in Asia, the Americas, and Africa in the fifteenth and sixteenth centuries, approximately a third of the world's people were foragers. Over the past five hundred years, the percentage of the world's population that forage for a substantial portion of their living dropped precipitously, in part because of the actions of states and because of changes in population density, economic opportunities, and state and international social and economic development policies.

The modern anthropological appreciation of hunting and gathering societies received significant impetus in April 1966, when seventy-five scholars from various parts of the world met at the University of Chicago at the "Man the Hunter" Conference (Lee and DeVore 1968). Twelve years later, the First Conference on Hunter-Gatherer Studies (CHAGS 1) was held in Paris, France (June 1978). This meeting included scholars from a dozen countries, one of whom was an indigenous Siberian, then the Dean of the Faculty of the University of Yakutia (Leacock and Lee 1982). A second CHAGS meeting was held in Quebec in 1980, and it, too, included representatives from hunter-gatherer societies, several of whom were Inuit.

The next two CHAGS meetings were held in Europe, one in Bad Homburg, Germany (CHAGS 3) in 1983 and the other, CHAGS 4, in London in September 1986 (see Ingold et al. 1988a, b). A major issue raised at the third CHAGS meeting was whether or not the concept "hunter-gatherer" is a valid one, given that these populations had been dominated by more powerful societies and that they were seen as part of a poverty-stricken, marginalized underclass in the societies in which they lived (Schrire 1984; see also Wilmsen 1989). There is no question that hunter-gatherers have been affected significantly by outside forces. In some cases, they became the proverbial "victims of progress," while others transformed themselves, engaging in activities such as specialized hunting or wild resource collecting, a process seen, for example, among some of the Adivasis (the "Scheduled Tribes") of India and among Southeast Asian foragers such as those in Thailand, Laos, and Malaysia.

The Fifth Conference on Hunting and Gathering Societies (CHAGS 5) was held in the Southern Hemisphere, this time in Australia in 1988 (Altman 1989; Meehan and White 1990). This meeting included a number of Aboriginals, some of whom were working on conservation and economic development issues. CHAGS 6 was held in another hunter-gatherer stronghold, Alaska, in 1990 (Burch and Ellanna 1994). Again, indigenous people, including Inuit, Aleuts, and Alaskan Indians, played significant roles in this meeting. Together, these meetings have provided a series of stimulating discussions of issues relating to hunting and gathering peoples involving both scholars and representatives of hunter-gatherer groups, and they have contributed to important theoretical developments in anthropology and archaeology. Topics such as politics, economics, social organization, gender, symbolism, and ideology were explored in detail.

The Seventh Conference on Hunting and Gathering Societies, which was held in Moscow in August 1993, was no exception. This meeting had significant representation of members of hunter-gatherer groups, many of them from the former Soviet North, who spoke about their resistance to state oppression and their internal political dynamics. They also outlined their roles in the growing activism of indigenous northern peoples in seeking self-determination and self-representation. This was a historic meeting, as it was the first extensive East-West scholarly exchange in anthropology since the demise of the USSR. There were discussions of the interactions between foragers and modern states, cosmology and worldview, ideology and consciousness. A related, significant area of debate at the conference was on hunter-gatherer aggression and peacemaking. Identity politics and the struggle for control of the development and political agendas were examined, as were themes that had long been important in various CHAGS conferences, including demography, ecology, and subsistence.

The essays included in this volume represent a sample of the papers that were presented at the meeting. The five major themes into which this book is divided are:

    I. Warfare and Conflict Resolution
    II. Resistance, Identity, and the State
    III. Ecology, Demography, and Market Issues
    IV. Gender and Representation
    V. World-View and Religious Determination

The themes of this volume—conflict, resistance, and self-determination—were echoed in each of the conference thematic sections.

Virtually all of the societies discussed at the conference and in this book have interacted with the state in a variety of ways. Most of them resisted efforts of states to assimilate them, and they sometimes engaged in direct conflicts with state institutions, including the military, and with private companies. An important factor affecting hunter-gatherer societies in the twentieth century has been the market, with efforts to both commercialize and conserve the world's biodiversity having significant impacts on the well-being of hunter-gatherers and other indigenous peoples.

Issues and themes selected for discussion at CHAGS 7 parallel theoretical developments that have given hunter-gatherer research scholarly direction (for a review of trends in the study of hunter-gatherers, see Myers 1988). They also reflect the increasing internationalization of hunter-gatherer studies and the expanding role of scholars from outside traditional Western academic centers in the study and analysis of hunter-gatherer societies. In order to assure smooth and open research opportunities as well as good communication, it was believed to be critically important to establish cooperative links across the international community, especially with researchers from developing countries and indigenous communities.

Ideas observed, tested, or refined with the study of hunter-gatherers have been among the most important areas of anthropological research. These ideas include much of the basis of modern evolutionary ecological theory (e.g., Smith 1991; Smith and Winterhalder 1992), the study of postindustrial societies from a humanistic perspective (Myers 1988: 274–76), and the analysis of the origins and impacts of social complexity (Keeley 1988; Price and Brown 1985).

Despite the long-standing incorporation of all circumpolar hunting and gathering societies into nation-states, the majority of them continue to practice foraging subsistence activities, most often within the social and ideological framework of a foraging ethos. As noted in the chapter in this volume by Peter Schweitzer, the recent opening of the former Soviet Union has added a vast area to international circumpolar research and has opened new venues for comparative studies. Political and social development among hunting and gathering societies of the Far North has a number of exemplary characteristics for other indigenous groups of the world, including land claims, local control of resource development, and subsistence hunting rights (Minority Rights Group 1994; Schweitzer, this volume; Smith and McCarter 1997; Young 1995).

Hunters and Gatherers: Definitional Issues

There are significant differences of opinion about whether or not "pure hunter-gatherers" still exist. On the one hand, there are those who say that there are sizable numbers of people who forage for at least part of their subsistence and income. On the other, there are those who argue that there are no people in the world today who fall into the "hunter-gatherer" category. It is crucial, therefore, that efforts be made to come up with criteria that allow researchers and development workers to determine the degree to which local people are dependent on wild resources. This is important because it will enable agencies and individuals to help promote the rights of foragers and former foragers in regard to (1) access to sufficient food and materials to meet their basic subsistence and material needs, (2) access to resources for purposes of generating income, and (3) access to resources viewed as socioculturally significant, such as wild plants and minerals used in healing rituals and other kinds of ceremonial or ideologically oriented activities.

It is extremely difficult to say how many hunter-gatherers there are in the world today. It has been estimated that there are some 400–500 million indigenous peoples, those peoples who are considered aboriginal, native peoples, Fourth World Peoples, or "first nations" (Bodley 1999; Hitchcock 1994; Maybury-Lewis 1997). Some of these groups obtain much of their food and income from wild sources. In India, for example, of the 68,400,000 people considered to be Adivasis in 1991, approximately 1,300,000 people from some twenty-five different groups were classified by D. Venkatesan (personal communication) as hunter-gatherers. Table I.1 contains data on the estimated numbers of hunter-gatherers in the contemporary world. We hasten to point out that the figures presented here are very rough and reflect information obtained from a variety of sources,

TABLE I.1 Estimated Numbers of the World's Indigenous Peoples Who Are or Were Hunter-Gatherers

Region	Country of Residence	Estimated Population
Circumpolar Region		
Inuit (Eskimo)	Russia, Greenland, U.S., Canada	100,000
Latin America (total*)		3,500
Ache (Guayaki)	Paraguay	400
Hiwi (Cuiva)	Venezuela, Colombia	800
Siriono (Yukui)	Bolivia	140
Huaorani (Auca)	Ecuador	1,250
Former Soviet Union		
Northern Peoples	Siberia, Russian Far East	200,000
South Asia (total)		2,000,000
Adivasis (foragers)	India	1,300,000
Andaman Islanders	India	600
East Asia		
Ainu	Japan	26,000
Southeast Asia (total)		600,000
Orang Asli	Malaysia	90,000
Penan	Malaysia	7,600
Australia		
Aboriginals and Torres		
Strait Islanders	Australia	300,000
Africa (total)		450,000
Batwa (Pygmies)	7 countries in Central Africa	200,000
San (Bushmen)	6 countries in southern Africa	105,000
Hadza	Tanzania	1,000
North America (total)		150,000
Indians, Aleuts	U.S., Canada	90,000
Grand Total (foragers and former foragers)		**5,219,500**

*This and other regional totals reflect the hunter-gatherer population for the area, with specific examples of hunter-gatherer groups listed below.

Sources: Data obtained from Barnes et al. (1995); Hitchcock (1994); Kelly (1995); Kent (1996); Lee and Daly (1999); Minority Rights Group (1994); Veber et al. (1993); Young (1995); as well as the International Work Group for Indigenous Affairs, Cultural Survival, Survival International, and this volume.

including national and local censuses, indigenous peoples' advocacy groups, general works on hunter-gatherers, anthropologists' reports, and data compiled by hunter-gatherer groups themselves. These figures are preliminary and are definitely in need of correction and refinement. We present them here in order to allow readers to have some idea of the range of variation in the distribution and numbers of people who have been classified by themselves or others as hunter-gatherers.

The concept "subsistence" is sometimes defined as "resource dependence that is primarily outside the cash sector of the economy" (Huntington 1992: 15–16). This economic definition is, in many ways, inadequate in the contemporary world context. The vast majority of the world's population is involved at least to some degree in the cash economy. Even if households do not take part directly in cash transactions, they often receive transfers in the form of cash or goods from relatives, friends, the state, or other sources. Subsistence activities link people into a complex network of interactions, reciprocity, and exchanges, some of which are culturally based and others of which are primarily economic in nature. A classic example of this linkage is in the manufacture, exchange, and sale of ostrich eggshell bead necklaces and bracelets that occurs in the Kalahari Desert region of southern Africa, which links people together in a complex system of delayed reciprocity and mutually beneficial interaction. In the Kalahari, the manufacture and sale of ostrich eggshell items is an important source of income for a sizable number of San households, especially for those that are female-headed. It is necessary, therefore, to broaden the definition of a subsistence producer to include those people who obtain wildlife and other wild natural resource products for meeting basic household subsistence *and* income needs.

Subsistence foraging is far more than simply a means of making a living for a segment of the world's population. It is also a complex system of obligation, distribution, and exchange that is crucial to the well-being of both subsistence producers and market-oriented producers. Today, the vast majority of people obtain their food from a variety of sources. In Alaska, northern Canada, and Siberia, the bush is still an important source of food. Yet even in these areas, the majority of people can be described as having mixed economies or diversified production systems. Foraging is a buffering strategy in many areas of the world today that serves as a fallback strategy in times of stress, as in cases where people have been affected by drought or conflict—as has been the case, for example, in Somalia and the Sudan.

Some of the characteristic features of those people who are defined as foragers are as follows: (1) they depend on wild natural resources for subsistence, income, and ideological needs; (2) they use human labor and fire as sources of energy; (3) they are kinship-based societies; (4) they have common property resource management systems; (5) they have close attachments to land and the resources on that land; (6) they are characterized by sophisticated and complex ideological systems; and (7) they have a world-view that combines both nature and spiritual phenomena.

There have been arguments over the issue of hunter-gatherer subsistence rights, with some people asserting that hunter-gatherers are getting preferential treatment. This argument is made by nonindigenous people in the northern United States (e.g., in Wisconsin and Minnesota and around the Great Lakes) and on the Northwest Coast (Fixico 1998). Certainly, there are cases in which foragers have been given privileges, especially as regards hunting. The Hadza of Tanzania, for example, are allowed to hunt using a Presidential License issued by the president of the country. In Namibia, the Ju/'hoansi San of eastern Otjozondjupa are allowed to hunt for subsistence purposes as long as they use traditional weapons (Biesele and Hitchcock, this volume).

An assumption about hunter-gatherers is that they are self-sufficient societies (i.e., they do not depend on outside agencies for any inputs). In fact, there are few people today who are totally exempt from the market. Some hunter-gatherers have been subsidized by the state, as was the case, for example, with Siberian hunters and trappers under the government of the former Union of Soviet Socialist Republics. There is also a fairly sizable number of people in the world today who engage in foraging on the larger economy through the collection and recycling of castoffs and other goods.

Some government officials define hunter-gatherers on the basis of the kinds of technology they use or even on the basis of the clothes that they wear. Department of Wildlife and National Parks officials in Botswana, for example, identified people as hunter-gatherers if they used traditional weapons such as bows and arrows or, alternatively, if they were wearing leather breechcloths. The problem with this approach was that those people who wore Western clothing, such as a pair of trousers and a shirt, for example, were subject to arrest for engaging in illegal activities if they were found hunting.

Hunter-gatherers have also been defined as people lacking domestic animals. Such a definition is problematic when one considers that many people who traditionally have been characterized as foragers, including Australian Aboriginals and Kalahari San, engage relatively extensively in livestock-related work on cattle stations and cattle posts, herding cattle and other stock in exchange for payments in kind (e.g., food, clothing, a calf a year) or cash. In Botswana, a significant portion of the national cattle herd is managed and overseen by Kua, Nharo, and other San (Hitchcock 1996). In Kenya, groups such as the Okiek and Dahalo have been able to accumulate sufficient livestock to be identified as pastoralists by government officials (Daniel Stiles, personal communication). It is interesting to note, on the other hand, that those groups who lose their stock are subsequently identified as hunter-gatherers. Thus, processes of livestock accumulation and loss affect the ways in which people are identified and presumably the ways in which government ministries and other institutions treat those populations.

An examination of the contemporary socioeconomic systems of foragers and former foragers in the contemporary world reveals that a sizable proportion of them are living at or below the absolute poverty level (APL). The APL can be defined as the income level below which a minimum nutritionally adequate diet plus essential nonfood requirements cannot be afforded. Some of the nonfood requirements include matches, candles, and soap. The Poverty Datum Line (PDL), or the "minimum income needed for a basic standard of living," is used by some economists as a means of determining household socioeconomic status. One way to deal with poverty among groups is to provide commodities to them, a system known as "rationing" in Australia. In Botswana and Namibia, San are provided with drought relief food, and they are allowed to take part in labor-based public works (LBPW) projects in which people are given food or cash in exchange for their labor. In Australia, The Community Development Employment Projects (CDEP) scheme, which is administered by the Aboriginal and Torres Strait Islanders Commission (ATSIC), provides grants to Aboriginal community councils, which then use the funds to create jobs in community development. The funds that Aboriginals and Torres Strait Islanders receive are calculated to be roughly equivalent to what they would get as unemployment benefits or entitlements from the Department of Social Security of the government of Australia (Altman and Sanders 1991). Some foragers and former foragers are uncomfortable with some of these schemes and argue that they should have the opportunity to earn their own subsistence and income rather than depend on what they consider handouts.

One theme of this volume relates to the interactions between foragers and the states in which they live. Some foragers have been fortunate or unfortunate enough to be in areas where mineral and petroleum resources have been found. Aboriginal communities have responded to these discoveries in a variety of ways. In Australia, for example, some groups have opposed mining activities out of hand, whereas others have sought to negotiate with mining corporations in the hopes of receiving substantial royalties. David Trigger describes Aboriginal strategies of resistance and accommodation, focusing his attention in part on the deliberations over the Century zinc mine in northwestern Queensland. While some Aboriginal groups maintain that their relations with the land preclude what they describe as routine commodification, others suggest that mining has its benefits, including jobs and compensation paid to

Aboriginal communities that they can then invest in local development. Clearly, the notions that all indigenous peoples are "one with nature" and that they are generally conservation-minded and broadly opposed to development are not correct in every instance.

There is no question that hunter-gatherers and other indigenous groups have opposed what they have felt to be environmentally destructive projects. The Penan of Malaysia, for example, have blockaded logging roads to prevent commercial timber exploitation by lumber companies, and the Hai//om San have prevented tourists from entering Etosha National Park in order to underscore their land claims in northern Namibia.

Several major events in the past few years have led to a significant increase in interest over issues involving hunters and gatherers and indigenous peoples generally. One event was the recognition of the quincentennial of the arrival of Christopher Columbus in the New World (October 1992), which was protested widely because of what indigenous leaders characterized as the genocidal actions of Columbus and his associates. The United Nations declared 1993 as The Year of the World's Indigenous People, with the theme, chosen by the General Assembly, as "Indigenous People—A New Partnership" (Anaya 1996; Barsh 1996). This was done in part to strengthen both grassroots and international cooperation for solving problems facing indigenous peoples and to attract additional funding for indigenous peoples' projects and activities.

Contributing to the awareness of the importance of indigenous concerns was the role played by indigenous peoples and their supporters at the United Nations Conference on Environment and Development (UNCED) held in Rio de Janeiro in June 1992. The text of Agenda 21, which grew out of the Rio Conference, addressed the importance of having indigenous peoples, among other groups, as active participants in decision-making processes concerning sustainable development. An important theme of Agenda 21 was the crucial importance of broad-based participation in decision-making regarding environmental, economic, and social issues.

Hunter-gatherers and former foragers have sometimes engaged in innovative strategies for promoting conservation and ensuring the long-term survival of ecosystems and sociocultural systems. Australian Aboriginals and Alaskan Native peoples have sought to enter into co-management arrangements with national park managers and government agencies to oversee parks and game reserves. The Ju/'hoansi San of Namibia have established community-based resource management programs that include tourism as a means of generating income while at the same time limiting the number of people who enter their area (Biesele and Hitchcock, this volume). The Ainu of Japan have engaged in cultural revitalization movements that have had as some of their goals self-determination and enhancement of Ainu cultural identity (Irimoto, this volume). The

Evenkis of Taimyr in Arctic Siberia, reported on in this volume by David Anderson, engaged actively in a process of ethnogenesis, utilizing both government-authorized identities and identities as they perceived them themselves in order to achieve their varied objectives. As Anderson notes, the vernacular ideas of "wildness," in dialogue with local, cultivated identities, suggest a powerful rhetoric of indigenous peoples' resistance to forces threatening to encapsulate and transform their hunting and reindeer-herding community. The Evenkis act as if they live in what Anderson describes as a "sentient ecology," in which their actions, motivations, and achievements are understood and acted upon by nonhuman entities ranging from weather to wild and domesticated animals.

The CHAGS conference volumes, including this one, are unique in part because they are not only compilations of analytical case materials but at the same time are summaries of trends in research and anthropological theory. One overarching theme involves the current science/culture controversy. The necessity to understand science as a form of culture is starkly underscored by historical polarities long existing in hunter-gatherer studies, in which, for example, optimal foraging strategy theory has lived side by side (and has often been intertwined) with ideological explorations for some decades. In fact, it may be argued that the relatively small size of the researcher base, along with the particular research questions shaped by holistic strains in these cultures themselves, may have created an early need in hunter-gatherer research culture to resolve disciplinary splits only now being addressed in some other areas of anthropology.

From research questions to methodologies to political concerns, the study of hunter-gatherers reflects this and other cutting-edge aspects of the entire discipline as it approaches the end of the millennium. Some of these concerns were summarized by Annette Weiner in a 1993 presidential address to the American Anthropological Association, in which she called for new interdisciplinary forms of engagement with "postmodern culture." Weiner urged anthropologists to heed not only the multivocal nature of cultural messages, but also "local and transnational sites, the representations of authors and informants, the changing velocities of space and time, the historical conditions in which capitalism is reshaping global power on an unprecedented scale, and the historical conditions of Western theory and practice" (cited in Franklin 1995).

Weiner's challenge was taken up by Franklin (1995) in the area of critical science studies, under which rubric the most important organizing features of recent attempts to bridge the gap between Snow's "two cultures" have been outlined. In this volume, the chapters by Briggs, Griffin, Trigger, Rival, Staniukovich, and Widlok, among others, reflect serious grappling with what Franklin (1995: 166) calls the "knowledge of knowledge, the nature of nature, the reality of reality, the origin of origins, the code of codes." Issues of the volume overlap to a great extent with those identified by Weiner and Franklin, as indeed they do with the productions of the informal colloquies on African civil society (Comaroff and Comaroff 1993) now taking place among graduate students and faculty at the University of Chicago. These concerns include the following: age, gender, and changing leadership issues; counterhegemonic moves in identity and assertion of ownership of resources of many kinds; the reproduction and transformation of exchange networks and social equity; competition and consensus in developing states; the performance of identity; and the problematics of collaborative research with former "informants." These contemporary issues are being used as a lens, looking both backward and forward in time.

Dowson's chapter on painting as politics among the San of southern Africa voices a rallying cry for the integration of symbolic and political issues in hunter-gatherer studies. It also takes rock art studies out of the impressionistic "never-never land" it too often inhabited, and gives it stature as a meaningful historic study. Showing that the artists who painted prehistorically were negotiating complex power relations humanizes prehistory in a new way—one that will, we predict, be determinative of important future approaches in both history and archaeology.

The chapter on contemporary Jahai of northern Malaysia by van der Sluys similarly pushes on academic boundaries. It presents an anthropological research strategy that grounds analysis in a set of structured ethnographic data concerning a culture's world-view, and demonstrates the way in which tropical rain forest hunters may be seen to make positive cultural choices based on their core cultural premises and values regarding well-being. In so doing, the study insistently humanizes our view of people who have previously been, like their prehistoric counterparts in Dowson's essay, relegated by anthropology to an unrealistically "simple" and often rote existence.

The Socioeconomic Status of the World's Foragers

Of the world's contemporary population, those designated by themselves and others as hunters and gatherers tend to be overrepresented in the categories of people who lack basic human rights, live below the poverty datum line, and work for others under exploitative or unjust conditions (Ingold et al. 1988a; 1988b; Leacock and Lee 1982; Lee and Daly 1999). They have also been the victims of genocide, ethnocide, and active discrimination in disproportionate numbers (Bodley 1999; Hitchcock and Twedt 1997; Maybury-Lewis 1997). For instance, sizable numbers of North American Indians and Inuit, Latin American Indians, and indigenous peoples elsewhere in the world have died out as a result of disease after contact with members of colonizing societies.

While hunter-gatherers exist in a variety of situations, many of them do have some similarities in terms of their socioeconomic status. A significant proportion of them are characterized by relatively high rates of unemployment, by low wages and incomes, and by poverty. They are very much affected by changes in prices, as noted in this book by Mitsuo Ichikawa in his assessment of the Mbuti in what is now the Democratic Republic of Congo (DRC) and by Volker von Bremen in his discussion of the Ayoréode of Paraguay. Many, if not most, hunter-gatherers experience considerable difficulties in getting access to and maintaining secure control over land, something noted in this volume by Thomas Widlok for the Hai//om of Namibia and Laura Rival for the Huaorani of Ecuador. Olga Murashko points out that one way of handling such complex situations is to employ the concept of an international ethnoecological refuge.

In terms of health, education, and welfare, many hunter-gatherers have moderate to poor health (though this varies considerably), are undernourished or experience seasonal or long-term nutritional stress, have relatively low literacy and education levels, and are characterized by lower degrees of access to social services than the majority of the population of the countries in which they live. A major reason for these situations relates to the ways in which states tend to place emphasis on high population density areas for development investment. States also have certain, often incorrect, perceptions of the lifestyles of hunter-gatherers and other indigenous peoples living inside their borders, so their strategies for promoting social and economic development are not always as effective at enhancing the well-being of local people as they might be. Barry Hewlett's discussion of Baka Pygmies and the perceptions about their development on the part of the government of the Central African Republic (CAR) and various nongovernment organizations (NGOs) underscores the importance of the ways in which hunter-gatherers are viewed and how this affects the kinds of development policies that are pursued.

From the standpoint of demography, hunter-gatherers were generally characterized by low to moderate population growth rates in the past, though these patterns have tended to change over time as a result of sedentarization and other processes (e.g., access to new kinds of foods that contain large amounts of carbohydrates). With increased access to immunization and other medical assistance, hunter-gatherers tend to live longer than they did in the past. In some cases, however, this is offset by new diseases such as HIV/AIDS, which is on the increase among foragers and former foragers, particularly in Africa. Fertility levels are changing, with population growth rates among some former foraging groups ranging from 2 to 3.5 percent per annum. The population pyramids of hunter-gatherers today thus exhibit a fairly sizable number of young people and older people. The question of whether or not hunter-gatherers are dying out, which is addressed by Dmitri Bogoiavlenskii with reference to Russia's northern indigenous peoples, is an important one. As Bogoiavlenskii's data show, the populations of northern indigenous groups are on the rise, something that is true among many other foragers and former foragers in other parts of the world.

Hunter-gatherers are often exposed to structural violence to a greater degree than members of other groups in the states in which they reside. In some cases, members of hunter-gatherer groups join resistance movements or are incorporated into the militaries of states ranging from Vietnam to India. The degree to which hunter-gatherers and other indigenous peoples and ethnic minorities receive poor treatment is related in part to their sociopolitical status, which generally is at the bottom of a several-tiered system in the countries that they inhabit. Members of hunter-gatherer groups tend to be given harsher jail sentences and fines in court, and in some countries, such as Botswana and Australia, individuals from groups with a history of hunting and gathering tend to be overrepresented in the prison system. In many states in the past, hunter-gatherers did not have the right to represent themselves in court, so they had nowhere to turn if they disagreed with the ways they were treated. As one Kua San put it when she was questioned about the status of her great-grandparents, "They did not have control over their own lives."

There is growing international recognition of the difficulties faced by hunter-gatherers. Their plight was underscored in 1994 with the killings of sizable numbers of Twa (Pygmies) during the genocidal massacres in Rwanda that led to the deaths of over 800,000 people. Hunter-gatherers themselves have done much to alert the world to what they are facing. At a meeting of the Human Rights Commission of the United Nations in March 1996, spokespersons from a number of indigenous groups, including the San of the Kalahari, called for protection of their land and resource rights, and recognition of their cultural and religious rights (Crosette 1996).

Indigenous peoples generally possess ethnic, cultural, religious, or linguistic characteristics that are different from the dominant or numerically superior groups in the countries in which they exist. They tend to have a sense of cultural identity or social solidarity, which many members attempt to maintain. In some cases, members of indigenous groups try to hide their identity so as not to suffer racial prejudice or poor treatment at the hands of others. In other cases, they proclaim their ethnic affiliation proudly and openly. Indeed, an important criterion for "indigenousness" is the identification by people themselves of their distinct cultural identity. Most indigenous people prefer to reserve for themselves the right to determine who is and is not a member of their group. A number of hunter-gatherer groups have sought actively to promote their own cultural identity as a means of enhancing their chances at what they see as cultural survival, one example being the Ainu of Japan.

African and Asian countries tend to take two different positions on the issue of indigenous populations within their territories: (1) they claim that there are no indigenous peoples whatsoever, or (2) they state that all of the groups in the country are indigenous. Botswana, for example, has argued that virtually all people in the country with the exception of Europeans are indigenous, whereas spokespeople for various San groups in the country maintain that only they are indigenous, since they have had a presence in the Kalahari for tens of thousands of years whereas others arrived only in the past two thousand years. Botswana uses a bureaucratic definition to cover resident populations along with others who share similar characteristics of residing in remote areas and being marginal in a socioeconomic sense (Hitchcock and Holm 1993). Multiracial states like Botswana, Indonesia, and Malaysia prefer not to differentiate specific populations that are targets of development programs, in part because they do not wish to be seen as practicing a kind of apartheid or separation on the basis of ethnic identification.

In many parts of the world, "indigenousness" has taken on added political and economic significance because it is used to claim title over blocks of land, certain types of resources, development assistance, or recognition from states and intergovernmental organizations. Indigenous groups have pressed hard for greater recognition of their rights, and they have been able to gain at least some control over parts of their original territories in a number of countries. There are still numerous challenges to be faced, particularly since a number of governments have begun to go back on some of the agreements that they have made about indigenous rights, as was seen recently in the case of Brazil.

Indigenous organizations, local leaders, and advocacy groups all maintain that it is necessary to gain not just de facto control over land and resources, but also de jure legal control. One way to do this is to negotiate binding agreements with states, while another is to seek recognition of land and resource rights through the courts. Indigenous peoples in Australia, Canada, and New Zealand have had some success in gaining state recognition of land and resource rights. There are only a handful of cases in which indigenous groups have gained political power in the countries in which they live, one example being Greenland. Obtaining greater civil and political rights, especially the right to participate in decision-making and policy formulation, however, remains a yet-to-be realized goal for most indigenous peoples.

The various indigenous organizations and their supporters have called for a new approach to political and economic development, one which is sustainable over the long term. In order for this to occur, however, changes will be necessary in the ways in which decision-making is handled. Indigenous groups and advocacy NGOs have argued vociferously for an approach to development and change that is participatory and equitable—one which "puts the last first."

Land and Hunter-Gatherers

Hunter-gatherer societies usually managed their land and natural resources on a communal basis. Under these systems of tenure, land could not be bought or sold, nor could it be pledged as collateral for a loan. Individuals had rights to land and property on the basis of customary law. Thus, hunter-gatherers tended to have de facto but not de jure rights to land. They had these rights on the basis of their membership of a specific social group. Land was held in the name of that group, and every individual in the group theoretically had the right to sufficient land and resources to support him- or herself.

Property in the form of land among hunter-gatherer societies consists of what one might describe as a bundle of rights. In many cases, the same piece of land can have a variety of claims on it for various purposes. It is not unusual, therefore, to have complex systems of land and resource rights that are spread widely throughout local communities. Overlapping rights and obligations are common in hunter-gatherer systems of resource tenure. Two of the primary factors in resource-related matters among foragers are kinship and social alliances. People are allocated land rights on the basis of group membership or, in some cases, through provision by an authority figure, usually, if not always, in accordance with public sentiment. Methods of obtaining rights to land include inheritance (birth rights), marital ties, borrowing, and clientship, in which an individual enters a patron-client relationship and is given access to land in exchange for his or her allegiance. In some cases, individuals and groups could get land through colonization, the movement into a nonutilized area and the establishment of occupancy. There were also cases in which territorial acquisition occurred through conquest. Land and resource rights could also be obtained through the investment of labor, such as digging a well, building a fence, or clearing an area around a hut.

Land is part and parcel of hunter-gatherer sociopolitical systems, and it is often perceived as a territorial dimension of foraging societies. Local entities have rights over blocks of land (e.g., a band in the case of a mobile desert foraging society, a lineage or other kind of descent group in the case of a complex hunter-gatherer group such as those on the Northwest Coast of North America). Among the Ju/'hoansi of northwestern Botswana and northeastern Namibia, as noted by Biesele and Hitchcock (this volume), a band averages around twenty-five to thirty people and resides in and utilizes an area ranging from 100 to 400 square kilometers. Rights in these areas, which are known as *n!oresi* (territories) are handed down from one generation to the next. These areas usually—but not always—contain sufficient resources to sustain a group over the course of a year.

Landlessness was not a major problem in most hunter-gatherer communities, in part because of the distribution mechanisms that existed. Conflicts between individuals and groups did occur in foraging contexts, particularly in those areas in which population densities were high, as was the case in northern California, along the Northwest Coast of North America, and in parts of South Asia. A basic principle involving land matters among foraging societies is that one cannot buy or sell land. There were cases, however, in which people transferred the rights to land to others, sometimes in exchange for goods and services.

A land market did not exist in most foraging societies, a situation which colonial and postcolonial governments wanted to change. A key approach to agricultural and economic development by the state was the privatization of land, a process which, it was argued, would provide individuals with the incentive to invest more labor and capital and, at the same time, to manage and conserve resources. This privatization process has led to the dispossession of hunter-gatherers in places as far afield as Australia, North and South America, Asia, and Africa. The process of land reform was done by declaring areas as *terra nullius* (empty land) (Bodley 1999). This is what occurred in Australia, for example. Another strategy was to declare land as state land, giving rights to the government, which, in turn, ceded portions of the land to private companies and individuals. In all of the cases in which the basis for land tenure was changed, people on that land, some of whom were hunter-gatherers, were dispossessed, and many of them were forced to relocate to new areas.

The common property management systems of hunter-gatherers provided them with a means of ensuring access to resources among group members even in periods of scarcity. At the same time, the communal land tenure systems became the object of attack by colonial and postcolonial governments bent on either creating private land tenure systems or turning the land into state land. British systems of common law saw the abrogation of hunter-gatherer land rights in areas as diverse as Australia, the New World, Africa, and South Asia. The establishment of the Soviet Union saw large amounts of indigenous land turned into state property. Large numbers of foragers were dispossessed as a result of these changes (see Table I.2).

The strategy of removing people from their traditional territories generally was done in most cases without the agreement of the people

TABLE I.2 Areas Controlled by Indigenous Peoples

Country	Area (sq. km.)	Percentage of Country
Greenland	2,125,600	100
Papua New Guinea	128,000	97
Ecuador	128,000	45
Sweden	137,000	33
Colombia	260,000	25
Canada	2,221,559	22
Australia	895,000	12
Mexico	169,000	8
Brazil	573,000	7
New Zealand	16,200	6
United States	364,500	4
Costa Rica	1,930	4
India	1,498	<1
Botswana	3,523	0.6
Namibia	6,300	0.08

Note: Data obtained from Bodley (1999); Durning (1992: 24, Table 3); Veber et al. (1993); Young (1995).

themselves. Even in those cases in which people did appear to agree, as occurred, for example, in the United States when treaties were signed (e.g., the Fort Laramie Treaty of 1868), the indigenous groups did not concur with the European notion that land would become private and thus off-limits to them for occupancy and use. The widespread process of dispossession and the establishment of native reserves (or, in the United States, reservations) had highly negative impacts on the well-being of hunter-gatherer peoples.

As state-induced settlement occurred, hunter-gatherers responded in a variety of ways. In some cases, they settled on the peripheries of trading stations (e.g., the Hudson's Bay trading posts of North America), forts (e.g., Fort Robinson in western Nebraska), and missions (e.g., the missions of California such as San Juan Capistrano and Santa Barbara). When hunter-gatherer populations had their mobility options limited and as a result became residentially stationary, they had to work out ways to continue to earn a living. In some cases, they worked for other people in exchange for food or cash. In other cases, they intensified their foraging efforts, going on long-distance hunting and gathering trips and procuring large amounts of goods that they either processed for storage or sold. Native Americans on the Great Plains such as the Cheyenne and Lakota, for example, engaged in extended buffalo hunts and sold some of the produce. Some of them entered into the formal economy, in a number of cases working as soldiers, as can be seen, for example, among the Crow of North America, the Montagnards of Vietnam, and the Kxoe and Vasekele San of Namibia.

A major factor affecting hunter-gatherers and other indigenous groups in various parts of the world was the provision of food and other goods by the state. This provisioning strategy was not always done out of humanitarian concerns; it was also a means of getting people to become increasingly dependent on the state, and of putting them in a position to be more easily assimilated. While the food given to indigenous groups was sometimes the difference between survival and starvation, there were serious costs to the peoples receiving that food, not least of which was the creation of a dependency syndrome in which indigenous people were tied more closely to the state. Household heads lost status, and there were tensions along lines of gender and age within families. Many of the people in the settlements faced severe problems in terms of poverty, hunger, unemployment, restricted housing access, and discrimination. As a consequence, some people migrated away from the relocation areas in order to find employment opportunities and a more satisfactory living situation elsewhere. It was often males who left home in search of new opportunities, leaving behind their wives and children who had to resort to depending on other people for food, income, and labor.

Most hunter-gatherers did not sit idly by while the state took their land or forced them into dependency situations. Australian Aboriginals, for example, fought hard to get recognition of their land and political rights. These struggles resulted in the passage of a major statute, the Aboriginal Land Rights (Northern Territory) Act of 1976. There were also important court cases, such as the *Mabo* decision of 1992, which recognized native title for the Murray Islanders in the Torres Strait (Young 1995). The Inuit and other First Nations in Canada have negotiated with the Canadian government for recognition of their land rights. One result of these efforts was the declaration of Nunavut (Our Land), a 770,000 square mile area that became Canada's third official territory on 1 April 1999. Hunter-gatherers are now in control of the political process in Greenland, where they are represented in the Greenland parliament.

Hunter-Gatherer Political Organization, Conflict, and Conflict Resolution

Arguments about why hunter-gatherers tend to experience greater degrees of deprivation than many other groups include that they tend to be small in number, live in relatively remote areas in many cases, and have social customs and traditions that are different from the majority populations of the countries in which they reside. Some hunter-gatherers in the past lived in small, coresidential groups of people known as bands that were widely dispersed across the landscape. The average group size was twenty-five to fifty people, approximately five to six families. These groups were united through bonds of kinship, marriage, friendship, and reciprocity, as outlined in this volume by Laura Rival, Robert Tonkinson, and Jean Briggs. Public policy was a product of extensive consultation and discussion among the members of hunter-gatherer groups. San, Hadza, and Australian Aboriginals tended to be egalitarian in their social and political organization, with individuals having relatively equal access to resources.

The politics of hunter-gatherer communities were such that individualism was tolerated and, in fact, was admired. Those people who were disruptive or who engaged in socially inappropriate behavior (stealing, fighting, adultery, and abuse) were usually dealt with by peers who intervened to stop fights and who remonstrated with them, urging them to stop acting in negative ways. Those people who continued to act in ways that were disapproved of by other members of their communities were subjected to social pressure, which usually took the form of comments and criticisms made by other members of his or her group. Individuals who continued to act inappropriately were ostracized. If an individual still persisted in unacceptable behavior, he or she might be forced out of the group. In extreme cases, that person might be put to death by other members of the group.

Many hunter-gatherers have customs that help them to avoid situations likely to arouse ill will and hostility among individuals within bands and between bands. These customs include meat-sharing, gift-giving, and extensive public discussion of events and ways to deal with issues of concern to the group. Among many hunter-gatherers, the meat of wild animals is shared among members of a group, usually along lines of kinship and friendship. The distribution is usually overseen by the individual(s) who procured the resource or who manufactured or had possession of the weapon that was used in the kill. Sharing is something that is seen by most if not all hunter-gatherers as an activity that is important to maintaining good social relations among people and to ensuring at least some access to resources among group members.

A prevailing assumption in the past about hunter-gatherers was that foraging communities lacked formal leaders and did not have organized political institutions. Discussions with hunter-gatherers, however, lead to the conclusion that virtually all communities had people whom they respected and whose suggestions they frequently chose to abide by. These leaders made decisions, adjudicated disputes, and represented the community in discussions with outsiders. In some cases there were groups of elders who formed what might be described as community councils. These people had a significant say in civil matters, such as how to handle disruptive individuals. They were also important in decision-making when people of other communities requested permission to enter their areas in order to use local resources. Complex hunter-gatherer societies—such as the Kwakiutl, Tsimshian, and Bella Coola of the Northwest Coast, as well as some northern California Indian groups—tended to mark their territories and engaged in activities to protect those territories (Kelly 1995: 163). It should be stressed, however, that enhanced territorial behavior was in some cases a response to competition for scarce resources, as was the case, for example, with furbearing animals in Canada.

There has been an ongoing debate in anthropology about war and peace among hunter-gatherers and other indigenous peoples (see, for example, Ferguson and Whitehead 1992; Keeley 1996). Warfare and conflict resolution was one of the themes of the CHAGS 7 conference. While it was noted by contributors to this volume such as Jean-Guy Goulet, Jean Briggs, Marcus Griffin, and Elena Batianova that hunter-gatherers place a high value on maintaining peace and tranquility and have various social and ritualistic strategies for promoting harmony and alleviating conflict, there is also evidence that aggression and conflict has occurred among foragers, sometimes at quite high levels. As Goulet notes, there were conflicting visions of peace and conflict among the Dene Tha of northwestern Alberta. While efforts were made to control hostility, there were socially sanctioned ways in which hostility and aggression could be expressed. Marcus Griffin takes note of rising levels of conflict and murder among the Agta of Eastern Luzon in the Philippines, and points out that violence has increased as the state and other groups have begun to play greater roles in the lives of the Agta. As Leland Donald notes, Northwest Coast hunter-gatherers engaged in conflict, sometimes in efforts to obtain people who would eventually wind up as slaves. Clearly, while hunter-gatherers, like other people, generally eschew violence, they do engage in it, and violence is sometimes viewed as a means, albeit a risky one, of dealing with the state and other agencies that move into hunter-gatherer territories and exploit the resources present there. The archaeological and ethnographic records reveal numerous cases of warfare and conflict, some of which were pursued for material or ideological purposes.

As noted by a number of authors in this volume, a major issue with which hunter-gatherers and indigenous peoples are concerned is that of sovereignty, or, as many indigenous leaders put it, "self-determination" (Anaya 1996; Bodley 1999). An examination of the sociopolitical statuses of indigenous peoples around the world reveals that very few of them are in control of the governments of the countries in which they reside, and most of them lack political power even at the regional level. A major reason for this situation is that many of them were designated by colonial governments as "wards of the state," lacking legal rights to participate in political decision-making or to control their own futures.

The past three decades have witnessed an intensification of efforts at both the international and grassroots levels to promote human rights for indigenous peoples, hunter-gatherers, and minorities. Yet these populations continue to be vulnerable to oppression and exploitation. International conventions and instruments on indigenous and minority rights often go unenforced, and, as a result, the members of these groups have their rights violated with impunity by states, international agencies, and private companies and individuals (Hitchcock 1994; Minority Rights Group 1997).

Today, there are literally hundreds of indigenous grassroots organizations and institutions that are seeking to enhance their livelihoods and gain greater control over their areas. Some of them are engaged in sustainable development activities, carrying out ecotourism and rural industrial projects, social forestry programs, and soil and water conservation activities. Indigenous peoples are engaged not only in community-based conservation activities but also in social movements aiming to bring about social and environmental justice (Durning 1992). By doing regional networking and organizing civil demonstrations, native peoples in Australia, Canada, Colombia, Bolivia, and Ecuador have taken some important steps toward gaining government recognition of their land and political rights. They have also formed regional organizations, such as the Inuit Circumpolar Conference, and international organizations like the World Congress of Indigenous Peoples (WCIP). These organizations have played important roles in getting both governments and international agencies to agree on developing policies and programs that are more socially and environmentally sustainable. Indigenous and environmental groups have enhanced their impacts through their collaborative efforts, which ultimately could lead to international recognition of a communal right to a healthy environment.

The right to a healthy environment has been a major concern of hunters and gatherers, who have experienced what they perceive as more than their fair share of environmental disasters and habitat destruction, sometimes at the hands of influential private companies. Such problems occurred in the ecologically rich Oriente region of Ecuador, where the Huaorani live. As Rival points out in her chapter, oil companies, including Texaco and Maxus, have had spills and have left toxic wastes in Ecuador, reducing the quality of life for the people there. Similar problems can be seen for the inhabitants of Prince William Sound in Alaska, where the Exxon Valdez went aground a decade ago. These issues received considerable attention at the CHAGS 7 conference from the indigenous peoples living in the Russian Far North (which includes Siberia and the regions to the east of the Urals) and the researchers working with them. These peoples, who have been termed the "Numerically Small Peoples of the North," have been heavily impacted by the expansion of timber, mining, and oil company activities in their areas, especially in the past several decades. Violence, both ritual and nonritual, is on the increase, as noted here by Elena Batianova.

Like many other areas of the world, the Russian Far North has seen the rise of indigenous political and environmental movements. But in the remote, difficult reaches of the Arctic, only the larger-scale industrial investments can turn a profit; hunter-gatherers and other smaller-scale groups tend to have little option but to work for others or to try and survive by foraging and selling their produce to anyone who is fortunate enough to have the cash to buy it. As one member of a Siberian indigenous group put it, "We are living in a land which has been fouled by oil companies, and we are on the verge of starvation while they make huge profits."

Hunter-Gatherers in Russian and Western Anthropology

The Seventh Conference on Hunting and Gathering Peoples (CHAGS 7) was noteworthy for having been held in Moscow at a time when Russian/Western academic contacts were still relatively few in anthropology. It also added to a short but significant list of international conferences that have given participants from many parts of the world the chance to reflect upon their own academic traditions in the light of very different ones current in Russia. Among these had been the small conference at Burg Wartenstein in 1976, which resulted in the publication of *Soviet and Western Anthropology*, edited by Ernest Gellner (1980), and the larger CHAGS 6 held in Fairbanks, Alaska, in 1990, which brought a substantial number of Russian scholars to the United States for the lively interchange that served as the impetus for the 1993 CHAGS 7 in Moscow.

To put some of the differences in academic traditions into perspective with regard to the present volume, it is worthwhile to look briefly into areas like folklore and historicity (for other subject areas, see Chapter 1 by Schweitzer), and to assess how these developed in the former Soviet Union versus the ways they are regarded by Western anthropological scholarship. The essays in this volume are themselves illustrations of greatly varying attitudes toward the utility of folkloric and linguistic materials in the ethnography of ethnic difference. In particular, we draw attention to the fundamental ways in which Russian and Western anthropology differ as disciplines. The Russian discipline (*etnografiia*), although institutionally distinct from linguistics, archaeology, and physical anthropology, was always very inclusive in its practice, comprising history, archaeology, and even philosophy, among other fields, within its scope. Perhaps even more importantly, to quote Gellner, *etnografiia* also "reflects or expresses the manner in which the intellectuals of the Soviet Union think about some of the deepest problems within their own society, and about its place in the scheme of things and in world history" (Gellner 1980: ix). Getting enmeshed in the Marxist debates that this comment initiates is beyond the scope of this introduction. But a few relevant remarks may be made about the different attitudes toward cultural studies that are implied, particularly in an area that has long been an uneasy one in the West—that of overlap or collaboration between anthropology and folklore studies.

According to Bromley (1975: 603–4), contemporary ethnic groups manifest their specific ethnic features through "spiritual culture" rather than through material or organizational infrastructure. This "spiritual culture" includes the profound legacy of oral folklore, which extended through all strata of Russian society until far into this century. The techniques of structural linguistic analysis are thus routinely and confidently used by Russian researchers as methods by which ethnographic analogies enter the historical past.

Oral traditions, particularly views of the historical past held by specific peoples, have been the object of extensive methodological writing by Russian scholars. Though there exist similar approaches in Western traditions (e.g., Jan Vansina's *Oral Tradition: A Study of Historical Methodology*, 1965), it is only recently that Western anthropologists and archaeologists have taken it very seriously, such as in current research being carried out in the Kalahari by Andrew Smith and Richard Lee.

Then there is what Dragadze (1975: 604) calls "the most striking and baffling feature of Soviet anthropology—the historical dimension ... each society ... containing elements of the past and moving towards some new form." It is clear to a Western folklorist how aptly suited such a perspective is to investigation through structural rules for expressive cultures such as those elaborated by Vladimir Propp in his book *Theory and History of Folklore* (1984). But this perspective has been less clear for Western anthropology as a whole, which has long regarded folklore studies as a kind of stepchild, and finds itself obscurely embarrassed by otherwise "serious" works that rely even to a small degree on folklore methodologies and materials. A persistence of this attitude might cause the enthusiastic Russian use of such sources and approaches to be regarded as quaint or worse; we therefore feel it is important to point out the deep disciplinary precedents for the use of oral ideological materials in the study of cultures.

It is equally important to remember, as Roman Jakobson points out in his commentary on Afanas'ev's *Russian Fairy Tales* (Jakobson 1945), that Russian folktales were first recorded and published, not in their homeland and not in their native tongue, but in English, in English translation. Russian folktales remained unwritten so long in Russian because of the Russian Church's dominance over written literature. This domination extended to all classes, so that oral transmission long remained the only medium for the diffusion of "a copious, original, manifold, and highly artistic tradition" based upon a shared and ancient orality. What brings this reverence for and reliance on folk tradition right up to the moment in the intellectual traditions of the Russian social sciences is the equally strong emphasis in Russian academic life on the integration of what the West would call separate disciplines, including literary studies, history, archaeology, and anthropology.

Aleksandr Nikolaevich Afanas'ev, by education a lawyer, became one of the few scholars in Russian anthropology to play such a profound role in the history of a national culture. But other Russian scholars of oral literature in society—like Meletinsky (1974) and of course Propp himself—have, through their work, profoundly affected the course of analytic trends in Russian social science. The semiotic approaches of structural linguistics have thus become an irrevocable part of the substrate of cultural studies in Russia in a way they have not in Western anthropology in general. There are, of course, exceptions to this statement in various of the European traditions, but overall it may be said that the Western disciplines of comparative literature, folklore, and history (narrowly conceived) have benefited more from the infusion of theory on the rules of cultural creativity and transmission than has Western ethnography up to this point.

In this volume, the contributions of Alekseenko and Kim serve to underscore the expansion of hunter-gatherer study that is possible with the inclusion of cultural detail usually associated in Western anthropology with linguistics and folklore. Alekseenko presents a contextualized account of time in the Ket traditional world-view by showing its embeddedness in details of the Ket bear cult. The cyclicity of time in Ket and other Siberian cultures is closely connected not only to outcomes in the enterprise of hunting but to human relationships with the world of the dead. Amassing such integrated detail allows Alekseenko to approach an area of human life—that of emotional states regarding important rites of passage—that has been rarely touched on in Western anthropology.

Alexandra Kim outlines the linguistic complexities of the life of the soul in Sel'kup conception. Because the spiritual traditions of most hunting-gathering cultures have existed in oral form, they have remained relatively inaccessible to researchers, and in fact have been regarded as somehow "lesser" than those "great" religious traditions of the world known through texts and codices. Kim's investigation of the Sel'kup lexicon regarding religious life and its grounding in the Sel'kup physical and social environment is profoundly humanizing in its great detail and etymological connectedness. This chapter also fearlessly opens an enormous cultural question that social scientists have skirted for years—that of abstract ideas. Because this issue is, after all, basic to anthropological inquiry, the essay forms a fitting end to our anthology. It leaves readers with a challenge in world understanding that should stimulate further humanizing research with foragers—and perhaps enable us to better know ourselves.

References

Altman, J. C. 1989. *Emergent Inequalities in Aboriginal Australia*. Sydney: Oceania Monographs.

Altman, J. C., and W. Sanders. 1991. "The CDEP Scheme: Administrative and Policy Issues." *Center for Aboriginal Economic Policy Research Discussion Paper 5*. Canberra: Center for Aboriginal Economic Policy Research.

Anaya, S. J. 1996. *Indigenous Peoples in International Law*. New York and Oxford: Oxford University Press.

Barnes, R. H., A. Gray, and B. Kingsbury, eds. 1995. *Indigenous Peoples of Asia*. Ann Arbor, Mich: Association for Asian Students, Inc.

Barsh, R. L. 1996. "Indigenous Peoples and the UN Commission on Human Rights: A Case of the Immovable Object and the Irresistible Force." *Human Rights Quarterly* 18: 782–813.

Bodley, J. H. 1999. *Victims of Progress*. Mountain View, Calif.: Mayfield Publishing Company.

Bromley, Y. V. 1975. "Reply to Ernest Gellner's 'The Soviet and the Savage.'" *Current Anthropology* 16: 603–4.

Burch, E. S., Jr., and L. J. Ellanna, eds. 1994. *Key Issues in Hunter-Gatherer Research*. Oxford and Providence: Berg Publishers.

Comaroff, Jean, and John Comaroff. 1993. *Modernity and Its Malcontents: Ritual and Power in Postcolonial Africa*. Chicago: University of Chicago Press.

Crosette, B. 1996. "Rising Variety of Groups Vie for Attention at U.N. Rights Forum." *The New York Times*, 31 March.

Dragadze, T. 1975. "Reply to Ernest Gellner's 'The Soviet and the Savage.'" *Current Anthropology* 16: 604.

Durning, A. T. 1992. *Guardians of the Land: Indigenous Peoples and the Health of the Earth*. Washington, D.C.: World Watch Institute.

Ferguson, B., and N. Whitehead, eds. 1992. *War in the Tribal Zone*. Santa Fe: School of American Research Press.

Fixico, D. 1998. *The Invasion of Indian Country in the Twentieth Century: American Capitalism and Tribal Natural Resources*. Niwot, Colo.: University Press of Colorado.

Franklin, S. 1995. "Science as Culture, Culture as Science." *Annual Review of Anthropology* 24: 163–84.

Gellner, E. 1975. "The Soviet and the Savage." *Current Anthropology* 16: 595–617.

Gellner, E., ed. 1980. *Soviet and Western Anthropology*. London: Duckworth.

Hitchcock, R. K. 1994. "International Human Rights, the Environment, and Indigenous Peoples." *Colorado Journal of International Environmental Law and Policy* 5: 1–22.

_____. 1996. *Kalahari Communities: Bushmen and the Politics of the Environment in Southern Africa*. Copenhagen: International Work Group for Indigenous Affairs.

Hitchcock, R. K., and J. D. Holm. 1993. "Bureaucratic Domination of Hunter-Gatherer Societies: A Study of the San in Botswana." *Development and Change* 24(1): 1–35.

Hitchcock, R. K., and T. M. Twedt. 1997. "Physical and Cultural Genocide of Various Indigenous Peoples." In *Century of Genocide: Eyewitness Accounts and Critical Views*. S. Totten, W. S. Parsons, and I. Charny, eds. 372–407. New York and London: Garland Publishing Company.

Huntington, H. P. 1992. *Wildlife Management and Subsistence Hunting in Alaska*. Seattle: University of Washington Press.

Ingold, T., D, Riches, and J. Woodburn, eds. 1988a. *Hunters and Gatherers: Volume 1: History, Evolution, and Social Change*. New York and Oxford: Berg Publishers.

_____. 1988b. *Hunters and Gatherers: Volume 2: Property, Power, and Ideology*. New York and Oxford: Berg Publishers.

Jakobson, R. 1945. "Commentary." In *Russian Fairy Tales*. A. N. Afanas'ev, ed. New York: Pantheon.

Keeley, L. A. 1988. "Hunter-Gatherer Economic Complexity and 'Population Pressure': A Cross-Cultural Analysis." *Anthropological Archaeology* 7: 373–411.

_____. 1996. *War Before Civilization*. New York and Oxford: Oxford University Press.

Kelly, R. L. 1995. *The Foraging Spectrum: Diversity in Hunter-Gatherer Lifeways*. Washington, D.C.: Smithsonian Institution Press.

Kent, S., ed. 1996. *Cultural Diversity among Twentieth Century Foragers: An African Perspective*. Cambridge: Cambridge University Press.

Leacock, E., and R. Lee, eds. 1982. *Politics and History in Band Societies*. Cambridge: Cambridge University Press.

Lee, R., and R. Daly, eds. 1999. *The Cambridge Encyclopedia of Hunters and Gatherers*. Cambridge: Cambridge University Press.

Lee, R. B., and I. DeVore, eds. 1968. *Man the Hunter*. Chicago: Aldine.

Maybury-Lewis, D. 1997. *Indigenous Peoples, Ethnic Groups, and the State*. Boston: Allyn and Bacon.

Meehan, B., and N. White, eds. 1990. *Hunter-Gatherer Demography: Past and Present*. Sydney: Oceania Monographs.

Meletinsky, E. 1974. "Structural-Typological Study of Folktales." In *Soviet Structural Folkloristics*. P. Maranda, ed. The Hague: Mouton.

Minority Rights Group. 1994. *Polar Peoples: Self-Determination and Development*. London: Minority Rights Group International.

_____. 1997. *World Directory of Minorities*. London: Minority Rights Group International.

Myers, F. 1988. "Critical Trends in the Study of Hunter-Gatherers." *Annual Review of Anthropology* 17: 261–82.

Price, T. D., and J. A. Brown, eds. 1985. *Prehistoric Hunter-Gatherers: The Emergence of Cultural Complexity*. Orlando, Fla: Academic Press.

Propp, V. 1984. *Theory and History of Folklore*. A. Y. Martin and R. P. Martin, trans. Minneapolis: University of Minnesota Press.

Schrire, C., ed. 1984. *Past and Present in Hunter-Gatherer Studies*. New York: Academic Press.

Smith, E. A. 1991. *Inujjuamiut Foraging Strategies: Evolutionary Ecology of an Arctic Hunting Economy*. New York: Aldine de Gruyter.

Smith, E. A., and J. McCarter. 1997. *Contested Arctic: Indigenous Peoples, Industrial States, and Circumpolar Development.* Seattle: University of Washington Press.

Smith, E. A., and B. Winterhalder, eds. 1992. *Evolutionary Ecology and Human Behavior.* New York: Aldine de Gruyter.

Vansina, J., ed. 1965. *Oral Tradition: A Study of Historical Methodology.* Chicago: University of Chicago Press.

Veber, H., J. Dahl, F. Wilson, and E. Waehle, eds. 1993. "… *Never Drink from the Same Cup": Proceedings of the Conference on Indigenous Peoples in Africa, Tune, Denmark, 1993.* Copenhagen: International Work Group for Indigenous Affairs and Center for Development Research.

Wilmsen, E. N. 1989. *Land Filled with Flies: A Political Economy of the Kalahari.* Chicago: University of Chicago Press.

Young, E. 1995. *Third World in the First: Indigenous Peoples and Development.* London: Routledge.

Chapter 1

SILENCE AND OTHER MISUNDERSTANDINGS

Russian Anthropology, Western Hunter-Gatherer
Debates, and Siberian Peoples

————————=◆=————————

Peter P. Schweitzer

Introduction

The present book is the first post–*Man the Hunter* volume devoted to the
study of hunting and gathering societies that includes a significant number of case studies dealing with Siberian peoples.[1] This fact alone, or—
even more so—its novelty, seems to require explanation. In addition, as
readers will undoubtedly discover for themselves, the issues addressed
and the perspectives chosen in the articles on Siberia differ from what
Western anthropology has established as the mainstream treatment of
hunter-gatherers over the last thirty years. Thus, this chapter intends to
provide one possible reading of these recognizable differences.

As a first approximation to the topic, I want to relate a personal example of how I experienced the unified neglect by Western and Russian
anthropology of Siberia, an area that historically was inhabited largely by
hunter-gatherers. As a graduate student in the early 1980s, I became
intrigued by the growing body of literature on hunter-gatherers but, at
the same time, dismayed by the complete absence of Siberian data in
these discussions. Arriving in 1986 in Leningrad, eager to work on a dissertation topic designed to partially rectify this situation and expecting to
be met cheerfully by Soviet colleagues, I soon realized that hardly anyone
among the Siberian specialists seemed interested in my glaringly Marxist-
sounding topic "Foraging Modes of Production in Northeastern Siberia."

It turned out that neither my lack of experience in Siberian ethnography nor the fact that contemporary Siberian peoples could hardly be classified as "pure hunter-gatherers" was responsible for this reserved reception. Instead, over the years I began to realize that differences in research traditions and approaches, some of which I will discuss below, lay at the heart of this failed cross-cultural encounter. To conclude the narrative of my quest for the hunter-gatherer debate in Siberia, my final thesis retained little of the initial "big questions." Instead, it became an ethnohistoric treatment of a narrowly circumscribed area in northeastern Siberia, with hardly recognizable allusions to Western hunter-gatherer debates in unsuspicious places. This change of mind was to a large degree triggered by my Soviet colleagues, and I never had reason to regret it.

Since I believe that there is more to this story than a private anecdote of scholarly miscommunication, in the following pages I will explore a number of different temporal and topical aspects of several relationships. On the one hand, Western anthropology's interest and disinterest in Siberian peoples as hunter-gatherers will be portrayed and tentatively explained.[2] More emphasis, however, will be put on illustrating and understanding the relationship of Russian/Soviet anthropology in general, and Siberian studies in particular, to the study of hunting and gathering societies. This "preference" seems to be justified in a publication addressing primarily an English-speaking audience and will be of relevance in contextualizing the Siberian chapters of this volume. Thus, there will be two distinct but related questions addressed in the following pages:

1. Why did Western anthropology neglect data about Siberian hunter-gatherers until the recent past?
2. Why did Soviet/Russian anthropologists working in Siberia rarely, if ever, address issues that had been raised in Western debates about hunter-gatherers?

Both issues/questions have to be put into historical perspective, i.e., before discussing possible reasons we have to locate these tendencies of neglect in time. This chronological view leads inevitably to the present and the future and, thereby, to the question as to how these relations will develop from this point in time.

The Roots of Silence

Western Anthropology and the Peoples of Siberia

A comprehensive treatment that examines if and how non-Russian anthropology incorporated Siberian data is clearly beyond the scope of this essay; it would require a separate article, if not a book. However, it is possible to make the general statement that pre-twentieth-century scholarship outside of Russia was reasonably well informed about Siberian peoples (many early ethnographers of Siberia were non-Russians, and Germans were especially numerous among them). If we focus our attention on the social/cultural anthropology of the twentieth century, it becomes obvious that the early decades of this century were particularly productive in providing information about Siberia in languages other than Russian. On the one hand, the Jesup North Pacific Expedition (1897–1902), under the direction of Franz Boas, resulted in an unprecedented level of Russian-American cooperative research and publications, part of it situated in northeastern Siberia (see, e.g., Bogoras 1904–09; 1910; 1913; Jochelson 1905–08; 1910–26; Laufer 1902).[3] On the other hand, a significant number of other researchers (both Russians and non-Russians) made their results of Siberian research available in Western languages (see, e.g., Donner 1933; Findeisen 1929; Lehtisalo 1932; Shimkin 1939; Shirokogoroff 1929; 1935; Steinitz 1938; Zolotarev 1937). Finally, a number of comparative studies, based on Russian and non-Russian sources on Siberia, were published in Western languages (see, e.g., Czaplicka 1914; Hallowell 1926; Harva 1938; Nioradze 1925; Ohlmarks 1939; Stadling 1912). While none of these works consciously addressed issues of hunting and gathering, most of them provided data on the subject.

A cursory look at a few English-language texts (and textbooks) of the time reveals an ambiguous picture. Some authors used Siberian examples extensively in illustrating certain issues of general anthropology (see, e.g., Forde 1934; Lowie 1934). Daryll Forde's *Habitat, Economy, and Society* is particularly relevant for our purposes, since the author's ecological perspective led him to organize his case studies by subsistence categories; under "Food Gatherers" Siberia is represented by the Yukagirs, and the northern Tunguses (Evenks and Evens) figure under "Pastoral Nomads" (Forde 1934). Other contemporary authors, however, completely neglected the available information on Siberian peoples (see, e.g., Radin 1932; Wissler 1929). Most importantly, Julian Steward—who was to become one of the founding fathers of the modern Western discourse on hunter-gatherers—belonged to the latter camp. In none of his writings, including his seminal "The Economic and Social Basis of Primitive Bands" (Steward 1936), could I detect any substantial discussion of Siberian materials.

While before World War II the incorporation, or neglect, of Siberian data seems to have been determined largely by idiosyncratic preferences of individual authors, the situation changed dramatically after the war. Between the 1950s and 1980s, Siberia was almost entirely absent from the indexes of British and American textbooks and of general anthropological treatises. There are at least three well-known circumstances that might explain the post–World War II ignorance of Siberia:

1. There were hardly any possibilities for Western fieldwork in Soviet Siberia.
2. Very few Western anthropologists spoke or read Russian; thus the available Soviet literature was left unutilized.
3. Cold War attitudes made interest in Soviet Siberia suspicious if it was not directed toward the critique of Communist crimes.

However, several counterarguments to these "common-sense explanations" should be raised:

1. The few Westerners who were able to conduct fieldwork in Siberia during the late 1960s and 1970s (e.g., Caroline Humphrey and Marjorie Mandelstam Balzer) were unable to attract a larger anthropological interest in their work before the late 1980s. Balzer's research among the Khantys especially should have made students of hunting and gathering societies curious about her results.
2. The language argument is not very convincing, because—as we see today—the Russian language is studied when there is interest in Siberia (and, thus, the lack of Russian-language competence is an effect and not a reason of disinterest). There are even a few examples of useful Western articles based entirely on non-Russian sources.[4] Restricting myself to Chukotka for this purpose, three such contributions come to mind (Ingold 1986; Leeds 1965; Libby 1960). Particularly, Ingold's 1986 article, "Hunting, Sacrifice and the Domestication of Animals," while almost entirely based on works by Bogoras published at the beginning of the century, is one of the most interesting treatises on Chukchi society. Ingold's analysis of the differences between reindeer-herding and hunting/gathering Chukchi social and economic relations as expressed through world-view and ritual is compelling. Thus, one dares to wonder what results could have been possible if Western anthropologists had incorporated Russian-language data.
3. The Cold War argument definitely has its strong points. The general political atmosphere certainly led to a level of suspicion and distrust against any information coming from the Soviet Union. However, as the active postwar collaboration regarding questions of the peopling of the New World between North American and Soviet archaeologists and physical anthropologists shows (see Krupnik 1998), these sentiments and attitudes could be overcome when there was recognition of mutual scholarly benefit (especially, after the 1950s).[5]

Thus, in addition to the issues already addressed, we will have to turn to specific aspects of the Western anthropological discourse. Modern Western hunter-gatherer debates effectively got under way during the 1960s. Elman Service's concise summary statement *The Hunters* (Service 1966) not only defended Steward's "patrilocal band hypothesis," but also continued the latter's neglect of Siberia. Wendell Oswalt's technology-centered evolutionary account of hunting, *Habitat and Technology* (Oswalt 1973), displays an "empty quarter" where Siberia is located on its map of cases discussed, while Carleton Coon manages to mention the Chukchis, Koriaks, and Itel'mens a few times, mainly in conjunction with American Eskimos, in his *The Hunting Peoples* (Coon 1971). However, the most influential statement of these years stems from the conference and subsequent publication *Man the Hunter* (Lee and DeVore 1968). Although the entire book does not contain a single substantial reference to Siberian hunter-gatherers, it contains a highly interesting passage explaining why this is the case. "Elder statesman" George Peter Murdock, in his "The Current Status of the World's Hunting and Gathering Peoples" (Murdock 1968: 16) declared:

> The non-agricultural peoples of Siberia have long since been converted to a pastoral mode of life in the interior, or, on the coast, have come to depend primarily upon fishing and have adopted a relatively sedentary settlement pattern. The only two Siberian peoples who seem to meet our strict definition of hunters and gatherers are the Ket ... and the Yukaghir.... Both tribes have doubtless been so altered by Soviet acculturation policies that further field work among them is unlikely to yield rewarding results.

Murdock's statement contains three distinct points, which—taken together—eliminate all Siberian peoples from the category of "eligible hunter-gatherers":

1. Many Siberian groups have, long prior to the twentieth century, adopted reindeer herding and are thus pastoralists and not hunter-gatherers. However, Murdock does not mention that interior (or taiga) reindeer herders of Siberia have historically used domesticated reindeer as beasts of burden in hunting pursuits. The herders were in many respects similar to "mounted hunters" (although rather few groups actually rode these animals).
2. Siberian hunter-gatherers, whose subsistence was traditionally based on seasonally sedentary fishing and/or sea mammal hunting, are not "real hunter-gatherers." Murdock's "strict" definition excluded also "mounted hunters" and "incipient tillers," which left him with a short list of "twenty-seven surviving groups of hunter-gatherers" (Murdock 1968: 15).

3. The only two Siberian groups to make it through categories (1) and (2), the Kets and Yukagirs, are finally eliminated because of the effects of Soviet acculturation policies. It should be noted, however, that Murdock's list of twenty-seven contained North American groups, such as the Apache, California Indians, and northwestern Athapaskans, among several others. That the underlying assumption—i.e., that any of these groups was, in the 1960s, less affected by mighty acculturative pressures than the Kets and Yukagirs—could be taken seriously is difficult to imagine, even during the heyday of Cold War distrust against everything Soviet.

While these three distinct criteria seem to address three different realms of taxonomy and definition, points (1) and (2) can be understood as voicing a common concern, namely the definitional boundaries of the hunter-gatherer category. While the statements under point (3) can be criticized easily, the two other points cannot be contested factually. Nevertheless, it is appropriate to question the usefulness of any given definition as a heuristic device. Already the volume *Man the Hunter* violated Murdock's strict definition, e.g., by including articles on Northwest Coast societies and on the Ainus, which, according to point (2), fell outside the range of the permissible sample. Subsequent books and articles on the subject have continued to disregard Murdock's criteria. Not only "sedentary fishermen/sea mammal hunters" outside of Siberia became part of the emerging "hunter-gatherer discourse," but also part-time pastoralists—in obvious violation of point (1)—were included in these considerations (it should suffice to mention the "Great Kalahari debate" and its forerunners). Still, Siberia remained outside of these discussions.

In order to give Murdock's strict definition a positive spin, it might be said that by excluding Siberia, he focused attention on a core group of nomadic, "simple," and egalitarian hunter-gatherers (though the "California Indians" seem somehow odd as a part of this group). At the same time, it becomes immediately obvious that this narrow focus eliminated the possibility of exploring the full range of the "foraging spectrum" (Kelly 1995), something that has become increasingly important in recent years (e.g., Kent 1996; Shnirelman 1992). It seems that this "purist" approach to delineating the boundaries of the category "hunter-gatherer" has to do with viewing hunter-gatherers as "our contemporary ancestors" or "our primitive contemporaries." Murdock himself had given the latter phrase wide recognition by using it as the title for one of his early textbooks (Murdock 1938).

However, it was not George Peter Murdock's evolutionary comparativism that triggered the "new hunter-gatherer debate" of the 1960s and 1970s. Instead, it was a broad movement—which hereinafter will be labeled "neoevolutionism," which includes "cultural ecology," "cultural materialism," etc.—that overcame the cautious Boasian paradigm by proposing a (natural) science perspective on human behavior. One of the implicit or explicit assumptions was that "real" contemporary hunter-gatherers could provide better clues about the "human condition" than other kinds of societies (Lee and DeVore 1968: ix). This perceived possibility called for new "scientific" methods of counting and measuring; subsequently, these data had to be procured anew and could not just be extrapolated from somebody else's research. The "degree of acculturation" was also a concern, although none of the studies conducted in the 1960s and since were able to pretend that any of the groups under consideration were foragers in a world of foragers. Thus, the experimental and evolutionary aspects of the new approaches disqualified Siberia, either on the grounds of fieldwork access or acculturation.[6]

Instead of presenting a single-factor explanation, we have to conclude the present section by acknowledging a multitude of factors at work. Nevertheless, it seems possible to arrange them somehow hierarchically, thus indicating that they are not of equal relevance in understanding the questions at hand. The fact that World War II seems to mark a dividing line in the Western treatment of Siberia indicates the undeniable consequences of Cold War attitudes on our subject. However, it is impossible to assign all Western anthropologists to the camp of stern anti-Soviet believers (as it is likewise impossible to assume that every Soviet anthropologist was a convinced ideological enemy of the West). Thus, the theoretical and methodological inclinations of the neoevolutionist paradigm have to be given appropriate consideration. I believe that only the combination (and mutual reinforcement) of these two factors can explain most of the neglect under discussion. The other factors mentioned seem to be secondary, that is, they are likely to be effects of the first two. For example, the widespread unwillingness to examine and interpret Soviet sources instead of conducting one's own fieldwork can be explained by the prevalent distrust of Soviet sources *and* by the long- dominant approach that "real contemporary hunter-gatherers" offer a privileged window into human nature and (pre)history. Ironically, there was a significant number of politically leftist scholars among the American neoevolutionists. Thus, we are confronted with a strange alliance of distrusting anti-Communists and leftist believers in the scientific study of social evolution that succeeded in excluding/silencing a significant number of human societies from the developing hunter-gatherer discourse.

Soviet Anthropology and the Study of Hunter-Gatherers

In the preceding pages, I speculated about reasons why a particular anthropological tradition excluded a certain region of the world, Siberia, from its discourse. This section intends to tackle the question of why a particular taxonomic device, the category "hunter-gatherers," was so rarely utilized in another anthropological tradition, the Russian/Soviet tradition. However, after addressing the question from the general perspective of Soviet anthropology, I will also turn to Siberia, since I believe that there were specific reasons at work in excluding Siberian societies from what was the Soviet equivalent of hunter-gatherers.

The chronological aspect of the question under consideration is relatively easy to answer. Starting in the mid-1930s, when Marxist-Leninist dogma became firmly established in Soviet anthropology, the category "hunter-gatherers" rarely was assigned any theoretical significance. Previously, that is, in the general works of early Russian anthropologists from the 1880s onwards (who were mostly evolutionists and/or materialists), the category was used quite frequently as an organizational device in presenting materials from around the globe (see, e.g., Kovalevskii 1906; Kropotkin 1902; Maksimov 1913; Ziber 1883). However, since it made little sense to speak of a hunter-gatherer "debate" or even "discourse" at the time, the use of the term did not necessarily indicate a particular theoretical position. Still, what comes closest to a hunter-gatherer debate of the time, i.e., the deliberations of German/Austrian economic anthropologists about distinct types of hunting societies and on whether pastoralism could have emerged directly from hunting (see, e.g., Grosse 1896; Hahn 1891; Koppers 1915–16), were evidently closely followed in Russia.

The relatively unambiguous timing of the disappearance of hunter-gatherers from Soviet anthropological horizons also provides a straightforward explanation for it: Marxist-Leninist anthropology dismisses the category "hunter-gatherer" as a low-level analytical category (it is just a "mode of subsistence") and replaces it with the dialectical notions of "mode of production" and "social formation." The social formation closest in content to the category "hunter-gatherers" is *pervobytnoe obshchestvo* (literally "primordial society"; generally rendered as "primitive society").[7] *Pervobytnoe obshchestvo* is a category that includes all preclass societies; while many members of the class are hunting and gathering societies, (classless) agricultural societies belong there as well. At the same time, hunter-gatherers with pronounced social and economic stratification are in danger of falling out of *pervobytnoe obshchestvo*.

This model of categorization follows rather directly from the writings of Marx and Engels on the nature of the relationship between economy and other aspects of society. More specifically, Rosa Luxemburg, in her critique of Grosse's attempt to correlate family forms with modes of subsistence, had already stated, "if we only know that a community lives by hunting, herding or agriculture, we still do not know anything about the proper nature of 'production' and its relation to other aspects of culture"

(Luxemburg 1925: 108). The particular difficulties that arise when one tries to correlate hunting and gathering with a particular "mode of production" became evident during the 1970s and 1980s, as scholars of hunting and gathering societies informed by Western Marxism provided such attempts (e.g., Ingold 1988; Keenan 1977; Lee 1980).

Thus, it could be argued that Soviet anthropology merely studied hunter-gatherers under a different label from that of its Western counterpart. This is to a certain degree true, since hunting and gathering societies were in no way excluded from the scope of the discipline. They were extensively cited in the key texts about *pervobytnoe obshchestvo* (e.g., Bromlei 1982; 1986; Kosven 1953; Pershits 1982), as examples of a (mostly bygone) chapter of human history. One might expect that this view of hunter-gatherers as representatives of early humanity should have brought Soviet anthropology in close contact with Western neoevolutionists. However, Soviet anthropology generally displayed an ambiguous fascination with neoevolutionism: it was the subject of disproportionately many Soviet reviews, which generally acknowledged its "attempts to overcome the theoretical impasse into which the historical school had led" (Petrova-Averkieva 1980: 53), but at the same time declared that the only real alternative was Marxism.[8] In addition to these general concerns, there were also more specific theoretical reasons for rejecting the new Western approaches to hunter-gatherer studies; among them were the following:

1. By concentrating on the specific qualities of hunting and gathering societies, Western anthropology had to put much emphasis on the "Neolithic revolution" as a dividing line in human history. For Soviet anthropology, on the other hand, still following Engels, the emergence of class relations remained the basic qualitative transition in social evolution.[9]

2. The reemphasis on the study of bilateral kinship systems, beginning in the West in the 1960s and 1970s, threatened the Soviet concept of *rod* (best English translation "lineage," "exogamous clan," or—in Engels's terms—"gens"). The *rod* held a very prominent place in the Soviet theory of primitive society. The assumption that social evolution is characterized by the subsequent stages of matrilineal and patrilineal kinship organization was transformed into dogma in Soviet ethnography since the 1930s.[10] This was to a large extent connected with Engels's work *The Origin of the Family, Private Property and the State* (Engels 1972), which gave priority to the notion of "lineage" over the notion of "community" (*Gemeinschaft*), still very much used by Marx.

3. The notion of the "original affluent society," coined at the "Man the Hunter" conference, is in fundamental contradiction to the

Marxist-Leninist concept of *pervobytnoe obshchestvo. Perbvobytnoe obshchestvo* is conceptualized as being unable to produce surplus, due to the low development of the forces of production. The argument of the "original affluent society" threatened the "prime mover" of the Soviet concept of social evolution, which is based on the linear development of the forces of production.[11]

So far, we have established why Soviet anthropology made little use of the analytical concept of hunter-gatherers and have looked at some of the specific reasons that separated it from Western research of the 1960s and 1970s. However, we still have to clarify whether Soviet anthropology merely practiced hunter-gatherer research under a different label. In doing so, I will concentrate on the example of Siberian hunter-gatherers, since they are the prime focus of our inquiry.

One defining characteristic of the Soviet study of *pervobytnoe obshchestvo* was that it was not merely one research perspective being investigated by anthropologists working in their regional areas of expertise. This was succinctly stated by Gellner's dictum that *pervobytnoe obshchestvo* "is an important, restricted and above all heavily theory-loaded term" and "anyone who fails to note this will altogether misunderstand Russian anthropological discussions" (Gellner 1988: 12). In addition, we have to keep in mind that, while most anthropologists at the Moscow Institute of Ethnography were working in regional sectors (e.g., Siberia, Africa, non-Soviet Asia), anthropologists dealing with *pervobytnoe obshchestvo* had no official regional specialization. As a rule, they were theoreticians who made use of data collected by regional specialists, archaeologists, historians, etc. At the same time, regional specialists (of Siberia or elsewhere) were not "authorized" to address the big questions of *pervobytnoe obshchestvo* and kept to problems of regional culture history instead. This division of labor, which characterized Soviet science organization but is no longer in place, is still recognizable in many aspects of post-Soviet anthropology.

While the aforementioned applies as much to Africa as to Siberia, there were more specific reasons for rarely combining the category hunter-gatherers (or *pervobytnoe obshchestvo*, for that matter) with Siberia as a region. Most historical, pre-Soviet Siberian societies were classified as belonging to a stage labeled "disintegration of *pervobytnoe obshchestvo*," which marked the final phases of *pervobytnoe obshchestvo*. Ethnographically, the classical locus of *pervobytnoe obshchestvo* has remained Australia and Tasmania throughout the Soviet period. At the same time, contemporary Siberian societies were supposed to be socialist (or, at least, firmly embarked on the way to socialism). Where ethnographic realities had not already prevented anthropologists from putting *pervobytnoe obshchestvo* and Siberia together, political dogma surely succeeded in doing so. Thus,

Siberian societies were both of marginal theoretical interest and inherently dangerous to the student of *pervobytnoe obshchestvo*.

In 1972, an edited volume was published that counteracted much of what has been said above. Entitled *Hunters, Gatherers, Fishermen* (*Okhotniki, sobirateli, rybolovy*; Reshetov 1972), it is, to my knowledge, the only book in the Soviet tradition dedicated entirely and solely to hunter-gatherers. In the introduction (p. 10) there is a specific reference to *Man the Hunter* and *Contributions to Anthropology: Band Societies* (Damas 1969), the basic works of the emerging Western discourse. It also contains five articles on Siberian hunter-gatherers, written by anthropologists with long-time field experience in the area they were writing about (Alekseenko 1972; Khomich 1972; Liapunova 1972; Taksami 1972; Vasilevich 1972). However, with the exception of Vasilevich's article, the Siberian contributions do not differ substantially from other works on Siberia at the time, i.e., they are detailed investigations devoted to particular problems of the culture history of a restricted area. Vasilevich's chapter stands out, since her careful historical analysis leads her to reject an earlier Soviet dictum about the localization of Evenk clans and the prior existence of tribes and phratries among them. In addition, the reader contains one article on the Neolithic of northern Eurasia (Khlobystin 1972), which rejects the then dominant view in Soviet anthropology that the Siberian past (as that of any part of the world) was characterized by matriarchy and matrilineality. Instead, he suggests something like a duolineal totemic organization.

The other parts of the book contain theoretical contributions and case studies from Southeast Asia, Australia, and Africa. Many of them present careful revisions of Soviet representations of hunter-gatherers, without openly criticizing the dominant models. In any case, the volume stands out as a singular event in the history of Soviet hunter-gatherer studies. Instead of speculating which particular academic or political conditions might have enabled its publication, I just want to draw attention to the fact that the volume was published in Leningrad, which was also home to most of its contributors. In contrast, the standard works on *pervobytnoe obshchestvo* were generally produced by members of the Moscow Institute of Ethnography, which also housed the institute's section on theoretical problems.

One author of the volume, Vladimir R. Kabo, has before and since continued to express "dissident" ideas concerning the socioeconomic structure of hunters and gatherers much informed by the Western debate.[12] His major work on the topic *The Primordial Pre-Agricultural Community* (*Pervobytnaia dozemledel'cheskaia obshchina*), published in 1986, gives a good synthesis of his approach. One of Kabo's main arguments runs counter to the Soviet tradition of conceptualizing "primitive society." He contrasts the "gens" with the *obshchina* (literally, "community"). The *obshchina*, as used by Kabo, is close to the term "band," more common in English-language writings on the topic. Without denying the existence of lineages or exogamous clans, he regards the *obshchina* as the basic unit of primitive socioeconomic organization. Thus, Kabo comes close to positions of materialistic Russian ethnographers of prerevolutionary times, like Ziber (1883) and Maksimov (1913), who had little official recognition during Soviet times, as well as to Western concepts putting the "band" at the core of socioeconomic relations.

Kabo characterizes the community as follows (1986: 258–61): it consists of families, economic groups, and task groups; it is connected to a more or less defined territory. The number of the members of a given community depends on various factors: ecology, technology, and social relations. The community is adaptable to various ecological environments. The land and its resources are common property, while personal property rights are exercised on objects of individual use. The division of labor within the community is based on age and sex, with emerging individual specialization, while sharing distributes the products. Various forms of exchange connect different communities or parts of them.

However, Kabo's book does not deal with Siberian hunter-gatherers. Besides the fact that some of them do not fit his model, there appear to be additional reasons. At the time, Siberia was still under the almost exclusive domain of Soviet ethnographers and was thus also a stronghold of the concept of lineage-based (*rodovaia*) organization. A critical reevaluation of Siberian social organizations might have caused strong opposition to this work. But it should be recalled that there is an earlier article by Kabo, based on fieldwork among the Nivkhs, which can be seen as an application of his theory to a Siberian society (Kabo 1981). He demonstrates that even in this society famous for its lineage-based (*rodovoi*) kinship system, the local group (*obshchina*) is the dominating feature. Kabo's approach remained rather singular in Soviet anthropology. However, his major book on the topic wasn't published until 1986, when things slowly started to change. At that point, other books—with similar "hunter-gatherer topics"—started to appear; e.g., one of Kabo's students, Olga Artemova, published a study on the complex interplay between personality and social norms among Australian Aborigines (Artemova 1987), while Viktor Shnirel'man— who was to become a leading figure in post-Soviet hunter-gatherer research—presented a theoretically sophisticated treatise on the "origins of the producing economy," that is, he dealt with the "Neolithic revolution" which turned hunter-gatherers into farmers (Shnirel'man 1989). This leads us to the next chapter of Soviet/Western relations regarding hunter-gatherer studies.

After the Silence

Since the late 1980s, many of the conditions described above have changed. Western anthropologists are crowding the Siberian field, and Russian anthropologists seem to abandon old dogmas and to actively search for new approaches. Because a comprehensive survey of these ongoing activities is impossible in the confines of this chapter, I will use recent Conferences on Hunting and Gathering Societies (CHAGS) and the present volume as my major point of reference.

CHAGS 6 at Fairbanks in 1990 was the first of all conferences on hunting and gathering societies to include the active participation of Soviet scholars, most of them presenting on Siberian societies. Reportedly, there was a seventeen-member delegation from the Soviet Union; five of their papers were on Siberia, which constituted 6 percent of the overall number of presentations (Smith 1991: 73). Smith's "Western" conference report mentions two Soviet papers on Siberia by name and contains the general remark that "many of the Soviet papers were descriptive by contemporary Euro-American standards and reflected the isolation of Soviet scholarship" (Smith 1991: 73). Not surprisingly, the single Soviet/Siberian paper that made it into the published volume of the conference (Shnirelman 1994) addresses issues of the Western debate (such as "original affluence") to a larger degree than the other Soviet papers that were presented. Shnirel'man's (1990) own "Soviet" conference report is, by the way, unique in that it hardly mentions the Soviet presentations.

At CHAGS 7 in Moscow, there were more than twenty-five Siberian papers scheduled for presentation, although approximately ten presenters were unable to participate, mainly due to financial reasons. Most Russian papers dealt with Siberian hunter-gatherers and were presented by scholars with long experience in Siberian studies. However, for the first time there were also several papers by Western anthropologists based on fieldwork in Siberia. In the current volume, Anderson's article provides an excellent example of new approaches entering the field.

Giving a brief and general characterization of Western research in Siberia, studies of contemporary sociopolitical processes can be said to prevail (e.g., the analysis of indigenous political movements, of international dependencies, etc.). The traditional focus of Western anthropology on synchronic data observable in the present, and the dramatic social, economic, and political transitions that are taking place all over the former Soviet Union make this tendency understandable.

Russian research on Siberian hunter-gatherers is naturally more diversified. On the one hand, there is a continuation of traditional research topics, while on the other hand, contemporary issues that were once considered "sensitive" have become very prominent. So-called applied research, especially on ethnopolitics, demographics, and social planning, is flourishing. The articles by Murashko and Bogoiavlenskii (this volume) exemplify this tradition very well.

Areas of Russian research that were well represented at the CHAGS 6 and 7 conferences, as well as in the present volume, are world-view, mythology, and ritual. The case studies by Alekseenko (this volume), Batianova (this volume), Fedorova (this volume), and Kim (this volume) are excellent examples of this approach. Western and southern Siberia specifically have been covered well by detailed studies (see, e.g., Gemuev 1990; Gemuev and Sagalaev 1986). One important facet of the spiritual and ritual aspects of these societies is their complicated and multilayered structure. Contacts with other complex societies of Eurasia, migrations, and influences from world religions and other widespread belief systems date back long before the encounter with European colonialism. We are thus reminded that the mental expressions of hunter-gatherers cannot be reduced to Stone Age economics.

Future Prospects: Convergence or Conscious Maintenance of Differences?

In the original version of this essay (Schweitzer 1993), I had argued for the convergence of Western and Soviet/Russian approaches to hunter-gatherer studies in order to ensure better mutual understanding. While I still believe that such developments could be fruitful (see below), I also recognize that it is not very likely to happen. While it was naive to assume that long-standing research traditions would change overnight, on a more general level this recognition is reflected in the changing relations between Russia and the West since the early 1990s. Though the early postperestroika years were characterized by Western expectations that Russia as a whole (and Russian social science in particular) would swing over to Western models and by Russian fascination for everything bearing the label "Western" (signifying the antithesis to previous official models), things have changed considerably since then. Russia, recognizing that the West is not a homogeneous construct of theory and action, has overcome its simplistic adoration of Western ways of life and thought (sometimes even leading to pronounced anti-Western sentiments). At the same time, Western interest in Russia has declined over the years, especially since it has become obvious that renouncing dictatorial Soviet state socialism is not the same as embracing Western liberalism. In the fields of hunter-gatherer and Siberian studies, this has resulted, to a certain degree, in "business as usual" on both sides.

However, one significant development has occurred, namely, the resurgence of Siberian fieldwork by Western anthropologists. Over the last

ten years, more Western anthropologists have worked in Siberia than during all the decades following the Russian Revolution taken together. As of
1998, I am aware of at least ten Ph.D. dissertations based on Siberian work
in the field of social/ cultural anthropology that were defended at Western
universities during the 1990s. Although none of them has made issues of
hunter-gatherer research the focus of their attention, it will become
increasingly difficult for Western students of comparative hunter-gatherer
studies to ignore Siberian data. The requirements of Ph.D. fieldwork in
the Western (especially British) anthropological tradition, i.e., prolonged
field stays of a year or longer, differ from the Soviet/Russian model of several shorter (two to three months) visits, mainly during the summer.[13]
Without implying that it is necessarily better, the Western model of fieldwork can be expected to yield different results.

Despite my reservations, voiced above, against easy recipes of "meld-
ing" Western and Russian approaches, I will proceed with a few suggestions regarding research agendas, which might become influential
in one direction or the other; the selection is obviously noncompre-
hensive and largely determined by my personal interests and view-
points. Needless to say, I am not arguing for a critiqueless abandoning
of one or the other anthropological tradition, but for a widening of
both horizons.

Starting with what I consider the strong points of Soviet/Russian
research traditions in Siberian studies, I would like to pick "history." As
mentioned above, Soviet anthropology was considered a "historical science." Beyond the Marxist-Leninist notions of that dictum, this means
that there exist published ethnohistorical investigations for most areas of
Siberia. This research tradition can be traced back to at least the 1950s
and was generally conducted under the labels "ethnogenesis" (*etnogenez*)
and "ethnic history" (*etnicheskaia istoriia*). There has been recent criticism of this approach from within Russia (e.g., Shnirelman 1993), which
brings forward charges that these often nationalistically tainted reconstructions of a people's history were primarily intended to distract attention from the fact that the present political and other realities of this
particular group (as part of the Soviet Union) were far removed from the
romanticized past. Although I certainly agree with Shnirelman's critique
of the political misuses of this research, the "ethnogenetic approach" as
such should not be discredited. Among its positive aspects is that it calls
for a combination of several anthropological subdisciplines and neighboring disciplines. The articles by Chindina, Golovnev, and Kim (all this
volume) demonstrate the creative integration of archaeology, cultural
anthropology, linguistics, and oral history. Unlike the American tradition, in which the unity of the "four-field approach" is often more an ideological statement than a fact in actual research practice, the Russian

tradition of cross-disciplinary research is necessitated by historical questions that could not be answered otherwise.

Questions such as who a particular group of hunter-gatherers is and how they became who they are have become crucial in recent theoretical clashes within the hunter-gatherer debate. While the interpretations of historical information continue to be hotly disputed,[14] most scholars will probably agree that the use of history has become inevitable in hunter-gatherer research. In the case of Siberia, there is not only a rich legacy of work already conducted by Russian and Soviet scholars, but also an extremely vast record of written sources, dating back to the sixteenth century in the case of Russian sources, and even much further in the case of Chinese and Mongolian sources. Thus, Siberia offers unique possibilities, since the historical study of hunter-gatherers can be pushed further back than in many other regions of the world.

Due to the multitude of research perspectives and agendas that have informed recent Western anthropological studies, it is decisively more difficult to reasonably discuss Western approaches that could or should be applied to Siberian studies. Since Soviet/Russian anthropology is less specialized and diversified than its Western counterpart, certain subfields probably have not developed due to limited resources. In restricting myself to "classical fields" of anthropology, the insufficient development of Siberian studies of kinship and political organization is noteworthy. While in Western anthropology the fields of kinship and studies of political organization have been viable and dynamic throughout most of the twentieth century, early Soviet anthropology was satisfied with the framework provided by Lewis Henry Morgan in the 1870s. In the case of kinship studies, this meant that the statement that a certain people uses a classificatory kinship terminology was often considered sufficient. Consequently, the elaborate terminology of Western kinship studies had no Russian equivalent.

In the late 1960s and early 1970s, a new generation of Soviet anthropologists attempted a new look at kinship, providing thereby a more refined terminology, new schemes of the evolution of kinship terminology, and better ways of representing them. However, the facts that these new approaches have been infrequently applied to Siberia (with the exception of Chlenov 1973, 1978 and some reports by younger scholars, published in "gray literature") and that the focus has been rather on kinship terminology than on kinship as a complex set of concepts and practices leaves much to be done. Political anthropology emerged very late in the Soviet branch of the discipline and was largely restricted to African studies (e.g., Kubbel' 1988). Only recently have Russian anthropologists—beyond the analysis of current political affairs—turned to closer examinations of issues of "power" in Siberian societies (e.g., V. Popov

1996). Kinship and power in their past and present expressions among Siberian hunter-gatherers, and in their interrelations with other socio-cultural domains, certainly deserve more attention in the future.

In addition, there are a number of general characteristics of Siberian societies that could influence the overall tenor of hunter-gatherer debates, no matter if conducted within Western or Russian research traditions. For example, the fact—once lamented by Murdock—that many Siberian peoples have fully or partially adopted reindeer-herding offers a variety of important research agendas. The questions why and how hunter-gatherers become pastoralists, how hunter-gatherers and pastoralists interact, how they differ, etc., are important enough to pose, even if they cannot be answered in a straightforward way. Another category of hunter-gatherers, excluded by Murdock from his *Man the Hunter* survey, are seasonally sedentary sea mammal hunters and fishermen. In recent years, Western scholars have placed much research attention on the "otherness" of these hunter-gatherers in contrast with nomadic foragers. The Far Eastern part of Siberia in particular offers in this respect extensive comparative research opportunities. For example, the specialized fishermen of aboriginal Kamchatka, the Itel'mens, contrasted vividly with those from the Canadian Northwest Coast in their social and economic organization despite similar ecological conditions.

The latter point is directly related to the issue of "complex hunter-gatherers." While the original formulation of the concept of two distinct types of hunter-gatherers ("lower" vs. "higher hunters"—Grosse 1896) was largely ignored by the English-language literature of the 1960s and 1970s, Soviet anthropology continued to operate with this concept (Shnirelman 1992). Today, Western anthropology seems to have adopted various bipartite conceptualizations of hunter-gatherers (e.g., Begler 1978; Woodburn 1980; Testart 1982; Price and Brown 1985). As most Siberian hunting and gathering societies can be characterized as "complex," our presently insufficient understanding of complex hunter-gatherers could be greatly enhanced by more research in Siberia.

Thus, it becomes evident that the inclusion of Siberian peoples into a global sample of hunter-gatherers has a number of conceptual advantages to offer, in addition to moving beyond the textbook stereotype that hunter-gatherers are an African phenomenon.

Finally, in addition to the possibilities outlined above, there is clearly the option—proposed by David Anderson in the context of "knowing the land" on Taimyr—that "the heuristic vessel of The Hunter is best set aside" (Anderson, this volume). Not only does Anderson's case study provide convincing region-specific reasons for doing so, but it has implications for other areas of Siberia and beyond. To a certain degree, his proposal could be seen as a call for adopting a Russian/Soviet terminology, which—as we have seen—rarely applied the concept "hunter-gatherers" to Siberia. However, it seems obvious that such a conclusion does not make more than superficial sense, if only for the reason that Anderson's dismissal of ethnic categories for understanding environmental relations sharply contradicts Russian/Soviet anthropological practice. Instead, I want to use his argument as a reminder that there is more to be done than "business as usual" and "making approaches compatible." There is clearly a need for new conceptual tools and perspectives, inside and outside of Siberia. Part of the task is to question whether our core anthropological categories enable us to understand increasingly complex relations, or whether they just obstruct our view. This exploration applies as well to the term "hunter-gatherer," even in a volume that carries this very notion in its title.

Notes

I would like to thank Megan Biesele, Evgenii Golovko, Igor Krupnik, Igor Osipov, Petra Rethmann, Nikolai Ssorin-Chaikov, and Nikolai Vakhtin for valuable comments on an earlier draft. Stacie McIntosh provided much needed editorial assistance.

1. Actually, the volume resulting from CHAGS 6 (held in Fairbanks, Alaska, in 1990; Burch and Ellanna 1994) was the first to contain an article on Siberia (Shnirelman 1994). The current volume contains nine articles on Siberia.

2. In the following, "Western anthropology" will serve as a convenient shorthand label for English-language anthropology. Other traditions of Western anthropology I am familiar with, such as French- and German-language contributions, fit into the overall pattern of what will be said below, although significant differences—which are beyond the scope of this chapter—with English-language contributions exist.

3. See Krupnik (1998) on the transnational, collaborative aspect of this venture.

4. At the same time, translations of relevant Soviet works into English, such as A. Popov's famous *The Nganassan* (1966), which contains detailed information about hunting techniques and technologies, were entirely neglected. Strangely enough, in 1987, after twenty years of neglect by scholars of the neoevolutionistic persuasion, an "evolutionistic" book appeared that used Popov's materials for one of its case studies (Johnson and Earle 1987).

5. Official Soviet postwar attitudes can be subdivided into two distinct phases: before the mid-1960s, when access to the country and to information about it was severely limited, and after the mid-1960s, when access became partially possible. In this context, it is interesting to note that Moscow hosted the Seventh International Congress of Anthropological and Ethnological Sciences in 1963, during which many Western anthropologists visited the Soviet Union for the first time. Even if the Congress itself did not contribute to a change of attitudes, it was at least an indicator of such changes.

6. Other approaches to the subject, such as Eleanor Leacock's critical ethnohistoric inquiries, would thus have been possible within the given research possibilities in Siberia at the time. However, Leacock's approach was rather marginal than mainstream within the overall picture of Western hunter-gatherer research.

7. Ernest Gellner has suggested to translate *pervobytnoe obshchestvo* as "primordial community" (Gellner 1988: 19). While I agree with his argument that the Russian term denotes a condition, rather than a residual negative category or a doctrine, I believe that the alternative suggested by him is likely to cause other misunderstandings.

8. Evidently, there was and continues to be a significant difference in how Soviet/Russian and Western readers understood such passages. Soviet readers typically ignored the unavoidable "party-line jargon" of such official statements and focused their attention on the few pages or paragraphs that contained the "real" information. Western readers, however, tended to take the compulsory confirmations of dogmas too seriously; thus, their attention was distracted from the "real" content, which might contain new and provocative information and interpretation.

9. Due to limited time and space, this characterization of Soviet anthropology has to remain oversimplified, although I am aware of the existing variability even prior to *glasnost* and *perestroika*.

10. In this context, the extensive Soviet usage of the concept of "survivals" (*perezhitki*) deserves to be mentioned. Survivals are cultural elements considered to be remnants of a past social formation and were utilized in reconstructing the local phases of general social evolution.

11. See Rumiantsev (1987: 115–17) for a critique of Kabo's use of the concept of the "original affluent society."

12. See Kabo (1983; 1985) for English-language versions of his main arguments.

13. Long-term "stationary fieldwork" was an intrinsic component of early Soviet anthropology, under the leadership of Vladimir Bogoraz and Lev Shternberg. After World War II, this practice was abandoned. Obviously, financial and administrative factors had their role in this development (research institutes had to be staffed during the academic year, and repeated two-month trips were easier to accommodate within yearly budgets). To my knowledge, however, detailed research on the subject has not been conducted (*pace* the short note by Llobera [1977] with the promising title "Soviet Anthropology and Fieldwork").

14. For example, a "revisionist" protagonist of the "Great Kalahari Debate," Edwin Wilmsen, interprets the results of extensive historical research as calling for the abandonment of the category of "hunter-gatherers," as a Eurocentric ahistorical construct (Wilmsen 1989). Solway and Lee (1990) make a radically different point by using similar historical sources.

References

Alekseenko, E. A. 1972. "K voprosu o roli faktora rodstva v sotsial'noi zhizni ketov." In *Okhotniki, sobirateli, rybolovy. Problemy sotsial'no- ekonomicheskikh otnoshenii v dozemledel'cheskom obshchestve*. A. M. Reshetov, ed. 172–86. Leningrad: Nauka.

Artemova, O. Iu. 1987. *Lichnost' i sotsial'nye normy v ranne-pervobytnoi obshchine*. Moscow: Nauka.

Begler, E. B. 1978. "Sex, Status and Authority in Egalitarian Societies." *American Anthropologist* 80: 571–88.

Bogoras, W. 1904–09. *The Chukchee*. Publications of the Jesup North Pacific Expedition; 7. Leiden: E. J. Brill.

_____. 1910. *Chukchee Mythology*. Publications of the Jesup North Pacific Expedition; 8(1)—Memoir of the American Museum of Natural History New York; 12. Leiden: E. J. Brill.

_____. 1913. *The Eskimo of Siberia*. Publications of the Jesup North Pacific Expedition; 8(3)—Memoir of the American Museum of Natural History New York; 12. Leiden: E. J. Brill.

Bromlei, Iu. V., ed. 1982. *Etnos v doklassovom i ranneklassovom obshchestve*. Moscow: Nauka.

_____. 1986. *Istoriia pervobytnogo obshchestva. Epokha pervobytnoi rodovoi obshchiny*. Moscow: Nauka.

Burch, E. S., Jr., and L. J. Ellanna, eds. 1994. *Key Issues in Hunter-Gatherer Research*. Explorations in Anthropology. Oxford: Berg.

Chlenov, M. A. 1973. "K kharakteristike sotsial'noi organisatsii aziatskikh eskimosov." Paper presented at the Ninth International Congress of Anthropological and Ethnological Sciences, Chicago, 1973.

_____. 1978. "Geography of Kinship Systems of the Peoples of Siberia and the Soviet Far East." *Problems of the Contemporary World* 72: 161–69.

Coon, C. S. 1971. *The Hunting Peoples*. Boston, Mass.: Little, Brown.

Czaplicka, M. A. 1914. *Aboriginal Siberia: A Study in Social Anthropology*. Oxford: Oxford University Press.

Damas, D., ed. 1969. *Contributions to Anthropology: Band Societies*. Bulletin; 230. Ottawa: National Museums of Canada.

Donner, K., ed. 1933. *Ethnological Notes about the Yenisey-Ostyak (in the Turukhansk Region)*. Mémoires de le Société Finno-ougrienne; 66. Helsinki: Suomalais-ugrilainen Seura.

Engels, F. 1972. *The Origin of the Family, Private Property and the State*. With an introduction and notes by Eleanor Burke Leacock. Trans. Alec West. New York: International Publishers.

Findeisen, H. 1929. *Reisen und Forschungen in Nordostsibirien. Skizzen aus dem Leben der Jenissejostjaken*. Berlin.

Forde, C. D. 1934. *Habitat, Economy and Society: A Geographical Introduction to Ethnology*. London: Methuen.

Gellner, E. 1988. *State and Society in Soviet Thought*. Explorations in Social Structures. Oxford: Basil Blackwell.

Gemuev, I. N. 1990. *Mirovozzrenie mansi: Dom i Kosmos*. Novosibirsk: Nauka.

Gemuev, I. N., and A. M. Sagalaev. 1986. *Religiia naroda mansi. Kul'tovye mesta (XIX–nachalo XX v.)*. Novosibirsk: Nauka.

Grosse, E. 1896. *Die Formen der Familie und die Formen der Wirthschaft*. Freiburg i. B.: Akademische Verlagsbuchhandlung von J. C. B. Mohr.

Hahn, E. 1891. "Waren die Menschen der Urzeit zwischen der Jägerstufe und der Stufe des Ackerbaues Nomaden?" *Das Ausland* 64: 481–87.

Hallowell, A. I. 1926. "Bear Ceremonialism in the Northern Hemisphere." *American Anthropologist (n.s.)* 28: 1–175.

Harva, U. 1938. *Die religiösen Vorstellungen der Altaischen Völker*. FF Communications; 125. Helsinki.

Ingold, T. 1986. "Hunting, Sacrifice and the Domestication of Animals." In *The Appropriation of Nature: Essays on Human Ecology and Social Relations*. 243–76. Manchester: Manchester University Press.

_____. 1988. "Notes on the Foraging Mode of Production." In *Hunters and Gatherers: History, Evolution and Social Change*. T. Ingold, D. Riches, and J. Woodburn, eds. 269–85. New York: Berg.

Jochelson, W. 1905–08. *The Koryak*. Publications of the Jesup North Pacific Expedition; 6(1–2)—Memoir of the American Museum of Natural History New York; 13. Leiden: E. J. Brill.

———. 1910–26. *The Yukaghir and the Yukaghirized Tungus*. Publications of the Jesup North Pacific Expedition; 9—Memoir of the American Museum of Natural History New York. Leiden: E. J. Brill.

Johnson, A. W., and T. Earle. 1987. *The Evolution of Human Societies: From Foraging Groups to Agrarian State*. Stanford, Cal.: Stanford University Press.

Kabo, V. R. 1981. "Obshchina i rod u nivkhov." In *Puti razvitiia Avstralii i Okeanii. Istoriia, ekonomika, etnografiia*. K. V. Malakhovskii, ed. 198–219. Moscow: Nauka.

———. 1983. "Society and Culture of Hunters and Gatherers: The Common and the Specific." In *Studies in Ethnography and Anthropology: Part 2*. 32–38. Moscow: USSR Academy of Sciences.

———. 1985. "The Origins of the Food-Producing Economy." *Current Anthropology* 26: 601–6.

———. 1986. *Pervobytnaia dozemledel'cheskaia obshchina*. Moscow: Nauka.

Keenan, J. 1977. "The Concept of the Mode of Production in Hunter-Gatherer Societies." In *The Anthropology of Pre-Capitalist Societies*. J. S. Kahn and J. R. Llobera, eds. 2–21. London: Macmillan.

Kelly, R. L. 1995. *The Foraging Spectrum: Diversity in Hunter-Gatherer Lifeways*. Washington, D.C.: Smithsonian Institution Press.

Kent, S., ed. 1996. *Cultural Diversity among Twentieth-Century Foragers: An African Perspective*. Cambridge: Cambridge University Press.

Khlobystin, L. P. 1972. "Problemy sotsiologii neolita Severnoi Evrazii." In *Okhotniki, sobirateli, rybolovy. Problemy sotsial'no-ekonomicheskikh otnoshenii v dozemledel'cheskom obshchestve*. A. M. Reshetov, ed. 26–42. Leningrad: Nauka.

Khomich, L. V. 1972. "Nekotorye osobennosti khoziaistva i kul'tury lesnykh nentsev." In *Okhotniki, sobirateli, rybolovy. Problemy sotsial'no- ekonomicheskikh otnoshenii v dozemledel'cheskom obshchestve*. A. M. Reshetov, ed. 199–214. Leningrad: Nauka.

Koppers, W. 1915–16. "Die ethnologische Wirtschaftsforschung. Eine kritisch-historische Studie." *Anthropos* 10/11: 611–51; 971–1079.

Kosven, M. O. 1953. *Ocherki istorii pervobytnoi kul'tury*. Moscow: Izdatel'stvo Akademii nauk SSSR.

Kovalevskii, M. M. 1906. *Rodovoi byt*. Moscow.

Kropotkin, P. 1902. *Mutual Aid: A Factor of Evolution*. London: William Heinemann.

Krupnik, I. I. 1998. "Jesup Genealogy: Intellectual Partnership and Russian-American Cooperation in Arctic/North Pacific Anthropology. Part I. From the Jesup Expedition to the Cold War, 1897–1948." *Arctic Anthropology* 35(2): 199–226.

Kubbel', L. E. 1988. *Ocherki potestarno-politicheskoi etnografii*. Moscow: Nauka.

Laufer, B. 1902. *The Decorative Art of the Amur Tribes*. Memoirs of the American Museum of Natural History; 7(1). Leiden: E. J. Brill.

Lee, R. B. 1980. "Existé"il un mode de production 'fourrageur'?" *Anthropologie et Sociétés* 4: 59–74.

Lee, R. B., and I. DeVore, eds. 1968. *Man the Hunter*. New York: Aldine Publishing Company.

Leeds, A. 1965. "Reindeer Herding and Chukchi Social Institutions." In *Man, Culture and Animals: The Role of Animals in Human Ecological Adjustments*. A. Leeds and A. P. Vayda, eds. 87–128. Washington, D.C.: American Association for the Advancement of Science.

Lehtisalo, T. 1932. *Beiträge zur Kenntnis der Renntierzucht bei den Juraksamojeden*. Instituttet for Sammenlignende Kulturforskning, Serie B: Skrifter; 16. Oslo: H. Aschehoug & Co.

Liapunova, R. G. 1972. "K voprosu ob obshchestvennom stroe aleutov serediny XVIII v." In *Okhotniki, sobirateli, rybolovy. Problemy sotsial'no- ekonomicheskikh otnoshenii v dozemledel'cheskom obshchestve.* A. M. Reshetov, ed. 215–27. Leningrad: Nauka.

Libby, D. 1960. "Three Hundred Years of Chukchi Ethnic Identity." In *Men and Cultures: Selected Papers of the Fifth International Congress of Anthropological and Ethnological Sciences, Philadelphia, September 1–9, 1956.* A. F. C. Wallace, ed. 298–304. Philadelphia: University of Pennsylvania Press.

Llobera, J. R. 1977. "Soviet Anthropology and Fieldwork." *Man (N.S.)* 12: 177–78.

Lowie, R. H. 1934. *An Introduction to Cultural Anthropology.* New York: Farrar & Rinehart.

Luxemburg, R. 1925. *Einführung in die Nationalökonomie.* Paul Levi, ed. Berlin.

Maksimov, A. N. 1913. *Teoriia rodovogo byta.* Moscow.

Murdock, G. P. 1938. *Our Primitive Contemporaries.* New York: MacMillan.

_____. 1968. "The Current Status of the World's Hunting and Gathering Peoples." In *Man the Hunter.* R. B. Lee and I. DeVore, eds. 13–20. New York: Aldine Publishing Company.

Nioradze, G. 1925. *Der Schamanismus bei den sibirischen Völkern.* Stuttgart: Strecker und Schröder.

Ohlmarks, Å. 1939. *Studien zum Problem des Schamanismus.* Lund and Copenhagen: C. W. K. Gleerup and Ejnar Munksgaard.

Oswalt, W. H. 1973. *Habitat and Technology: The Evolution of Hunting.* New York: Holt, Rinehart and Winston.

Pershits, A. I., A. L. Mongait, and V. P. Alekseev. 1982. *Istoriia pervobytnogo obshchestva.* Moscow: Vysshaia shkola.

Petrova-Averkieva, J. P. 1980. "Der Neoevolutionismus in der gegenwärtigen Ethnographie der USA." In *Kultur und Ethnos. Zur Kritik der bürgerlichen Auffassungen über die Rolle der Kultur in Geschichte und Gesellschaft.* B. Weissel, ed. 39–57. Berlin: Akademie-Verlag.

Popov, A. A. 1966. *The Nganassan: The Material Culture of the Tavgi Samoyeds.* Bloomington: Indiana University Press.

Popov, V. A., ed. 1996. *Simvoly i atributy vlasti. Genezis. Semantika. Funktsii.* St. Petersburg: Muzei antropologii i etnografii im. Petra Velikogo (Kunstkamera) Rossiiskoi Akademii nauk.

Price, T. D., and J. A. Brown, eds. 1985. *Prehistoric Hunter-Gatherers: The Emergence of Social Complexity.* Studies in Archaeology. Orlando, Fla.: Academic Press.

Radin, P. 1932. *Social Anthropology.* McGraw-Hill Publications in Sociology. New York: McGraw-Hill.

Reshetov, A. M., ed. 1972. *Okhotniki, sobirateli, rybolovy. Problemy sotsial'no- ekonomicheskikh otnoshenii v dozemledel'cheskom obshchestve.* Leningrad: Nauka.

Rumiantsev, A. M. 1987. *Pervobytnyi sposob proizvodstva. Politiko- ekonomicheskie ocherki.* Moscow: Nauka.

Schweitzer, P. P. 1993. "Rediscovering a Continent: Siberian Peoples and the Hunter-Gatherer Debate." Paper presented at the Seventh International Conference on Hunting and Gathering Societies (CHAGS 7) in Moscow, Russia, August 1993.

Service, E. R. 1966. *The Hunters.* Foundations of Modern Anthropology Series. Englewood Cliffs, N.J.: Prentice-Hall.

Shimkin, B. D. 1939. "A Sketch of the Ket, or Yenisei 'Ostyak.'" *Ethnos* 3/4: 147–76.

Shirokogoroff, S. M. 1929. *Social Organization of the Northern Tungus.* Shanghai: Commercial Press.

_____. 1935. *Psychomental Complex of the Tungus.* London: Kegan Paul, Trench, Trubner.

Shnirel'man, V. A. 1989. *Vozniknovenie proizvodiashchego khoziaistva: Problema pervichnykh i vtorichnykh ochagov.* Moscow: Nauka.

_____. 1990. "Ot edinstva k mnogoobraziiu: smena paradigm v izuchenii obshchestv okhotnikov, rybolovov i sobiratelei." *Sovetskaia etnografiia* 6: 135–43.

Shnirelman, V. A. 1992. "Complex Hunter-Gatherers: Exception or Common Phenomenon?" *Dialectical Anthropology* 17: 183–96.

_____. 1993. "Archaeology and Ethnopolitics: Why Soviet-Archaeologists Were So Involved in Ethnogenetic Studies." Paper presented at the International Symposium "Interpreting the Past," Israel, 30 May–4 June 1993.

_____. 1994. "*Cherchez le Chien*: Perspectives on the Economy of the Traditional Fishing-Oriented People of Kamchatka." In *Key Issues in Hunter-Gatherer Research*. E. S. Burch, Jr. and L. J. Ellanna, eds. 169–88. Oxford: Berg.

Smith, E. A. 1991. "The Current State of Hunter-Gatherer Studies." *Current Anthropology* 32: 72–75.

Solway, J. S., and R. B. Lee. 1990. "Foragers, Genuine or Spurious? Situating the Kalahari San in History." *Current Anthropology* 31: 109–46.

Stadling, J. 1912. *Shamanismen i norra Asien. Några drag ur shamanväsendets utveckling bland naturfolken i Sibirien*. Populära etnologiska skrifter; 7. Stockholm: Cederquists Grafiska Aktiebolag.

Steinitz, W. 1938. "Totemismus bei den Ostjaken in Sibirien." *Ethnos* 3: 125–40.

Steward, J. H. 1936. "The Economic and Social Basis of Primitive Bands." In *Essays in Anthropology. Presented to A. L. Kroeber in Celebration of His Sixtieth Birthday, June 11, 1936*. R. H. Lowie, ed. 331–50. Berkeley: University of California Press.

Taksami, C. M. 1972. "Okhotniki, rybolovy i sobirateli Amurskogo basseina i Sakhalina." In *Okhotniki, sobirateli, rybolovy. Problemy sotsial'no- ekonomicheskikh otnoshenii v dozemledel'cheskom obshchestve*. A. M. Reshetov, ed. 187–98. Leningrad: Nauka.

Testart, A. 1982. "The Significance of Food Storage among Hunter-Gatherers: Residence Patterns, Population Densities, and Social Inequalities." *Current Anthropology* 23: 523–37.

Vasilevich, G. M. 1972. "Nekotorye voprosy plemeni i roda u evenkov." In *Okhotniki, sobirateli, rybolovy. Problemy sotsial'no-ekonomicheskikh otnoshenii v dozemledel'cheskom obshchestve*. A. M. Reshetov, ed. 160–71. Leningrad: Nauka.

Wilmsen, E. N. 1989. *Land Filled with Flies: A Political Economy of the Kalahari*. Chicago: University of Chicago Press.

Wissler, C. 1929. *An Introduction to Social Anthropology*. American Social Science Series. New York: Henry Holt.

Woodburn, J. 1980. "Hunters and Gatherers Today and Reconstruction of the Past." In *Soviet and Western Anthropology*. E. Gellner, ed. 95–117. London: Duckworth.

Ziber, N. I. 1883. *Ocherki pervobytnoi ekonomicheskoi kul'tury*. St. Petersburg.

Zolotarev, A. M. 1937. "The Bear Festival of the Olcha." *American Anthropologist* 39: 113–30.

PART I

WARFARE AND CONFLICT RESOLUTION

Chapter 2

VISIONS OF CONFLICT, CONFLICTS OF VISION AMONG CONTEMPORARY DENE THA

Jean-Guy A. Goulet

Introduction

This essay concerns the ways in which anthropologists propose different explanations for acts of aggression or the lack thereof among Northern Athapaskans or Dene without paying sufficient attention to the ways in which Dene themselves account for their behavior and that of fellow Dene.[1]

In Honigmann's summary of anthropological research in the Canadian subarctic, we are told that Athapaskan populations in the region, like their Algonkian counterpart, "normally controlled the release of hostility" and "vigorously checked any direct aggressive behavior, verbal or physical, toward other people" (1981: 736). The majority of authors attribute this general suppression of aggression in interpersonal relations to the respect for personal autonomy, a core value of subarctic indigenous populations. Hallowell (1938) and Slobodin (1960) express a dissenting view. They attribute the absence of aggression to fear, rather than to regard for personal autonomy. This is also the view with Helm (1961: 87) who writes that "the general diffidence and restraint exhibited in interpersonal contacts spring from a fear of conflict or unpleasantness." Helm (1961: 176) further remarks that "the respect for the autonomy of the other is, of course, ultimately for the individual a self-protective device, for to infringe on another's autonomy is to call down hostility upon one's self." According to this view, "pervasive anxiety" and "social distrust" characterize life in subarctic communities because individuals are constantly "afraid of what might happen should they infringe on the right of somebody else" (Honigmann 1981: 737).

Faced with these two conflicting visions regarding the possible cause for the suppression of aggression among indigenous populations in the Canadian subarctic, Honigmann suggests we simply conclude that fear motivates people to refrain from aggression, while "from an outside vantage point, Indians showed regard for one another's feelings" (1981: 737). This conclusion is unsatisfactory. It fails to consider the possibility that both fear of retaliation and regard for personal autonomy motivate Dene not to intervene in each other's life, and more importantly, it falls short of seriously considering the manner in which Dene actually construct their accounts of nonaggression and of aggression.

Before turning to such accounts we must take note of the fact that students of subarctic communities consistently report that after heavy drinking "normal" controls of aggressive behavior rapidly dissolve to give way to "flamboyant emotionality, ready expression of anger, and loss of other inhibitions" (Honigmann 1981: 737).[2] Under these conditions violent behavior frequently leads to serious injuries, attempted homicides, and even death, for which individuals consistently disclaim responsibility.

In its own brief to the Alberta Task Force on the Criminal Justice System, the Dene Tha Women's Society reports that "wife abuse on the Assumption reserve is very common. It is sometimes very violent. Women get slapped, punched, kicked, raped, beaten at times so badly, they have to be medivaced [sic] to High Level" (1990: 2), the predominantly Euro-Canadian town 80 kilometers east of Chateh. This abuse comes consistently from the hands of drunken husbands who would never be aggressive to their wives when sober. Similarly, Dene Tha men regularly suffer serious injuries at the hands of other drunken men. The sight one early morning of Peter, with a broken tooth, a bleeding nose, and a swollen black eye, staring out at empty space and sitting on the living room floor of his cousin's house, surrounded by his young (two- to five-year-old) nephews and nieces, or that of Luke rushed to the hospital with a severe abdominal wound following a shooting incident, come to mind. I also recall the conversation with Joan, as she wandered aimlessly on the road, her face swollen and her nose bleeding, telling me that her drunken daughters had beaten her up. There are many other similar disturbing recollections.

All across the subarctic, individuals and communities seem to alternate between two conflicting visions of life: one according to which they profess the highest regard for each other's autonomy, the other according to which they become each other's fiercest aggressors or unfortunate victims. The change involved is so drastic, "the wildness and chaos of uninhibited spree drinking" so "dismaying and terrifying," writes Brody, that "possibly this is something that has to be seen to be believed" (1981: 110). As noted by Savishinsky (1982: 118), young children "observe all aspects of drunken comportment, and they therefore become accustomed to its characteristics long before they begin to fully participate in drinking as teenagers."

This cycle of peaceful coexistence and open aggression against each other calls for an explanation. MacAndrew and Edgerton were the first to suggest that Native North American populations had learned to structure drunkenness in cultural terms after "the coming of the white man" (1969: 100). In the same vein, Honigmann (1981: 737) believes that Athapaskans and Algonkians give expression to their animosity and behave aggressively when drunk because they have come to "know that, within limits, drunkenness made such behavior expectable and socially excusable." Under such circumstances, it would seem that neither the respect for each other's autonomy nor the fear of others is sufficient to prevent acts of aggression.

Why is this so? Is violence random? Are there likely targets of a drunken individual's animosity? To answer these questions we must examine closely the relationships between the circumstances preceding acts of aggression and the environment in which they are played out. As this essay will demonstrate, we then discover that drunken Dene Tha choose the appropriate moment to direct their aggression against those whom they consider to be the legitimate objects of their anger. Dene Tha do so because although they fear the aggression of others, they also wish to retaliate against those who, they feel, have interfered with their goals.

This chapter therefore argues that under the cover of drunkenness individuals find the socially accepted conditions allowing them to engage in acts of aggression that infringe, within limits, each other's autonomy in a socially expected and permissible way. The discussion is based on numerous observations and on an examination of accounts of aggression among the Dene Tha, a Northern Athapaskan population of northwestern Alberta, Canada.[3] The argument proceeds in five steps. First, I show how Dene Tha social life alternates between the reliable, tranquil, often cheerful composure of adults and teenagers and the distressing, brutal outbursts of the same individuals who later claim they are not accountable for their actions since they did not know what they were doing when drunk. Secondly, I point out how the value of autonomy pervades Dene Tha socialization, and I link this form of socialization to the Dene strategy of withdrawal when faced with drunken individuals who are out of control. Thirdly, I examine another Dene Tha strategy of social control, that of calling upon non-Native third parties to check the violent behavior of a drunken spouse, kinsman, or relative. This strategy can also be seen to respect the Dene commitment not to interfere directly with someone else's actions. Fourthly, I document how Dene Tha weigh the consequences of interfering with someone else's behavior, precisely because they fear to become the object of that person's retaliation when that person becomes drunk. I also show how retaliation against abusive individuals proceeds under the cover of drunkenness. While individuals involved in acts of aggression may deny they knew what they were doing when drunk, in many cases, one cannot help but think with Lithman (1979: 119) "that people drink because they want to do what they can do when they are drunk." And lastly, I briefly focus on the Dene Tha notion of *echint'e*, "a power," that can be used by individuals to secretly retaliate against their enemies and cause them misfortune, and even death. While this notion instills deep fear among Dene Tha, I indicate how it also provides them with an interpretive tool to account for extreme cases of aggression by drunken relatives.

Dene Tha Accounts of Aggression

To read generalizations about patterns of behavior of distant "others" is not the same as coming face to face with individuals whose behavior fully fits the pattern. When I initiated fieldwork among the Dene Tha in 1980, two strongly built Dene Tha men in their early thirties came to visit me and have tea early in an afternoon. It was our first meeting as I was in the initial weeks of my first six-month long period of fieldwork. Full of laughter, they introduced themselves as very best friends and sat next to each other, shoulder to shoulder, on the living room sofa. I could not help but focus on the bluish, bruised face of one of the men, whose nose was covered with a wide bandage. The man immediately and spontaneously explained his recent injuries, telling me first that they had been inflicted by his friend sitting next to him. At this mention, both men immediately laughed and nudged each other with their elbows as they insisted they could not get angry over this incident because the blow had been unintended. The circumstances were as follows. While at a drinking party, the victim's drunken friend—with a large piece of lumber in hand—had waited behind a door to smash in the face of a foe expected to walk across the threshold. However, it was the friend, also drunk, not the foe, who had entered the room. To everyone's surprise, the premeditated blow had hit the face of an intoxicated friend. As they told me about this turn of events, both men broke into laughter. The broken nose and bruised face were really nothing at all, they said. The victim reiterated that his friend did not know who he was when he was hit. Laughing again, both men repeated how much they enjoyed each other's company. When the two men eventually walked away, I doubted it was possible not to feel anger toward someone, albeit a friend, who had inflicted such serious injury upon oneself.

The two men's account of the event made it clear that this was not a case of random violence. The aggressor and the intended victim were known to each other and had scores to settle. While the two men would never fight it out when sober (Dene never do so), retaliation was due. The appropriate moment presented itself when the two enemies were drunk in the midst of a large party. The aggressor had waited behind a door to smash a large piece of lumber in the face of a known foe, also drunk, who was expected to walk across the threshold. As the man stood behind the door he thought that the legitimate target of his aggression would soon be in sight. While the blow did not fall on the anticipated victim, the aggressor knew all along that he would not be held accountable for his act of aggression. He could always claim, according to generally accepted Dene convention, that when drunk one does not know what one does.

There are, however, acts of violence that appear to be random. As the following case illustrates, these actions are not directed at anyone in particular and cannot be constructed as an act of retaliation. Parents of a teenage son came to visit me to discuss their son having to appear in court to face a charge of having shot and seriously injured his brother (MZS). One of the first things the mother said was: "They say our son shot him; but who would shoot his own brother. *No, he was drunk, he did not know what he was doing.*" The father continued saying that the boy had shot through a door not knowing he would hit or miss someone. "He is just a little boy, he doesn't know, he was drunk when it happened and he did not know," added the mother. The parents pointed out further circumstantial evidence that removed the blame from their son. The rifle used by their son was normally disassembled and unloaded under their bed, precisely to prevent any accident in the house. Their son, his brothers, and other friends had gathered in their house to drink. In the course of the night, the brother who was to be shot, took the rifle from under the bed, reassembled it, and loaded it. The son later took the gun to chase after another friend who was going around the house imitating a duck. In the excitement of the mock hunting expedition, a first shot went off in the air. The young man imitating the duck sped away. The second shot went through a door and seriously injured the brother who was in the room. But, the father insisted, "He didn't know his brother was there." When the son realized what he had done, he told his mother: "Mammy I did not know, I am very afraid, I was drunk." Having informed me of the case they left for the court hearing. A few hours later they returned elated with the news that their son had been set free, under probation.

A good judge, other Dene Tha commented, is "one who listens." Referring to the Euro-Canadian judge who was hearing the case described above, another Dene Tha said: "This judge doesn't get mad, he listens, and even when someone stabs someone else, he listens, he doesn't send him to jail. He gives someone many chances." The reference to someone stabbing someone else was to a recent case in which a woman had been acquitted of stabbing and wounding her husband with a pair of scissors when the two were drunk. According to the Dene Tha, this woman, as well as the young man who had inadvertently shot his brother, had to be released because they had not known what they were doing while drunk. Under such circumstances, as the Dene Tha reminded me again and again, one is not accountable for one's behavior, and therefore one should not be punished.

At some level people hold the view that if someone behaves improperly, there is no need for human punishment; life itself will mete out the suitable punishment at the appropriate time. This view is expressed in the following story incorporated by the Dene Tha band in its "Submission to the Task Force on the Criminal Justice System and Its Impact on the Indian and Metis People of Alberta": "A man was bit by a mosquito and sought revenge by gathering a whole bunch of them which he placed in a bag. In the winter, he released them in the cold, saying: '*Xont'e uh sade*: eat me now.' The mosquitoes all died. Next summer, the man went hunting and was found dead, without blood, in the bush." The story expresses the Dene Tha concept of justice, rendered by the word *tandi*. According to this concept "if someone commits a crime, s/he will suffer the consequences. Life itself has a way of establishing justice even for the smallest form of life" (Dene Tha Band of Assumption 1990: 22). This view, as the following observations will show, also informs the Dene Tha way of socializing children. Children are largely expected to learn to behave properly from the consequences of their own actions.

Autonomy and Noninterference

Students of the Dene have often commented on the fact that Dene expect learning to occur through observation rather than through instruction, an expectation that is consistent with their view that true knowledge is personal knowledge, a theme that goes hand in hand with the premium they place on nonintervention in the life of others (Scollon and Scollon 1979: 185–209; Ridington 1987: 25; 1988: 46; Rushforth 1992: 485–88; Watson and Goulet 1992: 224–27). In the literature, the use of the term "noninterference" to characterize Dene social life comes from the fact that anthropologists do not see Dene adults intervene in instances in which Euro-North Americans would do so: e.g., stopping a year-old child from approaching a broken window pane; taking a chainsaw and a new pair of gloves from a boy before he destroys them; taking a child bitten by a dog to the nursing station; snatching liquor away from young children who are drinking it and becoming drunk; removing from a community hall drunken men who interrupt the community dance; and so on. In each of these cases, to state that Dene behavior consists of noninterference is to describe them as *not* acting as we would act. To engage in this kind of description is to miss the point that in behaving as they do the Dene promote *their* own values and view of life: they consistently maximize the number of occasions in which one can learn by oneself and for oneself what it is to live competently an autonomous life. Hence, I suggest that anthropologists write about the Dene ethical principle of "personal responsibility for one's own life," where in the past they would have used the expression "noninterference." Since it is the Dene world that we strive to grasp, the onus is on us to write as much as possible in a manner that conveys their world-view and their ethos.

The right to one's autonomy and the obligation to respect that of others—that is the obligation not to diminish other people's ability to realize their goals—are opposite sides of the same coin. These principles are nurtured and respected throughout one's entire life. The respect for one's autonomy is experienced by the year-old child who moves toward a broken window, climbs up into a chair, moves its hand through the gaping hole, feels the cold outdoor air, and safely withdraws its hand without touching the window pane's jagged edges. All along, the child's parents and grandparents quietly observe as they carry on with their own activities, while I, not believing my eyes, silently cringe at the thought of an impending injury. In old age, the consideration for one's right to accomplish one's goals on one's own is experienced by people who in their seventies pull themselves up and climb aboard pickup trucks all by themselves—something that may take them several minutes to do as they pull themselves partially up, slip down, and pull themselves up again, sweating and breathing heavily in the process. As they do so, able-bodied adults casually carry on with their conversation in the vehicle, while I wonder if it would not be more respectful, and easier for everyone, to give the elderly person a helping hand.

The differences between my spontaneous view and that of the Dene Tha reflect our very different upbringing. According to the Dene Tha, to interfere with the child's exploration of its environment would violate its right and ability to pursue and achieve its goals. According to my point of view, to stop the child from approaching the broken window is to protect it from possible injury. I must, however, acknowledge that over the years the accidents and injuries that I expected in the course of the children's free-ranging exploration did not occur. This fact, I believe, accounts for the relaxed attitude of Dene Tha adults, who quietly and silently supervise their children in their activities. Dene Tha parents know that at a relatively early age children can handle knives, axes, and chainsaws without getting hurt. The children proceed with confidence in their exploration, secure in the knowledge that no one will interfere with their activity. According to the Dene Tha, to offer an elderly person a helping hand to get into a vehicle would be insulting, for it would imply that he or she cannot climb on board the vehicle on his or her own. According to my point of view, to offer a helping hand to the elderly person would signify respect. To the Dene Tha, however, to do so would take away from the elderly person the opportunity to act autonomously.

To Be a Responsible Parent and Child

Everywhere the ethical principle of personal responsibility for one's own life informs the way parents raise their children. While I often heard Dene Tha parents tell a child "don't do this!" or "leave that!" I have never seen a parent impose his or her will on a child or take something away from a child. In the eyes of the Dene Tha, to be a responsible parent is to act in the knowledge that one's children are responsible for *their* actions, and thus to interfere minimally with their decisions. This view informs the way Dene Tha parents let their children make decisions that non-Dene parents or professionals would never consider letting them make. When a six-year-old girl was bitten by a dog, I expressed to the parents my concern about rabies and suggested that their daughter be taken to the nursing station for examination and, possibly, vaccination. If they wished, I could take them in my vehicle. The parents listened. We sat in silence for a few minutes. The parents then told me that while they agreed with my recommendation, their daughter did not want to go. They could not and would not take her for medical attention against her will. As they said so, the girl looked at me with a smile. She knew that it was up to her to make up her mind, and that having done so, everyone would respect her decision. I was not convinced that this was the best course of action, but a week later the wound had healed properly, and the girl could be seen merrily playing with her siblings and cousins. In Dene social interaction generally, and in Dene socialization of children in particular, we do not encounter the open exercise of power understood as "getting another to do something that s/he would otherwise not do" (Stets 1995: 130).

To Be Responsible for Oneself and for Others

It is a basic premise of Dene thought that one learns from the hard lessons of life. It is from this perspective that we can appreciate the Dene Tha approval of John's conduct when the young man had let his young cousins get drunk, while he himself was deciding to sober up and give up drinking. In their eyes, to take the liquor away from the children would have been irresponsible. I had met John one morning as I was in search of someone to instruct me in Dene Dháh, the local Dene language. I had entered his house to find it empty except for himself, sitting on his bed, half drunk. Two empty whiskey bottles and a dozen bottles of beer were scattered around the floor. I sat down on the bed next to him and asked how he was. He replied that he was happy because he had decided to stop drinking. "When was that?" I asked. "Last night," he replied. John had been drinking with friends and had returned home in his car, with beer bottles and two bottles of whiskey left to drink. Thinking that drinking was bad and that he should quit, he had nevertheless kept on drinking in his room, where he silently observed his younger cousins, children of eight and ten years old, get drunk as they helped themselves to some of his liquor. As he kept thinking to himself that drinking was bad, he eventually decided to sober up and rid himself of the remaining liquor, which he poured outside the house, after which he fell asleep. He had awakened a few moments before my arrival and was now resting, happy with his decision to cease drinking.

As I listened to him I thought of the contradiction between his words and his behavior, between his opinion that drinking was bad and his letting his young cousins get drunk with his liquor. In my view, his responsibility would have been to take the liquor away from the children and prevent them from getting drunk. Intrigued by his attitude, I decided to find out from other Dene Tha what they thought of John's behavior. Without revealing John's identity, I informed Dene Tha friends of what I had seen and heard. I told them I was intrigued. "What was the man doing?" I asked. The Dene Tha friends immediately answered: "He was setting an example." I asked how this was so, and they said: "This is how you stop." In their view John had acted in the most responsible of manners: "He wants them [his young cousins] to see how it was with him when he was drinking. He wants them to take some of the medicine he had. It's up to this certain person to make their mind; no one is going to make their mind."

Since the decision to drink or not to drink is one's own responsibility, to take the liquor away from the children would have been to make that decision for them, a most irresponsible thing to do from the Dene Tha perspective. I commented that in my experience this was the biggest difference between a Euro-Canadian family and a Dene family. "In our families, we would just take the liquor away from the children," I said. The wife and husband immediately responded: "Yeah, just like the missionaries did with us." They looked at each other, surprised at having pronounced the same words at the same time. There was much excitement in their voices. To stop drinking as this man had done, without anyone telling him to do so, was to set an example: if one stopped to think about it, one could stop drinking. In the view of the Dene Tha, the mere fact that John was now living a sober life was telling others—including his cousins—that it was also possible for them to do so. Others could draw this lesson from their observation of John's behavior without his having to tell them so in so many words.

The respect for other people's choices and the responsibility for one's own well-being explain the preferred strategy of Dene Tha to simply withdraw when in the presence of someone drunk who threatens them. Once, at two o'clock in the morning, I met a five-year-old girl walking on the road away from her home. I asked her where she was going. She answered: "To my grandfather's place. My parents are drunk and fighting." She would return home to her parents when they had sobered up. On another occasion, I met all of the women and children of a family in the house of their neighbors, where they had spent the night. They explained that as the father and his friends were drinking in their home, they had preferred to leave until the men sobered up. Similarly, one summer, when a few drunks were disturbing a Prophet Dance performance involving over one hundred fifty sober Dene Tha, people did not confront them. Rather, they stopped dancing and sat by quietly as they looked at the drunks acting up around the ceremonial fire. Half an hour went by. The drunks appeared determined to stay. People decided to pick up their things and return home. People said: "They are bothering us, better go home."

In brief, what outsiders see as noninterference in other people's lives Dene see as preserving each other's ability to truly live one's life to the fullest extent possible. It is this deeply held attitude experienced over the entire course of one's life that shapes the typical Dene Tha strategies of social control when faced with disturbing and threatening drunken individuals. Dene Tha invoke the individual's responsibility for his or her own life to justify not interfering in that individual's life, even if he or she is drunk and prone to violence. The responsible course of action, then, is to avoid being injured by the drunken party and wait for the moment when the person returns to his or her normal self.

"Call the Police!": A Dene Strategy of Social Control

In the face of drunks who are disturbed and threatening, Dene Tha may simply avoid confrontation by withdrawing to a safer place. Yet Dene Tha may also call upon a non-Dene third party to intervene and remove the threatening individual from their midst. In Chateh, this third party is invariably the local, non-Native police officer from the Royal Canadian Mounted Police (R.C.M.P.), known locally as *dene kuelehi*, literally, "the person who puts one inside," a clear reference to one's imprisonment in the local holding tank or in regional prisons. In the eyes of the Dene Tha, arrest and imprisonment by the police is not seen as a punishment of the intoxicated individual, but rather as a means to temporarily protect oneself and/or others from someone whose mind is gone.

It is noteworthy that the person who makes the decision to call the police asks a third party to make the call. In the words of an adult student: "Even my mom tells me: 'Your dad's drunk! Call the cops!'" (Dene Tha Band of Assumption 1990: 8). Over the years, many families asked me to call the R.C.M.P. on their behalf to come and remove a drunken parent or child from their homes. Since I would not do so, parents or grandparents would then ask another household member to place the call.

Failing a third party to call the police, one must of course then do so oneself. This was the case with a Dene Tha woman who told me: "[My husband] said he would kill me. At three in the morning I ran at the cops just in socks. When he drinks he thinks he is a man, he does all kinds of crazy things." The cops came to her house and arrested the husband before he could hurt anyone. The next day the man returned home sober, his angry words and threats of the previous night completely gone. In a sense, his wife had protected him from himself. In the years I spent in Chateh, abused women who had called the police to remove their drunken husbands from their homes refused to bring charges lest their abusive husbands retaliate later with more mistreatment. Abusive husbands could nevertheless be charged and brought before the judge by police officers acting in the name of the Crown. The responsibility for the resulting imprisonment, if any, would then rest with a non-Dene.

Alcoholic beverages are readily available to the Dene Tha, and on any given evening as many as fifty or more individuals may be drunk, especially on weekends and on days following the arrival of a paycheck or a pension check. There are therefore numerous occasions on which non-Dene police officers are called to arrest Dene Tha who are drunk and who threaten their spouses or other household members. Since there are many such calls, and since there is a contingent of five R.C.M.P. officers stationed in Chateh, who are prepared to work 17 to 18 hours a day (Dene Tha Band of Assumption 1990: 7), the level of incarceration is high. Out of a population of approximately one thousand, the majority of which is under twenty years of age, the Dene Tha averaged six incarcerations per day in 1989, for a total of 1,392 imprisonments on reserve, and 803 off reserve (Dene Tha Band of Assumption 1990: 2). Of the 1,392 short-term imprisonments on reserve, 935 were alcohol related. In 1990 the local band reported 518 instances of on-reserve imprisonment, an average of 4.3 per day, in the first four months of that year, most of them alcohol related. These individuals are in the great majority males under forty years of age. It is they who appear predominantly in the daunting criminal statistics generated by the justice system.

In Chateh, as in many other American Indian communities, a number of factors account in part for this "alarming" rate of alcohol-related arrests (Mail 1980; Heath 1991: 37). Dene Tha indicated that drunken individuals were rare in Chateh before the mid-1960s when the construction of a road intended to facilitate oil and gas exploration in the region connected the reserve to the nearby town of High Level (80 kilometers east). This road made year-round travel to and from High Level possible. The High Level bars and liquor store became a regular destination of more and more Dene Tha under the age of forty. It is they, more often than any other group, who use the cover of drunkenness to act aggressively against others in the ways discussed in this chapter, and who benefit the most from the social convention that one is not accountable for actions committed when drunk. This has become more so after the sporadic drinking of the past, when people would brew their own liquor, gave way to the regular heavy drinking of contemporary reserve life.

Drinking periods are tied to availability of funds, an economic limitation noted by Medicine (1983), Leland (1976), and Waddell and Everett (1980). In Chateh, higher levels of drinking also varied according to the flow of cash in the community. Such were the days after men returned from the firefighting season, for instance. Dene Tha men observed that firefighting money "is for the fire water." They did not, however, spend all of their money on drink. When they returned from firefighting with their paychecks, they would typically buy gifts for their parents and spouse (a piece of furniture, a major appliance, or a television, for instance), give some money to siblings and cousins, and keep some of the money for their own enjoyment for drinking in High Level and in Chateh.

When the drinking problems became more and more serious, the band council declared Chateh a "dry" reserve. The intention of the council bylaw was to prevent people from bringing liquor back to Chateh and drinking on the reserve. The bylaw means that possession of an alcoholic beverage on reserve makes one liable to arrest by the R.C.M.P. Being seen drunk on reserve also makes one suspect of having had liquor on the reserve and thus liable to arrest. As Dene Tha friends explained, "When they had this wet reserve, the drinking wasn't so bad; but when they started this dry reserve business that is when the drinking picked up. That's when the challenge began. There's nothing better to do, there's the challenge, you know, trying to evade the R.C.M.P., just the challenge." A Dene Tha woman told me, "There are lot of them around, bootlegger; they buy some booze, keep the money rotating." Her husband immediately added: "Just like stealing. They buy something at five dollars and sell it here at twenty to twenty-five; buy something at ten and sell it at forty or forty-five. They spend some money to drink and keep the rest to buy some more to sell." Even Dene Tha who had given up drinking would sometimes engage in bootlegging to raise quick cash when in need. When I confronted a Dene Tha couple who were doing so, asking them how they could peddle liquor when they themselves had given up drinking because of the pain it had brought to their home, they answered: "But if they choose to drink, that's their decision. It's up to them."

Fear of Retaliation/Wish for Retaliation

Among subarctic indigenous populations, as within other populations, social factors determine the forms of aggressive behavior, its targets, its frequency, and the contexts in which it is manifested. Conversely, the ways in which likely targets of aggressive behavior respond to a potential threat is also foreordained by social factors. The following accounts will establish that while individuals refrain from aggression out of both regard for one another's feelings and fear, people nevertheless use the cover of drunkenness to act aggressively against others and thus to settle scores in a socially permissible way.

Over the years, numerous observations and conversations with Dene Tha led me to see that in many instances these two contrasting states of affairs—the attentive and joyful climate of sober life on the one hand, and the uninhibited outbursts and violence associated with drinking on the other—are actually phases in a continuous, complex process of social interaction. Individuals who feel belittled or undermined by others live in the knowledge that, come the appropriate moment, they might always join a drinking party, vent their hostility, and attack their antagonists without being held accountable for their behavior. Conversely, when Dene Tha refrain from interference in other people's lives, they do so out of fear of eventual retaliation by a drunken party. Dene Tha employees at the local store, for instance, told me they did not report to their employer or to the police theft by fellow employees or by customers, for if they did so, it would only be a matter of time before they would suffer injury at the hands of the intoxicated individual they had reported. Dene Tha women abused by their drunken husbands told me how they would confide in their brothers when the latter were sober, and explained how these brothers, when drunk, would later appear at the homes of their brothers-in-law to beat them up. Growing accustomed to this logic, I spontaneously asked a Dene Tha woman who reported that the drunken son of her neighbor had slashed the four tires of her pickup truck: "What have *you* done?" She immediately replied: "I'm keeping my niece away from him. We might have to move to Edmonton for a while." In typical Dene fashion, withdrawal from Chateh with her niece, rather than confrontation or bringing charges with the police officer, was her preferred course of action. And so on. Many violent acts are acts of retaliation.

In many Dene Tha accounts, a close association is established between alcohol and violence without the assumption that this association is causal in nature. Dene Tha do not subscribe to the "malevolence assumption," the phrase coined by C. Hamilton and J. Collins, Jr., to refer to the tendency to assume "that alcohol is a cause of violence between family members" when they find "an offender with a drinking problem or the presence of alcohol in an incident of family violence" (1982: 26; in Gusfield 1992). Rather, in many cases, Dene Tha recognize drunkenness as providing themselves and others with a socially legitimate context to pursue objectives that they cannot seek when sober. Dene Tha recognize that, although drunk and "not knowing" what they are doing, individuals do turn against fellow employees who have denounced them, do beat up their brothers-in-law who have abused their sisters, or do destroy the property of those who stand in their way. In and out of drunkenness, Dene Tha operate within a complex system of management of self and of social relationships. It is clear from the above that if Dene Tha do not take justice into their own hands when sober, they are seen to do so in many cases by means of alcohol. Under the cover of drunkenness, Dene Tha can be seen to seek to achieve their own goals, even if at a considerable cost to themselves.

Covert Aggression

The foregoing observations are important for understanding the local dynamics of nonaggression and aggression. However, our discussion of whether Dene Tha account for their restrained behavior when sober in terms of fear of each other or in terms of respect of each other's autonomy would remain incomplete if we did not mention another source of fear, *echint'e*—"a power" or "a powerfulness" received from animals or other life forms while on a vision quest. Until very recently, almost everyone in Chateh experienced, before the onset of adolescence, encounters with animals that became their helpers and that gave them "a power" to heal specific illnesses. Today, many parents still encourage their young children to spend time wandering in the bush in the hope that they will come back with an animal helper. People "describe a vision as *mendayeh wodekeh* 'something appearing in front of someone' or *mba'awodi* 'something talking to or sounding for someone'" (Moore and Wheelock, 1990: 59). Because a vision often comes hand in hand with a song, a young person who is sent to seek a vision is often told, "Go for a song! *Shin kaneya!*" A person who encounters an animal while on his or her vision quest is known as *Dene wonlin edadihi*, "a person who knows an animal." "When they come back they are not supposed to tell you [what they saw and heard]; if they do, their power just goes away," confided one informant. Children who have found a helper in the bush hint at the identity of the animal concerned by, for example, not eating flesh of that species, but they may not be specific. In this fashion, individuals who know an animal engage in a complex process of indirectly revealing the source of their "power," until such day when they are asked by others to call on their "power" for healing purposes. The first successful healing thus publicly confirms one's relationship with one's animal helper (See Goulet 1982; 1989; 1994b; Watson and Goulet 1992).

Animal helpers are a source of concern because they may be called upon by Dene Tha to carry out acts of aggression or retaliation against fellow Dene Tha. To offend someone is to risk becoming the object of his or her evil thoughts. Speaking of elders, a Dene Tha man in his forties said: "Old people they are very bad, they know. But they are O.K. They don't bother you as long as you don't get them mad. You make them mad, they can hurt you [with their power]. If not, they can help you lots of ways." One man expressed a similar view in the following way: "Last night I went to [their] house to sing, but they were drinking. [He] wanted to fight me, but they told him to stop. I have power. He doesn't know but I could make him ill; I go to sleep and if I dream of him, I make him sick, it is very easy for me to do that. I would send my power over there, I would send it with my brain over there." The "power" would then overtake the mind of the intended victim. The targeted person would then be very likely to have an accident, most probably a very serious, if not deadly, one. Dene Tha would readily understand the teaching of Naidzo, the Bear Lake prophet, who told the Dogribs that "the worst thing you can do is to kill somebody whether it is by *ink'on* or with a club" (Helm 1994: 29). *Ink'on,* the Chipewyan and Dogrib equivalent to the Dene Tha *echint'e,* is indeed something to fear.

Dene Tha use the English term "medicine" to refer either to *yu* (various natural substances with medicinal properties) or to *echint'e,* "a power." It is in this sense that the term is most often used in the anthropological literature concerning "medicine fights" and "medicine power."[4] So central is this notion to Northern Athapaskan lives that over fifty years ago Mason (1946: 37) wrote that "Northern Athapaskan religion is practically synonymous with shamanism or the comprehensive term 'medicine.'" When a Dene Tha mother shared her concern over her children because "someone [was] throwing bad medicine around the school," I asked her to tell me this in Dene Dháh. She said "*edéhtl'éh koan woteh kíndi edu újon wonlin.*" The key concept here is "*kíndi edu újon,*" which means, literally, "someone's mind [or thought] is not good." The mother translated her statement back to English as "someone's bad thoughts are around the school"—someone's mind is the source of evil thoughts that wander around seeking an intended victim.

While a few Dene Tha spoke of "bad medicine" when speaking in English, others used the expression to curse someone. Dene Tha translated the expression "they placed a curse on him," as *"ede guchint'e t'ah giyech'ede,"* which they translated back to English as "they bother him with their spiritual beings." *Guchint'e*, which is most often translated as "their power," is glossed here as "their spiritual beings." The expression "to place a curse on someone" stands for the Dene expression *"giyech'ede,"* "they bother him." This is the same verb parents used to tell their children not to bother me when I was working on transcripts and translations of conversations in their homes.

Dene Tha often mentioned that extreme acts of aggression carried out while in a state of intoxication were due to the effect of "a power" sent by others to destroy the lives of their enemies. This is the case in the following account in which a woman draws on the notion of *echint'e* to explain her husband's extreme behavior. In an all too common bout of abuse, her husband had abandoned her outdoors where, unconscious and severely injured, she nearly bled to death. She recovered after intensive surgery and prolonged hospitalization. When she returned home, her first thought was to take her husband to a healer. The account begins with a reference to a visit to a first healer, and concludes with a healing ceremony performed on the occasion of a visit to a second healer:

> Bill [names her husband] can't drink anymore. A few days back he just about went crazy and we went to see that old man [names neighbor who is healer]. He told [Bill] he had to stop drinking or something would happen to him, like maybe he would die. Then this guy came to get [Bill] to get him for a ride. *I did not say anything, I knew it was up to him.* Like when old people tell us to do something and we don't do it, it can be really bad. Usually I send them away [friends who want to take her husband along to drink], but this time I did not. So he [Bill] went with him. He was gone four days in High Level. I stayed at my mom's. [Field notes, verbatim; my emphasis]

The speaker goes on to say that after her husband had returned from High Level they had a fight, after which he could not sleep at night:

> It was just like if he was afraid. He asked me to put on the light and he had a pain in his chest and in his back up near his neck. Then I remembered what [Bill's grandmother] told me before she died. She said: "If ever he gets like he's not himself, take him to see old [names local dreamer and healer]. I told [Bill]: "Tomorrow, Sunday, we go and see him." He said, "O.K."
>
> Then Sunday he did not want to go. He said: "We go Monday." Monday, he did not want to go. He said, "We go tomorrow." I told him: "Tomorrow never comes." I took the kids to my mom. We [Bill and her] brought with us a strip of beaver fur, a five dollar bill, and a piece of moose hide cut the size of the five dollar bill. [The wife of the first old man they had consulted] had told us to take that. [According to the Dene Tha such "gifts" are for the animal helper of the healer]. All the way he [Bill] kept saying: "Let's go back." I kept talking to him until we got there. I told him: "You have to ask yourself."

The speaker went on to describe how she and her husband sat in the elder's house, without her husband saying a word: "We sat and sat. Then I told him: 'We are going to sit here all night, I am not going till you ask.' Then I took him into the room where the old man was and he asked." The healing ceremony then went as follows:

> The old man began to take his things out [of his "medicine" bag] and he began to sing. He sang for a long time. Then he asked us what house we lived in. We told him [so and so's] old house. He asked Bill where it hurts. Then he put his head on Bill's chest and when he put his head up, he spat a sea shell and showed us what he got out of his chest. It was a black thing, the size of a quarter, it had a tiny head. He told us he was going to destroy it. [She explains that he swallows it and it becomes destroyed in his body.]
>
> He told us that our house was like an open mouth and that was the mouth of an animal. Maybe that mouth is closed and that is when Bill got crazy. He told us there were four men [their spirits] in our house, but they would soon leave. They are the ones that put that bad medicine on Bill. They used the grizzly bear. That thing he took out of Bill was a part of that grizzly's body. He told us: "I have 'power,' but there is a God who watches over us, and the power I have to help others come from him." "You must pray lots and make the children pray," he said. [Field notes, verbatim]

The woman concluded her account, saying: "If we don't do what he says, it is like if we are abusing this old man's 'power' and he will help us only when he knows that we are worthy of help. He told Bill: 'When you feel like drinking you come here and drink my tea, and I will talk with you.'"

It is noteworthy that the decision to seek this healer's help was the woman's. It is she who remembers the words of her husband's late grandmother: "If ever he gets like he's not himself, take him to see old [name of 'powerful' Dene Tha dreamer and healer]." The words of the grandmother cast the husband's excessive brutality when drunk in a new light. It is something he does when he is not himself. It follows that a curse must be involved, that someone else is responsible for the husband's extreme behavior. This is borne out by the Dene Tha healer. While the healer promises to neutralize the destructive "power" at work in Bill's life, the assurance of recovery is conditional on Bill and his family praying, and on Bill giving up his drinking habit. The elder puts the responsibility squarely into Bill's own hands: "When you feel like drinking you come here and drink my tea, and I will talk with you." Following this healing ceremony, Bill diminished but did not quit his drinking. Nevertheless, in the months and years that followed he never succumbed to the excessive brutality that had characterized his relationship with his wife. The recourse to the local healer was seen as successful (Watson and Goulet 1998).

Summary

The intention of this essay was to understand how and why the Dene Tha vigorously check any direct aggressive behavior when sober, and when drunk vent their hostility and attack individuals they resent. A close examination of the circumstances preceding acts of aggression and the environment in which they are played out led us to discover that in many cases, under the cover of drunkenness, Dene Tha choose the appropriate moment to direct their aggression against those whom they consider the legitimate object of their anger. Dene Tha do so because although they fear the aggression of others, they also on occasion wish to retaliate against people who, they feel, have either interfered with their goals or have inflicted injury on a close kin. Being drunk and having "lost their mind," individuals create the socially accepted conditions under which to engage in acts of aggression for which they will not publicly be held accountable.

I also showed how the value of autonomy that pervades Dene Tha social life is consistent with the two strategies they employ when faced with drunken individuals who are out of control: either withdrawal from the environment where the drunks are acting out, or reliance upon non-Dene third parties to temporarily incarcerate the threatening individual. Both strategies respect the Dene commitment to respect as far as possible each other's autonomy, including the right of each individual to give up drinking when he or she wants to make that decision. I thus supported Honigmann's view and that of the majority of students of Dene societies, that respect for each other's autonomy is a major determinant of Dene behavior. However, I also documented how Dene Tha refrain from interfering with someone else's behavior precisely because they fear to become the object of that person's retaliation when that person becomes drunk, and I examined cases of retaliation against abusive individuals that proceeded under the cover of drunkenness. I therefore concluded, contrary to what Honigmann says, that both regard for one another's feelings *and* fear motivate people to refrain from interfering with someone else's goals.

Finally, I briefly focused on the Dene Tha notion of *echint'e*, "a power" that can be used by individuals to secretly retaliate against their enemies and cause them misfortune and even death. An extreme case of abuse suffered by a woman at the hands of her husband illustrated that Dene Tha have recourse to the notion of *echint'e* to account for inordinate cases of aggression by drunken relatives. In this way Dene Tha again exonerate individuals who, having "lost their mind," have gone too far in their aggression against others. In words and in deeds, Dene Tha tell each other and themselves, "you can do crazy things when you are drinking," but you should do it in such a way that "there is nothing to worry about."

Acknowledgments
The extensive research time among the Dene Tha between 1980 and 1985 made possible by the Canadian Research Centre for Anthropology, Saint Paul University (Ottawa) is greatly appreciated, as are annual grants from the Social Sciences and Humanities Research Council from 1980 to 1984. I thank Christine Hanssens and Graham Watson for their comments on previous drafts of this essay.. And above all, I express my gratitude to the people of Chateh who shared with me their stories and welcomed me into their lives and homes.

Notes

1. This essay is a much expanded version of the first part of a paper, "Power and Medicine Fights among Contemporary Dene Tha," presented at the Seventh International Conference on Hunting and Gathering Societies (CHAGS 7), hosted by the Institute of Ethnology and Anthropology and the Russian Academy of Sciences, in Moscow, 18–22 August 1993 (Goulet 1994c). In its present form, this chapter is a condensed version of parts of two chapters of *Ways of Knowing: Experience, Knowledge and Power among the Dene Tha* (Goulet 1998).

2. Honigmann supports this characterization with references to Balicki (1963); Hallowell (1946: 207–8); Helm (1961); Helm and DeVos (1963); Helm, DeVos, and Carterette (1963: 127); Honigmann (1949: 250–58); Savishinsky (1971: 611); and Slobodin (1960), to which we may add Brody (1981: 249–53); Hammer and Steinbring (1980); Heath (1991: 27 and 38); Ridington (1988: 17); and the present essay concerning the Dene Tha.

3. In the anthropological literature, people of this community are referred to either as Slavey (Asch 1981: 348), as "The Hay River, Albertan Beaver Indians" (Mills 1982: 67), as "the Dene Tha branch of the Beaver Indians" (J. G. E. Smith 1987: 444), or as the "Hay Lakes Alberta Dene" (Helm 1994: 15). Chateh is the name of the reserve also known as Assumption (see map in Asch 1981: 338). The Department of Indian and Northern Affairs Canada (1987: 91) listed the reserve as Hay Lake with a population of 809 in December 1986. Linguistically, Dene Dha is a more appropriate spelling, but the people of Chateh have retained the old spelling, Dene Tha, and I follow suit. Fieldwork among the Dene Tha extended over five years (1980–84), six months a year, with regular, shorter visits since. Quotations of informants are verbatim. All individual names are fictive to protect anonymity.

4. The term "medicine fight" is not found in the index of volume 6 of the *Handbook of North American Indians*. Under shamans one finds two references to shamanic "contests." The first is from Steinbring (1981: 250), who refers to "shamanistic contests [the Salties of Lake Winnipeg] in which two rival shamans competing for power and authority would incite each other to the highest pitch of evil-doing sorcery." The second reference is from McClelland (1981: 502), who reports that Tutchone shamans or dream doctors "dueled with the spirit helpers of rival dream doctors from other groups." It was Ridington (1968) who first wrote of "medicine fights" as an instrument of local political process among the Beaver Indians, followed by D. Smith (1973; 1990, and 1993) and Sharp (1986; 1988) for the Chipewyan. See Krech (1981) for a review

of Northern Athapaskan accounts of misfortune suffered at the hands of fellow Northern Athapaskans in the early historic period, 1789–1860; and Helm (1994: 114–16) for accounts of how, in the same historic period, "powerful" Dogribs overtook their enemies' minds, including that of a Hudson Bay manager to make him extend credit, which he had to that point steadfastly withheld. Goulet (1994a and 1994b) examines the Dene Tha notion of "knowing with the mind."

References

Asch, M. I. 1981. " Slavey." In *Handbook of North American Indians*. Volume 6: Subarctic. J. Helm, ed. 338–49. Washington, D.C.: Smithsonian Institution.

Balicki, A. 1963. *Vunta Kutchin Social Change: A Study of the People of Old Crow. Yukon Territory*. NCRC 63–3. Ottawa: Department of Northern Affairs and National Resources. Northern Coordination and Research Centre.

Brody, H. 1981. *Maps and Dreams*. Vancouver: Douglas and McIntyre.

Dene Tha Band of Assumption. 1990. "Submission to the Task Force on the Criminal Justice System and Its Impact on the Indian and Metis People of Alberta." 12 June 1990. Manuscript.

Dene Tha Women's Society. 1990. "Submission to the Task Force on the Criminal Justice System and Its Impact on the Indian and Metis People of Alberta." 18 April 1990. Manuscript.

Department of Indian and Northern Affairs Canada. 1987. *Schedule of Indian Bands, Reserves and Settlements Including—Membership and Population, Location and Area in Hectares*. Ottawa.

Goulet, J.-G. A. 1982. "Religious Dualism among Athapaskan Catholics." *Canadian Journal of Anthropology* 3(1): 1–18.

_____. 1989. "Representation of Self and Reincarnation among the Dene-Tha." *Culture* 8: 3–18.

_____. 1994a. "Dreams and Visions in Other Lifeworlds." In *Being Changed by Cross-Cultural Encounters: The Anthropology of Extraordinary Experience*. D. E. Young and J.-G. Goulet, eds. 16–38. Peterborough, ON: Broadview Press.

_____. 1994b. "Ways of Knowing: Towards a Narrative Ethnography of Experiences among the Dene Tha." *Journal of Anthropological Research* 50: 113–39.

_____. 1994c. "Power and Medicine Fights among Contemporary Dene Tha." In *Hunters and Gatherers in Modern Context*. Volume I, Sixth International Conference on Hunting and Gathering Societies, Linda Ellanna, ed. 209–24. Fairbanks: University of Alaska Fairbanks.

_____. 1998. *Ways of Knowing: Experience, Knowledge and Power among the Dene Tha*. Lincoln and London: University of Nebraska Press and Vancouver: University of British Columbia Press.

Gusfield, J. R. 1992. "Listening for the Silences: The Rhetorics of the Research Field." In *Writing the Social Text: Poetics and Politics in Social Science Discourse*. R. H. Brown, ed. 117–34. New York: Aldine de Gruyter.

Hallowell, I. A. 1938. "Fear and Anxiety as Cultural and Individual Variables in a Primitive Society." *Journal of Social Psychology* 9: 25–47.

_____. 1946. "Some Psychological Characteristics of the Northeastern Indians." In *Man in Northeastern North America*. Frederick Johnson, ed. 195–225. Papers of the Robert S.

Peabody Foundation for Archaeology 3. Andover, Mass. (reprinted: pp. 125–50 in *Culture and Experience*, by A. Irving Hallowell, University of Pennsylvania Press, Philadelphia, 1955.)

Hamilton, C., and J. Collins, Jr. 1982. "The Role of Alcohol in Wife Beating and Child Abuse." In *Drinking and Crime*. J. Collins, Jr., ed. London: Tavistock.

Hammer, J., and J. Steinbring. 1980. *Alcohol and Native Peoples of the North*. Lanham, Md.: University Press of America.

Heath, D. B. 1991. "A Decade of Development in the Anthropological Study of Alcohol Use: 1970–1980." In *Constructive Drinking: Perspectives on Drink from Anthropology*. M. Douglas, ed. 16–69. Cambridge: Cambridge University Press.

Helm, J. 1961. *The Lynx Point People: The Dynamics of a Northern Athapaskan Band*. Anthropological Series 53, National Museums of Canada Bulletin 176. Ottawa: National Museums of Canada.

_____. 1994. *Prophecy and Power among the Dogrib Indians*. Lincoln and London: University of Nebraska Press.

Helm, J., and G. DeVos. 1963. "Dogrib Indian Personality: Rorschach, Thematic Apperception Test, and Observational Data Collected in 1959 and 1960, N.W.T., Canada." (Unpublished manuscript in Helm's possession.)

Helm J., G. DeVos, and T. Carterette. 1963. "Variations in Personality and Ego Identification within a Slave Indian Kin-Community." In *Contributions to Anthropology*. Part 2. 94–138. Anthropological Series 60, National Museums of Canada Bulletin 190. Ottawa: National Museums of Canada.

Honigmann, J. J. 1949. *Culture and Ethos of Kaska Society*. Yale University Publications in Anthropology, No. 40. New Haven, Conn.: Yale University Press.

_____.1981. "Expressive Aspects of Subarctic Indian Culture." In *Handbook of North American Indians*. Volume 6: Subarctic. J. Helm, ed. 718–38. Washington, D.C.: Smithsonian Institution.

Krech, S., III. 1981. "'Throwing Bad Medicine': Sorcery, Disease, and the Fur Trade among the Kutchin and Other Northern Athapaskans." In *Indians, Animals, and the Fur Trade: A Critique of Keepers of the Game*. S. Krech, III, ed. 73–108. Athens: University of Georgia Press.

Leland, J. 1976. *Firewater Myths: North American Indian Drinking and Alcohol Addiction*. New Brunswick, N.J.: Rutgers Center for Alcohol Studies.

Lithman, Y. G. 1979. "Feeling Good and Getting Smashed. On the Symbolism of Alcohol and Drunkenness among Canadian Indians." *Ethos* 44(1–2): 119–133.

MacAndrew, C., and R. B. Edgerton. 1969. *Drunken Comportment: A Social Explanation*. Chicago: Aldine.

Mail, P. D. 1980. "American Indian Drinking Behavior: Some Possible Causes and Solutions." *Journal of Alcohol and Drug Education* 26: 28–39.

Mason, J. A. 1946. *Notes on the Indians of the Great Slave Lake Area*. Yale University Publications in Anthropology, No. 34. New Haven, Conn.: Yale University Press.

McClelland, C. 1981. "Tutchone." In *Handbook of North American Indians*. Volume 6: Subarctic. J. Helm, ed. 493–501. Washington, D.C.: Smithsonian Institution.

Medicine, B. 1983. "An Ethnography of Drinking and Sobriety among the Lakota Sioux." Unpublished Ph.D. diss., University of Wisconsin–Madison. University Microfilm, Ann Arbor, Michigan.

Mills, A. 1982. "The Beaver Indian Prophet Dance and Related Movements among North American Indians." Unpublished Ph.D. diss., Harvard University, University Microfilm, Ann Arbor, Michigan.

_____. 1986. "The Meaningful Universe: Intersecting Forces in Beaver Indian Cosmology." *Culture* 4(2): 81–91.

Moore, P., and A. Wheelock. 1990. *Wolverine Myths and Visions: Dene Traditions from Northern Alberta*. Edmonton: University of Alberta Press.

Ridington, R. 1968. "The Medicine Fight: An Instrument of Political Process among the Beaver Indians." *American Anthropologist* 70: 1152–60.

_____. 1987. "From Hunt Chief to Prophet: Beaver Indians and Christianity." *Arctic Anthropology* 24(1): 8–18.

_____. 1988. *Trail to Heaven: Knowledge and Narrative in a Northern Native Community*. Iowa City: University of Iowa Press.

Rushforth, E. S. 1992. "The Legitimation of Beliefs in a Hunter-Gatherer Society: Bearlake Athapaskan Knowledge and Authority." *American Ethnologist* 19(3): 483–500.

Savishinsky, J. S. 1971. "Mobility as an Aspect of Stress in an Arctic Community." *American Anthropologist* 73(3): 604–18.

_____. 1982. "Vicarious Emotions and Cultural Restraint." *Journal of Psychoanalytical Anthropology* 5(2): 115–35.

Scollon, R., and S. B. K. Scollon. 1979. *Linguistic Convergence: An Ethnography of Speaking at Fort Chipewyan, Alberta*. London: Academic Press.

Sharp, H. S. 1986. "Shared Experience and Magical Death: Chipewyan Explanations of a Prophet's Decline." *Ethnology* 24: 257–70.

_____. 1988. "The Transformation of Bigfoot: Maleness, Powers, and Belief among the Chipewyan." Smithsonian Series in Ethnographic Inquiry, No. 9. Washington, D.C.: Smithsonian Institution.

Slobodin, R. 1960. "Some Social Functions of Kutchin Anxiety." *American Anthropologist* 62(1): 122–33.

Smith, D. M. 1973. *Inkonze: Magico-Religious Beliefs of Contact-Traditional Chipewyan Trading at Fort Resolution, NWT, Canada*. National Museum of Man, Mercury Series. Canadian Ethnology Service 6. Ottawa: National Museums of Canada.

_____. 1982. *Moose-Deer Island House People: A History of the Native People of Fort Resolution*. National Museum of Man, Mercury Series. Canadian Ethnology Service 81. Ottawa: National Museums of Canada.

_____. 1990. "The Chipewyan Medicine Fight in Cultural and Ecological Perspective." In *Culture and the Anthropological Tradition: Essays in Honor of Robert F. Spencer*. 153–75. New York: University Press of America.

_____.1993. "Albert's Power: A Fiction Narrative." *Anthropology and Humanism* 18(2): 67–73.

Smith, J. G. E. 1987. "The Western Woods Cree: Anthropological Myth and Historical Reality." *American Ethnologist* 14: 434–48.

Steinbring, J. H. 1981. "Saulteaux of Lake Winnipeg." In *Handbook of North American Indians*, Volume 6: Subarctic. J. Helm, ed. 244–55. Washington, D.C.: Smithsonian Institution.

Stets, J. E. 1995. "Role Identities and Person Identities: Gender Identity, Mastery Identity, and Controlling One's Partner." *Sociological Perspectives* 38(2): 129–50.

Waddell, J., and M. Everett. 1980. *Drinking Behavior among Southwestern Indians*. Tucson, Ariz.: University of Arizona Press.

Watson, G., and J.-G. A. Goulet. 1992. "Gold In, Gold Out: The Objectivation of Dene Tha Dreams and Visions." *Journal of Anthropological Research* 48(3): 215–30.

_____. 1998. "What Can Ethnomethodology Say About Power?" In *Qualitative Inquiry* 4(1): 96–113.

Chapter 3

WARFARE AMONG THE HUNTERS AND FISHERMEN OF WESTERN SIBERIA

━━━━━◄(◉)►━━━━━

Liudmila A. Chindina

Western Siberian hunters and fishermen inhabited the vast lowland composed of tundra, forest-tundra, taiga, and forest-steppe, extending from the Ural Mountains to the Yenisei River. Their economic and cultural systems were closely linked to environmental factors. As early as in the Neolithic, there were four types of subsistence economies, based predominantly on hunting or fishing, with different sorts of specialization: (1) mobile reindeer hunting in the tundra, (2) hunting of forest ungulates at the time of their migration east of the Ural Mountains and in the forested areas of the Upper Ob River, (3) sedentary fishing in the Lower Tobol River area, and (4) seasonal hunting and fishing in the forested areas along the Ob and Irtysh Rivers (Epokha bronzy 1987: 306).

These subsistence systems were highly dynamic in time and space, corresponding to technological developments, the sociopolitical environment, and environmental changes. Introduction of food production, mainly various forms of pastoralism, led to the formation of diverse economies and subsequent cultural changes. Environmental changes, causing aridity or humidity, continually altered natural zones (Shnitnikov 1957) and invariably affected economic and cultural adaptations. The formation of a marsh system in western Siberia stimulated paleoeconomic and demographic developments (Neishtadt 1971). The western Siberian taiga covers 141.9 million hectares, 70.4 million hectares being marshland (Evseeva and Zemtsov 1990: 159; Zemtsov 1976: 207). The marshes are growing rapidly (on average 45,000 hectares annually), invading biologically productive territories and causing their devastation. According to geomorphologists, two different intensive processes of marsh formation caused changes in the landscape and the carrying capacity of the taiga. The first dated to the Middle Holocene (ca. 4,500 years B.P. [B.P. meaning "before present"]), when the large, complex marsh systems of the Vasiugan and Surgut types were formed, and watersheds shifted. The second one occurred in the late Holocene (ca. 2,000–2,500 years B.P.), when marsh systems grew and formed ridge-lacustrine complexes (Vinogradov et al. 1969; Zemtsov 1976: 222–24). The most crucial ecological crises in prehistoric western Siberia took place in the early Bronze Age and in the early Iron Age.

Economic, cultural, and demographic transformations followed environmental changes. People had to move to new and more productive territories, and population density at hunting and fishing grounds increased. Two adjustments were made to these conditions. The first was the improvement of hunting and fishing technologies and adoption of elements of food production. It is thus not accidental that pastoralism and metalworking were introduced to western Siberia much earlier than to eastern Siberia. The second was the acquisition and exploitation of new territories accompanied by mass migrations away from traditional areas.

Historical, cultural, and ecological factors stimulated both aggressive and peaceful responses. In this chapter I will discuss the role of warfare among hunters and gatherers of the Middle Ob River basin in the Irtysh and Yenisei interfluency (the southern taiga zone), from the time of the first organized military actions up until the ethnographic present of the sixteenth and seventeenth centuries. Warfare, as a specific, organized form of attempted conflict resolution among western Siberian hunters and fishermen, was one of the most common, frequent, and decisive strategies of behavior. Numerous folk traditions, legends, and epics of western Siberia give evidence of the cultivation of a warrior spirit via the intentional instillation of military skills among boys—dexterity, strength, bravery, cunning, mobility, and know-how in handling weapons (Lukina 1990; Patkanov 1891; Pelikh 1972). Special *rites de passage* for a future warrior were practiced. For instance, the Sel'kups[1] held a small ritual in which a bow and an arrow were thrown into a lake when a newborn boy was first brought across it (Pelikh 1972: 333).

Judging from ethnographic data and from oral tradition, armed clashes had numerous causes, for instance, revenge for violation of traditional rules or any damage inflicted, such as the kidnapping of women or the appropriation of wealth or land. Wars could be waged according to certain rules (including declarations of war and formal duels) or without any rules (such as secret attacks on sleeping enemies, by treachery, or in the absence of men, etc.). Enemies could be either related clans or people of different ethnic groups. Some wars were contained and completed with a duel between two warriors and a peacemaking ceremony; others were particularly brutal and led to the extermination of a number of clans or families. Already one hundred years ago, S. N. Patkanov (1891) published an illuminating description of warfare, its leaders, weapons, and military techniques, as described in Khanty epics and narratives. G. N. Pelikh (1972) collected Sel'kup legends from the Middle Ob region that were filled with military information. "The warriors lived in the Ket River area" (Pelikh 1972: 319). "In former days people fought brutally with each other. The villages struggled; they used to slaughter everybody" (p. 323). Wars were waged in the past. "There was a strong man ... a warrior who visited the village and took a wife. Then all the community went to fight (against the warrior)" (p. 324). In the Ob region, "they fought since time immemorial. One man (a warrior named Pygynbalk) went to the Lower (River) and stole another man's wife ... the clansmen came and killed the warrior ... there was a large village in Kal'dge, they all were slaughtered" (p. 343). At Tym River, "warriors lived everywhere ... they fought ... the *Kveli kup* (birch people) lived at the lake. Now they are all gone; they were massacred in order to appropriate fishing grounds" (pp. 223–334). Sel'-kups by no means only fought with related groups. "Once a war came from Vakh River (from the Khantys). Only reindeer wool was left at the Tym River. All the people were slaughtered" (p. 338).

It is well established that before western Siberia was included into the Russian state and the local inhabitants were pacified, the Ob Sel'kups lived under conditions of perpetual warfare. They fought against the Nenetses, the Evenks, the Khantys, and various Turkic-speaking groups. In addition, they fought with each other (Istoriia Sibiri 1968: 360; Kastren 1860: 252; Pelikh 1981; Solov'ev 1987). As among adjacent peoples, war leaders— warriors (*sengir*) and princes (*kok*)—arose among the Sel'kups along with social inequalities. The roles of *sengir* and *kok* differed. The *sengir* was a patriarch; people lived permanently in his fortresses. His power was of a patriarchal nature. According to tradition, "he defended his site, his forest. He defended his people. If we lose our territory, what will the people eat? He defended the land for the sake of his people" (Pelikh 1981: 139). A *kok* had a temporary fortress. His power was of a forceful nature, as is evident from the term "*kok*"; *kokctpat* means "to beat" or "to offend" (Mal'tsev 1843), *gogiltigo* "to rule" (Erdélyi 1969: 74), and *kottigo* "to strike" (Kuper and Pusztay 1993: 64). A *kok*, whose authority was inherited, had special detachments of *liaks* (warriors), selected regardless of their kinship ties, who had high social status, were physically strong, and owned appro-priate weapons. In other words, specialized military detachments, each consisting from around fifty to three-hundred warriors (Bakhrushin 1935: 35), were formed in order to seize loot and to defend the *kok* and his territory (Pelikh 1981: 139–45). One can clearly see herein a form of private estate and a corresponding system for its protection.

Such social and political developments among the Sel'kups were strongly affected by external factors. Persistent raids by neighbors and rapid expansion of the fur trade disrupted traditional social patterns and strengthened the role of military power. New leaders gained power and replaced former clan aristocracy. When the Russians came to western Siberia in the sixteenth century, they encountered this militarized organization among the Sel'kups.

Thus, warfare as a purposeful and specialized strategy emerged very early among people of the West Siberian taiga. It seems very important to find warfare's roots and reconstruct its early forms and developmental stages in order to understand both relationships between particular hunter-gathering communities and the general nature of past cultural processes in the region. The absence of written sources among the indigenous peoples makes it difficult to reconstruct the Siberian past. The narratives of travelers are few, their chronological and geographical information very poor, and it is not easy to relate them to specific cultures of western Siberia. Archaeological sources thus play a crucial role by providing a vast variety of data to examine the problems in question. These data, although uneven in qualitative, quantitative, and chronological terms, include weapons, fortifications, military aspects of settlement patterns and burial rites, sanctuaries, and mobile art. Internal and external correlation of various artifact groups and their comparative analysis via complex multidisciplinary methodology reveal some characteristics of warfare among the West Siberian forest cultures in the Bronze Age and early Iron Age with which it is possible to reconstruct both tactics (means and ways of waging battles) and strategies (goals and direction of the military actions), as well as relationships among the winners and the losers.

The fortified Amnia I site at the Kazym River (eastern tributary of the Ob River) provides the earliest and only evidence of warfare among the West Siberian inhabitants in the Neolithic. It is a promontory site with three lines of fortification protecting eight houses. It covers an area of 1,260 square meters (Morozov and Stefanov 1989; 1993). Judging from the excavations, fortifications were developing at the time. Initially, only one house at the tip of the promontory was protected by a moat. Later, the original moat was filled in, two dwellings were built above it, a new moat was dug, and a palisade erected. A third outer moat was dug either simultaneously or somewhat later. The site has been broadly dated to the Neolithic, the last third of the fourth millennium and the first third of the third millennium B.C. (Morozov and Stefanov 1993: 168).

Polished stone arrowheads and axes could be loosely identified as weapons. In terms of contemporary West Siberian forest cultures, the variety of arrow points in Amnia is very impressive; the points differed from each other in shape, size, and design, and retouch was intensively used. That artifacts were used for hunting is well attested from the faunal data, which include reindeer, moose, and beaver, among others (Morozov and Stefanov 1993: 155). The Amnia 1 site can be provisionally[2] combined with the Sartyn'ia 1, Khulium-Sunt, Kirip-Vis-Iugan sites as composing one specific culture. This group emerged as a result of the northward migration of Trans-Ural people, who maintained many aspects of their original culture despite numerous transformations. It is possible that they introduced fortification in order to resist pressures from the alien cultural environment. However, one case is not enough to reach any decisive conclusions. The complex and effective fortification system of Amnia 1 is unique to northern Eurasia only and is not found in the Neolithic of Siberia or the Ural Mountains. Close analogies are known only in the Tripol'e culture of the Ukraine and Moldova. Promontory fortified sites are found among the West Siberian hunters and fishermen only in the terminal Bronze Age and early Iron Age (Borzunov 1992).

In the Samus'-Seimino period (between the late Neolithic and the early Iron Age), large reinforced dwellings were erected at some sites (Pashkinskii Bor I and Volvonchi I) at the Konda River. The excavators (Stefanova and Koksharov 1988: 163) assumed that banks and moats surrounding the dwellings indicated the evolution of fortifications. However, whether they were indeed military structures has been questioned by V. A. Borzunov (1992: 42), who suggests that the banks were used to strengthen the foundation of the walls, and that the moats served for drainage.

Nevertheless, despite the absence of fortifications, the development of military techniques among the hunters and fishermen of the southern taiga and taiga-steppe zones of western Siberia can be linked to the early Bronze Age. The Samus' cultural complex, which comprised several cultures and variants, was under formation there by the eighteenth and seventeenth centuries B.C. (Epokha bronzy 1987: 272–74; Matiushchenko 1973; Molodin and Glushkov 1989). As of now, the Tiumen', Middle Irtysh, and Tomsk variants have been identified (Kosarev 1981). The sites of Samus' 4, Krokhalevka 1, and Pashkin Bor 1 and the graveyards of Sopka 2 and Rostovka are most representative and well studied. One can deduce from the subsistence remains of the Samus' sites (i.e., from settlement patterns, dwellings and their interior features, artifacts, bone residues) and paleoenvironmental data (topography, landscape, flora and fauna, soils, climatic changes) that the Samus' were both hunters and fishermen. The Samus' economy certainly varied with local conditions, but in general it was a complex system composed of both hunting and gathering and food production. Hunting and fishing is evident from numerous arrow points, harpoons, net sinkers, fishhooks, and bone residues (see Table 3.1).

TABLE 3.1 **Bone Identifications from the Samus' Sites**

Fauna	Samus' 4	Pashkin Bor 1	Cherno-ozer'e 4	Krokha-levka 1	Baraba Lowland Sites
Goats and sheep	?		163	2	14
Cattle			7		8
Horse			29	2	21
Dog		1		1	3
Moose	+	3	3	3	21
Roe deer			+		8
Bison			+		
Reindeer		1			
Brown bear	4–5	1	5	2	12
Wild boar			+		2
Beaver				3	2
Fox			5		2
Sable					3
Hare			+		24
Wolf					3
Birds	+				15
Fish:	+	many		many	3
Roach				+	
Pike				+	
Sturgeon	+				
Siberian whitefish (Muksun)	+				

Legend: Numbers indicate the quantity of specimens; + indicates the existence of specimens; ? means "not exactly known."

Sources: Epokha bronzy 1987; Matiushchenko 1973; Molodin 1985; Molodin and Glushkov 1989; Stefanova and Koksharov 1988.

Although some aspects were highly conservative, the traditional hunting and gathering economies nonetheless underwent development in terms of artifacts and structural features. Hunting and fishing dominated in some areas depending on the natural environment and its carrying capacity. Though widespread, fishing was particularly important in the Lower Tobol River, where a distinct subculture emerged (Epokha bronzy 1987: 306). Seasonality became very important, and a special schedule was worked out: in fall and spring, big game hunting of moose; in winter, trapping and bear hunting; in spring and fall, waterfowl hunting; and in winter, forest bird hunting. In some areas mass fishing was practiced in spring and summer at special fishing grounds. This is documented by temporary hunting and fishing sites, as well as by faunal remains at permanent sites.

Subsistence techniques were highly differentiated depending on whether they were carried out by collective or individual efforts. The food-producing economy was comprised of pastoralism among Samus' groups. It was especially important in the Middle Irtysh and Tomsk areas (sites of Chernoozer'e 4, Krokhalevka 1, and—probably—Samus' 4; see Table 3.1).[3]

Bronze production flourished in the Samus' environment. Bronze artifacts and casting molds were excavated in the foundry workshops in Samus' 4, Pashkin Bor 1, Preobrazhenka 3, and Vengerovo 2, and metallurgists' burials were discovered in Sopka 2 and Rostovka. Bronze artifacts were typologically similar to the Turbinsk-Seimino ones well known from eastern Europe (Aspelin 1875; Bader 1964; Chernykh 1970; Gimbutas 1956; Gorodtsov 1915; Spitsyn 1893; Tallgren 1931). Either hunting and gathering and food production contributed roughly equally to the economy, or hunting and gathering dominated due to culture-historical factors and the geographical environment. The evolution of pastoral activity and metalworking among West Siberian south-taiga populations was related to influence from the steppe cultures. With the transition from the Neolithic to the Bronze Age and the introduction of new technologies, traditional multifaceted subsistence was less efficient in the steppe zone, and a pastoral economy became widespread (Epokha bronzy 1987: 312). By contrast, a multifaceted hunting-gathering/food-producing economy predominated in forest cultures. One of the driving forces behind the economic transformations in question was aridization (Shnitnikov 1957).

In response to aridization, development of steppe pastoral economics demanded the extension of inhabited territories, which was achieved through expansion into the northern river valleys. This caused clashes with local inhabitants and even between the pastoralists themselves for suitable pastures. On the one hand, the demographic situation was in flux among advanced hunters and fishermen, resulting in the redistribution of hunting and fishing grounds by force. On the other hand, the development of multifaceted economies (seasonal hunting and fishing, pastoralism, metalworking) demanded territorial stability regardless of group size. Growing socioeconomic contradictions led to the increase of aggressive strategies to solve critical problems. Thus, it is not accidental that there is extensive evidence of bloody clashes and military actions from the Samus' time on. Mass production of specialized weapons and armor emerged. Bronze arms for close combat were represented by large spears with a forking central ridge; bilateral and unilateral daggers with solid, sometimes decorated, handles; shaft-hole battle axes; and functionally universal axe-celts, variously decorated in a Samus'-Seimino style.

Long-distance arms included darts and compound bows and arrows. They are found frequently due to their universal functions. Metal darts were probably used exclusively for military goals. Bone tips of a compound bow were found in Krokhalevka 1 and Sopka 2 (Molodin 1983: 103; Molodin and Glushkov 1989: 23). A bowman had a set of arrows tipped with both bone and flint points of various shapes. A complete set of Samus' period military equipment is known from the Rostovka graveyard. It included armor bone plates from 15 to 45 cm in length (Matiushchenko and Sinitsina 1988: 7, 11, 47). Numerous plates of this sort were discovered in grave 33: 111 complete and thirty-seven broken ones. Judging from the number of plates and their size, the armor protected the entire torso and probably the arms as well. Along the sides the plates were evenly pierced with holes so that they could be tied together. An armored warrior was highly mobile and invulnerable.

The special significance of weapons for the Samus' was also expressed in ideology. Everything linked with weapons and their production was sacred and ritualized. This is clear from remains in both molder workshops and burial sites. Ritual pottery with solar, anthropomorphic, and zoomorphic decorations was discovered in the armor-producing workshop in Samus' 4. Implements used for polishing metal objects were frequently covered with anthropomorphic and phallic depictions, symbols of masculine power.[4] As a rule, purifying fires were used for warrior funerals, and special, isolated caches of weapons (maybe sacrifices or cenotaphs) were buried (Matiushchenko and Sinitsina 1988: 66; Molodin 1985: 81–83).

The wide variety of weapons employed in the Samus' period is understandable for it was a time of serious ecological and political turmoil in the zone of ancient civilizations, which resulted in mass migrations that reached the northern taiga. The introduction of complex technology for bronze production to the steppe and taiga zones of Asia was of no less importance and resulted in a wide variety of tin-bronzes, a highly sophisticated technology of point production, and the appearance of the famous Seimino-Turbino bronzes.

Military actions in the region were connected to the history of the Seimino-Turbino transcultural phenomenon evidenced in sites over a vast region inhabited by numerous different cultures. According to Chernykh and Kuz'minykh (Epokha bronzy 1987: 104), the original components of the phenomenon in question should be sought in the mountainous Altai region and among the hunters and fishermen north of the Sayan-Altai region. These united and aggressive tribes moved rapidly westward up to the Kama and Volga River areas and were superior to the local inhabitants in terms of weapons and means of transport. The aggressive tribesmen were horsemen who used chariots in warfare as well as strong hooks attached to Rostovka spears, which could stop their opponents' chariots by pulling the drivers out of the chariot or could stop horses by unseating their riders.

According to a number of authors (Epokha bronzy 1987: 105), these advantages resulted in the unimpeded rapid movement of the warriors-metallurgists. No doubt, there is some truth to this explanation, but one must also consider that the local inhabitants quickly switched to food production as well, adapting it to the local environment and traditions. Otherwise, it would be impossible to talk of any cultural entity, let alone such a strong one as Samus'.

A migration from the southwest occurred in the early Bronze Age (i.e., in the early second millennium B.C.) and appears to have been related to an economic and ecological crisis in this ancient agricultural region. The xerothermal maximum of the second quarter of the second millennium B.C. pushed farmers to new territories and forced some of them to switch to pastoralism. These developments were followed by an increase in aggressiveness, the erection of numerous fortresses, the development of weaponry, and the emergence of cultures with armored mounted troops (Dandamaev and Lukonin 1980; Masson 1989; Negahban 1964; Van den Berghe 1964), whose raids probably forced their northern neighbors to move to Upper Ob and Tomsk Ob areas. Interesting observations were made by Kiriushin (1994: 57–58) who revealed two different somatic types in the graveyards of the areas in question: (1) a Europoid ("Mediterranean") type arriving from the southwest; (2) a mixed local type with strong Mongolian features.

The first type was represented by men only, and the second one largely by women. There were many slain or mutilated skeletons in the graveyards; arrows were found among the bones, and severed limbs and skulls were discovered. Most skeletons belonged to men between twenty and thirty years of age. Apparently, men predominated among the migrants who occupied new territories in the course of heavy military campaigns and seized women for themselves.

In the late Bronze Age the bearers of comb pit ware, and later of crossed ware, moved in from the north, and Andronovo people moved in from the south. The latter were farmers and pastoralists who occupied territories that were unimportant to hunters and fishermen and maintained peaceful relationships with them. However, one should not exaggerate the peacefulness of their contacts. Competing cultural influences led to the breakdown of cultural and economic traditions, and serious territorial, marital, and ideological conflicts must have been settled by military means, which would explain the numerous weapons in two different cultural zones.

The Kulai culture developed in the Narym-Surgut Ob region between the fifth century B.C. and the fifth century A.D. One must distinguish two periods in its evolution: the early Kulai or Vasiugan stage (between the fifth and the second centuries B.C.) and the late Kulai or Sarovo stage (from the second and first centuries B.C. to the fifth century A.D.). The mass migrations of the Kulai in various directions began in the third century B.C. As a result, a vast cultural entity emerged, stretching from the mountainous Altai to the Arctic zone (Chindina 1984). The fates of western Siberian peoples were determined by the Kulai for many centuries. In ethnic terms, the migrations provided the basis for the formation of the Samoyedic ethnic group in the northern margins of Eurasia (Chernetsov 1963; Chindina 1977; 1978; 1984; 1991; 1992; Khelimskii 1983; Mogil'-nikov 1972; 1978; Vasil'ev 1979).

As a rule, migrations are caused by population growth accompanying local pressure on land or by political, ethnic, or ideological confrontation. Overpopulation, in turn, is a result of natural population growth or environmental decline. Thus, a contradiction emerges between population growth and capacity to provide ample subsistence in a traditional society with limited technological means. Excess population has to migrate in response. Rapid demographic growth in western Siberia was spurred by economic development in response to ecological crisis. Food-gathering technology was progressively improved in the region: for example, specialized trapping was introduced, and fishing methods became more diverse. Food production methods were also developing: horse breeds that were capable of retrieving fodder from under the snow were selected; special herd composition was established locally; and iron production was introduced with its rigid specialization. Bronze-working became widespread; in fact, each Kulai family practiced bronze casting (Chindina 1984: 135–46), which provided the material basis for population growth. Early Kulai settlement patterns were very impressive—huge sites emerged at that time covering up to hundreds of meters or even kilometers (for instance, Barsovo near Surgut and Stepanovo at Vasiugan). Separate kin communities used to settle close to each other, sharing a joint cult center and fortress.

Technological transformation came to an end at the Sarovo stage of the Kulai cultural development, when iron became the main raw material for weapon production. Firstly, this made the Kulai independent from the formerly highly restricted ore sources. There was plenty of raw material for iron production in the marshy areas of western Siberia, in contrast to the lack of copper ores. Secondly, it made labor more efficient and improved the well-being of the people. It is worth noting that the great bulk of the iron artifacts were weapons that corresponded perfectly with the needs of the Kulai sociopolitical environment.

Nevertheless, under predominantly hunting and gathering economic conditions and with limited technology, the productive forces, despite significant progress, could not support the rapidly growing population, which resulted in migration. With a predominantly hunting and gathering

TABLE 3.2 Osteological Data from the Kulai Sites

Sites	Vasiugan Stage				Sarovo Stage				
	Stepa-novo 1	Stepa-novo 2	Stepa-novo 4	Kamen-nyi Mys	Sa-rovo	Dubro-vinskii	Ust' Polui	Ust' Irmen'	Bolshoi Log
Fauna									
Horse	x		x	x	x			x	
Sheep				x		x		x	x
Cow				x		x		x	
Dog				x	x	x	x		
Moose	x	x	x	x	x	x	x	x	x
Reindeer					x		x	x	x
Roe deer								x	x
Brown bear	x								
Sable	x				x	x	x		
Beaver					x	x	x	x	x
Badger					x	x			
Wolverine					x	x			
Squirrel/fox					x	x	x		
Hare				x	x	x	x		
Birds	x			x	x	x	x		
Fish	x	x			x	x	x	x	?

Source: Chindina (1984: 130, Table 14).

economy (see Table 3.2), the Kulai were highly dependent on the surrounding natural environment. Severe ecological crisis caused by an increase in humidity and a fall in temperature took place in the late Holocene (ca. the fourth to first centuries B.C.). Tree species became less diverse, large tracts were flooded, and marshy areas grew extensively. Still, had the population been sparse, there would have been ample room for settlement.

The formation of marshes undermined the economic basis of the local inhabitants. Many riverine-lacustrine areas turned into a typically marshy environment. Lack of oxygen in the marshy waters caused massive fish death in wintertime. Marsh formation also resulted in a decline in soil fertility, stimulating the growth of plant species that are less appropriate for animal fodder, so animals had to look for richer pastures elsewhere. As the natural environment degenerated, people started to move to more favorable regions and to extend community territories. The complex processes in question were accompanied by drastic structural changes within the communities. In the Sarovo stage, subsistence grounds were divided between separate communities. The former large settlements disintegrated, patrilineally based communities spread widely all over the exploited territory, and community size shrank to three to five nuclear family dwellings and domestic structures.

Originally, people used to migrate to the south. As the taiga shifted southward at three to four degrees altitude (Krylov 1961: 69; Zubanov 1972: 182), a favorable environment emerged. When occupying such new areas, the Kulai used to remain within a familiar natural setting, i.e., within the taiga region. It is not accidental that all the Kulai sites were located only in mixed (coniferous-deciduous) forests in the vast region from the Upper Ob River to the Altay and Sayan mountain ranges. The Kulai then moved southward and to the southeast along the riverbeds or narrow passes between the marshy areas that were already occupied. As a rule, these movements were accompanied by bloody clashes between local inhabitants and the Kulai groups. The Kulai society then developed a high degree of militarism, which was by no means characteristic of hunters and fishermen in general. Intended to resist alien attacks, fortified sites became a widespread phenomenon that correlated with wars waged to seize and redistribute surplus. Among 130 known Kulai settlements, there are forty-five fortified sites, which were established both in Kulai territory and along routes leading to the alien grounds where many Kulai lived.

The Kulais produced weapons of a special style that differed from those of their steppe and forest-steppe neighbors. These weapons also served as valuable sacrificial objects and are found at all cult sites, where the best items were accumulated: swords, battle-axes, spears, and various arrows. Weapons symbolized strength and wealth. Judging from a depiction of a warrior from the Parabely cult site ("hoard"), as well as from rich weapons and dresses from other sites, a warrior-hero cult was emerging by the terminal Kulai period that became particularly pronounced in the Relka time.

The Kulai movement southward was accompanied by the destruction of local cultures. How was it that well-advanced cultures (Tagar, Sagat, and Bol'sherechensk) were defeated by these barbarians? In order to understand this issue, one must analyze the political situation among neighboring steppe inhabitants. The invasions of Alexander the Great in Central Asia at the end of the fourth century B.C. affected the entire Saka-Massagetic world. The Massagetae (Yüeh-chih) moved eastward to the Altai, the Upper Ob region, and the Minusinsk depression, where they mixed with local inhabitants (Chlenova 1994; Troitskaia 1979). Some new cultures emerged, in particular, the Tagar and Bol'sherechensk cultures. The political situation deteriorated in the east when in the late third century B.C. the Huns, headed by Shan-yüeh Mo-teh, destroyed Han China between 205 and 165 B.C. and defeated the Ting-lings (Tagars) and the Yüeh-chih, driving the latter to the west and conquering Sargat territories in the Irtysh steppe (Gumilev 1960; Mogil'nikov 1972). Differences in tactics and strategies of the opponents played a decisive role in weakening the southern tribes.

The Bol'sherechensk culture covered the Upper Ob territory and was one of the so-called Scythian-Siberian cultures (Troitskaia 1979: 6). From time to time the Bol'sherechensk warriors had raided the Tomsk Ob areas, and had overtaken the southern margins of their land by the third century B.C. There they came into conflict with the Kulai migrating from the north. The Bol'sherechensk warriors were less advanced militarily despite their association with the Scythian-Siberian entity. For instance, no weapons at all were found in 47 percent of the male burials, and short- and long-distance weapons were discovered in only 26 percent of the remaining graves (Troitskaia and Borodovskii 1994: 83). They were mounted bowmen armed with the typical Scythian bows and arrows with small points (Khazanov 1971; Meliukova 1964), which were effective for dense, unfocused shooting from horseback at an unprotected target. This tactic was well adapted for the open steppe, but did not work in a forest setting. In strategic terms, the Bol'sherechensk warriors had no plans to wage war against the forest tribes. They worried much more about steppe invaders like the Wu-sun or Yüeh-chih, which is probably why they had no fortified sites at all (Troitskaia and Borodovskii 1994: 81–82).

Kulai tactics, by contrast, were adapted to a diverse forest landscape. The Kulai used a heavy complex bow and arrows with large points, which penetrated easily and were accurate for longer distances (150–200 meters). Waging wars in small dispersed groups, the skillful hunters used hunting tactics (secret approach, tracking, and ambush) for military purposes. Therefore, the Kulai were lethal enemies for the Tagar and Bol'sherechensk people. The Kulai bone armor, designed to protect against heavy Kulai weapons, was virtually invulnerable to small Scythian arrows. After the Kulai conquered new territories, they erected fortresses immediately to defend themselves and their newly acquired lands. They exterminated or assimilated local inhabitants, who must have retreated to the steppe regions, for Bol'sherechensk or Sargat sites have not been found by archaeologists working in the southwest (Chindina 1984; Troitskaia 1979). The Kulai were particularly hostile toward the Sargat groups, judging from archaeological remains (Chindina 1984: 164–65).

The warrior cult first emerged in the western and southern territories. The new stage in military development was linked to the southern taiga Relka and Potchevash cultures dated between the fifth and ninth centuries A.D. Military organization was strengthened significantly as a result of socioeconomic differentiation and the necessity to settle internal conflicts during the period of private ownership formation, growth of an elite, and pressure from the Turkic states (Chindina 1991). Then the fortified sites were turned into permanent settlements intended for special military goals. A privileged warrior stratum is well attested, accompanied by a hero cult. Warriors' corpses were cremated with special ceremonies in clan or separate graveyards (Finno-ugry i balty 1987). Special warrior representations are present in mobile art with marks signifying rank—infantryman, rider, heavily and lightly armed warriors.

In contrast to previous cultures, the Relka and Potchevash cultures had different socioeconomic features resulting from a complex, multifaceted subsistence base. New climatic deterioration (falling temperature) began in the Relka period 1,500 to 1,000 years ago. However, Relka adaptive strategy differed from that of the Kulai: instead of vast migrations, they developed food-producing economics (pastoralism and some farming) together with metallurgy. Some economic activities were highly specialized, e.g., fur-trapping, iron production, and metalworking. The private sector grew, and egalitarianism declined. The cultures were composed of tribal alliances incorporating various ethnocultural components. Relationships within cultures and between neighbors were ambivalent: aggressive acts led to frequent armed conflicts, and in order to preserve cultural unity much energy had to be expended in peacemaking.

The clash with early civilizations put hunters and fishermen of the Middle Ob region into an unfavorable position; the dispersed groups of the Relka and Potchevash cultures' descendants, who were often in conflict with each other, could not resist the organized military pressure of the Turkut, Kidan' Yenisei Kyrghyz, and Kymak states. The southern areas of the Middle Ob and Irtysh region thus were incorporated into those states, and their inhabitants had to pay fur tribute (*iasak*). The Kulai-Relka military traditions were kept alive, but now they worked against the bearers of these traditions. The Turkic conquest stimulated the development of an unbalanced economy based on extensive hunting and trapping for furs, while food production became negligible. This economic structure was further strengthened by the military-political system of the late medieval period and resulted in cultural degradation.

The militarization of society was ideologically expressed in a hero cult and in heroic epics. Foot soldiers and mounted warriors as well as sacred war dances were widely depicted during Kulai and Relka times (Chernetsov 1953; Chindina 1991). Some images represented in the mobile art were very close to the mythical *Tialiakhyng-Kantup-Khule* (the person in the conical helmet) or *Mir-Susna-Khum* (the sky rider of Ugrian mythology) (Mify narodov 1988: 153–54). He is a hero named *Iche* (*Ii*), the sun's son of Sel'kup tradition (Donner 1915; Mify narodov 1987: 595). Such rich representational material addresses the issue raised by Karl Donner concerning the antiquity and originality of Samoyedic epic. All of the mobile art from the Middle Ob territory, beginning with the Kulai culture, contrasts with the mobile art of neighboring cultures in its explicit preference to depict moose. This can be seen in representations of mythical riders. In Samoyedic oral traditions, the moose symbolizes the link with the upper world. It is highly probable that the warriors riding on horse- or mooseback expressed the "ethnic coloration" of this ancient culture hero.

Notes

The original Russian text was translated by Viktor Shnirel'man; the translation was stylistically edited by Polly Wiessner and Megan Biesele. Roger Powers cross-checked the archaeological terminology, and Peter Schweitzer, in consultation with the author, provided the final edit.

1. Oral tradition and ethnographic data on Siberian (mainly western Siberian) indigenous peoples, especially those who lived in the given region by the seventeenth century, are extensively used in this essay. The Sel'kups (Narym Ostiaks) are Samoyeds who inhabited the Middle Ob as well as the Taz River valley in the seventeenth century. The Khantys (Ostiaks, Ob-Ostiaks) are Ugrians who lived in the Lower Ob River valley. The Nenetses (both forest and tundra ones) are Samoyeds who lived in the Lower Ob River valley. The Evenks (Tunguses) belong to the Tungus-Manchurian linguistic/cultural group; some of them moved between eastern Siberia and the Middle Ob River valley.
2. We have little data from the Lower Ob Neolithic. Amnia 1 pottery is highly peculiar and differs from the other sites.
3. There are some doubts concerning the stratigraphic position of the sheep bones in the Samus' 4 site.
4. Some authors (Kosarev 1981: 212; Molodin and Glushkov 1989: 127–28) identify these artifacts as millstones and link them to farming. This interpretation for Samus' groups in general seems doubtful because irons were found together with weapons or cast objects, and in technological terms they are inappropriate for grinding.

References

Aspelin, J. R. 1875. *Suomalais-ugrilaisen Myinaistutkinnon Alkeita (Die Anfangsgründe der finnischugrischen Altertumsforschung)*. Helsingfors.

Bader, O. N. 1964. *Drevneishie metallurgi Urala*. Moscow: Nauka.

Bakhrushin, S. V. 1935. *Ostiatskie i vogul'skie kniazhestva*. Leningrad.

Borzunov, V. A. 1992. *Zaural'e na rubezhe bronzovogo i zheleznogo vekov*. Ekaterinburg: Izdatel'stvo Uralskogo Universiteta.

Chernetsov, V. N. 1953. "Bronza Ust'-poluiskogo vremeni." *Materialy i issledovaniia po arkheologii SSSR* 35: 121–78. Moscow: Izdatel'stvo Akademii nauk SSSR.

_____. 1963. "K voprosu o meste i vremeni formirovaniia ural'skoi (finno-ugro-samodiiskoi) obshchnosti." In *Congressus internationalis Fenno-Ugristarum Budapestini Habistus, 20–24 September 1960*. Budapest.

Chernykh, E. N. 1970. *Drevniaia metallurgiia Urala i Povolzh'ia.* Moscow: Nauka.

Chindina, L. A. 1977. *Mogil'nik Relka na Srednei Obi.* Tomsk: Izdatel'stvo Tomskogo gosudarstvennogo Universiteta.

_____. 1978. "Kul'turnye osobennosti sredneobskoi keramiki v epokhu zheleza." *Iz istorii Sibiri* 7: 161–74. Tomsk: Izdatel'stvo Tomskogo gosudarstvennogo Universiteta.

_____. 1984. *Drevniaia istoriia Srednego Priob'ia v epokhu zheleza.* Tomsk: Izdatel'stvo Tomskogo gosudarstvennogo Universiteta.

_____. 1991. *Istoriia Srednego Priob'ia v epokhu rannego srednevekov'ia (relkinskaia kul'tura).* Tomsk: Izdatel'stvo Tomskogo gosudarstvennogo Universiteta.

_____. 1992. "The Interaction of Arctic and Taiga Cultures of Ural-Siberian Area in the Iron Age." In *Specimina Sibirica. Tomus 5: The Arctic Papers of an International Conference.* Savariae.

Chlenova, N. L. 1994. *Pamiatniki kontsa epokhi bronzi v Zapadnoi Sibiri.* Moscow: Nauka.

Dandamaev, M. A., and V. T. Lukonin. 1980. *Kul'tura i ekonomika drevnego Irana.* Moscow: Nauka.

Donner, K. 1915. "Samoedskii epos." *Trudy Tomskogo obshchestva izucheniia Sibiri* 3(1): 38–53.

Epokha bronzy. 1987. *Epokha bronzy lesnoi polosy SSSR.* Moscow: Nauka.

Erdélyi, J. 1969. *Selkupisches Wörterverzeichnis (Tas-Dialekt).* Budapest: Akadémiai Kiadō.

Evseeva, N. S., and A. A. Zemtsov, 1990. *Rel'efoobrazovanie v lesobolotnoi zone Zapadno-Sibirskoi ravniny.* Tomsk: Izdatel'stvo Tomskogo gosudarstvennogo Universiteta.

Finno-ugry i balty. 1987. *Finno-Ugry i balty v epokhu srednevekoviia.* Arkheologiia SSSR. Moscow: Nauka.

Gimbutas, M. 1956. *Borodino, Seima and Their Contemporaries: Key Sites for the Bronze Age Chronology of Eastern Europe.* Peabody Museum of Archaeology and Ethnology. Proceedings of the Prehistoric Society 22.

Gorodtsov, V. A. 1915. *Kul'tury bronzovoi epokhi v Srednei Rossii.* Otchet rossiiskogo istoricheskogo muzeia za 1914 god. Moscow.

Gumilev, L. N. 1960. *Khunnu.* Moscow: Vostochnaia literatura.

Istoriia Sibiri. 1968. *Istoriia Sibiri, vol. 2.* Leningrad: Nauka.

Kastren, M. A. [Castrén, M. A.]. 1860. *Puteshestvie po Laplandii, Severnoi Rossii i Sibiri.* Magazin zemlevedeniia i puteshestvii 6(2). Moscow.

Khazanov, A. M. 1971. *Ocherki voennogo dela sarmatov.* Moscow: Nauka.

Khelimskii, E. A. 1983. "Rannie etapy etnogeneza i etnicheskoi istorii samodiitsev v svete iazykovykh dannykh." In *Problemy etnogeneza i etnicheskoi istorii samodiiskikh narodov.* 5–10. Omsk: Izdatel'stvo Omskogo Universiteta.

Kiriushin, Iu. F. 1994. "Migratsionnye protsessy v Verkhnem Priob'e v epokhu eneolita i v bronzovom veke." In *Paleodemografiia i migratsionnye protsessy v Zapadnoi Sibiri v drevnosti i v srednevekov'e.* 5–8. Barnaul: Izdatel'stvo Altaiskogo gosudarstvennogo Universiteta.

Kosarev, M. F. 1981. *Bronzovyi vek Zapadnoi Sibiri.* Moscow: Nauka.

Krylov, M. F. 1961. *Lesa Zapadnoi Sibiri.* Moscow: Izdatel'stvo Akademii nauk SSSR.

Kuper, Sh., and Ia. Pusztay. 1993. "Sel'kupskii razgovornik (narymskii dialekt)." In *Specimina Sibrica.* Köszeg, Hungary: Péter Tillinger.

Lukina, N. V., ed. 1990. *Mify, predaniia, skazki khantov i mansi.* Moscow: Nauka.

Mal'tsev, F. G. 1843. "Slovar' russko-ostiatskii." St. Petersburg.

Masson, V. M. 1989. *Pervye tsivilizatsii.* Leningrad: Nauka.

Matiushchenko, V. I. 1973. *Drevniaia istoriia naseleniia lesnogo i lesostepnogo Priob'ia. Chast' 2: Samus'skaia kul'tura.* Tomsk: Izdatel'stvo Tomskogo gosudarstvennogo Universiteta.

Matiushchenko, V. I., and G. V. Sinitsina. 1988. *Mogilnik u derevni Rostovka vblizi Omska.* Tomsk: Izdatel'stvo Tomskogo Universiteta.

Meliukova, A. I. 1964. *Vooruzhenie skifov*. Moscow: Nauka.

Mify narodov. 1987. *Mify narodov mira, tom 1*. Moscow: Sovetskaia entsiklopediia.

Mify narodov. 1988. *Mify narodov mira, tom 2*. Moscow: Sovetskaia entsiklopediia.

Mogil'nikov, V. A. 1972. "K voprosu o sargatskoi kul'ture." In *Problemy khronologii v drevnei istorii ugrov*. 66–86. Moscow: Nauka.

_____. 1978. "K kul'turnoi kharakteristike Zapadnoi Sibiri v epokhu rannego zheleza." *Iz istorii Sibiri* 7: 175–89. Tomsk: Izdatel'stvo Tomskogo gosudarstvennogo Universiteta.

Molodin, V. I. 1983. "Pogrebenie liteishchika iz mogil'nika Sopka 2." In *Drevnie gorniaki i metallurgi Sibiri*. 96–109. Barnaul: Izdatel'stvo Altaiskogo gosudarstvennogo Universiteta.

_____. 1985. *Baraba v epokhu bronzy*. Novosibirsk: Nauka.

Molodin, V. I., and I. G. Glushkov. 1989. *Samus'skaia kul'tura v Verkhnem Priob'e*. Novosibirsk: Nauka.

Morozov, V. M., and V. I. Stefanov. 1989. "Issledovanie v basseine r. Kadym." In *Arkheologicheskie otkrytiia Urala i Povolzh'ia*. Syktyvkar: Nauka.

_____. 1993. "Amnia 1—drevneishee gorodishche Severnoi Evrazii?" *Voprosy arkheologii Urala* 21: 143–70.

Negahban, E. O. 1964. *A Preliminary Report of the Marlik Excavation*. Teheran.

Neishtadt, M. I. 1971. "Mirovoi prirodnyi fenomen—zabolochennost' zapadnosibirskoi ravniny." *Izvestiia Akademii nauk SSSR. Seriia geograficheskaia* 1.

Patkanov, S. K. 1891. *Tip ostiatskogo bogatyria po ostiatskim bylinam i geroicheskim skazaniiam*. St. Petersburg.

Pelikh, G. I. 1972. *Proiskhozhdenie sel'kupov*. Tomsk: Izdatel'stvo Tomskogo gosudarstvennogo Universiteta.

_____. 1981. *Sel'kupy XVII v. Ocherki sotsial'no-ekonomicheskoi istorii*. Novosibirsk: Nauka.

Shnitnikov, A. V. 1957. "Izmenchivost' obshchei uvlazhnennosti materikov severnogo polushariia." *Zapiski Geograficheskogo obshchestva SSSR* 16 (n.s.).

Solov'ev, A. I. 1987. *Voennoe delo korennogo naseleniia Zapadnoi Sibiri. Epokha srednevekov'ia*. Novosibirsk: Nauka.

Spitsyn, A. A. 1893. "Arkheologicheskie iziskaniia v Viatskoi gubernii." *Materialy po arkheologii vostochnikh gubernii* 1.

Stefanova, N. K., and S. F. Koksharov. 1988. "Poselenie bronzovogo veka na reke Konde." *Sovetskaia arkheologiia* 3.

Tallgren, A. M. 1931. "Zur Chronologie der osteuropäischen Bronzezeit." *Mitteilungen der Anthropologischen Gesellschaft in Wien* 61.

Troitskaia, T. N. 1979. *Kulaiskaia kul'tura v Novosibirskom Priob'e*. Novosibirsk: Nauka.

Troitskaia, T. N., and A. P. Borodovskii. 1994. *Bol'sherechinskaia kul'tura lesostepnogo Priob'ia*. Novosibirsk: Nauka.

Vinogradov, A. P., A. L. Devir, E. I. Dobkina, and I. G. Markova. 1969. "Novye datirovki pozdnechetvertichnikh otlozhenii po radiouglerodu." *Geokhimiia* 10.

Van den Berghe, L. A. 1964. *La necropole de Khurvin*. Leiden.

Vasil'ev, V. I. 1979. *Problemy formirovaniia severo-samodiiskikh narodnostei*. Moscow: Nauka.

Zemtsov, A. A. 1967. *Geomorfologiia Zapadno-Sibirskoi ravniny (severnaia i tsentral'naia chast')*. Tomsk: Izdatel'stvo Tomskogo gosudarstvennogo Universiteta.

Zubanov, V. A. 1972. *Paleogeografiia Zapadno-Sibirskoi nizmennosti v pleistotsene i pozdnem pliotsene*. Leningrad: Nauka.

Chapter 4

HOMICIDE AND AGGRESSION AMONG THE AGTA OF EASTERN LUZON, THE PHILIPPINES, 1910–1985

———=(0)=———

Marcus B. Griffin

Introduction

The Agta, according to the anthropological literature, are egalitarian in the extreme, enjoy a minimal gender division of labor, and have fathers who are significant caregivers of children (Estioko-Griffin 1985; P. Griffin 1981; Griffin and Griffin 1992; Rai 1990).[1] At the same time, they are reported to exhibit one of the highest homicide rates in the world (Headland 1986; Knauft 1987) and are also reported to suffer stress on many fronts (Headland 1985). In this essay, I suggest that the Agta value cooperation and nonaggression, while I develop the thesis that much of the homicidal violence reported can be explained as a result of new stresses tied to rapidly deteriorating social, economic, and political conditions.

The Agta, like many other decentralized, egalitarian societies, tend to avoid conflict. Group harmony is sought and cooperation is generally mandatory. Survival depends upon the quality and smoothness of interpersonal relations. Like many societies around the world that do not have an institutionalized legal system, the Agta rely upon public opinion and group mediation to settle their disputes. Grudges may be held and resurface in times of tension and then finally be resolved through violent action. Such attacks, in turn, may require revenge killing. Disputes are usually, however, tempered through reconciliation or avoidance.

Though homicides do occur, Agta rarely accept lethal violence as appropriate in maintaining group harmony and stability. Raiding among dialect groups has traditionally been the only prominent form of violence among the Agta; homicides within linguistically bounded groups have only recently become noteworthy. Considering several groups of eastern Luzon Agta and their special behaviors and circumstances, we may find important variation in the frequency and context of homicide and related lethal violence. One group, the Ilagen[2] Agta and other Agta nearby in northern Aurora and southern Isabela Provinces, may suffer the greatest homicide burden; another, the Agta of southeastern Cagayan Province, may have a low homicide rate (see Table 4.1).

By looking at each homicide profile and the trend in homicide types over the past century, one gets a clear picture that homicides occurred in particular contexts and are remarkable only over the last two decades and within a very small geographical area. In fact, two brothers of the Ilagen group account for 27 percent of known homicide victims, both Agta and non-Agta, since 1960. Other killings were reactions to the aggression of soldiers and drunken non-Agta. Alcohol consumption has played a pivotal role in inter-Agta homicide, with 31 percent of known cases since 1960. Prior to about 1960, the history of Agta homicide is mostly of sporadic inter-language group raiding of which three are reported since 1910, with a notable one in 1948.

Agta violence may be separated according to the cause or contributing factors leading to violence and according to how the antagonists are socially related. Intra-group homicide, extra-group raiding, and jealousy and spurned love form the first category while alcohol, confrontations with non-Agta, and military conflict form the latter. Prior to 1970, intra-group homicides usually stemmed from spurned love and jealousy. There are no recorded alcohol-related deaths prior to 1970. Since 1970, alcohol has drastically increased the number of homicides among blood relatives. Disputes between Agta and non-Agta over land and poor treatment have greatly added to the number of homicides among both groups. As with intra-group homicide, alcohol consumption has fostered conflict between Agta and non-Agta.

Violence among simple societies is frequently explained in terms of sociobiology and reproductive success, functionalism and fraternal interest or group solidarity, and socialization (Knauft 1987). The Agta case fits none of these categories but is best explained in terms of historical forces. The increase in homicides among the Agta since 1970 largely occurs within the alcohol-related and interethnic (Agta : non-Agta) categories of causation. There is no evidence for any change in traditional homicide rates, except that alcohol may provide new contexts for violence. Instead, what accounts for the rise in homicide rates is the introduction of nontraditional forces through (1) a reduction in foraging space, (2) a reduction in foraging resource quality, (3) the exchange of forest products for alcohol instead of traditional foodstuffs such as rice and maize, (4) the political incorporation of the Agta into the Philippine nation-state, and (5) the exploitation of the Agta for political and military ends by local government officials.

The Agta, like all groups of people, are affected by what goes on around them. Social structures and the environment interpenetrate each other, and therefore a discussion of each with attention to historical change, in the Agta case, is necessary before descriptions and explanations of homicide can be dealt with.

The Environment

The nature of and variation in the ecological and social environments seem to have a bearing on the Agta's increasingly violent response to problems. At a minimum, the differential exploitation of resources by Agta and non-Agta may have contributed to reactions favoring violence and aggression by both parties. Certainly one may argue that the existence of the Agta today is socially and ecologically precarious (P. Griffin 1991) and that stresses on their health and well-being are increasing. The fragile nature of the natural resources and the difficulty of social resources confounds what has in the past been a fairly stable adaptation; the frustrations of Agta seem to be a part of their new propensity for violence.

The Agta environment is rapidly changing. Primary forest has been heavily logged; immigrant farmers have cleared forests for agriculture. Fruit and nut trees are fewer every year. Many wild yams are not able to thrive in other than primary forest. Rattan harvesting has reduced animals' food resources. Rivers and littoral zones are being overharvested and destroyed through lowlander use of dynamite, pesticides, and sodium cyanide.

Game animals are suffering a similar decline. The lack of faunal abundance within these forest areas may have more of an impact on Agta well-being than the abundance of plant foods. The game most hunted by the Agta are pig, deer, and monkey. All three have been declining in population as primary forest has been destroyed. While secondary forests are not entirely useless to the Agta, they do not sustain exploitable starches. Agta hunters claim that game animals tend not to be found in recent secondary forests. The loss of fruiting trees adds to the hardship as surviving animals carry less fat. These unprecedented hardships bring the Agta into direct opposition among themselves and with neighboring immigrant settlers.

The Agta perception of this change includes attitudes of resignation and indignation. They do temper their frustrations with talk of persevering in a bad situation. At the same time, demand for pork and venison by low-landers has increased while Agta desire for rice and items such as liquor, coffee, and a variety of consumer goods is on the rise (P. Griffin 1991; Peterson 1985).

Kinship and Residence Groups

Agta say, "a man without kin is a dead person" (Rai 1990: 31). Given that relatives are crucial to Agta existence (see M. Griffin 1996 for a discussion and analysis of Agta kinship), the nature of kinship and homicide among relatives may be central to explaining some recent Agta violence. Raiding that occurred before the 1960s, and which may still occur on a very small-scale basis, never resulted in the murder of one's own kin. Some nonkin were, and continue to be, enemies or potentially dangerous people. Kinship ties determine, through descent phrased groupings, what territory an Agta may pass through unmolested. Movement among residential groups is also dictated by the relative affection of kinship ties.

An Agta's recognized kin remain somewhat few in daily life terms yet are potentially quite large. Generation is an important limitation. The Agta do not often consider kinship past three lineal generations. As older relatives die, including spouses, those affines previously considered kin are generally no longer recognized. Cousins, both cross and parallel, and especially cousins who frequently reside in the same residence areas as the speaker, enjoy bonds as close as siblings. Some affinal relatives likewise develop extremely close emotional and support ties and in fact may be affectively closer than some consanguineal kin. The degree of affective closeness is largely an artifact of years of proximity in residence.

Families in a residential group may disperse and relocate for a variety of reasons. Renewal of close friendships with particular kin motivates some to change residence; resource scarcity and deteriorating relations with non-Agta may hasten moves. A primary cause of residential moves may be group discord. When Agta heatedly argue, conflict is defused by those in opposition avoiding each other for a few months. This cause of dispersal has also been described among the Mbuti and Ik by Turnbull (1968: 135–36) and is a common forager response to social stress. While group disharmony may be a frequent cause of Agta changing residence, the choice of where to move and how long one may stay is, again, dictated by kin affinity (i.e., actual as opposed to potential group membership).

Aggression

There are differences in the amount and level of violence among Agta. The Cagayan Agta are clearly different in their expression of violence from the Isabela Agta. The facts need mentioning that the two populations traditionally raided each other and that each considers the other to be more *ebukid*, or aggressive and backward, than itself. The southern Agta of Isabela have a higher rate of homicide than the northern, or Cagayan, Agta. The disparity in homicide rates cannot be substantiated statistically, but is clear from a review of the field notes of Griffin, Estioko-Griffin, and Rai, and from the author's own experience living with both groups. The frequent contact with immigrant farmer and violent mountain tribal populations such as the Ilongot (Rosaldo 1980) that the southern Agta have had, unlike the northern Agta, may account for this disparity in violence. However, further quantitative data are needed to support this perception.

Eastern Luzon's history of being a haven for insurgent military groups and political dissidents may have affected the Isabela Agta. This may be especially so of the Casiguran-Palanan area, which has been a traditional stronghold of the New People's Army (NPA) and various lost (renegade) Philippine Army commands since the late 1960s and early 1970s. The Cagayan Agta have not had this history of insurgent activity. However, the 1980s saw an increase in military conflict in the north, which produced an increase in Agta:non-Agta homicide. The data are not available to discuss a possible increase in Agta to Agta homicide, but given the Isabela model, an increase in intra-Agta homicide is not hard to imagine. This is, of course, assuming that prior to several hundred years ago, both the northern and southern Agta experienced a similar intensity of homicide and violence.

Agta kill in retribution for some perceived slight. Many homicides develop out of heated arguments. As mentioned earlier, if arguments are not defused by nonparticipants, the situation may turn lethal. A homicide may not occur immediately after an argument; the insulted individual(s) may ambush the other in the forest while hunting or fishing. Agta usually assume that hunting accidents are not accidents at all but retribution murders for prior grievances. Spontaneous killing, when drunk and not arguing, may be the expression of hidden animosity. Homicides are usually among relatives and are not indiscriminate.

Homicides among the Casiguran Agta dramatically rose from the 1970s and 1980s with the cause attributed to alcohol-exaggerated tempers. The Cagayan Agta, until 1985, were not exposed to readily available alcohol. In fact, the Agta of Nanadukan-Malibu professed a preference for coffee in 1980. Logging surveyors in Cagayan frequently traded coffee, not alcohol, in exchange for fish and meat. Not until 1982, when a logging road reached Malibu, did the Agta request alcohol instead of coffee from the resident anthropologists. My guess is that alcohol was desired in order to "properly" entertain the more frequent non-Agta passing through the area. Certainly alcohol has exacerbated violent conflict among Agta and between Agta and non-Agta (P. Griffin 1991; Peterson 1985). To what extent alcohol has distorted traditional violence among the Agta of the Sierra Madre range is not entirely clear but may be explored to the extent data permit. In this chapter some attention is given to contrasting the forms of violence.

In order to release group tension and to realize social control, kin often bicker and argue about one another's behavior. These arguments have three levels of seriousness, the most common and least serious of which is bickering. If personal comments are made rather than just undirected criticism, bickering may escalate to more serious arguments in which the parties return insults rather than ignoring them. This level is eased by others in the group joking and teasing those who are arguing. If insults become particularly hostile, such as criticisms directed at one another's foraging competence or stinginess, events may turn lethal.

In August 1981 the arrival of a particularly "incompetent" man and his "fat, lazy" wife caused a fair amount of group tension among those residing in Nanadukan. Kalbo, a luckless hunter, was the brother of Busibus, who was a son-in-law of one of the two elder male siblings around which the residence group revolved. Kalbo did not, therefore, have dense kin ties in the group to gloss over his and his wife's inadequacies. The following is a conversation I recorded in my journal that many in the residence group participated in while Kalbo was on one of his few fishing trips with his wife. I was thirteen years old at the time.

"Markes, do you know what incompetent means?" my friend Lakas asked me one warm afternoon while we pounded arrows.

"Incompetent?" I feigned ignorance. He could not possibly be referring to my progress smithing steel arrowheads. He had to be referring to someone else for the word used was extremely offensive to Agta. We were gathered inside my parents' hut and those that were not off hunting were looking at our Agta photograph-census book or watching me shape an arrowhead.

"That heavy sow never leaves her hut. All she does is sit and watch us work," complained Karling, an unmarried young woman.

"That fat …" her younger cousin began.

"That's enough, Merli!" said Tonkris. Tonkris was Lakas's father and the elder of the residential group's sibling set. He turned to me and spoke slowly and deliberately to ensure that I would not misunderstand. What was occurring was serious.

"Pay attention to this, Markes," he continued in a low voice and moved over to sit so close as to be against me. "Kalbo is an incompetent man. He makes poor arrows. They break easily and do not fly straight. He can not track game, the animals hear him and run away. He can only catch small sucker-fish, not mullet when spearfishing in the river. Understand and write that in your book. Incompetent. That is very, very bad for an Agta."

"Make sure you don't marry a woman like Kalbo's wife!" Tonkris's wife broke in.

"Quiet! You speak too loudly." Tonkris reprimanded. The group became silent. The subject was quickly changed as Tonkris explained how to pound the flaws out of the arrowhead I was working on. The women went back to looking at photographs; the men chewed betel and watched Lakas and me craft arrows.

Kalbo and his wife left the camp a week later. The potential for serious strife over hard feelings and disproportionate food sharing was gone and with it the likelihood of harsh words said loudly.

Everyday bickering is not uncommon in any situation in which two people have to live with each other. Among the Agta, such bickering is performed usually by one person who, for one reason or another, is emotionally stressed or no longer has patience. Events to cause such stress may be the general lack of food, the quality of the water, incessant rain, bothersome children, or the nagging of another person. Bickering of this nature may be viewed as venting frustration, and few pay attention to what the person says since the comments are thrown out at everyone and at no one in particular. However, if someone gets irritated by another's bickering, then comments turn from general to specific between the irritated and the irritable. Often spouses of both parties will tell each other to "shut up" and the conflict will end with grumbling. One party may leave the camp on a subsistence activity in order to be alone and cool off.

One incident in the 1980 Nanadukan rainy season camp illustrates this situation. Three brothers, all aged fifty or more, continued an ongoing dispute over relations with lowlander farmers and their desire to buy farmland from the Agta. One brother adamantly opposed the sale or even the presence of the non-Agta. Another, a long-time resident at the location, favored sale. Several times after heated discussion, including threats to kill any incoming farmers (as well as the resident anthropologists, who were hosted by the "favorable" man), the angry person would take to the forest to cool off, as well as to mull over his opposition. Once he took his wife and children away for several days. Eventually he left, not to return again during the anthropologists' two-year residence.

Arguments may persist and heighten in vexation. Issues turn from general behaviors of a person to particular shortcomings. One may be called lazy or an incompetent forager and poor provider. The behavior of one's children may be called into play. Sexual virility and performance may be insulted. There are myriad insults.

Any such situation unfailingly gets the attention of the entire group. These arguments are deemed serious and require settling for fear of violence. At this point, relatives start to make fun of the arguers and the issues they are arguing about. Brothers-in-law from each side may mimic together the sexual behavior of each insulted party. This generally causes those fighting to laugh. Laughter is a critical tension-breaker among the Agta. If genitalia are the topic, older kin may discuss loudly the various characteristics of male and female genitalia and how those disputing appeared when young and adolescent. Comic hunting events, such as falling down while chasing game, or a wild arrow shot, or one's panicked tree climbing when pursued by an angry sow, are remembered loudly when one's competence is questioned. Laughter breaks the pace of the argument and diverts the attention of those fighting.

Following an argument, the camp usually splits, as mentioned in the above example. This is a common form of conflict resolution to prevent the offenders from getting in each other's way or creating further group discord. The side that has the least strong family tie will set up a new camp or join another camp, depending on the season and wishes of others also moving. The function is to maximally reduce the conflict. The parties may get back together within the year; although insults are not forgotten, their sting deadens with time and distance. There are no accounts of arguing parties splitting permanently since kinship bonds are strong among the Agta.

The following example comes from the field notes of Navin Rai, who conducted his dissertation research in 1978 among the Agta of San Mariano, Isabela. The case exemplifies a relatively minor hassle that was resolved by a temporary split of group members.

> The three unmarried girls and three unmarried boys did not return last night. People in the camp waited around. In the morning, the topic was brought up by the mother of one of the young girls. Another man was agitating the topic. A man and an old lady argued. The lady was angry, imitating sexual acts. The man was the father of one of the young men in question.
>
> Man: "Did you see them making love?"
> Old Lady: "Men are too much these days."
> Man: "Men are hot for women these days."
> The discussion continued.
>
> Other camp members stayed more or less neutral, as if they were not listening. A few joined in laughing. Later the wife of the man in the argument took part in the discussion. She took the side of the old lady. It was later taken as a big joke.
>
> The early morning resumed, with people following their everyday tasks of pounding rice, fixing lean-tos, and tending children. The old lady and some children played "cha-cha-cha" on a tape recorder. Eventually everyone started dancing.
>
> Later that morning, most of the Agta gathered around Kabang's lean-to and discussed the movement of camp. The offending youths returned at 8:36 A.M.

They were quiet and wary. The man that defended them earlier in the morning against the old lady commented to his son that the young man had a "wet penis." They all kept quiet.

The youths brought back whiskey, beer, and rice from the meat that they had traded the day before in Del Pilar *sitio*. The men immediately started drinking.

The fight and fuss over the girls of Digud camp and the boys from other camps that were visiting to court the girls continued. The six of them kept quiet while their parents discussed what was right and what was not right to do. Women were particularly pissed off. Then a fight over who owns which batteries broke out. The camp is splitting and moving.

If members of a group do not joke during an argument, events may turn lethal. Unlike the !Kung (see Lee 1979 for recent !Kung behavior), the Agta do not resort to fist fighting or wrestling. Agta reach for knives, guns, and arrows when insults become too much to bear. This is similar to !Kung behavior of the past about which an elderly man said, "a [fist] fight like we saw could not have happened among the San of the old days, because the grown men seeing the fight, their hearts would rise and the arrows would start flying" (Lee 1979: 381). The Agta do not fight with fists but settle insults with arrows. These arrows are almost always deadly, as the Agta rarely miss a shot and shots are made at close range. As late as the 1960s, the Agta were still using poisoned arrows. Arrows these days, however, are equally lethal, being made of metal rather than bamboo or palmwood.

Wives may or may not participate in their husbands' violent episodes. In one case observed within a residence group, a set of brothers and cousins began drinking. As soon as they started, their wives quietly hid their bows and arrows, knowing from bitter experience that among those particular men conflict was likely and potentially lethal. In another case, a domestic dispute ended with an angry husband chasing his wife around and out of the camp, pursuing her with a machete and curses. She came back a few hours later, knowing he was not really intent on doing bodily harm.

Homicide

I will now divide Agta homicide into two categories, traditional and contemporary. The dividing line starts roughly between 1970 and 1975. The Agta do not speak of any such division, but I do because of the extremely uncharacteristic nature of violence since 1970. I will tie this change to the wider political economy of the region and the changing social role the Agta have in this system.

The Agta of Casiguran in Quirino and southern Isabela Provinces had a homicide rate of 209 per 100,000 per year between 1977 and 1984.[3] The majority of homicides were between relatives. Prior to widely available alcohol, killings stemmed from arguments. Other homicides were premeditated and the result of long-standing feuds and grudges. Lethal violence from alcohol-induced spontaneous aggression is recorded only after 1970. The rapid influx of immigrant farmers and traders after World War II may have caused this new pattern of spontaneous homicide. A few cases were the result of immigrant agriculturalists pitting Agta against one another. This interference of Agta life by settlers has also resulted in a significant number of homicides between the two groups.

The accounts of homicide among Cagayan Agta are limited to deaths by raiding in past years and to murders through military conflict in more recent years. Among the Casiguran Agta, intra-group homicide is known in a fashion unseen in Cagayan. One may argue that the traditional *expressions* of violence among Agta are largely similar. The *frequency* of violence may be the difference between eastern Cagayan and Isabela Agta.

Feuding, Jealousy, and Spurned Love

Table 4.1 lists the non-alcohol-related Agta:Agta homicides that have occurred in Eastern Luzon. Case #13 is the only known case among the (Dupaningan) Cagayan Agta. Homicides were traditionally committed for a variety of specific reasons. The thirteen cases listed in this table are fairly representative depictions of the causes and contexts of murder. Eight cases involved estranged love, marital problems, and competition for a woman's attention. Three cases involved insults and heated arguments. One killing involved death in the forest under ambiguous circumstances; the "accident" may have stemmed from hidden animosity. One case involved the sanctioned (i.e., unrevenged) killing of an offensive and violent man.

Marital problems seem to be a major cause of intra-kin conflict. Although spouse fidelity is highly valued among the Agta, affairs are not infrequent, and reactions to infidelity differ. Some spouses do nothing, others divorce, while others kill. There is almost always talk of wanting to kill. For example, upon my return to Palanan in 1993, my childhood playmate's wife had run off to the forest with another man, abandoning her husband and four young children. My friend was very angry but more concerned about his children's well-being than what to do immediately about his wife. Although my friend said that he would have gone to kill the man his wife was with *if* they had taken his children, his older cousin had to be repeatedly restrained for several days to prevent him from dashing off into the forest with bow and arrow in hand. So, a wife's lover may or may not be killed; the lover may be killed and the wife taken back home; sometimes just the wife is killed; and sometimes no one is killed.

TABLE 4.1 Non-Alcohol-Related Agta:Agta Homicides, Eastern Luzon

Case No.	Killer	Sex	Victim	Sex	Year	Reason
1	Taun	m	Puktu	m	1920	revenge against his sister-in-law's lover
2	Dungas	m	Golgol	m	1940	Golgol had an affair with Dungas's wife
3	Suket	m	Munoy	m	1950	Munoy insulted Suket in front of a girl both wanted to marry
4	Gayak	m	Mungaw	m	1971	revenge for Mungaw killing Gayak's third cousin
5	Dimas	m	Tanduay	m	1966	the two brothers-in-law always argued
6	Rambat	m	Singgat	f	1970	Singgat would not leave her sick husband and 3 children so he killed her and the children
7	Aluping	m	Bulitug	m	1974	Bulitug married Aluping's mother and then often beat her
8	Kuton	m	Angaben	m	1976	"hunting accident," but some say the killing was over a grudge
9	Dandani	m	Abuhes	m	1977	Dandani felt his brother was not fair in distributing meat
10	Weswes	f	Amel	f	1982	Weswes was jealous of her new, younger cowife
11	Abuyug	m	Lawak	m	1983	Lawak had taken his eloped daughter back from Abuyug's son
12	Himat	m	Danda	f	1976	Danda ran off with Himat's cousin
13	Tanggay	m	Dodo	m	1974	Dodo allowed Tanggay's dog to be eaten by a crocodile

However, there are no records of a wife killing a husband over unfaithfulness. In the case of my childhood friend, after three months his wife and her lover "surrendered" ("surrender" is a term used for New People's Army insurgents, including Agta, who turn themselves in to local military authorities to proclaim an allegiance to Philippine society, government, and law).

Three cases from my data set depict such variation in response to adultery. In Case #1, Sakaya's[4] lover was killed while she returned to her husband. In fact, the one to avenge the affair was her sister's husband, not her own husband. This indicates the closeness that brothers-in-law may develop over time despite the principle of respect (*igalang*) that guides most in-law relationships. Case #2 describes Dungas having killed his wife's lover and bringing her home. On the other hand, Case #12 shows that Himat killed his wife and not her lover for the lover was his cousin.

Himat probably did not kill his cousin for reasons of blood affinity alone; undoubtedly the two men were closely bonded from childhood. As the data indicate, reactions to adultery depend upon the individual, and there are no strict rules for treatment of adulterers.

Competition over prospective spouses accounted for several of the documented homicides. Case #11 describes how the father of a new groom killed the bride's father for dissolving a marriage after the young couple eloped. In Case #6, Rambat killed Singgat and her three children for not running away with him. A second wife was killed in Case #10 by her jealous cowife. While Agta men may take a second wife if the first is unable to bear children, rarely does this result in homicide. While killings occur between men in competition for a woman, the death of a competitor usually involves the victim having insulted the perpetrator. A woman often has more than one suitor, but not all courtships involve suitors insulting one another. Emotional attachment and desire for a woman combined with personal offense tend to dominate as reasons to kill a competitor when insulted.

Family and group discord may bring about a homicide. One may view some of the aforementioned insult retribution killings as a form of reducing future conflict and promoting group cohesion. Little or no retribution is made against a person who kills when the victim is deemed a sorcerer or troublemaker. For example, in Case #7, a teenager shot his stepfather at the request of his mother because the man had often beat her. The victim was not avenged by his relatives for he was widely considered a bad man and they felt that he "deserved what he got."

Agta rarely accept deaths in the forest as accidental. Case #8 involved the death of a man in the forest under uncertain circumstances. Most Agta, but not all, believed Angaben accidentally shot Kuton with a rifle while the two were hunting together. But this case is an exception. As homicides frequently occur in ambush when the victim may be hunting, deaths in the forest are rarely believed to be accidental, and therefore may be revenged.

Alcohol and Intra-kin Homicide

Spontaneous aggression and lethal violence is a recent trend among the Casiguran Agta and invariably involves alcohol consumption. Due to alcohol-heightened passions and where prior grievances are not evident, an argument's intensity increases to the point that others are unable to stop the intoxicated antagonists. Table 4.2 gives an account of known alcohol-related homicides that are drawn from Tom and Janet Headland's personal records. There are no known alcohol-related murders among the eastern Cagayan Agta.

TABLE 4.2 Alcohol-Related Homicides among the Casiguran Agta

Case No.	Killer	Sex	Victim	Sex	Kin	Year	Reason
1	Kudham	m	Toblol	m	No	1976	drunken argument, no prior grievances known
2	Kallab	m	Saneg	m	?	1980	both were drunk, Kallab clubbed Saneg with no provocation
3	Basur	m	Imak	m	No	1980	self-defense, Imak attacked Basur while drunk
4	Apdit	m	Kuyog	m	Yes	1983	self-defense, Kuyog attacked Apdit while both were drunk and arguing
5	Kuso	m	Sugpu	m	Yes	1984	both got into a heated drunken argument
6	Dinuko	m	Buli	m	Yes	1984	drunken argument with no prior hostility
7	Piko	m	Mana	f	Yes	1984	husband and wife were drunk when suddenly Piko stoned Mana
8	Lapduk	m	Puli	m	Yes	1984	self-defense, Puli shot Lapduk in the upper left arm with an arrow but Lapduk managed to stab Puli five times in the chest

The four clubbing deaths indicate the spontaneous and irregular nature of alcohol-induced homicide. One victim was clubbed with a rifle butt, one with a large stick, and two with large stones. These are previously unrecorded methods of killing. The victims of these four attacks are also uncharacteristic of the Agta homicides previously described. Victims are usually not so closely related to one another. In one case, the victim and killer were good friends, in another a man beat his uncle to death, and a third man stoned his wife. The patterns of homicide previously described in Table 4.1, if related at all, usually involved affines, not blood relatives. This violence may be the reflection of Agta not being able to control stress and, when intoxicated, taking their frustrations out on the nearest person—usually a relative.

Data indicate that the attempt to take another's life instigates the reaction of killing the attacker rather than merely disarming him. This is demonstrated by Case #3 in which Basur dropped a heavy log on his attacker's head after he was knocked out with a bottle and no longer a threat. Aggression is met with aggression when the instigator does not maintain smooth interpersonal relations.

Conclusion

Most Agta men seem capable of homicide. Troublemakers do account for a sizable percentage of murders, however. Dimas and his brother Alokong are good examples of what other Agta label "bad Agta." In other words, a "bad Agta" is someone who is uncooperative and doesn't try to get along or persevere in the face of difficulty. There do not seem to be any prohibitions in principle against an Agta killing another. Of course, consequences of retribution are very prevalent and almost obligatory. A murderous Agta can count on being attacked in revenge at some point in the future and probably when most vulnerable. This may be the largest deterrent, excepting the Agta propensity for frowning upon aggression and lethal violence in general.

Killer-victim relationships may or may not be an expression of socialization; the data are inadequate to say either way with confidence. Weswes, the woman who partially decapitated her new cowife, was the daughter of Dimas, a man with many known homicides. However, since father-child relationships are not authoritarian or disciplinarian (see Griffin and Griffin 1992 for a discussion of father-child relationships) and girls tend not to use fathers as role models, Weswes's case is not representative. Although children do receive slaps for not obeying or for not tending younger siblings properly, with mothers generally doling out slaps more than fathers, displeasure with a child's behavior is more often expressed verbally than physically. Furthermore, older siblings provide the bulk of care and socialization for younger siblings.

Although socialization of children to be aggressive or violent seems unlikely in the Agta case, there has been a great deal of lethal conflict between Agta and non-Agta settlers, soldiers, and loggers that may result in a violent regional environment. While data do not exist to demonstrate conclusively a causative relationship, the violence stemming from insurgent warfare has undoubtedly spilled into Agta society. Murders involving Agta and non-Agta often occurred when either or both groups had been drinking. Other cases of homicide are vengeful in nature, especially in conflicts involving soldiers and Agta men. Agta helping soldiers may bring them into opposition with Agta helping insurgent forces. Agta receiving more material goods than others from lowlanders may cause resentment among relatives as norms of resource distribution at times may be ignored.

When harassed by non-Agta, Agta may resort to violence more readily than if an Agta were antagonizing them. This seems to be rooted in their complaint that while Agta can control the behavior of other Agta through kin-based social pressure, they are powerless to affect the behavior of non-Agta. Since Agta traditionally met personal insult with violent retribution, the frequent killing of non-Agta therefore is not surprising, given the frequency with which land is stolen by farmers and labor is demanded by soldiers. In 1982 at a logging station in the Ilagen area of Isabela, an Agta of renowned temper was offended by the station manager. Speaking to the anthropologists interviewing him, he said: "You see that man over there?" pointing at the station house thirty yards away, "You tell that man that if he looks at me like that again I'll kill him." His wife became alarmed, as did the station manager, for the Agta was taken very seriously. Many Agta, while valuing peace and cooperation, may be at the end of their rope and may develop a reputation of violence so that they will no longer be taken advantage of.

Scarcity of local and imported resources has caused the lowering of living standards and has resulted in intra-kin conflict as resource distribution patterns shift. With the forest no longer capable of supporting the Agta, the increasingly widespread use of Agta as wage labor brings unrelated Agta together in new systems of cooperation and conflict. Patterns of homicide will probably continue to increase and spread as long as non-Agta continue to antagonize Agta attempts to overcome exploitation and engage national society on more equitable terms.

Notes

1. This essay is a revised version of my 1991 senior thesis at the University of Hawaii at Manoa, which was also presented at the Seventh Conference of Hunting and Gathering Societies, hosted by the Russian Academy of Sciences, Moscow, Russia, August 1993. Much of the data has been provided by Janet and Thomas Headland and supplemented with my own field research. John Early and Thomas Headland (1998) have a published demography of the Casiguran Agta that is relevant to my discussion of Agta homicide.

2. The Ilagen Agta are one "river-drainage group" within, perhaps, the Casiguran Agta linguistic unit. Thomas Headland includes them in his census of Casiguran Agta. Other names might be applied; they just call themselves Agta and "from" the Ilagen river drainage.

3. The actual figure of Casiguran Agta homicide is unclear. Headland's Ph.D. dissertation (1986) states on page 391 that fourteen homicides occurred between June 1977 and May 1984 in a population of 4,340 (or two homicides per year in a population of 614 [p. 400].) This gives a figure of 326 homicides per 100,000 per annum ([2/6,140] x 100,000=326). However, Headland's personal data files indicate only twelve homicides occurred between these same years. The lower figure has been chosen to avoid potential error.

4. Names of people have been changed to protect their identities.

References

Early, J., and T. Headland. 1998. *Population Dynamics of a Philippine Rain Forest People: The San Ildefonso Agta*. Gainesville, Fla.: University Press of Florida.

Estioko-Griffin, A. 1985. "Women as Hunters: The Case of an Eastern Cagayan Agta Group." In *The Agta of Northeastern Luzon: Recent Studies*. P. B. Griffin and A. Estioko-Griffin, eds. 18–32. Humanities Series, No. 16. Cebu City, Philippines: San Carlos Publications.

Griffin, M. B. 1996. "Change and Stability: Agta Kinship in a History of Uncertainty." Ph.D. diss., University of Illinois at Urbana-Champaign.

Griffin, P. B. 1981. "Northern Luzon Agta Subsistence and Settlement." *Filipinas* 2: 26–42.

_____. 1991. "Philippine Agta Forager-Serfs: Commodities and Exploitation." In *Cash, Commoditisation and Changing Foragers*. N. Peterson and T. Matsuyama, eds. 199–222. Senri Ethnological Studies, 30. Osaka: National Museum of Ethnology.

Griffin, P. B., and M. B. Griffin 1992. "Fathers and Childcare among the Cagayan Agta." In *Father-Child Relations: Cultural and Biosocial Contexts*. B. S. Hewlett, ed. 297–320. New York: Aldine de Gruyter.

Headland, T. N. 1985. "International Economics and Tribal Subsistence: A Report of a Microeconomic Study of a Negrito Hunter-Gatherer Society in the Wake of the Philippine Crisis of 1983." *Philippine Quarterly of Culture and Society* 13: 235–39.

_____. 1986. "Why Foragers Do Not Become Farmers: A Historical Study of a Changing Ecosystem and Its Effect on a Negrito Hunter-Gatherer Group in the Philippines." Ph.D. diss., University of Hawaii.

Knauft, B. M. 1987. "Reconsidering Violence in Simple Societies: Homicide among the Gebusi of New Guinea." *Current Anthropology* 28(4): 457–500.

Lee, R. B. 1979. *The !Kung San: Men, Women and Work in a Foraging Society*. Cambridge: Cambridge University Press.

Peterson, J. T. 1985. "Hunter Mobility, Family Organization and Change." In *Circulation in Third World Countries*. R. M. Prothero and M. Chapman, eds. 124–44. London: Routledge.

Rai, N. K. 1990. *Living in a Lean-To: Philippine Negrito Foragers in Transition*. Anthropological Papers, Museum of Anthropology, University of Michigan, No. 80. Ann Arbor: Museum of Anthropology, University of Michigan.

Rosaldo, R. 1980. *Ilongot Headhunting, 1883–1974: A Study in Society and History*. Stanford, Cal.: Stanford University Press.

Turnbull, C. M. 1968. "The Importance of Flux in Two Hunting Societies." In *Man the Hunter*. R. Lee and I. DeVore, eds. 132–37. Chicago: Aldine.

Chapter 5

Conflict Management in a Modern Inuit Community

———=◉═———

Jean L. Briggs

This chapter examines what happens to traditional means of solving interpersonal difficulties when Inuit move from small camps into large communities.[1] Such moves, though they alleviate, even solve, some of the problems of camp life, create others in their stead. To put the situation in the simplest—perhaps oversimple—terms, nomadic Inuit, moving into a settlement, exchange physical hardship and (relative) social ease for physical ease and social hardship. On the physical side, no matter how inadequate the diet in the settlement is felt to be, there is no longer need to fear starvation; no matter how inadequate the housing, it is always heated somehow; no matter how ill people get, there are nurses and doctors to tend them; and if one has no means of earning money, welfare will, no matter how inadequately, provide. But on the social side, a great many unfamiliar and difficult situations are now encountered. Uncertainties with which Inuit had established ways of dealing have been replaced by uncertainties that they do not know how to manage.

How are conflicts resolved under these new circumstances? What has survived of old methods, and how have old and new been adapted to one another? I begin by briefly outlining some old ways of keeping and restoring peace in hunting camps, and how those strategies worked. Then I describe the new situation in one Canadian Arctic settlement and suggest reasons why the old mechanisms cannot work in that context. Finally, I discuss an interesting new way of dealing with tension that is developing in the community—a new way that both embodies and carries forward some aspects of traditional strategies.

In Nomadic Camps

The aim of traditional conflict management was to keep social relations smooth. People had several ways of averting conflict before it could arise. They were reluctant to express personal wishes, except through the most indirect of hints or exaggeratedly playful jokes, which allowed others to "not hear" if they so chose. At the same time, they were acutely sensitive to hints and jokes and even subtler signs of the existence of another's need, and they took pains to anticipate and fulfill those wishes, so that it was rarely necessary to make a request. If, in exceptional circumstances, someone did ask for something, the wish was granted if at all possible; and if it was not possible, careful excuses were made.

Unhappiness, discontent, and irritation were kept to oneself or formulated as cheerful jokes, partly because unhappy people were considered dangerous. It was thought that such individuals might resort to aggression in the attempt to change their situation or overcome their dissatisfaction or unhappiness. Indeed, stories were told of people who had killed, or threatened to kill, in grief following an accidental death. Alliances could be dangerous, too, creating factions and escalating conflict by spreading it more widely, so people did not ask one another for support when they were at odds. In general, people did not interfere with one another's actions and did not try to influence or even inquire into each other's intentions, plans, or motives. Above all, they refrained from criticism, except under special circumstances, which will be described below.

On the very rare occasions when people argued or quarreled, bystanders remained silent or melted away altogether, rather than taking sides.[2] But in difficult cases, the community as a whole might delegate someone to lecture the troublemakers in a public forum, such as a campwide feast (Muckpah 1979), or the catechist might pray for them during a campwide church service.[3] On the other hand, if the squabble was between children and was therefore not frightening, adults were likely to laugh, joke, and try to turn the dispute into play. Clearly, all these strategies were designed to defuse the conflict; to isolate it; if possible, to make play of it; and so to pacify the quarrelers.

One well-known and striking exception to the pattern of nonconfrontation in pre-Christian days was the song duel, but the ritualized confrontation of the song duel was at the same time an outstanding example of the same principles of indirection, denial of hostility, and pacification that governed nonconfrontational modes of dealing with conflict.[4] The song duel, like the public lecture, was resorted to in exceptionally troublesome cases, when the feelings of the antagonists ran too high to allow them to keep silent. In the duel, the two offended parties exchanged scathing songs while an amused audience looked on; but distance was created between the antagonists, and between them and their conflict, by means of several devices. First, the contests were held during festive gatherings, and the songs were easily confused with the good-humored, playfully insulting songs that friendly joking partners directed at each other in the same gatherings. Moreover, the dueling songs never focused clearly on the conflict in all its particular, controversial detail. A successful song created a smoke screen through the use of irony—or the ambiguous appearance of irony—as well as metaphor and allusions. In short, the duel embedded conflict in an artistic form, isolated it within a ritualized context, concealed it behind irony and an ambiguity of genre, and at the same time publicized it by focusing the attention of the entire community on it. The festivity, the ambiguity, and the presence of an unaligned audience allowed the antagonists simultaneously to confront each other in a safe context and to avoid confrontation—or more precisely, to pretend they were not confronting.

Another salient characteristic of the song duel was that the singers were required to avoid argumentation and self-justification. A countering song was not a rebuttal or a defensive statement, which might have escalated the quarrel; it was instead a counterattack on some other subject. Thus, the conflict never took the form of a logically linked series of propositions, which could have built to a firm conclusion concerning "right" and "wrong," with its residue of disgruntled "loser," nor did it explode into an all-out battle between factions competing to have their version of truth recognized and to destroy the opposition. These would have been unbalanced solutions; at the end, some people would have "belonged" to the community more solidly than others. In a song duel, performances were judged not according to the righteousness of the case, but by their artistic quality. When the duel or the feast was over, the conflict was supposed to be over, too, and the offenders were (ideally) reincorporated fully into the community.

Notice, now, some of the consequences of traditional ways of managing social conflict. First, attention was paid to the needs of others, on the one hand, and care was taken not to interfere, on the other hand, so that a high level of social responsibility was balanced with a great degree of personal freedom. Secondly, the same pattern of noninterference—which, as I have said, was very broadly defined to include nonintrusion into other people's minds, maintenance of one's own mental privacy, and physical withdrawal from difficult social situations—not only served to prevent confrontation but also created and maintained an emotional and social distance that helped to keep social relationships smooth, at least on the surface. Discretion may have worked on a more profound level, too, by preventing many frustrations and irritations from occurring at all. Thirdly, this emotional and social distance, which inhibited the flow of information, in addition to maintaining smooth surfaces, also created useful doubts about the intentions of other people and the meanings of their actions. On the one hand, these uncertainties allowed people generously to "give the benefit of the doubt" and to refrain from condemning hastily. But doubting also kept people alert to dangers—resentments and hostile intentions—that might be concealed beneath the surface; such alertness made it possible for people to soothe unspoken hostilities and to repair undisclosed troubling situations before they could break through. Doubt—ambiguity again—allowed people to see others simultaneously as friend and foe, as joking and insulting. There was no clean division between good people and bad. Finally, since people were not singled out as "bad people" in the social drama, they were neither isolated nor humiliated by being made the focus of critical attention but rather were kept integrated in the community. People were not rank-ordered according to their social worth, the bad being less socially accepted than the good—as happens when justice and retribution are the fundamental principles according to which conflicts are resolved.

These ways of managing conflict worked very well in the tightly interdependent world of a hunting camp or a small, homogeneous settlement. But in order for such dynamics to work, it is necessary to *have* a small, tightly interdependent community, composed of people who are well known to each other and who share many assumptions about what is to be valued and what behaviors mean. When these conditions obtain, people can agree on the issues in social life, without having to make them explicit and thus open to argument. They can imagine one another's needs accurately. When someone withdraws from interaction, they can guess the cause and remedy the situation. When someone drops a hint or makes a joke, others can draw from a limited range of possibilities to interpret the message.

In order for traditional strategies to work, people also have to want to fill each other's needs, because they are affectionately bonded to one another; and they must fear the sanctions of rejection and ostracism that may be imposed if they fail, because no alternative life situations are available. It is true that in extreme cases, a family—even an individual—could walk away from camp and set up camp somewhere else, alone. But both physically and emotionally, such a course of action would be very difficult to take.[5]

In Modern Settlements

In most Arctic communities today it is not possible to avoid conflict.[6] For one thing, many settlements are too large and too diverse in all manner of ways. The settlement under discussion here is of this sort. First, it is ethnically and linguistically diverse. Represented are not only Inuit and *Qallunaat* (Europeans and Euro-Canadians) but also, and perhaps equally troublesome, a number of different Inuit groups, who speak different dialects and suffer from a variety of usually unpleasant preconceptions about one another. There is economic and educational variation, too. Incomes range from a few hundred per month for people who are on welfare to the extremely high sums earned by artists and sculptors, a few of whom are millionaires. Amount of schooling ranges from none at all in older generations to several individuals who have teaching degrees from provincial universities and many who have high school education or vocational training of one sort or another. Experience outside the community also varies greatly. A few people have never traveled beyond the settlement and its hinterlands, while many others have visited, or even lived for a while, in southern Canada for medical or educational purposes; and some few—sculptors attending exhibitions of their works, or high school children on organized trips, or women married to Europeans—have visited Europe or Latin America. Of course, with or without formal education and travel, people vary with regard to the kinds and extent of expertise they have managed to acquire. Needless to say, all of this diversity results in a variety of lifestyles, values, and goals, with attendant social divisions and hierarchies of influence and power. I think we have always overgeneralized about the cultural "traits" shared by the members of a group, but now it is even more irresponsible than it was formerly to make general statements about what "Inuit" do, think, and feel.[7]

   Diversity and complexity is found also in the texture of a single individual's life. To take one example, Samuel [a pseudonym], a man of about forty, is a hunter, a sculptor, and a town official. When he is at home, he spends a great deal of time camping "out on the land," and one often finds an animal carcass lying on the kitchen floor, from which people help themselves when they are hungry, in the style of camp life. He ran for elected office, a new phenomenon, in his settlement, but his reason for wanting the office had strong traditional resonances: "If you love these people you have to help them." In addition, Samuel teaches sculpture to other native sculptors in a southern city. He speaks good English and good Inuktitut, a combination that is rare in this community. He also writes songs about strongly felt personal vicissitudes, as his grandparents and other old-time Inuit used to do. The words, often reflecting Christian religious beliefs, are in Inuktitut, and the tunes are "western," sometimes borrowed from hymns and sometimes created by Samuel himself on a country-and-western model. And as he bounces over the tundra in his four-wheel-drive truck, coming back from fishing, a Mozart quartet plays on his tape deck. He says he likes to play chamber music before he goes to sleep, too, because it is peaceful.

Needless to say, such an intermingling of traditions and lifestyles, both individually and socially in the community, creates a troublesome tangle of wishes and needs. People disagree about the legitimacy of any given expectation, and, thus, about whether it should be accommodated. Some of these disagreements are interpersonal, owing to divergent values. A traditionally oriented grandparent may think that a small child should be given what she wants, whereas a young parent influenced by Euro-Canadian child-rearing patterns may protest, "I don't want to spoil her." One person may feel offended when a kinsman, a friend, or even a neighbor asks for or offers money in exchange for some needed commodity, whereas others are offended if they are not offered money. Some people feel it is incumbent upon them to lend freely, when asked, any object, no matter how valuable, that they are not currently using—a boat, a snowmobile, a citizen's band radio—and at the same time, they resent being asked. Others refuse to lend for fear that the object will be damaged, and the person whose request is refused is outraged.[8] Problems also arise when people have consistently different resources at their disposal. A person on welfare may expect to be supported at need by a kinsman who has a job, while the latter, who has many financial obligations not understood by his have-not relative, may feel desperate at the drain on his funds.

Questions concerning the legitimacy of a need may also arise intrapersonally, that is, people may be ambivalent about their own goals, values, and so on, so that no matter how others try to assist, those who are helped perceive themselves to be unhelped. One woman of my acquaintance always wanted to be out on the land when she was in town and vice versa. When she was in town, she complained that none of her kin had offered to take her camping with them, and when she was out camping with some kinsman who *had* taken her, she complained that no one would come to pick her up and bring her home.

Another conflict-generating consequence of the diversity and size of the community is that there are just too many people who have needs to fill, and many of these people are not one's kin. This means that the bonds of affection and obligation that support prosocial behavior are much weaker in town than they were formerly on the land, and fear of sanction is also weaker. Moreover, as I have just suggested, even when people want to help others—kin or friends—their resources may well be inadequate because of competing claims. Here again is fertile ground for the breeding of frustration and resentment. The result of all these situations can be an acid bath of human relations, erosion of a sense of social responsibility, and proliferation of conflict.

Another problem, which generates a great deal of friction, is that individual freedom is eroded to the point where some people complain of feeling "caged." What causes Inuit to feel this way in a social context in which Euro-Canadians might experience increased opportunities for independent choice in thought and action, as compared with life in a hunting camp?

One part of the caged feeling is purely physical: some people find it hard to live in a house; they feel cooped up, uncomfortably enclosed. In such cases, periodic escape to "the land" is a real necessity, even if the "land" is only a tent pitched behind the house. But the cage is symbolic, too. It is not only that conflicts between incompatible lifestyles and goals, both (or all) intensely desired, make people feel bound or constricted: "I really want to live on the land, but I have to have a job to support my family." It is more than that. Town life entails contractual relations, which require unprecedented kinds of interference with the sort of spontaneous decision-making that was possible—indeed, mandatory—in the life of a hunter on the land. If one has a job, one has to make an explicit commitment to work, in a particular place and for a specific period of time defined in terms of hours, days, weeks, sometimes months. And if one wants to make an exception to this commitment—to take a day off, for example—one must publicly state one's intentions, sometimes even one's reasons. Worse, one must ask permission and subject oneself to the judgment of one's employer. It doesn't matter that one's child is sick and can't go to school and one has to find a babysitter, or that one has a hangover and overslept, or that the weather is fine for fishing and the larder empty of fish; one's employer considers it imperative, nevertheless, that one appears for work every day and on time. Any other behavior is "unprofessional" or "irresponsible," and employers tend to be very irritated when Inuit behave "erratically."[9] But the necessity to justify one's actions is an intrusion on what would be a legitimate sphere of privacy in camp life. Not only that, it places one in a subordinate and therefore demeaning status vis-à-vis another person. Moreover, when it is necessary to label intentions and reasons clearly and categorically, the safety screen of ambiguity, behind which so much of social life took place in camp, is peeled away, exposing one to others' judgments concerning the validity and legitimacy of one's actions and forcing confrontation.

There are also now community bylaws and other organizational regulations that have to be taken into account in planning one's activities. Like contracts, these universalistically formulated rules fail to take into consideration the contexts of action and the personal circumstances of an individual actor. Again, freedom of action is eroded and people feel caged and resentful—so much so that on one occasion the Inuit mayor of the community instructed the bylaw officer (who was not Inuit) to delay enforcing the laws that the Community Council (who were Inuit) had themselves formulated and approved.

In sum, life in a modern settlement both generates new sources of conflict and undermines old ways of managing it. Social order has to be renegotiated on a new basis, and new modes of communication more appropriate to life in a large and diverse community have to be found. Most importantly, those new modes have to involve *some* confrontation.

So what is happening? How is this difficult situation being met?

New Strategies for Conflict Management

Some, perhaps all, of the camp dwellers who moved into this settlement twenty or more years ago still fear aggressive confrontation. One man, for example, was reluctant to have me come to a meeting that he was chairing, because a controversial bylaw was to be discussed, and, as he put it: "We're going to argue." On the same subject, another person told me: "People won't come to meetings; they don't like to fight." I understood this reluctance when that same person told me about the violent fantasies she endured when she sat in meetings and heard people express views that she disagreed with. Again, a young woman told me that in order to avoid conflict with her mother, she did not speak to her for two years. And children regularly drop out of school when teachers criticize them.

Nevertheless, there is some recognition that old ways have become unworkable. Evidence of this is the wish (that is, advice) that was given by one older woman to her newborn namesake: "Learn to answer back—because *I* can't." New ways of dealing with interpersonal difficulties are also developing, ways that carry forward and combine with the new some elements of old, still active values and ways of interacting. In general, people recognize a much greater need to *talk* about issues and problems and *negotiate* solutions, and forums in which to engage in these activities are proliferating. For example, in the community under discussion there are more than twenty voluntary organizations, which play a great variety of roles: administering housing, overseeing the ecologically careful use of game, organizing recreational activities, consulting with troubled individuals, and so on. The forums are not all organizational, either. A number of people serve as informal advisors to their friends and relatives on domestic problems related to marriage and child-rearing—problems that never used to be discussed at all.[10]

I am going to limit my discussion here to just one of the new forums, one that I find exceptionally interesting in the way it combines old and new principles in managing social tensions. I observed its operation in only one community, but I am told that in one form or another it has developed in many other native settlements as well. I refer to local radio.[11]

There are actually two sorts of local radio in the settlement. One of these is citizen's band (CB), colloquially known as "red radio" because of the color of the instruments. Many, if not most, households have red radios and use them extensively, not only to keep contact between settlement and camp, or between camps when family members are out on the land, but also to communicate within the settlement, even when the people called on the radio also have telephones.

The other kind of local radio is the ordinary, centralized sort, with a "station" in a room of the local government building. I think this radio plays music for some hours every day, and perhaps there are other programs, too; but I never found anyone listening to any program other than the one I describe here. Most people seem to listen with religious regularity to this program, a phone-in hour that comes on twice a day, at lunch and supper time (noon and early evening). People who phone the host, a bilingual Inuk, either leave messages that the host relays to the community in both Inuktitut and English or speak their own pieces in either language, and—if it is a meeting notice or an announcement of some other public event, or in any case when the speaker requests it—the host will translate into the other language.

The phone-in hour is regularly used by settlement officers and organizational leaders of all sorts to make announcements and exhortations to the community at large. Meeting notices, promulgation of new bylaws, public health advice and warnings, reminders to individuals who have appointments to see visiting medical specialists, mundane school announcements, and lectures on the importance of sending one's children to school are all made through this channel, rather than on red radio, perhaps because almost all households have ordinary radios, whereas CBs, being more expensive, are more unevenly distributed.

While many of these organizational messages are "purely" practical, evoking a mundane response, others are likely to have emotionally charged connotations for some hearers: "The water in Fish Lake has been tested and has been found not safe to drink"; "Young people have to be at home by 11 o'clock on school nights"; "If hunters abandon animal carcasses they will be fined"; "Because of the danger of rabies, unchained dogs will be shot"; "Now that it's spring, we should clean up around the houses so that the town will look beautiful."

Both radios are used to send personal messages.[12] Some of these are practical, too—domestic requests, invitations—or simply informational: "Johnny, come home, your dinner's ready"; "Susie, come home and stay with the baby, I have to go to the store"; "I need a ride to the fishing lake"; "Michael, you're welcome to sleep and eat here if you want to"; "I had a phone call from Mary [in Montreal] today; she says a big hello to Michael and Ruby and Sally."

But again it is clear that such messages, though matter-of-fact on the surface, have a potential for communicating far more than the words themselves: "I care for you" and perhaps "You are heedless of that care";

"Why don't you ever stay home and be useful instead of running around town and neglecting your responsibilities?"; "Why don't any of my kin who have transportation ever think to offer to take me along?"; "My daughter and I forgive you for treating her badly"; "Mary's special friends are Michael, Ruby, Sally," and so on.

Other personal messages have more explicit emotional charges, both positive and negative, though they are phrased in general terms: "I am grateful to the people who helped me when my snowmobile broke down [out on the land]"; "I am an old man and it's hard for me to carry my groceries, nevertheless the young people of this town never offer to help me"; and "I don't like it when people come into my house, drunk, on Friday nights and make a mess."

Finally, some few messages are both highly charged and explicitly personal: A woman makes acid remarks about the defects of another's children; a mother pointedly asks her married daughter if she has taken an object belonging to her mother.[13] Most interesting of all, a daughter sends her mother a *loving* message that makes reference to the latter's recently deceased husband, and she tells me that her decision to use the radio was motivated by the fear that her mother would cry.[14]

Notice, now, how many of these messages are capable of generating conflict or just interpersonal discomfort. Troublesome on the community level are the promulgation of controversial bylaws and exhortations on divisive, symbolically loaded subjects[15]—indeed, exhortations on *any* subject, which, by attempting to influence, intrude on autonomy of decision-making and freedom of action. On the individual level, messages can cause difficulties not only by expressing antagonistic personal interests—making accusations, implied and explicit—but also, as my last example indicates, by raising the spectre of a painful past. Why broadcast all of this socially disruptive matter, especially the personal tensions, which, one might imagine, could be handled more discreetly on the telephone or more sensitively face to face? If the characteristics of radio and the ways in which the radio messages are formulated are compared with patterns of conflict management in camp life, I think some light may be shed on this question.

First of all, in camp life people feared and avoided confrontation, preferring to say nothing about disagreements, resentments, and other painful feelings, rather than risk social unpleasantness. Nevertheless, sometimes tensions built up in the camp to the point that it was difficult not to express them. I have tried to demonstrate that this dilemma exists in exacerbated form in the settlement. One still finds fear of confrontation, while at the same time, the diversity of lifestyles and the adoption of the European practice of living by rules and regulations, instead of by subtle interpersonal negotiation and silent adaptation, mean that matters certain to be controversial must frequently be expressed.

We have seen that in former days the dilemma was resolved—or at least addressed in extreme cases—by the public song duel, which allowed antagonists to express and conceal hostility at one and the same time. Radio, I shall argue, has some of the same characteristics as the song duel. I think particularly of publicity, ambiguity, and the complex role of the audience.[16]

Communications broadcast over radio are of course received by a large audience, either directly from the radio or indirectly via the gossip network. In the case of red radio, they are even heard in other communities and out on the land, in widely dispersed hunting and fishing camps. Eckert and Newmark (1980: 200–201) point out, with regard to the song duel, that the presence of an audience, whether visibly present or merely symbolic—referred to in vague terms in a song—can intensify both accusation and sanction by causing persons who may feel uncomfortable about their behavior to imagine that there are many critical eyes upon them. The public lectures and prayers that addressed the delinquent in a camp served the same purpose of isolating the offender in the presence of a phalanx of critics; today it is radio that provides the audience.

Eckert and Newmark (1980: 200) also point out that when the *community* is perceived as critical, some of the burden of responsibility for criticism is removed from the individual accuser. In this way, the confrontation is diluted and so made safer: for the accuser, who has the backing of the community; for the accused, who need not fear retribution at the hand of a single irate individual; and for the community, which can, more easily than an angry antagonist, reincorporate offenders and so reconstitute itself.

Reintegration following castigation is also facilitated when offenders, instead of being clearly identified, are left to imagine their own offense, real or potential, and to worry about its possible consequences.[17] Thus we come to the subject of ambiguity—an important quality of song duels, as mentioned earlier. There is ambiguity in the radio messages, too, though it is not created in the same way as in the song contests. The songs were art forms, shaped of metaphors and allusions, and the audience responded to them on this level. Moreover, they were often ironic, and they could easily be interpreted as joking. At the same time, by the very nature of a "duel"—and also because of the intimate, face-to-face nature of life in a camp—it was always clear to whom a song was addressed. None of this is true of radio. The ambiguity of a radio message is based, first, on the fact that speakers often refrain from naming both themselves and the people they are talking about, and, second, on the vague, general, or altogether implicit manner in which criticism is usually phrased. Of course, many of those who listen will recognize the voice of the speaker and will know to whom the messages are addressed, even when no names are mentioned; and some will take personally the criticism, explicit or implied. Nevertheless, speakers who have not named the individuals they have in mind can deny any personal reference.

Even when the intended recipient of the message is named, I have suggested that confrontation in the radio situation is diluted and controlled by the fact that the recipient is at a distance and need not be met face to face. Moreover, as in the song duel, the audience helps to control the uncomfortable situation by witnessing it and by implicitly judging both accuser and accused. The fact that all participants, both antagonists and audience, are sitting quietly and separately at home, addressing their critical comments only to fellow listeners in the household, inhibits both the dyadic escalation of hostility and the development of active factions.

Another point of comparison concerns the formulation of response to an emotionally charged message. Eckert and Newmark (1980: 192) have told us that in song duels, antagonists were required not to respond directly, defensively, but rather to counter with a statement on a different subject; and I have mentioned that in everyday camp life, too, argument was strongly proscribed. I noted only two instances of response to an item that was broadcast, and both demonstrate the enduring strength of old patterns in the new context and show us something of how radio works. In one case, a young woman, in her official capacity as representative of a community organization, had broadcast a message urging all young people to help with village cleanup. In the next session of the phone-in program, an elder picked up and repeated her message but without acknowledging or directly replying to it. The young woman was supported but a faction was not created and "autonomous" expression was preserved. The other case was that of a woman who repeatedly criticized the moral character of another woman's children. The woman who was the butt of the attacks told me that she refrained from replying for five years; then finally she turned the accusation back on her antagonist's children: "It's *your* children, not mine ..." And, said she: "She never said another word." So great is the fear of direct rebuttal.

In sum, in radio talk as in the song duel, conflict is embedded and isolated within a formal—one might say, ritualized—context, concealed behind ambiguity, and publicized before an audience, which can perform several functions: giving (imagined) support; providing (imagined) sanctions; creating safe distance between potential opponents; and, through all of the above, controlling antagonism and preventing actual conflict. Talking on the radio allows people in emotionally uncomfortable relationships to avoid speaking face to face or even on the telephone, either of which media would create a dangerously dyadic situation. As did the song duel, radio allows people to confront without confronting and to respond without responding. The value of the radio is indicated by the fact that in the socially stressful environment of the settlement, the public is called on, not just occasionally in rare and exceptionally troublesome cases, but every day. Indeed, twice a day.

Finally, radio does not serve the community only by airing trouble-some situations in a relatively safe mode; we have seen that it also provides a forum for the expression of warm and positive sentiments like gratitude, which can create and strengthen bonds among community residents. Not least in importance, the radio is a focus for participation in settlement life: almost everybody talks, and listens to their fellows talking, on one kind of radio or the other, or both. So radio, like the song duel, draws the diverse and fragmented community together in more than one way.

Nevertheless, lest this picture, complex though it be, leave too tidy an impression, I will conclude by mentioning that in this community there are—not surprisingly—traditionally minded individuals, even in younger generations, who disapprove of using the radio to "complain."

Notes

1. This chapter was originally a paper delivered at the CHAGS 7 conference in Moscow in August 1993. Sections of this revised version have been borrowed from another essay on Inuit conflict management in which traditional strategies are more compre-hensively discussed (Briggs 1994).

    The chapter is based on fieldwork in Canadian Inuit camps in the 1960s and 1970s, and two to three decades later in a modern Canadian Arctic community, where some of the camp members now live. I withhold more precise information to protect the identities of individuals.

    A more extended treatment of the same subject is found in W. C. E. Rasing's study of changes in Iglulingmiut social order between 1821 and 1989 (Rasing 1994). Rasing analyzes the historical processes that have "decivilized" (as he puts it) the Iglulingmiut in modern settlements by increasing social differentiation and decreasing integration and self-control (p. 279). His case material concerning instances of conflict is espe-cially interesting and instructive.

2. I once saw a woman have an asthma attack from fear when a man, accidentally struck in the face by a flying rope, said angrily to her husband: "That wouldn't have happened if you hadn't let go!" The woman in question was not a timid young thing, either; she was a daunting personage and widely respected. The man who had spoken went hunt-ing and did not return for several days.

3. The Inuit with whom I lived were all Anglicans.

4. The mechanisms through which the song duel worked in Central Canadian Inuit soci-ety are perceptively and subtly analyzed by Eckert and Newmark (1980: 191–211), and I draw heavily on their work throughout the account that follows. The Eckert and Newmark article is well worth reading in its entirety, as are two other fine studies by Phyllis Morrow (1990: 141–58; 1996: 405–23) on the fundamental philosophical con-cerns that underlie conflict management and much other behavior, too, in Inuit and Yupik societies.

5. In Greenland, today as in the past, people are believed occasionally to run away from society into the mountains. Such individuals are called *qivittut*—the word means "disappointed ones." "The *qivittoq* [singular form] is loneliness personified, the expression of all that is feared about rejection and isolation" and has no more social identity (Nuttall 1992: 114).

6. Sources of interpersonal and intercultural tension in modern Arctic settlements are outlined also in Briggs 1985.

7. The twin assumptions that cultures are constituted by shared traits and that the world's societies can be tidily described as culturally separate are widely criticized these days. See, for example, Fredrik Barth 1969; 1993, and Eric Wolf 1982.

8. Strong ambivalences about giving and sharing existed in camp life, too. However, in that environment the resulting tensions were commonly expressed in joking and hearty laughter, in acute watchfulness and a tendency to count and remember the neighbor's possessions, and in suspicious gossip. Goods were not often either directly requested or withheld unless a convincing pseudonurturant excuse could be concocted. ("The baby is hungry" was a particularly effective one.) But now, Euro-Canadians—and some Inuit—model possessive behavior, creating more opportunities for acting on feelings that were formerly covert, and resentment may be exacerbated.

9. Tensions between Inuit and Euro-Canadians in northern settlements, and the critical judgments that the latter make of Inuit are frequently mentioned in books and articles about the Canadian North today. An especially perceptive analysis is that of Hugh Brody (1975).

10. Similar phenomena are occurring in many Inuit, and also Yupik, communities. A plea that problems and feelings about problems should be openly discussed as a means of healing divided generations and troubled communities has been most eloquently made by an Alaskan Yupik Eskimo in a paper that he wrote while in jail and addressed to his fellow Yupiit (Napoleon 1992). Phyllis Morrow tells me (personal communication) that a Yupik friend once remarked to her that the "talking cures" now used to treat substance abuse are "very non-Yupik … but maybe new poisons require new cures."

11. I have found local radio programming in all the Canadian Inuit communities that I have visited, and Phyllis Morrow has told me (personal communication) that in the Bethel area of Alaska in the 1970s and 1980s, radio was used for many of the same purposes that I describe here, including the management of social tensions. For a discussion of the partly similar, partly different, uses of local radio in a Canadian Ojibwe Native American Indian community, see Lisa Valentine 1992 and 1995, especially pages 34–40 and 50–57.

12. I did not check whether there were systematic differences between the personal messages that were telephoned to the radio station and those that were sent via CB radio. The question—a cogent one—did not occur to me until I read Phyllis Morrow's prepublication review of this essay and (at Morrow's suggestion) Lisa Valentine's comprehensive study of the communicative patterns in an Ojibwe community (1995).

13. My field notes tell me that these two messages were sent by CB.

14. This message was sent through the radio station. I am not sure whether the daughter feared her mother would feel more pain if told in person and she wished to spare her that grief, or whether she thought her mother would cry in either case and she just preferred not to witness it. The point (to be elaborated below) remains the same.

15. The symbolic loads carried by everyday activities in modern Inuit communities are discussed in Briggs 1997.

16. For lack of space, I present only a partial and, I hope, provocative comparison here. A careful reading of Eckert and Newmark (1980) would suggest additional points of significant similarity and contrast.

Phyllis Morrow, in her prepublication review of this essay, pointed out yet another way in which communication by radio resembles traditional interaction patterns, though not specifically the song duel. Individuals "volunteer" both what they have to say and also the time of speaking, "rather than being asked, prompted, or confronted by another" (personal communication).

17. I have only touched in passing on the parallels between radio and other traditional mechanisms of social control. Concerning the crucial role of imaginary sanctions—warnings issued in the form of playful hints and jokes—in maintaining order in camp life, see Briggs 1994.

References

Barth, F., ed. 1969. *Ethnic Groups and Boundaries*. Boston: Little, Brown.

Barth, F. 1993. *Balinese Worlds*. Chicago: University of Chicago Press.

Briggs, J. L. 1985. "Socialization, Family Conflicts and Responses to Culture Change among Canadian Inuit." *Arctic Medical Research* 40: 40–52.

_____. 1994. "Why Don't You Kill Your Baby Brother? The Dynamics of Peace in Canadian Inuit Camps." In *The Anthropology of Peace and Nonviolence*. L. E. Sponsel and T. A. Gregor, eds. 155–81. Boulder, Colo.: L. Rienner.

_____. 1997. "From Trait to Emblem and Back: Living and Representing Culture in Everyday Inuit Life." *Arctic Anthropology* 34(1): 227–35.

Brody, H. 1975. *The People's Land*. Harmondsworth: Penguin.

Eckert, P., and R. Newmark. 1980. "Central Eskimo Song Duels: A Contextual Analysis of Ritual Ambiguity." *Ethnology* 19(2): 191–211.

Morrow, P. 1990. "Symbolic Actions, Indirect Expressions: Limits to Interpretations of Yupik Society." *Études Inuit Studies* 14(1–2): 141–58.

_____. 1996. "Yup'ik Eskimo Agents and American Legal Agencies: Perspectives on Compliance and Resistance." *Journal of the Royal Anthropological Institute* (N.S.) 2(3): 405–23.

Muckpah, J. 1979. "Remembered Childhood." *Ajurnarmat* International Year of the Child Issue on Education. N.p.: Inuit Cultural Institute.

Napoleon, H. 1992. "Yuuyaraq: The Way of the Human Being." *Northern Notes* 3: 1–36. Hanover, N.H.: Dartmouth College.

Nuttall, M. 1992. *Arctic Homeland: Kinship, Community and Development in Northwest Greenland*. Toronto: University of Toronto Press.

Rasing, W. C. E. 1994. *'Too Many People': Order and Nonconformity in Iglulingmiut Social Process*. Nijmegen: Katholieke Universiteit, Faculteit der Rechtsgeleerdheid.

Valentine, L. P. 1992. "Voix de nulle part: Le pouvoir négocié dans les causeries radiophoniques chez les Ojibway de la rivière Severn." *Anthropologie et Société* 16(3): 103–18.

_____. 1995. *Making It Their Own: Severn Ojibwe Communicative Practices*. Toronto: University of Toronto Press.

Wolf, E. R. 1982. *Europe and the People Without History*. Berkeley, Cal.: University of California Press.

Chapter 6

WARS AND CHIEFS AMONG THE SAMOYEDS
AND UGRIANS OF WESTERN SIBERIA

——=◉=——

Andrei V. Golovnev

A famous explorer of western Siberia, M. Alexander Castrén (Kastren 1860: 252), noted in the nineteenth century that "the savage peoples of Siberia" were skillful in warfare long before the Russians came, and that *bellum omnium contra omnes* was widespread, resulting in the emergence of "princes of power." He felt that this example answered the disputed question of whether warfare was predominant from the dawn of humanity as Thomas Hobbes thought, or whether "a noble savage" lived in peace according to Jean-Jacques Rousseau (for various explanations of "pre-state" warfare, see Ferguson 1989; McCauley 1990; Shnirel'man 1992).

Warfare has an accompanying "culture" comprising arrangement of battles and their conduct, norms of behavior toward both a "we-group" and enemies, diplomacy, strategy, tactics, and the like. Sometimes it is closely linked to norms and aspects of daily culture (hunting methods, means of transport, settlement building), and other times quite the reverse (what is considered crime among a "we-group" is considered valor when it is directed against "strangers"). On the one hand, warfare is a special state of culture in which a society's capital is used to whatever extent necessary to achieve victory. On the other hand, warfare is more than slaughter: it is a precondition for peace as well. Organization of public life and social status depend on success in war or on the readiness for it. Of course, one must consider the nature of war: local conflicts contained by cultural rules can stimulate cultural development; all-out warfare, particularly that between different cultures involving foreign invasion and political subjugation, can result in massive destruction.

Here I will analyze warfare among the Ugrians and Samoyeds of western Siberia. They share much in common with warfare among other traditional peoples in terms of their causes (revenge and procuring women), the importance of shamans, certain military preparations and actions, war rituals, special systems of military education, "Spartan ethics," and effects on male social status. There are also cross-cultural similarities in tactics (Burch 1974: 2–7; Ekvall 1964: 1136–38; Goldschmidt 1989: 17–23; Solov'ev 1987: 129–31).

Areas of Warfare

Narratives concerning war abound in the folklore of the Nenets, Khanty, Mansi, and Sel'kup peoples, telling of how all these groups clashed over territorial claims, attempts to procure women, and seizure of reindeer herds. There were also interclan wars among the tundra Nenetses, as well as among the Ostiak princes who headed sociopolitical groups in various taiga regions. The "stony" Samoyeds (Yamal-Ural Nenetses), the Ostiaks of the Koda towns (Ob'-Alym Khantys), the Pelym Vogul principality (southern Mansis), and the "Piebald Horde" (*Pegaia orda* in Russian documents of the late sixteenth century; the first recorded reference to the Narym Sel'kups) were especially warlike. The above-mentioned areas were probably the military-political centers of the indigenous peoples in the late medieval period (see Figure 6.1).

These local military alliances put up resistance to the Russian troops in the sixteenth and seventeenth centuries, resulting in important ethnic shifts. The Mansis moved to the Sos'va-Liapin area in the Transural region, the Khantys forced the Sel'kups out of the Vakh basin, and in turn the Sel'kups invaded the Enets area of the Taz and Turukhan Rivers. The Nenetses spread eastward up to the Yenisei River, assimilating the Gydan Enetses (Mantu); simultaneously, the Arctic Sikhirtia people disappeared because of Nenets pressure.

Armed conflicts, which persisted during the pre-Russian period, gradually ceased after the Russian administration was established. However, minor armed clashes continued during the rule of the Tsarist empire, even in the Soviet Union. The interethnic borderlands (forest-tundra and northern taiga), where the Samoyeds and the Ostiaks clashed, were especially troublesome. The Nenetses and the eastern Samoyeds (the Nganasans and the Enetses) competed in the tundra proper. The centers of conflict in the taiga coincided with the areas of the most intensive migrations (northern Transural and Taz-Turukhan areas).

FIGURE 6.1 Centers of Military Expansion in Western Siberia in the Sixteenth and Seventeenth Centuries

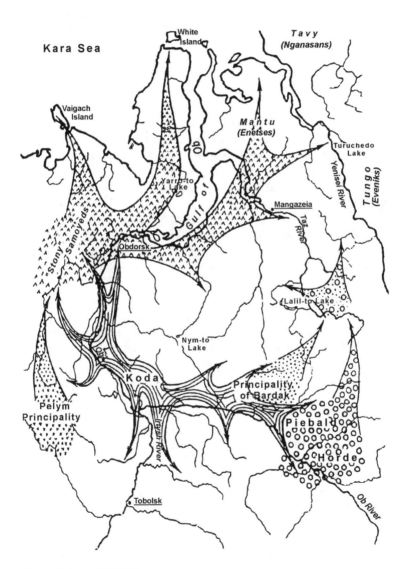

Source: Golovnev (1995: 99).

Military Norms and Customs

Each local culture had its own style of warfare as well as attitudes toward peace. The Nenetses preferred fast raids, the Ob-Ugrians, thoroughly organized campaigns, and the Sel'kups (at least when they were moving northward), skillful guerrilla tactics. Here I will compare and contrast warfare customs of the Nenetses, the Sel'kups, and the Ob-Ugrians, centering on norms and traditions.[1]

The Nenetses

Nenets legends generally give the number of warriors in symbolically "big" numbers, e.g., "three by ten tens," "seven by nine nines," etc. To describe large military arrangements, *mandalada*, metaphors are used, such as "an army like a living earth, like the buzz of mosquitoes." Each detachment was named after a clan or people—*si'iv iu Susoi* (seven by nine Susois), *si'iv Tungo* (seven Tungus). Witnesses usually mention a leader's name and the size of a detachment ("forty tents," "thirty sledges"). The Ob-Ugrian legends describe forces ranging from several (three to ten) to several dozens (thirty to forty) warriors or sledges. In legends recorded by Patkanov (1891: 71) the Samoyed detachments are said to be composed of up to two to three hundred persons.

The Nenets war leader was called either *saiu erv* (the head of the war or a hunting drive leader), *serm' pertia* (affairs conductor) or *nerm' pertia* (going ahead). The Ugrian tales call the Nenets chiefs *otyr, urt* (princes or warriors). I know of only one case in which a leader of the rebels was called *parangoda* (tsar). In the majority of the war tales, a leader is called simply by his personal name.

LEADERS, WARRIORS, AND ALLIES. It is often impossible to find a leader in Nenets tales until a war is over. In many cases there is a difference between one who first leads a detachment ("a clan elder") and one who wins a final victory (usually a "younger brother"). Moreover, a future winner is often described initially as helpless, silly, lazy, or sleepy. Probably this represents how real events develop as individuals rise to the cause. At the start of warfare, an actor knows only the enemy; allies join later. A strong warrior does not look for allies in advance; if allies are sought, then this is done by somebody else (often by a woman) for his sake.

A request for help from allies is often phrased as a demand. The younger Iabtonge (a hero of the *Niar Iabtonge* tale) sends his sister to Siudbia Pyriagi to ask for help. "He promises to give him half of his 10,000 reindeers in exchange for assistance and one of his sisters for free; but he also threatens to kill him if he refuses" (Kupriianova 1965: 418–19). A hero often relies on good fortune to get allies. In the tale *Si'ivda Noetsia*, a man who seeks revenge is persuaded by his grandmother to wait ("probably the earth will come to help you, and you will set off together"). In another legend the hero guesses, "Probably, my seven brothers touched the earth," i.e., they went to a war (ibid.: 62, 232, 741).

One person can be an initiator for armed actions, but he must be supported by brothers. Each involved party is invariably a group of clansmen—"two Mantu," "three Saner," "four Ngyivai," and the like. The "brother-chiefs" are usually supported by numerous *ngacheky* (guys) or *makboda* (workers, herdsmen). As a rule, commoners are depersonalized; they die quickly in battles so as not to interfere with descriptions of heroic deeds. A "serf" can very rarely become a key figure after his master's death. However, even if he is fairly strong, survives a severe battle, gets married to his master's widow and has children with her, a serf is still secondary in the biography of the main hero (Tereshchenko 1990: 22).

Among the "true people," the strongest person becomes first among equals. Sometimes this takes place in games before a war starts (Kupriianova 1965: 285–90). Usually, a leader also has shamanistic skills: he often resuscitates slain allies or returns to life himself. Superiority can also be expressed in the ability "to hold fast his gaze"; for example, in one tale a hero is victorious because his rival averted his gaze (Sherbakova 1984: 91).

Sometimes epic warriors defeat gods and take their place in the pantheon. Nenets heroes need no protection from ghosts. In the course of battle, they fly through the sky with the help of their bows or just by raising their legs (Tereshchenko 1990: 24). They can appear in black masks, with a silver shield before their chests (Kupriianova 1965: 738), or in three layers of chain armor of which only one layer remains by the end of the battle.

The warriors of Nenets epics are not specific clan heroes. For instance, the Serotetto clan tells tales of the legendary "Khariuchi elders" (the clan ancestors) and of "Iaptik elders" (heroes of the opposite phratry) with the same enthusiasm. Legendary heroes have the same fate—they become gods. Many of these heroes can be incarnated into the same character, one by one.

Thus, "heroism" is a temporary (almost accidental) state ranging between that of a sleepy younger brother and a god. Military status is also a temporary state; many warriors, even women, can occupy this status. For instance, shaman-women fight against enemies, hunt wild reindeer, and even drink wine in *siniakui* (a sacred place in the tent forbidden to women) together with men. A heroine, Amianako, is represented as a mighty mistress of the camp (Kupriianova 1965: 313, 314), while another legendary woman leads an enemy coalition.

It seems that military leadership was either nonexistent among the Nenetses or the potential to become a leader was open to all segments of society. To put it differently, leaders and heroes appeared to fill a need and disappeared when tensions ceased. The secret of invincibility of the tundra Nenetses was closely linked with the social ability to recruit a large number of warriors. Types of leadership depended to a large extent on the causes and goals of warfare.

CAUSES OF INTERNAL CONFLICT. Nomads of the tundra were (and still are) accustomed to meeting neighbors and even strangers. The appearance of a stranger drew curiosity rather than hostility. Relationships between people who met each other depended on respect for norms and ethics rather than on legal claims over territory, kin, or property. War could break out if a stranger fell in love with a girl without paying proper respect to her brothers. The brothers Piasia were offended by their neighbors, the three Tungo, who showed indifference to their intention to take their reindeer out of a joint herd. On their side, the three Tungo treated the rumpled hair of the elder Piasia as a challenge.

At first glance, such breaches of etiquette appear to be subsidiary rather than true causes for conflicts, but in fact such nuances of behavior signaled friendly or hostile relationships to those who held doubts and suspicions. In 1993 in Yamal, I was told the story of the five Iaptik brothers. The oldest of them was angry with a "nomad" who encroached on their hunting grounds with his reindeer herd. In order to make amends, the "nomad" attempted to give reindeer to the brothers. The insulted elder Iaptik ordered them to refuse the gift. They hit the reindeer on the ears (a very rude gesture), and the reindeer returned to the nomad's herd. Battle broke out in which the Iaptik brothers perished from blows to the skull. The story blames the elder Iaptik for his inhuman deed in response to the courtesy and generosity of the "nomad."

Blood revenge was the most frequent cause for conflicts. It was also used in retribution for the violation of ethics. Kupriianova (1965: 63) cites an example: "He kills sleeping people. We want to kill him asleep." However, as a rule, it was forbidden to kill sleeping people. A hero in the *Eva Piasia* tale knocks on a sledge near his enemy's tent and says: "Ngarka Piasia, you took my bride. Rise and prepare to fight."

In Nenets legends, women are not only a cause for hostilities, but also participants in military events as advisers, initiators, and even warriors. Nevertheless, disputes around marriage were frequently given as reasons for hostilities. If in response to a marriage proposal parents continually answered that a girl was too small and would not be able to build a tent at a new camp, this was considered reason enough to start a war (Tereshchenko 1990: 27). Often a marriage proposal, doomed to fail from the very beginning, was only a pretext to turn a hidden hostility into an open clash (Kupriianova 1965: 453).

EXTERNAL CONFLICT. All of the above-mentioned cases dealt with hostilities among the Nenetses themselves. Nenets ethical norms did not necessarily apply outside of the *Nenei Nenneche*'s (true people's) world. For an attack against the *Tavy* (the Nganasans) or *Tungo* (the Tunguses), their very existence could be the cause of war, since they were regarded as people of a different world. According to Zhitkov (1913: 226), "some forest people (the Tungus) are depicted as savages in contrast to the Samoyeds. They do not use fire and are afraid of it, wear clothes made of non-processed hides, and the like." The *Tungo* or *Tavy* are mentioned in the Nenets legends as enemies "by definition," against whom the heroes have to fight sooner or later and whom they try to exterminate by all available means.

Wars against strangers had pragmatic reasons as well—to seize women and reindeer to demonstrate power, to weaken rivals by depriving them of reindeer transport, and to strengthen one's own herd. Neighbors had their own ambitions, and borderlands were persistently an area of revenge.

RAIDING TACTICS. Military tactics depended on the nature and cause of conflict. When dealing with the Ob or Irtysh forest inhabitants, the Samoyeds could limit themselves to fast plundering raids or could besiege an Ostiak town. Winter was the most appropriate time for raids, though they could go upriver by boat in summer as well. Rapid movement was their main tactic. In winter, if resistance was strong, they "quickly disappeared, seizing the Ostiak wealth, wives and reindeer herds." In summer, if the Ostiaks were too numerous, the Samoyeds disappeared rapidly in their light boats, and the Ostiaks could not pursue them in their heavy wooden boats (Patkanov 1891: 71).

The establishment of Russian rule weakened the Ugrian principalities, so that Nenetses could plunder them easily. Firstly, they would send a scout into the camp that was to be invaded. The Khantys from the Trom'egan River still tell stories about the adventures of Nenets scouts (*Avus ekh*). Once a woman went to feed a dog, but found it dead and saw legs in "fine boots" protruding out of the dog's house. She did not alarm people but instead went to bed. That night somebody shouted loudly, and the *Avus ekhs* surrounded the tent. They killed the husband and took the woman and reindeer with them. The tale concludes that one had to kill an enemy scout to prevent an *Avus ekh* attack.

The targets of Nenets nighttime raids were usually wealthy villages of reindeer herders (especially when the men were away during the winter hunting season). According to a Kazym Khanty legend, once forty sledges of Nenetses attacked a village at night. First, they destroyed bows and broke the arrows; they even destroyed those weapons that were kept in the sacred sledges. Afterwards, they collected all of the reindeer, put the women into the sledges, and went north. When the Khantys heard what had happened, they pursued the Nenetses and recovered their reindeer and women with great difficulty. Women were by no means only captured. Among other incidents, the Kunovat Khantys tell of a fortress defended by women who were all slaughtered when the fortress fell to the Nenetses.

Thus, the Nenetses used to plunder the inhabitants of the Ob forests. In contrast, their movement eastward to the Gydan, Taz, and Yenisei tundra represented territorial expansion. There they clashed with the Enetses (Mantu) people, who were related to them and led a similar way of life. The Nenetses' advantage was their numerous reindeer herds, whereas the Mantu were largely wild reindeer hunters with only a few domesticated reindeer.

A conquest of tundra territories by no means implied territorial occupation. The Nenetses knew very well that a reindeer herder could easily return and take revenge. Victory and success on the tundra involved seizure of the reindeer, rather than land, and so reindeer herds in the eastern Ob tundra were captured for the sake of power rather than out of greed.

The legendary Mokhopcho Iaptunai was the first Nenets reported to have attacked the Enetses at Gydan. Only two Enetses survived. Fleeing toward the Yenisei River, they met relatives, and came back and killed Mokhopcho and other Iaptunais (Simchenko 1975: 111). However, other Nenets attacks followed, according to the legend, and the last Enets was killed by Nenetses at the Olenii Island where his head still lies on a hill named *Mantu-yar* (sandy place of Mantu).

After that a battle at Turuchedo Lake took place. The legend is told in two parts, one concerning the Nenetses' movement toward the Yenisei, and the other describing the battle itself, which lasted two to three days. When the Nenetses (Iuraks) came to the Yenisei River, they saw a man in a sledge moving from the Mantu side. "He saw the Iurak warriors, was frightened and turned back. They pursued him and followed him for a long while. One of his reindeer became tired and he cut the bridle-rein. He did not sit in the sledge, but jumped from side to side so as not to be hit by an arrow. They could not overtake him. Then the Iuraks reached Turuchedo lake" (Vasil'ev 1977: 124).

This description is typical for fighting in the tundra, in contrast to the forest battle at the Turuchedo Lake. Several times I was told about similar contests in reindeer sledges. For instance, the younger Iaptunai pursued his enemy: he tried to take better aim in order to kill him with an arrow, but he did not shoot since he thought, "What if I hit a reindeer?"

All similar narratives demonstrate the pursuit of enemy in sledges. A specially trained team of battle reindeer played the main role in this phase of attack; their value was not lower than their master's life. It is not accidental that many stories begin with the depiction of the hero's reindeer team, and the hero's attentiveness toward them.

The Turuchedo battle was an exceptionally complex, rule-bound military event. First, there was a meeting of the clan chiefs and shamans arranged by a major chief. Then, a male reindeer was sent to the enemies as a declaration of war, after which the enemies began to recruit warriors and to build a palisade. A scout was sent to the enemy, and a model tent was erected by the Enetses at the proposed battle site. Finally, an elder envoy went to the Yenisei tribes with a proposal of seven war rules. These were:

1. Representatives, who had diplomatic immunity, would be appointed from each side for the war negotiations. Their sledges had to be led by two reindeer, each bearing red banners identifying them as such.
2. Turuchedo Lake was to be the battlefield.
3. The battle should start the next morning.
4. In order to define distance between sides for the beginning of the battle, the sons of the war leaders had to shoot from both sides.
5. The size of the forces had to be equal for the first attack (fifty persons in this case), but the reserves, located 200 meters from the battlefield, could be limitless.
6. Fighting would be pursued each morning at the point where it had stopped the previous day (one should not fight at night).
7. In order to cease battle for the night, the appointed representatives would intervene from both flanks.

Peace was made following special negotiations:

1. Losses had to be calculated every day; reserves had to be used to restore the number of warriors.
2. In case of a defeat, a Nenets chief had to send his war bow with seven arrows as well as a battle dagger to a leader of the Enetses and the Nganasans.
3. The end of the war had to be signaled by large red banners raised behind a frontline detachment.
4. Representatives from both sides had to then circle their troops three times shouting, "Our troops won/lost the battle and are the winners/losers, the war is over!"
5. The war leaders had to choose sites for burials, and two collective graves (for both sides) had to be dug.
6. Fires had to be made near the graves at which both war leaders would make speeches concerning the victory, the defeat, and the necessity to live in peace.
7. The losers had to leave their bows, arrows, and daggers at the grave, and return to their homeland (Dolgikh 1961: 89–96; Khomich 1966: 144–46).

Actually this version, presented by an Enets named P. Bolin, contrasts with other legends describing Samoyed wars that I know. A version documented by Vasil'ev (1977: 124) seems closer to the Samoyed pattern: "The Mantu stood at the opposite side of Turuchedo and the Iuraks at this side. Both armies descended to the ice and the war started. The Iuraks killed a son of the Mantu leader, and the Mantu said: 'We will not fight any more. We will rather give you our most beautiful girl.' They stopped fighting."

Traditional Nenets battle stories do not describe "offensives against strangers." When news of an imminent attack was received, neighbors met and formed a joint camp. They attempted to attack enemies somewhere along the latter's way so as not to let them reach the campsite (Kupriianova 1965: 294).

A fast, preventive offensive was considered the best way to defend oneself. In a forest Nenets story, *Ni Nyiavu*, a Nenets woman who was married to a Mantu man noticed that her husband's relatives were making preparations to go to war against her brothers. She went to her native camp where she found her brothers off guard. She informed them that the Mantu were planning to attack them. They answered: "We do not care. This countryside is a flat plain. One cannot hide anywhere. Stay with us for a night." On the next day the woman came back to her husband's camp and found all the Mantu slain.

If the enemies came unexpectedly at night, they conformed to war ethics that proscribed destroying, burning, or shooting into a tent. They had to knock on the pole of a sleeping enemy's tent and say: "Come out so you will not think that we killed you by chance. We have not come to do good." A true warrior rose to fight immediately, even if he did not have enough time to put on his armor. In legends, battles lasted for several years, destroying the area. Bows and arrows, axes, and whipping sticks with metal spear-like tips were the main weapons.

THE WINNERS AND THE LOSERS. If a war did not end in a draw (in which case a sister exchange followed), the loser could survive only if he begged for mercy (Kupriianova 1965: 116, 142). In a ritual sense, "preservation of life" could mean keeping the corpse intact, rather than displaying mercy. Nenetses believed that a mighty enemy could ultimately be killed only through magical means. In one story, a hero hung the loser's head from the top of a high tree and his heart and lungs from the branches (Tereshchenko 1990: 24). The younger Piasia impaled Pariko Tungo's head with a whipping stick. The heads of two other enemies were taken. An influential relative saved a scoundrel, Ne Lekhechi, saying: "After her mother's and father's deaths, I nourished her with reindeer milk. Cut her ears, cut her nose, but do not kill her." Sala Ian-tetta also did not kill all of his enemies. He sliced the ears and kneecaps of two of them and forced them to fetch water for three years. During that time, their ears and knees healed, and he sent them away.

In order to get rid of an enemy once and for all, one had to give his corpse to a water spirit. Sometimes it was impossible to finish killing an enemy. For instance, the hearts of the defeated enemies were believed to have gone under the ground with the intention of harming people in the future. It was impossible to destroy the younger Tungo since he had no heart (it was "hidden somewhere"). The severed heads of sorcerers were thought to be able to grow back onto their bodies after they rolled around a circle. Only the sorcerer's sister could render him harmless forever by stepping over him or by staring at him. "I laid Iav Nerkykhii on the ground and took a knife out of his head. I cut off his head and it grew back on, I cut open his chest but the wound healed. Then I called for his sister. She jumped over her brother. I cut off his head and blood came out. I threw his head under a dirty sledge" (Kupriianova 1965: 606–7). Mass slaughter of everybody in a camp appears to have occurred as well. For example, one story tells how the elder Ngader exterminated everybody, including dogs, in the camp of the "seven Tungus."

The Sel'kups

The Sel'kup legends describe a time when they were ruled by warriors, and when "the tsar was not recognized." These warriors were said to have taken the place of the tsar. Seven warriors lived around Napas (on the Tym River) (Pelikh 1981: 136). The warriors, or princes, were called *miuty-kok* (war chief) and *marg-kok* (big war leader) (Castrén 1855: 101; Pelikh 1981: 133). At that time, fortified settlements were constructed by the Sel'kups and called *koch* (*ketty*) or *kor* (*kora*). According to archaeological data, the fortresses were erected in the hills or on river banks. Fortification consisted of a rampart, a moat, and a palisade (Dul'zon 1966: 53; Pelikh 1981: 137–38).

Prior to the very early seventeenth century, when the Piebald Horde (*Pegaia orda*) was defeated by Russian-Khanty troops, its princes deserved the honorable Turkic title *kok*, since they maintained independence from their mighty southern neighbors and were in diplomatic contact with them. The Horde's last prince, "proud" Vonia, "could recruit up to 400 warriors" (Butsinskii 1893: 8). Probably as a result of a serious defeat in the early seventeenth century or of division into two factions, the Sel'kups no longer engaged in any large-scale military or political activity in their original territory, the Narym Ob River area, and their proud princes disappeared. It is possible that the better part of Vonia's followers retreated to the north, to the Taz-Turukhansk region, where "a new Sel'kup history" began.

SURVIVAL TACTICS. If the entire Horde (about five hundred people) had moved to the Taz River instead of fighting against the Russians and the Khantys, it could easily have broken the resistance of the local Enetses (Nenetses), built fortresses in the hills, and established an appropriate order. However, the Horde survived only in narratives, and only three men reached the Taz River, one of them being killed shortly after.

Deprived of their territory, the Sel'kups lost not only the ancestral graves, sanctuaries, and subsistence grounds, but, more importantly, they lost the communication system that allowed them to assemble an army in a short time, to equip it substantially, and to meet at a designated place. Since the Sel'kups had inhabited the Ob River region for as long as their history recalls, they were experienced in defending their own land rather than exploiting new areas. After the seventeenth-century events, they had to make adjustments in order to survive when they moved north.

According to legend, the Sel'kups came to the Taz River knowing nothing about reindeer-herding or constructing tents. They built subterranean dwellings and moved by skis (in winter) and by boat (in summer). Soon they learned how to use reindeer for transport and became able to compete with the Enets reindeer herders. It is easy to imagine how vulnerable these formerly settled hunters would have been to the nomads' arrows, if they had not adopted such practices.

However, the Sel'kups did not turn into nomads but rather built permanent settlements, adopting two different types of reindeer transport, the Evenk packing and riding style and the northern Samoyed harness type. They both constructed subterranean dwellings and erected tents side by side at their settlements. Sometimes they even dug subterranean dwellings under their tents in order to hide their wives and children in case of a sudden Nenets (Enets) attack.

It is possible that complex subterranean structures, like those used by the Sel'kups at the Ob River, were used rather than common one-chambered domestic structures like *chui mot* or *noi mot* (see Lezova 1991: 101–7). For instance, based on oral tradition, Prokof'eva (1947: 200) has reconstructed an old Sel'kup subterranean structure, which included subterranean corridors and an exit toward the river. According to Pelikh (1981: 136), there were even "two-story" subterranean dwellings with holes in the walls for defense with bows and arrows called *miuty-mate* (military house). In legends it is said that "in the past the Sel'kups lived under the ground" in subterranean caves dug in the riverbanks (*karamo*) (Prokof'ev 1940: 69–71).

River barrages, which, judging from the data on Ob battles, the Sel'kups could construct, were by no means enough to defend a settlement, since the enemy, the northern Samoyeds, preferred terrestrial movements. In order to defend their forest areas, the Sel'kups used "passive" hunting techniques: "In order to drive the Iuraks back, the Ostiaks used ambushes at their routes and met them with arrows" (Tret'iakov 1869: 384). This method was effective since the Nenetses (Enetses) themselves did not use traps with tightened bows or deadfalls (that could result in the killing of freely roaming domesticated reindeer) and were not skillful in their discovery.

There were, probably, not many open clashes between the Sel'kups and the local people since, firstly, the Sel'kups were not numerous enough for that, and, secondly, it was not easy for them to recruit allies (Kets and Evenks)—a battle at Keli Mach at the Tol'ka River was probably the only case. The Sel'kups won the battle at Tol'ka due to their skillful bow usage for which they were well known. In the old Sel'kup tradition, a *liak* (derived from *lokka, lakka* [friend; Castrén 1855: 131; Prokof'ev 1928: 27] or *laka* [war arrow; Wilkuna 1950: 346]) is a warrior in "an iron dress" (*kyzy-porg kum*), who can repulse an arrow with a stick. Up to ten or thirteen bowmen hid themselves behind him and shot from behind his back (Pelikh 1981: 133, 140–42). It is possible that this Sel'kup practice made a great impression on the northern nomads. Probably, the Sel'kup and the Tungus warriors also used some shamanistic means to support their efforts. Although the fighting at the Tol'ka River took place on a large scale, it did not put an end to warfare. Numerous small-scale clashes followed in which guerilla tactics were employed.

THE LESSONS OF "SLY ICHA." Icha is a culture hero in Sel'kup mythology. He is depicted as a hunter pursuing the Sky Elk, as the youngest son of the Creator, as a slaughterer of the monsters, and as a trickster. The northern Sel'kups appreciated him most of all as a fighter against the wealthy reindeer herders, the Nenets nomads. In one legend, Icha's mother once picked up reindeer intestines and a stomach, thrown away by a *tytta* (a wealthy reindeer herder), brought them home and wanted to eat them. Icha took them from her, tied the reindeer stomach to his mother's chest and asked her to pretend that she was sick. Then he invited neighbors "to see a dying person," and when they came, he thrust a knife into the reindeer stomach. The guests thought he killed his mother. He then addressed the knife: "You killed my mother, now make her alive!" The mother returned to life immediately. The surprised neighbors spread the rumor concerning Icha's wonderful knife. A *tytta* heard about it and came to Icha asking him to give him the knife. Icha agreed but on the condition that the *tytta* would test the knife only on wealthy persons. As a result, the *tytta* stabbed all the rich people and asked his servant to kill him and to say afterwards: "You killed all these people, now make them alive!" The servant followed his orders but to no avail. Icha redistributed all their wealth, reindeer, and fine clothing among the poor Sel'kups.

Similar exploits are attributed to Nemai Porga, a famous Sel'kup chief. A legend tells of his coming to the Taz area (the land of the Nenetses or Enetses, called by the Sel'kups *Kelek Tamdyr*), where he saw large reindeer herds and understood that the locals were a strong and wealthy people. Since the Sel'kups were not numerous, Nemai Porga avoided attacking Kelek camps openly. He raided them when the men were hunting elsewhere, killing everybody including women and children and capturing their reindeer and sledges. Since Kelek camps were situated far apart and many Keleks knew nothing about the Sel'kup invasion, Nemai Porga visited their camps as a guest. He would enter the central tent and ask all the men to come for a talk. At this very time, his companions exterminated residents of the peripheral tents, after which they attacked the central tent and slaughtered the rest of the men, who were usually unarmed. In other cases, the Sel'kup chief burned the Kelek camps and killed fleeing residents with arrows or sticks.

In another legend, Nemai Porga went for winter fishing. He noticed water swaying and realized that the Nenetses were traveling somewhere nearby. He rushed home and ordered his daughters-in-law to cover the roof of his house with bark and dry grass. When the Nenetses came, he sent his daughters-in-law outside to receive them as guests and to invite them into his house. When Nemai Porga left the house, the Nenetses started to get out after him, but they were cut down by the daughters-in-law who were waiting for them outside with axes. Nemai Porga set fire to the house, which burned down together with the Nenetses.

The Nenetses (Enetses) were appalled by the actions of the Sel'kups and their chiefs. They were not surprised by slaughter and brutality, but they could not understand the slaying of women, the main form of wealth among the Nenetses. The capture of women was in fact the goal of Nenets wars. They were confused by the ingenuity of their enemy, for instance, by their use of hidden reindeer traps. So the nomads retreated. However, the armed clashes did not cease. They were continued by indigenous Taz inhabitants who moved westward (i.e., the forest Nenetses). Another party, provisionally identified as Enetses, was driven to a trans-Yenisei territory by the Sel'kups and by the tundra Nenetses who moved eastward. Soon the Nenetses adopted "Sel'kup rules of the game," and a series of mutual attacks started, accompanied by extreme brutality.

A forest Nenets legend tells of a *Tasym Khapi* (Sel'kup) raid on a Nenets camp and the seizure of a wife and son of a man who was absent. The Nenets man, Enatlia, and his relatives produced bows and arrows, boats and chain armor, and went to Sel'kup land to rescue the prisoners. At the Taz River they met a Sel'kup shaman with her little son. Enatlia severed the child into two parts, and drowned the woman with paddles. The Nenets warriors stopped at the Taz riverbank opposite a large Sel'kup settlement. They sent an envoy to the enemy to propose a peaceful resolution of the conflict through competition between bowmen.

A Sel'kup warrior had to shoot a kite on the Nenets side, and a Nenets had to shoot an eagle on the Sel'kup side. The Nenetses won the competition and wanted to return home, but the Tasym Khapis "wanted to fight." Arrows flew above the river for several days and, "only a few people survived among the Sel'kups, blood running from the settlement to the river like a brook." Finally, the Nenetses won and returned to their native camps (Lezova 1993: 55–56).

In the Sel'kup legend "Two Brothers" (recorded by the author from F. N. Kalin in Tol'ka in 1988) the conflict between Sel'kups and Nenetses is presented differently:

> There were two brothers. The elder one had a wife and a newborn child. The brothers lived together, built a trap at the river and checked it every morning. The wife went to the forest to gather berries. When she came back, she brought hazel grouses or wood grouses. Her husband asked her: "How do you manage to kill these birds?" The wife answered: "See, they are without wings. I throw a stick, a stone, or a knife at them."
>
> One day the brothers and the woman sat in the tent around the fire drinking tea. The younger brother said to the elder brother's wife: "It seems to me that many people are impressed on your face." She replied: "Oh, where do all the people on my face come from? Probably, something will happen to me soon." The younger brother said to the elder one: "Bring war attire into the tent, a war will break out soon." The elder brother did so. Then everybody went to bed but a child kept crying. The elder brother wanted to put on war attire, but his wife stopped him: "Put it away. The child is crying because he is afraid of your war attire." In fact, the child was crying because the mother placed a twig under its back, and it kept crying till midnight. When the brothers fell asleep, the woman did what the Nenetses had ordered her to do [when pretending to gather berries, she used to visit the Nenetses who intended to kill her husband and brother-in-law]. She dressed the child and left the tent. She heard birds cry, and at that very moment arrows flew and made numerous holes in the tent. The woman thought: "Probably everything is over and they are dead."
>
> But the younger brother, who climbed a pole, survived. When the Nenetses entered the tent, he escaped, reached a river, and jumped into it. The Nenetses shot at him, but only one arrow hit his heel. He bound it with a splint and went to the nearest camp. When he arrived he began to shout: "I am nude, bring me clothes." They brought him clothes. He dressed, went to the tents, and told what had happened. The Sel'kups organized an army and went along both riverbanks. Every time they reached a turn, they saw waves from the Nenets boats. When they reached the seventh turn, there were no waves. They hid themselves there and waited. Then they saw three boats, two close to the banks and a third one in the middle of the river. There were two men in each of the former, and a Nenets chief with a woman in the latter. The younger brother cried: "Onia [the elder brother's wife]! Lift up your husband's war dress so that it will not get soaked when I start shooting." The Nenets chief said: "Let me put on my war attire." But when he raised his head the younger brother shot and killed him. The woman cried: "Do not kill me. Let us live together!"
>
> The Sel'kups killed all the Nenetses. They dragged out the woman with the elder brother's war dress to the bank. The younger brother said to her: "You got wet, and I got wet when I pursued you. Make a fire, we will dry ourselves and go home. Also cut a tall thin birch tree and sharpen it at both ends. I will

bend it, and we will dry our clothes. I will rest until then." The woman did everything. The younger brother stood up, took the long thin birch pole, and impaled the woman with the sharp end in such a way that the top reached her head. After that he hung her above the fire. He cut out her lips, nose, and eyes and put them into the fire.

After that he released the army and went home to see the brother. He came into the tent and saw his brother cut open without liver, kidney, heart, and tongue. The younger brother thought that if he had brought the woman alive with him to replace his brother's body parts with hers, that he would come to life. The younger brother killed a dog and put the liver, kidney, heart, and tongue into the brother's corpse. The wounds closed and opened again. They did that many times. Finally, when the wounds closed once again the elder brother said: "A dog cannot rescue me. Bury me, but put me upon the *pore* [platform] rather than in the ground." The younger brother went and called for help. People came, made a *pore*, and put the elder brother upon it. There he died.

This terrible story needs almost no comment. It describes the level of hostilities and the territorial proximity between the Sel'kups and the Nenetses. Its heroes are shaman-brothers, who were the common war chiefs among the Sel'kups (the younger brother is a shaman because he can "read a face" and restore a corpse, and the elder one because he is buried upon the *pore*). The main theme of the story is that revenge is inevitable against enemies and traitors.

The Ob-Ugrians

The Khanty terms for the war leaders (princes, warriors) were *ior, ur,* and *urt,* and the Mansi ones, *oter* and *ater.* "The princes were a special war caste, who had to defend the land against the outside enemies. They took part in wars not only as war leaders, but due to their military abilities, they played a decisive role in the clashes with the enemies" (Patkanov 1891: 8, 9, 13, 43). There was a detachment of fifty to three hundred persons in every Ostiak principality (Bakhrushin 1955). In order to defend his town from Bogdan Briazga in 1582, the prince Demiian (Nimniian) assembled up to two thousand Ostiaks and Voguls. In that very year, the Cossacks killed prince Samar and his eight allied princes near the Samarov Iam (Miller 1937: 242, 246).

In some traditions, warriors' trips start and finish in a town. Probably, the main goal of this kind of war was upgrading the political status of town-principalities rather than the seizure of lands or even of wealth. That is why an arrangement of fortresses and the towns' preparations for warfare are stressed in legends.

TOWN DEFENSE. An improvement of fortresses is treated as a very important undertaking in Ob-Ugrian heroic epics: "On the eve of the war the citizens ... fixed the ramparts, deepened the moats, and erected new palisades" (Patkanov 1891: 68–69).

The military status of the residents was expressed in whether a fortress was built on an open site (commonly on a high riverbank) or whether it was hidden in the lowlands. Only "a hero" who could repulse a direct attack built a town on a riverbank. Those who had much stronger enemies were hiding in the lowlands. Moreover, "only the prince himself, his relatives, servants, and a few citizens lived in the upper town; common people could hide themselves there only in case of serious danger. The majority of the population lived in nearby villages ..., which were often situated at the foot of the hill." Commoners were thus called *mygdat-iakh* (ground people) (Patkanov 1891: 13, 17).

The lower status of the lowland people comes across in a Khanty legend in which the local inhabitants hid themselves in the subterranean dwellings during *Avus ekh* attacks and "did not go out all winter." The eastern Khantys built subterranean dwellings "in hidden places" and dug special underground exits toward the river (Kulemzin and Lukina 1992: 42). A Vasiugan Khanty story portrays an extreme case: an Ostiak, in order to hide himself from enemies, entered his subterranean dwelling only through "a hole" by the riverbank, and he hid his dug-out canoe there as well. Since a sandpiper was considered to herald war, when the Ostiak saw one, he immediately fled to "the hole," sat down in the canoe and waited till the danger passed (Kulemzin and Lukina 1978: 27).

Underground corridors were not specific to lowland sites. For instance, a fortified town was built on a hill along the Upper Voikar River. In case of a *Khurun ekh* attack, its inhabitants hid themselves in subterranean dwellings supplied via underground corridors. Nevertheless, underground corridors are not mentioned in the narratives on "highland" defense. However, if Prince Evr would have had these corridors in his fortress, he would not have had to starve while under siege and would not have been killed in a counterattack (Patkanov 1891: 70).

The "icy" town people practiced a highland-type defense. They poured water on the hill slopes, so that the enemy could not climb them. Moreover, they sometimes rolled logs down on the attackers (Patkanov 1891: 69).

The "openness" of a town did not necessarily imply accessibility. Special platforms were erected on high poles for patrols who warned of enemy attack. They also watched for alarm signs from other towns, for in the event of attack, red banners were raised above the fortresses. A water route leading to a town was commonly strung with a rope or a wire, and an alarm sounded if it was broken (Patkanov 1891: 16, 64, 68, 70).

The rule was that if a visitor did not employ special codes and practice required ritual actions, he was considered an enemy and could be killed immediately. In the Vakh River area, "A traveler had to ascend a high hill not far from the village and to shout loudly to announce his arrival with peaceful intentions. Later, adorned with a special headband, he had to descend to his boat and go to a pier where he was met by the hosts. He then had to take off the headband at the bank and hang it on a tree already decorated with similar items" (Dmitriev-Sadovnikov 1916: 11).

Travel along the taiga rivers was dangerous if one did not respect these rituals. In one Khanty legend, people of the Konda River erected a wooden palisade to stop the Samoyeds from coming in birch boats. They started shooting from the riverbank when the boats stuck fast or sunk. In this way "a mighty old woman" who lived on the hill slaughtered thirty warriors in birch boats.

It is not accidental that Emder warriors used to stop "near high points along their route to prince Nangkhush's town. The local people gave them prestige drinks as if they were gods and brought sacrificial animals" (Patkanov 1891: 63). The warriors' visit to the town was highly ritualized. They "demonstrated their skill in boating, forcing their vessels to wriggle like otters, and whistled with thin and thick throat to show their high morale. They stopped boats at a bow shot distance and, leaning on the bows, jumped to the bank, fearing no treachery" (ibid.: 64).

This preventive ritual served as a sort of "pre-defense" that helped people to recognize and even exterminate enemies in good time. Its complexity expressed the importance of preventing sudden attacks under the condition of open and sedentary town life.

OFFENSIVE STRATEGIES. In view of the fact that an enemy could not arrive unnoticed and would be killed immediately, attackers would pretend to be guests. One commonly used strategy was to come on the pretext of arranging a marriage, and this is one of the reasons why war raids were commonly identified with searches for brides. There is an interesting detail in a story of the Emder princes. Despite the guests' respectful behavior and Prince Nangkhush's purposeful generosity, both sides preferred to have guards at night. The old prince's sense of danger was reasonable. War had broken out often among the Emder and Konda warriors (Patkanov 1891: 64).

An attack on a town could be long in duration. In 1585 a large Ostiak force surrounded a Russian town at the mouth of the Irtysh and attacked it throughout the day; it was by no means easy for the Russians to repulse the attack. The Ostiaks retreated by night, but they prepared for an even more ferocious attack before dawn (Miller 1937: 267). In northern Khanty stories, the bellicose "people of the towns" attacked the towns at night.

The wooden palisades were the main obstacles for the attackers, who were endangered with arrows and rolling logs. When they reached the palisades, the warriors started to hack them up with their large axes. Sometimes a town surrendered after a short siege since the Ostiaks had no food stores for longer sieges (Patkanov 1891: 69).

Psychological means were used at the ritualized opening of an attack in which the chiefs' war regalia played a role. Sacred ceremonies were organized at first sight of the defenders. Before attacking the Russian town, "the Ostiaks brought a famous *shaitan* (idol), put it on a tree in full view of the town, and made sacrifices to it, asking it to help them be victorious over the Russians" (Miller 1937: 267).

In order to capture "unassailable fortresses" various measures were taken: scouts were employed and false retreats were organized in order to lure the defenders out of the town. In this way, the Emder warriors destroyed Prince Evr's "copper town." The most successful attacks took place "in the field" when the enemy left town for some reason. "Usually the Ostiaks attacked small numbers of enemies suddenly, shooting them with numerous arrows. If resistance was strong, they dispersed, reassembled rapidly, and attacked once again. Commonly the weaker side lost heart and fled. If the enemy was strong but located at an unfortified place, the Ostiaks preferred a surprise attack to an open battle. They first sent scouts in to gather information. If the information was favorable, a detachment went forward very cautiously … the Ostiaks launched a battle with a wave of arrows to inflict as much harm on the enemy as possible, after which they engaged in hand-to-hand fighting … they did not fight in rows, so they fought in a helter-skelter manner. Everyone sought to duel with an individual enemy" (Patkanov 1891: 64–65).

The raids could take place during any season, but preferably in summer, for the Ob-Ugrians (especially Khantys) considered themselves to be invulnerable on the rivers, in contrast to the Samoyeds who preferred winter campaigns because of their reindeer transport. The northern Khantys have narratives describing river battles against the "people of the towns." It was also dangerous to leave a town in winter because of possible Samoyed attacks. Thus, the Ugrians preferred to fight in summer, and the Samoyeds in winter.

WAR MORALE. In order to win a victory against a particularly strong and experienced enemy, a sudden attack was by no means sufficient. Morale factors like self-confidence and enthusiasm were of paramount importance. It was this morale that could allow a few attackers to force a formidable crowd of defenders to flee or surrender. Good morale was an advantage of attackers.

The warriors roused their morale at home before a campaign started. The ability to arouse warriors was probably one of the princes' essential skills. A lifestyle in which men competed frequently in races and war games kept a fighting spirit alive. Such games included shooting, wrestling, jumping over belts put before poles, skiing, and throwing large boulders with the help of feet. It is thus not surprising that the warriors could dodge an arrow having heard a bowstring sound (Patkanov 1891: 43, 65).

The rituals intended to develop a war morale (like "a dance with arms" described by various authors, see, Abramov 1851: 6–7; Kastren 1858: 308–310; Shavrov 1871: 11–12), were held at "a dancing square," and possibly in some dwellings. Particularly interesting is the night dance with sabers and spears, which was organized by a shaman. The Ostiaks "swayed from side to side, shouted with various tones of voice, sometimes occasionally and then frequently, one after another. The utterances and movement continued for about an hour, and the more the Ostiaks cried and swayed, the more they flew into a rage" (Abramov 1851: 7).

The lead warrior was a source of morale in epics; the rest of the men are described as faceless followers of a prince. When a chief of an attacking faction was killed by an arrow, a large army of followers then lost soon after: only a few survived to take flight. In turn, sometimes the defenders were overwhelmed by the sight of numerous enemy, and would have been unable to fight were it not for the prince's courage (Patkanov 1891: 41, 69).

HOSTILE MAGIC. An enemy was treated as a "nonhuman" who deserved brutality. Probably this was a ritual rule rather than "the nature" of the fighters. In order to convince an enemy (and oneself) that he was "nonhuman," it was necessary to kill him in a "nonhuman" way. While killing an enemy in a subtle way, the winner affected magically those who still survived. It is well known from war history that "prodigious brutality" was the best way to convince people of enemy strength.

A Polui Khanty story tells with sympathy of an ingenious host who gathered enemies around the fire, bolted the door with a log, and burned the dwelling together with the guests. In a Tromegan Khanty story, Khanty and Nenets chiefs competed in bow-shooting before a battle broke out, the winner having the privilege to start shooting in the battle. Two rafts, one with the mother of the Khanty chief Salak and one with the mother of the *Avus ekh* chief, were lowered into a lake. The competitors took aim to hit cedar cones put on the women's heads. Salak shot, splitting the cone on his mother's head in two. But the Nenets chief failed and killed his own mother. While in battle, the *Avus ekh* violated the agreement and started to shoot first. Their chief's arrow hit Salak, who staggered and retreated three steps. Then he shot and his arrow pierced the enemy's chief's chain armor. Salak "smashed the other Nenetses' heads against ice," and the rest of them asked for mercy, promising never to encroach on Khanty land again.

An ideology of rejection of anything "alien" (Golovnev 1991) begins with artificial opposition. A Nenets bowstring is made of reindeer hide, while a Khanty one is of cedar root impregnated with sea mammal fat. The Nenetses shoot raising their bows high above their heads, while the Vakh Khantys keep them level with their bodies (Kulemzin and Lukina 1978: 31). The Nenetses are said to be afraid of bears, while the Tromegan

Khantys hunt them; the Nenetses do not eat pike, while many Khantys eat them. Sometimes minor differences are mentioned to distinguish close neighbors. For example, arrow plumage is of wood grouse wing among the Ob Khantys, and of squirrel tails among the Maloiugan Khantys (Kulemzin and Lukina 1978: 41). Opposition can express itself in nicknames. The Ostiaks call the Samoyeds *N'ara noga teda khor iaranet* (the reindeer Samoyeds who eat raw meat) (Patkanov 1891: 36). The forest Nenetses call the Pim Khantys *Paritschtea* (blacks) (Kastren 1860: 244).

Behavioral norms are also important. "The Ostiaks did not touch Samoyed clothes and other possessions, and if they took anything from them, they did so across a fire. They then smoked the objects with beaver fur" (Kushelevskii 1868: 150). Hostility is manifested in attitudes toward "alien" norms as well. In the Sel'kup view, swans are sacred birds: it is forbidden to kill them (Lukina 1985: 150). In contrast, the Vakh Khantys considered that "it is possible to break and throw away swans' bones" (Kulemzin 1984: 103). Under war conditions, attitudes toward "aliens" can be underwritten by magic: long ago, the Vakh Khantys used to cut a cross in the ground in order to stimulate the local Nenetses to die off (Kulemzin 1984: 115–16). In order to weaken their enemy, the Vakh Khantys stole the "Agan goddess" of the Avus-Iaun Iakh. "In order to have glory and to humiliate enemies, the winners (the Ostiaks) used to take skin from their heads (*ukh-sokh*) … in their view, the soul of a decapitated man eventually dies … the more enemy scalps a prince had, the more respected he was" (Patkanov 1891: 66, 67). The Mansis also took scalps (Gondatti 1886: 64).

A winner took the armor of a slain enemy. Sometimes a loser cast it to the winner by himself in order not to be robbed after death. There is evidence that warriors ate hearts of the defeated enemy in order to obtain their strength. In response to numerous raids on their lands by an Altym warrior named Sengepov, the Irtysh Ostiaks started a war against him though he was already dead. They were told that an evil spirit in a bird resembling a loon flew through him. "Then they went to the graveyard where he was recently buried, dug him out, cut out his heart strong as a stone, cut it into pieces, and ate it" (Patkanov 1891: 66–67).

PEACE OATHS. Concepts concerning peace are similar to those for warfare, since peace is made with the enemy. Thus, it is not surprising that oaths for peace include the same beliefs as those for aggression. Thus, warriors used to say that if any of them violated the oath, skin would be taken from his head. While saying that, they kissed "pike nose and fire" (Patkanov 1891: 66). In a Pim Khanty story, in which the Khantys decided to make peace with the *Avus ekh*, they brought a pike and an *Avus ekh* chief cut off its upper jaw saying: "We will not fight until the pike grows a new jaw."

It was by no means easy to make peace with the enemy (especially, for winners to make peace with losers). Usually, revenge followed defeat. Nevertheless, each side made peace in its own way, but with spirits rather than with the enemy. For the winners, that meant obtaining power over the seized territory. For instance, after a victory over the Nenetses, the three Ostiak brothers established three sanctuaries in the areas won.

Conclusion

Former military experience was used by the northern peoples during revolts against Soviet authorities in the 1930s and 1940s (Golovnev 1995: 163–94). These were large-scale revolts in which shamans participated actively and traditional brutality was practiced. It is worth noting that all these recent events took place in the nomadic areas, whereas permanently settled inhabitants were not involved. It was reindeer-herding that provided groups with economic and social autonomy and made them not only independent of the state but even able to withstand it.

Since its emergence, large-scale reindeer-herding played a defensive role in the conflict between the indigenous populations and the Russian state. Both in the nineteenth and twentieth centuries, cultural differences between the groups in question were a source of permanent conflict between them, since the Russian state attempted to subjugate local communities, whether by Russian Christianization or Soviet collectivization. In the course of explicit or implicit resistance against the Russian influence, the reindeer became a symbol of independence for indigenous peoples. This was reflected in a sacralization of domesticated reindeer and in an attitude toward reindeer-herding as a symbol of ethnic life. The aboriginal intention to be independent of new authorities was undoubtedly a major stimulus for the emergence of nomadism in the tundra. That was why large-scale reindeer-herding emerged throughout the Siberian tundra—from Yamal to Chukotka—in the seventeenth and eighteenth centuries, and was also a reason for the "pathological" passion of all warriors and rebels to seize reindeer.

The social structure was drastically altered in northwestern Siberia after intergroup and interethnic wars, as well as military-political chiefdoms, disappeared. The taiga peoples (the Mansis, Khantys, and Sel'kups) were the most strongly affected, for their warriors had formed a special "caste." The tundra Nenetses with their "democratic chiefdoms" were less affected.

On the one hand, the former northern wars can be regarded as brutal and unjust. On the other hand, they stimulated the development of handicraft, transport, fortification, physical culture, and intellectual self-awareness. The conflicts also encouraged the internal unity of ethnic groups and helped maintain stable ethnic boundaries. However, the "spirit of war" did not know ethnic boundaries. Whenever wars broke out somewhere in the huge territory ranging from west of the Ural Mountains to the Yenisei River, they would eventually affect the entire region. In general, the direction of aggression was from west to east; the taiga and tundra regions along the Yenisei River still witnessed conflicts in the nineteenth century, which had originated—and long died down—in the Ural and Irtysh areas. Thus, in the early twentieth century, oral traditions about wars were still cast in the form of historic accounts in the east, while they had taken on the form of heroic epics in the west.

Notes

The original Russian text was translated by Viktor Shnirel'man and edited by Polly Wiessner, Megan Biesele, and Peter Schweitzer.

1. Descriptions of military norms and customs are mostly based on folklore and oral history, which date back to late medieval times when the Russian state initiated its conquest of Siberia, i.e., in the sixteenth and seventeenth centuries. However, similar features were revealed in the latest indigenous wars and revolts, occurring in the mid-1800s and even up to the 1930s and 1940s.

References

Abramov, N. A. 1851. "O vvedenii khristianstva u ostiakov." *Zhurnal ministerstva narodnogo prosveshcheniia* 72(10–12).

Bakhrushin, S. V. 1955. "Ostiatskie i vogul'skie kniazhestva v XVI-XVII-vv." In *Nauchnye trudy*. Vol. 3, Pt. 2: 86–152. Leningrad.

Burch, E. 1974. "Eskimo Warfare in Northwest Alaska." *Anthropological Papers of the University of Alaska* 16(2): 1–14.

Butsinskii, P. N. 1893. *K istorii Sibiri: Surgut, Narym i Ketsk do 1645 g.* Khar'kov.

Castrén, M. A. 1855. *Wörterverzeichnisse aus den samojedischen Sprachen*. St. Petersburg: Kaiserliche Akademie der Wissenschaften.

Dmitriev-Sadovnikov, G. M. 1916. "Na Vakhe." *Ezhegodnik Tobol'skogo gubernskogo muzeia* 26: 1–15.

Dolgikh, B. O., ed. 1961. *Mifologicheskie skazki i istoricheskie predaniia entsev*. Moscow: Izdatel'stvo Akademii nauk SSSR.

Dul'zon, A. P. 1966. "Zemlianka epokhi bronzy na Srednei Obi." *Uchenye zapiski Tomskogo gosudarstvennongo pedagogicheskogo instituta* 16.

Ekvall, R. B. 1964. "Peace and War among the Tibetan Nomads." *American Anthropologist* 66: 1119–48.

Ferguson, R. B. 1989. "Anthropology of War: Theory, Politics, Ethics." In *The Anthropology of War and Peace: Perspectives on the Nuclear Age*. P. R. Turner and D. Pitt, eds. 141–59. South Hadley, Mass.: Bergin & Garvey.

Golovnev, A. V. 1991. "'Svoe' i 'chuzhoe' v predstavleniiakh khantov." In *Obskie ugry (khanty i mansi)*. 187–224. Moscow: Institut etnologii i antropologii RAN.

———. 1995. *Govoriashchie kul'tury: traditsii samodiitsev i ugrov*. Ekaterinburg: Institut istorii i arkheologii, Ural'skoe otdelenie RAN.

Goldschmidt, W. 1989. "Inducement to Military Preparation in Tribal Societies." In *The Anthropology of War and Peace: Perspectives on the Nuclear Age*. P. R. Turner and D. Pitt, eds. 15–31. South Hadley, Mass.: Bergin & Garvey.

Gondatti, N. L. 1886. "Sledy iazycheskikh verovanii u man'zov." *Trudy etnograficheskogo otdeleniia Imperatorskogo obshchestva liubitelei estestvoznaniia, antropologii i etnografii pri Moskovskom universitete* 7: 49–73.

Kastren, M. A. 1858. "Etnograficheskie zamechaniia i nabliudeniia Kastrena o lopariakh, karelakh, samoedakh i ostiakakh, izvlechennye iz ego putevykh vospominanii 1838–1844." *Etnograficheskii sbornik rossiiskogo geograficheskogo obshchestva* 4.

———. 1860. "Puteshestvie po Laplandii, Severnoi Rossii i Sibiri, 1838–1844, 1845–1849." *Magazin zemlevedeniia i puteshestvii* 6(2).

Khomich, L. V. 1966. *Nentsy. Istoriko-etnograficheskie ocherki*. Leningrad: Nauka.

Kulemzin, V. M. 1984. *Chelovek i priroda v verovaniiakh khantov*. Tomsk: Tomskii gosudarstvennyi universitet.

Kulemzin, V. M., and N. V. Lukina. 1978. *Materialy po fol'kloru khantov*. Tomsk: Tomskii gosudarstvennyi universitet.

———. 1992. *Znakom'tes': khanty*. Novosibirsk: Nauka.

Kupriianova, Z. N. 1965. *Epicheskie pesni nentsev*. Moscow: Nauka.

Kushelevskii, Iu. I. 1868. *Severnyi polius i zemlia Iamal*. St. Petersburg.

Lezova, S. V. 1991. "Zhilishche severnykh sel'kupov." *Eksperimental'naia arkheologiia* 1: 101–7.

———. 1993. "K istorii tazovskogo regiona." In *Problemy etnicheskoi istorii samodiiskikh narodov, chast' 2*. 53–56. Omsk: Omskii gosudarstvennyi universitet.

Lukina, N. V. 1985. *Formirovanie materialnoi kul'tury khantov (vostochnaia gruppa)*. Tomsk: Tomksii gosudarstvennyi universitet.

McCauley, C. 1990. "Conference Overview." In *The Anthropology of War*. J. Haas, ed. Cambridge: Cambridge University Press.

Miller, G. F. 1937. *Istoriia Sibiri*, Vol. 1. Moscow-Leningrad.

Patkanov, S. K. 1891. *Tip ostiatskogo bogatyria po ostiatskim bylinam i geroicheskim skazaniiam*. St. Petersburg.

Pelikh, G. I. 1981. *Sel'kupy XVII veka. Ocherki sotsial'no-ekonomicheskoi istorii*. Novosibirsk: Nauka.

Prokof'ev, G. N. 1928. "Ostiako-samoedy Turukhanskogo kraia." *Etnografiia* 2: 96–103.

———. 1940. "Etnogoniia narodnostei Ob'-Eniseiskogo basseina." *Sovetskaia Etnografiia. Sbornik statey* 3: 67–76.

Prokof'eva, E. D. 1947. "Drevnie zhilishcha na rekakh Tym i Ket." *Sovetskaia etnografiia* 2: 199–202.

Shavrov, V. 1871. "Kratkie zapiski o zhiteliakh Berezovskogo uezda." *Chteniia v obshchestve istorii i drevnostei rossiiskikh* 2.

Sherbakova, A. M., ed. 1984. *Nenetskie skazki*. Vologda.

Shnirel'man, V. A. 1992. *Voina i mir v traditsionnykh obshchestvakh (po materialam zapadnykh issledovanii)*. Moscow: Institut etnologii i antropologii RAN.

Simchenko, Iu. B. 1975. *Zimnii marshrut po Gydanu*. Moscow: Mysl'.

Solov'ev, A. I. 1987. *Voennoe delo korennogo naseleniia Zapadnoi Sibiri. Epokha srednevekov'ia*. Novosibirsk: Nauka.

Tereshchenko, N. M. 1990. *Nenetskii epos. Materialy i issledovaniia po samodiiskim iazykam.* Leningrad: Nauka.

Tret'iakov, P. 1869. "Turukhanskii krai." *Zapiski Imperatorskogo rossiiskogo geograficheskogo obshchestva po obshchei geografii* 2.

Vasil'ev, V. I. 1977. "Problema formirovaniia eniseiskikh nentsev (K voprosu ob etnicheskoi prirode etnograficheskikh grupp v sostave sovremennykh narodnostei Severa)." In *Etnogenez i etnicheskaia istoriia narodov Severa.* 111–47. Moscow: Nauka.

Wilkuna, K. 1950. "Über die obugrischen und samojedischen Pfeile und Köcher." In *Commentationes fenno-ugricae in honorem Y.H. Toivonen.* Helsinki: Suomalais-ugrilainen Seura.

Zhitkov B. M. 1913. "Poluostrov Iamal." *Zapiski Imperatorskogo rossiiskogo geograficheskogo obshchestva po obshchei geografii* 49.

Chapter 7

RITUAL VIOLENCE AMONG THE PEOPLES OF NORTHEASTERN SIBERIA

———————•◎•———————

Elena P. Batianova

When the Cossacks and traders first encountered the Chukchis, Koriaks, Itel'mens, and Siberian Yupiks of Chukotka and Kamchatka in the seventeenth century, they noted that indigenous inhabitants practiced "inhumane and criminal" (from the point of Christian morals) customs and rites involving severe forms of violence such as homicide, beating and even physical mutilation, violent capture of women, and the like. Ritual violence among these peoples included blood revenge, human sacrifices, ritual infanticide, and "voluntary suicide" of the elders. In the eighteenth century, members of expeditions of the Russian Academy of Sciences reported the same.

In the present chapter I examine the social and historical roots of these rites among the Chukotka and Kamchatka peoples, drawing particular attention to current practices and attitudes. The premise of the essay is that it is best to take a functional approach to the understanding of ritual violence as a culturally stipulated means of resolving tensions between groups. I will base my discussion on literature sources, archival data, and on my own field studies.[1]

Let us start with infanticide. The famous traveler Ferdinand Wrangell (Vrangel' in Russian), who visited the Chukchis in 1820, described these customs in the following way: "They maintained a non-natural, inhumane custom of killing infants who were born weak or with physical defects as well as old people who could not sustain the rigors of nomadic life any more" (Vrangel' 1841: 345). Many other sources contain notes on the ritual killing of children among the Chukchis; for instance, the diaries of the Billings expedition of 1785 to 1793 relate that the Chukchis "dispose of their infants born with defects or injured limbs" (Sarychev 1802: 109). According to V. G. Bogoraz (1934: 28), Chukchi mothers who had delivered a child but were not feeling well would sometimes strangle the newborn in order to escape their own death. If a woman died during childbirth, the newborn child was strangled and disposed of in the tundra together with the deceased mother. Bogoraz (1939: 178) noted that the Greenland Inuit practiced a similar custom; they buried newborn infants together with the deceased mother if there was no foster-mother. Shashkov (1868: 77) mentioned similar facts. Obviously, such killings were not regarded as violence in archaic societies.

A newborn child was not perceived as a "true human being" until rituals were performed to transform him or her into a person, such as naming ceremonies and the like (Baiburin 1993: 41, 102).[2] Before these "humanizing" rituals were completed, a child was considered a part of the mother's body. That is why a mother's death meant the child was dead as well. Furthermore, people killed deformed infants, twins, or babies born under conditions that were believed to herald disaster such as thunderstorms (Krasheninnikov 1949: 77).

The customs in question are no longer practiced in Kamchatka and Chukotka, though they live on in Chukchi and Eskimo ritual beliefs handed down over generations. A young Eskimo girl from Lavrentiia, Chukotka, told me that in the former days the Eskimos used to kill the newborn infant by piercing the head with a needle.[3] In contrast, I have never heard of ritual killings of children among the Koriaks. However, Koriaks did regularly cremate their dead. On 27 March 1930, the newspaper *Izvestiia* noted that "a deceased Koriak woman together with her living daughter were burned in the fire according to a barbaric tradition" in the village of Paren'. Later on, this fact (it is not clear whether real or fictitious) was played up by the Bezbozhnik publishing house (Kosokov 1930: 74). It is possible that the story was fabricated in order to prosecute proponents of the old customs during a struggle against indigenous religion.

I could not find any traces of the custom of killing twins among the Koriaks. On the contrary, a "twin cult"—elements of which still survive—precludes any violence toward twins: one cannot punish twins, belittle them, or even address them in a low voice. There are didactic stories in family narratives illustrating that twins can die because of careless treatment. The birth and death of twins was accompanied by special rituals. One had to make small wooden or stone figurines of wolves (protectors of twins) after twins were born; the twins themselves were then called wolves. If twins died, they were to be cremated. For example, in 1984 a thirty-five-year-old woman from the village of Ossora complained that her deceased twin children were not cremated according to tradition, and thus they would be taken by wolves. Moreover, she believed that after she died she would turn into a she-wolf herself.

Another custom which is worth noting deals with senilicide or "voluntary death," well known in ethnography. It was observed among the Koriaks and even more frequently among the Chukchis (Bogoraz 1900; 1934; 1939; Zelenin 1937). According to this custom, old and sick people could be ritually killed by their relatives at their own request. This custom was first reported during the eighteenth century by an expedition under the command of the Captains Billings and Sarychev. Gavriil Sarychev observed that among the Chukchis "a son kills a father without mercy, if the latter cannot be useful to the family because of his old age, disease or senility. It often happens that the sick person asks for it, like for a favor, wishing to die in a heroic way" (Sarychev 1802: 109). The ritual had rigid rules; a person willing to die had to invite relatives and to make this wish known using a formula such as, "I turned into a wild reindeer" or "treat me as game." They themselves chose "assistants" or "companions" who were supposed to kill them. According to Avgustinovich (1878–79: 43), they made a special garment for "a voluntary death," produced of the best reindeer skins and wolf fur, that was similar to those of Chukchi battle dress. Other sorts of homicide were also practiced and passed down as tradition. In 1984 the reindeer Koriaks of Tymlat village (eastern Kamchatka) told me that an old Chukchi woman, who had joined them for the summer, had fallen ill and had asked them "to help her to die" by piercing her temple with a large old-fashioned needle. Her husband had requested the same.

The custom of voluntary death included several prohibitions. For instance, if one had spelled out the willingness to die according to the custom, one could not reverse the decision, or else the deceived spirits could take one's relative instead. A chosen "assistant" could not refuse to serve, since he or she was also considered to be "chosen by the spirits."

Many Siberian peoples—for example, the Evenks, the Kets, the Buriats, and the Tofas—hastened the death of those who were incapacitated by age and/or illness, but their customs did not involve active killing. People destined to die were abandoned in the tundra, taiga, or barren lands and were provided with some food as a token chance of survival. I think that the more brutal custom among the Chukchis and the Koriaks can be explained by its links with sacrifice. This connection is evident from one of Wrangell's descriptions, which tells about the epidemics among the Chaun Chukchis in 1814. At that time, the local shamans declared that the spirits would cease causing disaster only if an old man named Kochan were sacrificed. People did not consent, but when the epidemics continued, the shamans insisted that their plan be carried out. Kochan then declared publicly that for the sake of the well-being of others he was ready to sacrifice his life. After that his son, "softened by requests and threatened by curses, plunged a knife into his father's chest and gave the corpse to the shamans" (Vrangel' 1841: 346–47).

This voluntary death carried out in the context of sacrifice was not a unique case. In a story entitled "Aivan," Pugachev (1960: 35) mentions "a voluntary death" recommended by a shaman that was demanded by "a wind spirit," which was in fact a sacrifice. Bogoraz (1934: 109) also stressed the relationship between the "voluntary death" custom and sacrifice. Zelenin (1937: 57) was obviously wrong in objecting to Bogoraz's view and in attempting to construct a sharp contrast between "voluntary death" customs and sacrifices. Rather, these two forms of ritual violence— voluntary death and voluntary sacrifice—were derived from the same world-view and were intertwined both ritually and ideologically. Many observers emphasized a functional basis for the "voluntary death" custom in the harsh environment of the Far North. An American member of the Siberian detachment of the Western Union Telegraph expedition, George Kennan, ascribed a rationality to the custom in question in the following words: "A wandering life made sickness and infirmity unusually burden-some to both sufferers and supporters; and this finally led to the murder of the old and sick, as a measure both of policy and mercy ... these customs ... are the natural development of certain circumstances, and only prove that the strongest emotions of human nature ... are all powerless to oppose the operation of great natural laws" (Kennan 1871: 215).

Indeed, a sick person living together with the rest of the family did endanger the health and life of others, causing discontent and fear among neighbors. This very situation was described by a writer, Semushkin, who worked in the Far North in the 1920s. In his famous novel *Chukotka*, he describes, in particular, a severely ill eighty-year-old woman in a tent at Cape Ryrkaipii: "There was a stench inside the tent. Her disease affected other family members, but she did not ask to die and so was left alone." The old lady's son asked Semushkin: "What should I do? One must strangle the old woman but she does not ask for it." He expressed his discontent and intolerance with the following words: "You do not understand. Friends stopped visiting me, they are afraid of falling ill. Everybody thinks that an evil spirit has settled in my tent" (Semushkin 1939: 195). It was important that old people declared their own willingness to die, avoiding any implication that the relatives no longer wanted to care for a helpless person. Recovery of old people sometimes caused fear, rather than joy, among the relatives since they believed that the spirits would then take a younger person instead (see Kosokov 1930: 63). There were different means of carrying out requested homicide, depending on local tradition. Use of a spear was probably closely associated with sacrifice, since until recently a spear was used in the ritual slaughter of animals. Also, death by spear was accompanied by rigid rules; for instance, a woman could not take part in such a killing.

The custom of voluntary death was difficult to eradicate. In the early nineteenth century Vrangel' (1841: 345) noted: "Despite all the efforts of the authorities and clergy, this awful custom was practiced persistently." The missionary Argentov, who conducted a census among the Chukchis of the Chaun area, stated that the old Chukchis rarely died a natural death since "custom did not provide for that" (Argentov 1850: 16). Business correspondence between the Gizhiga police chief and the military governor of the Primor'e region, which was found by V. N. Ivanov in the Yakutsk archives (Ivanov 1960), provides evidence that the custom was widespread among the Chukchis in 1880:

> The anticipation of suicide with the help of a relative is widespread in the region, except for a few areas: the town of Gizhiga, the villages of Anadyrsk, Penzhinsk and Naiakhansk, the fortresses at the Penzhina inlet, and the nomadic camps of the Yakut. In the rest of the territory this kind of death is common for both men and women, and suicides probably account for no less than 25 percent of deaths, and possibly more. One tells a close relative (a son, a brother, or a nephew) of the willingness to die, and this wish is fulfilled in the presence of family members and all tent residents (usually, several families inhabit one tent). It is considered impossible to reverse such a decision. The appointed executioner thrusts a spear into the bare chest of the person, and the corpse is burnt afterwards. The most recent cases of this sort occurred last November at a small Chukchi camp at the Upper Paren' River. First, a wealthy Chukchi named Atakhai requested others to kill him because of illness, the second was his sister, and the third to die was a poor Chukchi, who hoped to receive a reindeer herd with silver horns in the other world.... All three homicides were committed according to tundra customs and were recognized by the relatives of the deceased as not demanding blood revenge. (Ivanov 1960: 172–73)

Kennan wrote about voluntary death among the Koriaks in the mid-nineteenth century:

> the Koraks murdered all their old people as soon as sickness or the infirmities of age unfitted them for the hardships of a nomadic life ... all Koraks are taught to look upon such a death as the natural end of their existence, and they meet it generally with perfect composure. Instances are rare when a man desires to outlive the period of his physical activity and usefulness. (Kennan 1871: 214)

In the Soviet period, the "voluntary death" custom became illegal and its participants were charged with homicide, but nevertheless it was maintained by the Chukchis. The ethnographer of the Koriaks, Stebnitskii (n.d.), wrote in the 1930s: "Among the Koriaks the custom of killing old people has disappeared now," but "among the Chukchis it was practiced until very recently. Many employees of the Chukchi National Okrug are struggling against it even now."

The custom survived until recently, and may still exist today. During six short field trips to the Chukchis and Koriaks between 1984 and 1990, I managed to document more than ten "voluntary death" cases. However, people talked about them as if they had taken place several decades ago. In Ust'-Belaia (Anadyr' region, Chukotka) an old woman told me that during her childhood she witnessed the voluntary death of her uncle, who was known as a shaman. She said: "He did not die, but requested death in Chukchi style." On the eve of the event she noticed that the residents of her uncle's tent were preparing a ceremony. They took out festive clothes and killed a reindeer, and relatives arrived. At night the girl was taken to another tent to sleep, and by the morning everything had come to an end. She was told that her uncle had gone to another world.

Sometimes a ritual had been performed just prior to our arrival. Thus, in summer 1987, one of the reindeer-herding leaders was "voluntarily" killed in the Kanchalan tundra (Anadyr' region). A young girl from Kanchalan told me about this case: "In July an old man was brought to the tundra. He was severely ill and could no longer tolerate the suffering. His physician had sent him away. The old man felt that he could not survive, and requested that people kill him. They did so and buried him in the traditional way. The best reindeer were slaughtered because he was a leader of the herders. All his relatives had died in a similar way, and he wanted to die like his ancestors."

In 1980, an influential local Chukchi "chief" who lived on Aion Island ended his life in a similar way. His daughter told me the following story:

My father died in 1980. He was 70 years old. He had a hard life. In 1947 his entire clan died of measles. All the people died, adults and children. My father survived because he was out with a herd together with his nephew. Collectivization was taking place at the time and a literate Chukchi was there. He made reports to the NKVD [forerunner of the KGB] about everybody. After his report was submitted, my father and his friend were prosecuted. They were deprived of their reindeer herd and resettled from the forest to Aion Island, where they lived by hunting. They had to remain there until they received special instructions. In 1953 Stalin died. The literate Chukchi who reported them went away. My father was appointed leader of the herders. They obeyed, feared, and respected him. He punished alcoholics, beating them with a stick. People understood him without words. They knew him all over the tundra, in the Bilibino area, the Chaun area. They invited him for races and he won every time. He hoped to restore the large markets that existed in Chukotka in former times. Father did not understand the Soviet power. He was offended by it. He used to say: "I achieved everything by myself, why did they take my reindeer? Why was it illegal to have them?" He was against everything that was Russian.

He never stated that life took a turn for the better after the Russians came. He forbade the consumption of Russian food during holidays. He took canned food away from us. He shouted at me: "It will be a disgrace if you marry a Russian." He respected traditions, and felt that one must follow them. He loved children. He treated everything told or made by a child as something sacred. Once a girl gave him a necklace, put it on his neck, and he never took it off, for he felt that it should be left on. He was very harsh, but we felt his love. When he fell ill with cancer, he wanted to die according to tradition. He assembled everybody and asked his daughter to come. Then he said: "Leave me here on the island. You cannot move because of me, I hinder you." We told him: "Not at all," but he persuaded us. "When I die, I will be constantly with you like the wind. I will turn into grass, into nature." He suffered terribly, could not eat, was hungry for almost two months, and became very thin. We found a lonely place near Kuz'michikha River. There my elder sister and one of my brothers killed him.

It should be noted that people usually hide their participation in the "voluntary death" ritual and are not inclined to talk about it. They practice it secretly since they can be prosecuted; the law does not distinguish between ritual and nonritual killing. According to witnesses and practitioners, this custom is still practiced in order to save people from suffering and to allow people to die in an honorable way following tradition. Interestingly enough, contemporary Chukchis link the ancestors' strength and courage to this custom, since it allowed old people to demonstrate courage while being killed and command the younger to fulfill their will: "Our elders gave orders. They used to assemble people and say: 'You and you!' The younger men tried to be strong, not to lose heart. They only asked: 'How?'" (Tymlat, Kamchatka).

Persistence of the custom in question was, above all, a result of traditional evaluations of life and death categories. Thus, in the Chukchi view, death is always caused by violence: the Chukchis do not believe in a natural death.[4] One dies at the hand of another through witchcraft or direct physical violence; it is better to die at the hand of a relative than of a stranger or evil spirit, i.e., of disease. Captain Sarychev pointed out in the eighteenth century that "they [the Chukchis E.B.] consider a natural death a disgrace, which, in their view, is good only for women" (Sarychev 1802: 109). Fear of dying from disease was and is a reason to choose "voluntary death." According to Anna Sirina (personal communication, 1993), during her fieldwork in the Lower Kolyma River region of Yakutia in 1993, S. I. Sleptsov (an Even born in 1948) told Sirina that his mother, in her youth, lived along the Lower Kolyma River, where the Chukchis roamed. She related how an old Chukchi man who caught influenza "was afraid" to die from the illness and asked relatives to kill him. In the morning he sharpened a knife for the purpose and tested it. His own wife then killed him with this knife in the afternoon.

The belief in the superiority of a voluntary death is embedded in Chukchi mythology. For instance, in the Chukchi view, people who die voluntary deaths obtain the best positions in the world of the deceased. They are thought to live in the red fire of the northern lights and to get reindeer with silver horns as a reward, among other benefits. The Chukchis speak of the deceased as follows: "He died a good death." I heard that many times during my field trips.

The tradition of "voluntary death" reverses the usual status of murderer and victim: a victim is treated as dominant—one who enforces his will—and the murderer, as a victim of moral pressure. Thus, people who were asked to be "assistants" or "companions," i.e., the murderers, were often considered by society as being punished for ill-treatment of the elders or for other misbehavior, such as laziness, ill will, and the like. An old Chukchi woman in Tymlat told me that, when she was living with her husband's family, she was permanently afraid that her sick mother-in-law—who had already prepared a special rope made of reindeer sinew—would want her to be the "assistant." However, the old woman chose her son and the eldest daughter-in-law, "the most unfriendly" one, to be "a companion." Another Chukchi woman explained to me why it is necessary to be good to old people: "One should not offend old people, since the time may come when he or she would call on you and say, 'It is you!'" According to Chukchi belief, another reason why a person who chose voluntary death was in command was that such a person disseminated danger. Having declared his or her will to die according to tradition, he or she was in close contact with the spirit world and thus dangerous.

Sometimes killing was committed without any ritual. While describing three "voluntary death" cases, the famous explorer of Chukotka, N. Kalinnikov, noted that one case deviated from custom. "It involved the killing of a sick wife who was shot with a gun by her husband. She had been sick for some years ... and asked her husband continuously to put an end to her sufferings. The husband avoided it for some time but then agreed. He shot her with a new gun, brought her corpse to the barren ground, left her there together with the gun, and was miserable for a long time" (Kalinnikov 1912: 87). In the Soviet period, when the custom was performed in secret, and often in a hurry, it lost many traditional elements and became closer to a common murder "by request" rather than a ritual killing. A thirty-six-year-old woman from Billings village told me: "A woman was sick and could not eat. She asked another old woman to kill her. The latter put a towel around her neck and strangled her."

The Chukchis and the Koriaks had a "light" attitude toward death, since they believed in the cyclical nature of time and in rebirth. Widespread suicides were linked with this belief. Krasheninnikov (1949: 368) wrote of the inhabitants of Kamchatka: "Suicide was the last pleasure for them." Bogoraz also noticed widespread suicides among the Chukchis. Among reasons for suicide, he mentioned offense, insult, grief over a relative's death, or a special psychological state such as unwillingness to live. According to sources of the eighteenth and nineteenth centuries, collective suicides or suicides involving the extermination of an entire family did occur. "If they were afflicted by a disaster or by pain, they preferred to overcome it by suicide, killing their wife and children in advance" (Zapadnyi bereg 1852: 141). In the archives of Anadyr', there is a case of a Koriak suicide committed in 1943. A head of a collective farm, who was afraid of punishment for losses to a jointly owned reindeer herd, chose to commit suicide. Prior to that he killed his wife and five children.

Zelenin (1937: 48) criticized Bogoraz, Steinmetz, and others for having "mixed voluntary death customs with a common suicide" and argued that one had to distinguish between these completely different phenomena. However, though different, all had common roots in beliefs about life and death. In addition, suicides were sometimes caused by ritual etiquette. Thus, if most camp members died due to an epidemic, the fortunate survivors had no right to live; they were not accepted by other camps and were forced to commit suicide since they were considered to be victims of the spirits. Bogoraz (1939: 139) noted that a fifteen-year-old boy from "the dead camp" came to his uncle who met him with a gun and ordered him to return immediately. "Go and hang yourself or stab yourself," the old man shouted from a distance. "You belong to the *Kelet* [harmful spirits, Chukchi, pl.], go away." Thus, suicides among the Koriaks, the Chukchis, and many other Siberian peoples were a cultural tradition rooted in accepted psychology and world-view.[5] Frequent suicides among these peoples today must be considered in the context of this orientation.

Let us now turn to Chukchi and Koriak beliefs about murder. Two categories of murder were distinguished: murders committed by one's own people (relatives or family members) and those committed by strangers. The former were not punished at all and were treated as "purely familial matters." Zibarev (1990: 107), referring to Beretti (1929: 19), mentioned a case in which "the Chukchi elders refused to arrest a Chukchi who had killed his two wives, a nephew and a son, while stating that, according to their customs, he did not commit any crime." Sometimes a family itself used to sentence one of its members to death because of hostile and aggressive behavior that endangered the others. Even if a person committed a murder without obvious motives, it was often justified by the rationale that he or she had been bewitched by evil spirits. A young Chukchi woman from Markovo (Anadyr' region) told me that her aunt was killed by her own husband, and that she felt sorry for the husband rather than blaming him. In her view, he was only guilty in that while coming back from the tundra he "did not purify himself of the spirits," "did not shake them off," and as a result they forced him to commit a murder. Traditionally, any murder except a ritual one committed within a kin group was considered a great misfortune, a punishment for disrespect toward spirits. It was linked to the curse of a shaman or spirit. Argentov documented the following legend amongst the Chaun Chukchis in 1844 (Argentov 1850: 54): "A founder of the humans had a wife, a large worm. He was angry with her, beat her, and threw her into the fire. She fell on her back and said before dying, 'You are killing me. As a result your descendants will fight with each other and kill each other.'"

By contrast, if a stranger was the murderer, blood revenge followed: "If one murdered somebody he would be killed by the deceased's relatives" (Krasheninnikov 1949: 372). Several published and archival sources of the late nineteenth century mention a case of blood revenge among the Oliutorsk Koriaks that occurred when one man killed another during the sharing of game meat. The relatives of the latter set fire to the subterranean dwelling of the murderer, burning all the inhabitants to death. I was told of the same case during my field trip to the Karaga region of Kamchatka. Interestingly enough, D'iachkov (1893: 64; see also Stebnitskii n.d.: 183; Ivanov 1960: 174), who described this very case, pointed out that since the relatives of the deceased were Christians, they initially did not take revenge but rather decided to appeal to the law. The local authorities, however, did not understand and advised them to punish the murderer in the traditional way. They ultimately did so.

Usually, blood revenge ceased when the relatives of the deceased punished the murderer. Moreover, people preferred material death compensation to bloody revenge. "A big payment is always better than blood," Chukchi informants told Bogoraz (1934: 185). Conflicts among the Chukchis, Koriaks, and Siberian Yupiks could also be settled by duels—so that revenge was not required in the case of an evil spirit. Stebnitskii (n.d.: 6), who collected Koriak shamanistic folklore, documented a case in which an evil spirit, a *kalaku*, attacked a shaman. Undaunted, the latter challenged the spirit to a drum competition and won. Witchcraft causing sickness or death was treated as the worst sort of violence that had to be revenged. Being charged with witchcraft was the most frequent reason for prosecutions against shamans in the 1920s and 1930s. In 1987, a local physician (a young Chukchi girl) in Vaegi complained that it was not possible to deal with a local shaman, and that the majority of patients in the hospital were victims of his witchcraft, which the physicians were not able to counter.

Bogoraz described how the methods of Chukchi witchcraft closely resembled those of other peoples. They included various actions involving corpse flesh, use of human skulls in preparation of medicine to do harm with the help of animals, and spells and the like. In the view of

Vaegi inhabitants, a shaman's saliva and whisper were especially dangerous. It should be noted that witches and shamans are proud of their "evil
deeds." "Do you remember the plane that crashed a year ago?" an old
Koriak woman, who was famous as a shaman, once asked me. "I do not
remember, but why do you ask?" "It happened because of my spells," she
said proudly.

It is as if society has licensed shamans to use violence, especially in the
form of witchcraft. However, sources also mention that the Chukchis
killed a shaman if in their view he abused his position. The most recent
cases of human sacrifice among the Chukchis are dated to the very early
nineteenth century (see above). Argentov (Val'skaia 1961: 178–79) noted
that at the Chaun River in 1812 an Orthodox missionary was about to
fall victim to a ritual sacrifice when the Chukchis "in wolves' hats and
armed with spears, surrounded the unarmed old man and wanted to kill
him as a sacrifice to the earth." One of the Chukchi elders "rescued him
from the killers." The decisions of shamans were not uncontrolled, for
shamans also claimed leadership in the "voluntary death" custom. Special forms of ritual violence, "the shaman tests," were used against shamans themselves, when, for example, a shaman sentenced a person to
death and people doubted that the spirits had really demanded it. If after
long tortures (sometimes lasting several days) a shaman insisted on his
decision, people finally agreed with him (Vrangel' 1841: 346). George
Kennan wrote:

> The natives themselves, however, seem to doubt occasionally the priest's pre-
> tended inspiration, and whip him severely to test the sincerity of his profes-
> sions and the genuineness of his revelations. If his fortitude sustains him
> under the infliction without any exhibition of human weakness or suffering,
> his authority as a minister of the evil spirits is vindicated, and his commands
> obeyed. (Kennan 1871: 213)

There was one more type of ritual violence that was for the most part
symbolic—violence against women, as practiced in bride abduction.
Bogoraz wrote of Chukchi abduction:

> In the past, a group of boys used to catch a girl in the tundra, tie her hands and
> feet, and bring her to the tent of him who had chosen her as a wife. Even rela-
> tives, for instance cousins, used to do that. Such abductions did not result in
> severe hostilities between the families. The girl's parents demanded ransom
> from the abductors. A woman from the abductor's family was then given as
> compensation. The contemporary Chukchis consider this marriage custom as
> a traditional one. (Bogoraz 1934: 127)

There were symbolic fights between men and women that could also
be observed in games. For instance, among the Vaegi Chukchis, two

teams, one male and the other female, participated in tug of war or a ball game. This fight of the sexes was symbolized even in a kind of checkers game; half of the checkers represented women and the other half, men.

Ritual symbolic violence against women was particularly noticeable in the Itel'men and Koriak custom of "bride capture," which was a usual part of wedding ceremonies. A boy who wanted to marry a certain girl obtained a right to "seize" a bride after a period of service to her father. The girl was guarded and actively defended by her relatives, who beat and scratched the groom severely. This violence against the man was further-more a form of initiation accompanying the boy's passage to the new sta-tus of being a husband. Kennan (1871: 202) observed this ritual among the Koriaks in Kamchatka in the mid-1860s and interpreted it as "An infringement upon the generally recognized prerogatives of the sterner sex." Violence against women was also evident in the spouse-exchange tradition that is still practiced among the Chukchis. Sometimes men make an alliance with other men that permits intercourse with their respective spouses without permission of the women, leading to female protest. Bogoraz (1934: 137) mentioned that a Chukchi woman com-mitted suicide in protest against this custom. A young Chukchi girl from Vaegi complained to me that her mother treated her badly and consid-ered her a stranger, since the girl had been fathered by an unwanted "spouse-exchange partner," with whom the mother was forced by her husband to have intercourse.

In conclusion, one must note that ritual violence constitutes a specific mechanism to curb aggression. Among the peoples of northeastern Siberia, rituals moderated violence, set limits for it, and prevented its escalation. Many conflicts and tensions were resolved through constrained violence associated with a spirit of competition. Even one who was doomed to a "voluntary death" would say to the appointed killer, "Let us wrestle with each other."

Ritualization of violence was an attribute of a social ecology, a way to settle tensions between the generations (voluntary death), between the sexes (capture of the bride, spouse exchange), and between groups and individuals in real or potential conflict with each other (various duels and competitions). Some of these customs or elements of them have been maintained into the present, due to the cultural concepts that the peoples of northeastern Siberia hold toward life, death, time, good, and evil.

Notes

The original Russian text was translated by Viktor Shnirel'man; the translation was reviewed by Lydia Black, Patty Gray, and Nikolay Ssorin-Chaikov, and edited by Polly Wiessner, Megan Biesele, and Peter Schweitzer.

1. The field studies on which this essay is based were carried out between 1984 and 1990 in Koriak, Chukchi, and Chuvan settlements of Chukotka and Kamchatka. In the Koriak Autonomous Okrug, research was conducted in 1984 (settlements of Tymlat, Karaga, and Ossora in the Karaga region), 1985 (villages of Palana and Lesnaia in the Tigil' region), and in 1987 (settlement of Palana). In the Chukchi Autonomous Okrug, fieldwork was conducted in 1987 in the Anadyr' region (settlements of Tavaivaam, Kanchalan, Markovo, and Vaegi), in 1988 in the Bilibino region (village of Aniuisk with a visit to reindeer camps in the tundra), in 1989 in the Chaun region (settlements of Aion and Pevek with visits to reindeer camps), and in 1990 in the Anadyr' region (villages of Ust'-Belaia and Tavaivaam).
2. There is a proverb in Russian that translates roughly as, "a nameless child is a devil."
3. However, one should not exclude the possibility that contemporary information of this sort stems from ethnographic publications.
4. The main question that the Chukchis ask a deceased person at the ritual of divination before his or her funeral is: "Who made that?" i.e., "Who is guilty of the death?"
5. A similar attitude toward suicide was described for the Khantys: "The Ostiaks do not consider suicide a sin, they say 'scrym' ekhtys' (death has come)" (Materialy 1993: 140).

References

Argentov, A. 1850. "Pervaia narodnaia perepis' chukchei, naseliaiushchikh Chavanskii krai." Unpublished manuscript in the archives of the Russian Geographical Society, St. Petersburg; razriad 64, op. 1, N. 32.

Avgustinovich, F. M. 1878–79. "O plemenakh, naseliaiushchikh Kolymskii okrug." *Izvestiia obshchestva liubitelei estestvoznaniia, antropologii i etnografii* 31: 41–43.

Baiburin, A. K. 1993. *Ritual v traditsionnoi kul'ture. Strukturno-semanticheskii analiz vostochnoslavianskikh obriadov.* St. Petersburg: Nauka.

Beretti, N. N. 1929. *Na krainem severo-vostoke.* Vladivostok: Vladivostokskii otdel gosudarstvennogo Rossiiskogo geograficheskogo obshchestva.

Bogoraz, V. G. 1900. *Materialy po izucheniiu chukotskogo iazyka i fol'klora, sobrannye v Kolymskom okruge. Chast' pervaia, obraztsy narodnoi slovesnosti chukoch.* St. Petersburg: Imperatorskaia Akademiia nauk.

———. 1934. *Chukchi. Chast' 1: Sotsial'naia organisatsiia.* Leningrad: Izdatel'stvo instituta narodov Severa TsIK SSSR.

———. 1939. *Chukchi. Chast' 2: Religiia.* Leningrad: Izdatel'stvo Glavsevmorputi.

D'iachkov, G. 1893. *Anadyrskii krai. Rukopis' zhitelia sela Markova.* Vladivostok.

Ivanov, V. N. 1960. "Interesnyi dokument ob obychaiakh chukchei XIX veka." In *Iakutskii arkhiv, vyp. 1.* 171–75. Yakutsk.

Kalinnikov, N. F. 1912. *Nash krainii Severo-Vostok.* St. Petersburg: Tipografiia morskogo ministerstva.

Kennan, G. 1871. *Tent Life in Siberia.* New York: Putnam.

Kosokov, I. 1930. *K voprosu o shamanstve v Severnoi Azii.* Moscow: Bezbozhnik.

Krasheninnikov, S. 1949 [1755]. *Opisanie zemli Kamchatki.* Moscow: Izdatel'stvo Glavsevmorputi.

Materialy. 1993. *Materialy po iuridicheskoi etnografii malykh narodov Severa.* Tomsk: Izdatel'stvo Tomskogo gosudarstvennogo universiteta.

Pugachev, N. 1960. *Chukotskie rasskazy.* Magadan: Magadanskoe knizhnoe izdatel'stvo.

Sarychev, G. A. 1802. *Puteshestvie flota kapitana Sarycheva po severo- vostochnoi chasti Sibiri, Ledovitomu moriu i Vostochnomu okeanu, v prodolzhenii vos'mi let ... Vol. 2.* St. Petersburg.

Semushkin, T. 1939. *Chukotka.* Moscow: Sovetskii pisatel'.

Shashkov, S. 1868. "Detoubiistvo." *Delo* 4: 69–118.

Stebnitskii, S. N. n.d. "Ocherk etnografii koriakov." Unpublished manuscript in the archives of the State Museum of Anthropology and Ethnography of Peter the Great, St. Petersburg; f. K-1, op. 1, N. 50.

Val'skaia, V. A. 1961. "Puteshestvie Andreia Argentova na severo-vostok Sibiri v 1851 godu." *Strany i narody Vostoka* 2: 172–87.

Vrangel', F. 1841. *Puteshestvie po severnym beregam Sibiri i po Ledovitomu moriu, sovershennoe v 1820, 1821, 1823 i 1824 gg.* St. Petersburg.

Zapadnyi bereg. 1852. "Zapadnyi bereg Kamchatki po opisiam Ushakova i Elistratova." *Zapiski gidrograficheskogo departmenta* 10: 136–55.

Zelenin, D. K. 1937. "Obychai dobrovol'noi smerti u primitivnykh narodov." In *Pamiati V. G. Bogoraza (1865–1936). Sbornik statei.* 47–78. Moscow: Izdatel'stvo Akademii nauk SSSR.

Zibarev, V. A. 1990. *Iustitsiia u malykh narodov Severa (XVII–XIX vv.).* Tomsk: Izdatel'stvo Tomskogo gosudarstvennogo universiteta.

Chapter 8

PATTERNS OF WAR AND PEACE AMONG COMPLEX HUNTER-GATHERERS

The Case of the Northwest Coast of North America

————»◦«————

Leland Donald

The peoples of the Northwest Coast culture area are the best known ethnographic cases of complex hunter-gatherers. In this chapter I describe traditional patterns of intergroup conflict and its resolution among these peoples. I will also briefly compare these patterns with those of some horticulturists who are organized at similar levels of sociocultural complexity and with other foragers who are not "complex." Northwest Coast warfare will be shown to conform to most of the patterns suggested by Vayda (1960) as typical of warfare practiced by tribal horticulturists. The most unusual feature of Northwest Coast warfare was the practice of taking captives, most of whom became slaves.[1]

By the Northwest Coast I mean those aboriginal inhabitants of the north Pacific Coast of North America from roughly Yakutat Bay in the north to the mouth of the Columbia River in the south. There was considerable variation within the culture area in most domains of culture including warfare, therefore in this essay my statements about war and peace apply particularly to the north and north-central parts of this region: the Tlingit, Haida, Tsimshian, the best known of the Wakashan speakers (Kwakwaka'wakw and Nuu-chah-nulth), and the Nuxalk.[2] Warfare was a prominent and important activity everywhere on the coast, but the data on war and peace are much better for these groups than for those further south, and space limitations suggest concentrating on the groups where the data are best.

The Prehistory of Northwest Coast Warfare

From the earliest contacts with Europeans (the 1770s), considerable intergroup violence has been noted in the historic and ethnographic record for the culture area. Before discussing this record, I will consider what archaeological research tells us about the possible time depth of warfare in the region.

As with other social phenomena, archaeology has been able to uncover only a fragmentary and uncertain prehistory of war in the culture area, and much necessary excavation is yet to be done. Nevertheless, a useful, if partial, picture can be reconstructed.

Based largely on his interpretation of evidence found in sites in the Prince Rupert Harbour area (Tsimshian territory, ethnographically), Mac-Donald suggests that "warfare has been an organized and relatively extensive activity since approximately 1000 B.C." (1989: 4). Mitchell (n.d.) has recently made a good case that in the Queen Charlotte Strait area (Kwakwaka'wakw territory, ethnographically) between 500 B.C. and A.D. 300 probable Wakashan speakers replaced probable Salishan speakers. Although there is not direct evidence that this large-scale expansion of the Wakashan at the expense of the Salish was the result of warfare, this seems likely.

Skeletal remains recovered at a number of sites in the culture area have a high frequency of spinal and limb fractures, which have been interpreted as injuries resulting from warfare. The incidence of such fractures is particularly high in northern sites (ethnographically, Tsimshian and Heiltsuk) and considerably lower in sites from areas that were Coast Salish in historic times (Cybulski 1990: 58).

Moss and Erlandson (1992: 83), in a recent consideration of forts and defensive sites, make a reasonably strong case that fortified sites began to appear in various parts of the culture area between about A.D. 400 and 700 and that there was a dramatic increase in the number of forts in use between about A.D. 900 and 1400.[3] Their estimate of well over one thousand fort sites for the culture area is consistent with both the archaeological and ethnographic picture of fairly intensive warfare.

Altogether, the archaeological evidence suggests that warfare was well established throughout the culture area by A.D. 500 or so and that its incidence may well have increased around A.D. 1000. Two distinctive types of defensive sites (fortified rocky headlands or small islands and trench embankments) and the near confinement of one type (trench embankments) to Salish territory and its environs suggest some variation in patterns of and responses to warfare as well. Many of the artifacts recovered from sites throughout this time period are similar to those used historically in warfare. Taken together, the archaeological evidence suggests that historic warfare was a continuation of patterns and practices that had a lengthy time depth in the culture area. I recognize, of course, that contact and trade with Europeans brought technological and other changes to intergroup fighting as they did to other aspects of Northwest Coast culture.

Ethnographic/Historic Warfare

Strategy and Tactics

RAIDS. The principal strategy of a Northwest Coast war leader was to secretly get his party of warriors to an enemy settlement and to stage a surprise attack, usually at dawn or at night. Open, frontal attacks on villages were rare but did occur. A few ritualized battles may have occurred, but they were probably uncommon.

Scouts were sent out to locate the enemy settlement (if this was not already known), to determine the strength of the enemy forces, and to gain as much detail as possible about the exact sleeping locations of important enemy warriors and titleholders. Men were assigned to attack each enemy dwelling and even to kill particular leading men. The attack was launched against a hopefully sleeping enemy who were killed as quickly as possible. Ideally, all adult males in the settlement would be killed along with some women and children, while the remaining women and children would be taken prisoner—most to eventually wind up as slaves. Desirable property was plundered, houses burned, and canoes destroyed, and then the raiders attempted to make their escape before a counterattack or a pursuit could be organized.

Such a war party was under the command of an important titleholder, often described as a chief warrior or head warrior. Command structure was underdeveloped and weak. The leader had good control of his men if they were all from his descent unit or local group, but allies from other communities were very unreliable. If the leader was killed, the attackers—even if on the verge of success—might very well give up the attack, often retreating in near panic. Elaborate tactics, especially if they involved the coordination of several groups from different communities, often failed, leading to victories of considerably reduced scope or even to defeat for the attackers. Discipline was weak on the defenders' side also; sentries were often slack in their attention to their duties, allowing successful surprise attacks even when communities had taken reasonable precautions. In the event of a surprise attack, a coordinated defensive response was often impossible to organize as a consequence of the panicked reaction of the victims.

Ethnographic accounts (which are almost entirely the result of memory ethnography) emphasize ritual rather than practical preparations for war. The sources probably overemphasize the ritual side of war, but it should not be overlooked. Not only the warriors made special preparations, but also the remainder of the community undertook ritual precautions, especially the warriors' wives.[4]

SUPERNATURAL MEASURES. Intergroup hostilities were also fought by supernatural means. Only Tlingit war parties seem to have regularly included shamans. At times, Tlingit shamans from opposing groups would conduct spirit battles, and a particular episode might end with the supernatural victory of one group's shamans, no physical violence having taken place (see Olson 1967: 111). Regular participation in war expeditions by shamans is not noted for other groups, but it is clear that shamans were not infrequently called upon to lend their powers to the waging of a conflict. They might, for example, attempt to launch spirit attacks against an enemy from their home village, as when the residents of a Twana community hired a shaman to harm another community through use of his spirit powers (Elmendorf 1960: 474). In addition, witchcraft, which was frequent in intra-group conflicts, could also be used across community lines. The point is that conflict was waged with all of the tools at hand, and opponents might well employ both the dawn raid with war clubs and shamans' spells.

The Technology of Warfare

WEAPONS AND ARMOR. Prior to European contact, the principal weapons were the dagger, spear, war club, and the bow and arrow. Even before contact it is probable that some daggers, particularly in the north, had metal blades.[5] Armor, also common throughout the culture area, was most elaborate in the north. Most of the armor in museums was collected from the Tlingit. The fully armed Tlingit warrior wore an untanned moosehide shirt or shift underneath his armor proper, which was made of rods or slats tied together with leather. His body was covered from the neck to about the knees, with his head and neck protected by a wooden helmet and collar. Helmets were usually elaborately carved, often with grotesque, ferocious human faces. Shields were also used by warriors in some groups. Armor became less elaborate farther south in the culture area, frequently consisting of elk-hide or moose-hide tunics or shifts alone. Because of the great need for armor, moose and elk hides were important items of trade (both species had limited distribution on the coast proper). During the maritime fur trade period (1780 to about 1825), they became important items in the inventory of many European ships. The ships' crews traded for bales of "clammons" (tanned elk hides) around the mouth of the Columbia River and brought them north to trade for furs (Gibson 1992: 230–31).

Although bows and arrows were used in war as well as for hunting, most fighting was hand-to-hand rather than at bowshot range. This meant that the most important weapons were the dagger for stabbing and slashing and the club for inflicting the crushing blow.

The canoe must not be overlooked in any discussion of the technology of war on the Northwest Coast. Raiding parties rarely approached their target communities by land. The terrain and the heavy forest that covered most of it combined to make land travel difficult for any purpose. These were maritime- and riverine-oriented cultures whether the activity was subsistence, trade, or war. The dugout canoe was made in a great variety of sizes and styles throughout the culture area. The largest and most useful canoes for war were made from red cedar and could be over twenty meters long. Such canoes could carry as many as thirty men and their equipment. Canoes brought the attacking force to and from the community of their opponent, but the actual encounters usually happened on land, most frequently on beaches near villages or in the villages themselves, although sea battles did occur.

FORTIFICATIONS. As has already been noted, fortified sites constitute some of the best evidence regarding the prehistory of warfare on the Northwest Coast. Although no one has done a thorough, systematic study of ethnographically and historically known fortifications, hundreds are mentioned in the literature. It is probable that, at least in the northern and central parts of the culture area, every major settlement had an associated fortification. Fortifications are rarer in the southern part of the culture area, although they are certainly not absent there.

Most of the fortifications are best described as refuges—easily defended fortified bits of high ground to which the inhabitants of a community could retreat in anticipation of or as a result of an attack. Since no attacking force could sustain itself in the field for more than a few days, such refuges did not have to be built or organized to withstand long sieges. Usually some rocky island or headland near the village was chosen, and its natural defenses (steep cliff faces) were enhanced with log barriers at the top of the natural barricades. Often these enhancements followed the principles that are used in successful fortifications throughout the world: a platform might be built along the top of the rocks that extended well beyond the edge of the rocks, giving the defenders the capacity to fire or drop objects directly down onto their attackers.

Most villages do not seem to have been fortified themselves, their inhabitants relying on refuges of the type described. But some archaeological fortified sites are large enough to contain—and some do contain—house depressions, and some historically known villages were also fortified. Such fortified villages were most common among the Tlingit, Tsimshian, and Haida, although not all communities of these peoples were fortified. It is also possible that fortified villages became more common during the historic period and were used as strongholds rather than merely refuges. Strongholds are designed to protect an entire community and its goods, to withstand longer periods of attack, and to offer active means of defense. The increasing trend in the north to fortified villages, if this indeed was a trend, may reflect the growing prosperity of some communities during the fur trade period and the need to hold their ground at strategic points. Some of these walled communities were quite large. An illustration of the winter village at Sitka, originally drawn in 1804, shows fourteen large houses surrounded by an extensive log palisade (reproduced in MacDonald 1989: 14). However, at least among the Tlingit, the entire community might not be included within a single fortification. In some communities, individual houses or groups of houses belonging to the same clan might have their own fortifications. This is consistent with the fact that intercommunity warfare among the Tlingit often involved only portions of the warring communities.[6]

One final type of fortification should be mentioned briefly. This is the trench embankment, which is found largely in Coast Salish territory in the south-central and southern parts of the culture area. Trench embankments were of two kinds. For one kind, the builders chose a small raised point or peninsula and dug a trench about two meters deep to separate the point from the main body of land. The fill from the trench was used to build a supporting base for a palisade on the seaward side of the trench. For the other kind, a semicircular trench was dug and a steep cliff face supplied the fourth side of the fort. Both types of trench embankments seem to have been refuges rather than strongholds.

Motivation

The usual motivation for attacks on other groups was revenge: the attackers sought a death to balance the death of a member of their own group. If that death had occurred as a result of actions by members of a different group, that group was the usual target of the attack, but a death by any perceived cause might be an occasion for an attack. Not infrequently, if those seeking revenge encountered persons belonging to a group different from the offending group, one or more deaths there would satisfy the avengers, who would return home with their grief assuaged.[7] One might distinguish between revenge and consolation, although they flow into each other. Revenge seeks to kill a member of equal rank in the offending group. This may be more important than killing the actual killer if the killer was of lower status than the victim. Consolation seeks a death (or deaths) to wipe out the grief that the relatives of the dead feel. It may also be expressed as offering some sort of consolation to the deceased as well. For example, the Kwakwaka'wakw seek a victim to be a "pillow" for the deceased, and the Nuu-chah-nulth seek a "death companion" (Boas 1966: 109; Drucker 1951: 333–34).

Other motivations were also present: wars were fought that led to the capture of important resource sites by the victor; rights to incorporeal property were taken in war; the capture of slaves was the dominant motive in some post–European contact wars, though whether or not this was the case prior to contact is unclear. The desire to capture important resource sites has been well documented for the Nuu-chah-nulth (Swadesh 1948). Given that the outcome of some fighting in most parts of the area (and especially the north, which is the focus here) was a change in the control of important resource loci (see below), the importance of territorial gain (resource base improvement) has probably been underestimated as a motive in the culture area.[8]

Outcomes

A successful attack on an enemy community meant a number of deaths in that community and few or no deaths in the attacking party. It also meant returning safely to the home community.

A dramatic illustration of the outcome of a successful raid can be seen in Paul Kane's painting of a Makah war party returning from an attack on a Clallam village. Kane (1968: 159–61) did not actually witness any of the events, but reconstructed the scene from the accounts of Clallam participants. The raid, which occurred in early 1847, was the result of a quarrel over a dead whale that had beached near a Clallam village, although it had been struck and killed by the Makah. (Historically, the Makah were whalers, but the Clallam were not.) The Clallam succeeded in preventing the Makah from securing their prey. A few months after this incident, the principal titleholder of the Makah and four other men went to the Hudson's Bay Company post of Fort Victoria. Their journey carried them past the Clallam villages, and on their return the Clallam attacked the party, killing the titleholder and one of his men. Upon learning of these deaths, the titleholder's younger brother immediately led a war party of twelve large canoes (that many canoes would have contained about two hundred men altogether). They attacked the heavily fortified Clallam village and forced the defenders out of their fortifications by setting fire to the wooden structure. Altogether, the Makah took eight heads and eighteen prisoners, most of whom were women. The painting shows the returning Makah canoes with five Clallam heads being displayed in triumph.[9]

Such successes were often transitory, however. The next installment in the fighting might see the roles of the two communities reversed. Only the complete extermination of a group would be likely to lead to an unbalanced, permanent termination of hostilities between two groups. A successful raid would lead to new deaths to be avenged, and even if the attacked community was virtually wiped out, kin of deceased community members would almost certainly be found in a number of other communities. These kin were potential and sometimes active revenge-seekers.

Achieving a balanced end to hostilities involved some kind of peacemaking and will be discussed under that heading.

If the attackers inflicted significantly more casualties than they received (a common but not inevitable event), they could consider the deaths that they sought consolation for to be avenged (such revenge seems nearly always to have been a part of warfare even if other motives were present or even dominant).

The number of deaths could be, given the size of the populations involved, quite large—most winter villages contained less than one thousand persons and many fewer than five hundred persons. Reasonably circumstantial accounts list deaths in the twenties and thirties; accounts of one hundred or more casualties are common, although all large numbers must be viewed with some skepticism.

In addition to deaths, most successful raids also included the taking of prisoners, which were almost exclusively women and children. A few of these captives might be ransomed by their relatives, but most became slaves (Donald 1997).

Other plunder might include boxes, canoes, dancing and ritual paraphernalia, and food, as well as incorporeal property. Important titleholders were particular targets because their deaths demoralized the enemy and because of the prestige one acquired on taking their lives. However, an additional reason for killing such men was that the killers were often able to take over their victims' names and ritual prerogatives. Indeed, one important way that new rituals, dances, and songs diffused was through their capture in war.

Finally, if the defeated group was exterminated, or virtually so, their territory—or at least important resource loci within it—might be appropriated by the victors. For the Nuu-chah-nulth there is explicit documentation that acquisition of desirable resource loci was a conscious motivation for some wars. This motivation is much less well documented for other groups, but we do know that for many groups resources did in fact change hands as a result of warfare. Some Kwakwaka'wakw local groups, for example, are known to have significantly increased the value of their salmon resources by the capture of rich salmon streams from their Kwakwaka'wakw neighbors (Dawson 1887). Probably in the eighteenth century, some Haida expanded from their Queen Charlotte Islands homeland and succeeded in displacing the Tlingit from Dall Island and a large part of Prince of Wales Island (Langdon 1979: 103).

Opponents

By definition, Northwest Coast war entailed conflict and fighting between members of two different local communities. But this tells us relatively little about who fought whom. Members of different local communities from within the same language/cultural group fought each other. For example, most Nuu-chah-nulth wars were with other Nuu-chah-nulth, Tlingit often fought Tlingit, and so on. Wars also cut across language and cultural boundaries, but the local community was not necessarily the warring unit. Tlingit clans from different local groups fought each other, often without involving other clans from their villages of residence. Indeed, an attack on the members of one clan in a Tlingit village would not necessarily lead to the involvement of other clans in the village. Even fighting across language and cultural boundaries might also be relatively specific: a particular group of Haida or Tsimshian, for example, might seek to attack and kill only members of a specific Tlingit clan rather than Tlingit in general.

The three northern ethnolinguistic groupings (Tlingit, Haida, Tsimshian) had particularly complex interrelations. All three were matrilineal, and their phratry/moiety/clan systems were aligned with each other (Dunn 1984). Titleholders married titleholders across as well as within ethnolinguistic boundaries. The groups also traded with each other and were invited to each other's feasts. In addition, there was also a lot of fighting and bad relations, and raids and counterraids could go on for years.[10] Affines were also frequently once and future enemies. Prisoners, especially important ones, were often ransomed, but many became and remained slaves. (For example, the Tsimshian word for "slave" is the diminutive of Tlingit.) This created a complex set of fragile relationships: in disputes both across ethnolinguistic boundaries and within ethnolinguistic boundaries many participants had consanguines and affines on all sides.

Peacemaking

On occasion, hostilities between groups ceased when one group had been completely exterminated by the other. This must have been rare, though, because even a badly defeated group usually had a few survivors who took up residence as refugees with kin in other groups. Even if they lacked the military power to retaliate quickly against the victors, they (and their descendants) remained to form the nucleus of a set of people with a desire to avenge the deaths of their kin. Less complete defeats might still lead to one group's retreat or withdrawal from disputed territory and to its seeking safety elsewhere, but still the goal of eventual retaliation remained.

Mechanisms that, in theory, did ensure a permanent peace between warring groups existed, but in order to come into effect, a balance had to obtain between the two groups. That is, the losses on one side had to match the losses on the other. This did not simply mean an equal number killed on each side, for the rank of those killed was taken into account as well, and the loss in rank had to balance. If a balance had not been achieved during the period of fighting, then transfers of goods and slaves could sometimes accomplish it.

Peace ceremonies usually involved the exchange of goods, including slaves; sometimes involved the ransoming of important prisoners held by one or both sides; and often involved an exchange of hostages, who remained as honored guests to help maintain peaceful relations during the initial months of peace between the groups. All of the northern and north-central groups had such peacemaking practices.[11] One obvious sign of peacemaking was the use of bird down in the ceremonies.

Peacemaking was supposed to lead to permanent peace between warring groups, but as the years passed, incidents between members of the two formerly adversarial groups might well lead to renewed hostilities.

It should be noted that many of the groups that fought also traded and feasted each other, and that titleholders from the groups were often intermarried. This meant that the incentives for peace were strong, even as incidents regarded as provocation led to retaliation.

Conflict with Non-Natives

My concern here is primarily with indigenous conflict, but because virtually all of our information on this topic is post-European contact, I will briefly consider conflict with non-Natives. Native behavior in these conflicts tells us something about indigenous warfare and reminds us that we have to consider possible changes due to contact circumstances when reviewing ethnographic and historic sources.

Although there were some contacts with non-Natives before the late-eighteenth-century incursions into the area by the Russians, Spanish, and British, and later others, nothing definite can be said about the character of contacts before those with Europeans. Most of the initial relations were relatively nonviolent, but Northwest Coast Native Americans did not passively accept European actions.[12] There was swift reaction to perceived slights and insults and to practices that did not result in balanced exchanges. The Europeans' firepower gave them an advantage, but not necessarily a decisive one in particular encounters. The principal Native tactic was the same as that employed in indigenous warfare—the surprise attack—and the motives were similar as well: to avenge deaths and slights to important persons, and to plunder. If an attack against a ship was successful, the European vessel was plundered and some of its crew might be enslaved—again consistent with indigenous patterns. As in the Native pattern, the offender might not be the one attacked—the next European vessel to put into a village harbor might well be the recipient of the violence earned by its predecessor.

The principal advantage of the Europeans was not the musket (Natives soon obtained a supply of these), but rather ship-borne cannon: a village could be destroyed in a matter of hours, if not minutes. Although the maritime fur trade period (up to about 1825) was sprinkled with attacks on vessels and some successful Tlingit attacks on Russian land bases, relations were generally peaceful, if often tense, throughout this period. The land-based fur trade period and subsequent colonial periods saw increasing European control—and an increasingly effective use of naval power to enforce this control—but no major protracted Native resistance emerged. This is not to say that the locals were always passive; coastal titleholders struggled to keep control of their inland trade routes, for example. Some Tlingit even attacked and destroyed as late as the 1850s an inland Hudson's Bay Company post that threatened such a trade route (Oberg 1973: 107).

Another effect on fighting patterns during the land-based fur trade period occurred with the establishment of trading forts, which became attractants for large groups of Natives from a wide area around the forts. More Natives were brought face to face under tense conditions than was usual before these posts were built (rum added significantly to the volatile mix). At Fort Simpson, for example, Tsimshian, Haida, and Tlingit renewed and intensified their long-standing relationships, which were both hostile and friendly. The establishment in the early 1840s of Victoria on the southern tip of Vancouver Island drew inhabitants even of the Queen Charlotte Islands and Tlingit country to the north. These and other northerners often both fought and feasted their way to and from Victoria. Such mid-nineteenth-century practices have established the idea that long-distance raids were typical of Northwest Coast fighting. Before places such as Victoria offered both goals and refuges far from home, however, most raiding and fighting took place much nearer the aggressors' home territories.[13]

Ferguson and Whitehead (1992) have suggested that when peoples like those on the Northwest Coast come into contact with expanding or intrusive states, indigenous patterns of warfare are "transformed." From the mid-1770s representatives of European states played an increasingly important and intrusive part in the lives of Northwest Coast peoples. The earliest contacts quickly developed into an important fur trade, at first maritime- and then land-based. As the nineteenth century wore on, fur trade activities were increasingly replaced by settlement, missionization, and finally full incorporation into the nation-states of Canada and the United States. By the 1870s, indigenous warfare had been suppressed. As the earlier parts of this section have indicated, the fur trade in particular had an impact on many aspects of indigenous warfare. But the evidence from archaeology and oral tradition strongly suggests that intergroup and intercommunity conflict were both prevalent and thoroughly integrated into Northwest Coast cultural patterns long before European contact, direct or indirect, became important for these peoples.

Comparisons with "Tribal" Agriculturalists and with Other Hunter-Gatherers

Vayda (1960: 1–2) has suggested that certain general features define a type of warfare that is widespread among nonstate societies: "smallness in the scale and shortness in the duration of active hostilities, the poor development of command and discipline, the great reliance upon surprise attacks, and the importance of the village community or local group in the organization of war parties." Vayda's examples of this type of warfare, drawn from every continent, are all practiced by agriculturalists to some extent. Indeed, his description could be considered the classic pattern of warfare among "tribal" agriculturalists. Clearly Northwest Coast warfare is of this type also.

If more detailed comparisons are made between Northwest Coast intergroup conflict and intergroup conflict among the Maori and among various New Guinea groups (especially in the highlands), the similarities are striking.[14] This is true across most warfare variables, including motivation, strategy and tactics, outcomes, and opponents. The most important differences between the Northwest Coast and New Guinea peoples include the taking of captives who become slaves by the Northwest Coast peoples and the lack in the Northwest Coast of the formalized, almost ritual battles that are found in some parts of New Guinea. Another important difference may be the Northwest Coast practice of transferring important ritual property and prerogatives by killing their current owners.

The general conclusion must be that in comparative terms Northwest Coast warfare conforms to "tribal" patterns. This cluster of complex hunter-gatherers shares not only such features as clans and lineages with tribal agriculturalists, but styles of fighting as well.

How does Northwest Coast warfare compare with intergroup conflict among less complex hunter-gatherers? Simple hunter-gatherers, most often described as band societies in the literature, are generally held to be peaceful or at least relatively so. Is this in fact the case, or do band societies fight wars also? In confining my comparisons to band/band fighting, I find that even though warfare between bands and more complexly organized societies tells us about band societies' capacity to resist the incursions of larger-scale societies, it does not tell us about their relations with similarly organized groups.[15]

Although the material is spotty and often minimal, the available ethnographic and ethnohistoric data suggest a moderately high degree of intergroup conflict among North American Arctic and subarctic hunter-gatherer bands. Burch (1974) on northwest Alaska Eskimo warfare, Fienup-Riordan (1990) on Yup'ik Eskimo warfare, and Slobodin (1960) on Kutchin warfare describe warfare patterns that are very similar to those outlined here for the Northwest Coast. Samuel Hearne's eyewitness account (1971: 148–63) of Chipewyan attacks on Inuit camps could easily describe raids by Northwest Coast warriors (these date in the 1770s). The principal difference is the lack of interest in taking captives. Other Arctic and subarctic groups did, however, take captives from time to time, although the scale of captivity and hence slavery never reached that found on the Northwest Coast. The Arctic and subarctic North American material also suggests that warfare there did not normally lead to territorial gains, i.e., to the capture of additional resources. This may be a difference between the Northwest Coast and these two culture areas or may simply reflect the sketchy nature of the record on warfare in the Arctic and subarctic. We should also keep in mind that territorial/resource gain as a motivation/ cause of warfare has been questioned for the Northwest Coast and also remains a topic of some controversy for places like New Guinea as well (Knauft 1990).

Conclusions

Warfare was a frequent, not a rare, event in traditional Northwest Coast cultures, and was also very well integrated into the cultures of the region. The same communities, kin groups, and individuals not only fought each other at times, but also intermarried, participated in each other's ceremonies, and engaged in trade. Warfare was an important mechanism for territorial change, the diffusion of ritual practices and paraphernalia, and the shifting of people from one group to another (via slavery).

Northwest Coast warfare falls well within the range of fighting practices of "tribally" organized peoples. This is true of the strategy and tactics involved, the motivations for fighting, and the types of opponents. From the perspective of tribal warfare, the most unusual feature of Northwest Coast warfare is the taking of captives who usually become slaves.

When Northwest Coast warfare is compared to that found in much of northern and aboriginal North America, the similarities are more common than the differences. This is true of North American "bands" as well as of other North American "tribes." The major differences relate to the taking of captives/slaves, the seizure of incorporeal property by killing its owners, and the probable waging of war for the control of resource loci.

The archaeological evidence and oral traditions strongly suggest that warfare was both frequent and a well-integrated feature of Northwest Coast cultures prior to contact with Europeans. Nevertheless, contact initiated new trade relations and goods, and introduced new technologies that probably intensified warfare. In particular, control of fur trade routes by strategically situated middlemen became increasingly worth fighting for, and raids with slaves as their principal object probably increased.

Notes

1. I gratefully acknowledge the financial support that this research has received from the Social Sciences and Humanities Research Council of Canada and the University of Victoria Faculty Research Committee. I also thank my colleague Donald Mitchell for his continued advice and insights on matters of the Northwest Coast and for his specific comments and suggestions about this chapter.

2. The contemporary descendants of several ethnographically and historically well-known Northwest Coast peoples now prefer names of their own choosing. Where I am aware of these preferences and where the preferred name is widely accepted in the appropriate Native community, I have used it here. For the benefit of those who are not regional specialists, the older names and their replacements are provided here: "Kwakiutl" is now "Kwakwaka'wakw," "Nootka" is now "Nuu-chah-nulth," and "Bella Coola" is now "Nuxalk."

3. Some fortified sites may be even earlier, but there are too few of them known at present to definitely establish a widespread presence.

4. Examples of descriptions of warfare in the ethnographic sources for north and north-central groups include Boas (1966: 105–19) on the Kwakwaka'wakw; Drucker (1951: 332–65) on the Nuu-chah-nulth; McIlwraith (1948: 338–77) on the Nuxalk; Garfield (1939: 266–71) on the Tsimshian; and de Laguna (1972: 579–604), Emmons (1991: 324–58), and Olson (1967: 69–82) on the Tlingit. Examples illustrating my otherwise undocumented generalizations can be found in these accounts. The most accessible, relatively full description of warfare in a southern group is Elmendorf (1960: 465–79; 1993: 126–64) on the Twana of Puget Sound.

5. The source of the metal would have been drift metal from shipwrecks. For illustrations of weapons and armor, see Feest (1980: 58–59, 62, 80, 82), De Laguna (1990: 217, 218), and Arima and Dewhirst (1990: 401).

6. For brief descriptions of fortification types and possible changes over time, see Moss and Erlandson (1992: 74–75). For illustrations of some historic forts and a reconstruction of an important Tsimshian fort, see MacDonald (1989: 12–15, 67–72).

7. See, for example, McIlwraith's (1948: 370–71) account of an intended Kwakwaka'wakw expedition against the Nuxalk. On their way to Nuxalk country, the raiders encountered some Heiltsuk who were acting as messengers to deliver potlatch invitations to a number of communities. After some indecision (potlatch messengers were not supposed to be harmed), the Kwakwaka'wakw attempted to kill all the Heiltsuk messengers. Only one escaped. After these killings the Kwakwaka'wakw abandoned their plans to attack the Nuxalk and returned to their villages. For a Kwakwaka'wakw version of the same events, see Boas (1966: 114–15).

8. For a general treatment of motives and causes of Northwest Coast warfare see Ferguson (1984), and for slave raids in particular, see Donald (1997: 113–16, 231–33).

9. This painting is reproduced in Feest (1980: 31). Kane collected his account of the raid during a brief visit to the Clallam village in May 1847.

10. For a long sequence raid and counterraid between several Tsimshian and Haida groups, see Boas (1916: 380–88). For complementary versions of a historically late sequence involving several Tsimshian and Haida, see Boas (1916: 388–92) and Swanton (1905: 384–89).

11. Such ceremonies are probably best described for the Tlingit. See, for example, Olson (1967: 81–82). For peacemaking ceremonies across ethnolinguistic boundaries, see the end of the account mentioned in note 7.

12. For a discussion of European/Native hostilities with documentation, see Cole and Darling (1990: 126–28).

13. For documentation and fuller discussion of the increasing distance of raids in the land-based fur trade period in the context of slave raiding, see Donald (1997: 106–12).
14. For Maori warfare, see Vayda (1960). For New Guinea warfare, see Heider (1991), Meggitt (1977), and the many studies cited in Knauft (1990).
15. Warfare among non-North American bands is very poorly described. I have not found much focused discussion of it in the literature. Therefore, I confine myself to North American cases, of which I am much better informed, but see Robarchek and Robarchek (1992) and Dentan (1992).

References

Arima, E., and J. Dewhirst. 1990. "Nootkans of Vancouver Island." In *Handbook of North American Indians*. Volume 7: Northwest Coast. W. Suttles, ed. 391–411. Washington, D.C.: Smithsonian Institution.

Boas, F. 1916. *Tsimshian Mythology*. Thirty-first Annual Report of the Bureau of American Ethnology: 29–1037.

_____. 1966. *Kwakiutl Ethnography*. Chicago: University of Chicago Press.

Burch, E. S., Jr. 1974. "Eskimo Warfare in Northwest Alaska." *Anthropological Papers of the University of Alaska* 16(2): 1–14.

Cole, D., and D. Darling. 1990. "History of the Early Period." In *Handbook of North American Indians*. Volume 7: Northwest Coast. W. Suttles, ed. 119–34. Washington, D.C.: Smithsonian Institution.

Cybulski, J. S. 1990. "Human Biology." In *Handbook of North American Indians*. Volume 7: Northwest Coast. W. Suttles, ed. 52–59. Washington, D.C.: Smithsonian Institution.

Dawson, G. M. 1887. "Notes and Observations on the Kwakiool People of the Northern Part of Vancouver Island and Adjacent Coasts, Made During the Summer of 1885: With a Vocabulary of about Seven Hundred Words." *Transactions of the Royal Society of Canada* 5(2): 63–98.

De Laguna, F. 1972. *Under Mount Saint Elias: The History and Culture of the Yakutat Tlingit*. Smithsonian Contributions to Anthropology 7.

_____. 1990. "Tlingit." In *Handbook of North American Indians*. Volume 7: Northwest Coast. W. Suttles, ed. 203–228. Washington, D.C.: Smithsonian Institution.

Dentan, R. K. 1992. "The Rise, Maintenance, and Destruction of Peaceable Polity: A Preliminary Essay in Political Ecology." In *Aggression and Peacefulness in Humans and Other Primates*. J. Silverberg and J. P. Gray, eds. 214–70. New York: Oxford University Press.

Donald, L. 1997. *Aboriginal Slavery on the Northwest Coast of North America*. Berkeley: University of California Press.

Drucker, P. 1951. *The Northern and Central Nootkan Tribes*. Bureau of American Ethnology, Bulletin 144.

Dunn, J. A. 1984. "International Matri-moieties: The North Maritime Province of the North Pacific Coast." In *The Tsimshian: Images of the Past, Views for the Present*. M. Seguin, ed. 99–109. Vancouver: University of British Columbia Press.

Elmendorf, W. W. 1960. *The Structure of Twana Culture*. Washington State University Research Studies, Monographic Supplement 2.

_____. 1993. *Twana Narratives: Native Accounts of a Coast Salish Culture*. Seattle: University of Washington Press.

Emmons, G. T. 1991. *The Tlingit Indians*. Ed. F. de Laguna. New York: American Museum of Natural History.

Feest, C. 1980. *The Art of War*. London: Thames and Hudson.

Ferguson, R. B. 1984. "A Reexamination of the Causes of Northwest Coast Warfare." In *Warfare, Culture, and Environment*. R. B. Ferguson, ed. 267–328. New York: Academic Press.

Ferguson, R. B., and N. L. Whitehead. 1992. "The Violent Edge of Empire." In *War in the Tribal Zone: Expanding States and Indigenous Warfare*. R. B. Ferguson and N. L. Whitehead, eds. 1–30. Santa Fe, N.M.: School of American Research Press.

Fienup-Riordan, A. 1990. "Yup'ik Warfare and the Myth of the Peaceful Eskimo." In *Eskimo Essays: Yup'ik Lives and How We See Them*. 146–66. New Brunswick, N.J.: Rutgers University Press.

Garfield, V. 1939. "Tsimshian Clan and Society." *University of Washington Publications in Anthropology* 7: 167–336.

Gibson, J. R. 1992. *Otter Skins, Boston Ships, and China Goods: The Maritime Fur Trade of the Northwest Coast, 1785–1841*. Montreal: McGill-Queen's University Press.

Hearne, S. [1795] 1971. *A Journey from Prince of Wales's Fort in Hudson's Bay to the Northern Ocean*. Edmonton: M. G. Hurtig Ltd.

Heider, K. 1991. *Grand Valley Dani: Peaceful Warriors*. 2d ed. Fort Worth, Tex.: Holt, Rinehart and Winston.

Kane, P. 1968. *Wanderings of an Artist among the Indians of North America*. [orig. 1859] Edmonton: Hurtig.

Knauft, B. M. 1990. "Melanesian Warfare: A Theoretical History." *Oceania* 60: 250–311.

Langdon, S. 1979. "Comparative Tlingit and Haida Adaptations to the West Coast of the Prince of Wales Archipelago." *Ethnology* 18: 101–20.

MacDonald, G. F. 1989. *Kitwanga Fort Report*. Hull, Quebec: Canadian Museum of Civilization.

McIlwraith, T. F. 1948. *The Bella Coola Indians*. Toronto: University of Toronto Press.

Meggitt, M. 1977. *Blood Is Their Argument: Warfare among the Mae Enga Tribesmen of the New Guinea Highlands*. Palo Alto, Cal.: Mayfield.

Mitchell, D. n.d. "Changing Fortunes: Kwakiutl-Salish Frontiers of the Central Northwest Coast." Manuscript in possession of author.

Moss, M. A., and J. M. Erlandson. 1992. "Forts, Refuge Rocks, and Defensive Sites: The Antiquity of Warfare Along the North Pacific Coast of North America." *Arctic Anthropology* 29: 73–90.

Oberg, K. 1973. *The Social Economy of the Tlingit Indians*. Seattle: University of Washington Press.

Olson, R. L. 1967. *Social Structure and Social Life of the Tlingit in Alaska*. University of California Anthropological Records 26.

Robarchek, C. A., and C. J. Robarchek. 1992. "Cultures of War and Peace: A Comparative Study of Waorani and Semai." In *Aggression and Peacefulness in Humans and Other Primates*. J. Silverberg and J. P. Gray, eds. 189–213. New York: Oxford University Press.

Slobodin, R. 1960. "Eastern Kutchin Warfare." *Anthropologica* n.s. 2: 76–94.

Swadesh, M. 1948. "Motivations in Nootka Warfare." *Southwestern Journal of Anthropology* 4: 76–93.

Swanton, J. R. 1905. *Haida Texts and Myths, Skidegate Dialect*. Bureau of American Ethnology, Bulletin 29.

Vayda, A. P. 1960. *Maori Warfare*. Maori Monographs, No. 2. Wellington, New Zealand: Polynesian Society.

PART II

RESISTANCE, IDENTITY, AND THE STATE

Chapter 9

THE CONCEPT OF AN INTERNATIONAL ETHNOECOLOGICAL REFUGE

=••••=

Olga Murashko

Modern Legal Status of Societies of Hunters, Gatherers, and Fishermen of Russia

In Russia, ethnic groups whose subsistence depends on hunting, gathering, and fishing are grouped under the title "numerically small peoples of the North." Since 1928, they have had a special legal status. Unfortunately, the right of these peoples to lead independent and traditional lives, as proclaimed by the original documents of the 1920s, had already been violated in the 1930s. The modernization and industrialization of the regions occupied by the indigenous peoples of the Russian North, especially over the last thirty years, have endangered these peoples' cultures.

The idea of the creation of international ethnoecological refuges as a means to preserve traditional cultures of indigenous peoples was born several years ago, the result of discussions about ways to effect the realization of the International Convention of Independent Countries on Indigenous Peoples. The Convention (hereafter referred to as Convention 169) was signed by twenty-six countries in July 1989. At that time, the legislative and executive branches of the Russian government adopted the declaration, necessitated by the ratification of Convention 169, the resolution of the Supreme Soviet, and the president's decree on the organization of the territories of traditional subsistence and their prioritized usage by the indigenous peoples of the North (April 1992). The following legislative bills securing the mechanism for the realization of Convention 169 were written and debated:

1. Legislative bill "On the Protection and Rational Usage of the Land and Other Resources on the Territories Occupied by the Numerically Small Peoples of the North" was written in the fall of 1991. It addressed the problem of defining the territories of traditional usage.
2. Legislative bill "Organizing Principles of the Legal Status of Indigenous Numerically Small Peoples of the North" was written by scholars of the Department of Northern Studies of the Institute of Ethnology and Anthropology.
3. Several legislative bills on the creation of self-governing administrations of Northern peoples were written by the Institute of the Problems of Numerically Small Peoples of the North in Yakutsk, which addressed the problem of legal status of ethnic districts, regions, settlements, and communities.

All of the legislative bills created in the style of Convention 169 were ready in the summer of 1992. However, as of today none has been adopted. In July 1993, the Supreme Soviet of the Russian Federation adopted a law of the Russian Federation: "Organizing Principles of the Legal Status of the Numerically Small Peoples of the Russian Federation." However, the law was not signed by the president. Article 24 of this law states: "To preserve the habitats of the numerically small peoples and to facilitate the development of the traditional forms of subsistence, territories of traditional subsistence may be formed with the initiative of these peoples. Such territories are the inalienable part of these peoples and cannot be used for industrial or other development, which is not part of their traditional subsistence, without their consent" (K publikatsii zakona 1992: 63). Unfortunately, this law specifies neither the criteria of defining the boundaries of such territories nor the sources of funding for their formation.

As indicated by the 1992/93 correspondence between the Russian section of the "International Work Group for Indigenous Affairs" and the regional associations of the peoples of the North, the administrations of the regions that are inhabited by the peoples of the North have not yet implemented the president's decree, issued on 22 April 1992, and have not organized territories of traditional subsistence. Similarly, the communities of Northern peoples are not registered or are put under such conditions that their existence is difficult to sustain.

The proposed federal law "Organizing Principles of Legal Status of the Indigenous Numerically Small Peoples of Russia" was adopted by the State Duma several times, but was always rejected by the Council of the Federation and by the president. Instead, the law "About Guarantees of the Rights of the Numerically Small Peoples of the Russian Federation" was signed by the president in May 1999. The law has the character of a declaration and carries no enforcement measures. Other laws on the rights of indigenous people have not even been debated. At the same time, under the conditions created by this legal vacuum, the traditional natural re-sources of the indigenous peoples are being alienated from them through privatization and consequent destructive exploitation of hunting grounds, fishing areas, and traditional reindeer pastures. The indigenous people of Russia are being impoverished during this process as they no longer receive state subsidies at the same time that they are losing their natural resources.

The other side of this process appears more positive: the conditions of impoverishment and neglect encourage communities of indigenous peo-ple of the North to revitalize their traditional forms of subsistence. The early 1990s saw a revival of small-scale reindeer-herding, cooperative sea mammal hunting, and fishing using the old means and techniques; usage of dog sleds for transportation purposes; revival of traditional forms of self-government; sharing; and teaching young children traditional sub-sistence techniques. The importance of traditional knowledge and tradi-tional world-view is growing.

The Difficulties of the Realization of Ethnic Rights

To my knowledge, Convention 169 has been ratified by only two coun-tries out of the twenty-six that signed it. Russia, like many other countries that signed the Convention, began to work out its own legislation on the rights of indigenous people. Why has Convention 169 been neglected, considering the amount of time and effort put into it by all of the coun-tries involved? Obviously, there are difficulties with defining both the sub-ject of law—"indigenous peoples and peoples leading traditional life"— and the object of law formulated by Article 14 of the Convention as fol-lows: "Appropriate ethnic groups have the right to own lands which they traditionally occupied."

The task of securing special rights for any ethnic group is difficult the-oretically as well as practically. On the theoretical plane, the problem is defined by the existence of two diametrically opposed concepts of the ethnic group, the first one being a statistical unit (Bromlei 1983), and the second being an abstract concept utilized in political discourse (Anderson 1983). In terms of practical difficulties, we can mention the situational and processual character of the development of an ethnic identity for the indigenous peoples, which is conditioned by the social stratification of ethnic groups, degree of integration of various strata into modern society, dispersion of occupancy, and other factors (Bourdieu 1984).

This problem is further complicated in Russia due to the fact that the ethnic identity of individuals is registered on their passports. Current broad discussions concerning the possibility of having ethnic rights caused many people of mixed heritage, who once chose to register them-selves as belonging to the dominant ethnic culture (for example, as Russian or Yakut/Sakha in Yakutia), to seek legal means to prove their Native ethnicity. In addition, in Siberia there exist traditional groups of a mixed ethnic background that do not have the status of "numerically small peoples of the North" and are eager to obtain it, since many members of these groups are integrated more into the traditional subsistence systems than into modern industrialized society.

There are also difficulties in defining the boundaries of the territories "traditionally occupied" by these peoples. Firstly, since some ethnic groups are full-time or part-time pastoralists, they presently occupy territories that are far away from the lands which they occupied only two hundred years ago. Secondly, many ethnic groups occupy different ecological/subsistence zones of the same territories: for example, sedentary fishermen live in the river basins while watersheds are occupied by pastoral reindeer herders. Thirdly, the modern distribution of indigenous peoples is the result (among several others) of their forced displacement by the government. Today, their "traditional" territories are occupied by some other ethnic group. When an ethnic group that traditionally occupied a territory but was displaced from it now tries to claim its right to the territory, the ethnic group currently occupying the land fights for its right to the territory. The attempts to reconstruct the ethnohistoric equilibrium by giving indige-nous people the right to establish national-ethnoeconomic autonomies, and the failures to account for the modern socioeconomic foundations of the relationships between social subgroups inside of an ethnic group, as well as interethnic relations, may lead to socioeconomic conflicts over the resources under the banner of the ethnic rights movement.

It is obvious, then, that the subject of law should be defined not only according to ethnic affiliations, but also according to socioeconomic affil-iations. The basic right guaranteed by Convention 169 is an economic one—the right to own land and its resources—and should be given to the economic subjects. A tribal group by itself is not an economic subject. Indigenous peoples are therefore not the subject of law in this case. In-stead, the subject is ethnosocial and territorial-subsistence groups that sus-tain traditional ways of life. This definition coincides with the definition given by Convention 169 but refers not to indigenous peoples in general, but rather to territorial-subsistence groups of indigenous peoples.

Indigenous people who are already involved in the paradigm of mod-ern industrialized and urbanized society need other measures for the protection of their rights. They must be able to freely express their eth-nic affiliations, use their native languages, maintain their cultures, estab-lish ethnic units according to ethnic affiliation, and develop ethnic institutions of self-governance. In other words, indigenous people need to exercise the rights that are guaranteed by international agreements (such as the final document of the Vienna meeting between the countries/members of the Council on Safety and Cooperation in Europe, and others) and that are included in the system of legal norms of extraterritorial ethnic autonomy.

Ethnoecological Refuge: Shelter and Preserve for Everybody

At the center of the concept of ethnoecological refuges lie the rights and obligations of the people occupying the territories that have a special ecological and historical-cultural value. This value is determined by the fact that some part of the population of such territories continues to maintain a historically formed, long-term, and ecologically balanced way of coping with the environment in a manner that utilizes only renewable resources. Such territories, as parts of the anthrobiosphere, are valuable for the whole of humanity as they are natural preserves of specific forms of human culture. Their preservation is a way of maintaining various forms of the development of humanity. The following elements belong to the natural, ethnoecological, and cultural heritage of ethnoecological refuges:

- The environment, with its flora and fauna, which supports traditional subsistence
- Systems of special and seasonal distribution of population, procurement territories, and networks of seasonal camps
- Systems of seasonal and spatial combination of various subsistence modes; for example, in Siberia there is a combination of hunting, fishing, gathering, and reindeer-herding
- Social institutions and folk knowledge that guarantee long-term use of renewable natural resources and a transfer of valuable ecological and ethnic information; for example, systems of procurement taboos, land taboos or sacred lands that prohibit subsistence usage of a territory for a certain period of time to preserve its resources, local subsistence calendars, knowledge of edible and medicinal plants, domestication of animals, ways of obtaining and processing various resources, organizational structures of subsistence groups, forms of distributing land and resources, domestic crafts, child-rearing practices, and many others

Ethnoecological refuges must be territorial and have a special regime of environmental protection. Traditional resource usage in these refuges will be determined by the normative rules that are developed by the organizations responsible for carrying out demographic and ecological monitoring of the territories in cooperation with their populations. Any other type of activity that is not a traditional form of subsistence should be prohibited or reduced to bare minimum in the territories of the refuges. These normative rules mean that the right to exploit renewable resources on a given territory may be granted to a limited group of people. It will be fair to take into account the ethnic origins of these peoples, the length of their occupation of a given territory, their knowledge of traditional subsistence systems, and their previous types of occupation when defining the aforementioned limited group.

Ethnoecological refuges will be organized by the country on whose territory the refuge is situated if there is an initiative on behalf of the indigenous peoples and other ethnic groups currently occupying the territory, and if there is an agreement with the regional administrations. An indigenous people referendum will resolve arguable cases. After the examination of requests by a committee, the refuge will be registered by the International Ethnoecological Refuge Fund organized under the United Nations. An ethnoecological refuge represented by a self-governing organization elected by its population must be recognized as a legal entity. A refuge will be subsidized by the government, the Fund and other sources.

These suggestions in regard to ethnoecological refuges are close to the statements of the 1972 Convention on Protection of World Cultural and Natural Heritage. The fact that ethnoecological refuges are a part of the world's cultural and natural heritage has not yet been included in the statements of the Convention, which define "objects of heritage." Article 12 of the Convention suggests broadening the list of such "objects of heritage."

The Convention on Protection of World Cultural and Natural Heritage differs from Convention 169 on the rights of indigenous peoples in that it suggests establishing the World Heritage Fund and finding ways to assist countries in the protection of their heritage.

Society's Reaction to the Establishment of Ethnoecological Refuges

The idea of ethnoecological refuges does not enjoy wide popularity. I discussed my suggestions on the establishment of such refuges with different audiences in Russia. Federal agencies, as we have seen, declare beneficent intentions in regard to the indigenous people of Siberia and in regard to solving ecological problems, yet they are in no hurry to adopt ecological laws or laws that would guarantee the rights of indigenous peoples to lead a traditional way of life. Local administrations behave similarly; moreover, when it comes to carrying out specific projects, they take an openly hostile position.

Just such an attitude was adopted by the administration of the Chukchi Autonomous Okrug regarding the creation of the Beringia international park, which was proposed to preserve traditional forms of subsistence of the area's indigenous peoples, the Chukchis and Siberian Yupiks. The negative reaction of the regional administration toward this ecological project can be explained by its desire to have complete freedom to intensively exploit the natural resources of the region, to eliminate potential hindrances to the industrial development of the region, and to define the borders of the national park in such a way as to use its territory according to the administration's own agenda.

Neither does the idea of ethnoecological refuges excite populations that have relatively recently migrated into regions traditionally occupied by Native groups. Under conditions of low economic development, a large part of the rural population and the populations of small Russian towns have had to resort to traditional forms of subsistence: hunting, gathering, and fishing. These populations represent the majority of industrial migrants in Siberia, and for them traditional forms of subsistence as listed above are a very important part of the family budget.

For these migrant populations, the idea of establishing preserves, such as those that existed in Europe in the Middle Ages to protect hunting and fishing grounds, is alien. Discussions of ecological problems and the necessity of giving priority in these types of activities to indigenous people are viewed by the "migrants" as an attempt to violate their own human rights. However, there is no consensus on this issue among the migrants. Those who have lived in Siberia for about twenty years and intend to stay there take ecological issues very seriously and sympathize with indigenous people. However, such people are, unfortunately, a minority.

In addition, the concept of international ethnoecological laws is met with distrust by all of the aforementioned groups. The thought that Siberia is an ecological resource for all of Eurasia, in a global world-view, and that traditional ways of its exploitation by indigenous people are the ethnoecological heritage of all humanity, opposes the idea of national sovereignty. Similarly, this concept contradicts the stereotype that Russians have learned in schools since the times of Lomonosov: "Russia will be rich through the resources of Siberia." Siberia is seen as a huge, bottomless "storage pit" whose treasures belong only to Russia. It is believed that the Russian government must be in control of the exploitation of these resources. The majority of the population views the idea that international laws should regulate the usage of these resources and the relations between the state and the indigenous populations not just as unnecessary, but as dangerous.

The idea of ethnoecological refuges is met with some degree of distrust even by certain leaders of ethnic rights movements who see establishment of ethnic-territorial autonomies as the only means of preserving indigenous peoples' cultures.

The organization of preserves of natural environment and indigenous cultures by international law is supported only by indigenous people themselves. In these ideas they see some hope of preserving what remains of their native environment and some defense against deforestation, mining, and outside hunters.

The establishment of ethnoecological preserves is not new. Many countries have created reservations for their indigenous populations. In Russia, seeing territories of traditional subsistence as cultural preserves was first introduced in 1822 in "Statutes on *Inorodtsy*" (people of foreign origin; more specifically, indigenous people) by the prominent Russian political leader of the nineteenth century, M. N. Speranskii (Ustav 1830). The statutes of 1822 stated that the Russian government would not interfere in the internal life of the indigenous societies of Siberia. The borders of indigenous territories were defined according to traditional definitions of the Siberian Natives themselves. The statutes prohibited non-Natives from migrating into Siberia to enter territories possessed by the indigenous peoples, from carrying out activities that are carried out by the Natives, or from mining the indigenous territories (Murashko 1991).

The establishment of the International Ethnoecological Refuges Fund indicates a new attitude toward traditional indigenous cultures as world ethnoecological heritage. Preservation of this heritage is important for all humanity as variation in the forms of adaptation is necessary for the survival of humanity. The objects of natural and cultural heritage are already protected by the international community. It is now important to protect ethnoecological heritage and its bearers, whose numbers are diminishing.

A quick glance at opinions about granting indigenous people the right to preserve their traditional ways of subsistence and the territories of traditional resource use shows that this topic deserves a separate investigation. It is necessary to conduct a poll of all interested parties on the following questions, among others:

- What part of the indigenous population wishes to preserve and develop traditional forms of subsistence; what is the age and gender composition of each group?
- How do indigenous people envision this process: as whole groups or as individuals; conservation or modernization of traditions?
- What do they think about the limitations imposed by the status of preserved territory; how are they going to raise their children; how do they see their relationship with the rest of the world?
- How do various ethnic groups that border the territories occupied by indigenous people see ways of regulating relationships with them?

- What do these ethnic groups think about the limitations imposed on them by bordering preserves or by living in such a preserve?

The majority of the territories where indigenous people lead a traditional subsistence lifestyle are located in Third World countries, which attempt to cope with socioeconomic problems by intensively exploiting their natural resources. Everywhere (including some developed countries) the exploitation of resources is hasty and rapacious. However, global natural and cultural processes resulting from the "death" of yet another refuge for many species of plants and animals and many forms of unique human culture are matters of concern for the ecological and cultural future of all humanity.

Note

The original Russian text of the article was translated by Irina Dubinina and stylistically edited by Megan Biesele. The final edit was provided by Peter Schweitzer, in consultation with the author.

References

Anderson, B. 1983. *Imagined Communities: Reflections on the Origin and Spread of Nationalism*. London: Verso.

Bourdieu, P. 1984. "Espace sociale et genese des classes." *Actes de la recherche en sciences sociales* 52.

Bromlei, Iu. V. 1983. *Ocherki teorii etnosa*. Moscow: Nauka.

K publikatsii zakona. 1992. "K publikatsii zakona." *Etnopoliticheskii vestnik Rossii* 2: 56–70.

Murashko, O. A. 1991. "Pravo na svobodu etnicheskoi identifikatsii i razlichnye formy etnicheskogo samosoznaniia." In *Mezhdunarodnyi simpozium pravo i etnos. Materialy dlia obsuzhdeniia*. 112–23. Moscow.

Ustav. 1830. "Ustav ob upravlenii inorodtsami 1822 goda." In *Pol'noe sobranie zakonov Rossiiskoi Imperii s 1649 g*. Vol. 38 (1822–25). 396–417. St. Petersburg: Tipografiia Ego Imperatorskogo Velichestva kantseliarii.

Chapter 10

ABORIGINAL RESPONSES TO
MINING IN AUSTRALIA

Economic Aspirations, Cultural Revival,
and the Politics of Indigenous Protest

———≡◉≡———

David S. Trigger

Aboriginal responses to large-scale mining projects have been subject to increasing public attention in Australia during recent decades. Concomitantly, a literature has gradually emerged which presents various analyses of, and commentaries upon, what are often broad conflicts between indigenous groups, companies, and governments (see, e.g., Connell and Howitt 1991; Howitt et al. 1996). While the overwhelming focus in such studies is on a conflict of interest between resource developers and Aboriginal people, there is an occasional acknowledgment of the importance of an arena of internal politics and diversity of responses within and between Aboriginal communities (Dixon and Dillon 1990; Keen 1993).

My concern in this chapter is to address somewhat contesting Aboriginal views about mining. Among some groups, mining is opposed because it is regarded as the antithesis of indigenous cultural relations with land, yet among others, such large-scale resource developments are embraced because of the potential economic benefits they may bring. After some general comments on this issue that pertain to a nationwide debate, I focus upon the case of negotiations over the new Century zinc mine in northwest Queensland, having been involved closely in working for a range of Aboriginal groups as they have sought to develop responses throughout the 1990s. In conclusion, I will seek to encompass this case study within a more general argument about Aboriginal resistance and accommodation in this region of the Australian Gulf country.

Mining as the Bearer of Cultural Intrusion or Economic Benefits? National Discourses

At the level of national discourses focused upon Aboriginal issues, there are certainly those who speak against mining, some claiming that as a form of land use it is foreign to, and inconsistent with, relationships to land within Aboriginal cultures.

From among many available statements of this kind, we can consider the example of an introductory comment by an influential Aboriginal radio journalist on his weekly national program dealing with indigenous issues. In introducing an interview with a well-known Canadian environmentalist, he contrasted Aboriginal values with what he termed "Western values" concerning land, suggesting they are "like chalk and cheese—Western values are driven by the dollar and materialism while indigenous values relate to spirituality and the land" (*Speaking Out*, ABC Radio National, 18 October 1992). The stress on spirituality is a common theme in Aboriginal discourses about land that circulate through the national media.

To take a second example (*Encounter*, ABC Radio National, 22 November 1992), a senior man, often reported publicly as a major figure in maintaining traditional "law" in the Kimberley region of Western Australia, put his point in the following way: "The whole of Australia is our museum. All our history—these trees and mountains, creeks, rivers—that is our history. And we [are] the caretakers of looking after them … that is our Dreaming, our birthrights and our responsibility and our [way of being] honorable to the land." By this view, mining is regarded as sacrilegious. The point was made directly by another interviewee on the same program. While he comes from a less traditional background than the Kimberley speaker just quoted, and proclaims a Christian religious commitment together with his Aboriginality, this person discussed his view that Aboriginal people feel much greater spiritual connection with the landscape, as compared to other Australians. Thus, he commented on how mining is inconsistent with an indigenous perspective: "It's not just that there's going to be holes in the ground and maybe there might be some tailings or whatever that's left behind, pollution of some type, but it's the tearing apart of some relationship of ours." Such assertions reflect a widely held view across both urban and remote indigenous communities in Australia, namely, that the nature of Aboriginal relations with land precludes its routine commodification; indeed, the relation with land is arguably conceived as of the same philosophical order as relations with kin (Trigger 1996).

However, there are other Aboriginal people who state quite unambiguously that their communities are not, in principle, against mining or other resource developments. The director of the Northern Territory's biggest Land Council wrote in 1982 (Lanhupuy 1982: 55–56): "The Northern Land Council has often expressed its opinion that it won't stand in the way of development, unless we are totally ignored in respect of social factors that must be taken into account." The problem was, then, as he saw it, in the way that development was being implemented. Similarly, in the Western Australian context, the director of the Aboriginal Legal Service has commented: "Aboriginal people are definitely not against mining development, despite any impression that may have been created" (*West Australian*, 24 August 1991).

A major issue in negotiations is whether economic benefits will flow to local Aboriginal groups who reside near mining projects. For example, in 1992, the chairman of the Northern Land Council explained the position of his organization regarding a new, large lead-zinc mine (McArthur River) in the Northern Territory (see Figure 10.1): "We're not blocking any development. We're asking for equality in the treatment of Aboriginal people for the land lost to the mining development and fair compensation for what they've lost to the mining company" (*Green & Practical*, ABC Radio National, 21 November 1992). He went on to suggest that the

FIGURE 10.1 Century Mine, Showing Pipeline Route Options

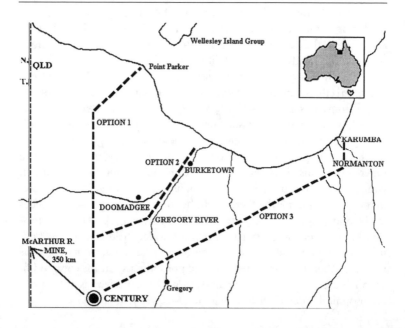

company should negotiate to assist the regional Aboriginal community "in the way of tourism and other projects, fishing industries and so on," that is, to develop some economic viability.

By 1996, with McArthur River mine in full operation, an Aboriginal man was interviewed on national television about local fears concerning the marine environment at the nearby ship loading facility. He expressed a similar sentiment to that given four years earlier by the Land Council chairman, stressing the benefits of jobs and wages as against any potential damage to the traditional landscape. When asked whether he had been concerned about pollution of Gulf waters, he replied: "We were worried about it for a couple of years, but it turned out O.K. Now we can see, y'know, something [economic benefits] coming back to the community" (*Sunday Program*, Channel 9, broadcast 21 July 1996). Yet, in the context of my discussion about a diversity of views among Aboriginal people, it is relevant to note that this man was reportedly prominent among a group who successfully tendered for a contract to transport minerals as part of the mining operation. Just whether he was a local "traditional owner" of the land involved and the extent to which his position might be shared across the regional Aboriginal community were left unclear from his public statements. Certainly, it is questionable whether a wide proportion of the local community would be involved closely in his particular enterprise, and those who do not feel that they are receiving economic benefits directly may well be less inclined to voice approval for the large McArthur River project.

It is this complexity of diverse indigenous views about mining that can be portrayed in the case of Century, destined to be one of the biggest zinc mines in the world and located within the same region of northern Australia as McArthur River, some 350 km to the southeast (see Figure 10.1).

Century Mine: Concerns about Environmental Pollution and the "Integrity" of Country

Century is a major zinc deposit located within a region in which some four thousand Aboriginal people reside in a number of different communities. News of the mine began filtering through to these townships from the end of 1990. The mine was proclaimed by government and industry spokespersons as a great potential benefit to all Australians, including Aboriginal people. However, indigenous responses to the rhetoric of pro-development ideology have encompassed a range of concerns about potential negative implications of the mine, apart from a simultaneous acceptance among some people that economic benefits can be expected to flow to indigenous groups.

In particular, some members of Aboriginal communities—resident on offshore islands and the mainland coast near various sites where a shipping port facility has been proposed—have stated repeatedly that they are opposed to this aspect of the development, primarily because of their fears about its potential environmental effects on the marine resources they continue to hunt. Over the years of meetings and discussions, there have been many statements emphasizing the importance of the continuity of these traditional hunting and fishing practices; the highly prized foods of dugong and saltwater turtle have been particularly mentioned as at risk from potential spillage of zinc or simply from newly intrusive, large-scale shipping activities. Threats to the cultural and symbolic significance of the marine domain have also been a focus for concern. As a spokesperson for people at Normanton (where the slurry pipeline from the mine is likely to end) put the matter: "We live off those seas, for our food, and also we have very strong beliefs that come from those rivers, that come from those seas. Now you affect those rivers, you affect those seas, you are killing us … no question about it" (*Sunday Program*, Channel 9, broadcast 21 July 1996).

Similarly, on the mainland, nearer the actual mine site some 150 km inland, there have been strong apprehensions about leakage from the slurry pipeline that will pass under rivers; and about whether the seasonal flow of waters down Gulf rivers will be affected by the pumping of very large quantities of water out of an open-cut mine pit that will be nearly 1.5 km along its longest diameter and some 340 meters deep.

This kind of concern about environmental damage has melded into a broader critique from some Aboriginal people that rests on a perception of the mine as inappropriately intrusive into what we might term the "integrity of country," including the spiritual, as well as material, properties of the landscape. As people have gradually become aware of the planned scale of disturbance at the mine site itself, their sense of apprehension about the land being so drastically modified has grown. To quote one man's comment, such a deep pit would in his view inevitably "wake up that Rainbow Snake," i.e., disturb a major spiritual force that is far underground; from his perspective, this was a danger regardless of whether the pit were to be dug in an area where surface features of topography are particular foci of "sacred sites."

In a similar vein, we can note statements from a woman at a public meeting in 1992. After listening to company spokespersons outlining the nature of the project, she asked them why they had come back to request again about site clearance work on the coast, when an earlier decision by Aboriginal people had been to reject any possibility of agreeing to a port facility in that area. She went on to comment that "digging up the land" was not part of Aboriginal cultural practices in the past: "They never [did not] dig up ground for money." This speaker likened this reluctance to "open up ground" to cultural practices evident in the Bible among "the descendants of Abraham." On the occasion of the meeting, held at a large local Aboriginal community, she received some applause and positive acknowledgment for expressing these sentiments about core values of Aboriginal "culture."

Probably the strongest version of this type of view is that, *in principle*, such large-scale mining developments as Century should not proceed on traditional Aboriginal lands. To quote from one of the more forthright (women) speakers at the same meeting in late 1992:

> Aboriginal people have a spiritual connection with the land, and anything that goes through there [traditional lands] that's man-made, that's pushed through by Europeans is foreign to their way, and it's not right ... you're see-ing it only from a European's point of view, y'know like there'd be more money, more jobs and things like that. But Aboriginal people say, just let us have our land, let us get back into our culture, we've been taken away from it for so long, we want to get our children back into it, we want them to become strong and identify as Aboriginal people, you know just leave us alone and let us be. (Tape-recorded at Doomadgee, 25 November 1992)

The speaker was an unusual member of the Gulf Aboriginal communi-ties, in that she had lived for several decades away from the region of her birth, and had generally participated widely in the broader Australian society. In fact, with her return to the area, coincidentally around the time of the first discussions about Century Mine, she brought a highly politi-cized consciousness about indigenous rights to a community whose members do not generally participate routinely in the national Aborigi-nal political movement.

Together with a relatively small number of others, this woman op-posed the mine (especially the pipeline) very actively; several individuals engaged in effective media appearances, led a "sit-in" demonstration at a national park near the mine site, and generally politicized the conscious-ness of their peers. The *in principle* opposition to mining of this group can be regarded as bound up with what we might term a *politics of indi-genism* (Beckett 1994), i.e., with the task of reproducing and recuperating indigenous "culture" in the context of an intensely politicized struggle with the wider Australian society. The struggle is seen to have both mate-rial and symbolic dimensions among these activists, and encompasses the sort of political consciousness entailing "symbolic opposition" to the broader society that has been written about for certain Canadian Native communities of the 1960s (Schwimmer 1972). Thus, the mine becomes symbolic of the continuing process of Euro-Australian colonization. To this extent, opposition to it is regarded as resistance against the sort of commercial enterprises that originally drove the process of Aboriginal dispossession. "We will be dispossessed again!" exclaimed the chairperson of an Aboriginal negotiating team when addressing the media about the prospect of the mine (*7.30 Report*, ABC Television, broadcast 8 July 1996).

The more the rhetoric of government or industry or media commentators touts the great value of this "biggest zinc mine in the world"—a project with "the potential to generate absolutely massive wealth of the State and the nation," in the words of the Queensland premier in 1996 (*Sunday Mail*, 31 March 1996)—the more opposition to it assumes symbolic importance as a form of Aboriginal resistance. After predicting negative social impacts such as "racial" conflicts with "redneck miners" and the prostituting of "our young women for alcohol," the coordinator of the regional Land Council told one journalist exactly what he thought of pro-development rhetoric: "Is that something we should accept, just in the interests of the nation, more degradation to our culture?" (quoted in Wear 1996: 35).

Yet such politicized views are hardly shared by all residents of the Gulf communities. Just as those opposed to the mine lodged native title applications as a basis for negotiating about potential cultural intrusions and environmental damage, others made counterclaims over the land in order to ensure that the mine can proceed and produce economic benefits.[1] An exchange between the activist woman quoted above and another person serves to illustrate these differing positions. The activist attacked a company man who was addressing the 1992 public meeting I have described; she stated that he obviously had no capacity to understand the significance to Aboriginal people of the area on the coast being proposed as a possible site for the port facility. However, another woman who had previously spoken about the importance of economic benefits that might flow from the mine, loudly denounced this attempt at asserting the sacredness of the coastal site as an impediment to any development occurring there. She angrily shouted that the area was being used by Aboriginal people to transport "sly grog" from the mainland across to Mornington Island. "Now, does that shock you?" she asked, mocking the previously expressed sentiments about the sacredness of the country. "That's nothing to do with the White man!" she continued.

Her point was to emphasize the disarray among young people within the Aboriginal communities and the importance of addressing this fact through realistic attention to problems such as unemployment and alcohol abuse. This view surfaced in the meeting as in conflict with the politics of indigenism and broad anti-Euro-Australian sentiments implicit in the first woman's attack on the company representative. As the decorum of the meeting began to break up temporarily because of this argument, the earlier speaker fired back a response consistent with her original point about Euro-Australian culpability and insensitivity: "Who brought the grog?" she demanded of her accuser, implying that it was introduced to Aboriginal people by the colonizing society, and thereby restating the need to fight the wider society to achieve justice for indigenous people.

Century Mine as the Bearer of Economic Benefits?

From the perspective of those who stress the value of what appear to be promises of substantial economic benefits (employment, training for young people, funds for new business operations), it is pointless and wrong-headed to ignore the opportunities that the mine presents. To quote the reported words of a spokesperson for one of the incorporated indigenous associations: "The reality is this mine is going to go ahead whether we like it or not, and if we are not careful we will lose what they have offered us now" (*Courier Mail*, 4 April 1996, p. 4). In the words of the chairman of the elected Aboriginal Council administering local government services at Doomadgee (the largest community in the region), the mine represents "our bread and butter"; this was so, he suggested, especially in light of possible future cuts to government funding for benefits such as unemployment payments. Similarly, at a meeting at an outstation community in August 1996, one visiting woman from Doomadgee linked her support for the mine and pipeline to improving the circumstances of young people. "I'll support the jobless," she commented forcefully.

In taking this position, such people risk being defined as "greedy for money" among those for whom dangers of environmental pollution and/or the cultural integrity of the landscape are paramount. For example, they are "jumping on the bandwagon of greed," according to one local man quoted in a newspaper report during June 1996 (*Courier Mail*, 28 June 1996, p. 3). In a social world in which intense webs of interpersonal relatedness are monitored according to a broadly egalitarian ideal (Martin 1995: 6), stressing the importance of economic advancement for Aboriginal people constantly risks being denigrated as simply a disguised form of personal acquisitiveness. "He's working for the company" is thus the sort of accusative dismissal directed at an individual perceived to be in close liaison with industry or government personnel seeking to establish the project. At least, this is so among those opposed to cooperation with building the new mine; their condemnation rests on the assertion that such individuals simply hope to gain benefits for themselves and their immediate families and thereby cut themselves off from the broader networks of relatedness and obligation with other Aboriginal people. Perhaps the most extreme accusation of this sort has been that "corruption" is involved; that is, that certain Aboriginal people have been "bribed" or "paid off" by the company and the Queensland government to manufacture their assent to the project (see statements made on *Sunday Program*, Channel 9, broadcast 14 July 1996).

Yet the responses of persons attacked in this way can be equally disparaging about their critics. Those seeking to oppose the project completely may in turn be labeled as selfishly pursuing their own personal agenda of political protest and thereby undermining attempts to realistically negotiate "some good things" for the wider population of Aboriginal people. This type of condemnation rests on the broad proposition that activist opposition to the project is manufactured by only a small number of individuals who are accused of not consulting with or listening to others (see, for example, comments to this effect on *Sunday Program*, Channel 9, broadcast 14 July 1996). The implication is that adequate consultation would recognize that the majority of people support the mine because it will bring economic advancement.

Nevertheless, this latter assertion is not always easy to demonstrate; over recent years, there has been no shortage of occasions on which some individuals have vigorously expressed cynicism about the notion that the mine will bring jobs and associated improvements in health and other social problems. Furthermore, opponents of the mine are seen by their supporters as making a strong point by suggesting that government should address the material needs of indigenous communities, thus obviating the necessity to accommodate a negotiated agreement with the mining company. Thus, what some regard as sensible embracing of economic opportunities, others decry as a form of blackmail. "Why should we have to sell our souls for a house?" was a question raised by an impassioned speaker at a meeting with Queensland government personnel during September 1996.

Responses to the Mine from Senior "Law" Experts: A Politics of Reputation

While these broadly divergent positions, which I will label "oppositional" and "accommodationist," encompass substantial sectors of the indigenous population, it is important to address specifically the distinctive situation of senior men and women known to hold traditional and historical knowledge of the landscape and of those with rights to it. For these older people, both the emergent self-conscious politics of indigenism and the details of working out economic benefits remain somewhat remote. They are commonly focused upon a local arena of Aboriginal politics in which their reputations are made and sustained (for a discussion of this domain of politicking at Doomadgee in the early 1980s, see Trigger 1992: 111–18).

The cultural knowledge they control is a key form of "currency" made central to negotiations over rights to land or future resource developments; however, they themselves are often more concerned with what we might term a vibrant politics of reputation *within* Aboriginal communities, than with either the assertion of cultural difference as part of a politics of opposition to Euro-Australian domination or the imperative to achieve regionwide economic advancement.

On occasions, I have witnessed senior "law" experts seek not to oppose or protest against various Euro-Australians involved in negotiations, but rather to *impress* them, thereby drawing them into an acknowledgment of the authority of the "old people," a high-status category to which the "law" experts can claim to belong. This has occurred especially when influential senior individuals come to feel that general control over dealings involving "country" is being coopted by younger people less knowledgeable about "culture." In these circumstances, significant tensions can develop.

In the Century Mine case, it is arguable that the actions of both certain company personnel and a Queensland government department's officers have exacerbated these tensions through attempts to forge an alliance with Aboriginal elders. They have sought to achieve this outcome partly by appearing to acknowledge the asserted decision-making seniority of these individuals, and also through energetically making a display out of talking about and looking after their material needs, e.g., by transporting them around the region, assisting them with shopping, ensuring that they receive adequate food at meetings, and so on. In such contexts, apparently helpful outsiders also tend to become embroiled within the inevitable discourse of complaint from the old people about whether they have been looked after adequately by Aboriginal organizations such as the Land Council, whose employees arrange facilities and transport associated with consultations and meetings.

While the motives of company or government officers at times may well be genuinely oriented to the straightforward task of ensuring that older people are looked after properly, the consequence is that the officers' benevolence breeds considerable personal goodwill toward themselves as individuals: "They look after you just like you family, make you real welcome," commented one man in his sixties about the experience of visiting the mine site for discussions on several occasions during 1995/96. This type of sentiment can clearly influence Aboriginal people to agree to company propositions in negotiations over the mine, at least partly on the basis of personal feelings toward individuals, rather than through considered assessments of hard facts to do with economic benefits or environmental safeguards. To this extent, the pattern of benevolence tinged with a proclaimed respectfulness on the part of some industry or government people could be said to inflame emergent tensions between particular senior holders of cultural knowledge and younger people opposing the mine.

One illustrative case must suffice here as an ethnographic example of the way such tensions can be played out. At a meeting in 1995, a young Land Council officer argued aggressively with a company man who had transported important old people the long distance from the major regional town (Mt. Isa) to the remote location for the discussions. At a particularly heated moment, the young activist sought to include other Aboriginal people present in a deliberate insult directed at the company man. "Anybody want to keep talking to this *juga?*" he exclaimed, thereby using the term for "young uninitiated boy" to address the company officer clearly much older than himself.

The younger man had only recently been initiated under the supervision of the most senior lawman present,[2] and this authoritative traditional leader was clearly not impressed with the young activist's aggression and attempted insulting behavior. As the meeting broke up and the lawman was about to return to Mt. Isa (along with his family, in the company man's vehicle), he expressed to me considerable condemnation of what had transpired: "We've never had meeting like that before!" Following that incident, the old man refused to support the Land Council officer. On a television interview filmed some months later, he stated with reference to this person's opposition to the mine: "He's doing the wrong thing" (*Sunday Program*, Channel 9, broadcast 14 July 1996).

In the same interview, the senior law expert restated what he had been saying for some time, namely that the mine location does not impinge upon any Dreaming site: "It's all right. I tell everyone [about] that one, mine [is] away from that place [i.e., from an important Dreaming site]." However, my interpretation of this pronouncement is that it is embedded firmly within a regional politics of reputation, such that this very respected man is particularly concerned to maintain his acknowledged authority on matters of "country" and its significance. While he knows that younger activists and their supporters would rarely (if ever) criticize him overtly, he is also aware that a major arena of Aboriginal action (through the media and as part of the general discourse with government and company personnel) tends to marginalize senior people such as himself. His detailed knowledge of the totemic geography of the mine area can, from his perspective, appear to be left out of the politics of protest being controlled by younger and less knowledgable people.

From the viewpoint of those opposed to the mine, suggesting quietly that such older respected individuals may be "confused" is to imply that in their intense focus upon the local arena of a politics of reputation, senior people may ignore the wider issues of economic benefits, environmental impacts, and the general struggle with government and industry to achieve positive outcomes for indigenous communities. The suggestion is that older people may be influenced by the fact that company or government personnel (or journalists) appear to listen attentively to their pronouncements (at times, we must assume, without the language fluency to understand much of what is being said). While it is doubtless a tactical error (and locally bad etiquette) for people engaged in protest against what the mine represents to marginalize senior law experts, the notion that the old people are not always fully aware of what is involved in the mining development cannot be regarded as completely without foundation. In the case I have outlined, several questions are apposite. Does the old man realize how very deep and wide the open-cut mine pit will be? And does he know how much stone artifact material is located on top of one of the hills marked for destruction (a hill too steep for him to climb, at least on the occasion during which I was present)? If his pronouncements about such culturally significant materials during visits to other sites in the region are any guide, his statement made during the television program that proceeding with the mine poses no threat to the cultural integrity of "country" might well be qualified in light of his gaining more information.

Conclusion: Resistance and Accommodation in Aboriginal Responses to Mining

For some time, my research concerning the Gulf communities discussed in this essay has focused upon the emergence of indigenous responses to a diverse history of Euro-Australian intrusions beginning around the 1860s. This has involved Aboriginal people becoming enmeshed within a struggle over ideas, as well as over their land and labor. Thus, I have depicted a complex mix of resistance and accommodation that has produced the pattern of Aboriginal life and identity in recent decades (Trigger 1992).

This interplay between resistance and accommodation is apparent in the diverse responses to large-scale mining projects that I have outlined in this chapter. Though I began by recounting the strongly expressed arguments that circulate at the level of national discourses (variously opposed to or in favor of large resource developments), against the background of a detailed case study, it would appear simplistic to build an analysis solely on such general politicized pronouncements. One-dimensional characterizations of a single indigenous position—positing either that mining is regarded as antithetical to core values in Aboriginal culture or that it will necessarily be embraced as providing a way out of poverty—are themselves part of a political discourse that requires careful analysis.

In attempting to pursue such a fine-grained investigation through a case study, I have argued that there are genuine substantial differences of opinion among Aboriginal people about whether the huge new Century Mine in northwest Queensland will produce overall positive or negative consequences for their communities. While, as has been suggested by some writers (e.g., Martin 1995: 11), "wealth" for Aboriginal people lies substantially in "social forms of capital," i.e., in maintaining intense patterns of social relationships, in this region at least, perceived potential economic benefits from the mine play a major role in shaping the responses of many individuals, families, and groups.

This view is contested by others who stress the importance of sustaining the emergent recuperation of indigenous culture against what they see as dangers posed to the environmental and cultural integrity of "country." As a result, quite severe social tensions have developed that tend to be incorporated into wider axes of dispute operating in the life of communities in which conflict is given routine public expression. While such tensions are by no means related solely to differences over the Century Mine issue, the question of responding to the new development and of framing associated native title claims has become a key factor in Aboriginal political life of the past decade.

Understanding the complexities of *internal* dynamics within Aboriginal communities thus becomes essential to any analysis of indigenous responses to large mining projects like the one I have examined. The implications of this essay suggest that attention should be turned toward local level conceptions of cultural revival—what I have termed a "politics of indigenism," whereby what is stressed is the recuperation of indigenous culture as an alternative to accommodating new resource developments. However, the challenge is to clarify the relation between this emergent form of "resistance" and a pattern of broad-based aspirations seeking to achieve economic advancement and a realistic way out of poverty and major social problems.

Notes

1. Under the federal *Native Title Act* of 1993, indigenous groups can make applications to a tribunal, asserting that they hold native title over particular lands. In the case of proposed development projects to occur on those lands, these groups thereby establish a "right to negotiate" with both the company carrying out the development and the government granting use of the lands for the project. In the case of Century Mine, there have been seven native title applications over lands involved in the project.

2. This had occurred at a community across the border in the Northern Territory. Initiation ceremonies are no longer common in the region of northwest Queensland in which the mining development is to proceed.

References

Beckett, J. 1994. "Review of 'Stars of Tagai: The Torres Strait Islanders.'" *Canberra Anthropology* 17(2): 128–30.

Connell, J., and R. Howitt. 1991. *Mining and Indigenous Peoples in Australasia*. Sydney: Sydney University Press.

Dixon, R., and M. Dillon. 1990. "Introduction." In *Aborigines and Diamond Mining: The Politics of Resource Development in the East Kimberley, Western Australia*. R. Dixon and M. Dillon, eds. 1–4. Perth: University of Western Australia Press.

Keen, I. 1993. "Aboriginal Beliefs vs. Mining at Coronation Hill: The Containing Force of Tradition." *Human Organization* 52(4): 344–55.

Howitt, R., J. Connell, and P. Hirsch, eds. 1996. *Resources, Nations and Indigenous Peoples: Case Studies from Australasia, Melanesia and Southeast Asia*. Melbourne: Oxford University Press.

Lanhupuy, W. 1982. "Aboriginal Perspective of the Land and Its Resources." In *Aboriginal Sites, Rights and Resource Development*, R. M. Berndt, ed. 53–58. Perth: University of Western Australia Press.

Martin, D. 1995. "Money, Business and Culture: Issues for Aboriginal Economic Policy." Discussion Paper No. 101, Center for Aboriginal Economic Policy Research, Australian National University, Canberra.

Schwimmer, E. 1972. "Symbolic Competition." *Anthropologica* 14(2): 117–55.

Trigger, D. S. 1992. *Whitefella Comin': Aboriginal Responses to Colonialism in Northern Australia*. Cambridge: Cambridge University Press.

_____. 1996. "Kinship, Land Rights and Aboriginal Culture in Australia." In *Contemporary Cultural Anthropology*, 5th ed. M. C. Howard, ed. 184–86. New York: Harper Collins.

Wear, P. 1996. "Loudmouths Rule, OK?" *The Bulletin* (26 March 1996).

Chapter 11

POLITICAL MOVEMENT, LEGAL REFORMATION, AND TRANSFORMATION OF AINU IDENTITY

━━◦◉◦━━

Takashi Irimoto

Introduction

This chapter analyzes the impact of states on, and the responses of, indigenous peoples when forced to interact with governments, with special reference to the Ainu of Japan. The purpose of this essay is twofold: first, to assess significant aspects of Ainu relationships with the government, within the Japanese social and cultural milieu; second, to contribute to the general study of ethnic identity by clarifying dynamic mechanisms in the relationships between ethnic identity and cultural revitalization movements. I shall then point out how distinct or similar the Ainu situation is from other contemporary northern hunter-gatherers in Alaska and Canada.

The viewpoint of this essay is, as far as is possible, objective and without political biases, and conclusions are based on analysis of empirical data. Research material includes historical documents, meeting reports, and published newspaper articles as well as my own observations made during periods of interaction with contemporary Ainu.

The Ainu of the eighteenth century lived in Hokkaido, Sakhalin, and the Kuril Islands, depending mainly on salmon, deer, and wild plants for subsistence, although some cultivation was practiced in the southwestern part of Hokkaido. The Ainu origins, according to recent studies in physical and genetical anthropology, are Mongoloid, and their phylogenesis is based on the Jomon people who inhabited the Japanese archipelago from

8,000 B.P. to the second century B.C. The physical and cultural characteristics of the Ainu have developed, then, as a result of their relative geographical, cultural, and political isolation from mainland Japan. As early as 1454, the Ainu began to interact with the Japanese nation when a land lord set up residence in southern Hokkaido. One of his subordinates later became founder of the Matsumae clan, through which the Tokugawa Shogunate began to control Hokkaido in 1604. After a period of open resistance by the Ainu, especially in 1699, the feudal government completely subdued the Ainu. By this time, Ainu life had undergone a process of change characterized by a formalized trading economy and feudal relationships with the Shogunate (Irimoto 1987; 1992). After the Meiji Restoration in 1868, the new government started to develop Hokkaido by sending immigrants there, and by including the Ainu as full members of the nation. Since government policy at that time was to encourage agriculture, the Ainu life was drastically changed from hunting/gathering to agriculture, particularly with the 1899 Protection Law for Former Natives in Hokkaido, by which private ownership of land that had been reserved by the government was offered to the Ainu for the purpose of agriculture (Irimoto 1991).

The estimated population of the Ainu was 16,136 in 1854, compared to 24,381 in 1986. Today, the Ainu remain a minority group in modern Japan, constituting 0.02 percent of the total Japanese population. Moreover, genetic mixing has occurred to the point that even in 1962 only 0.9 percent of the Ainu population in Hidaka District were pure Ainu (Government of Hokkaido 1965: 17). Of course, the term "genetically pure" may be only hypothetical considering the development of the Ainu.

The impact of Japanese politics on the Ainu over the years since the 1899 Law seems to have resulted in not only the economic and social assimilation of the Ainu, but also the loss of their culture. The current Ainu response to their situation is a desire for the restoration of their identity as Ainu in the context of modern Japan. Worldwide movements of indigenous peoples and movements for ecological issues are driving forces for the Ainu political movement. Furthermore, the Ainu cultural revitalization movement—including Ainu cultural exhibitions, revival of rituals, and Ainu language schools—aims to reaffirm Ainu identity and to support the establishment of a new law to replace the 1899 Law.

Political Movements and Legal Reformation

In order to understand the political movement clearly, it is necessary to analyze the process of change in the Ainu movements in historical context. In each period, appeals and activities of the Ainu varied according to social systems on national and international levels, as well as to internal conditions of Ainu life. The political structure of Japan itself was transformed from the Tokugawa feudal system to the imperial system through the Meiji Restoration in 1868, and then to the democratic system after the conclusion of World War II in 1945. During this time, the major focus of the Ainu movements has shifted from welfare to cultural preservation, and from assimilation to ethnic independence.

In this essay, the process of change in the Ainu movement is divided into the following five phases. The first phase of the movement started from around 1899 up through 1929, during which a cogent application of the 1899 Protection Law for Former Natives in Hokkaido was demanded by the Ainu on a local basis. The second phase ran from 1930 to 1944, when a revision of the 1899 Law was demanded by a newly established Ainu organization in Hokkaido. This objective was accomplished in 1937. The third phase of the movement took place from 1945 to 1960. Ainu organizations reformed and then appealed in vain to obtain an exception to the Agrarian Reform Act, which was being enforced on postwar Japan by the General Headquarters of the United Nations. The fourth phase started in 1960 when Ainu organizations reorganized and made a demand to the government that a fund be established for Ainu welfare. At the same time, the organization declared support for the 1899 Law. Then, Ainu opinion split on the question of maintenance versus abolition of the Law. During this period, worldwide revolutionary movements were a developing trend within the international political framework of the U.S.-Soviet Cold War. The Ainu movement was activated in part by this trend. Finally, the fifth phase started in 1984 when Ainu organizations strategically changed their line of policy from assimilation to ethnic independence, and proposed a new law for the Ainu. This movement was activated by the worldwide movement of indigenous peoples. Cultural revitalization movements were also noticeably accelerated during the last two phases. In the rest of this section, the relationships between the Ainu political movements and legal reformation in each phase will be examined.

The first phase of the Ainu movement began in Asahikawa in 1899 due to the Ainu being relocated from reserved land. They protested against relocation by organizing the Former Natives' Union for Staying and Living, which was supported by the Constitutional Party. They achieved their purpose. However, again in 1902, difficulties arose due to inappropriate operation of the tenant system for their land, a problem that remained unsolved until the 1934 Legislation for Measures of Protected Land for Former Natives in Asahikawa (Arai 1972: 52–55; 1983: 27–40; Kita 1987: 187–98; Matsui 1971: 249–58). In Tokachi District, another movement started, led by a Japanese philanthropist who was working as a government official and was also the president of Kyokumei Sha (The Morning Sunlight Society: MSS), as well as a member of the Hokkaido Ainu Kyokai

(The Hokkaido Ainu Association), which will be described later. MSS was originally established in Tokachi District in 1922, and aimed for the improvement of the Ainu economy in this region (Kita 1967: 2–32). Their activities, which were funded by membership fees and donations, included guidance and encouragement of agriculture, improvement of housing, small-scale funding for employment, reformation of customs such as the prohibition of drinking and promotion of saving, and the management of community halls. The Society was at the time connected with Dr. John Batchelor of the Church Missionary Society of London, who was devoted to Ainu welfare through missionary activities. These first phase movements were regionally based efforts to solve problems caused by the improper implementaion of the 1899 Law and to improve the Ainu economy, which had not adjusted well to new social and economic situations.

However, despite its local origins, the issue of the 1899 Law became generalized and affected all Ainu in Hokkaido, leading to a second phase of movements that started in 1930 when the first meeting of Ainu in Hokkaido was held in Sapporo. The aim of the meeting was a resolution for revision of the 1899 Law. The meeting was successful, and was in fact promoted by MSS. At the same meeting, the Hokkaido Ainu Kyokai (The Hokkaido Ainu Association: HAA) was established. The president of MSS also occupied the presidency of the newly formed HAA. Both organizations were private, although they were supported by government officials.

The 1899 Law contained eleven articles that were designed to promote the self-sufficiency of the Ainu economy and the integration of Ainu society into the nation-state through agriculture, welfare, and education. By this law, private ownership of land, which had been reserved by the government, was offered to the Ainu (Irimoto 1991: 1–51). However, over the fifty years following the Meiji Restoration and the thirty years after the law's enactment, the 1899 law had been revealed to be inappropriate for the conditions of the Ainu. Their society was totally destroyed, and many of them had failed to function in the agricultural economy. The points of the demanded revision were as follows: financial assistance for Ainu who engaged in business, industry, and fisheries; release from restrictions on the transfer of ownership of allotted land; allowance for scholarships; improvement of housing by state subsidy; abolition of segregated elementary schools for Native students, and replacing them with general elementary schools. HAA and MSS politically cooperated to promote the movement for revision of the 1899 Law, which was achieved in 1937.

During this period, HAA published a journal called *Yezo no Hikari* (The Light of Hokkaido). The complete set of three volumes, along with a fourth additional printing, were released from 1930 to 1933 (HAA 1930; 1931a; 1931b; 1933). The journals were used by the HAA to circulate

information on current situations and opinions among the Ainu community in Hokkaido, and at the same time to present them to the general
public. The HAA president addressed the journal as a means of training
and educating the Ainu youth (Kita 1930: 2). Major issues in journal articles written by the Ainu themselves concerned the need to awaken the
Ainu population to the necessity of adapting to their new social and political situation as full members of the nation-state. Standing at the parting
of ways between assimilation and independence, they decided to choose
the way of assimilation, since independence was economically and socially impossible due to the destruction of Ainu society and to the reality
of prejudice. Moreover, they stressed the importance of new education
and even of doing away with Ainu culture. In this context, they also presented their opinions on the 1899 Law, which was seen as useless and
even harmful because it segregated Ainu from Japanese. Thus, this issue
of segregation fueled the demand for the abolishment of the 1899 Law
(Hiramura 1930: 24–26; Kaizawa 1931: 23–24; Mukai 1930: 15–17; Ogawa
1931: 20–21; Onobu 1930: 8–10; Yoshida 1931: 10).

The Law was revised in 1937 almost as requested, after seven years of
struggle for legal reformation. Thereafter, the Law was again revised: in
1946, 1947, and 1968. In the process, matters on welfare, public health,
and education were transferred and became measures under general
Japanese law, and articles of the former law relevant to these matters were
successively deleted over time. As a result, the 1899 Law today has almost
no effective value, other than providing financial assistance for necessary
Ainu facilities under Article 7.

The third phase of the Ainu movement started in 1945, after a period
of inactivity during the state of emergency caused by World War II. This
time, the major issue was the protest against the application of the Agrarian Reform Act on their plotted land, which was being enforced by the
General Headquarters (GHQ) of the United Nations on postwar Japan.
Since many Ainu had let out their plotted lands on lease, they stood to
lose their lands because the Act classified them as absentee landowners, a
designation which gave the government authority to expropriate.

The HAA organization was reformed in 1946 and designated as the
Shandan-hojin Hokkaido Ainu Kyokai (Corporation, Hokkaido Ainu
Association: CHAA). The former HAA was a private organization, but the
newly established CHAA was a corporate body officially recognized by
the National Government. In this guise, Ainu advocates appealed for an
exception to the Agrarian Reform Act. Simultaneously, MSS incorporated
with CHAA and took similar action by petitioning the Ministry of Agriculture and Forestry and the GHQ in Tokyo. They claimed that the 1899
Law was a special law and was prior to the Act. Additionally, the Government of Hokkaido also applied an exception to the application of the Act

to the Ainu. In Asahikawa, the Ainu and tenant farmers jointly founded the Committee for Liberation for Common Land of Former Natives in Asahikawa in 1948. They requested an equitable solution to the problem, including a demand for abolishment of the 1899 Law, a position which was also supported by the city mayor. However, the GHQ did not agree with the proposal, and the purchasing plan was carried out in 1948 without making exception for Ainu plotted land. As a result, 2,318 hectares of over one thousand landowners was purchased, which represented 26 percent of the original plotted land. At this point, the policy of encouraging agriculture, practiced since the Meiji Restoration, ended for practical purposes. Some interesting statistics of the 1978 census show that out of an original 9,061 hectares of plotted land, 7,705 hectares were lost due to confiscation for testing, the Agrarian Reform Act, selling, and transfer (Advisory Group for the Utari Problem 1988: 12–13; Kita 1967: 32–38; Matsui 1971: 274–75).

In the postwar social environment, which experienced the spiritual uplift of postwar democracy, some Ainu ran for election: two for the House of Representatives, one for the governor of Hokkaido, and one for the Assembly of Hokkaido Government in 1947. However, all were unsuccessful (CHUA 1984: 20). In 1948, CHAA again published its journal, this time under the name of *Kita no Hikari* (The Light of the North) (CHAA 1948). The tenor of argument was the same as that in the former *Yezo no Hikari* journal published by HAA. In fact, the leading directors of CHAA largely overlapped with the former HAA, though the chief director at this time was Ainu. Since the chief director's regular profession was that of a pastor, the CHAA's argument was rather directed toward self-enlightenment and toward urging the Ainu to reconsider their former habits that had prevented them from adapting to the new economic and social life. Also, the CHAA insisted that their objective was general improvement and the improvement of the welfare system for the Ainu, as was stated in the association's charter. Thus, the association was defined as a social work organization rather than a political organization. This definition has been, at least officially, continued through the present. The CHAA has advocated the importance of education and of unity to improve Ainu life, with the goal of reaching the same quality of life as that of the general Japanese public (Mukai 1948: 4–6; Ogawa 1948: 6–10). In the meantime, MSS reformed as a corporate organization, though its assets had been taken over under the Agrarian Reform Act, presenting management with severe difficulties. Moreover, the activity of CHAA also became stagnant. Thus, the Ainu movement in this phase slowed down considerably.

The fourth phase started in 1960, when the Ainu organizations were reconstructed. In 1961 the CHAA's name was officially changed to Shadan-hojin Hokkaido Utari Kyokai (Corporation, Hokkaido Utari Association:

CHUA). The term "Utari," literally "the fellow" in Ainu language, was preferred when referring to the Ainu. This was a cultural construction used to avoid the racially biased view contained in the term "Ainu" (CHUA 1991a: 951–52; Kaizawa et al. 1972: 188). At the same time, the definition of Utari is somewhat broader than a genetic term for the Ainu, since the term refers to "the people who are thought to be descended from the Ainu on the basis of the generally accepted idea of a local society, and persons who became members of Ainu society through marriage, adoption and so on" (Government of Hokkaido 1986: 1–2). As such, the name change of the association reflected social conditions of the Ainu population at the time.

During the 1960s and the early 1970s, worldwide revolutionary movements were a developing trend. Communists and revolutionary organizations, harnessing student power, protested against capitalism and imperialism along the line of Marxist-Leninist theory. Some of this uprising involved the Ainu problem since it was thought that the Ainu fit the revolutionary model of the liberation of colonial people (Ota 1973). The Ainu movement was activated again in 1968 when the Hokkaido Government celebrated its centennial. Ainu protested against government policy and against academic and social discrimination. Thus, some Ainu formed the political organization of the Ainu Kaiho Domei (Union for Ainu Liberation: UAL), and they came to see the 1899 Law as a law of colonial policy. Further, they decided to assert their rights and make a claim for damages that had occurred in the past (Yuki 1971: 443–46). However, through a series of bomb outrages in 1972, 1975, and 1976 in Hokkaido, UAL activists separated themselves from Japanese radicals.

In Asahikawa, immediately after the 1972 explosion that occurred there, the Asahikawa Ainu Kyogikai (Asahikawa Ainu Council, AAC) was founded, declaring that they were not associated with the attack (Arai 1983: 39; *Hokkaido Newspaper*, 27 October 1972). After the 1976 explosion at the Hokkaido Government Building, the UAL declared their separation from indiscriminate terrorism. They claimed that the phrase "Ainu revolution" was applicable only to the Ainus and further stated that *Ainu moshir*, literally, "the human world," was a world only Ainu could reach through their ethnic consciousness (Yuki 1980: 158–59). They defined their ethnic identity in a historical perspective; the boundary between Ainu and non-Ainu Japanese was drawn based on an Ainu ethnic consciousness molded by the sharing of common historical experiences. Although the policy of their movement was not accepted by the majority of the Ainu at that time, it may have affected them, for the theoretical base of today's claim follows the same reasoning but in a democratic way.

During this period, CHUA devoted its activity to eliciting a government fund to be used to raise the economic standard of the Ainu, which was in fact the original goal of the association. The Ministry of Public Welfare appropriated a fund of welfare measures for the Utari in the 1961 budget, and the Hidaka branch of the Hokkaido Government conducted a survey on living conditions of the Ainu in 1962 for the 1963 budget (Government of Hokkaido 1965). The office of the CHUA was established at the Department of Folk Life in the Hokkaido Government Building in 1964. In 1970, the CHUA passed a counterresolution against the abolishment of the 1899 Law, insisting that a positive aspect of the 1899 Law was still in use and that it was the only law that could protect the Ainu. However, its abolishment had now been a long-time goal of the Ainu and was also advocated by the Administrative Management Agency in 1964 and by the All Mayors' Association of Hokkaido in 1970 (CHUA 1988: 12, 55; *Hokkaido Newspaper*, 18 June 1970; National Library 1987: 5). The counterresolution, therefore, made a rift between CHUA and the Asahikawa Ainu Council (AAC). The root of this difference lies in the fact that each of them had been established by historically different processes of movements on regionally specific problems. The policy of the AAC had been to consistently declare unconditional, and to demand immediate abolishment of, the 1899 Law. They even entertained doubt about demanding compensation for the past and the wisdom of leaning on this type of hope (Arai 1983: 39–40).

Starting in 1971, CHUA planned to establish a welfare fund for the Ainu to be funded by the National Government and supported by the Liberal Democratic Party, which was in power. Then in 1972, the Hokkaido Government conducted an investigation on conditions of Ainu life and subsequently implemented the Utari Welfare Measures, which have been in effect since 1974. Subsequently, AAC changed its policy to accept the fund, an action caused by some members joining CHUA to get fund monies and by an internal crisis that threatened to split the AAC (*Hokkaido Newspaper*, 8 December 1974). In addition, since 1974 the charter of CHUA has been revised to restrict membership to the Utari and their families, excluding people who had been previously eligible (CHUA 1991b: 985; *Hokkaido Newspaper*, 28 July 1973). The government's current seven-year plan (the fourth consecutive seven-year plan: the first plan ran from 1974 to 1980; the second, from 1981 to 1987; the third, from 1988 to 1994; and the fourth runs 1995 to 2001) includes projects for promotion of education, culture, living, and industry (CHUA 1988: 55–56; Government of Hokkaido 1990: 22; Irimoto 1991: 11). In fiscal year 1989, for instance, total expenditure for Utari Welfare Measures was 3,110 million yen (U.S. $22.5 million at an exchange rate of $1 = 138 yen), with 50.9 percent allotted by the National Government, 34.6 percent by the Hokkaido Government, and 14.5 percent by municipal governments (Government of Hokkaido 1991: 132;

Irimoto 1991: 11). These developments led to an increase in the number of households possessing CHUA membership, from 420 in 1963 to 3,561 in 1984 (CHUA 1984: 21).

Starting in 1978, the CHUA again began examining the issue of whether or not the 1899 Law should be abolished, which led to a report on the issue and a push for new legislation at the general meeting in 1982. Experiences that CHUA members had during visits to China, Alaska, Canada, and Scandinavia, from 1976 to 1982, to contact other minorities and indigenous peoples (Kayano 1991: 96–99; Nomura 1984: 132) may have affected their ideas and influenced them to move from a policy of assimilation to one of ethnic independence under the claim of an indigenous right. In the 1970s, a cultural revitalization movement also occurred, especially after the 1971 opening of the Ainu cultural museum at Nibutani. There, the revitalization of Ainu culture developed into a device for political movement. Consequently, political, economic, and cultural demands were all integrated into the issue of establishing a new law to replace the 1899 Law. In a 1984 general meeting, the CHUA agreed on a draft for a new law concerning the Ainu, which would replace the 1899 Law.

In the fifth and final phase, from 1984 up to the present, those in the Ainu movement have continued their efforts to realize new legislation. A private advisory group to the governor of Hokkaido, including the president of CHUA and other associated individuals, was established in 1984. In 1985 it was tasked with examining the proposal to replace the 1899 Law. In 1988, after three years' examination, the advisory group reported to the governor that the old law should be abolished and a new one established. The proposed new law includes:

1. A declaration of respect for the rights of Ainu people
2. Enforcement of applicable laws and regulations to ensure protection of human rights
3. Promotion of Ainu culture
4. Establishment of a fund for self-dependence
5. Establishment of a new deliberative council including Ainu representatives (Advisory Group for the Utari Problem 1988; CHUA 1988: 26–30; Government of Hokkaido 1990: 24–25; Irimoto 1991: 19)

In 1988, the governor of Hokkaido and the Assembly of Hokkaido Government, based on the advisory group's report, requested that the National Government enact the new law. CHUA also passed a resolution to accept the advisory group's report at a general meeting, and then petitioned the National Government to enact it into law.

Transformation of Ainu Identity

As described in the previous section, the Ainu identity is ethnic consciousness molded by the sharing of common historical experiences. When it is presented to others, identity becomes political, whether it is intended or not by the possessor. Identity can be complex, especially in the situation of ethnic syncretism as in the Ainu case. It is significant that ethnic identity can be changed through generations. In other words, there is a conscious decision to choose and to make one's own identity depending on social, cultural, and economic factors. The dynamism of Ainu identity rests solely on this fact.

The ethnic identity of the Ainu has fluctuated between two extreme poles, that of Ainu and of Japanese. The maximum variations possible in defining identity by an individual are determined by social, cultural, and economic settings, as well as by physical characteristics. Since the physical differences are relatively minor between the Ainu and Japanese, especially after the extensive genetic intermixing and the near elimination of cultural and economic disparity, ethnic identity becomes rather subjective, on an intellectual level. This fact gives flexibility to the issue of Ainu ethnic identity and forms an insecure ethnic boundary between Ainu and non-Ainu Japanese.

In this unique setting of the Ainu in Japan, the dynamic processes of change and transformation of ethnic identity through generations is presented. The first generation to come into direct contact with the Japanese, which occurred in the Meiji Era starting in 1868, retained their identity as Ainu and maintained the Ainu culture. Ainu in the second generation, although they were intimately familiar with Ainu culture and language, denied their ethnic identity as Ainu. They were bicultural and bilingual; however, they decided not to pass on the Ainu culture, especially Ainu language, to their children. This stemmed from a belief that it was best for their descendants to be fully Japanized, and that the Ainu culture was useless in this endeavor. The Ainu in the second generation were the backbone and foundation of the Ainu movement toward assimilation in its earliest phase, as described in the section on political movements, and they were the founding members of MSS and HAA, founded in 1922 and 1930 respectively. The childen of the second generation, who were the third generation and the rising youth of that time, also supported assimilation, and took on a Japanese identity by denying the Ainu identity. The Ainu in the third generation learned Japanese in school but did not learn Ainu at home from their parents. Although they may have picked up some Ainu words from their grandparents, who could speak only Ainu, most of them abandoned the Ainu. Although the third generation had neither Ainu cultural experiences nor an inherited Ainu identity, they became the nucleus of today's cultural revitalization movements. The Ainu in the third generation are the core members of CHAA and CHUA, founded in 1946 and 1961 respectively. They strategically took on a new Ainu identity, and changed Ainu policy from assimilation to ethnic independence during the last two phases of political movements. Further, they tried to pass on Ainu culture to future generations, an action that they came to believe would be useful for their descendants. Some in the fourth and fifth generations have now joined the revitalization movement. Since they have a total lack of experience in the so-called traditional Ainu culture, some have become students at Ainu language schools that have opened in recent years (Irimoto 1994). However, their identity is still uncertain.

The above account shows a transformation of identity through self-definition, depending on particular social, cultural, and economic environments in each period. The transformation is also seen as an adjustment to Ainu ideology in the process of syncretism of two different systems of human life. The more recent identity transformation can also be seen as a countermovement that developed at the point in time when assimilation had almost been completed. In this transformation, the loss of Ainu culture was positively correlated with the remaking of Ainu identity and the initiation of a cultural revitalization movement. On the other hand, in the former generation (the second generation) the experience of Ainu culture was negatively correlated with a presentation of Ainu identity.

Aniu identity, as analyzed in the fourth phase of political movement, was realized on the basis of an ethnic consciousness and was presented in the form of political opposition. The same process may be observed in the cultural revitalization movements. When the Ainu came to view the collection of Ainu artifacts by Japanese scholars as plundering, the ethnic boundary between Ainu and non-Ainu was formed into consciousness. Thus, the establishment of a museum led by the Ainu, even though it was funded by the government, has special meaning for the Ainu. An identical feeling of pride exists among the Ainu for the linguist Mashiho Chiri. Even though there were many Japanese linguists studying the Ainu language, most did not receive much attention by the Ainu. The fact that Mashiho Chiri was an Ainu who studied the Ainu made him meaningful to the Ainu. This formation of an ethnic boundary was based on the historical negative perception of the Ainu and on the Ainu's perception that they were treated as merely a study subject by non-Ainu scholars. The cultural revitalization movement was motivated by the idea of the Ainu restoring Ainu culture. It is particularly meaningful that the Ainu of the third generation, who had no experience in the traditional Ainu culture and initially rejected its perpetuation, started today's cultural revitalization movement by transforming their identity to Ainu.

A significant factor in contemporary Ainu movements is the transformation of the Ainu identity from a negative connotation to a positive one. The negative identity of the Ainu in the past was formed by social prejudice and prevented the Ainu from asserting themselves as a culture. In fact, they had willingly embraced assimilation into the nation-state. However, this process was interrupted by an ethnic boundary formed due to the negative perception of Ainu identity. Since economic and social assimilation have proceeded, this negative image has become inconsistent with the reality of the modern Ainu. Consequentially, the Ainu started to create a new image for their culture that reflects a positive identity of the Ainu. This is a cultural revitalization movement with an underlying political agenda.

The strategy used to form a positive identity was twofold. The first goal was the elimination of negative stereotypes, which produced a negative identity; the use of such stereotypes in textbooks, schools, and tourism was attacked. Secondly, the propagation of Ainu culture in a positive light was used to establish a positive identity. This was achieved through museum exhibitions, education in schools, and public lectures.

In order to create a positive image of the Ainu culture, operations were conducted to promote positive elements from the traditional culture, or to reinterpret positively cultural elements that were adapted in more recent history. These emphasized cultural elements came to function as symbols of Ainu identity. For instance, the traditional system of food distribution in hunting-gathering societies, in which the hunter gives meat to everyone, is interpreted as a humanistic custom in Ainu society. Similarly, the *charanke*, a traditional conflict- solving procedure using a contest that may have lasted several days with arguments being exchanged until one side gave up, is reinterpreted as an example of democracy in Ainu society. Finally, the custom of leaving a portion of wild plants untouched during harvest time is seen as a behavior derived from the idea of protecting natural resources by thanking the spirits and coexisting with nature.

Ainu culture and society, interpreted in this manner, would be a peaceful, democratic, and humanistic world coexisting with nature in harmony. This type of statement, with the Ainu living happily with nature, was the crux of a poem narrated by Yukie Chiri (1923), which ignored the actual disappearance of Ainu culture. As a result, the image, though some points may be true, projects an ideal utopian world.

> Hokkaido was once a land of freedom for our ancestors. Embraced by the natural beauty of this vast land, they enjoyed peaceful lives like innocent children. They were truly favored by nature. How happy they must have been!
>
> In winter, in defiance of the freezing cold, they would search for bears by plowing through deep snow covering the mountains and forests. In summer, with chirping sea gulls as their companions, they would fish all day on boats

floating on an emerald sea like leaves swaying to cool breezes. In spring, when the land is filled with flowers, they would spend day after day singing with the birds and picking butterburs and mugworts under soft sunlight. In evenings tinted with autumnal colors, after the bonfires lit for trapping frogs died out, they would admire a full moon over Japanese pampas grasses rustling in the strong wind, listening to the sounds of deer calling for their friends in the valley. What a pleasant life they lived!

These peaceful days are gone. Decades have passed since all the dreams were shattered. Rapid development swept the land, changing mountains into villages and villages into towns.

This utopian image is accepted by the Ainu, as well as by the non-Ainu Japanese, as a positive image of Ainu culture. For the Ainu, this image functions as a justification to support their pride in an Ainu identity. Therefore, the image becomes a common code for communication between Ainu and non-Ainu Japanese. By dropping a negative identity and creating a positive identity, the previously existing ethnic boundary is dissolved. Thus, in this instance making an ethnic identity is not meant to form an ethnic boundary, but rather to break down an existing boundary.

Although it may seem contradictory to assert that by making an ethnic identity, ethnic boundaries can be broken down, such a statement can be supported because the image used here as a symbol for Ainu culture is not specific to Ainu culture but rather is a general idea for contemporary Japan. The idea of a utopian world can be easily accepted by either Ainu or Japanese. The ethnic identity created by the Ainu in cultural revitalization movements draws on the presentation of an Ainu culture similar to contemporary ideal Japanese culture. As a result, the ethnic boundary may be weakened by stressing the commonality between the two cultures.

Conclusion

As revealed in the section on political movements and legal reformations, the significant aspect of Ainu relationships with the Japanese government was its interdependence. The ideas behind this interdependence were not based on dual opposition, but on mutual dependence. The various Ainu organizations described here have been formally or informally dependent on the government and its agencies. These organizations function as a device for the adjustment of claims to solve problems.

The process of transformation of the Ainu identity was presented in this chapter to demonstrate that the loss of Ainu culture correlated positively with the remaking of an Ainu identity and the initiation of a cultural revitalization movement. Despite the general agreement that creating ethnic identities reinforces ethnic boundaries, the making of an Ainu ethnic identity has rather broken down the ethnic boundary. The reason is that the symbolic representation and its interpretation of Ainu culture stress the basic commonality between the Ainu and Japanese. In conclusion, it is the transformation of ethnic identity from negative to positive, with the support of a cultural operation, that has made a demand for legal reformation possible.

Finally, I would like to compare the Ainu political movement with recent movements of northern hunter-gatherers in Alaska and Canada. In the case of the Ainu, the Protection Law for Former Natives in Hokkaido, which was concerned with the Ainu people, including occupations, land, medical care, and education, had already been established in 1899, approximately a century ago. This may seem similar to the state of the Native Americans in the contiguous United States, but in the case of the Ainu the basic policy regarding relations between the nation-state and the indigenous people promoted syncretism, not separatism, as seen in the reservation/reserve systems in the U.S. and Canada.

As a matter of course, it is common in Japan and Western democratic countries that ethnic minorities and indigenous peoples in nation-states take political measures based on democratic principles to satisfy their political, social, and economic demands. Nevertheless, the specific demands of these groups vary, depending on the historical background and present social and economic situation of a given people. In this sense, recent moves by the Ainu to establish a new law in line with worldwide indigenous peoples' movements was characterized by their practical goal of achieving ethnic dignity through a cultural revival, not by demanding lands and various rights for subsistence, as seen in Alaska and Canada. This cultural goal was achieved when the Law Concerning Promotion of Ainu Culture and Dissemination and Enlightenment of Knowledge about Ainu Traditions was enacted in 1997. The law is intended to realize a society in which the pride of Ainu people is respected and ensures that the expression of Ainu ethnic identity and their cultural activities are socially recognized and financially supported, through positive comprehension of Ainu culture.

Change in ethnic identity is seen not only in the Ainu case described in this chapter, but also in the changing of names of indigenous peoples in Canada and Alaska: "Eskimos" to "Inuit," and "Indians" to "Natives," "Denes," and "First Nations." The process of negotiation between nation-states and indigenous peoples, however, greatly depends on the culture to which they belong (e.g., Japanese culture, Western culture), and results have varied from culture to culture. In Alaska and Canada, lines are drawn between "selfness" and "otherness," based on conscious and subconscious thinking that favors dualistic oppositions, and cultural value is placed upon cultural and individual uniqueness and independence. In

Japan, on the contrary—probably due to a long process of syncretism involving many peoples since the prehistoric ages—commonality rather than dissimilarity among people is emphasized, and cooperation rather than confrontation is considered important in conflict resolution. This idea serves as a common cultural code when settling problems between the Ainu and the nation-state.

Consequently, in contrast to indigenous peoples' movements in Alaska and Canada, which claim both land and sovereignty and proceed on to separation and independence, the Ainu movement is practically directed toward syncretism and symbiosis.

References

Advisory Group for the Utari Problem (Utari Mondai Konwa-kai). 1988. *Ainu Minzoku nikannsuru Shin-po Mondai nitsuite* (On the Problem of the New Law for the Ainu). Sapporo: Department of Folk Life, Hokkaido Government.

Arai, G. 1972. "Ouji no Ainu to Gendai" (Ainu: Past and Present). *Hoppo Bungei* 5(2): 49–59.

_____. 1983. "Hokkaido Kyudojin Hogo Ho to Tatakatte Yanseiki" (One-Half of the Century Battled with the Protection Law for the Former Natives in Hokkaido). In *Ekashi to Fuchi*. 27–40. Sapporo: Sapporo Television Co.

CHAA (Corporation, Hokkaido Ainu Association). 1948. *Kita no Hikari* (The Light of the North).

Chiri, Y. 1923. *Ainu Shinyo Shu* (A Collection of Ainu Yukars). Sapporo: Konando Shoten.

CHUA (Corporation, Hokkaido Utari Association). 1984. *Ainu-shi Sousetsu* (Abstract of the Ainu History). 1–24. Editing Committee for the Ainu History.

_____. 1988. *Ainu Minzoku no Jiritsu eno Michi* (A Way to Self-Support of the Ainu). Sapporo: CHUA.

_____. 1991a. "Showa 36 Nendo Hokkaido Ainu Kyokai Sokai Kiroku" (A Record of the General Meeting of Corporation, Hokkaido Utari Association in 1961). *Ainu Shi Shiryo-hen* (The Ainu History, Materials) 3: 947–55.

_____. 1991b. "Shadan-hojin Hokkaido Utari Kyokai Teikan" (The Memorandum of Corporation, Hokkaido Utari Association, 1972 with 1974 revision). *Ainu Shi Shiryo-hen* (The Ainu History, Material) 3: 984–94.

Government of Hokkaido (Hokkaido-cho). 1965. *Hidaka Chiho niokeru Ainu-kei Jumin no Seikatsu Jittai to sono Mondaiten* (Living Conditions and Problems of the Ainu Inhabitants in the Hidaka Region). Urakawa: Hokkaido Hidaka Shicho.

_____. 1986. *Showa 63 Nen Hokkaido Utari Seikatsu Jittai Chosa Hokokusho* (The Investigative Report on the Life of the Utari in Hokkaido). Sapporo: Hokkaido Minsei-bu (Department of Folk Life).

_____. 1990. *Ainu Minzoku wo Rikaisuru tameni* (For the Understanding of the Ainu). Sapporo: Hokkaido Seikatsu Hukushi-bu (Department of Life and Welfare).

_____. 1991. *Hokkaido no Seikatsu Hukushi* (Life and Welfare in Hokkaido). Sapporo: Hokkaido Seikatsu Hukushi-bu (Department of Life and Welfare).

HAA (Hokkaido Ainu Association). 1930. *Yezo no Hikari* 1 (The Light of Hokkaido).

_____. 1931a. *Yezo no Hikari* 2 (The Light of Hokkaido).

_____. 1931b. *Yezo no Hikari* 3 (The Light of Hokkaido).

_____. 1933. *Yezo no Hikari* 4 (The Light of Hokkaido).

Hiramura, Y. 1930. "Ainu toshite Ikiruka? Hatamata Shamo ni Doukasuruka?" (Whether Living As the Ainu, or Being Assimilated to the Japanese?). *Yezo no Hikari* 1: 24–26.

Hokkaido Newspaper. 18 June 1970. "Do Utari Kyokai wa Hantai/Kyudojin Hogo Ho no Haishi" (Opposition by the Corporation, Hokkaido Utari Association against the Abolishment of the Protection Law for Former Natives in Hokkaido). *Ainu Shi Shiryo-hen* (The Ainu History, Materials) 4: 985–86.

_____. 27 October 1972. "Bakuha niha Mukannkei/Asahikawa Chikabumi Ainu ga Kogi" (Being Not Concerned in the Explosion, A Protest Meeting by Chikabumi Ainu in Asahikawa). *Ainu Shi Shiryo-hen* (The Ainu History, Materials) 4: 990–92.

_____. 28 July 1973. "Ishiki Toitsu no Kuno Mazamaza/Do Utari Kyokai Sokai" (Sufferings to Make Accord in General Meeting of Corporation, Hokkaido Utari Association). *Ainu Shi Shiryo-hen* (The Ainu History, Materials) 4: 1005–6.

_____. 8 December 1974. "Asahikawa Ainu Kyo Rosen Tenkan he" (Changing Policy of the Asahikawa Ainu Council). *Ainu Shi Shiryo-hen* (The Ainu History, Materials) 4: 1013–15.

Irimoto, T. 1987. "A Cultural Anthropological Analysis of Historical Data on the Ainu of the Saru River Region: C. 1300–1867 A.D." *Bulletin of the Institute for the Study of North Eurasian Cultures* 18: 1–218. Hokkaido University [with English summary].

_____. 1991. "Economic, Social and Political Prospects of the Ainu." International Conference on the Indigenous Peoples in Remote Regions: A Global Perspective, University of Victoria, Victoria, pp. 1–51.

_____. 1992. "Ainu Territoriality." *Bulletin of the Institute for the Study of North Eurasian Cultures* 21: 67–81.

_____. 1994. "Ainu Go Kyoshitsu to Ainu Bunka" (Education of Ainu Language and Ainu Culture). In *Ainu Go no Tsudoi—Chiri Mashiho wo Tsugu* (Talks on the Ainu Language). O. Miyaoka et al., eds. 215–24. Sapporo: Hokkaido Shuppan Kikaku Center.

Kaizawa, T. 1931. "Dojin Hogo Shisetsu Kaisei nitsuite" (On the Revision of the Institution for Protection of Natives). *Yezo no Hikari* 2: 23–24.

Kaizawa, T., et al. 1972. "The Contemporary Problems." In *Asu ni Mukatte* (Toward Tomorrow). M. Gonai et al., eds. 185–214. Tokyo: Maki Shoten.

Kayano, S. 1991. "Senju Minzoku tono Koryu no Tabi" (Visits for Communication with Indigenous Peoples). *Jishu heno Michi* (A Way of Independence) 43: 95–115.

Kita, M. 1930. "Kantogen" (Forward). *Yezo no Hikari* 1: 1–2.

_____. 1967. *Ezo Minzoku Shadan Kyokumeisha 50 Nen Shi* (A Fifty Years' History of Kyokumeisha). Obihiro: Tokachi Kyokumei Sha.

_____. 1971. "Fifty Years with the Protection Law for Former Natives." In *The Remnant of Kotan—An Aspect of the History of Human Rights of the Ainu.* 367–436. Asahikawa: The Association of the Members of the Committee for the Protection of Human Rights in Asahikawa.

_____. 1987. *Ainu Enkaku Shi* (History of the Ainu). Sapporo: Hokkaido Shuppan Kikaku Center.

Matsui, T. 1971. "The Origin and the Result of the Problem on the Ainu Land in Chikabumi." In *The Remnant of Kotan—An Aspect of the History of Human Rights of the Ainu.* 233–84. Asahikawa: The Association of the Members of the Committee for the Protection of Human Rights in Asahikawa.

Mukai, Y. 1930. "Kyoiku naki Mono wa Horobiru Ainu-jin niwa Kyoiku ga Kyumu" (Men without Education Will Be Ruined: Pressing Need of Education for the Ainu). *Yezo no Hikari* 1: 15–17.

_____. 1948. "Zen Do Utari Shoshi ni Tsugu" (The Notice for All of the Utari in Hokkaido). *Kita no Hikari* 1: 4–6.

National Library. 1987. "The Law for the Ainu." Issue Brief Number 0016; 31/01/87. 1–23.

Nomura, G. 1984. "Kokunai Shosu Minzoku no Jinken—'Ainu Minzoku nikanuru Horitsu' Seitei wo Motomete" (Human Rights of the Minority in the Nation-State—Toward the Legislation of "Law Concerned with the Ainu"). In *Jinken Hakusho: Hisa-betsusha no Tachiba yori 1984* (White Paper on Human Rights). Committee for Declaration of World Human Rights, ed. 113–45. Osaka: Kaiho Shuppan Sha.

Ogawa, S. 1931. "Zento no Komyo wo Mokuhyo ni" (Light for Goal in Future). *Yezo no Hikari* 3: 20–21.

_____. 1948. "Ainu Kyokai Sonritsu no Shushi to Shimei" (The Object and the Mission for Establishment of the Ainu Association). *Kita no Hikari* 1: 6–10.

Onobu, K. 1930. "Dozoku no Kanki wo Unagasu" (Demand for Awakening for the Ainu). *Yezo no Hikari* 1: 8–10.

Ota, R. 1973. *Ainu Kakumei Ron: Yukara Sekai heno Taikyaku* (A Theory of Ainu Revolution: Retreat to the World of Yukar). Tokyo: Shin-sen Sha.

Yoshida, K. 1931. "Shakai Jigyo no Taisho toshiteno Ezo Minzoku" (The Ainu as the Subject for Social Undertaking). *Yezo no Hikari* 3: 3–10.

Yuki, S. 1971. "Write to the Utari—The Way of Ainu, the Natural Man." In *The Remnant of Kotan—An Aspect of the History of Human Rights of the Ainu*. 437–47. Asahikawa: The Association of the Members of the Committee for the Protection of Human Rights in Asahikawa.

_____. 1980. *Ainu Sengen* (The Ainu Manifesto). Tokyo: San-ichi Shobo.

Chapter 12

TRACKING THE "WILD TUNGUS" IN TAIMYR
Identity, Ecology, and Mobile Economies in Arctic Siberia

———◅●▻———

David G. Anderson

In his presentation at the Seventh Conference of Hunting and Gathering Societies, Peter Schweitzer confessed his surprise at arriving in Moscow in 1986 expressly to study hunters and gatherers in Siberia only to be advised by professional state ethnographers, perhaps with a polite smile, that his quest was properly an archival one (Schweitzer 1993). The explanation that Schweitzer no doubt heard was that although wild reindeer were still hunted and Arctic fox were still trapped, the persona of the "hunter-gatherer" had long been replaced in this socialist state by more respectable rural professionals such as the "fly-in/fly-out" reindeer rancher or the salaried state hunter. The view of Soviet state ethnography, as many Western scholars were to learn, was that hunting and gathering persisted but that these activities were far from subsistence undertakings, having been authorized by highly trained managers and supported by an intricate net of social security benefits within a complex institutional structure. Schweitzer argued, correctly in my view, that the initial puzzlement that both groups of scholars experienced stemmed from fundamentally divergent ethnographic priorities.

Simply put, Western scholars were eager to find hunter-gatherers in order to embrace them as the long lost relatives who would share with them important lessons about equality and ecology. By contrast, in the Soviet tradition, any purported relationship between urban scholars and their rural kin only served to underscore how much better life had become for the city folk since they had left the insecurity of the chase for the guarantees of a planned society and complex division of labor. To bridge these traditions Schweitzer practically suggested combining the best of both outlooks. Thus, in his view, the well-developed Soviet tradition of linking reconstructive ethnology to an analysis of the "ethnogenesis" of complex social formations naturally complemented the ahistorical tendency of Western scholars to make ideal types out of actually existing hunting contexts that were nonetheless evocative in their analyses of kinship and social power. Thus, Schweitzer argued, the structural model of a hunting and gathering society could be heuristically retained and enriched through the study of how it changes over time.

Schweitzer's opening observations in Moscow in 1993 marked for me the conclusion of an initial year of field research in a mixed Evenki and Dolgan state farm in a relatively remote area of Arctic Siberia.[1] During my journey to the settlement Khantaiskoe Ozero in the southwestern corner of the Taimyr (Dolgano-Nenets) Autonomous District, I too had to stubbornly push on with my quest despite friendly but authoritative warnings that not only had all indigenous hunters of the region long since drank away their heritage ("they have been spoiled by civilization"), but that the people with whom I had wanted to meet—Evenkis—had long since vanished. At the conclusion of my journey, I found that not only did Evenkis persist and that local wild reindeer hunting and Arctic fox trapping were vibrant and lucrative activities, but that those Evenkis who did live on the tundra practiced evocative rituals of reciprocity with one another and within what would be best described as a sentient ecology. Although my notebooks recorded many examples of social, economic, and symbolic organization common to other rural hunting contexts worldwide, I continue to be puzzled by a significant anomaly that has led me, among others, to question the usefulness of a concept that unites these aspects through a single productive strategy (see, for example, Feit 1994; Myers 1988). This was the simple fact that those who practiced the most elaborate relationships of reciprocity on the land described themselves *not* as hunters but as Evenkis (*evenkil*), "locals" (*mestnye*), or, more commonly, "people of the tundra" (*tundroviki*). Turning this anomaly into a paradox was the fact that those who were most proud and vociferous of the appellation of "hunter" (*okhotnik, promyslovik*) tended to be equally proud of the fact that they were Russians (*russkie*) and were highly dismissive of some of the more "inefficient" behaviors of the "locals."

To write about living on the land in terms of a single subsistence strategy in this context would mean to anticipate one of two conclusions: either that the hunting enterprise here was submerged within a complex array of socioprofessional categories such that "the Evenki laborer is *actually* a hunter at heart" (see Bird-David 1983), or that the *real* uncorrupted hunting society was to be found in another time or place just beyond the horizon of current social memory or the next river drainage. Both conclusions would necessarily imply that the local view of what it means to live on the land must be ignored for the sake of protecting a useful comparative model. Instead, this chapter argues that taking the local view seriously offers equally promising insights for comparisons between most rural circumpolar sites and more generally between other contexts worldwide in which the relationship between people and animals is of primary importance. I will write narrowly of this one place in Taimyr, but my reading and travels in Siberia suggest that my conclusions can be applied generally throughout Inner Asia. Here I will emphasize the local use of relational identities; however, notions of time (Feit 1994), cosmology (Scott 1989), and the ethics of interacting with nonhuman persons (Fienup-Riordan 1994; Hallowell 1960) are as significant here as in the circumpolar world generally. Finally, while generally stressing the robustness of localized "ways of knowing," I wish to show how an overly idealized and rationalized category of the "hunter" in the minds of urban planners (and ethnographers) has actually created a social situation wherein young people must actually forgo hunting in order to practice the craft of attending to the land and its animals. In the context of Taimyr, the ideal-typical concept of hunter (and the associated concepts of herder and fisherman) seems to be the biggest threat to the survival of the "tundra-person."

What's in a Name? The Politics of Nationality in Taimyr

In the anthropological literature, Evenkis are known as hunters and reindeer herders who occupy an unusually wide territory from Central Siberia through Mongolia, Manchuria, and Zabaikal'ia, and then northwards along the Pacific coast of the Russian Far East. Taimyr represents their most northerly and westerly homeland—in fact, so much so that many ethnographers in Russia are surprised to learn that they live there. The English-language literature on Evenkis emphasizes the performances of their ritual specialists—*samanil* (shamans)—under their official prerevolutionary ethnonym of Tungus (Anisimov 1963; Shirokogoroff 1935). Russian language works also explore Evenki shamanship but also offer rich studies of their "national" history,which explore such innovations as the domestication of the reindeer (Pomishin 1990) or the reasons behind their wide dispersal (Tugolukov 1985; Vasilevich 1969). The preferred ethnographic present is usually the end of the nineteenth and start of the twentieth century, wherein Evenkis are represented as living in multifamily mobile groupings using domesticated reindeer for transport and to hunt coveted furbearers (sable, ermine) and wild game (moose, wild reindeer).[2] Richer families in northern areas might be described as holding up to one thousand head of reindeer, but in general, most ethnographers and travelers describe limited reindeer holdings ranging from three to one hundred animals. The Evenki mobile economy was one of reindeer-facilitated hunting, trapping, fishing, and trading. Large-scale ranching of reindeer for the sale of meat was a recent invention—in many places as late as the 1960s. In general, those Evenkis who specialized in one or another economic strategy were thought of in extreme terms: thus, both full-time fishermen (*menederil* "squatters") and full-time trappers (*batraki* "workers") were thought of as "poor" (Vasilevich 1969).

The term "Evenki" comes from the word used in this Tungus-Manchu language to describe their people as a whole (*evenki* singular, *evenkil* plural). The final vowel coincidentally preadapts the word into a plural for Russian speakers making the pair *Evenk* and *Evenki* somewhat of a standard in Russian and in English translations of Russian texts. Tsarist administrators used the term "Tungus" (*tungusy* plural)—a word derived from the Yakut language (*Tungus* singular, *tungustar* plural)—to refer to people generally classified today as Evenkis and Evens.[3] This prerevolutionary term has great currency in the literature today because the majority of the records consulted to reconstruct the preferred pre-Soviet ethnographic present are the records of Tsarist tribute-takers. As we shall see, the meaning of "Tungus" is also important in contemporary speech situations. An implicit ethnographic tradition of attributing unquestionable authority to administrative records has given Evenkis a somewhat seamless national identity despite the very great territories that they inhabit and their own skills as traders and middlemen.[4] It is not rare for Evenkis of the older generation today to speak several languages—one of which is usually Yakut. Until recently, there has been little exploratory work on the range of terms actually in circulation in Evenki communities. My own fieldwork and reading of the literature suggests that clan and territorial appellations have been found to be much more useful in day-to-day life for Evenkis than the collective identifier in their own language (Anderson 1995: chapter 3). Furthermore, as Shirokogoroff (1935: 124) noted long ago, Evenkis are aware and wise enough to produce the term that a tribute-taker or an ethnographer is most likely to understand.

Understanding the difference between authorized identifiers, such as those used by state officials, and vernacular identifiers in Siberia is not so much important to adopt "politically correct" terminology as it is to understand the channels of politics itself. The Russian Empire, like other colonial powers, placed great emphasis on correct classification of peoples so as to correctly calibrate their regional politics (see Raeff 1956). Soviet state managers wished to liberate their Siberian comrades from their tributary status and make them full citizens of a multinational state. Hence, all Tsarist identifiers were "corrected" with careful attention given to the reports of linguists on vernacular terms in instances that did not contradict the design of administratively convenient boundaries between nations. Although Soviet-era national appellations are often very close to some vernacular terms, the logic of the redistributive economy was not flexible enough to capture the richness of the way that these terms were used in everyday life. Thus, to this day, Siberian citizens must choose only one nationality for themselves during the rite of passage of receiving their internal passports and do not have the option of changing that identity easily on a year-to-year (or day-to-day) basis, or of living two or three national identities simultaneously. To a Western reader this may seem like common sense and a fairly regular administrative practice, but in a society in which one's nationality determined the affirmative action programs for which a person was eligible or what kind of external development assistance might be sent to a village, how one "registers" oneself has important implications for one's life course (Anderson 1996a). In a varied multinational and multilingual region like Taimyr, the tailoring of social identities in order to facilitate social development necessarily trimmed down some of the spaces in which local identities were reproduced.

One of the most important institutions linked to nationality and one's authorized identity from the point of view of both citizens and state managers is the district in which one lives. In the 1920s, the Soviet Union began experimenting with territorial forms of indigenous self-administration that arguably foreshadowed indigenous land claims in other parts of the world and definitely foreshadowed the eruption of nationalism in the regions after 1989 (Kaiser 1994). The Taimyr (Dolgano-Nenets) National Okrug (district) and its Evenki twin to the south were formed in 1932 as two of the last special enclaves in Siberia established expressly to focus the energies of the state on improving the lives of the indigenous population that happened to be within their borders (Forsyth 1992; Slezkine 1994). Although the system of national districts distinguished itself from North American reservations by allocating massive territories nominally to sparse indigenous populations, the representative branches of these districts were quite weak.[5] Trained indigenous *kadry* were recruited to work in special educational and economic ministries, which drafted programs tailored directly for the economies and languages of local peoples. Although the number of indigenous peoples in responsible positions is still impressive, these cadres did not have much flexibility to question the manner in which programs were administered or what goods were distributed. Thus, the national or autonomous districts are best thought of as legal territories cordoned off on the bureaucrat's wall map for special executive attention.

Before the creation of a special territorial vessel within which new authorized nationalities could focus their energy on participating in Soviet society, the range of vernacular identity and the extent of movement across the tundras were quite wide. According to official state ethno-graphic sources (and using russified ethnonyms), Taimyr is the homeland to seven aboriginal nationalities: Evenki, Dolgany, Yakuty, Entsy, Nentsy, Nganasany, Krest'iane (Dolgikh 1963). The range of social intercourse between these people roughly followed "the edge of the forest" from the Ob River drainage through the Yenisei River drainage to the Lena drain-age (some 1,500 km) along special trading "roads" (Anderson 1996b). The effect of special administrative attention for native peoples in Taimyr was a dramatic improvement in education, health care, and the supply of trade goods within relatively restricted "orbits" around administrative posts exclusively authorized to provision schooling, medicine, and am-munition (and eventually transport) to people of one or another autho-rized nationality. The curious ecological impact of this transition will be explored in a section below.

The establishment of discrete territories had a limiting impact on the currency of one's identity as well. Depending on the resolution of one's ethnographic lens, the seven indigenous groups of the region either col-lapsed into two main groups or shattered into a kaleidoscope of lineages with allegiances to one or more "nations." The preference of state admin-istrators is for a simpler picture, thus only two of these official nationali-ties (Dolgany and Nentsy) are thought to be hegemonic and feature conspicuously in the title of the political district.[6] However, for those who experiment with different resolutions, Taimyr is famous for clouding their ethnographic gaze. The famous state ethnographer of Nias (*nganasan*) Andrei Aleksandrovich Popov, for example, upon arriving in Taimyr wrote an excited and exuberant letter to his supervisor Bogoraz-Tan:

> This frontier strikes [one] as a wondrous mosaic made up of entirely different peoples [*narodnostei*]; each completely unstudied. For some strange play of circumstance they have been left outside of scholarly attention. Usually on the ethnographic maps these nationalities are known by the broad terms of the Tungus, the Samoyed and so forth. But upon closer acquaintance with them, they divide themselves into many different groups [*gruppy*] often differing very sharply from each other in language and lifestyle. I sincerely would like to believe that the All-Union Academy of Sciences … will devote its attention to the colorful and dappled nationalities [living] in this forgotten oasis between the Yenisei and the Lena [Rivers].[7]

In contrast, the exasperated field correspondent for a doomed ethno-graphic atlas of Central Siberia confessed: "In practice there are constant difficulties for administrators and missionaries to divide one or another family between *dolgan, yakuty*, or finally *tungus*. It is sufficient only to start to talk to a *tungus* and then to learn with surprise that he counts himself as *dolgan*."[8] A very common ethnographic technique for bridling the evocative nature of identity in the region was to identify certain inter-mediary groups that gravitated to one or another legitimate nationality.[9] One of the more curious artifacts of this process is that people using the vernacular appellation *sakhalar* (or *hakalar*) and a similar language are officially called Dolgans, Sakhas, or Yakuts depending upon whether or not they are registered in the Taimyr Autonomous District, the Sakha Repub-lic, or the Evenki Autonomous District.[10] This curiosity becomes mysteri-ous when one traces sudden jumps and falls in the population of Yakuts in Taimyr over time (Anderson 1996b) or realizes that representatives of each nation can often be siblings. What inspired my own fieldwork was the fact that although certain groups had been tagged as "dying out," or were alter-nately "russified," "yakutized," or "dolganized" at various times in the Soviet era, in 1992 and 1993 they still had the audacity to persist.

On the Track of the "Wild Tungus"

The spring thaw of 1993 had been anxiously awaited by Nikolai Savel'e-vich Utukogir, the brigadier of the Number One Reindeer Brigade of the Khantaiskii *sovkhoz* (state farm). As if by some cruel fate, the winter sea-son had blown in many unexpected challenges. The weather had been unusually harsh with a combined snowfall some three times the norm necessitating a daily search for accessible forage for the herd—a task that took its toll on the health of the calving cows. To make matters more dif-ficult, the meddlesome yet, up to now, reliable surveillance flights of state farm officials had been grounded by the general collapse of central state financing. Life on the tundra was possible without bimonthly helicopter visits by veterinarians, sport hunters, or bootleggers from the city—espe-cially with a reindeer herd approaching one thousand head. However, the absence of butter, batteries, and most importantly ammunition with which to hunt for wild reindeer (or to keep wolves at bay) made life on the land less enjoyable than it could be. The sudden break in the gale-force blizzards and the beginning of constant sunlight brought another chal-lenge. Should the expected *sovkhoz* flight not arrive, it would soon be impossible to reach the settlement due to the rate at which the rivers were swelling and the extreme distance from the settlement at which the brigade was moving.[11] Early one morning, for precipitous reasons that were unclear to me, it was decided to make a break "on the light" (*na legke*) for the settlement. Within three hours, an *argish* (caravan) was assembled of eight sleds and some forty harnessed reindeer with a min-imum of supplies (axes, rifles, matches, outdoor clothing, one side of wild meat). In three days, all somewhat stunned by snow blindness and lack of sleep, our entourage of five impatient adventurers had reached the settlement only several hours after the anticipated helicopter had come and gone.

The purpose of the *argish* was far from urgent but it broke the long routine of daily tending the troublesome state herd—a herd that the *pastukhi* (herdsmen) had noted was becoming wilder and wilder every year. Moreover, it allowed our pathfinder, the senior son Vitia Nikolaevich, to show off his knowledge of the land and its routes by using it—which is arguably what makes life on the reindeer brigades most attractive to young men. Our way back for the most part followed what was known as the "old road"—a trajectory through the angled front ranges of the Pultoran Mountains, which at one time linked Lake Khantaiskoe to the colonial capital of Turukhansk (and earlier still, the Cossack fort of Mangazeia). At places, the "road" was diverted due to the fact that portions of it had been submerged by the Khantaiskoe hydroelectric reservoir since 1972. We traveled without compass or without reference to my American tactical navigation map, which was found to be useless for its reliance upon invisible coordinates rather than the tangible features that tell people where the road lies. In this tundra, tangible landmarks are not built features such as cabins or cut-lines but rather inclines indicating river courses, the alternation of thickly treed places and open tundra patches (*laida*), and the whisper of the prevailing wind.

Our journey also enabled us to visit kin presently assigned to the Number Four and Number Three brigades. "Performing a visit" (*gostovat'*) is an old Evenki institution that facilitates the communication of news, the exchange of reindeer, and at one time the negotiation of alliances and marriages (Karlov 1982). Because of the great distances placed between brigades since the beginning of the 1970s with the development of "productive" reindeer-breeding, it is not now an institution that enlivens the life of the tundra-person as much as it once did. The biggest news sought from the distant neighbors was the fate and movement of a family of wolves between the three brigades. A constant subject of discussion was the movement of wild reindeer (expected soon to stream northwards to their coastal breeding grounds)—the hunt of whom was a constant source of enjoyment and interest for "locals" who live on the land. Whether or not this somewhat arduous *argish* was strictly necessary was not a matter for consideration by members of the Number One Reindeer Brigade. Although the director of the collective farm found these sudden voyages irritating, the herdsmen of this brigade prided themselves on being the *most* Evenki of all the brigades, which in a way almost obliged them to continue living a lifestyle of effortless motion through the landscape punctuated by occasional visits—irrespective of the constraints that a rationalized productive structure had placed upon them.

I was introduced first to the *most* Evenki brigade since it was thought that my quest for Evenkis would eventually bring me to them. The idea of some labor institutions being more Evenki than others was initially interpreted by me to be a statistical observation (i.e., that there were more Evenkis in the composition of this brigade than in others). However, eventually it became apparent that this idea was an interval variable: one person could display more or less Evenkiness at different times of one's life and in different contexts. As I got to know my eight comrades better, it soon became evident that they were not unambiguous Evenkis. The matron of the brigade, Liuba Feodorovna, in fact had been registered as three different nationalities at different times of her life (Sakha, Dolgan, Evenki). She spoke at least three languages well: Russian, Yakut, and Evenki. Similarly, one of the more charismatic younger members spoke Yakut and Russian fluently but did not understand Evenki—and yet registered himself as Evenki. All members of the brigade would take offense at the word "Tungus." Listening carefully to the way Evenki was spoken here, and with some comparative help from Leonia, an expert *khempo-evenki* reindeer herder born on the Left-Bank of the Yenisei, I found out that many expressions were creolizations of Yakut, Evenki, and Russian.[12] When I queried and fumbled my way through these small anomalies that might indicate a *lack* of Evenkiness, my suggestions were either laughed off or rebuked. My somewhat temperamental tent-mate Vova would often throw Yakut expressions into his speech partly to complicate my weak attempts to learn Evenki, but also to force me to see the larger picture. The *chumrabotnitsa* (tent-keeper) Liuba Feodorovna was the most articulate in explaining this complex ethnoscape. She once patiently explained, no doubt referring to her own life, that one could "tune into" (*nastroit'*) being Evenki or Dolgan as one could tune a radio between channels. In moments of exasperation, she would sharply denounce any contrafactual examples on my part by exclaiming that any Evenki who did not understand Yakut was no better than a wild beast (*dikar*) raised in isolation from more cosmopolitan circles of conversation.

Unlike the tidy picture presented in statistical renderings of nationality, identity on the tundra, like the character of a reindeer, tended to be treated not as an attribute of nature but as an attribute of cultivation. This became clearer in the second day of our *argish* as we tried to locate the infamous Number Three Brigade in order to exchange news (but also to retrieve a half-dozen harness reindeer "borrowed" a year earlier). Finding this brigade proved to tax the skills of our own junior brigadier Vitia. Within the collective, Number Three had the reputation of being *partizany*—an image from the ubiquitous genre of World War II adventure stories of the surreptitious but presumed loyal guerrilla fighter. Number Three often traveled without two-way radios or neglected to file paperwork on time.

As we broke trail through seemingly endless thick groves of larch forest, one member of our *argish* (who had once been the head of the Party-controlled trade union) remarked: "[This brigadier] is the *real* 'wild Tungus.' Following his trail is like following a bear." The image seemed to express the consensus of the whole exhausted group. When we finally found the remains of Number Three's last campsite, consisting of packed sleds and even a smoking campfire, the trail left by the reindeer herd and its associated tenders seemed to suggest that the whole brigade had recently escaped our arrival by scaling a nearly vertical incline. We abandoned our search at that point and directed our energies toward forcing our flagging harness reindeer to carry us the remaining seventy kilometers to the settlement.

The image of the "wild Tungus" in this region is an idiom replete with several generations of literary and political overtones. Since all Siberian hunters and herders today have a high degree of literacy, the root association comes from the Russian poet of the Golden Age A. S. Pushkin.[13] Balancing this literary allusion is the fact that most Dolgans and Yakuts in the settlement use the word *tongus* as a tough pejorative for Evenkis. As one Evenki women explained, "It seems to mean that we are lower somehow." The image of the "wild Tungus" also carries the powerful overtones of the civil war, implying the problem of whose culture would become canonized as the standard-bearer of Soviet civilization. Although Dolgans/Yakuts spearheaded an active campaign of resistance against the Bolsheviks to the extent of fomenting an uprising at the Taimyr trading post of Volochanka in 1932 (claiming the lives of twenty Party workers and wounding fourteen, according to Troshev 1993), they were in the end chosen as the best recruits to restructure the local economy. In the words of A. A. Popov, they were the "most advanced [*peredovoi*] people in terms of culture."[14] Evenkis in this region of Siberia, by contrast, cooperated with Bolshevik organizers by "donating" their more modest stocks of reindeer to early collective *artely* but nevertheless were constantly represented in Party reports as "poor" or "weakly developed." "Wildness" in early Party documents was directly associated with fiercely autonomous bands of producers who managed to weave themselves, their families, and their herds in between the authorized state administrative stations well into the late 1950s.[15] The Taimyr resettlement schemes of the 1960s were directly designed to match more developed peoples to less developed; hence Dolgans and Yakut-speaking Evenkis were deliberately relocated to the Evenki settlement of Khantaiskoe Ozero to "raise" the latter's level of culture. In the current context of privatization, the "unloyal" element of the wild equation has become invigorated as Dolgan newcomers clamor to gain private land-hold tenures over fishing spots and traplines that "local" Evenkis consider to be their birthright. To bring the idiom back to the journey at hand, the brigadier of the Number Three Reindeer Brigade was not reputed to be a wild privatizer, but his actions suggested those of the early renegade travelers who evaded the grip of the state administration (and perhaps a little too blatantly borrowed other people's reindeer).

Although Soviet state managers and their Russian Federative heirs have used national identifiers in order to measure the needs of their client populations, the vernacular meanings of these terms preserve a certain degree of relativity, which takes into account a person's biography, behavior, and loyalty to both place and collective. The two authorized identifiers in this context, Dolgan and Evenki, and one older identifier, Tungus, are applied in an economic and political field in a manner that suggests that they are earned despite what the central registries record. Official national identifiers have been incorporated locally in a war of position within an administrative distributive apparatus. As one resettled elderly "Tungus" was heard to cry out to a pair of Yakut-speaking youths: "So you guys register yourselves as Evenkis—that's good! Don't sell out your people!" The ideas of wildness and cultivation here, much as in Amazonia (Gow 1993) or Highland Burma (Leach 1964), signify the degree to which a particular person participates in a cultural project. They subtly indicate how a person mixes solidarity to an official political program with respect for local ethical imperatives within a varied and demanding landscape. This pragmatic conception of identity goes some way in explaining why a local view of Evenkiness as a sort of rare and untarnishable creed allows the identity to persist in spite of creolization, radical administrative reorganizations, and the expectation on the part of some urban-based ethnographers for Evenkis to disappear within a flood of "Dolganization" (Dolgikh 1963).

Identity and the Sentient Ecology of Taimyr

The vernacular ideas of "wildness" in dialogue with loyal, cultivated identities immediately suggest a powerful rhetoric of resistance to forces threatening to encapsulate and transform this hunting and herding community. Such a view implies that spontaneous and unregistered movement and the "taking" of animals is fundamentally opposed to a strict, compartmentalized, division of labor administered from the multistory office complexes in Dudinka and Moscow. To a large degree this is true. As the conclusion to this chapter will show, the multiple "perestroikas" in this area of Siberia (Grant 1995) have taxed the energy of individuals and of animals to such an extent as to threaten the continuation of local ecological traditions. However, positing this situation in a dualist framework does not help us understand what the local ideal of "living on the land" entails (Descola and Palsson 1996). In fact, the idea of radical deregulation, of "giving the tundra back to the Tungus," which is now the dominant policy paradigm in Russia, misses the subtleties of the local view of community and threatens to escalate already high levels of unemployment, sickness, and alcoholism.

Similar to many areas of the circumpolar Arctic, the primary way that life on the land is described by local state hunters and reindeer herders in the Khantaiskii state farm is through "knowing" (*znat'*) or "attending" (*sobrazit'*) to "land" (*tundra; buga*) and animals. Knowing the land is achieved not through formal scholarly training but rather by being with animals, by moving on the land, and by observing the skills of more knowledgeable "teachers" (*uchitelia*). Demonstrating a proper, respectful relationship to animals and to the land is demonstrated through conservation (not hunting unless needed and consuming all meat "taken") and through reciprocity (giving "gifts" to the land). Richer descriptions of ritual and of attitudes to land in this rural context are elaborated in Anderson (1995; 1998). For comparative purposes, the idea of people existing in a relationship with "natural" entities and specific animals mediated by attention and reciprocity seems to be as strong here as in other rural aboriginal contexts (Bjorklund 1990; Feit 1986; Fienup-Riordan 1994; Scott 1989; Tanner 1979).

The local interpretation of relationships on this tundra is special for two aspects (although these may be general Inner Asian ideas). First, people act as if they live in a "sentient ecology" in which their actions, motivations, and achievements are understood and acted upon by nonhuman entities. These entities can range from weather to specific animals, both wild and tame. Living in a sentient ecology implies adherence to very strict ethical guidelines, which Harvey Feit (1994) has eloquently shown to be an "enduring present" where present behavior implies future success or failure. Feit uses this ethical idea to show that the dichotomy of planning versus spontaneity cannot be used to distinguish a hunting and gathering society from a pastoral or even an agricultural society. Within a political economy that gave a whole new meaning to the idea of the "plan" and to the multitude of latent and irrational consequences of provisioning an "enduring future," I would concur that the pragmatics of "the hunt" are not that much different from the way that Muscovite shoppers describe the way that they "hunted down" (*dobil*) or "gathered" (*dostal*) deficient commodities in a harsh consumerist landscape. Second, although for Taimyr tundra-people there is a very complex understanding of the behavioral differences between wild reindeer, wolves, and foxes as opposed to domesticated reindeer and dogs, the category of "attentiveness" can be applied in both domesticated and wild contexts. In fact, as we established in the previous section, wildness is an attribute that can be displayed by people much as cultivated behavior can be attained by certain individual reindeer or wolves. Within the debate at hand, this desiccates the "rubicon" dividing hunters from herders.[16] "Attentiveness" and "love" also characterize the relationship between people and fish—but that is another story.

The legacy of sixty years of intensified applied ethnographic research and development assistance in Taimyr adds a further layer to the relationship between people, land, and animals. Although the most favored construction of the traditional society for Evenkis suggests a fairly cosmopolitan mixture of hunting, herding, fishing, and trading invigorated by "knowing," the last three generations who became involved in building an alliance with the Soviet state adopted not only official national identifiers but also official professional designations. Unlike in the North American Arctic, where fur-trapping and reindeer hunting are marginalized with respect to the national economy through the category of "subsistence," Soviet planners had a very clear vision for the socialist reindeer herder, the socialist hunter, and the socialist fisherman. In Taimyr, as all over Siberia, these professions had regulated salaries and pension benefits, Heroes of Labor, professional congresses, as well as their own professional feast days (i.e., "Day of the Reindeer Herder"). These professional designations, much like the national designations so carefully pruned by state ethnographers, were designed to be officially free of any ambiguity of practice. Thus, reindeer herders were supposed to display twenty-four-hour vigilance over their herds in order to guarantee the planned reproduction ratio of the animal stocks. Hunting wild reindeer was seen as a "lack of labor discipline" (see Syroechkovskii 1984). Similarly, hunting in the area of one's authorized fishing point, unless specifically licensed and limited by quota, was considered to be "poaching."[17]

Despite these significant changes, it does not seem appropriate to retire Evenki relationships with wild animals to an archival past. There has been much written on the difference between living on the land in an industrial mode ("productive nomadism") and living on the land in a nonmodernized, subsistence "nomadic way of life" with the stress being put upon a fundamental difference between the two (Lashov and Litovka 1982; Vitebsky 1992). Again, an etic view does suggest great differences between the use of a "shift method" to take salaried workers from the settlement to the herd (and back again every two weeks) and large families raising their children on the tundra with an eye to reading tracks on the snow, not characters on a page. However, as with the case of national identities, there are many vernacular innovations that mediate these strict, official professional designations. Thus, "everyone knew," including the director of the state farm, that if individual appropriation of furs was not tolerated, no one would agree to hunt for the state. Similarly, no *tundrovik* would consent to work, or in fact survive, as a herder if he or she had to subsist on airborne shipments of rice, condensed milk, and canned pork. In the twenty years that productive nomadism was instituted throughout rural Siberia, tundra-people and villagers (*poselkovye*) still experienced their tasks as a continuity and not a "leap from the Stone Age to the Space Age." The *pastukhi* of the Number One Reindeer Brigade all saw their task as "feeding the village" (and not meeting quotas), enlivened by a social community more characterized by interaction with animals than with people. In moments of irritation at the lack of attention given the brigade by "those who sit" in the farm offices, the brigadier and his wife would boast that there would not have been any village without the reindeer herd.[18]

For our purposes, the most important link between the local understanding of the sentient ecology and "productive nomadism" is the idea of "attending to animals generally" and the ability to deliver produce to the community. As all treatises on the "crisis" in reindeer-herding tend to note, the best herders are in fact the people with the most knowledge about animals in general. This has been a historic necessity in Taimyr. Domesticated reindeer differ in size and color from wild reindeer, but what keeps them living next to people is their cultivated behavior. In Taimyr, all authorized "pastures" for domesticated reindeer are swept twice yearly by immense populations of wild reindeer moving between their wintering grounds deep within the Pultoran Mountains and the calving grounds on the coast. These migrations were understood and "managed" locally by moving herds of domesticated reindeer up and down mountainsides, occasionally out of the path of the "wild ones" and occasionally into their path in order to "take wild ones." The difference between holding a herd of domestic reindeer and hunting a population of wild reindeer hinged upon understanding the behavior of both sorts of reindeer—and was not a matter of how one's activity was codified by the state economist. Holding animals "close to home" was a choice of strategy that many *pastukhi* agree was positive for building communities but in essence was not different from "knowing" reindeer generally.[19]

Although the compartmentalized version of the Evenki mixed economy of hunting, herding, fishing, and trading is founded ultimately upon a local understanding of a sentient ecology that confounds all of these distinctions, the regulated version has led local relationships with animals to upset the web of reciprocity. Since 1960 reindeer herds have become so large that *pastukhi* can no longer give each member of the herd an individual apprenticeship in cultivation ("knowing the rope"). According to the members of the Number One Brigade, the result is that herds increasingly are going "wild." Similarly, the lack of sustained hunting of wild reindeer has led to the result that the "wild ones no longer come back"—or that wild reindeer have become "completely wild." Elaborating on the local view, it would seem that reduced predation, combined with the industrialized culling of the migrating wild cows, has altered the social structure and the age structure of the wild reindeer population such that the coherence of their regional microgroupings has been disrupted. This can be linked to chaotic changes in migration routes and an unprecedented explosion in wild reindeer populations that have coincided with the introduction of Soviet agricultural reforms in the mid-1960s (Syroechkovskii 1984).

My view is that the overlap between resettlements, professional specialization, and the standardization of rural development policy toward specific nationalities is not coincidentally related to the dramatic changes in the behavior of migratory wild reindeer, although this is difficult to prove using the tenets of positivistic wildlife biology. Whatever the root cause of the chaotic migrations, it is a fact that domestic reindeer have been retained only in Khantaiskoe Ozero, the Left-Bank Yenisei native communities of Taimyr, and the Dolgan communities along the far eastern border with the Sakha Republic. All other Evenki, Dolgan, and Ngo communities have lost their domestic reindeer altogether and thus the possibility of being "productively nomadic herders" or, for that matter, hunters. This somewhat apocalyptic state of affairs points to a relationship between people and animals that has become out of balance to a large degree because of the rationalized way reindeer-herding has been interpreted by planners and state ethnographers. It does suggest the twilight of a particular moment in the sentient ecology of the region—but this is an epitaph that has been proclaimed many times over for native peoples in Siberia. At the very least, scholars should be skeptical of recognizing overly strict divisions of social practice, such as the divisions between "hunting," "herding," and "fishing." As the same radical skepticism is currently being applied to bureaucratic modes of regulation within Russia as a whole, the political context may now be ripe to clear a space for a balanced relationship between communities of people and animals.[20]

Conclusion

The contemporary ecological challenges of people in Taimyr bring us to the central question of this chapter: in what way can an interpretative understanding of identity help us to understand a society of hunter-gatherers (if at all)? Through giving a history of the state-led rationalization of national identity, professional identity, and finally the identity of migratory and domesticated reindeer, I have suggested that the sentient ecology of Taimyr has been dramatically transformed. The change in the behavior of animals, not to mention the behavior of bureaucrats, has now raised the question as to whether "living on the land" can continue in the same terms as it was previously understood. This leads us to a categorical paradox. In order for locally based production to continue to support the settled kin of the tundra-people and to continue to light and heat the homes of the settlement, fur-trapping, industrial fishing, and perhaps a newly commodified form of reindeer tenure must be intensified. This intensive and rationalized relationship to the land and its animals would imply some overhunting ("taking what can not be consumed immediately") and perhaps slaughtering some animals with whom one does not have a relationship of "attentiveness." Such cynical and directed relationships are exactly what have guided Evenki youth into the arduous profession of reindeer-herding and away from becoming "hunters." The promise of the profit of such relationships is what makes many "newcomers" proud to be productive hunters. As the director of the state farm explained, Evenkis just do not produce enough fur to justify hiring them as state hunters.

An etic view of the situation must inevitably come to the conclusion either that the Evenki hunting and gathering society "died out" in 1890, 1932, or 1965, or that the existing hunting and gathering society composed of a mixture of state hunters, reindeer ranchers, and industrial fishermen must now be understood without the components of reciprocity, "attentiveness," and a relationship between people and animals that blurs the distinction between wild and cultivated. A somewhat paradoxical corollary of this view is that the existing hunting and gathering society in this region is primarily Russian. An emic view of this hunting and gathering context is that though people may sport various authorized labels, such as *pastukh* (herder) or Evenki, what makes their lives evocative and meaningful are the attributes of codified practices as Evenki or as herder that allow them to respect what I have called the sentient ecology. The attributes of attending to animals, whether wild or tame, and of taking animals in order to build settlements and human relationships within them can be seen to be common to many rural contexts worldwide that are characterized by mobile economic strategies and elaborate reciprocity with nonhuman persons.

Rather than privileging one subsistence strategy as the cultural core of a society, taking the local view seriously helps to avoid the paradox that Evenki herders practice a more evocative relationship to animals than do Russian hunters. The clearest term uniting the ideas of mobile economy and identity is the local word *tundrovik*. The idea that certain people, irrespective of professional qualifications or national designation, "know" the land better than others creates a common space for solidarity between Evenkis, Dolgans, Russians, and perhaps anthropologists. As one elder

Evenki explained, the term *tundrovik* (or *tiaa* in Yakut) means "this is all of the people ... kind of everyone out there ... the tundra people both *evenki* and *dolgan* ... it's everyone together." A concept that privileges how people interact with the land "out there" does not necessarily lose rigor if we are sensitive to important moments in this relationship. This chapter suggests that local vernacular meanings of "wildness" and of "knowing" provide important comparative clues that help to link this community of tundra-people to other communities worldwide. To explore these links, the heuristic vessel of the "hunter" is best set aside.

Notes

1. This chapter is based on a conference paper given in 1993 at the Seventh Conference of Hunting and Gathering Societies in Moscow. The field research for the paper was made possible by a doctoral fellowship from the Social Sciences and Humanities Research Council of Canada. Special thanks is due to Nikolai Savel'evich Utukogir of the Number One Reindeer Brigade, Khantaiskii State Farm for inviting me to stay with his family. This essay has benefited indirectly by comments from Tim Ingold.
2. For representative descriptions of "traditional" Evenki society in Central Siberia and Zabaikal'ia, see Shirokogoroff (1935), Vasilevich (1969), Karlov (1982), and Turov (1990).
3. This is a heuristic oversimplification. The Tsarist term "Tungus" also collapsed a variety of local appellations ranging from *orochen* to *hamnigan* to *bail*. It could also be employed to refer to people who would today be called Yakuts or Dolgans (Ermolova 1992; Gurvich 1962; Terletskii 1951).
4. In terms of its vast range and heuristic usage, the term "Evenki" has much in common with designators for Algonquian peoples. As many authors have noted, "Cree" is a much overgeneralized appellation having more reality in the mind of linguists than for the people themselves (Brightman 1993; Morantz 1983: 12–14; Preston 1975: 1–7). In terms of the relationship between Evenkis and Yakuts, which tends to be more of a continuum than a division, the best model in North America is that of the "linguistic convergence" of Chipewyans and Crees (Scollon and Scollon 1979).
5. All national districts were renamed "autonomous" districts in 1975, a constitutional move that heralded the start of one of the largest rural development initiatives in the circumpolar region. It would not be unfair to say that the rapid expansion of cities and the influx of highly paid urban workers from European Russia removed both the "national" and the "autonomous" quality of the enclaves (see Chichlo 1981; Grant 1995).
6. It is interesting to note that just five years before informed opinion selected Dolgans (*sakhalar*) and Nenetses (*nenets*) to be titular nationalities, there was one proposal to have Taimyr be a continuous portion of one pan-Tungus district (Severnyi 1930) or to have the population divided between Samoyeds, Yakuts, and Tunguses (Dolgikh 1929: 76).
7. Letter to V. G. Bogoraz-Tan from A. A. Popov, Dudinka, November 1930, fond 14 opis 1 delo 149 list 6, Archive of the Museum of Anthropology and Ethnography, St. Petersburg (hereafter cited as AMAE).

8. Manuscript by A. Ia. Tugarinov "Poianitelnaia zapiska k etnograficheskoi karte Turuk-hanskogo kraia," Archive of the Russian Academy of Sciences—St. Petersburg Division, 1923, fond 135 opis 2 delo 305.

9. This technique is perhaps best known through Jochelson (1926) who in a lengthy ethnography identified a long list of Yukagirized, Tungusized, and Yakutized nationalities. In Taimyr, Nias (Nganasan) ethnogenesis is commonly argued through the fate of a Nganasanised Tungus clan (Dolgikh 1952). Other Nias clans form bridge groups to Nenetses. Enetses appear and disappear as a people over several censuses (Anderson 1996b). "Within" (or between) Enetses is a distinct people called *hempo* who intermarry with Evenkis (Tugolukov 1985: 211; Vasil'ev and Simchenko 1963:38).

10. This picture becomes more convoluted when official identifiers are tracked over time. In a period of high Soviet hegemony, for example, in 1950, related Yakut-speaking individuals would have been officially called Sakhas in Taimyr, Yakuts in Evenkiia, and "reindeer Yakuts" in the Yakut Autonomous Republic (Gurvich 1977). After the wave of regional independent movements in 1991, the same triad are named Dolgans in Taimyr, Yakuts in Evenkiia, and Sakhas in the Sakha Republic. Feeling a little manipulated by all of these permutations, and some alienation from the "central Yakuts," Yakut-speaking reindeer herders in the western part of Sakha are coining the new ethnonym "Dolgano-Asia" (V. Alekseev, personal communication). For a heated controversy on the question of who is Evenki and who is Yakut in Western Sakha Republic, see Michael (1962: chapters 1–5).

11. In part due to heavy-metal pollution from the Noril'sk Alpine Metallurgical Factory and in part due to the exhaustion of pastures around the settlement Khantaiskoe Ozero, the Number One Reindeer Brigade orbited some 250 km to the southwest of the settlement in a territory that was nominally part of the Igarka Industrial District (and thus out of Taimyr).

12. This language was called the *govorka* ("the talk") by Popov (1934). It was also analyzed by the linguist Ubriatova (1985) as the foundation of the Western "Dolgan" dialect.

13. In his "Unto Myself I Raised a Monument" (1836) Pushkin wrote: "The rumor of my fame will sweep through vast Russia/ And all its peoples will speak this name/ Whose light shall reign alike/ For haughty Slav and Finn and wild Tungus/ And Kalmyk riders of the plain." This is a particularly famous phrase, often carved on statues of Pushkin in central cities, that assured Evenkis a place in Russian high culture.

14. A. A. Popov. "Doklad orgkomitetu kompleksnoi ekspeditsii issleodovanii A. N." Manuscript in the Krasnoiarsk Centre for the Preservation and the Study of the Most Recent History (Krasnoiarsk Party Archive), fond 28 opis 1 delo 24 list 1.

15. These autonomous collectives can be found mostly in archival records such as reports of the Noril'sk area "Wild Co-op" (*Dikii Artel*) (AMAE K2-1-128: 77; 14-1-134) or of the presence of "nationalist bandits" living with the "wandering Tunguses" in the mountains above Volochanka (State Archive of Krasnoiarsk *Krai* R2275-1-144: 245). Personal communication from the head of the Department of Agriculture in Dudinka, S. Ia. Palchin, indicates that many Nenets families in the coastal tundra regions have never been counted or registered, nor have they had any part in collectivization. These *edinolichninki* (independent entrepreneurs) were common among Evenkis in the region of Igarka until the mid-1960s.

16. Interestingly, one advocate of state rationalized reindeer ranching did not think that the level of cultivation of the relationship between Siberian native peoples and reindeer was nearly sophisticated enough to be considered "herding." In his view, herding in Taimyr bordered upon hunting (Andreev 1958). I would tend to agree with the conflation of hunting and herding, but for different reasons.

17. It can not be emphasized often enough that the radical compartmentalization of national identity and of professional practice was a post-1960s invention. Before 1964,

the collective farm at Khantaiskoe Ozero (then called "Red Trapper") raised reindeer in order to provision both fishermen and trappers with transport (and to feed the teachers in the very small settlement).

18. Until 1992 this was literally true, since all central state subsidies for the maintenance of the power station and the central heating plant were calibrated to the delivery price of reindeer meat. After 1992, reindeer meat was often bartered to hungry city workers in exchange for spare parts for settlement machines.

19. The blurring of "wild" and "tame" is also illustrated more unambiguously by different moments in the relationship between people and reindeer. Sometimes young wild calves were captured and taught "to know the rope." More recently, domesticated reindeer have "gone wild." The identity implicit in understanding the behavior of living things in general is signified in the words used to stand for relationships with animals. Wild animals are not killed but "taken." One does not hunt but "takes the wild ones" (*dikovat'*). One does not "herd" but "gathers reindeer together."

20. Recent events on this front are not encouraging. A publication by the World Wildlife Fund for Nature has marked the largest wild reindeer herd in Eurasia as a monument worthy of strict protection through a system of natural preserves (WWF 1993). Similarly, an anonymous Russian reviewer of a development report I wrote for a consortium considering commercial development of the Arctic Sea Lanes (Anderson 1996b) offered the view that native hunters and herders were not advanced enough to benefit from the free market unless to offer their furs for sale to foreign buyers.

References

Anderson, D. G. 1995. *National Identity and Belonging in Arctic Siberia: An Ethnography of Evenkis and Dolgans at Khantaiskoe Ozero, Taimyr Autonomous District.* University of Cambridge, Department of Social Anthropology [Distributed by University Microfilms International].

_____. 1996a. "Bringing Civil Society to an Uncivilised Place: Citizenship Regimes in Russia's Arctic Frontier." In *Civil Society: Challenging Western Models.* C. M. Hann and E. Dunn, eds. 99–120. London: Routledge.

_____. 1996b. "The Aboriginal Peoples of the Lower Yenisei Valley: An Ethnographic Overview of Recent Political Developments in North Central Siberia." *Polar Geography and Geology* 19(3): 184–218.

_____. 1998. "Property as a Way of Knowing in Evenki Lands in Arctic Siberia." In *Property Relations: Renewing the Anthropological Tradition.* C. M. Hann, ed. Cambridge: Cambridge University Press.

Andreev, V. N. 1958. *Perspektivy razvitiia olenevodstva na severe Vostochnoi Sibiri.* Noril'sk: Tipografiia Noril'skogo kombinata.

Anisimov, A. F. 1963. "The Shaman's Tent of the Evenki and the Origins of Shamanistic Rite." In *Studies in Siberian Shamanism.* H. N. Michael, ed. 199–238. Anthropology of the North: Translations from Russian Sources, 4. Toronto: University of Toronto Press.

Bird-David, Nurit. 1983. "Wage-Gathering: Socio-Economic Changes and the Case of the Food-Gathering Naikens of South India." *Rural South Asia: Linkages, Change, and Development.* P. Rolob, ed. 83: 57–87. London, Curzon Press.

Bjorklund, I. 1990. "Sami Reindeer Pastoralism as an Indigenous Resource Management System in Northern Norway: A Contribution to the Common Property Debate." *Development and Change* 21: 75–86.

Brightman, R. 1993. *Grateful Prey: Rock Cree Animal-Human Relationships*. Berkeley: University of California Press.

Chichlo, B. 1981. "Les nevuqaghmiit ou la fin d'une ethnie." *Etudes/Inuit/Studies* 5(2): 29–47.

Descola, P., and Palsson, G., eds. 1996. *Nature and Society: Anthropological Perspectives*. New York: Routledge.

Dolgikh, B. O. 1929. "Naselenie poluostrova Taimyra i prelegaiushchego k nemu raiona." *Severnaia Aziia* 2: 49–76.

_____. 1952. "Proiskhozhdenie nganasanov." In *Sibirskii etnograficheskii sbornik 1*. L. P. Potapov and M. G. Levin, eds. 5–87. Trudy instituta etnografii AN SSSR (novaia seriia), tom 18. Moscow: Izdatel'stvo Akademii nauk SSSR.

_____. 1963. "Proiskhozhdenie dolgan." In *Sibirskii etnograficheskii sbornik 5*. B. O. Dolgikh, ed. 92–141. Trudy instituta etnografii AN SSSR (novaia seriia), tom 84. Moscow: Izdatel'stvo Akademii nauk SSSR.

Ermolova, N. V. 1992. "Evenki: problema etnicheskikh razlichii i lokal'nykh grupp." In *Etnosy i etnicheskie protsessy. Pamiati P.F. Itsa*. V. A. Popov, ed. 97–106.

Feit, H. 1986. "Hunting and the Quest for Power: The James Bay Cree and Whitemen in the Twentieth Century." In *Native Peoples: The Canadian Experience*. R. B. Morrison and C. R. Wilson, eds. 171–207. Toronto: McClellan & Stewart.

_____. 1994. "The Enduring Pursuit: Land, Time and Social Relationships in Anthropological Models of Hunter-Gatherers and in Subarctic Hunters' Images." In *Key Issues in Hunter-Gatherer Research*. E. Burch and L. Ellanna, eds. 421–40. Oxford: Berg.

Fienup-Riordan, A. 1994. *Boundaries and Passages: Rule and Ritual in Yup'ik Eskimo Oral Tradition*. Norman: University of Oklahoma Press.

Forsyth, J. 1992. *A History of the Peoples of Siberia: Russia's North Asian Colony 1581–1990*. New York: Cambridge University Press.

Gow, P. 1993. "Gringos and Wild Indians: Images of History in Western Amazonian Cultures." *L'Homme* 33(2–4): 327–47.

Grant, B. 1995. *In the Soviet House of Culture: A Century of Perestroikas*. Princeton, N.J.: Princeton University Press.

Gurvich, I. S. 1962. "The Ethnic Affiliation of the Population of the Northwest of the Yakut ASSR." In *Studies in Siberian Ethnogenesis*, H. N. Michael, ed. 2–23. Anthropology of the North: Translations from Russian Sources, 2. Toronto: University of Toronto Press.

_____. 1977. *Kul'tura severnykh yakutov-olenevodov*. Moscow: Nauka.

Hallowell, A. I. 1960. "Ojibwa Ontology, Behaviour, and World View." In *Culture in History: Essays in Honour of Paul Radin*. S. Diamond, ed. 12–52. New York: Columbia University Press.

Jochelson, W. 1926. *The Yukaghir and the Yukaghirized Tungus*. American Museum of Natural History Memoir, 9. Leiden: E. J. Brill.

Kaiser, R. J. 1994. *The Geography of Nationalism in Russia and the USSR*. Princeton, N.J.: Princeton University Press.

Karlov, V. V. 1982. *Evenki v XVII-nachale XX v. (khoziaistvo i sotsial'naia struktura)*. Moscow: Izdatel'stvo Moskovskogo gosudarstvennogo universiteta.

Lashov, B. V., and O. L. Litovka. 1982. *Sotsial'no-ekonomicheskie problemy razvitiia narodnostei Krainego Severa*. Leningrad: Nauka.

Leach, E. R. 1964. *Political Systems of Highland Burma: A Study of Kachin Social Structure*. London: Athlone Press.

Michael, H. N., ed. 1962. *Studies in Siberian Ethnogenesis*. Anthropology of the North: Translations from Russian Sources, 2. Toronto: University of Toronto Press.

Morantz, T. 1983. *An Ethnohistorical Study of Eastern James Bay Cree Social Organization, 1700–1850*. Canadian Ethnology Service Paper, 88. Ottawa: National Museums of Canada.

Myers, Fred R. 1988. "Critical Trends in the Study of Hunter-Gatherers." *Annual Review of Anthropology* 172: 61–82.

Pomishin, S. B. 1990. *Proiskhozhdenie olenevodstva i domestikatsiia severnogo olenia.* Moscow: Nauka.

Popov, A. A. 1934. "Zatundrinskie krest'iane." *Sovetskaia etnografiia* 3: 77–86.

Preston, R. J. 1975. *Cree Narrative: Expressing the Personal Meaning of Events.* Canadian Ethnology Service Paper, 30. Ottawa: National Museums of Canada.

Raeff, M. 1956. *Siberia and the Reforms of 1822.* Seattle: University of Washington Press.

Schweitzer, P. 1993. "Rediscovering a Continent: Siberian Peoples and the Hunter-Gatherer Debate." Paper presented at the Seventh International Conference on Hunting and Gathering Societies (CHAGS 7) in Moscow, Russia, August 1993.

Scollon, R., and. S. B. K. Scollon. 1979. *Linguistic Convergence: An Ethnography of Speaking at Fort Chipewyan, Alberta.* New York: Academic Press.

Scott, C. 1989. "Knowledge Construction among Cree Hunters: Metaphors and Literal Understanding." *Journal de la Société des Americanistes* 75: 193–208.

Severnyi kruzhok Instituta Narodov Severa. 1930. *Taiga i tundra sbornik No. 2.* Leningrad: Izdatel'stvo kraevedcheskogo kruzhka INS.

Shirokogoroff, S. M. 1935. *Psychomental Complex of the Tungus.* London: Kegan Paul, Trench, Trubner.

Slezkine, Y. 1994. *Arctic Mirrors: Russia and the Small Peoples of the North.* Ithaca, N.Y.: Cornell University Press.

Syroechkovskii, E. E. 1984. *Wild Reindeer of the Soviet Union.* New Dehli: Amerind Publishing Co.

Tanner, A. 1979. *Bringing Home Animals: Religious Ideology and Mode of Production of the Mistassini Cree Hunters.* St. John's, Newfoundland: Institute of Social and Economic Research.

Terletskii, P. E. 1951. "Eshche raz k voprosu ob etnicheskom sostave naseleniia Severo-Zapadnoi chasti Yakutskoi ASSR." *Sovetskaia etnografiia* 1: 88–99. Newfoundland

Troshev, Z. 1993. "Taimyrskaia tragediia: fragment rukopisi." *Krasnoiarskii rabochii* vyp. 12-go oktiabria.

Tugolukov, V. A. 1985. *Tungusy (evenki i eveny) Srednei i Zapadnoi Sibiri.* Moscow: Nauka.

Turov, M. G. 1990. *Khoziaistvo evenkov taezhnoi zony srednei Sibiri XIX–XX.* Irkutsk: Irkutskii gosudarstvennii universitet.

Ubriatova, E. I. 1985. *Yazyk noril'skikh dolgan.* Novosibirsk: Nauka.

Vasilevich, G. M. 1969. *Evenki. Istoriko-etnograficheskie ocherki (XVIII– nachalo XX v.).* Leningrad: Nauka.

Vasil'ev, V. I., and Iu. B. Simchenko. 1963. "Sovremennoe samodiiskoe naselenie Taimyra." *Sovetskaia etnografiia* 3: 9–20.

Vitebsky, P. 1992. "The Crisis in Siberian Reindeer Herding Today: A Technical or a Social Problem?" In *Modern Siberia: Social and Economic Developments.* A. Wood and W. Joyce, eds. London: Routledge.

WWF-Arctic Programme. 1993. *Nature Reserves on Taimyr.* Oslo: WWF- Norway.

Chapter 13

MARGINALITY WITH A DIFFERENCE, OR HOW THE HUAORANI PRESERVE THEIR SHARING RELATIONS AND NATURALIZE OUTSIDE POWERS

———=◦《◉》◦=———

Laura Rival

The Huaorani, a small group of Amazonian hunters and gatherers,[1] inhabit the heart of the Ecuadorian Amazon, between the Napo and Curaray Rivers. Before their "pacification" by an evangelical mission, the Summer Institute of Linguistics (SIL) in the early 1960s, they lived in highly dispersed, semiautarkic, and transient collective dwellings located on hilltops away from rivers. Traditional longhouses—of approximately ten to thirty-five members—were typically composed of an older couple (often a man married to one, two, or three sisters), their daughters (with, when married, their husbands and children), and their unmarried sons. Each of these self-sufficient and dispersed residential units formed strong alliances with two or three others, while avoiding contact with all others houses. In this way, allied houses formed regional groups within which most marriages took place.

The Huaorani number 1,370 today (they were no more than 600 fourteen years ago), and 55 percent of the present-day population are under the age of sixteen. Two percent of the population is still uncontacted and lives in hiding. Although the advance of oil prospecting and the civilizing actions of SIL missionaries have resulted in sedentarization and riverine adaptation with the concentration of 80 percent of the population on less than 10 percent of the traditional territory (called the Protectorate), it is still through hunting and gathering in the forest that people secure their daily subsistence and retain their distinctive way of apprehending the world. Forest resources represent the bounty created by the daily consumption activities of past generations. The "natural abundance" of forest resources thus represents the exogenous creation of wealth. Like the trees associated with forebears that continuously provide for the living (Rival 1993b), foreign organizations such as the SIL, the oil companies prospecting on Huaorani land, and state schools are perceived as giving agencies. As such, they are expected to meet people's modern needs *without asking anything in return*. The Huaorani population has adjusted to demographic growth and increased population density by tapping new sources of food. Former enemies[2] in mixed communities are willing to share with each other as long as sharing neither creates obligations nor requires the management of scarce resources.

One way of presenting the Huaorani is to say that they are marginal, impoverished, decultured, exploited by other social groups (including indigenous peoples with a longer historical experience of interethnic contact), and, above all, dominated by—and entirely dependent on—powerful transnational companies exploiting oil in their territory. Such portrayals can be found almost daily in Ecuadorian newspapers or environmental NGO bulletins. This chapter will explain interactions between Huaorani people and the dominant society, taking the Huaorani social philosophy as a starting point. What seems to many environmentalists and indigenous leaders struggling for the recognition of indigenous territorial rights and for indigenous control over natural resources as childlike or beggarlike behavior[3] may be understood as a form of resistance. To substantiate this assertion, I provide an overview of the political economy of the Amazon region of Ecuador in which Huaorani society is now enclaved and summarize Huaorani dealings and interactions with "The Company."[4] I then turn to the traditional political strategy of fierce isolationism to examine its nature in the light of inter- and intraethnic social dynamics, as well as of the central cultural concept of "natural abundance."

The ONHAE-Maxus Friendship Agreement

On 13 August 1993, the ONHAE (Organización de la Nacionalidad Huaorani de la Amazónica Ecuatoriana, the Organization of the Huaorani Nationality of the Ecuadorian Amazon) signed an "Agreement of Friendship, Respect, and Mutual Support" with Maxus Ecuador Inc.[5] for a term of twenty years. This "agreement of good faith" binds the oil company to provide assistance to the Huaorani Nation in areas of education, health, and community development and to program "specific nondependency creating actions that will enhance the Huaorani's capacity for self-management." The treaty stipulates that Maxus, in addition to providing the goods and services requested by any Huaorani community,[6] offering vocational training, and giving Huaorani men employment priority in Block 16, has the prime responsibility of coordinating all scientific research on the Huaorani population and on the territory they inhabit, including the Yasuni National Park. The agreement is signed by the general manager of Maxus Ecuador Inc. and by the president of ONHAE. The witnesses of honor are: the president of Ecuador, Ecuador's minister of energy and mines, Ecuador's minister of national defense, and the executive president of PetroEcuador (Maxus 1994).

This agreement, which, in more than one respect, deserves to be compared with agreements and treaties signed between Native Americans and Euro-American commercial institutions in the course of history, raises a number of questions. The first two to come to mind are: Under what circumstances has an oil company, whose headquarters are located in Dallas, Texas, and whose primary obligation is to increase the company's profits by exploiting oil fields throughout the world, decided to turn itself into a scientific research station, as well as an NGO? Can a population of less than 1,400 living in a country of almost eleven million inhabitants, which signs a treaty with a powerful North American transnational company in a ceremony where the guests of honor are no less than this country's president and the official executives of its two most powerful ministries, really be considered marginal? These two questions cannot be answered without considering the Huaorani's encounter with the oil industry, or sketching the political economy of the "Oriente" (the name Ecuadorians give to their country's Amazon Region).

The Political Economy of a Key Marginal Region

Over 99 percent of Ecuador's oil comes from the Oriente (Ortiz and Varea 1995: 75). Oil revenues represent 18 percent of the GDP, provide 67 percent of Ecuador's export earnings, and account for 57 percent of the national budget. Despite the alarming depletion of oil reserves and falling prices on the world market, the national economy's dependency on this nonrenewable resource is not likely to diminish in the years to come. Ecuador now produces more oil of lesser quality, which sells at a lesser price, than when it was a member of OPEC. It specializes in heavy crudes, now imports fuel oil for its domestic consumption, and is planning to exploit all of the Oriente's deposits, no matter how reduced their size or heavy their crude. The demand for oil and oil derivatives is always increasing, and even oil exploitation in remote jungle areas has become profitable.

The largest part of Ecuador's oil revenues is used to repay the international debt and to import fuel oil. Oil revenues are also crucial to government funding for public services, particularly health and education. The oil industry, which was initially placed under the firm control of the army and of the state-owned company CEPE (Corporación Estatal Petrolera Ecuatoriana, the State Petroleum Corporation of Ecuador), is now almost entirely dependent on foreign investments and controlled by transnational companies, a large percentage of which is North American. Ecuador has granted concessions (each generally consisting of 200,000 hectares of indigenous land and/or primary rain forest) to foreign companies who assume the financial risk of exploring the forest subsoil and who are given the right to exploit profitable fields.[7] As reserves of petroleum are expected to last only fifteen years, foreign companies have an incentive to build the productive infrastructure as cheaply and quickly as possible and extract all the petroleum they can before the contract ends (see Kimerling 1991). Recent articles by oil engineers (Narvaez 1996) and economists (Acosta 1996) have argued that Maxus, whose costs of operation have been abnormally high and who received unique concessionary favors from former governments, has made profits in exploiting the heavy crudes of Block 16 not by creating new wealth, but rather by despoiling the national company PetroEcuador from two of its best wells in the area.

Although it is Amazon petroleum that has opened the longest and greatest period of economic growth in the history of Ecuador, the Oriente has benefited very little from it (World Bank 1990). For instance, while its population, which is growing at a rate of 4.9 percent per year (against 2.5 percent in the country as a whole), represents almost 4 percent of the national population, it receives only 2 percent of the national public sector investments. Furthermore, despite new legislation, the Oriente remains one of Ecuador's most marginalized regions. The weakness of the state in the Oriente, coupled with a number of international processes, such as those linked to the ratification of the biodiversity treaty and other international agreements for environmental protection and the defense of indigenous rights, has led some oil companies to take on the responsibility of directly and actively involving themselves in the social development of indigenous communities. The ONHAE-Maxus "Agreement of Friendship, Respect, and Mutual Support" is a good example of this new type of company policy.

However novel the model, it is not without precedents. A social fund[8] for the purchase of light equipment and the construction of community buildings in rural areas close to CEPE operations was created in 1984. CEPE social policy was primarily a response to organized protests against the fact that oil revenues did not benefit those who lived where oil was extracted. The following pattern summarizes these conflicts and their resolution. An extractive company develops its activities without consulting the local population, which either is native to the area and sees its property rights violated, or is colonist, very poor, and entirely dependent on the company and the frontier economy it creates.[9] The local population interferes with the company's activities in order to obtain social benefits that it should normally obtain from the state. As even the slightest disruption of drilling operations quickly amounts to thousands of dollars in losses, the company agrees to cover the cost of providing goods and services to the community as an economical solution. A consensus emerges between the two parties as the company accepts the responsibility to compensate the community for damages caused by petroleum development, and as the locals agree that such support to community development fairly redresses the societal prejudice and neglect they have suffered.

During the 1990s, the idea that social and environmental considerations should go hand in hand has given shape to a model of community development fund whose objectives are: (1) to control the negative impact of petroleum development on the environment, (2) to give impulse to the socioeconomic development of the communities affected by petroleum industry, (3) to project a positive corporate image, and (4) to support scientific research. With PetroEcuador replacing CEPE (PetroEcuador is itself fragmented into a number of subsidiaries and is the contractor of numerous transnational companies), the responsibility of designing and implementing a social and environmental policy has devolved to each block's main operator. This measure institutionalizes the fact that the state devolves the task of administrating the Oriente's populations living on concession land to the oil companies. As the Maxus community relations program amply illustrates, the model of development used by an oil company need not be different from the national and dominant state paradigm. The goal remains to give "impulse to socioeconomic and cultural change for the total incorporation of the indigenous sector into modernity and economic development" (Milton Ortega, personal communication, June 1994).

Working for "The Company"

Close to 90 percent of all Huaorani adult men worked for "The Company"[10] as unskilled laborers (to be more precise, as "macheteros" opening seismic trails) on short contracts between 1985 and 1992. Today, less than 10 percent work for wages in the oil sector. This is because oil exploration, the most labor-intensive phase in petroleum development, is almost over now, especially in Huaorani land, where Ecuador's new major fields have been under production since 1994. Although the period of significant employment was short and has now ended, it reveals key features of Huaorani responses to the oil frontier, including the initial systematic invasion and looting of oil camps located on their hunting grounds.

During my first period of fieldwork in 1989–90, I observed that Huaorani men were notified of the start of a new seismic program by radio. They would then discuss the matter among themselves, evaluating each other's intentions of enrolling. Although the final decision was always left to the individual, a clear—albeit diffuse and informal—consensus always arose as to who would leave or stay in the community. What made men decide to work on a particular contract was not so much a need for cash, but the timing, location and composition of the work team. Before deciding whether to enroll, they would check whether close kin living in other communities were going to be among the crew. Companie Générale de Géophysique's (CGG) files on Huaorani workers showed that the common pattern was for groups of agnatic kin to work in areas once occupied by their ascendants, that is, hunting territories that had been abandoned by their parents or themselves when the SIL came to relocate them westward in the "Protectorate" (Rival 1996). Informal conversations with workers both in the camps and in their homes confirmed my hypothesis that by opening seismic trails in a particular area, men felt they were reclaiming particular stretches of forest and securing their groups' territorial rights against potential encroachments or counterclaims. Finally, even though they would rarely enroll for contracts longer than eight weeks, married men would leave their communities only if their houses were in good condition and their wives had sufficient food supplies.

It is worth adding that Huaorani men had employment priority for all the exploration programs taking place on Huaorani land and the adjacent Yasuni National Park. This measure had been suggested to the companies by the missions, especially the Capuchino Mission in Coca.[11] Moreover, Huaorani men were allowed to terminate their contracts before the end, an option that a significant proportion (around 30 percent) took up. I should also mention the fact that a number of companies prospecting in the vicinity of Huaorani villages ended up modifying their usual work planning so as to treat these villages as additional camps to be serviced and supplied, a decision that outraged the remaining companies, which experienced a recrudescence in camp looting.[12] I came to realize that the pressure exercised by married women (via reported gossip of marital unfaithfulness or unorthodox long visits to kin living in other communities) was often the reason why men chose to shorten their stay with the company. It was also women who pressured the company to send helicopters with food supplies, which they saw as a minimum compensation for the temporary loss of access to their husbands' productive activities.

The work Huaorani men perform as macheteros—clearing the forest with machetes and axes—is more intense and harder than, but not different from, garden clearing work. As a matter of fact, the same term (*omëre quëqui*, "doing in the bush") is used for both activities. When referring to their "work journeys" for CGG or Geosource, men say that they were "busy land doing in the company," with the connotation of going on long treks in the forest and having to carry heavy loads back. The term *tabado*, from *trabajo*, the Spanish word for "work," is used for the long-term salaried occupations of young schooled men, for instance, the public relations jobs offered by Maxus to ONHAE leaders.

In the camps, although Huaorani men socialize with non-Huaorani workers, they tend to stick together, and at a safe distance from the rest of the crew. They always sleep, bathe, and eat together and apart from the Quichua, Shuar, or mestizo workers. What they enjoy the most about their work experience is to be in parts of the forest they have never visited before. As the camps move along seismic lines every two or three days, by the end of a full contract, they have known firsthand about 1,200 km of forest tracks. They also enjoy flying in helicopters, acquiring a whole range of objects, and having meals cooked for them. Helicopters are often the only possible means of transport between camps. Given the prohibitive cost of transporting camp equipment (tents, plates, cooking pots, blankets, containers, etc.) and seismic survey equipment (electric wire, tubes, iron sheets, etc.), these materials are simply left behind, most often for the Huaorani's exclusive use, as no other worker would venture back into the forest to get the discarded gear.

Camp visiting blends smoothly within foraging activities and nomadic movements, and Huaorani workers are frequently visited by their relatives. Visitors sometimes stay several days, fascinated by the camp's food organization, and particularly captivated by the food supplies brought by helicopter to the camps every few days. Visitors ask the cooks who prepare the crew's daily meals to give them some food. If this is refused, they simply take everything, justifying their action on the ground that all the cooks have to do is send a radio message to the main camp near Coca to get a helicopter back with replacement stocks.

After the company's departure, seismic trails are used for hunting, and helicopter landing sites (heliports) become garden clearings. Huaorani men feel they work for themselves as much as for the company, and for food and raw materials rather than for wages. If they do not see the rationale for opening thousands of kilometers of trails or for detonating tons of explosives in the forest, they appreciate the company's efficiency and material wealth. The company has chainsaws, outboard motors, trucks, and helicopters; it has good kitchens, plenty of food and clothes; it works fast and moves about swiftly. The high technology performance is taken for granted as the company's intrinsic quality. I suspect that no one really believed my statement that when my grandmother's mother was born, oil had just been discovered; engines did not exist; and cars, planes, and helicopters had not yet been invented.

In addition to seismic prospection, Huaorani people have seen the drilling of numerous exploratory wells throughout the 1980s and the 1990s. Before a well is drilled, service companies (several of which work on the site for four or five months) clear the site, which buzzes with noise and activity, the sky crisscrossed with helicopters and the ground cluttered with heavy machinery. These sites become the centers of intense village disputes. For example, when the platform for PetroCanada's exploratory well was built in the spring of 1989, about one hundred Huaorani from four villages (Dayuno, Huamono, Zapino, and Golondrina) were employed for two months. Fierce competition developed between the four villages, each claiming exclusive rights over the well site and the goods it contained. Each village wanted the company to give it food, clothes, tools, outboard motors, and chainsaws in exchange for the right to work on Huaorani land without disruption or disturbance. But villagers could agree neither on who had the legitimate right to make such a demand, nor on equally sharing the benefits between the four settlements.

These ethnographic facts lead me to conclude that the Huaorani have largely been successful at fitting oil prospection activities into their overall "economy of procurement"[13] (Bird-David 1992). They have used the work they were asked to perform to reinforce specific kin ties and make claims on new territories; they have sold their labor force on their own terms; and, finally, they have used the companies to strengthen traditional patterns of intraethnic alliance and enmity.

The Sharing of Natural Abundance

There is no word in Huaorani to translate literally what I call "natural abundance," but this does not mean that the term does not capture the indigenous representation of the relationship between living people, the forest, and past generations. A number of superlatives, emphatic suffix markers, adverbial forms, and, above all, speech diacritics (tone of voice, wordless exclamations, gestures) are used to convey the ravished pleasure and enthusiastic excitation caused by the sight—or the recall—of an abundance of objects, particularly useful resources and foodstuff. But products of what we would call human labor do not cause such admiration and enthusiasm. For example, none of the aforementioned superlatives would apply to a large manioc garden under production, a hip of hunted game, or collected nuts. A peccary herd passing by may cause much excitement ("they were so many, many, many of them!"), but no one would exclaim "They are so many of them!" at the sight of twenty hunted, dead peccaries waiting to be butchered and cooked. Similarly, a palm grove with ripening fruit will cause the ravished exclamation, "There is so much fruit, it is ripe!" but no one will marvel at the five or six big jars of fruit drink lining the longhouse wall. However, in the summer of 1996, when I arranged the seventy-five bush knives I had brought as presents for my adopted *nanicabo* (longhouse group) and its allies on the longhouse floor to dry, my classificatory father yelled in joy: "There are so many of them, so many that I can't count."

Although our conception of human labor is multilayered, the meanings deposited by Greek philosophy, Christianity, Hegel with his principle of domination and objectification, and Marx with his theory of increasing socialization through the intentional transformation of nature, are all converging to form the deeply rooted Western idea that labor is the quintessential expression of human nature,[14] the most social and powerful means for self-realization. This conception of work, which has rendered difficult the task of recognizing foraging as a productive—hence social—activity (Ingold 1988), prevents us from understanding Huaorani antiproductivism.

What makes Huaorani thinking so different from our own is their representation of the natural environment as comprising elements that are the direct manifestations and concrete objectifications of *past* human labor. The presence in the forest of abundant resources is thought to result from the daily productive and consumptive activities performed by people who died long ago. A hilltop is covered with producing palms because "the grandparents used to live there, they built their longhouse, they lived together without splitting up, and made gardens to feast with the enemies … do you see this fish poison vine? My grandmother must have made it grow here, look, there used to be a creek down there, she fished in it." Those are remarks I heard over and over again while walking through the forest with informants. In the course of living, a residential group hunts, gathers, and manages a whole range of useful plants along hunting trails and streams. People cook and eat, discard fruit seeds, throw away roots, and cut down trees, providing light for other tree species to grow. People are totally aware of these processes and of the intimate, symbiotic connections between their being alive (i.e., producing and consuming) and the state of the forest. They are also conscious that their present activities are the necessary conditions for future activities.

This representation of the forest as a giving environment is therefore quite straightforward and apparently devoid of ideological connotations. It is almost like an observation denoting sound ecological knowledge. There is no exchange with the dead, for they do not ask for anything. What they "give" to the living is not really a gift, anyway. It is more like a byproduct, a consequence of the fact that they spent their lives giving to, and receiving from, each other. Today's useful resources are the legacy of their sharing economy. So the living owe nothing to the dead. As a matter of fact, if the living can recognize in the landscape the activities of past people, they can never be sure of whom they were. My informants would invariably say that such a plant was put in such a place by those belonging to the longhouse of ..., and they would cite the name of a remembered (great-) grandfather or (great-) grandmother, somewhat hesitantly as if aware of the conjectural character of the allegation. How can we know with certainty whose activities have created abundance when residential groups are so mobile, and when so many different historical groups (not all Huaorani) have lived in the anthropogenized parts of the forest? What is important is that human work can be recognized in the landscape, and identified as *the* source of abundance for the living.

The longhouse residential group (*nanicabo*), which shows no age or sex segregation and which may number between ten and thirty-five members, constitutes the basic unit of Huaorani society. Most *nanicabo* members hunt and gather every day, generally alone. The goal of each "procurer" is to obtain enough food to feed her- or himself and to share with coresidents. Even young children make sure they always possess enough foodstuff, not only for their own consumption, but to give away—especially to their grandmothers, mothers, and elder sisters. Personal autonomy, a core value, is best expressed as the individual's ability to extract from the forest and carry back to the longhouse fairly large quantities of food. As most productive activities are performed individually, social life is organized around the collective sharing of food individually procured. In other words, whereas the longhouse economy is structured by the sharing of forest food individually obtained by each member, the *nanicabo* is reproduced as a collectivity based on nonreciprocal relations, in which givers do not become creditors, or receivers, debtors.

Relations of sharing at the level of the longhouse residence unit must be understood in the light of both autarkic closure and relative hostility between longhouse clusters. When demographically stable, the overall population is divided into dispersed networks of intermarrying longhouses separated by vast stretches of unoccupied forest. For greater security and autonomy, longhouse residential groups tend to isolate themselves from most other groups. Marriage alliances create solidarity and unity between longhouses exchanging marriage partners. These loose aggregates, sometimes called *huaomoni* (we-people), maintain relations of latent hostility with all other groups, which they call "others" or "enemies"(*huarani*). Members of longhouses that are not related by marriage avoid meeting and often ignore each other's exact location. However, their isolation from each other is relative, as they are connected through personal relationships, at least potentially. Kin living in nonallied longhouses reactivate their ties whenever spouses are scarce, or social disruptions caused by warfare are too acute. Huaorani society could not continue to exist as a separate entity without the periodic renewal of intraethnic alliances. By contrast, the rift between Huaorani (the word literally means "true human beings") and Cohuori, i.e., all other ethnic groups (literally, "cannibal predators") is absolute and unbreachable. The Cohuori are exterminators who prey unilaterally on the Huaorani, their victims. The Huaorani attribute their survival to their assertive and drastic isolationism. For centuries, they have lived in the interstices between greater and more powerful ethnic groups as nomadic and autarkic enclaves fiercely refusing contact, trade, and exchange with their powerful neighbors.

Drinking ceremonies or dance and song festivals are organized whenever there is an abundance of fruit, mainly peach palm (*Bactris gasipaes*) and banana (*Musa sapientum*). In their songs, feast-goers identify with birds gorging themselves on seasonal fruit. The chants they endlessly repeat throughout the night tell of birds gathered on a tree covered with ripening fruit. The vivid lyrics describe the colors, noises, and movements of the flying creatures, as well as the sweetness and abundance of the juices that compel them to congregate. When no fruit is left, they all leave and fly away, each bird going back to its own business. In this collective representation of the feasting group, the emphasis is on individual freedom and independence. The only thing that binds feast-goers together is the pleasure of consuming abundant and delicious food. No obligations or rights make them dependent on each other. If food is abundant, there is congregation and sharing. Food sharing at feasts, however, is not comparable with *nanicabo* food sharing, characterized by repetitive giving away that crystallizes enduring social units. Feast-goers do not share food; they jointly and liberally consume products from a natural source, a tree.

Manioc drinking ceremonies make for an interesting variant, for they result from *created*, rather than natural, abundance. The preparation of manioc into ceremonial drink, which entails far more work than the preparation of banana or palm fruit, requires furthermore its symbolic transformation into fruit. Manioc drinking ceremonies are planned by, and organized under the leadership of, a married couple called for the occasion *ahuene* (literally "of the tree") or owners of the feast. Their hard work and role in coordinating the collective production of food surplus is hidden behind symbolic imagery equating them with trees whose abundant fruit result from growth and maturation processes that can be traced back to the daily procuring activities of dead people. I have discussed elsewhere (Rival 1993a; 1993b; 1998a) the political significance of such ceremonies.

Ceremonial consumption, particularly in the case of manioc drinking celebrations, points to the structuring significance of the host-guest relationship, which is constituted by unilateral giving within a social field comprising not only human actors, but also living organisms and artifacts (Rival 1996). The Huaorani word for guest is *ne eñaca*, "the one who is born," while the word for host is *ne ocöinga*, "the one who is at home." Hosts are in the house, or of the house, and as such are required to give to their guests, unilaterally and upon request. A host, by giving away to the guest without expecting anything in return, is like a reproductive couple, a nurturing parent, a tree. In analytical terms, the host is like the *ahuene* who ritually create the conditions for natural abundance, and like forebears who continue to provide even after their death. Guests, on the other hand, are pure consumers, just like newborn babies. They are exogenous to the *nanicabo* they visit, but would slowly become part of it if they were to prolong their visit. A visitor is entitled to anything she or he sees and would like to have. But if the visitor stays on for more than a day, she or he must start giving away as much as she or he receives, thus entering the ambiguous category of half-visitor, half-refugee resident. This is why visiting patterns are highly restrictive, especially for women.

Who Are the Guests?

The host-guest relationship consists of the dynamic interaction between providers of "natural abundance" and the consumers who request it, and operates in everyday social life, as well as in the ritual context. It puts in relation categories of kin (especially across generations), the living and the dead, and groups of people with certain classes of animals and plants. Children start their social life as their parents' guests (Rival 1998b); visitors are guests; coresidents, busily engaged in continuous giving and receiving acts, are simultaneously guests and hosts; old people, who receive more than they can give away, progressively become their children's guests, until they die. Pets, the surviving offspring of hunted animals, are the guests of the longhouse in which they reside. The endogamous feast group celebrating a marriage in the palm grove that has grown on the dwelling site of their ascendants is in a way their guest. On the symbolic and representational level, the dynamism of unilateral giving turns sources of wealth (parents, hosts, or forebears) into natural objects (trees), and seekers of wealth into human consumers.

The propensity to turn unilateral givers from providers of natural abundance into natural objects partly explains the ways in which Huaorani people have reacted and adapted to outsiders, particularly corporate ones. Missions and companies are impersonal donors with the unlimited capacity to create abundance, that is, to provide enormous quantities of food and manufactured goods upon demand. The SIL missionaries, who, from the mid-1960s to the mid-1970s, prompted the Huaorani to relocate on their mission base, have progressively introduced new garden crops, shotguns, dogs, and Western medicine, as well as the intensive use of air transport and radio contacts (Rival 1994; 1996; Stoll 1982; Wallis 1971). Moreover, they have habituated the population to a sedentary existence in communities organized around airstrips and led by powerful outsiders whose ability to "attract" large flows of free manufactured goods secures unity and stability. Today, the powerful outsiders work for Maxus.

The SIL missionaries legitimated their presence and Bible translation work by presenting themselves as the relatives (wives and sisters) of the five missionaries killed by the Huaorani (Stoll 1982; Wallis 1971). Maxus legitimates its presence and industrial activities by signing an "agreement of friendship and mutual support," which turns its employees into welcome guests. On one level, the end result is identical, for both corporate organizations engage, often against their primary intention, in large-scale distributive actions and social engineering activities. However, their respective claims for legitimacy are, I wish to argue, accepted on slightly different grounds.

The legitimacy of the evangelical missionaries is founded on the life-long relationship between a Huaorani woman, Dayuma, and a North American missionary, Rachel Saint, a relationship sealed in the death of their brothers.[15] Dayuma had lived for many years with the Cohuori (hence taken for dead) when she eventually came back with Rachel to live among her people. Dayuma and Rachel, both legitimate outsiders, founded the largest Huaorani community by attracting and retaining followers through the control they exercised over marriage alliances, and through their ability to provide continuous fluxes of goods and foodstuff.

The staff members of Maxus, on the other hand, have no personal connections or kinship ties to offer; they are "friends" and "guests." The irony of the situation is that while they use the terms with reference to Western meanings (the relationship between friends is based on trust, equality, and free choice; the relationship between hosts and guests is based on the latter's respect of the former's rights of ownership and lead), they seem to be unaware of an inherent contradiction: Westerners do not treat friends as guests, and the guests we invite over are not necessarily friends. In any case, the Huaorani guest-host relationship is entirely different from the Western one. Guests are not friends, but a particular category of relatives. The relation between guests and hosts is not mutual, but structured by demand sharing, with hosts as "givers" and guests as "demanders." Since the relation between hosts and guests, fraught with ambiguity and dormant hostility, must be punctual, in no way can Maxus staff be defined as invited guests. Moreover, the mutualism envisaged between the company and the Huaorani population is not based on comparable benefits. Maxus does not need anything from the Huaorani; it is basically paying for peace. The underlying reasoning goes something like: "We are here to do a job. Please let us do our job. If you do not disturb us, we'll give you things you want." It could be argued that the Huaorani do not need anything from Maxus either. They are searching for an inexhaustible source of outside goods and foodstuff, whatever its origin or form. It follows that it is not Maxus, but the Huaorani, consumers of natural abundance, who are the guests.

It can be argued that the impersonal source of wealth represented by Maxus is likened to that which makes the forest a bountiful environment, i.e., the activities of long dead people. But however impersonal, the activities of a transnational company take place in the present and hence are attributable to some form of contemporary agency. This is why Maxus's wealth is perceived as being ambiguous. It is in part a source of natural abundance (i.e., of the same nature as the productive landscape, which results from past human action), and in part a source of created abundance (i.e., like the artificial abundance brought about by the work of the *ahuene*). Like the givers of a manioc feast, the company operates on contested terrain. Both clear the forest to establish rights over new territories, and both give away large quantities of goods to their guests, who may become allies or enemies. Both present themselves as producers of "natural abundance" (hiding the fact that it results from intensified productive activities), and treat their guests as overconsumers.

Compared to what it was less than forty years ago, Huaorani society has expanded enormously, both demographically and spatially. It has also, despite the present situation of intense contact, achieved a remarkable degree of isolation. The present Huaorani state can be described as one in which units of sharing are reproduced with their egalitarian and antiproductivist structures, and this, fairly independently from each other. Each unit maintains its autonomy and self-sufficiency by securing its own direct access to the new sources of natural abundance. Huaorani society is constituted on the basis of shared experiences of consumption. Huaorani people create and reproduce their separate and autonomous identity by devaluing their participation in social relations of production and giving priority to nonproductive forms of sociality. Concomitantly, they treat powerful outsiders and dominant forces as sources of endlessly renewable wealth.

Maxus has succeeded neither in silencing the Huaorani, nor in circumscribing their demands. Maxus wanted to be the respectful guest allowed to pump oil out of Huaorani land without being disturbed. But the Huaorani consider themselves to be the guests, and their vastly inflated demand-sharing requests can hardly be fulfilled. They may have little power over the future development of the oil industry in the Oriente, but by naturalizing the oil companies and denying all form of exchange or trade with them, they have reduced the power the companies may have over them to the precarious power of a feast-giver whose generosity is artificial and short-lived.

Notes

1. I have argued elsewhere (Rival 1993b) that Huaorani gardening is exceptional. Manioc and plantain are cultivated incipiently and sporadically for the preparation of ceremonial drinks, while daily subsistence is traditionally secured through hunting and gathering.

2. From the mid-1960s to the mid-1970s, the SIL missionaries prompted the Huaorani to relocate on their mission base. Relocated sometimes hundreds of kilometers away from their traditional lands, long-feuding bands have had no choice but to coexist and intermarry. Missionaries vehemently advocated monogamy, sexual modesty, and praying, while strongly discouraging feasts, chants, and dancing. Their influence, combined with the "mixing" of traditionally antagonistic groups and the high number of monogamous marriages between former enemies, put an end to warfare.

3. They contrast the Huaorani's ambivalent and complacent attitude toward oil companies with that of the Canelo Quichuas who, after years of fierce opposition to petroleum development, have taken on the role of political actors capable of negotiating on equal terms with the state and transnational oil companies the terms under which natural resources are to be managed and exploited on their land.

4. "The Company" is the generic term the Huaorani use for the fifty or so subsidiaries and subcontractors operating on Huaorani land.

5. Maxus Ecuador Inc. is a subsidiary of the Texan Maxus Energy Corporation, with headquarters in Dallas and operations in the United States and twelve other countries around the world.

6. Wherever they are located, including outside of Block 16, Maxus's operation block.

7. The contracts, called "service contracts with venture capital," contain a clause by which, during the exploitation phase, the Ecuadorian government, represented by PetroEcuador (formerly CEPE), is required to make two types of payments to the foreign companies it grants a concession to. One is a service fee, and the other a full reimbursement of investment and extraction costs. Both payments are usually collected in crude rather than in cash. It is agreed that the operation will revert to PetroEcuador after twenty years.

8. It is administered by the Unit for Environmental Protection since CEPE became PetroEcuador in 1989.

9. It is misleading to explain the condition of these unauthorized settlers, like that of the thirty thousand colonists who have migrated along the Via Auca, as resulting from poverty and lack of land in the Sierra. The colonists are, in fact, oil workers who do a little bit of agriculture between two contracts. The oil companies build their camps on the plots cleared by the colonists. They buy or rent these plots as if they were private properties, paying high prices to their colonist-workers, who build bars, brothels, and

stores near the camps. They do not make a living by growing coffee or raising cattle, but rather fully depend on the oil companies. They could not possibly be living along an empty road, a road with no Texaco truckdrivers stopping to buy their produce, with no oil workers stepping in to buy their drinks and cigarettes, with no electricity, and no medical care and other services provided free by the oil companies. Without oil companies, there would simply be no colonist living down the Via Auca.

10. Between 1985 and 1992, Huaorani men worked mainly for the two prospecting companies that did most of the seismic surveying in the area, the French CGG (Companie Générale de Géophysique) and the North American Geosource.

11. Coca's Bishop, who belonged to that mission and was the companies' principal adviser on Huaorani affairs, was killed in July 1987 by the Tagaeri, a group of Huaorani who wished to remain uncontacted and deeply resented the presence of oil crews in the forest.

12. When operating on Quichua, Shuar, or colonized land, oil companies may be forced to fund a community development project, but they never have to deliver regular supplies of food to the villages, or fly their sick to the evangelical mission's hospital in Shell-Mera.

13. Bird-David (1992: 40) argues that the subsistence-related activities of hunter-gatherers are neither productive (in the sense of controlling and intentionally transforming the environment), nor foraging (which implies a form of biological determinism). They are activities of "procurement," that is of careful management and acquisition informed by the awareness resulting from actively engaging with the natural world.

14. What Marx actually intended regarding the primordial character of labor and the primacy of production in all societies is far from clear or consistent. As Balbus (1982: 16) points out, Marx sometimes conceives of production as a transhistorical, universally applicable theoretical category, and equates the human condition with production; at other times, he is careful to stress that the category of production is more relevant to characterize *some* historical periods only, particularly the rise of capitalism. This leads him to argue (Balbus 1982: 30) that the ambiguity of Marx's formulation comes from the fact that Marx tends to equate the process of production as a whole with productive activities and the social relations of production. This is highly problematic for noncapitalist societies in which the determination exercised by the mode of production may, in practice and for each, mean something radically different.

15. Dayuma's brother, who speared Rachel's brother to death, was injured by a bullet Rachel's brother shot before dying. He died from the injury about a month later.

References

Acosta, A. 1996. *El Fracaso de los Contratos de Prestación de Servicios*. Quito: ILDIS.

Balbus, I. 1982. *Marxism and Domination: A Neo-Hegelian, Feminist, Psychoanalytic Theory of Sexual, Political, and Technological Liberation*. Princeton, N.J.: Princeton University Press.

Bird-David, N. 1992. "Beyond the Hunting and Gathering Mode of Subsistence: Observations on Nayaka and Other Modern Hunter-Gatherers." *Man* 21(1): 921–47.

Ingold, T. 1988. "Notes on the Foraging Mode of Production." In *Hunters and Gatherers: History, Evolution and Social Change*. T. Ingold, D. Riches, and J. Woodburn, eds. 269–85. Explorations in Anthropology, Vol. 1. New York: Berg.

Kimerling, J. 1991. *Amazon Crude*. New York: NRDC.

Maxus. 1994. *Procedural Manual for the Waorani Territory*. Quito: Maxus Ecuador Inc.

Narvaez, I. 1996. *Poder Etnico, Poder Transnacional. Huaorani vs Maxus*. Quito: Abya-Yala.

Ortiz, P., and A. Varea. 1995. "Introducción." In *Marea Negra en la Amazónia. Conflictos Socioambientales Vinculados a la Actividad Petrolera en el Ecuador*. 15–24. Quito: ILDIS.

Rival, L. 1993a. "Confronting Petroleum Development in the Ecuadorian Amazon: The Huaorani, Human Rights and Environmental Protection." *Anthropology in Action* (BASAPP) 16: 14–15.

_____. 1993b. "The Growth of Family Trees: Huaorani Conceptualization of Nature and Society." *Man* 28(4): 635–52.

_____. 1994. "The Huaorani Indians in the Ecuadorian Consciousness: Otherness Represented and Signified." In *Imagines y Imagineros. Representaciones de los Indigenas Ecuatorianos-Siglo XIX & XX*. B. Muratorio, ed. 253–92. Quito.

_____. 1996. *Hijos del Sol, Padres del Jaguar, los Huaorani Hoy*. Quito: Abya Yala.

_____. 1998a. "Domestication as a Historical and Symbolic Process: Wild Gardens and Cultivated Forests in the Ecuadorian Amazon." In *Principles of Historical Ecology*. William Balée, ed. 232–50. New York: Columbia University Press.

_____. 1998b. "Androgynous Parents and Guest-Children: The Huaorani Couvade." *Journal of the Royal Anthropological Institute* 4(4): 619–42.

Stoll, D. 1982. *Fishers of Men or Founders of Empire? The Wycliffe Bible Translators in Latin America*. London: Zed Press.

Wallis, E. 1971. *Aucas Down River*. New York: Harper & Row.

World Bank. 1990. "Ecuador's Amazon Region: Development Issues and Options." World Bank Discussion Paper 75; prepared by James Hicks et al. Washington, D.C.

PART III

ECOLOGY, DEMOGRAPHY, AND MARKET ISSUES

Chapter 14

"INTEREST IN THE PRESENT" IN THE NATIONWIDE MONETARY ECONOMY

The Case of Mbuti Hunters in Zaire

————=◈=————

Mitsuo Ichikawa

Forms of State Impacts on the Mbuti Society

The impacts of the state on hunting and gathering societies are imposed in both direct and indirect ways. Direct state intervention is obvious, for example, in the state policy for administering hunting and gathering societies. One of the most important problems of African countries is to incorporate hunting and gathering peoples into the newly formed nation-state system. Although African countries are relatively slow in this attempt, they have been trying in various ways to involve such hitherto neglected small-scale societies in nation-building processes.

As far as the Mbuti in the Teturi area of Ituri Forest are concerned, the former Zairian government[1] tried in the early 1970s, after president Mobutu's proclamation concerning "émancipation des pygmées," to sedentarize them along the major roads in order to incorporate their society into the state system. They were induced to build rectangular mud houses of a villager's type and to cultivate the fields around their newly settled villages. Some of them were even given machetes and seeds for cultivating fields of their own. Also, they have recently become subject to government taxation, from which they were previously exempted as *premiers citoyens* (first citizens) of the Zairian nation-state (Grinker 1994). Most of the Mbuti men now hold national identity cards, and occasionally vote in national and local elections. The Mbuti band also has a representative, called the *kapita*, who serves as a liaison with the government administration, helping the census takers, announcing the arrival of tax collectors, and transmitting various demands of government officers.

These forms of participation in the state system are, however, felt as a burden by the Mbuti. They do not feel benefited by the government in a visible way, and call the tax collector *mwizi* (thief) behind the scenes. They may pay the tax in fear of imprisonment, which they know eventually requires more money. Likewise, they are reluctant to go to an election that has no obvious *faida* (benefit). It is the *kapita* who suffers most from such burdens required by the government. If the administrative demands are not met, the *kapita* is ordered to attend the local office and is asked about it. The *kapita* system itself was introduced by external forces for administrative reasons and does not derive from Mbuti social relationships in any sense. Recently, however, the prestige of the *kapita* is being gradually acknowledged by the Mbuti in some areas; this prestige comes not through accumulating wealth or power, but through such sufferings.

In addition to these administrative and political requirements, there are also extra demands on the Mbuti. When the local chief and his police, gendarmeries, tax collectors, and other government officers are traveling in local areas, they usually demand of the Mbuti (and villagers as well) meat, transportation, and other services. The easy access to their settled villages on the roadside has resulted in increased contacts with these government officers. The 1970s sedentarization program failed shortly after its initiation, and most Mbuti have moved their settlements back to the forest behind the major roads. There are various reasons for this failure. One reason may be the underestimation of the Mbuti nomadic hunting and gathering life, which has been maintained for centuries through their interdependent relationship with the villagers. The Mbuti's own explanation was, however, that they wanted to escape from exploitative local agents of the government.

Thus, the direct intervention of the state has not so far attained significant success in integrating Mbuti society into the nation-state system. Nevertheless, Mbuti society has changed considerably during the last forty years through another channel of contact with the wider society. There have been increasing economic impacts through the commoditization of forest products and of the Mbuti labor force with the spread of the capitalist monetary economy. The influence of the state is also discernible in these changes.

The impacts of the state often take indirect forms in economic activities. One of the most systematic forms of such indirect intervention is the currency system, which is based on the state credit and financial systems. As is often emphasized, currency is one of the key economic elements of an independent state. This is reflected in the currency itself, which has the name of the issuing state printed on it. Establishing its own currency system is usually one of the first economic tasks of a newly independent state. To use the currency, therefore, means to follow the value system of the state that issues the currency. This does not mean much to the people who, since they use the currency every day as a matter of fact, are accustomed to see the values of things as the monetary prices. But for the people less dependent on the currency, it may mean something, particularly when the state value system is different from their own traditional value system. I will discuss in this chapter such a discrepancy between the economy of a hunting and gathering society and the state monetary economy, taking an example from the Mbuti Pygmies in the northeastern part of former Zaire.

Interest Oriented to the Present

It is often stated that egalitarianism is one of the important characteristics of hunter-gatherer social life. Apart from some North American societies, there is not much social stratification developed in most hunting and gathering societies, nor much inequality found in their wealth, prestige, and power. According to Woodburn (1982), such "equality is achieved through direct, individual access to resources and means of coercion and mobility ... and through the procedures that prevent saving and accumulation and impose sharing"; that is, through the system that he calls "an immediate return system." People living in this system are not concerned much about past debt relationships, nor are they interested in investment for the future. Their interest is primarily oriented to the present, rather than to the past or future. Such an instantaneous attitude toward life seems to be prominent among most of the present-day hunter-gatherer societies in Africa, whether or not the attitude has been formed through the impoverished and marginalized status imposed on these people by more powerful systems of a wider society.

The Mbuti in the Ituri Forest are also interested more in the present. The animals captured in the forest are cooked immediately after they have been carried back to the camp, and consumed in a day or two. Mbuti seldom preserve meat for their own consumption, except when it is used for exchange with the villagers and the meat traders. Their concern about immediate needs is also prominent in their agricultural practice. Even before the sedentarization program in 1970s, some Mbuti practiced small-scale agriculture around their base camp near the village. They plant, however, only plantain, cassava, and other vegetatively propagated crops, and have not so far grown rice and other seed crops in substantial quantities. This is because they cannot eat plantain suckers and cassava branches used for planting, whereas the seeds are in themselves edible, and actually eaten up when obtained from the villagers. The seeds would otherwise produce tens of times more food, but the Mbuti find it difficult to wait for several months for this reason at the expense of their immediate desire for consumption. As Turnbull (1983) pointed out, "If it is not here and now, then it is of no significance."

It should be noted, however, that the Mbuti have long been comprising a part of a much wider society. There are Bantu agricultural peoples who have been, for many centuries, keeping a close exchange relationship, often called a patron-client relationship, with the Mbuti. The elephant ivories hunted by the Mbuti comprised one of the most important export items to the world market in the early twentieth century. Some of them have also been providing the mining and plantation workers with meat, which has been hunted in the forest since the Belgian colonial days. In these ways, they were involved, though indirectly through the intermediary of their village patrons, in the economy of a wider society (Ichikawa 1991).

The Mbuti today obtain various goods manufactured in Europe, Asia, and other countries in the world, and are thus connected with the worldwide capitalist system. Since the 1950s, they have been keeping direct contact with people who live in a market-oriented society. The various goods brought by these people from outside the forest can be obtained only through commodity exchange, that is, through direct exchange at a more or less fixed exchange rate (Ichikawa 1991). It is therefore necessary for the Mbuti to adapt their life in some way to this market-oriented system, in order to obtain material benefits from the system. The problem is, therefore, to examine how the Mbuti are coping with the commodity economy of the contemporary world, while maintaining their own economy of an immediate return system.

Infiltration of Commodity Economy into the Mbuti Society

The Mbuti have long been keeping a *kpara* relationship (a so-called patron-client relationship) with neighboring agricultural villagers. They call each other by kinship terms, and in former days, the exchange between them mainly took the form of reciprocal gift-giving. Direct exchange of mutual products was also made from time to time, mostly between the Mbuti and nonpatron villagers (see Terashima 1986), and this probably provided the basis for the later development of commodity exchange. The exchange items in precolonial days were mostly confined to cultivated food, forest products, iron implements, and other local and regional products.

It was the ivory trade that first brought the Mbuti into contact with the world market. The ivory trade was first introduced by Arab slave traders in the late nineteenth century and was intensified by Europeans in the colonial period (Jewsiewicki 1983). In the Ituri Forest, rubber and ivories once comprised major forest products for export, as reported by a British traveler, Captain Powell-Cotton, who spent two years with his newly married wife in the Ituri Forest at the beginning of the twentieth century (Powell-Cotton 1907). While rubber was collected by the forced labor of the villagers, ivory was supplied by the Mbuti as well as by the villagers' elephant hunting (Grinker 1989). However, in those days, Mbuti contact with the market economy was still mediated by patron villagers. When a Mbuti killed an elephant, he brought the tusks to his patron villager, who sold them at a trading post. The Mbuti then obtained salt, tobacco, cloths, and agricultural food from the villagers, sometimes through approved looting (Ichikawa 1982).

The most important factor that directly influenced the Mbuti economy was the introduction of the commercial meat trade. The hilly country to the east of the Ituri Forest is blessed with rich soil of volcanic origin and comprises one of the most densely populated agricultural regions in central Africa. As colonization proceeded, there formed several population centers in this region. The meat from the Ituri Forest was expected to provide the people in these towns with animal protein. Moreover, these people were rapidly losing contact with the "wilderness" of the forest, as the forest was disappearing in the area. The meat from the forest was valued by these town people also as the source of "wild power," which could not be obtained from fish or domestic animals.

The meat trade was first introduced to the area by the Nande, the interlacustrine Bantu people from the eastern hill country, in the late 1950s (Hart 1978). At first, the traders were simply waiting at the patron villagers' houses for the Mbuti to bring the meat. They soon realized, however, that this was inefficient, because the Mbuti were more interested in satisfying their own immediate needs than the demands of traders who were not present at the forest camp. The traders then began to travel to the hunting camp themselves in order to get a better exchange rate and a quick supply of meat. They carried to the camp the Mbuti's favorite food (rice and cassava flour), tobacco, and cloths, and exchanged them for meat at fixed rates. Through such barter transactions with meat traders, the Mbuti became directly involved in a market economy for the first time.

From the late 1920s to 1950s, major roads were constructed, penetrating the forest from west to east, and north to south. Both the villagers and the Mbuti, who had been dispersed in the forest until then, were concentrated along these major roads. Plantations and small gold mining operations were opened along these roads and in other parts of the forest. The colonial government had also encouraged the cultivation of cash crops since the early 1950s, which resulted in further land shortages in the already densely populated hill country to the east of the forest. The Nande people living in this region began to migrate to the west into the forest areas, first as plantation and mine workers, then to seek gold and new land for cultivation. As the newly immigrating Nande people had no patron-client relationship with the Mbuti, they secured Mbuti labor by introducing a new form of employment, *para juru* (derived from *par jour* in French), in which Mbuti labor was directly exchanged for a certain amount of food, local beer, etc., on a daily basis. Such a form of employment soon became common in the central and southern parts of the Ituri Forest.

In these ways, the commoditization of both forest meat and the labor force had been initiated by the 1960s. This has considerably weakened the traditional interdependent relationship between the Mbuti and the villagers, since the meat trade and labor force comprised the important economic basis for their relationship.

Stable Exchange in an Unstable National Economy

The commodity economy has been rapidly developing since the end of the Simba Rebellion, which swept over the Ituri Forest from 1964 to 1965. Particularly since 1981 when gold dust mining, which had been prohibited since independence in 1960, was liberalized, the population of the Teturi area in central Ituri has swelled to more than double. As purchasing power increased, large quantities of commodities of different kinds flowed into this region and were sold at the local shops of the Nande merchants. Also, a local market was opened at Teturi village twice a week mainly for selling local foodstuff to the gold prospectors and their families who did not have enough fields for cultivation.

Although commodity exchange has been promoted in this way, the Mbuti dependence on cash is still very low. They do not usually go to shops or local markets to buy things there. While the Mbuti depend for as much as 60 to 80 percent of their food on agricultural products (Ichikawa 1986), most of this is not purchased for cash, but rather obtained from barter or from payment in kind. They actually get agricultural food either through *para juru*, day-based labor at the villagers' fields and settlements, or in exchange for meat hunted in the forest. Iron implements, used clothes, and other items are obtained in a similar way.

When employed for cash, the daily wage of the Mbuti in 1987 was 30 to 50 zaires, equivalent to about 25 to 40 U.S. cents. They rarely receive cash, however, except when they need it for some specific purpose, such as for paying taxes, fines, and bridewealth. When Mbuti men are employed for clearing the forest for cultivation, they are usually given, for every six men, 25 liters of banana beer costing 300 zaire, which is approximately the same as the wage for six men. However, when women work in planting, weeding, harvesting, or food processing, each of them is usually given 10 to 15 kg of raw cassava, which costs about 100 to 150 zaire, if purchased for cash at the market or directly from the villagers. In this case, the exchange value of the Mbuti labor force differs by more than double, depending on whether it is paid in cash or in kind. While both cassava and the Mbuti labor force are commoditized and exchanged for cash in this area, the inconsistency in the exchange rates suggests that the Mbuti labor force is not enmeshed in a single, unitary exchange system.

The discrepancy in exchange rates is more clearly seen by comparing the diachronic change in cash prices with that in the rates of barter exchange. Except for a brief period immediately after independence, the Zairian national economy has been worsening since independence. In spite of the devaluation and change of currencies attempted several times, the prices of commodities rose by as many as sixty times during the fifteen years from 1960, the year of independence, whereas the real wage dropped to a quarter during the same period (Young and Turner 1985). The excessive issue of paper currency made the economic condition even worse. The annual inflation rate from the late 1970s to 1980s was almost a hundred percent. In spite of the very sharp rise in commodity prices, the real wage considerably decreased in the capital city Kinshasa (Ohbayashi 1986). The political unrest that started in the early 1990s has caused virtual hyperinflation and accelerated further deterioration of the national economy. Under such economic conditions, people, wage laborers in particular, could hardly survive if they were to depend solely on the cash economy of the formal sector.

In the Teturi area, the prices of commodities also rose by several hundred to a thousand times during the twelve years from 1975 to 1987. The wage of the Mbuti, however, rose only 250 times over the 1975 level, which means a considerable change occurred in the relative price of labor to other commodities. In spite of such changes in cash prices, the amount of food the Mbuti receive for a day's labor has remained fairly constant.

The exchange rate was also maintained in the trade of meat, the most important trade item of the Mbuti. In meat trading, there is a unit of exchange comprised of one front or hind leg of a medium-sized duiker or one gutted blue duiker without a head. The former, weighing from 1.5 to 2 kg, was exchanged in 1987 for four (front leg) or five (hind leg) bowls of cassava flour, weighing 1,440 g and 1,800 g, respectively. The latter, weighing from 2 to 2.5 kg, was exchanged for six bowls (2,160 g) of cassava flour. The average exchange rate in 1975 was one unit of meat for

1,800 to 2,000 g of cassava flour (Ichikawa 1991).[2] The exchange rate, therefore, did not actually change during this period.

Until the late 1980s, the exchange rate for cloths had also remained stable. Printed cloths (sarongs) for women are one of the most attractive trade items to the Mbuti. A piece of woman's cloth had been exchanged in 1975 for five units of meat, that is, one medium-sized duiker (comprising four units) and one blue duiker. Although the cash price for cloth had been fluctuating considerably, the exchange rate had remained fairly stable, at least until the late 1980s (Ichikawa 1991).[3] However, as the supply of cheap cloths increased due to the rise of East African trade, the exchange rate changed in 1989 to one piece of cloth for three units of meat. This shows that the exchange rates for imported commodities are less stable than those for local or regional products.

Further Implications of Barter in the Contemporary National Economy

One of the reasons for the persistence of barter is that it ensures a stable exchange rate. The national economy of Zaire has been getting worse year by year since the early 1970s. Facing high rates of inflation and the sudden invalidation of paper currency, many Zairians in remote rural areas have lost trust in cash and prefer barter exchange. Barter markets in Zaire are, therefore, not just the remnant of an older type of economy prior to the introduction of cash economy. The fact that barter thrives in this country can be understood as a people's response to the unstable national economy (Ankei 1986; Ichikawa 1991).

Particularly for the Mbuti, it is not the profit itself, but rather the use values that they want to acquire from the exchange. The major items they obtain from barter are agricultural food and other consumer goods that are used immediately after acquisition. They want cash only when they need it for some specific purpose. In this sense, cash for them is not different from other commodities obtained from the exchange. They are not interested much in money for general purchasing power, nor in storing or accumulating it for future use. It seems natural, therefore, that they prefer barter to cash sales. Barter also conforms to their economy, which is based on "an immediate return system."

Next, I will examine some further implications of the barter economy for the ecology and political economy of the area. First, such a stable barter exchange served as a buffer against the impacts of market economy on the local ecology. If there had been no such buffer, the Mbuti would have been faced with difficulties, particularly when the relative cash price of meat went down. They would have hunted more animals in order to obtain a similar amount of food or other goods from the exchange. Moreover, like other peoples deeply involved in a cash economy, they might have pursued maximization of the hunting yield. They would have tried, for example, to hunt as much meat as possible, beyond their immediate need, and keep what was unnecessary in the form of cash. If the Mbuti had been caught up with such an infinite desire for profit, hunting pressure on the animal resources would have been accelerated, and this might have led to the deterioration of the resource base and to the collapse of the ecological balance of the forest. This might well have occurred, because the Mbuti have no authorized right over the forest, which would otherwise enable them to exert a collective control over the forest resources.[4] If everyone were to pursue maximum yields from hunting under competitive conditions, the result, as the theory of "tragedy of the commons" goes, would be the depletion of the resources (Hardin 1968).

There is a marked difference in the use of resources by the forest people like Mbutis and by the commercially oriented peoples of the capitalist system. The Mbuti use a diversity of forest resources, both directly and indirectly, for spiritual as well as material purposes. Their culture itself depends on the diversity of forest resources (Ichikawa 1996). Crucial to their life is stable and balanced use of forest resources, which conforms to the ecological principle of the tropical rain forest. In the capitalist market economy, by contrast, only a small number of resources with commercial values are exploited for acquiring profits as much as possible. To put it another way, while socioecological stability is essential to the former, maximization of production and productive efficiency is pursued by the latter.

Therefore, the stable exchange rate for acquiring concrete use values has served as a buffer for avoiding the adverse impacts of the capitalist market economy on the local ecosystem, which is maintained by the delicate balance of a diversity of its elements and is essentially incompatible with the capitalist economy. We may recall here that in the mid-1970s, nearly twenty years after the introduction of meat trading into the area, the hunting pressure on forest duikers by the Mbuti in the study area was estimated at only 10 to 15 percent of the standing stock, which seems well within the sustainable level (Ichikawa 1996).

Secondly, the Mbuti have maintained their economy relatively independent from the Zairian national economy. In a monetary economy, the value of any commodity can be expressed, in principle, by a unitary value system of money, and as such it is strongly influenced by the economy of a wider society. For example, the cloths available in the Ituri Forest are either foreign products or printed in Zaire with imported materials. The amount of cloths available and their prices, therefore, change considerably depending on the foreign exchange reserve and the exchange rate of

Zairian currency. Even the wage of Mbuti in the remote forest is influenced by the national economy and the international economic system behind it: the Mbuti wage is determined by the wage level of plantation workers in the Ituri region, and plantation workers' wage is in turn subject to the Zairian wage system. The wage in Zaire is no doubt influenced by the international division of labor under the world capitalist system, which seeks cheap labor and primary products in Africa. The relationship of the Mbuti wage to such an international system is reflected in the fact that their wage showed a similar rate of increase as that of the foreign exchange rate during the twelve years from 1975 to 1987.

The rate of barter exchange has been fairly stable, despite the change in cash prices. It seems to be supported by a sound value system and the local sense of balance of the living standard between the Mbuti and the villagers, and is not easily affected by short-term fluctuations in cash prices.

Conclusion

The local Mbuti economy based on barter sometimes contends with the national economy, and with the world capitalist economy behind it. I do not think that the Mbuti are conscious of these eventual effects of bartering. They simply prefer goods to cash, because the former can be used immediately when acquired. Largely because of such an instantaneous attitude toward life, the Mbuti are protected from being totally incorporated into the nationwide monetary economy.

The situation seems similar to what Hyden (1980) called "uncaptured peasantry" when describing the agrarian societies in Tanzania. According to Hyden, the reason for the difficulty in achieving development goals in Tanzanian rural societies is not only that they are marginalized and exist in an induced underdevelopment state due to the world capitalist system; there exists another, noncapitalist economy that contends with the capitalist system. Hyden (1980) called it an "economy of affection," which resists the penetration of the state policy oriented to the "economy of value" of the capitalist system.

We need not, however, consider this only as a negative factor impeding development. Take, for example, the case of wage laborers in Zaire. The real wage had dropped to a quarter of its former level during fifteen years after independence. If there had been no such "economy of affection," which enabled them to help each other (or, to hang on to wealthier relatives), they could not have survived this economic crisis. While the capitalist system, the "economy of value," allows only a minority of people to win the competition and become prosperous, an "economy of affection" enables the majority to survive. The difference between the haves and have-nots is systematically minimized in the latter. In other words, while the capitalist system pursues growth, or maximization of production or productive efficiency through competition, the bartering system results in social stability and the coexistence of the majority in a society.

Although the Mbuti have contacts with the market economy, their economy still remains "uncaptured" by the nationwide monetary economy. It also serves as a barrier to the unstable capitalist economy, and eventually helps the Mbuti to maintain relative autonomy in an economically and politically "encapsulated" situation (Woodburn 1988).

It is often asserted that the world capitalist economy integrated the local economies that had been isolated from each other. We should note, however, that the unification of economies by the capitalist system was usually associated with the destruction of relatively stable local economies that have their own value system. This point is particularly relevant to an area like the Ituri Forest, because it seems more important here to establish or maintain a stable life than to aim at hasty development; otherwise, the unstable, fluctuating national economy would impose hazardous influences on the Mbuti. In an economic situation as experienced in former Zaire, I think it is necessary to understand the role of "interest in the present" and the potential of the local economic system based on the exchange of use values.

Notes

1. While the name of the state changed from Zaire to Democratic Republic of Congo after the defeat of the Mobutu regime in 1997, I use the name Zaire in this chapter, since it deals with the period when the state was still called Zaire.

2. There was not a difference in the exchange rate among different units of animals in 1975. A gutted blue duiker was equivalent to one unit of front or hind leg of a medium-sized duiker.

3. When the exchange rate of cloths for meat was considerably disadvantageous, the traders did not bring new cloths for exchange, unless cheaper or used cloths were available. The exchange rate had been maintained in this way.

4. While the Mbuti have a loose territorial system among themselves (Ichikawa 1978), this does not always exclude other Mbuti from having access to the resources, nor does it affect the villagers who also depend on the forest resources.

References

Ankei, Y. 1986. "The Fish as 'Primitive Money': Barter Markets of the Songola." *Senri Ethnological Studies* 15: 1–68.

Grinker, R. R. 1989. "Ambivalent Exchange: The Lese Farmers of Central Africa and Their Relations with the Efe Pygmies." Ph.D. diss., Harvard University.

_____. 1994. *Houses in the Rain Forest.* Berkeley: University of California Press.

Hardin, G. J. 1968. "The Tragedy of the Commons." *Science* 162: 1243–48.

Hart, J. 1978. "From Subsistence to Market: A Case Study of the Mbuti Net Hunters." *Human Ecology* 6(3): 325–53.

Hyden, G. 1980. *Beyond Ujamaa in Tanzania: Underdevelopment and an Uncaptured Peasantry.* Los Angeles: University of California Press.

Ichikawa, M. 1978. "The Residential Groups of the Mbuti Pygmies." *Senri Ethnological Studies* 1: 131–88.

_____. 1982. *The Forest Hunters: The Life of the Mbuti Pygmies.* Kyoto: Jinbun-shoin.

_____. 1986. "Ecological Bases of Symbiosis, Territoriality and Intraband Cooperation of the Mbuti Pygmies." *Sprache und Geschichte in Afrika (SUGIA)* 7(1): 161–88.

_____. 1991. "The Impact of Commoditisation on the Mbuti of Zaire." *Senri Ethnological Studies* 30: 135–62.

_____. 1996. "The Co-Existence of Man and Nature in the Central African Rain Forest." In *Redefining Nature: Ecology, Culture and Domestication.* R. Ellen and K. Fukui, eds. 467–92. Oxford: Berg Publishers.

Jewsiewicki, B. 1983. "Rural Society and Belgian Colonial Economy." In *History of Central Africa.* D. Birmingham and P. M. Martin, eds. 95–125. London: Longman.

Powell-Cotton, P. H. G. 1907. "Notes on a Journey through the Great Ituri Forest." *Journal of the African Society* 25: 1–12.

Ohbayashi, M. 1986. *Agriculture in Zaire.* Tokyo: Association for International Cooperation of Agriculture and Forestry (AICAF).

Terashima, H. 1986. "Economic Exchange and the Symbiotic Relationship of the Mbuti Pygmies and Neighboring Farmers." *Sprache und Geschichte in Afrika (SUGIA)* 7(1): 391–405.

Turnbull, C. 1983. *The Mbuti Pygmies: Change and Adaptation.* New York: Holt, Rinehart and Winston.

Woodburn, J. 1982. "Egalitarian Societies." *Man* (n.s.) 17: 431–51.

_____. 1988. "African Hunter-Gatherer Social Organization: Is It Best Understood as a Product of Encapsulation?" In *Hunters and Gatherers 1: History, Evolution and Social Change.* T. Ingold, D. Riches, and J. Woodburn, eds. 31–64. Oxford: Berg Publishers.

Young, G., and T. Turner. 1985. *The Rise and Decline of the Zairian State.* Madison: University of Wisconsin Press.

Chapter 15

DYNAMICS OF ADAPTATION TO MARKET ECONOMY AMONG THE AYORÉODE OF NORTHWEST PARAGUAY

━━━◄●►━━━

Volker von Bremen

Introduction

Hunting and gathering societies are considered extremely sensitive to changes in their surrounding environment and, consequently, particularly vulnerable to colonial invasion of their territories. Indeed, many of them have suffered complete physical extermination either as a result of intentional colonial aggression or, more indirectly, by the destructive effects of such things as contact with previously unknown diseases, the reduction of their territory, and introduced ecological transformations. Those who have survived have done so because the destructive forces of the dominant, colonizing society have for some reason been mitigated. Today, there is no indigenous society met by anthropological researchers that has not felt the repercussions of clashes with colonialism and domination (cf. Wolf 1982). Nevertheless, there exists strong evidence that societies with a hunting and gathering tradition have a dynamic adaptive potential that enables them to resist the destructive powers of a world system predicated on market economy.

To illustrate and examine this thesis, I will present data of my research amongst the Ayoréode of Paraguay. Up to the end of the 1950s, the southern groups of the Ayoréode lived as traditional hunter-gatherers, occupying vast parts of the northern Gran Chaco near the Paraguayan-Bolivian border. Of all the Chaco indigenous groups, the Ayoréode are the group that resisted permanent contact with colonizing society for the longest time. Today, there remains only a fraction of one of the traditional local groups that continues its active resistance. The rest of this people, with a total population of about six thousand persons, is now part of the regional market economies of the Paraguayan and Bolivian Chaco.

As simple wage laborers, they search for work on either the mission stations or the cattle and agricultural enterprises of the descendants of nonindigenous colonists. Most of the Ayoréode ride bicycles in the settlements of their employers, they communicate with relatives in other settlements by cassette recorders, have radios, and wear Western clothes. About 97 percent of them have been baptized, some of them even twice by both Roman Catholic and fundamentalist Protestant missionaries.

Dependent on market and missionaries, they belong to a peripheric region of the world system described by Immanuel Wallerstein (1986). Within this peripheric region, which is the Gran Chaco of South America, the rural population as a whole is divided into culturally quite heterogenous groups.

Like the vast majority of the indigenous societies in this area, the Ayoréode were already inhabiting the northern Chaco well before European colonization reached this area. They basically possess neither cultural nor historical ties with the dominant Paraguayan society. Furthermore, even though the marginal status of the landless and small farmer mestizo population puts them in a similar sociopolitical position to the indigenous population, those of the latter category with a hunter-gatherer tradition are clearly distinguished from the former by a completely different system of reproduction, values, and social organization.

In order not only to understand but also to explain (cf. Jarvie 1985) the way that the Ayoréode are adjusting to modern living conditions, I consider it necessary to study their system of religious beliefs. While Renshaw, who analyzed the economic integration of the indigenous population of the Chaco into the national economy, focuses on those factors that are observable within socioeconomic relations (Renshaw 1988), the consideration of religious beliefs helps to understand the basic motivation of indigenous people for present-day behavior. Here we can find the logic of explanation, prediction, and control of space-time events (cf. Horton 1971: 94; Jarvie 1964; Jarvie and Agassi 1967; Lukes 1974; Duerr 1979). Considering this system, we discover indications to principles of a whole way of life, since to the Ayoréode—like other indigenous peoples—there is no human activity that cannot assume religious significance (cf. Burridge 1969: 4).

History and the Concept of Time

The Ayoréode understand contemporary time and the world they are living in by means of concepts that include the idea of an originating time and world. Indeed, the two worlds/times are closely related. However, the most important aspect of originating time is quite clearly and definitely separated from contemporary time.[1]

In the world that existed prior to what it has now become, there was no distinction between the human being and its surroundings. All and everything were ancestors, anthropomorphic beings that incorporated all of the characteristic features of natural and cultural phenomena, both abstract and concrete. As *jnanibajade* (ancestors) they already possessed the name of the being that exists today. The ancestors lived in the same manner as the contemporary Ayoréode, but with one crucial difference: it was in their world/time where/when all of the things that are important and necessary for life today were either discovered or created. For this reason, the time of the *jnanibajade* can also be considered as the time of origin.

Every myth includes a description of the original ancestors and those circumstances and events that led to the coming about of today's world. However, this was not the result of the creative action of a single divine personality nor of a cultural hero.

Basically, there are two possible explanations of the origin of the contemporary world in the mythical time of the ancestors (cf. Bórmida 1984):

1. by metamorphosis of the ancestor, generally caused by some kind of conflict within the original community that led the ancestor to withdraw from the community and to transform to what he or she is today;
2. by an originating act of the ancestor. In general, this form of creation is restricted to some objects that are goods of culturally determined production. (For example, the owl *Bujote* made the cloth for women's skirts.)

It is important to clarify, therefore, that for the Ayoréode contemporary objects are not derived from human invention, creation, or design. The "producer" does not possess innovative potential, but rather has the object presented to him. His action is restricted to "finding" the original model again and to bringing it to the present by renewing the original prototype. Therefore, there is no object that is the product of an inventing initiative of the individual human being.[2]

This is exactly the dividing line between original and contemporary time. In contemporary time, originating actions are no longer possible, since everything that exists has existed ever since the creative time of origin of the ancestors (for further information, see von Bremen 1991). The system described makes it feasible to continually reorder the forever metamorphosing external world without having to alter the essential mythological structure on which it is predicated. The division between originating and contemporary time is definite and absolute, since originating time belongs to a completed past and is, logically, always prior to contemporary time. However, it would be wrong to assume that this order is composed of a set of rules and regulations given once and for all that must always be followed. Here, it is necessary to contradict those classical positions in the research on myth which state that mythical thinking implies a distrust against innovation and historical change (cf. Lincoln 1983: 13).

Although originating time always remains in the completed past and prior to contemporary time, the border between the two is constantly shifting—consider the diachronic dimension characterizing historical time experienced, for example, with the passing of the generations. The term *jnanibajai* includes all those that have disappeared from historical time, the limit of which is formed by the grandparents or great-grandparents. As they disappear, so the border of historical time moves on. Within the lifetime of an individual, there is a constant adaptation to one's own particular present, which enables one to locate oneself within one's surroundings. This adaptation is well illustrated by the change of name that occurs with the birth of a child and, again, with the birth of a grandchild. Consequently, it is very seldom that one finds an Ayorei that remembers the birthnames of his or her grandparents.

It is, therefore, quite likely for experiences of relatively recent historical time to become integrated into the myth system, which is itself characterized by a lack of chronological order. As a result, there is no diachronic view of history, and the development of a historical consciousness of progressive sequences is prevented. Even though the framework within which originating acts and events can happen is well determined, there is no limit on what can continually be integrated into originating time. Indeed, everything that *is* has already been, and everything that *will be* also will have already been. The origin always stays in the past and can only be reconstructed retrospectively.

Integration of New Phenomena into Culture

With the establishment of permanent contact with the colonizing society, the Ayoréode have become aware of an abundance of new, strange objects and phenomena that they do not know how to deal with. However, the ignorance and uncertainty that they experience as they relate to the new does not threaten the existing explanatory system. In the same way that they deal with traditionally known phenomena, they apply the myth system to the new world and its objects by employing the following essential reasoning:

1. The new phenomena are intimately related to the nonindigenous people, the so-called *cojñThe*, who know how to "find" and use them.

2. The origin of these phenomena is located in originating time, since the Ayoréode cannot conceive of anything actually new—only things that might be unknown to some people.
3. Since these phenomena, like all others, are assumed to be related to a myth, ignorance of this myth makes them difficult to deal with.
4. The close relationship of the *cojñone* to these new and strange phenomena implies that they know how to deal with them, and that, consequently, they know the myths on which they are predicated and which determine their existence and the correct means of relating to them.

Consequently, the Ayoréode have a fundamental interest in discovering the myths of the new phenomena. This includes not only material goods but also things of the immaterial world. As the Ayoréode experience it, those myths can be discovered within the whole complex of Christian religion, writing, mathematical system, diagnosis and treatment of unknown diseases, cooperativism as practiced by Mennonite colonists, etc.[3]

The specific problems of the contemporary Ayoréode do not consist primarily in the danger of not being able to maintain their ethnic identity or their right of self-determination. In their view, it is rather their still existing ignorance about the origin of the new phenomena and their concomitant inability to contact the related ancestors. It is this contact that they regard as an essential precondition for successful living in the present world, since the ancestors always accompany the contemporary phenomena.

Adaptation

Although missionaries, employers, and other representatives of the dominant society have their own ideas about the role the Ayoréode and other indigenous people should play in the regional development process, these are not necessarily shared by the Ayoréode themselves, who act according to their own concepts. Within the prevailing economic conditions, they occupy certain roles such as wage laborers; a target group of development projects; or merely poor, ignorant, or needy people.

In general, there is a great deal of frustration among those development workers in the Gran Chaco who deal with indigenous peoples with a hunting and gathering tradition. Long-term projects invariably not only suffer changes during their implementation, but also fail to fulfill their objectives since the target group does not participate in the way expected and defined by the project management. The dynamic potential that enables the Ayoréode to deal with all of the changes forced on them by colonization is not limited to the ideological concepts mentioned above.

By acting in accordance with their traditional economic principles, the Ayoréode can also intervene as social actors in their present-day living conditions, and not remain as mere objects of external decisions on economic development. Since hunter-gatherer societies exhibit a high degree of dependence on nature as a productive and reproductive force, they are obliged to adapt, often quite dramatically, to the surrounding ecological conditions. According to Ayoreo concepts, the goods that are required to satisfy the basic needs do not have to be produced by investing human productive force; rather, they exist already. It is just a matter of "finding" them.

This basic concept is also applied to present-day living conditions. There is no conscious productive action that is directed toward a goal-oriented, planned transformation of nature and the environment. Instead of changing the environment by production, human beings look for ways to integrate themselves as a part of the already given conditions by getting to know the forces that maintain them and their environment and with which there exists a relationship of interdependence. As described already, the "production" of these forces, that is, the creation of a phenomenon by an intentional and conscious act of transformation, has already happened in the past.

While historically the mechanisms of adaptation were applied almost exclusively to an external, natural environment, today's environment is one that is greatly determined by the existing socioeconomic conditions and that has been changed by active human (colonist) intervention. Despite this, since the Ayoréode do not distinguish between natural and cultural phenomena, they perceive the new environment as one that is given and to which they have to adapt. There is no fundamental questioning of the ruling socioeconomical and political conditions, since they belong to the environment in the same way as the natural, ecological conditions. For this reason, the Ayoréode accept the existing work conditions as adequate mechanisms of behavior and action. For example, wage labor is one way to acquire the new resources essential for reproduction, and, in the process of becoming aware of these mechanisms, the Ayoréode perceive the confirmation of the existence of new gathering and hunting grounds.

External strategies, developed and implemented by missionary and development organizations, are also accepted as given by the Ayoréode. Since their integration into mission settlements was combined with an exodus from their traditional territory, adaptation to a new environment became a necessity. The planning and decision-making of missionaries are not questioned, since they also belong to the given external environment and do not arise from the intentional action of human beings.

In contrast, the concepts of change managed by the external agents stress the transformational capacity inherent in all human beings. This consciousness of the productive potential of the human being to transform the environment through specific intentional action is understood to be a global characteristic inherent in all peoples. Consequently, there is a fundamental conflict between the concept of change that stresses the intentional and decision-making capacity of the human being and the concept managed by the Ayoréode that considers change as something imposed from the outside to which one must adapt. Therefore, instead of assuming, as do development strategists, that change is possible because of the productive potential of the human being, the Ayoréode regard change as an adaptation to an already transformed environment by means of establishing effective social relations with the ancestors. The process of adaptation meant that the Ayoréode became dependent on the "hunting ground of wage labor/mission/development projects." Yet within this conception it is possible for them to continue living according to their own belief system.

Acquisition

Since the origin of the environment and the creation—or "production"— of all phenomena by an intentional, conscious act of innovative change is understood as located in a completed past, the interest of the Ayoréode in the sphere of economic action is concentrated on the acquisition of already existing and given objects for their own consumption. In contrast to other modes of subsistence, a great deal of work input is directed exclusively to the goal, the returns. This is referred to by Woodburn as "immediate returns" on labor (1982: 432).

For social reproduction, it is important to know the means of acquisition. Success in hunting and gathering is dependent on the successful application of a combination of practical skills and magic techniques. This implies both a profane and spiritual knowledge of nature and the environment, as well as the capability to adequately implement practical skills and techniques.

According to this system, the existence of a rifle, a bicycle, and all other new phenomena is considered as a quantitative expansion of the ancestors and their actions. Confronted with a large number of new phenomena, such as different diseases, weapons, tools, machines, books, "land" as property that is privately owned, or even different types of human behavior, the Ayoréode aim to obtain the knowledge that explains the existence of these phenomena, without which it is not possible to deal with them effectively.

The Ayoréode have one basic economic strategy for dealing with the external programs that aim to solve the problems of indigenous peoples by integrating them into the dominant society: they adapt to imposed economic activities (e.g., projects, development aid, and wage labor) by acquiring ("gathering") the resources connected with these activities in such a way that they are able to follow their own interests and satisfy their own needs. However, the techniques of hunting and gathering have changed: begging, agriculture, and wage labor are three of them, and all are practiced according to the same underlying premises, even though, in the eyes of the dominant society, they differ quite considerably.

Agricultural development, as it is planned and implemented within development projects, is generally connected with some kind of "food for work" program or food credit system, and consequently lends itself very well to fulfilling the interests of the Ayoréode in acquiring goods immediately. Work content is of secondary importance; the principal motivating factor for working is the access it gives to consumer goods, either through immediate distribution, credits, or payment.

Wage Labor and Money

Wage labor is the most common form of present-day work. It is carried out as a technique of acquisition that corresponds in the best way to the Ayoréode living conditions. The Spanish word *trabajo* is exclusively iden-tified by the Ayoréode as wage labor, that is, both the activities for which they receive wages as well as the work relations that permit the acquisition of market products.

Adopting foreign terms, such as *trabajo*, *plata* (money), and *cuenta* (credit account), to identify new means of acquisition has been necessary because the traditional context did not include sufficient symbolic images with which to interpret these new forms of acquisition. Other productive activities, such as hunting, gathering, gardening, and even the production of handicrafts for sale, are not considered as *trabajo*. Rather, as traditional subsistence activities they are considered "looking for prey," "doing things," or "planting/sowing." *Trabajo* is always reduced to an activity with the aim of acquiring market products that depends on wages, paid by an employer.

By adapting to this externally imposed form and organization of work, it is possible to succeed relatively quickly in acquiring new products. Therefore, under the transformed conditions, *trabajo* came to be quite closely identified with the traditional subsistence strategies. Furthermore, although traditional economic activities are still practiced, *trabajo* came to be, along with development programs, the most common form of imme-diate acquisition of goods. The importance of *trabajo* is not only due to the fact that wage labor is encouraged by development programs and the pre-vailing market economy in the region, but that it also helps the Ayoréode fulfill a variety of other aims. Although it is the amount of money that ulti-mately determines the access to the market and the limits of consumption, *trabajo* as a relationship between employer and employee is a key that opens the door to other services, especially within the Mennonite colonies. These include health services, the possibility of borrowing tools from the employer, and the use of certain transportation facilities.

The Ayoréode also connect the *cuenta* system, which gives direct access to consumer goods without the requirement of having to previously earn money, with *trabajo*. The Spanish word *cuenta*, used in this context, means "credit," and the meaning the Ayoréode impute to it is the result of their work experience in the Mennonite colonies. In all of the stores in these colonies, members of the cooperative system and other account holders can buy on credit. The Ayoréode cannot observe any transaction involving money. The "buyer" seems to receive the goods without paying, although in fact the monetary transaction takes place at the end of the month. Practical experience has convinced the Ayoréode that the possesser of a credit account has immediate access to all goods available in the stores. There was a time when many of the indigenous groups interpreted this as the principal causal factor for the difference of wealth between them and the Mennonites, since the former always have to pay with money.

Cuenta in the sense of a cumulative credit account is frequently used by the missionaries and other employers in their economic relationship with the Ayoréode. At the beginning of a work contract, the employed workers usually receive an advance payment. While working, they continue to hold a *cuenta* with the patron, frequently adding to it as they receive more goods. Therefore, the *cuenta* can be understood as a debt account that exists as long as the worker has not paid off the debt.

However, within the traditional system of distribution there are no debts. One can only distribute what one actually has at one's disposition, and less than nothing does not exist. Relatives or other persons that have a relationship of mutual obligation to distribute cannot demand from partners things that they do not have. However, under contemporary living conditions, there is a major problem in that the Ayoréode find that there is a great abundance of goods among nonindigenous colonists that they themselves do not have access to, despite the close relationship between the Ayoréode and the settlers. Since the dominant social conditions obviously do not permit the application of the traditional principles of distribution in the relationship with nonindigenous settlers, the Ayoréode are obliged to discover other principles that will permit their participation in the distribution of the settlers' goods.

According to their interpretation, the *cuenta* system is one such gateway; it permits access to market products without the obligation to simultaneously transfer money. Linked as it is to a *trabajo* relationship, it speeds up the acquisition process and permits access to market products even though, in a strict sense, this access has still not been earned in the work process. It offers the chance of flexibility managing work input and acquisition of market products.

Work is interpreted, among other things, as a means of opening a *cuenta* relationship, one that guarantees an "immediate return" on labor. Therefore, the availability of products is not connected exclusively to the work accomplished and to the wages earned, but also to the disposition of the employer to accept a *cuenta* relationship with the employee. Consequently, the Ayoréode criticize those employers who refuse to give contracts on a *cuenta* basis, saying: "Without *cuenta*, the money earned within a week is not enough."

Promoting the *cuenta* relationship is another attempt—like the development programs—to include nonindigenous peoples in the system of distribution that exists in Ayoreo society. Although the representatives of the dominant society present labor as *the* mechanism that permits access to market products, the Ayoréode's own experiences have given them a different perspective. When participating in certain development programs, they receive, without charge, food and other essentials (cf. von Bremen 1987). They also observe that the Mennonite colonists continue to possess greater quantities of goods than the Ayoréode, despite the fact that they have been working for them for years. Indeed, Mennonite access to goods would seem to be increasing. As a result of these experiences, the Ayoréode deduce that, in addition to wage labor, the sale of handicrafts, and development programs, there are other important mechanisms required to guarantee the "successful hunt."

They have still not discovered many of these mechanisms, and so it is certain that they will continue to experiment and evaluate their experiences of contact with the dominant society.

Conclusion

The historical experience of colonization in the Gran Chaco provides evidence to support the thesis that indigenous peoples with a hunter-gatherer tradition, despite being technologically inferior to other types of societies and having suffered from territorial expansion of—and military and economic submission to—the colonizing society, do, nevertheless, possess a dynamic potential that enables them to survive in the modern era.

The Ayoréode seem to be very conservative, since they accept the present-day circumstances as given ones that, therefore, are not to be questioned. However, they do not play the role of passive observers who are the mere objects of decisions that others determine. By a consequent application of those principles that were developed under the circumstances of traditional life as hunter-gatherers, the Ayoréode are able to adapt to the new and heavily changed living conditions, which require the transformation of many aspects of their cultural settings. Despite these adaptations, basic principles and structures of social organization and religious belief are maintained, since their dynamics permit them to reorganize new elements from the dominant society within these structures. As Jarvie and Agassi have noted in another context (Jarvie and Agassi 1967), the strength of this religious conception consists of the fact that it is a complete conception of the world, by which it is possible to explain all and everything—including developed technology met under the changed conditions of living.

Notes

1. It is my intention in this study to stress the relationship between originating time and existence of the ancestors on one side, and historical, contemporary time on the other side. I do not deal with "dream time," which exists parallel to historical, contemporary time (cf. Duerr 1979).
2. It is worthwhile to mention the different view that Overing has analyzed for the Piaroa, among whom there seems to exist a concept for hunting as a *productive* activity (see Overing 1991: 8).
3. In the Paraguayan Chaco, the colonies of Mennonite settlers of European descent form the main market for the indigenous population of the area. These colonies are organized economically on individual farming and cooperative trading.

References

Bórmida, M. 1984. "Como una cultura arcaica concibe su propio mundo." *Scripta Ethnologica* 8.

Bremen, V. von. 1987. *Moderne Jagd- und Sammelgründe: Entwicklungshilfe- projekte unter Indianern des Gran Chaco.* epd-Entwicklungspolitik, Materialien III/87. Frankfurt/M.: epd.

———. 1991. *Zwischen Anpassung und Aneignung—Zur Problematik von Wildbeuter-Gesellschaften im modernen Weltsystem am Beispiel der Ayoréode.* Munich: Anacon-Verlag.

Burridge, K. 1969. *New Heaven, New Earth: A Study of Millenarian Activities.* Oxford: Basil Blackwell.

Duerr, H. P. 1979. *Traumzeit.* Frankfurt/M.: Syndikat.

Horton, R. 1971. "African Conversion." In *Africa* 41(2): 85–108.

Jarvie, I. C. 1964. *The Revolution of Anthropology.* London: Routledge and Kegan Paul.

———. 1985. "Comment on M. K. Taylor's 'Symbolic Dimensions in Cultural Anthropology.'" In *Current Anthropology* 26(2): 176.

Jarvie, I. C., and J. Agassi. 1967. "The Problem of the Rationality of Magic." In *The British Journal of Anthropology* 18: 55–74.

Lincoln, B. 1983. "Der politische Gehalt des Mythos." In *Alcheringa oder die beginnende Zeit*. H. P. Duerr, ed. 9–25. Frankfurt/M., Paris: Qumran-Verlag.

Lukes, S. 1974. "Some Problems about Rationality." In *Rationality*. B. R. Wilson, ed. 194–213. Oxford: Basil Blackwell.

Overing, J. 1991. "Contesting Markets—Wandering in the Market and the Forest." Unpublished manuscript.

Renshaw, J. 1988. "Property, Resources and Equality among the Indians of the Paraguayan Chaco." In *Man* 23(2): 334–52.

Wallerstein, I. 1986. *Das moderne Weltsystem*. Frankfurt/M.: Syndikat.

Wolf, E. 1982. *Europe and the People Without History*. Berkeley, Los Angeles, London: University of California Press.

Woodburn, J. 1982. "Egalitarian Societies." In *Man* 17(3): 431–51.

Chapter 16

Can Hunter-Gatherers Live in Tropical Rain Forests?

The Pleistocene Island Melanesian Evidence

Matthew Spriggs

Rather than take on directly the arguments of Tom Headland (1987) and Robert Bailey and his colleagues (1989) concerning the viability of hunter-gatherer settlements in tropical rain forests in the absence of associated agricultural groups, I will discuss the evidence we have for Pleistocene subsistence in the Island Melanesian region from 35,000 years ago to about 10,000 years ago. I argue that these earliest settlers of the region were certainly "hunter-gatherers" in conventional parlance, but behaved in possibly unconventional ways in order to live in what were difficult rain forest conditions.

The constraints of a short essay mean that the Pleistocene evidence for mainland New Guinea has had to be left out of consideration. The relevant issues there are considered for the New Guinea Highlands by Hope and Golson (1995) and Mountain (1991a; 1991b), and for New Guinea as a whole by Groube (1989). Only Island Melanesia will be considered, consisting of the archipelagoes to the east and southeast of New Guinea: the Bismarck Archipelago (New Britain, New Ireland, and Manus), the Solomon Islands, Vanuatu, and New Caledonia. The archaeology of this region is considered in detail in Spriggs (1997), and pertinent information is given only in summary here.

Any constraints imposed on a hunter-gatherer existence in New Guinea are multiplied considerably in Island Melanesia. If early hunter-gatherers could live in Island Melanesia rain forests, then they could certainly live in

New Guinea. This is because of the relative poverty of the natural flora and fauna of Island Melanesia compared to New Guinea. The boundary between the latter island and New Britain marks the end of the distribution of primary division freshwater fish. Some 265 extant bird species found on the east coast of New Guinea are reduced to 80 in New Britain, and very few terrestrial mammals crossed the same gap unassisted by humans. The flora is also considerably depauperate compared to New Guinea.

Within Island Melanesia there are two further major biogeographic boundaries: that between the main Solomons and the Santa Cruz group to the south, and that between Vanuatu and New Caledonia. Beyond the main Solomons chain, all terrestrial mammals except bats have been humanly transported, thirty genera of extant land birds and 162 genera of seed plants find their eastern limits, and major disjunctions occur in the natural distribution of other fauna and flora. This boundary has led archaeologist Roger Green to talk of two Pacific Island regions: Near Oceania and (beyond the main Solomons and including Polynesia and Micronesia) Remote Oceania (Green 1991).

Even more significant in terms of seed plant distribution is the boundary between Vanuatu and New Caledonia, but this may be moot in terms of human settlement as no preagricultural human settlement has been found anywhere in Remote Oceania. The boundary between Near and Remote Oceania formed, on present evidence, an absolute boundary for Pleistocene settlement in the Pacific.

The area inhabited by humans in the Pleistocene, the Bismarck Archipelago and the main Solomons, was almost certainly rain forest throughout that period of human settlement, although this may not have been the case for the Vanuatu and New Caledonia islands further south. In the Bismarcks and Solomons we are within a few degrees of the equator, and it has been postulated that there was no major difference in the Pleistocene from the weather systems existing today (Enright and Gosden 1992). There would still have been an equatorial band of shelter between cyclone belts. Warm air would still have risen in the region of the equator, drawing in wind from north and south. The rotation of the earth created the same prevailing trade winds. The faunal and limited pollen evidence from the region also suggest continuity in rain forest habitat from the Pleistocene to the last few thousand years.

A Pleistocene human history for Island Melanesia was first established in 1981 with a terminal Pleistocene date for the inland cave of Misisil on New Britain (Specht et al. 1981; 1983). In 1986 a sequence back to 33,000 B.P. (B.P. meaning "before present") was established for New Ireland (Allen et al. 1988). In 1987 dates back to 29,000 B.P. were established for the Solomons, extending the known human history of this archipelago tenfold (Wickler and Spriggs 1988). Finally, in 1990 Pleistocene dates were recorded for Manus Island in the Manus or Admiralty Islands group (Fredericksen et al. 1993). Settlement of Manus involved a minimum open ocean crossing of 200 km, the longest attested open sea voyage in the Pleistocene world.

An extensive archaeological project in Vanuatu in the period between 1994 and 1996, led by the author, has failed to find any evidence that the Remote Oceania barrier beyond the main Solomons was breached during the Pleistocene or early Holocene, and similarly intensive research in New Caledonia has also failed to confirm earlier hints of an early, preagricultural settlement there (Sand 1995; and Christophe Sand, personal communication 1996).

There are at present less than ten Pleistocene archaeological sites known in the Island Melanesian region and so our reconstructions of lifestyle are tentative. All of the sites except one are rock shelters, and only four are any significant distance from the coast.

Before looking at the evidence from these sites, it is worth considering the frameworks for interpretation of what we might find. In previous publications (Spriggs 1993; 1996a) I have gone into the terminological distinctions needed to consider the range of behaviors that occur between the poles of simple foraging and intensive agriculture, that gray area where live Zvelebil's (1986) "complex hunter-gatherers" and Guddemi's (1992) "hunter-horticulturalists."

I have largely followed the lead of David Harris's discussions (1989; 1996) on the subject. Rather than seeing the presence of domesticated plants and animals as the important threshold between hunter-gatherers and agriculturalists, I consider that it is important to identify—for any given cultural sequence—when dependence upon agriculture began, defined in terms of the creation of agroecosystems that limit subsistence choice because of environmental transformation or labor demands. This threshold has greater implications for changes in human behavior and organization than whether cultivated plants are "domesticated" in the morphological sense or whether indeed some form of cultivation of crops is being carried out.

In my analysis none of the sites discussed below has crossed the agricultural threshold during the period under consideration. A fully agricultural lifestyle did not come into being in Island Melanesia until after 3500 B.P.

Settlement and Subsistence Prior to 20,000 B.P.

For the Bismarck Archipelago, the pre-20,000 B.P. fauna of New Ireland is the best known. The island's vertebrate fauna consisted of a narrow range of edible species of lizards and snakes, a single large rat species (*Rattus sanila*) of 500–1,000 gm weight, a small rat (*Melomys rufescens*) of 70–100 gm, and an unknown number of species of birds (Flannery 1995: 38–39). Exploitation of various local species of bats completes the list of hunted mammals. Some of these were quite large, such as the fruit bats *Pteropus neohibernicus* at 1,000–1,500 gm and *Dobsonia anderseni* at 200–300 gm (Flannery 1995: 190–91, 271). At 2 to 4 kilograms, the biggest of the lizards, *Varanus indicus*, was one of the largest-sized land animals around, and its importance as a protein source should not be underestimated. The rest of the Bismarck Archipelago was probably comparably endowed in edible terrestrial fauna.

The Solomon Islands were considerably better provided with edible species, with a rich fauna of bush rats including the endemic genus *Solomys*. These rats and various fruit bats, lizards (including *Varanus indicus*), snakes, and birds would have provided valuable protein sources for the archipelago's early human inhabitants. The reasons for this difference in natural endowment are unclear, although the Solomons chain appears to have received some of its species from an Australian source. Both the Bismarcks and the Solomons have a comparatively rich marine fauna, similar in many ways to New Guinea and tropical Asia and therefore familiar to the first colonists.

Only four sites older than 20,000 B.P. have been investigated: Yombon on New Britain, Matenkupkum and Buang Merabak on New Ireland, and Kilu on Buka in the northern Solomons. The Pamwak site on Manus may date back to this period but the lower layers remain undated, and so the site will only be discussed in the next section.

Three of the four archaeological sites belonging to this early period of settlement are cave or rock shelter sites. The fourth is an open site consisting of a series of localities on ridge tops in the vicinity of Yombon village and airstrip in New Britain. Yombon is at about 500 m altitude, some 30 km inland of the south coast of the island in an area of very high rainfall (over 6,350 mm annually) and generally dense rain forest. Over most of the airstrip and around the present village are dense scatters of chert artifacts, which were first reported in 1966. Excavations by Specht in the late 1970s revealed occupation levels dating from the Mid-Holocene, but research by Pavlides in 1991 and 1993 has extended the sequence back to 35,000 B.P. (Pavlides 1993; Pavlides and Gosden 1994).

Successive ash falls from Mount Witori to the northeast have blanketed the deposits and aided in their buildup and preservation. The lowest of these tephra deposits is just younger than 14,310 B.P. and seals a carbon-rich, sticky brown clay deposit with three radiocarbon dates between 32,630 B.P. and 35,570 B.P. from two localities 500 m apart. The associated twenty-seven artifacts consist of locally available chert flakes and fire-cracked chert pieces.

The significance of the site is not in the sparse stone tools themselves, but in their mere presence at this very early time in an inland area densely covered by tropical rain forest. Limits to settlement supposedly set by an impoverished fauna and flora were obviously not enough to deter exploration and use of this inland region as early as the dates for human occupation anywhere in Island Melanesia.

The cave site of Buang Merabak on the east coast of New Ireland is a 30 m long tunnel, some 10–14 m wide, with further chambers behind. It is about a kilometer inland at approximately 150–200 m altitude up a steep slope behind the village of Kanangusngus. Excavation was undertaken near the cave entrance, and bedrock of a large boulder was reached in one square at 165 cm (Rosenfeld 1997). Some anomalous radiocarbon dating results render interpretation difficult, but a determination from near the base gave an age of 31,990 B.P., and from 25 cm above it came a date of 20,350 B.P. This suggests a very slow buildup of the deposits resulting from very sporadic use of the cave. The deposits of this time period consist of mainly marine shell midden with small quantities of animal bone and stone flakes of chert.

The other cave on New Ireland, Matenkupkum, has been reported in more detail. In faces southeast, seaward, and is some 15 m above sea level in limestone on an old marine terrace. It is dry and airy, some 18 m long by 10 m wide. A 10 m by 1 m trench was excavated in 1985, and further excavation was carried out in 1988 (Gosden and Robertson 1991). The lowest two layers (6 and 7) were deposited between 35,400 B.P. and 21,300 B.P. on top of a very ancient, sterile beach sand (see Allen 1994: 341 for discussion of the earliest date).

During this period, the buildup of deposits was slow, with 50–60 cm of sediment laid down in 10,000 years. This suggests that the cave was used only sporadically during this period, when shellfish, fish, and animal bone were deposited, along with fairly undistinguished stone tools. Various steep-edged flakes and cores provided a variety of sharp edges for accomplishing a number of tasks, such as cutting up and cleaning animals and processing plant foods. The large size of individual shells and the narrow range of species exploited suggest little pressure on what were presumably pristine shell beds at the beginning of the occupation. A similar pattern was found at Buang Merabak.

The fish bone is notable in "Guinness Book of Record" style as the earliest evidence of sea fishing in the world, but as Allen points out there are not many fish represented in quantity in the Matenkupkum cave, and the species are all ones that would not require any specialized technology such as nets, lines, poisons, or even fish spears: "Fortuitous accidental or deliberate trapping or spearing on reefs on outgoing tides would account for the evidence to hand" (Allen 1993: 144). The poor variety of other animal bones might reflect the poverty of the New Ireland forests, or merely that only the immediate vicinity of the cave was the source for animals brought back to it. The reef itself appeared to be the main focus for the early inhabitants, mobile coastally focused foragers who lived an apparent "strand looper" existence, dealing with basically the same sorts of resources as they had been accustomed to much further west.

The problem is that shells, and to a lesser extent bones, survive, but until recently it was believed that plant remains rarely did. Is our coastal forager model a function of the visibility of particular kinds of remains and the ease of studying them? The evidence from Kilu cave, the fourth site of this period, suggests that it may be so. Kilu is near the southern end of Buka Island, which during the Pleistocene was the northern peninsula of Bougainville. At times of lowest sea level, Bougainville itself was joined to a series of other islands down through the Solomons chain as far as Nggela, with Guadalcanal being separated only by a narrow strait from this "Greater Bougainville." This island was considerably larger at 46,400 sq. km than even the Pleistocene size of New Britain.

Kilu is a cave at the base of a 30 m high limestone cliff, some 65 m from the sea and currently about 8 m above the high tide mark. It consists of a large, dry front shelter where excavation took place and a damper smaller cave chamber behind. The main shelter is 33 m by 17 m and well lit (Wickler 1990; Wickler and Spriggs 1988). The bottom portion of the present deposit dated to between 28,700 B.P. and 20,100 B.P., about 75 cm being built up over the 8,000 or so years. As at Buang Merabak and Matenkupkum, this seems to represent only very sporadic, low intensity use.

The rather ad hoc stone tools were examined by Tom Loy for residues of material adhering to them, which could give clues as to the function of the tools. A sample of forty-seven tools were examined under the microscope, from both Pleistocene and Holocene levels. Of these, some twenty-seven had evidence of use in the form of polish or starch grains and other plant material stuck to the tool surface. Seventeen of the tools from the Pleistocene levels had starchy grains identifiable to genus—fourteen from *Colocasia* taro and three from *Alocasia* taro. They were probably used to cut and scrape raw taro in preparation for cooking (Loy et al. 1992).

This work and similar studies that have subsequently taken place represent a major breakthrough in the archaeological study of subsistence. It has always been accepted that plants must have played an important role in early economies, but until recently it has not been possible to identify which plants were actually involved. We were limited to the elements of the economy that were more obvious in the archaeological record, such as bones and shells. Had we been similarly limited in our considerations of Kilu, then the interpretation of the site might have resembled that given by the excavators of Matenkupkum: a reef-focused strand looping economy.

Yet the Kilu evidence suggests a real focus on plants that later formed the agricultural staples of the region.

Colocasia taro was probably naturally distributed throughout the Bismarcks and the Solomons, but human selection produced the forms with large edible tubers. The amount of residue on individual tools suggests that this selection process had started and that forms with large tubers were already available. The source of the taro may have been the local stream or areas of natural swamp. It is unknown what level of management there was of this resource. The distribution throughout the deposit of tools with residue on them suggests that a regular supply was available, which would require some degree of cultivation.

A dense shell midden and the presence of marine fish bone, as at Matenkupkum and Buang Merabak, show that the adjacent coast was not neglected, but high visibility and bulk of shells does not necessarily equate with dominance in the diet. Kilu also produced a much greater quantity of bones from land animals than the two New Ireland sites. Five species of endemic Solomon Island rats were found, including two new species—the noble *Solomys spriggsarum* and the much smaller and less noble *Melomys spechti* (Flannery and Wickler 1990). These would have formed a rich forest source of protein that was unavailable in the Bismarcks. Bats and a range of reptiles, including a large skink, a varanid or monitor lizard, and snakes, were also part of what seems to have been a more varied diet than was available on New Ireland. Nearly all of the bones found appear to have resulted from human consumption rather than that of other predators such as owls, and the range of body parts present show that whole animals were brought to the site, and butchered and eaten there. Analysis of the small sample of bird bones recovered suggests that several species have become extinct over the 29,000 years of human occupation of the island (Wickler 1990: 141).

It is clear that our knowledge of this critical formative period of settlement of Island Melanesia is very scant at present. Gosden (Enright and Gosden 1992: 173; cf. Gosden 1995) has put forward an interesting overall model of this period, based in part on certain contrasts with the period that succeeds it. He noted that despite the lack of land resources, the early colonists would have had two factors in their favor: by moving into an uninhabited area they could live where they liked, and they could balance the poverty of the land resources with the richness of those of the sea.

Gosden argues that for the first few thousand years, the sea was important for the mobility it allowed in moving between scarce resources, as well as being an important food source. Low population densities would have given people room to move through the landscape between its dispersed resources, and at the same time would have made human contacts extremely important for securing necessary marriage partners and for keeping in touch with the wider world. The lack of land resources may have been more apparent than real, given the Kilu evidence for plant exploitation, or there may have been a real difference between the Solomons and the Bismarcks in this respect. The richer fauna of the Solomons may have provided a less precarious existence for its human inhabitants at this period.

It was mentioned earlier that preagricultural settlement does not appear to have extended south of the main Solomons. Although it is harder to get to Vanuatu and New Caledonia, these islands may not have been outside the technological ability of Pleistocene voyaging. The real problem was lack of food. Wild relatives of major food plants such as *Colocasia* and *Cyrtosperma* taros do not occur in Vanuatu forests. In the absence of introduced plants and animals, sustained human occupation of Remote Oceania may have been impossible. Bailey et al.'s (1989) judgment on tropical rain forests in general applies most forcefully to Vanuatu. As far as the early inhabitants of Island Melanesia were concerned, the archipelago may indeed have been a green desert.

Cultural Change in the Period 20,000 to 10,000 B.P.

The three cave sites we have been considering show a break in occupation at about 20,000 B.P. Kilu on Buka was abandoned between about 20,000 and 10,000 B.P. The lack of evidence for any sustained use of Matenkupkum on New Ireland between 20,000 and 16,000 B.P. is compensated for by the site of Matenbek some 70 m away in the same cliff line. This now partially collapsed cave revealed evidence of use from about 20,000 B.P. on (Allen et al. 1989: 550–52).

Matenbek, like Matenkupkum, is a relatively large shelter with a main front chamber 30 m by 20 m and some 6 m high. Near the entrance, the excavatable deposits proved to be 1.5 m deep. The earliest cultural material dated from 20,430 to 18,560 B.P. The layer above dates to the early Holocene and suggests reoccupation after a considerable hiatus.

At Buang Merabak on New Ireland, there was a date of about 20,900 B.P. from 60 cm depth and 10,800 B.P. from 40 cm, with a stratigraphic change at 55 cm. Either total abandonment or extremely ephemeral use is indicated for the period between these two dates (Rosenfeld 1997).

Other sites of interest for which we first have evidence of use after 20,000 and before 10,000 B.P. are Panakiwuk and Balof on New Ireland, Pamwak on Manus, and Misisil on New Britain.

Panakiwuk is a limestone rock shelter, roughly the same distance from the east and west coasts at a point where New Ireland is only about 8 km wide (Marshall and Allen 1991). It is situated in a rain forest at 150 m altitude. Given the steepness of the offshore slope, even at the time of lowest sea level the shore of the east coast would have been only a further 600–700 m away, just less than 4.5 km. At the base of the cultural deposit was a hearth dated to 15,140 B.P. with very little other material, which "only fleetingly reflects human presence" (Marshall and Allen 1991: 67). The next identified unit is associated with an episode of roof-fall built up between about 15,000 and 13,000 B.P., representing sparse human occupation during this period. The dates for the next cultural unit are somewhat confused, but span the period 10,300 to 8000 B.P. The densest concentrations of all classes of artifactual remains occur in the lower part of this unit, suggestive of a more constant use of the site during the terminal Pleistocene and early Holocene.

Initial occupation of the Balof shelters occurred at about the same time as that at Panakiwuk (White et al. 1991). This rock shelter complex is in a secondary forest not quite 3 km from the coast at an altitude of 80 m. Offshore, the lagoon is only 150 m wide, and so, even at times of lower sea level, Balof would not have been significantly further from the east coast. Distance coast to coast is about 10 km at this point. Balof 2 shelter is about 17 m by 14 m. Human occupation here goes back to about 14,240 B.P. Buildup of sediment was extremely slow until about 10,000 B.P., and somewhat faster from then until 8400 B.P. The dating is not fine enough to tell if there were significant gaps in occupation during this time. It is clear that the pre-10,000 B.P. occupation must have been very sporadic, and in this Balof 2 mirrors Panakiwuk.

The Pamwak site on Manus is the richest of the Pleistocene sites in terms of number and variety of stone artifacts and also the deepest, with approximately 4 m of cultural deposit sitting on limestone bedrock (Fredericksen et al. 1993). It is a large overhang shelter at the base of a limestone cliff in a secondary forest some 4 km inland from the south coast, at about 30 m altitude. The area within the drip line is some 89 sq. m. Unlike the sites already discussed, Pamwak has at times been considered further away from the sea than it is now. At times of lower sea level, it would have been up to 10 km from the sea, whereas now it is only 4 km distant.

The bottom meter or so of the deposit is now a clay, which formed in situ from cave earth. Artifact densities are as high as in later levels, but all bone, shell, and most other organic materials have been leached out of this bottom layer. Therefore, it has not yet proved possible to date the beginning of human occupation at the site. The earliest date obtained so far is an age of 13,000 B.P. at 1.7 m depth, marking a major change in artifact raw material from local chert to imported obsidian. The major period of occupation occurs around 10,000 B.P. when new artifact types appear.

A significant site dated to this period on New Britain is the inland cave of Misisil, the first Pleistocene site to be investigated east of New Guinea

(Pain and Specht 1985; Specht et al. 1981; 1983). It is the most inland of our Pleistocene sites, situated 30 km in from the south coast of New Britain and a kilometer or so away from Yombon. Misisil is near the top of a limestone ridge at about 500 m elevation. The cave is a simple cleft or enlarged joint, with a large entrance to the south, which is 20 m wide and 20–25 m high. It runs back into the hillside for about 30 m. The basal layers are sterile, but Layer 6 yielded a thin layer of grey-brown soil with charcoal and five small obsidian flakes. Two radiocarbon dates have been obtained from this layer, one of 11,400 B.P. and another of 9000 B.P. This early occupation is extremely ephemeral and perhaps represents occasional visits separated by thousands of years. There is no clear evidence that the nearby site of Yombon was occupied in the period from 20,000 to 10,000 B.P.

From the base of the excavated deposits at Matenbek, we find bones of the marsupial opossum *Phalanger orientalis* (Gosden 1995: 811), which has an average weight of about 2 kg. The absence of this animal in the earlier sites and the lack of speciation from its New Guinea progenitors suggests that it only arrived on New Ireland about this time. There is no evidence that it can cross sea gaps of its own volition, so a human introduction seems most likely, either as pets that escaped or as a deliberate "game park" strategy to stock the forests with easily caught game (Flannery and White 1991: 108). The result was the same. In the areas of the Island Melanesia where it occurs, the phalanger has become (apart from wild pigs, which were introduced much more recently) the commonest prey of hunters and a favored source of protein away from the coasts. It was the earliest of several such introductions to Island Melanesia and appears to be the earliest documented example of the deliberate movement of an animal by humans anywhere in the world.

The early occurrence of the phalanger is somewhat spotty in the New Ireland sites. In Matenkupkum it appears with reoccupation (or at least more than very ephemeral use) at 14,000 B.P. It occurs at Panakiwuk at about 13,000 B.P., but the earlier occupation at that site is very ephemeral. At Balof 2, however, it does not appear in the record until 10,000 B.P. Information on its distribution within Buang Merabak is not yet at hand. No bone remains have been reported from Misisil on New Britain and so it is a complete blank, although phalangers are common enough on the island today and it is the obvious conduit for introduction to New Ireland. *Phalanger orientalis* appears never to have reached Manus. Instead, the phalangerid there is *Spilocuscus kraemeri*, with an average weight of 2.5 kg (Flannery 1995: 104–5). There is evidence that *Spilocuscus kraemeri* was introduced to Pamwak at about 13,000 B.P. (Corrie Williams, personal communication).

A single *Phalanger orientalis* bone was found amid the rich faunal collections from the Holocene levels at Kilu on Buka, but none has been found in Pleistocene deposits. In unconsolidated deposits it is very easy for items such as bones to be displaced from upper levels during excavation, which may have happened in this case. Alternatively, it may signify an occasional introduction from New Ireland to the Solomons without the establishment of a breeding population. Phalangers are common today throughout the main Solomons chain, but have never otherwise been found in pre-3500 B.P. contexts. They have never been present in Vanuatu or New Caledonia.

As well as producing early phalangerids in the form of *Spilocuscus kraemeri*, Pamwak provides evidence for another Pleistocene marsupial introduction, the bandicoot, *Echymipera kalubu*. Commonly hunted on Manus today and a bit smaller than a phalanger at just less than 1 kg average weight (Flannery 1995: 68–69), it also appears suddenly among the animal bones at about 13,000 B.P. and quickly becomes the most dominant feature of the faunal remains at the site. Today it is found on New Britain as well, but its antiquity there is unknown. It has never been found on New Ireland or in the Solomons. A direct introduction to Manus from mainland New Guinea seems most likely, given that there is no evidence of contact between Manus and the rest of the Bismarcks throughout this period.

There are hints of the exploitation of, and in some cases evidence for the later extinction of, various bird species. No full report of the bird fauna from any of these sites is yet available, although it would seem that the extinctions occurred after 3,500 years ago. Low levels of predation on the forest birds continued throughout this period without apparently leading to the extinction of species. Reptiles, particularly lizards, continued as part of the human diet during this period, but never attained the importance of phalangers.

Useful plants, particularly the important nut tree genus *Canarium*, also appear to have been among the human introductions from New Guinea. Fragments of *Canarium* almond shell have been identified in Pleistocene and early Holocene Melanesian sites from burned remains that retain the distinctive shape and features of the nut. Yen has suggested (1990: 262, 268; 1995: 838–39) that the edible *Canarium* species was most likely introduced to the Bismarcks and Solomons from New Guinea, where they might have been naturally widespread. *Canarium* often forms an important food resource in Island Melanesia because it can be stored. If Yen is correct, then it must have been deliberately planted, tended, and harvested from at least the terminal Pleistocene onwards, on evidence from Pamwak shelter on Manus and from Kilu cave on Buka.

Other plant remains that have been identified in these sites do not occur in any quantity, except seeds of the native elm *Celtis*, a natural part of the lowland forests of Melanesia. The seeds are found in Buang Merabak,

Matenkupkum, and Panakiwuk, and in very large quantities in Pamwak. They are particularly resilient—surviving without being burned because of the uptake of calcium carbonate into the seed casings—and need not represent human use at all.

There are also finds of coconut, certainly used by people but again naturally dispersed in the region, and occasional plant parts of forest trees and ferns. *Colocasia* taro continues as an identifiable residue on the Kilu tools in the Holocene levels there. At Matenkupkum a preliminary residue analysis of thirty-six obsidian flakes from 12,000–10,000 B.P. levels revealed four flakes with unidentifiable plant residues (Gosden and Robertson 1991). Interestingly, a similar study of the Panakiwuk stone tools revealed that many carry blood and collagen residues (Marshall and Allen 1991).

A study by Huw Barton of residues on six obsidian and fifteen fine-grained stone flakes and twenty-one fragments of shell knives or scrapers from Balof 2 reveals that all three classes of material were used almost exclusively in processing starchy plants. *Cyrtosperma* and/or *Alocasia* taro residues were identified on tools from the beginning of occupation at 14,000 B.P. onwards, and yam, *Dioscorea bulbifera* or *D. nummularia*, on a tool in levels dating to 10,400 B.P. (Barton and White 1993).

From about 20,000 years ago we have the first evidence for exchange of stone resources with the movement of obsidian from the Talasea and Mopir areas of New Britain to Matenbek and Buang Merabak, a straight-line distance of some 250 km involving a sea crossing. This latter is not surprising in itself but does demonstrate the repeated practice from that time of sea transport between New Britain and New Ireland, as movement of obsidian between them continued down to the beginning of the twentieth century.

Obsidian is an extremely sharp but brittle black, glass-like volcanic rock. There are only four source areas for it in this region: New Britain, the Manus Group, the Banks Islands in northern Vanuatu, and the Fergusson Islands off Goodenough Bay in New Guinea (Bird et al. 1981). All of the obsidian from sites on New Britain and New Ireland in the period prior to 3500 B.P. can be sourced to New Britain. In the earliest New Ireland sites, the most favored source was Mopir, which is to the east of the major concentration of obsidian sources on the Talasea Peninsula and adjacent islands and nearer to New Ireland by some 30 km or so.

At Matenkupkum, the apparent date of the first appearance of obsidian has been reassessed in the light of the Matenbek evidence as occurring at 16,000 B.P. (Summerhayes and Allen 1993). Obsidian occurs back to 10,400 B.P. at Balof 2 (White et al. 1991).

Just to the south of Manus Island is the second major concentration of obsidian sources in Island Melanesia—in the Pam Islands (Pam Lin and Pam Mandian) and on Lou Island. Despite Pamwak's proximity to the obsidian sources some 35 km away, no obsidian occurs at all in the bottom 2.3 m of cultural deposit there. Instead, all of the stone material appears to consist of local chert, obtainable as river cobbles. When obsidian first appears at about 12,000 B.P., from both Pam and Lou sources, it almost immediately replaces these local materials as the material used in stone flake manufacture.

This situation is paralleled at Balof 2 where obsidian replaces fine-grained stone as the main raw material at about 10,400 B.P., again with virtually no overlap in stratigraphic distribution. The same process occurs at the same time at Matenbek (Gosden 1995: 814). At Buang Merabak there is a change in raw material selection at about 10,800 B.P. In the lower levels a wider range of materials was used, including chert. In the upper levels chert is virtually abandoned, and almost all of the worked stone is basalt. The stone industries at these sites, allowing for raw material differences, are generally similar. There are a high proportion of simple flakes suitable for a range of cutting and scraping tasks, and very few formal tool types.

At about 10,000 B.P. onwards a range of more formal tools do occur at Pamwak. These include edge-ground axes of volcanic rock, and knives and scrapers of pitchstone. At least one of these axes is waisted and reminiscent of the smaller but sharper Sahul forms, rather than the large and blunt ones from the Huon Gulf terraces of New Guinea. The lack of manufacturing debris for these materials suggests that these tools were made elsewhere and curated. At Balof 2 an edge-ground axe fragment was found in a level which dates to approximately 10,000 B.P. Apart from occasional pieces of worked and cut shell, other non-stone artifacts are rare in these sites. An important artifact class limited at present to Pamwak is the *Tridacna,* or clamshell adze, of which fourteen examples were found in excavation. All of the adzes except one are from the hinge portion of the shell. Again, the lack of manufacturing debris would suggest that they were made elsewhere.

The distinctiveness of Pamwak in this and in other regards might be interpreted as cultural difference, but it could just as easily reflect a difference in site function. Pamwak is much bigger than the other sites under consideration, especially if the area of all of the associated overhang shelter sites is taken into account, and it may have formed the base camp for a comparatively large group of people. This function might mean that a wider range of activities was carried out there than at the other sites, and that curated artifacts were more likely to be cached there.

Gosden's model of contrast between the archaeological record before and after 20,000 B.P. is the starting point for a consideration of economic change during this period. In the earlier period he detects a strategy whereby people moved themselves between scarce resources. In the later period there is evidence that resources were being moved, possibly between more settled groups. Allen (1993: 146) puts it succinctly: "It is possible to see in the data a progression from initial, coastally-oriented, low intensity occupation to more intensive and more extensive human use of the region. Matenbek at 18,000 looks archaeologically different to Matenkup-kum at 32,000; Balof 2 and Panakiwuk reflect different and more intensive usage at 8000 B.P. than at 14,000 B.P."

The major changes were the apparently deliberate introduction of wild animal species such as *Phalanger orientalis* into the New Ireland forests from 20,000 B.P. onwards and a different species of phalangerid and a bandicoot into Manus before 13,000 B.P., the transplantation of nut trees such as *Canarium* to New Ireland and Buka by the end of the Pleistocene and perhaps much earlier in Manus, and the movement of obsidian from New Britain to New Ireland from 20,000 B.P. on and from offshore islands to the Manus mainland from 13,000 B.P.

Making a conscious move to re-create the richer environment of the New Guinea forests, or at least to compensate for the poverty of the ones they settled in, the early Island Melanesians overcame the natural productivity limits of the forest environment and took an active part in shaping it.

Although moving from foraging to wild food production as a sequence demonstrates a continuum rather than a sharp break, it is clear that the system from 20,000 B.P. represents the latter kind of economy. The economy of the first settlers may also have gone beyond simple foraging by necessity, but the evidence is much clearer for this later period.

If we look at the period from 10,000 B.P. to the first evidence of an agricultural lifestyle in the region after 3500 B.P., we find that agriculture did not represent an inevitable development from what had gone before. There was no period of "incipient agriculture" leading up to the adoption of agriculture in the region. It arrived with new migrants who brought domesticated animals and samples of plants with them from Southeast Asia, but, more importantly, who had a totally different attitude to the landscape and the place of humans within it. These were the makers and users of Lapita pottery and its associated material culture (Spriggs 1996b). Their environmental impact was sudden and dramatic, quickly transforming Island Melanesian landscapes so that a hunter-gatherer lifestyle was no longer sustainable for the region's inhabitants. Subsistence choice rapidly narrowed to a fully agricultural economy throughout Island Melanesia.

Conclusion

The Island Melanesian rain forests of the Bismarcks and Solomons were occupied during the Pleistocene and early Holocene by groups of hunter-gatherers. Their ranges included both coastal and inland areas, in the case of Yombon on New Britain up to 30 km inland. Clearly, hunter-gatherers could live in these tropical rain forests, even allowing for Bailey et al.'s (1989) exaggerated criteria for "real" rain forests (see discussion in Spriggs 1996a). Bailey et al. correctly draw attention to the fact that tropical forests have never been the Gardens of Eden that they are often portrayed as. Their view of early human responses to the challenges posed by living in such forests, however, suggests far too passive a picture.

In the depauperate forests of Island Melanesia, the transplanting of useful plant species from more productive habitats may have been necessary from initial occupation of areas beyond the coastal fringe. Thus, there may never have been true foragers in the region's rain forests, a condition of regular exploitation being a form of wild plant food production from the beginning. The overall effect of this and the introduction of wild animal species beyond their natural range was to mimic the diversity of the New Guinea forests from whence the early settlers presumably came.

Bailey and his colleagues therefore may be right in one sense. Perhaps foragers could not have lived in these forests, but people did not have to wait for the advent of agricultural colonists to open up the canopy by clearing spaces for gardens. Wild plant food production and cultivation may have been developed early on as a set of strategies to allow occupation of the forests, starting with initial settlement in Island Melanesia (cf. Groube 1989 for mainland New Guinea).

To some it might seem that scholars such as Headland and Bailey have opened up Pandora's box by examining possible limits to hunter-gatherer occupation in tropical regions. Looked at superficially, it may appear that categories such as hunter-gatherer and agriculturalist are becoming so blurred as to put the former category in danger of disappearing altogether. One could read the foregoing discussion willfully to suggest that the movement of wild species of animals and plants and the deliberate planting of the latter are already beyond anything that could be described as hunting and gathering. I once did so, suggesting Pleistocene agriculture for the Island Melanesian region (Spriggs 1993). But this would be too mechanistic an interpretation of the evidence.

There is a vast difference in lifestyle and in attitude toward the environment implied by the terms "hunter-gatherer" and "agriculturalist." The Pacific Islands are a good place to demonstrate this. When fully developed agriculture did reach the area with Lapita culture, patterns of settlement, population density, land use, degree of human impact on the environment, and material culture were radically changed. The obvious continuities in Island Melanesian cultural sequences from at least 20,000 B.P. onwards until the moment of agriculture at about 3500 to 3000 B.P. and the radical reassortment that followed are eloquent witness to the gulf between two very different ways of life.

Note

This essay has benefited from the comments of the Moscow CHAGS 7 participants, and additional information has come from discussions with Christophe Sand and Corrie Williams. Its genesis comes from discussions with colleagues at the Australian National University and elsewhere in Australia, the United Kingdom, and Hawaii. The original conference paper was prepared while I was a Visiting Fellow at Clare Hall College, Cambridge, and I acknowledge the support of the President and members of the College during my time there. Professor Gerald Matiushin, Victor Shnirelman, and Andzey Tchepalyga were most hospitable during my stay in Moscow, and Jonathan Friedman, Kajsa Ekholm-Friedman, and Soren Lund were very accommodating on my way there and back.

References

Allen, J. 1993. "Notions of the Pleistocene in Greater Australia." In *A Community of Culture: The People and Prehistory of the Pacific*. M. Spriggs, D. E. Yen, W. Ambrose, R. Jones, A. Thorne, and A. Andrews, eds. 139–51. Canberra: Department of Prehistory, Research School of Pacific and Asian Studies, Australian National University.
———. 1994. "Radiocarbon Determinations, Luminescence Dating and Australian Archaeology." *Antiquity* 68: 339–43.
Allen, J., C. Gosden, R. Jones, and J. P. White. 1988. "Pleistocene Dates for the Human Occupation of New Ireland, Northern Melanesia." *Nature* 331: 707–9.
Allen, J., C. Gosden, and J. P. White. 1989. "Human Pleistocene Adaptations in the Tropical Island Pacific: Recent Evidence from New Ireland, a Greater Australian Outlier." *Antiquity* 63: 548–61.
Bailey, R.C., G. Head, M. Jenike, B. Owen, and R. Rectman. 1989. "Hunting and Gathering in Tropical Rainforests: Is It Possible?" *American Anthropologist* 91: 59–82.
Barton, H., and J. P. White. 1993. "Use of Stone and Shell Artifacts at Balof 2, New Ireland, Papau New Guinea." *Asian Perspectives* 32: 169–81.
Bird, J. R., W. R. Ambrose, L. H. Russell, and M. D. Scott. 1981. *The Characterisation of Melanesian Obsidian Sources and Artefacts using the Proton Induced Gamma Ray Emission (PIGME) Technique*. Lucus Heights: Australian Atomic Energy Commission Research Establishment.
Enright, N. J., and C. Gosden. 1992. "Unstable Archipelagoes: South-West Pacific Environment and Prehistory since 30,000 B.P." In *The Naive Lands: Prehistory and Environmental Change in Australia and the South-West Pacific*. J. Dodson, ed. Melbourne: Longman Cheshire.
Flannery, T. F. 1995. *Mammals of the South West Pacific and Moluccan Islands*. Sydney: Australian Museum and Reed Books.
Flannery, T. F., and J. P. White. 1991. "Animal Translocation." *National Geographic Research and Exploration* 7: 127–39.
Flannery, T. F., and S. Wickler. 1990. "Quaternary Murids (Rodentia: Muridae) from Buka Island, Papua New Guinea, with Description of Two New Species." *Australian Mammalogy* 13: 127–39.
Fredericksen, C., M. Spriggs, and W. Ambrose. 1993. "Pamwak Rockshelter: A Pleistocene Rockshelter on Manus Island, PNG." In *Sahul in Review: Pleistocene Archaeology in Australia, New Guinea and Island Melanesia*. M. Smith, M. Spriggs, and B. Fankhauser,

eds. Canberra: Department of Prehistory, Research School of Pacific and Asian Studies, Australian National University.

Gosden, C. 1995. "Arboriculture and Agriculture in Coastal Papua New Guinea." *Antiquity* 69: 807–17.

Gosden, C., and N. Robertson. 1991. "Models for Matenkupkum: Interpreting a Late Pleistocene Site from Southern New Ireland, Papua New Guinea." In *Report of the Lapita Homeland Project.* J. Allen and C. Gosden, eds. 20–45. Canberra: Department of Prehistory, Research School of Pacific and Asian Studies, Australian National University.

Green, R. C. 1991. "Near and Remote Oceania: Disestablishing 'Melanesia' in Culture History." In *Man and a Half: Essays in Pacific Anthropology and Ethnobiology in Honour of Ralph Bulmer.* A. Pawley, ed. 491–502. Auckland: The Polynesian Society.

Groube, L. 1989. "The Taming of the Rainforests: A Model for Late Pleistocene Forest Exploitation in New Guinea." In *Foraging and Farming: the Evolution of Plant Exploitation.* D. R. Harris and G. C. Hillman, eds. 11–26. London: Unwin Hyman.

Guddemi, P. 1992. "When Horticulturalists Are Like Hunter-Gatherers: The Sawiyano of Papua New Guinea." *Ethnology* 31: 303–314.

Harris, D. R. 1989. "An Evolutionary Continuum of People-Plant Interaction." In *Foraging and Farming: The Evolution of Plant Exploitation.* D. R. Harris and G. C. Hillman, eds. 11–26. London: Unwin Hyman.

_____. 1996. "Domesticatory Relationships of People, Plants and Animals." In *Redefining Nature, Ecology and Domestication.* R. Ellen and K. Fukui, eds. 437–63. Oxford: Oxford University Press.

Headland, T. 1987. "The Wild Yam Question: How Well Could Independent Hunter-Gatherers Live in a Tropical Rain Forest Ecosystem?" *Human Ecology* 15: 463–91.

Hope, G., and J. Golson. 1995. "Late Quaternary Changes in the Mountains of New Guinea." *Antiquity* 69: 818–30.

Loy, T. H., M. Spriggs, and S. Wickler. 1992. "Direct Evidence for Human Use of Plants 28,000 Years Ago: Starch Residues on Stone Artefacts from the Northern Solomon Islands." *Antiquity* 66: 898–912.

Marshall, B., and J. Allen. 1991. "Excavations at Panakiwuk Cave, New Ireland." In *Report of the Lapita Homeland Project.* J. Allen and C. Gosden, eds. 59–91. Canberra: Department of Prehistory, Research School of Pacific and Asian Studies, Australian National University.

Mountain, M. J. 1991a. "Bulmer Phase 1: Environmental Change and Human Activity through the Late Pleistocene into the Holocene in the Highlands of New Guinea: A Scenario." In *Man and a Half: Essays in Pacific Anthropology and Ethnobiology in Honour of Ralph Bulmer.* A. Pawley, ed. 510–20. Auckland: The Polynesian Society.

_____. 1991b. "Landscape Use and Environmental Management of Tropical Rainforest by Pre-Agricultural Hunter-Gatherers in Northern Sahulland." *Bulletin of the Indo-Pacific Prehistory Association* 11: 54–68.

Pain, C. F., and J. Specht. 1985. "Tectonic Stability of West New Britain, Papua New Guinea: Evidence from Cave Sediments." 1(15): 343–44.

Pavlides, C. 1993. "New Archaeological Research at Yombon, West New Britain, Papua New Guinea." *Archaeology in Oceania* 28: 55–59.

Pavlides, C., and C. Gosden. 1994. "35,000 Year Old Sites in the Rainforests of West New Britain, Papua New Guinea." *Antiquity* 68: 604–10.

Rosenfeld, A. 1997. "Excavation at Buang Merabak, Central New Ireland." *Bulletin of the Indo-Pacific Prehistory Association* 16: 213–24.

Sand, C. 1995. *Le Temps d'Avant: La Préhistoire de la Nouvelle-Calédonie. Contribution à l'Etude des Modalités d'Adaptation et d'Evolution des Sociétés Océaniennes dans un Archipel du Dud de la Mélanésie.* Paris: L'Harmattan.

Specht, J., I. Lilley, and J. Normu. 1981. "Radiocarbon Dates from West New Britain, Papua New Guinea." *Australian Archaeology* 12: 13–15.

_____. 1983. "More on Radiocarbon Dates from West New Britain, Papua New Guinea." *Australian Archaeology* 16: 92–95.

Spriggs, M. 1993. "Pleistocene Agriculture: Why Not?" In *Sahul in Review*. M. A. Smith, M. Spriggs, and B. Fankhauser, eds. 137–43. Canberra: Department of Prehistory, Research School of Pacific and Asian Studies, Australian National University.

_____. 1996a. "Early Agriculture and What Went Before in Island Melanesia: Continuity or Intrusion?" In *The Origins and Spread of Agriculture and Patoralism in Eurasia*. D. R. Harris, ed. 524–37. London: UCL Press.

_____. 1996b. "What Is Southeast Asian about Lapita?" In *Prehistoric Mongoloid Dispersals*. T. Akazawa and E. Szathmary, eds. 328–48. Oxford: Clarendon Press.

_____. 1997. *The Island Melanesians*. Oxford: Blackwell Publishers.

Summerhayes, G. R., and J. Allen. 1993. "The Transport of Mopir Obsidian to Late Pleistocene New Ireland." *Archaeology in Oceania* 28: 144–48.

White, J. P., T. F. Flannery, R. O'Brien, R. V. Hancock, and L. Pavlish. 1991. "The Balof Shelters, New Ireland." In *Report of the Lapita Homeland Project*. J. Allen and C. Gosden, eds. 46–58. Canberra: Department of Prehistory, Research School of Pacific and Asian Studies, Australian National University.

Wickler, S. 1990. "Prehistoric Melanesian Exchange and Interaction: Recent Evidence from the Northern Solomon Islands." *Asian Perspectives* 29: 135–54.

Wickler, S., and M. Spriggs. 1988. "Pleistocene Human Occupation of the Solomon Islands, Melanesia." *Antiquity* 62: 703–6.

Yen, D. E. 1990. "Environment, Agriculture and the Colonization of the Pacific." In *Pacific Production Systems: Approaches to Economic Prehistory*. D. E. Yen and J. M. J. Mummery, eds. 258–77. Canberra: Department of Prehistory, Research School of Pacific and Asian Studies, Australian National University.

_____. 1995. "The Development of Sahul Agriculture with Australia as Bystander." *Antiquity* 69: 831–47.

Zvelebil, M. 1986. "Mesolithic Societies and the Transition to Farming: Problems of Time, Scale and Organization." In *Hunters in Transition: Mesolithic Societies of Temperate Eurasia and Their Transition to Farming*. M. Zvelebil, ed. 167–88. Cambridge: Cambridge University Press.

Chapter 17

THE JU/'HOANSI SAN UNDER TWO STATES

Impacts of the South West African Administration
and the Government of the Republic of Namibia

————⫸⟪◉⟫⫷————

Megan Biesele and Robert K. Hitchcock

Introduction

Hunter-gatherers have faced numerous challenges in the twentieth century. They have struggled for survival in the face of expansion of state
systems, multinational corporations, and individuals who were anxious
to exploit their lands, labor, and resources (Burch and Ellanna 1994;
Burger 1987; Leacock and Lee 1982). In many cases, foragers and former
foragers were subjected to discriminatory policies that denied them
access to employment, educational opportunities, and land. This was
particularly true in those states that practiced apartheid ("apartness") or
separate development. Under national legislation, people of color in various southern African countries such as Namibia, South Africa, and Zim-
babwe were not allowed to live where they wished or travel from one area
to another without express permission of the state. High-paying jobs and
productive land were reserved for Europeans, while African members of
the population were often relegated to native reserves where economic
and educational opportunities were few (Bixler 1992; Green et al. 1981;
Gordon 1992).

Those peoples who were subjected to these inequitable policies and
practices expended tremendous energies in resisting the mistreatment
(Mermelstein 1987). Part of this resistance took the form of organizing
efforts at the grassroots, regional, national, and international levels. The
formation of the African National Congress (ANC) in South Africa in

1912 and the South West African Peoples Organization (SWAPO) in what is now Namibia in 1960 underscored the desire of local people to chart their own course and to seek more equitable treatment from the governments of the states where they lived.

This chapter outlines the growth of a grassroots movement among the Ju/'hoan San called the Nyae Nyae Farmers Cooperative (NNFC). Dedicated to securing land tenure and development in Nyae Nyae, formerly Eastern Bushmanland (now Otjozondjupa) in Namibia, for its two thousand or so members, this cooperative has had substantial success in areas ranging from communal land rights to educational and linguistic self-determination. Issues of political enfranchisement and self-awareness, sovereignty and self-determination, and creative cultural survival of an egalitarian society are examined here in the light of apartheid-era politics and the policies of the postapartheid Namibian government.

Established in 1986, four years prior to Namibia's independence, in tandem with concerned nongovernment organization (NGO) activity and an increasingly convergent world agenda on multiculturalism and indigenous peoples' rights, the NNFC's major theme has been community self-education through community communication programs. Changing circumstances and changing realizations have dictated flexibility of leadership and communication modes since the organization began. The development of a cooperative grassroots movement is a relatively new phenomenon among the San (Bushmen, Basarwa) of southern Africa (Hitchcock 1996; Hitchcock and Holm 1993). It has meant the rapid spread of confidence and competence with which to tackle contemporary challenges of ethnicity and identity. Ju/'hoan voices have now been brought directly into the global dialogue on cultural survival of indigenous peoples. These voices, far from demanding only mainstream rights, form a fresh chorus of locally informed, environmentally and socially responsible suggestions and possibilities.

The San of Namibia

The San peoples of Namibia are receiving special attention in many areas of human rights from the new government of Namibia (Biesele 1994; Hitchcock 1996; Republic of Namibia 1991; 1992). Long before independence in March 1990, the leaders of SWAPO were aware that they would be inheriting a difficult legacy in minority rights from the previous apartheid government. Dr. Kaire Mbuende, now Deputy Minister of Agriculture, Water and Rural Development, noted in a preindependence SWAPO position paper that the San were particularly disadvantaged among Namibian societies due to the violence with which apartheid had transformed them. Since coming to power, President Sam Nujoma and his government have pursued vigorous affirmative action policies toward the San peoples in an attempt to redress offenses (Republic of Namibia 1991; 1992).

However, practical considerations like the fragmentation and dispersal of most San communities due to land dispossession have made affirmative action very difficult to implement. One exception is the Ju/'hoansi San of the Nyae Nyae region in northeastern Namibia. Ironically, the apartheid practice of setting aside blocks of land for specific ethnic groups actually protected a portion of the ancestral land of the Ju/'hoansi, who were able to remain on that land in relatively intact communities (L. Marshall 1976). Many of the more positive human rights statements that can be made about San in Namibia today apply only to this group. The Ju/'hoansi are aware of their historically privileged status (due to geographical isolation and other factors) and have taken an exemplary role with regard to other San in the country.

Until recently, little research had been done on the conditions of life among the dispossessed San, many of whom work as ill-paid laborers on European or African farms, or live as squatters in rural or urban slums. Knowing what to do about the human rights of these people would be much easier if systematic surveying work was carried out in areas like Gobabis and Aminius, Tsintsabis, the Grootfontein farm district, etc. For now, the well-documented situation of the Nyae Nyae Ju/'hoansi, living in their original communities around the administrative center at Tjum!kui (Tsumkwe), provides baseline information (and an example for the future) on the human rights status of the Namibian San minority.

Issues regarding human rights may be divided into the following categories: land rights, political rights, economic rights, and cultural rights. The discussion below provides an update in these areas for the San minority in general and the Ju/'hoansi in particular. The difficulty of generalizing about the Namibian San is underscored by the fact that at least half a dozen San languages are used in different San communities (Gordon 1992; J. Marshall 1989). At an international conference held in Windhoek in June 1992 to bring together San peoples, government officials, and NGOs involved in San welfare, nine groups from Namibia participated. They were from Drimiopsis, M'kata, Omatako, Okongo, Tsintsabis, Bagani, Mangetti Block, Rundu, Corridor #17, and Tjum!kui (Nyae Nyae). Yet even this sizable group failed to represent many other San who live in dispersed small groups on the farms and in and around the communities of other groups in Namibia, something that the representatives at the meeting took note of in their discussions (Republic of Namibia 1992).

The Ju/'hoansi (Ju/Wasi) San with whom this chapter deals are sometimes referred to as !Kung (see Barnard 1992: 39–41; Lee 1979:

37–38; L. Marshall 1976: 15–18). Numerically, they are the second largest San group in Namibia, with an estimated population of 7,000; the largest group, the Hai//om, have an estimated population of 11,000 (Axel Thoma, Thomas Widlok, personal communications). The Ju/'hoansi are found in various districts of eastern and northern Namibia, including Tsumeb, Grootfontein, Otjozondjupa (formerly, Eastern Bushmanland), and the Gobabis farming area in Omaheke region.

The primary focus of this essay is on the Nyae Nyae region in what is now the Otjozondjupa region of Namibia (see Figure 17.1). In 1991, according to the Namibian national census, the population of Eastern Otjozondjupa was 1,493. As of 1997, there were some 1,500 Ju/'hoansi living in thirty-seven dispersed communities in this region, which today covers an area of 6,300 square kilometers. Most of the Ju/'hoansi in this region survive through employing a diversified set of subsistence and income-generating strategies, including foraging, food production, reliance on income from craft sales and salaries, and, in some cases, pensions from the Namibian government.

The land tenure situation of San peoples in Namibia has been very precarious for many decades. The great majority of San groups were completely dispossessed by incoming settlers—both European and African—or deprived of their traditional foraging grounds by the previous government's Directorate of Nature Conservation (Gordon 1992; Hitchcock 1992; J. Marshall 1989). Many, such as the Khoe of West Caprivi and the Hai//om of Oshikati and Kunene regions, were peremptorily resettled out of game reserve areas into new areas where they did not know the wild food resources and had little or no access to land on which to make an independent living (Hitchcock and Murphree 1995; Widlok, this volume). The Ju/'hoansi were faced with similar pressures at various times in their history, but they were able to hold onto a fraction of their old land by defeating during the 1980s a nature conservation plan to create a game reserve for tourists in their area (J. Marshall 1989).

Until the National Conference on Land Reform and the Land Question held in Windhoek in June–July 1991, the major preoccupation of the NNFC was establishing the security of their land tenure. They did this in various ways: They asked anthropologists, missionaries, and government workers to speak on their behalf to the government of South West Africa and later the government of the Republic of Namibia. They sought to dig wells and take over boreholes that had been drilled in their area in the hopes that this would give them de facto land use rights in the vicinity of the water points.

In the early 1980s, groups of Ju/'hoansi began to leave the administrative center at Tjum!kui and reestablish themselves on their traditional territories, or, as they are known to the Ju/'hoansi, their *n!oresi* (sing.

FIGURE 17.1 Ju/'hoan Settlements in the Nyae Nyae Region, Namibia

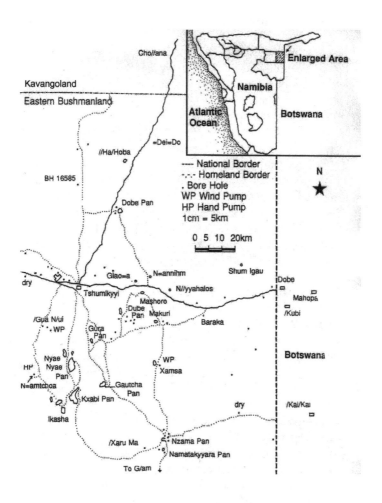

Source: Bixler (1992).

n!ore). This decentralization trend picked up steam after 1982–83, when three groups moved out to their *n!oresi* (Marshall and Ritchie 1984). By the mid-1990s, there were some thirty-seven Ju/'hoan groups living in areas to which they had long-standing customary rights (Biesele 1994; Jones 1996; Wyckoff-Baird 1996).

In the decentralized settlements, the Ju/'hoansi supported themselves through a mixed economic system involving some hunting and gathering, livestock-raising, crop production, sales of crafts, and, in some cases, wage-paying jobs (Biesele et al. 1993; J. Marshall 1989). In 1992, there were over forty people employed by the NNFC and the Nyae Nyae Development Foundation of Namibia (NNDFN), the nongovernment organization that provides technical support to the NNFC (Hitchcock 1992). Some individuals worked for the Department of Veterinary Services and the Ministry of Wildlife Conservation and Tourism (MWCT), now the Ministry of Environment and Tourism (MET). Four out of five households (80 percent) had livestock, and over 90 percent of the households engaged in crop production. Botelle et al. (1994: 141) maintain that Ju/'hoan households in the Nyae Nyae region are generally better off economically than many other Namibian San households.

The status of Ju/'hoan women, who contributed a significant proportion of the daily food supply and did a great deal of the household work, was high (Lee 1979; L. Marshall 1976). The elderly, both female and male, were respected for their knowledge and experience, and older people played important roles in Ju/'hoan society, doing numerous domestic tasks, taking care of children, and passing on knowledge to younger generations.

The Ju/'hoansi exhibit some significant features in terms of population and health. In the 1960s, the Ju/'hoansi had one of the world's slowest rates of population growth (Howell 1979; Lee 1979). The number of children born to women was between four and five. The average number of children who survived was slightly over two, meaning Ju/'hoan fertility was holding the population at the replacement rate. Infant mortality rates were moderate. The reproductive health of women was relatively good, though there were cases of venereal disease and infertility (Howell 1979).

Hunting-gathering Ju/'hoansi had very low serum cholesterol, low blood pressures that do not increase with age, and little in the way of heart disease. Ju/'hoansi were very active, going on forays for foraging and visiting purposes, carrying infants, and engaging in extensive work activities both in their camps and in the bush. Their nutritional status was relatively good, was high in vitamins and nutrients, and was diverse, with as many as 150 species of plants and over 40 species of animals consumed (Lee 1979). There were periods when people went hungry, especially during the late dry season, and undernutrition was a problem that the Ju/'hoansi had to contend with (Wilmsen 1989).

Over the past two decades, the Ju/'hoansi have undergone major social, economic, and demographic changes that have followed the shift from nomadic foraging to sedentary crop and animal raising. Population growth rates have risen to the point where some Ju/'hoan groups are increasing at a rate of 2.5 percent per annum (which would cause the population to double in twenty-eight years). Some of the hypotheses proposed for the increased growth rates range from changes in patterns of breast-feeding and female activity levels to dietary and physiological shifts. Ju/'hoansi are taller and heavier now than they used to be. Diets today are higher in carbohydrates and refined sugars, and there are indications that adult-onset diabetes is on the increase among Ju/'hoansi, a process not dissimilar to that among Native American populations after the establishment of reservations and the provision of government food. Cardiovascular disease is more common today than it was in the past among the Ju/'hoansi and other San (Trefor Jenkins, personal communication, 1985).

It is useful to compare data on living standards of San in Namibia generally and those in Eastern Otjozondjupa specifically over time. Table 17.1 provides information on San demographic and socioeconomic characteristics in Namibia as a whole in the early 1980s with data on Eastern Bushmanland under the South West African Administration in 1981 and in Eastern Otjozondjupa under the government of the Republic of Namibia in 1998 (for additional information on the latter, see also Wiessner 1998). It can be seen that the Ju/'hoan death rate has declined, although this may change with an increase in HIV/AIDS and other diseases. An increased life span is an example of some of the positive factors Ju/'hoansi have experienced since they have changed their nomadic life for a settled one.

Because of the higher calories diet, the reduced physical demands of settled life, and the availability of Western-style health care, more Ju/'hoan elders are living into their seventh and sometimes eighth decade of life. A large number of elders may prove to be particularly important for this transitional population. Older people remember the former nomadic life and have a better knowledge of the diversity of plants and animals and the different areas of the Kalahari in which they were found. As the Ju/'hoansi and other populations become more aware of the fragility of the environment, the knowledge that only elders have of a lifestyle that was in harmony with nature will become more valuable as time passes.

The Ju/'hoansi may be suffering more from the "diseases of development"—cancer and heart problems (Nurse et al. 1985; for further information see Howell 1979)—but this situation is offset by the fact that they now have greater access to health services. There is a clinic in Tjum!kui, and mobile medical assistance has been provided periodically by government and private entities and/or local people's organizations. The Ministry of Health is now in charge of that set of activities. Health education

TABLE 17.1 Comparative Data on Living Standards of San in Namibia
Generally and Eastern Otjozondjupa Specifically

	Namibia[1]	Eastern Bushmanland, 1981[2]	Eastern Otjozondjupa, 1998[3]
San population	2,245	2,800 (1,826 Ju/'hoansi)	2,059 Ju/'hoansi
Crude birth rate (CBR)	45.0 (1982)	32.6	38.0
Crude death rate (CDR)	34.4 (1982)	33.7	18.0
Tjum!kui population	552	716 (922 army)	225 Ju/'hoansi
Income per capita	R64/month or R768/year	R19/month, R280 year	N$12/month, N$144/year
Economy	salaries, rations	salaries, rations	salaries, pensions, food production, foraging, craft sales
Employed men	343	188	42
Unemployed men	787	269	378
Employed women	0	0	8

1. François Marais (1981).
2. Marshall and Ritchie (1984).
3. Nyae Nyae Development Foundation (1990–98).

programs, covering such topics as preventative health, family planning, women's reproductive health, and nutritional surveillance are on the increase. The HIV/AIDS rate among Ju/'hoansi is much lower than in the general population of Namibia, which is estimated by some analysts to be as high as 20 to 30 percent. As a result, efforts are being made to promote wide-ranging AIDS education in Eastern Otjozondjupa as well as elsewhere in Namibia. Overall, the socioeconomic and health situation of the Ju/'hoansi is higher than is the case for other San in Namibia.

Changes over Time in Northeastern Namibia

According to Marshall and Ritchie (1984: 6), the year 1970 marked a major turning point in the history of the Ju/'hoansi, as it was the year that the recommendations of the South West African government's Odendaal

Commission of 1964 were put into effect. This commission was aimed at establishing apartheid-style homelands for various ethnic groups in Namibia. Large portions of the traditional territory of the Ju/'hoansi, which they themselves estimated at around 70,000 square kilometers, was given to other groups, especially to Herero and Kavango. The Herero are a stock-keeping people who lived to the south and east of the Ju/'hoansi and who have had long-standing interactions with them, including having the Ju/'hoansi assist in herding their livestock in exchange for milk and sometimes clothing and tobacco (Biesele et al. 1989; Lee 1979; Wilmsen 1989). Some Herero brought cattle into what is now Eastern Otjozondjupa in the 1950s but were forced out by the South West African government (L. Marshall 1976: 13). Subsequent attempts were made by Herero to establish themselves in Ju/'hoan land, in part because of the grazing potential and the fact that it lacked *mogau* (*Dichapetalum cymosum*), a plant poisonous to cattle. Efforts were made by the Ju/Wa Farmers Union (JFU), established in 1986, to convince the Hereros to leave the area. This was not an easy task because some of the Ju/'hoansi had close links with Herero and were able to benefit from their presence.

Bushmanland had been declared formally as a homeland in 1976 under Proclamation 208 of South West Africa. This same proclamation called for the establishment of a Bushman Advisory Council, the membership of which was to be made up of individuals elected by San groups (Ritchie 1987: 67). The members of this council were supposed to serve as liaisons between San and the administration. In fact, according to Ju/'hoan informants, the individual who was their representative tended to take the side of the government and mainly told them what the government wanted them to do.

Changes that occurred in Bushmanland over time included the increased sedentarization of the Ju/'hoansi, nearly all of whom eventually moved into the settlement of Tjum!kui after it was established in 1960. By the late 1970s, Tjum!kui was considered "the place of death" by the Ju/'hoansi because of the high rates of conflict, spouse abuse, and infant mortality there (Marshall and Ritchie 1984; Ritchie 1987). In 1978, Bushmen Battalion 36 was established in Bushmanland when the South African Defense Force (SADF) began to recruit Ju/'hoansi into the army in earnest. The militarization of the Ju/'hoansi had profound impacts, with Ju/'hoansi soldiers receiving substantial salaries for what was decidedly high-risk work. The money that they earned was sometimes spent on their families, but it was also used for the purchase of alcohol and luxury goods (Marshall and Ritchie 1984).

By the time John Marshall and Claire Ritchie arrived in Tjum!kui in July 1980, there were major social cleavages among the Ju/'hoansi that had developed because of the destabilizing presence of the military, inequitable access to resources, and high population densities in Tjum!kui (J. Marshall

1989; Marshall and Ritchie 1984; Ritchie 1987). Many Ju/'hoansi were impoverished, unhealthy, malnourished, and despondent. It was for this reason that so many Ju/'hoansi wished to leave Tjum!kui and to resume their former lifestyles. As it turned out, the amounts of land that they had available to them were reduced substantially by the establishment of the Kaudum Game Reserve in the north and Hereroland to the south as well as the resettling of !Kung, Khwe, and Vasekela San from Angola and the Caprivi Strip in Western Bushmanland (Hitchcock 1992; J. Marshall 1989).

The lengthy struggle of the South West African Peoples Organization (SWAPO) and its allies against the South African Defense Force (SADF), which was seen as an occupation force in a country held illegally by South Africa from the time of the defeat of Germany in World War I, combined with international pressures exerted on the governments of South West Africa and South Africa, led eventually to a United Nations-assisted peace and independence process. Though under UNTAG (United Nations Transition Assistance Group) the San peoples were positive targets of the information campaign regarding the first Namibian election, their dispersal and generally low school attendance and literacy rates made it hard for them to be informed about their political rights. Some farmers in isolated areas who employ San laborers did not try to help them become better informed, preferring that they remained in ignorance so that they would not agitate for better wages or other benefits. The Ju/'hoansi sought to engage directly in the political process in order to gain greater recognition of their land and resource rights and to have a greater say in political decision-making and policy formulation.

The Ju/Wa Farmers Union, later called the Nyae Nyae Farmers Cooperative, experienced several major advances in political awareness by its membership. One of these was the first genuine election of a chairperson. Tsamkxao ≠Oma had been the chairman since the organization began in 1986, but he was in a way chairman by default, as few Ju/'hoansi at that time were bold enough to be politically articulate. /'Angn!ao /'Un's election in early 1991, then, was a real turning point for the NNFC. Observers, indeed, remarked at that time that the NNFC had taken on a life of its own (apart from its friends and NGO partner). Public statements made by the new chairman around that time reveal the growing sense of empowerment in the NNFC, as indicated in the following quotation:

> We have understood that if two people who have an interest in one area do not speak to each other but just think they each have the authority, it will work to our disadvantage. But if we work as cooperating neighbors, one coming from this direction and one from another, we will listen well to each other. So let's proceed calmly and say what we really want to have happen in our area, say all the things we want to have and to create there, because it is right that we should have the authority over our own place.... We must make straight the

direction we are going.... Our land has long ago been spoilt and made small. What spoilt it was the previous government, and now we're caught in the middle of a problem.... If we eventually have many cattle they will trample the grass and ruin the bush foods so we won't be able to find anything to eat, nor will our children. We have to plan together to have our gathering places and our hunting places. No-one should be closed off from his food by someone else; everyone should have free access to the wild foods he knows are his.... To accomplish this today we need a young person who can read and write so we can hold fast to what we have, sending papers to Windhoek.... We need an office, and a bank that is ours also.... It's our living, and that is a very big thing. These days we have to work with our own heads, because in the past it was someone else's head that got us into trouble. (/'Angn!ao /'Un)

Like a drone note in the developing rhetoric, the abuses of the preindependence regime continued to surface in public talk through these years. But during this period the NNDFN and the NNFC experienced substantial achievements made possible by the normalizing political environment in Namibia since independence on 21 March 1990. Among these achievements were the establishment and implementation of an ambitious wild resources survey and an opinion polling process for land use planning carried out by the NNDFN, NNFC, and the Namibian government's Ministry of Wildlife and Nature Conservation in 1991. A new training center, which was funded, built, and began operation in the early 1990s at Baraka, Nyae Nyae, acted as a base for agricultural and vocational training, health education, and adult literacy programs as well as housing the staff of the NNFC and NNDFN.

The NNFC blossomed as the voice of the people in both local and national forums, and came to be recognized as the "local traditional authority" in matters of settlement and land tenure in the Nyae Nyae region (Biesele 1994). At the National Conference on Land Tenure and the Land Question, the NNFC, assisted by the NNDFN, made presentations that led to the formal recognition by the Namibian Ministry of Lands of their traditional *n!ore* system as the basis for land allocation in the future. There was also an informal assurance to the NNFC by then Minister of Lands, Resettlement, and Rehabilitation (MLRR) Marco Hausiku that the *n!ore* system would provide the basis for land allocation in the Nyae Nyae area in the future, and that in other San areas, though they might have different systems, similar attention would be paid to traditional land use patterns (Republic of Namibia 1991).

Several questions were put by the NNFC delegates to the Lands Ministry, to President Nujoma, and to the leader of SWAPO, Moses Garoeb, after the Land Conference, regarding the implementation of resolutions. These questions touched on how the government would assure that the "special protection" promised by the conference for San land rights would not be co-opted in future on grounds of economic expediency. In other words, the Ju/'hoansi stressed that legislation is crucial, and that communal land rights must be as secure as those for any other landholders in Namibia.

Questions were also raised about what actual protection (ordinances, police action, etc.) would be given to local communities in the event of land encroachment by people who, for instance, have much larger herds of cattle, and about what measures were to be taken to ensure the San adequate representation on Land Boards once these are established. At this writing, no definite answers have been received. A "Technical Committee" was set up after the Land Conference to investigate the implementation of conference resolutions. This committee dealt primarily with commercial and not with communal lands. Thus, the legal status of Nyae Nyae, as of all other communal lands in Namibia, remains precarious in spite of the fact that a Communal Lands Bill was drafted in 1994–95. Noting the difficulties in communal land issues, a number of nongovernment organizations established a Working Committee on Land Reform, and held a "People's Land Conference" in Mariental, Namibia, on 4–8 September 1994, which made recommendations to the Namibian government for greater protection of people residing in communal areas of the country. This was especially important given the fact that land-hungry people were moving into many communal areas of Namibia in the 1990s, and serious land use conflicts were on the increase.

One important practical precedent regarding illegal settlement on communal lands was set, however, shortly after the 1991 Land Conference. President Nujoma said during a visit to Nyae Nyae that anyone wishing to settle in a communal land must receive the permission not only of the Ministry of Lands, Resettlement, and Rehabilitation but also of the traditional leaders in the area. The NNFC had the opportunity to test whether the government would back up this assurance late in 1991 when settlers from nearby Hereroland came to three Ju/'hoan communities without permission and began to water their cattle from community boreholes. After a full process of consultation with the illegal settlers, the NNFC was able to escort them peacefully back to the Herero border with the promised, but not necessary, backup of the local police and the regional commissioner. Minister Hausiku affirmed in *The Namibian* newspaper in 1991 that this action was legal and had the support of his Ministry.

It must be said, however, that this slim assurance, as yet unwritten anywhere in legislation, represents only a shadow of the security of tenure that the Ju/'hoansi feel they need in regard to land. The more fragmented San communities, representing the great majority of the San population, lack land access and tenure assurances even more. Information-sharing on political rights has been better organized in the Nyae Nyae area due to the grassroots organizing efforts and the presence of an active community-based organization there (Biesele 1994; J. Marshall 1989; Marshall and Ritchie 1984). But even in Nyae Nyae prior to the first elections, disinformation campaigns by warring political parties threatened the establishment of informed political enfranchisement.

A significant event in the early 1990s period was the acceptance by the Namibian Ministry of Education of a Ju/'hoan (San) language minority literacy program under its new Basic Educational Reform Program. The NNDFN was subcontracted to the government to provide this educational service for the first four years of education for Nyae Nyae children. A community-based health education program, inaugurated by the NNFC in February 1991, has trained village health workers at all of the thirty-seven "outstation" or decentralized villages in the Nyae Nyae region. There has also been institutional capacity-building done by the NNFC, the NNDFN, and the Living in a Finite Environment (LIFE) Project of the U.S. Agency for International Development (USAID) and the government of Namibia, which has served to enhance the leadership and has helped to formalize the institutional structure of the Ju/'hoansi's community-based organization (Hitchcock and Murphree 1995; Wyckoff-Baird 1996).

Cultural continuity and educational language rights are a bright spot of hope in Namibia at this writing. What is now the Namibian Ministry of Basic Education and Culture (MBEC) has made a substantial commitment to minority-language education for the first four years of school under its Basic Educational Reform Program. In this commitment it echoes sound educational policy over much of the developing world today, which holds that the best route to full literacy lies through learning literacy in the mother tongue, then generalizing this skill to English (or other national languages) after three or four years. The Ju/'hoan language is included in basic education reform as a pilot project, and its example will be used for educational programs in other San communities and language groups in other areas.

San school attendance rates have been the lowest in the nation, and current Namibian government policies aim to improve this situation quickly and substantially. Affirmative action hiring of a few San teachers has greatly improved the profile of national education in terms of attractiveness to San students and their parents. Literacy classes are being established in San communities as part of the national attempt to raise literacy rates, and San people of all ages have expressed interest in taking part.

Natural Resource Management among the Ju/'hoansi

The Ju/'hoansi have worked closely with the representatives of the NNDFN and various aid agencies in locating and mapping the boundaries of their territories and in coming up with rules for how the land and its resources should be managed within these areas. They have also worked out methods for discussing issues facing local communities such as agricultural labor allocation, distribution of livestock, and maintenance of physical infrastructure. The participation of women in the leadership of the NNFC was encouraged, and a number of the members of the management committee were women. It should be stressed, however, that a number of Ju/'hoan women maintained in interviews that they were underrepresented in the NNFC management body, something that was a concern of the cooperative management since they were under a certain amount of pressure from funding agencies to ensure gender equity.

Both Ju/'hoansi women and men have stressed the importance of maintaining "the health of the land" in northeastern Namibia. A potential environmental problem predicted by Namibian government planners was that the livestock owned by Ju/'hoansi would begin to have negative effects on the range and the wildlife populations in Eastern Otjozondjupa. Thus far, this has not happened in most areas, in part because herd sizes were relatively small, ranging from 16 to 77 per community and totaling less than 400 for the Ju/'hoansi in the 6,300 square kilometer area. There was, however, the problem of Herero cattle being brought into the area through arrangements between individual Ju/'hoansi and Herero cattle owners. Usually these arrangements included the promise of the use of the animals for milk and sometimes payment of cash or provision of food and clothing. In 1997 it was estimated that there were some 500 cattle belonging to Herero in Eastern Otjozondjupa (Barbara Wyckoff-Baird, personal communication, 1997).

A concern expressed by some government nature conservation officials was that the subsistence hunting activities of the Ju/'hoansi posed a threat to the game in the Nyae Nyae region. Some species were definitely on the decline, including reedbuck and eland. There were other species, such as elephants, leopards, cheetah, and small cats that apparently were on the rise. Not surprisingly, these trends were considered a mixed blessing by the Ju/'hoansi. One the one hand, they liked having substantial numbers of game animals in the region, while on the other, they would prefer that those animals be ones that do not cause problems for them.

The problem facing the Ju/'hoansi and other local people under the South West African government was that they had no say whatsoever in matters concerning wildlife that have effects on their domestic animals and water points. Decisions on the conservation status of wild animals and the setting of wildlife quotas for hunting were made by the Ministry of Wildlife, Conservation, and Tourism with no input from Ju/'hoansi or other local people. Wildlife resources were in the hands of the state, and the Ju/'hoansi had little, if any, say about how wildlife matters were handled. This was particularly problematic with respect to so-called "problem animals," those animals such as elephants that destroyed water points and gardens or predators such as lions, leopards, and hyenas that killed people's domestic animals. Complaints about problem animals were not responded to quickly by the Ministry of Wildlife, Conservation, and Tourism, according to Ju/'hoan informants, and the result was that all too often the animal that was shot was not the one that caused the damage to the fields, water points, or livestock.

Under Namibian law, Ju/'hoansi were not allowed to shoot lions even if they had killed some of their cattle or chased people. They were quick to point out that those people who paid large amounts of money to come into the Nyae Nyae region with a safari company *were* allowed to hunt lions. The irony of this situation was vexing to the Ju/'hoansi, who claimed that they were being discriminated against. Lions were a common topic of discussion among people interviewed in the Nyae Nyae region (Hitchcock 1992; J. Marshall 1989). As the former head of the NNFC noted in one interview, "Lions are the dogs of Western conservation." The conflicts between people and wild animals were a major source of contention both under the government of South West Africa and under the Namibian government.

Another natural resource-related issue that the NNFC had to deal with, and which came up frequently during the course of the environmental survey of Eastern Otjozondjupa in January 1991, was the use of some of the boreholes in the Nyae Nyae region for game. Some communities noted that they disliked having water points for wildlife so close to them. Others said that they would not mind having boreholes set aside specifically for game as long as they were long distances from existing communities. A number of people said that they worried about the idea of the NNFC setting aside boreholes for game because they thought that this strategy could lead to limitations being placed on livestock and farming activities. Clearly, very careful thought had to be given by the NNFC to land use and natural resource planning and management issues in the Nyae Nyae region.

The NNFC discussed a number of different strategies for dealing with wild animals and other natural resources in the Nyae Nyae region. One way to deal with wildlife, according to some of the members of the NNFC, was to gain the right to establish quotas for the numbers and types of animals that could be exploited for themselves. Such a strategy required closer cooperation between the cooperative and the Ministry of Environment and Tourism. It also necessitated greater understanding on both sides as to the reasoning behind decisions made about off-take rates and which animals should have limits placed on hunting. A second strategy was for the Ju/'hoansi themselves to monitor the wild animal numbers and distributions and on that basis make decisions themselves about which animals should be placed off limits in addition to the restrictions set by the government. It was decided at one of the NNFC meetings, for example, that roans would be declared as prohibited animals so that the roan population would have the opportunity to expand. A third strategy that the NNFC opted for was to request that the government of Namibia not give a safari hunting concession license to the safari company that had long operated in the area; in late 1992, the government of Namibia agreed to withdraw the safari concession license of Anvo Safaris.

In spite of some of the successes of the NNFC's efforts to get ministry officials to recognize their concerns, there were still some tensions between the Ju/'hoansi and the government. Many Ju/'hoansi were unclear about the Namibian government hunting regulations, especially those outlined in the Nature Conservation Amendment Act of 1986. It was not uncommon for people to be arrested for hunting from horseback with spears or to be apprehended and jailed for having killed a conserved animal. It was abundantly clear from discussions with people in the Nyae Nyae communities that there was a fair amount of antipathy toward the government's conservation officials (Hitchcock 1992; Hitchcock and Murphree 1995). This was particularly true in places where large numbers of men had been arrested for hunting violations. In one community, the entire adult male population had been arrested, causing tremendous social and economic disruption. In another case, a woman from Middle Pos was struck by a wildlife official when she complained about his dog destroying her garden.

Officials from the Ministry of Environment and Tourism sometimes failed to inform local people about the specific laws they were accused of having broken when they arrested them. When asked by the NNFC for copies of the laws, individuals from the Ministry of Wildlife Conservation and Tourism and later the Ministry of Environment and Tourism refused to provide them. The NNFC has pressed the government of Namibia to provide the Ju/'hoansi with copies of the laws, and has asked that government personnel conduct workshops to explain the implications of those laws. In the past several years, as the NNFC has worked more closely with government officials, efforts have been made to meet these requests.

A significant event in the history of the Nyae Nyae Ju/'hoansi was the establishment of a community-based natural resource management program with assistance from various NGOs and donor agencies. In 1995, the Ju/'hoansi of the Nyae Nyae region formed a committee and applied for so-called conservancy status of the Eastern Otjozondjupa region. Under current legislation in Namibia, a conservancy is an area of land in which communities have control over natural resource management and utilization (Jones 1996). The request for the establishment of the conservancy over Eastern Otjozondjupa met with success, and in November 1997, the first conservancy on communal land (which makes up over 40 percent of the country) was implemented. The NNFC is managing the area with the assistance of a group of community rangers, who serve not only as natural resource monitors but also as liaisons between local communities and the management committee of the NNFC. Some of the villages in the Eastern Otjozondjupa region have embarked on community-based tourism activities, and one of them, Makuri, has established a community campsite where tourists can stay (Ashley and Garland 1994). The money for such activities is distributed among community members who participate in the activities.

One of the advantages of having conservancy status is that the conservancy committee and the cooperative have greater control over who comes into their area. Nowadays, tourism and safari hunting companies are supposed to negotiate with the representative body of the Ju/'hoansi before they undertake tourism activities in the region. Regulations governing tourism have been drawn up by the Ju/'hoansi, and efforts have been made to let tourism companies and individual tourists know what they should and should not do when the visit the Eastern Otjozondjupa region, such as not swimming in the water tanks of local communities and cleaning up their campsites before they depart. Funds from tourism and from filmmaking have served to enhance the well-being of a fairly sizable number of Ju/'hoansi in Eastern Otjozondjupa.

Conclusion

The efforts of the Ju/'hoansi to speak out about natural resource management and land and human rights issues not only have served to enable them to gain recognition of those rights, but also have given representatives of the NNFC the confidence to work cooperatively with other groups from across the country in efforts to set up a working group aimed at enhancing their socioeconomic and political status. In January 1996, the Working Group of Indigenous Minorities in Southern Africa (WIMSA) was established in Namibia. This was done at the request of the Ju/'hoansi and other San in order to provide them with a platform to express their problems, needs, and concerns and to allow them to exchange information and ideas with other concerned individuals and groups—both San and non-San. The chairperson of the NNFC is also the head of WIMSA. One of the activities of WIMSA has been to lobby for the recognition of traditional San leaders in Namibia, something that helped provide the impetus for the Namibian government to name traditional San authorities in 1998.

The Nyae Nyae development program of the Ju/'hoansi has become the first pilot project in land use planning and community-based natural resource management in Namibia. Its efforts are serving as a model for similar kinds of work going on in the new South Africa, Botswana, Lesotho, and Swaziland. It should be emphasized, however, that the process has by no means been easy. Rights in regard to regional politics, at least in the Nyae Nyae area, potentially could have been dealt a substantial blow with the 1992 announcement by the Delimitation Commission of Namibia that Tjum!kui was to be lumped with much of Hereroland in a newly created Otjozondjupa region. Though for population reasons the Nyae Nyae area could not have hoped for regional autonomy, the very different land use and leadership patterns included in the one region could prove to be problematic. San groups included in other new regions will also experience difficulty in establishing a local political voice. Not only are there very low numbers and large distances to contend with, but also language differences and the very salient differences in cultural style regarding making community voices heard through representative leadership.

The NNFC model of decision-making and resource management had its utility, but it was not easily transferable to other areas, and it had its own complexities. Tensions sometimes arose between people in the Ju/'hoan settlements and the NNFC over issues such as the presence of Herero livestock at local communities and the frequency of visits by the cooperative management to the various settlements. Complaints were made by some people that the cooperative management personnel were not as responsive to their needs as they should be. Some Ju/'hoansi were distinctly uncomfortable with the idea of representative government, saying that they should have the right to speak for themselves at meetings and to make decisions at the community rather than the regional level. It was only after they realized that the large meetings in which all of the people in the region took part were very hard to arrange logistically and were very costly in terms of time and effort that they began to support the idea of having a kind of government by committee.

The Ju/'hoansi are sometimes taken to be "fiercely egalitarian" by anthropologists and development workers, a characterization supported by the understanding that they have very particular kinship-based altruism and resource distribution patterns. Nevertheless, they were expected by the "development" world and the government of Namibia to make a quick transition to representational leadership and a regional political vision of sharing, once the obstacles of colonialism and apartheid were cleared away. Formerly, the Ju/'hoan *n!ore kxaosi*, the oldest male or female core-group siblings in whom stewardship of resources and habitation area was vested, maintained coordinating relationships with other *n!ore kxaosi* that involved balancing the acts of giving—and strategically withholding—key environmental accesses.

With independence in Namibia, both national and developmental expectations were that these leadership and resource management attitudes would vanish overnight and give way to smoothly functioning "democratic" structures and attitudes of commitment to the health of the region as a whole. The application of an international stereotype of leadership and community management in the Ju/'hoan area of Nyae Nyae was a long and subtle process. Briefly stated, its effects have been confusion of various sorts among the *n!ore kxaosi* and their communities, between newly elected leaders and their constituencies, and, perhaps most tellingly, between the struggling new "Ju/'hoan" polity and the space tenuously saved for it in the Namibian governmental arena. As a specific example, there was a potentially dangerous feud over land and power that was fostered between the extended families of two formerly cooperating *n!ore kxaosi* by the very process of selecting leaders for the NNFC and defining leadership roles. Worse, as the cooperative became in the eyes of the Namibian government the "local traditional authority" in the absence of a headman tradition, the political representation structure for the area as a whole was threatened by this same process.

It may have been unrealistic to anticipate that Ju/'hoan leadership would rally without conflict to a regional or even ethnic cause. New Ju/'hoan leaders have been expected to transcend both the long-tenured social attitudes of their relatives toward non-self-aggrandizement and their own traditional altruism patterns as they forged new public selves and organizational functions. Individuals have suffered mightily in this process, and communities' early faith in the new leaders was eroded by the vision of the widening gap between old and new social values.

Yet the pressure to conform to outside expectations of efficiency and altruism increases every day. The danger of "distortion by expectation" must be taken into account as we assess the well-intentioned mentoring processes now becoming widespread in development efforts among indigenous peoples (for a discussion of participation processes among indigenous peoples, see Davis and Soefestad 1995). Unconscious models as well as conscious ones can affect developing local political structures, and in some cases could spell disaster for peoples with internal governance still functioning. Fortunately, in the case of the Ju/'hoansi, this has not happened, in part because of the level-headed practical approach of the Ju/'hoan people to conflict management and social problem resolution.

There is no question that a politicization process has been going on among Namibian and other San peoples (Hitchcock 1996; Thoma and Piek 1996). It has been led to some extent by the example of the Nyae Nyae Farmers Cooperative, since the NNFC has managed to gain a voice in local and national forums and to inform itself substantially about securing government services and funding. This process is in line with the contemporary realization by other world indigenous minorities that they can and must demand their political rights by becoming vocal on their own behalf (Burger 1987).

The politics of translation are also, as they should be, looming large for Ju/'hoansi today. There is a great mutual truth that is discovered over and over by indigenous peoples and their friends, but seems now to be growing ever surer. In the favorable human rights climate, at least at this moment in Namibia, we have "only to ask" Ju/'hoansi and other San people what they think. Enfranchisement of their own language's political voice and acceptance of their growing facility with the new national language, English, in both oral and written form, are finally moving them toward equality in discourse. This is a far cry indeed from apartheid and its distorted modes of communication.

Attention to better communication and to addressing the historically created conditions of unfairness that characterized the South West African administration under South Africa will have to take place on a massive scale. Nowhere are injustice and cultural blundering more apparent than in the tragic inability of the Roman-Dutch legal system still reigning in Namibia today to address the needs and sensibilities of Fourth World groups such as the Ju/'hoansi. Like former foragers everywhere in a world of agriculture and industry, San frequently run afoul of this system because it defines out of existence some of their very bases of survival. It is hoped that as their political and legal expertise increases, the Ju/'hoansi will be able to hold their own in the complex socioeconomic environment of southern Africa today.

References

Ashley, C., and E. Garland. 1994. "Promoting Community-Based Tourism Development: Why, What, and How?" Research Discussion Paper Number 4. Windhoek, Namibia: Directorate of Environmental Affairs, Ministry of Environment and Tourism.

Barnard, A. 1992. *Hunters and Herders of Southern Africa: A Comparative Ethnography of the Khoisan Peoples.* Cambridge: Cambridge University Press.

Biesele, M. 1994. "Human Rights and Democratization in Namibia: Some Grassroots Political Perspectives." *African Rural and Urban Studies* 1(2): 49–72.

Biesele, M., M. Guenther, R. Hitchcock, R. Lee, and J. MacGregor. 1989. "Hunters, Clients, and Squatters: The Contemporary Socioeconomic Status of Botswana Basarwa." *African Study Monographs* 9(3): 109–51.

Bixler, D. S. 1992. "Parallel Realities: Ju/wasi of Nyae Nyae and South African Policy in Namibia 1950–1990." M.A. Thesis, University of Nebraska, Lincoln, Nebraska.

Bixler, D., M. Biesele, and R. Hitchcock. 1993. "Land Rights, Local Institutions, and Grassroots Development among the Ju/'hoansi of Northeastern Namibia," *IWGIA Newsletter* 93: 23–29.

Botelle, A., R. Rohde, and I. van Rhyn. 1994. *Those Who Live on the Land: Land Use Planning in the Communal Areas of Eastern Otjondjupa: A Socio-economic Baseline Survey.*

Windhoek, Namibia: Ministry of Lands, Resettlement, and Rehabilitation (MLRR) and the Social Science Division (SSD), University of Namibia.

Burch, E. S., Jr., and L. J. Ellanna, eds. 1994. *Key Issues in Hunter-Gatherer Research.* Oxford and Providence: Berg Publishers.

Burger, J. 1987. *Report from the Frontier: The State of the World's Indigenous Peoples.* London: Zed Press.

Davis, S. H., and L. T. Soefestad, 1995. *Participation and Indigenous Peoples.* Washington, D.C.: World Bank.

François Marais. 1981. *Survey of the Bushmen Population in South West Africa.* Windhoek, Namibia: Office of Development Coordination and South West African Administration.

Gordon, R. J. 1992. *The Bushman Myth: The Making of a Namibian Underclass.* Boulder, Colo., and London: Westview Press.

Green, R., M.-L. Kiljunen, and K. Kiljunen. 1981. *Namibia: The Last Colony.* Burnt Mill, Harlow, Essex: Longman.

Hitchcock, R. K. 1992. *Communities and Consensus: An Evaluation of the Activities of the Nyae Nyae Development Foundation and the Nyae Nyae Farmers Cooperative in Northeastern Namibia.* Windhoek, Namibia: Nyae Nyae Development Foundation, and New York: Ford Foundation.

_____. 1996. *Kalahari Communities: Bushmen and the Politics of the Environment in Southern Africa.* IWGIA Document No. 79. Copenhagen, Denmark: International Work Group for Indigenous Affairs.

Hitchcock, R. K., and J. D. Holm. 1993. "Bureaucratic Domination of African Hunter-Gatherer Societies: A Study of the San in Botswana," *Development and Change* 24(2): 305–38.

Hitchcock, R. K., and M. W. Murphree. 1995. *Report of the Field Assessment Team, Phase III of the Mid-Term Assessment of the LIFE Project, USAID/Namibia Component (690–0251.73).* Windhoek, Namibia, and Washington, D.C.: U. S. Agency for International Development.

Howell, N. 1979. *Demography of the Dobe !Kung.* New York: Academic Press.

Jones, B. T. B. 1996. "Institutional Relationships, Capacity, and Sustainability: Lessons Learned from a Community-Based Conservation Project, Eastern Tsumkwe District, Namibia, 1991–1996." Research Discussion Paper No. 11. Windhoek, Namibia: Directorate of Environmental Affairs, Ministry of Environment and Tourism.

Leacock, E., and R. Lee, eds. 1982. *Politics and History in Band Societies.* Cambridge: Cambridge University Press.

Lee, R. B. 1979. *The !Kung San: Men, Women, and Work in a Foraging Society.* Cambridge, Mass.: Harvard University Press.

Marshall, L. 1976. *The !Kung of Nyae Nyae.* Cambridge, Mass.: Harvard University Press.

Marshall, J. 1989. *The Constitution and Communal Lands in Namibia: Land Rights and Local Governments. Helping 33,000 People Classified as "Bushmen," The Ju/Wa Case.* Windhoek, Namibia: Ju/Wa Bushman Development Foundation.

Marshall, J., and C. Ritchie. 1984. *Where Are the Ju/Wasi of Nyae Nyae? Changes in a Bushman Society, 1958–1981.* Center for African Studies, University of Cape Town, Communications No. 9. Cape Town: University of Cape Town.

Mermelstein, D., ed. 1987. *The Anti-Apartheid Reader: South Africa and the Struggle Against White Rule.* New York: Grove Press.

Nurse, G. T., J. S. Weiner, and T. Jenkins. 1985. *The Peoples of Southern Africa and Their Affinities.* Oxford: Clarendon Press.

Nyae Nyae Development Foundation. 1990–98. *Annual Reports of the Nyae Nyae Development Foundation.* Windhoek, Namibia: Nyae Nyae Development Foundation of Namibia and Nyae Nyae Farmers Cooperative.

Republic of Namibia. 1991. *National Conference on Land Reform and the Land Question, Windhoek, 25 June–1 July 1991, Volume 1: Research Papers, Addresses, and Consensus Document.* Windhoek, Namibia: Government of the Republic of Namibia, Office of the Prime Minister.

_____. 1992. *Regional Conference on Development Programs for Africa's San Populations, Windhoek, Namibia, 16–18 June 1992.* Windhoek, Namibia: Government of the Republic of Namibia, Ministry of Lands, Resettlement, and Rehabilitation.

Ritchie, C. 1987. "The Political Economy of Resource Tenure in the Kalahari: San Survival in Namibia and Botswana." M.A. Thesis, Boston University, Boston, Mass.

Thoma, A., and J. Piek. 1996. "Customary Law and Traditional Authority of the San." CASS Paper No. 36. Windhoek, Namibia: Center for Applied Social Sciences.

Wiessner, P. 1998. *Population, Subsistence, and Social Relations in the Nyae Nyae Area: Three Decades of Change.* Windhoek, Namibia: Nyae Nyae Development Foundation and Nyae Nyae Farmers Cooperative.

Wilmsen, E. N. 1989. *Land Filled with Flies: A Political Economy of the Kalahari.* Chicago: University of Chicago Press.

Wyckoff-Baird, B. 1996. "Democracy: Indicators from the Ju/'hoan Bushmen in Namibia," *Cultural Survival Quarterly* 20(2): 18–21.

Chapter 18

RUSSIA'S NORTHERN INDIGENOUS PEOPLES

Are They Dying Out?

=◉=

Dmitrii D. Bogoiavlenskii

The ethnic heterogeneity of the population of the former USSR has often been noted in the literature (Andreev et al. 1992; Bondarskaia 1977; Darskii and Andreev 1991). But the indigenous peoples of northern Russia stand out as an exception to this demographic diversity. Although they are not a homogeneous group, they are united by their small numbers,[1] their unique traditional economy (based on reindeer-herding, hunting, and fishing), the prevalence among them in the past (and even in some cases today) of a nomadic and semi-nomadic way of life, their limited socioeconomic development, and their cultural structure. All of the above allows us to refer to them as peoples of the Fourth World. One more aspect unites them: for over one hundred years the peoples of the North have been inseparable from the notion of being "almost extinct" (or "dying out").

In the second half of the nineteenth century, scholars came to the conclusion that the peoples of the North were dying out, based on materials gathered on some peoples, on some territories, and in some periods. They thought this loss of population resulted from the collision of aboriginal peoples with those from more technologically advanced societies. But Patkanov's precise 1911 calculation, based on extensive census materials, showed that there was no clear answer as to whether the indigenous population of the North was falling (Patkanov 1911). Moreover, based on the results of the 1926 census, Krasil'nikov declared that "the biggest part of the circumpolar peoples live in favorable conditions for natural increase, so there is no question of their dying out" (Krasil'nikov 1928). Nevertheless, the idea that the northern aborigines were doomed to die became very strong in Soviet northern literature between the 1920s and the 1980s. This literature, however, emphasized that the northern peoples were doomed in Tsarist Russia, and, of course, were saved by the October Revolution in 1917.

The peoples of the North became an object of special Soviet policies in the 1920s that were intended to quickly integrate their economy, culture, and way of life into a so-called "family of peoples, national in form, socialist in content." We will discuss neither the character of the state policy toward the peoples of the North—sometimes "traditionalist" or "modernizing" or "paternalistic"—nor the degree of force used in its administration. Rather, we will limit ourselves to the remark that one of the criteria of the success of this policy, at least in public documents, became growth in population (see Table 18.1). Now the post-Communist literature insists that it was during the Soviet time that these peoples were doomed. In any case, because of this widespread belief that the northern peoples were dying out, population growth among the peoples of the North became one of the most important indices of Soviet politicized ethnic statistics.

This chapter examines the population dynamics of northern Russia's indigenous peoples over the past thirty years. Before discussing these dynamics, the quality and peculiarities of census statistics, which are the basis for all population accounts, should be discussed. The possible inaccuracies in census reports of northern peoples can be explained by the following factors:

1. *Underenumeration of population.* In the past, underenumeration in distant northern regions could be substantial because of the people's nomadic way of life and widespread illiteracy. The likelihood of underenumeration is not so great now, but it is still a possibility.
2. *Changing or wrong definitions of ethnic groups in different censuses.* For example, the Chuvans, Oroks, and Enetses were not defined as distinct ethnic groups in the 1959, 1970, and 1979 censuses. Evenks and Evens were sometimes mistaken because their names sounded so much alike. There are many other examples of such inaccuracies.
3. *Overenumeration of population.* The northern peoples could also have been overcounted, because of the special attention focused on them, and because the census and its results in the former USSR were more political than statistical.

As a result, it is better to study the numbers of each ethnic group in the territories where they live rather than in the country as a whole (Tables 18.1 and 18.2). First, one can see the diversity of dynamics among different peoples. Some ethnic groups are growing rapidly: we can call the

TABLE 18.1 **Population Dynamics of the Indigenous Northern Peoples (of the former USSR; by population censuses)**

Peoples	1959	1970	1979	1989
All peoples	131,111	153,246	158,324	184,448
Nenetses	23,007[1]	28,705[1]	29,894[1]	34,665
Evenks	24,151[2; 9]	25,149[9]	27,294[9]	30,163[9]
Khantys	19,410	21,138	20,934	22,521
Evens	9,121[9]	12,029[9]	12,523[9]	17,199[9]
Chukchis	11,727[3]	13,597[3]	14,000[3]	15,184
Nanais	8,026	10,005	10,516	12,023
Koriaks	6,287	7,487	7,879	9,242
Mansis	6,449	7,710	7,563	8,474
Dolgans	3,932	4,877	5,053	6,945
Nivkhs	3,717	4,420	4,397	4,673
Sel'kups	3,768	4,282	3,565	3,612
Ulchis	2,055	2,448	2,552	3,233
Itel'mens	1,109	1,301	1,370	2,481[10]
Udeges	1,444	1,469	1,551	2,011[11]
Saamis	1,792	1,884	1,888	1,890
Siberian Yupiks	1,118	1,308	1,510	1,719
Chuvans	...[4]	...[4]	...[4]	1,511
Nganasans	748	953[11]	867	1,278[11]
Yukagirs	442	615	835	1,142
Kets	1,019	1,182	1,122	1,113
Oroches	782[5]	1,089[5]	1,198[5]	915
Tofas	586[11]	620	763[11]	731
Aleuts	421	441	546	702
Negidals	...[6]	537	504	622
Enetses	...[7]	...[7]	...[7]	209
Oroks	...[8]	...[8]	...[8]	190

1. Together with Enetses.
2. Together with Negidals.
3. Together with Chuvans.
4. Were counted as Chukchis.
5. Together with Oroks.
6. Were counted as Evenks.
7. Were counted as Nenetses.
8. Were counted as Oroches.
9. In every census, some Evenk groups were registered as Evens, and vice versa.
10. In 1989, about 500 Kamchadals of the Magadan region registered as Itel'mens; before they were registered as Russians.
11. Some other ethnic groups were incorrectly added to them.

Sources: Chislennost' (1985: 72–73); Itogi (1973: 10); Natsionalnii sostav (1991: 6); unpublished GOSKOMSTAT (State Statistical Department) data.

TABLE 18.2 **Population Dynamics of the Indigenous Northern Peoples in Native Regions**

Peoples	Native Regions	1959	1970	1979	1989	Annual Growth Rate (%)[1]		
						1959–69	1970–78	1979–88
Nenetses, Enetses	ARK, TUM, KRS	22,073	27,518	28,241	32,579	2.0	0.3	1.4
Evenks, Evens	YKT		13,042	15,568	17,347	23,096	1.6	1.2	1.9
Evenks, Evens	KHB	5,071	5,053	5,057	5,610	0.0	0.0	1.0
Evenks[2]	KRS, IRK, BUR, CHT, AMU	9,785	10,534	10,268	11,037	0.7	-0.3	0.7
Evens[3]	KMC, MGD	4,027	4,825	4,871	5,569	1.7	0.1	0.3
Khantys	TUM, TOM	18,703	20,443	19,821	21,175	0.8	-0.3	0.7
Chukchis/ Chuvans	MGD, KMC, YKT	11,499	13,213	13,613	15,551	1.3	0.3	1.3
Nanais	KHB, PRI, SKL	7,726	9,607	9,850	11,180	2.0	0.3	1.8
Koriaks	KMC, MGD	6,008	7,147	7,132	8,203	1.6	0.0	2.6
Mansis	TUM	5,829	7,025	6,727	7,268	1.7	-0.5	0.8
Dolgans[4]	KRS	3,895	4,574	4,643	5,460	1.5	0.2	1.6
Nivkhs	KHB, SKL	3,613	4,218	4,221	4,394	1.4	0.0	0.4
Sel'kups	TUM, TOM, KRS	3,669	4,186	3,319	3,346	1.2	-1.5	0.1
Ulchis	KHB	2,007	2,272	2,311	2,733	1.1	0.2	0.7
Itel'mens[5]	KMC	985	1,077	1,184	1,441	0.8	1.1	2.0
Udeges	KHB, PRI	1,329	1,288	1,275	1,463	-0.3	-0.1	1.4
Saamis	MUR	1,687	1,715	1,565	1,615	0.1	-1.0	0.3
Sib. Yupiks	MGD	1,079	1,203	1,341	1,531	1.0	1.2	1.3
Nganasans	KRS	694	789	789	1,128	1.2	0.0	3.6
Yukagirs	YKT, MGD	419	549	725	925	2.5	3.1	2.5
Kets	KRS	964	1,093	994	994	1.0	-1.0	0.0
Oroches, Oroks	KHB, SKL	600	859	785	840	3.3	-1.0	0.7
Tofas	IRK	429	507	515	630	1.5	0.2	2.0
Aleuts	KMC	332	344	365	390	0.3	0.7	0.7
Negidals	KHB	...	454	459	502	...	0.1	0.9

The abbreviations for the regions are: MUR = Murmansk, ARK = Arkhangelsk, TUM = Tiumen, TOM = Tomsk, KRS = Krasnoiarsk, IRK = Irkutsk, BUR = Buriatia, CHT = Chita, AMU = Amur, KHB = Khabarovsk, PRI = Primorskii krai, SKL = Sakhalin, KMC = Kamchatka, MGD = Magadan, YKT = Yakutia.

1. A negative number indicates a population decrease.
2. With Evenk groups in these regions.
3. With Even groups in these regions.
4. Without Dolgans of YKT, who were registered only during the latest census.
5. Without Itel'mens of MGD, who were registered only during the latest census.

Sources: Chislennost' (1985: 76–101); Itogi (1962: 312–37); Itogi (1973: 63–150); Natsional-nii sostav (1990: 102–52); unpublished GOSKOMSTAT (State Statistical Department) data.

growth of the Yukagirs "explosive," while the Evenks and Evens of Yakutia, the Nenetses, the Nanais, and the Tofas are all expanding in number. Then there are groups that are not growing and are even declining, such as the Evenks and Evens of the Khabarovsk region, the Saamis, the Sel'kups, and the Kets. There is, however, one thing common to the population dynamics of all the northern peoples: the period of the 1970s differed greatly from the 1960s and the 1980s for all groups (Table 18.2). The 1970s witnessed a dramatic decline in the population growth rate among the peoples of the North. A demographic analysis shows that although this decline was brought about by a decrease in fertility (together with increased assimilation into the non-Native population, mostly Russians), the low natural increase of the population itself was also determined by the extremely high mortality rate. Before we describe that situation, a few words about the nature of the statistical information have to be said. All data in this chapter are taken from official Soviet and Russian state statistical materials and the files of Registrars' Offices, which are characterized by incomplete data recording, especially in the 1960s.

Mortality

Of all demographic measures, the high death rate most strikingly distinguishes the northern peoples from almost all other peoples of the former USSR. Even such a rough index as the crude death rate was for a long time significantly higher for northern people than for the average Russian resident. This difference became slightly less only during the second half of the 1980s.

But by applying more sophisticated and accurate indexes—like the average life expectancy or standardized death rate—one can get a more exact picture of the situation. Thus, in 1978–79, the average life expectancy among northern peoples was almost eighteen years less than the national average; in 1988–89, it was ten years shorter than that for the whole population of Russia (Table 18.3).

In spite of the general stability of crude death rates in the 1960s and 1970s, the breakdown of deaths by age and by cause changed significantly. Infant mortality was slowly declining, as was child mortality, to a lesser extent (Table 18.4). But the death rate among the middle, or so-called working-age, groups was increasing. It is among these working-age groups that the mortality rate of northern people by far exceeds the rate for the entire former USSR. The standardized crude death rate among northern peoples of all ages was 2.6 times higher than that for the USSR as a whole in 1978–79. But for ages 25 to 30, the death rate among northern peoples was six times the national average, and for ages 35 to 50 it was four or five

TABLE 18.3 Life Expectancy (at birth; in years)

		1978–79	1988–89
Russia: Total population[1]	male	61.7	64.5
	female	73.1	74.4
Indigenous northern peoples[2]	male	44.3	54.0
	female	54.1	65.0

1. Demographic Yearbook (1994: 83).
2. My computations from unpublished GOSKOMSTAT (State Statistical Department) data and from my collection.

TABLE 18.4 Infant Mortality (per 1,000 live births)

	Official 1 yr[1]	Author's 5 yr[2]	Total Russian[3]
1965	68	120.0	26.6
1970	75	104.3	23.0
1975	58	81.5	23.7
1980	48	62.1	22.1
1985	46	47.3	20.7
1986	37	44.3	19.3
1987	33	40.0	19.4
1988	36	37.4	18.9
1989	30	35.6	17.8
1990	34	35.0	17.4
1991	29	35.0	17.8
1992	31	34.7	18.0
1993	36	35.6	19.9

1. Computed from unpublished GOSKOMSTAT (State Statistical Department) data.
2. My estimates (5-year average).
3. Demographic Yearbook (1994: 343).

times the national average. In fact, the probability of dying at a working age was higher for peoples of the North in the late 1970s than it was for Russians at the end of the last century (1896–97).

The breakdown of deaths by cause also changed. In the late 1950s, the main causes of death among northern people were infections and parasitic diseases, primarily tuberculosis. By the 1970s, death from these causes was dropping, and the leading causes of death had become traumas, accidents, and intoxication. Home and occupational traumas, homicides, and suicides (hereafter injuries) caused 30 to 60 percent of all deaths among peoples of the North (Table 18.5).

S. M. Navasardov calculated in 1985 that if we could have somehow eliminated deaths due to four classes of causes—diseases of the circulatory and respiratory systems, neoplasms (cancers), and infectious diseases—the

TABLE 18.5 Deaths by Causes (percentage of total number of deaths)

Indigenous Northern Peoples	Years	Infec- tion	Can- cer	Card./ vasc.	Respi- ratory	Injur- ies	Others and Unknown
Kamchatka Oblast'[3]	1958–62	24.7	7.6	7.6	14.2	17.8	28.0
Chukotka Okrug[2]	1958–59	40.9	9.4	4.5	10.1	9.4	25.7
Kamchatka Oblast'[3]	1968–72	12.4	10.7	13.7	11.4	36.5	15.2
Kamchatka Oblast'[3]	1978–82	5.7	9.6	15.3	12.0	47.8	9.5
Chukotka Okrug[2]	1978–79	6.1	15.4	18.4	16.4	35.9	7.8
Kamchatka Oblast'[3]	1988–92	4.0	12.1	29.8	5.9	36.9	11.3
Chukotka Okrug[3]	1988–89	5.9	19.7	24.1	14.2	23.5	12.6
6 Northern Regions of Russia[3]	1988–89	6.2	13.2	26.7	10.7	30.0	13.2
Total population of Russia[1]	1981	1.8	15.2	52.6	7.8	15.0	7.6
Total population of Russia[1]	1988	2.1	17.5	57.3	5.8	10.4	6.9

1. Demographic Yearbook (1994: 268).
2. Navasardov (1985).
3. My computation based on my collection.

average life expectancy of the indigenous population of Chukotka would have increased by 8.1 years (above what it was in 1978–79). But a hypothetical elimination of death by only one class of causes—that is, injuries (accidents, suicides, and homicides)—would have increased the average life expectancy by 10.9 years (Navasardov 1985). The increase in the death rate among working-age people, its decline among children, and the numerous cases of violent deaths all point to a social rather than a climatic or ethnic phenomenon.

The invasion of the North by companies "developing" its riches and the government's policy of encouraging agriculture—both of which led to a dramatic loss of fishing and hunting grounds and reindeer pastures—had severe consequences for the indigenous populations: Villages that were considered to have no economic futures were merged. Industrial activities damaged the land. Many indigenous people left their traditional industries. Young people were brought up in boarding schools, away from their families and traditional households, and were not inclined to spend their lives on the tundra or in the taiga. In large villages, where all of the jobs that require any special qualifications were taken by newcomers, large groups of indigenous people either took unskilled, undesirable, low-paying jobs, or had no jobs at all. Widespread poverty, loss of much of their traditional culture, and alienation from the newcomers' culture took a heavy toll on the indigenous peoples. Alcohol abuse and crime rose (Bogoiavlenskii 1987).

The high number of homicides and suicides among the northern peoples illustrates this social disintegration. In the six northern regions (Tiumen, Krasnoiarsk, Yakutia, Khabarovsk, Kamchatka, and Magadan), the suicide rate among indigenous people in 1988–89 was about 60 per 100,000 inhabitants and the homicide rate about 30 per 100,000 inhabitants. By comparison, among the entire population of the former USSR, the suicide rate was 20 per 100,000 and the homicide rate 8 per 100,000 (for the Russian Federation, the rates were 25 and 11).

However, since 1985 there has been a significant decline in deaths caused by accidents, intoxication, and injuries—a decline directly related to the anti-alcohol campaign in recent years. The number of deaths through violent causes has decreased generally, and the crude death rate has dropped significantly. The crude death rate fell to its lowest point in 1987, after which it began to slowly rise again. But as of today, this rate is still considerably lower than it was in the late 1970s. The difference in the average life expectancy between the northern people and the total population of the country also dropped from 18 years in 1978–79 to 10 years in 1988–89. The main reason for the lower average life expectancy of the indigenous northern peoples continues to be deaths caused by accidents, intoxication, and injuries. These deaths account for 6 of the total 11-year difference among men and for 3 of the 9-year difference among women.

Fertility

The second component of population growth is the birth rate. Changes in the birth rate among northern peoples can be explained largely by three factors: (1) widespread adoption of birth control; (2) structural changes in the population such as demographic waves, which change the number of women of childbearing age; (3) changes in the political and economic situation, which may include changes in governmental policy toward children, birth rates, and families, and in economic incentives.

The drastic decline in the number of births at the end of the 1960s and in the first half of the 1970s, as shown in Table 18.2, can be explained by the relatively small number of women of childbearing age, compounded by the introduction of birth control. In those years, the main group of childbearing women comprised those born in the 1940s and in the first half of the 1950s. There were few women of that age, because the death rate among northern people had been catastrophically high during the 1940s and early 1950s. In the second half of the 1970s, women born in the late 1950s and 1960s came of childbearing age. The number of newborns, as well as the crude birth rates, began to increase. This growth rate accelerated even more in the early 1980s, when the state adopted measures in support of large families and families with small children. That tendency lasted until 1987.

So population growth in recent times can be explained partially by structural changes and partially by political factors, especially the government's demographic policy. In addition, a significant increase was observed in the birth rate among young women, the majority of whom were not married. For instance, of the children born to Koriak and Even women in the Karaginsk and Penzhinsk areas of the Kamchatka district from 1983 to 1986, more than 50 percent were born out of wedlock (as compared with 16 percent among the nonindigenous population of Kamchatka).

Many nonindigenous residents of the North believe that the birth rate among indigenous peoples is high and uncontrollable. But that's not true. Although the birth rate among indigenous peoples is high compared with that of newcomers, it is far lower than that of the peoples of Central Asia (see Table 18.6). Sociological studies have noted that the desired number of children has decreased among younger indigenous women (Boiko 1977; Pika and Bogoiavlenskii 1988; Tomskii 1980). However, that number is still relatively high. This makes the present situation unstable, and, under certain conditions (strengthening of national identity, increased prestige of traditional occupations and crafts, and the pro-birth policy of the government, for example), some growth in the birth rate is possible. Structural changes will promote a decrease in the birth rate in the 1990s.

Marriage

One feature characteristic of northern peoples today is the low marriage rate. The dominant demographic factors contributing to this low rate are the relatively late average age at which northern people marry, the instability of ethnically mixed marriages, and the large number of widows, explained by the high death rate among indigenous men. Therefore, even though there are relatively few indigenous women who never marry, in 1978–79 the maximum share of indigenous married women reached a rate of only 75 percent in the 30 to 34 age group. That compared with 82 percent among same-age women in the entire USSR, and 82 to 88 percent among nonindigenous northern women.

The low marriage rate among some northern peoples (for instance, the Saamis and Mansis) and the late age at which they married were noted even in the last century. But among other peoples (ethnic groups in the Amur River area, and also among the Koriaks and Chukchis), it is a new phenomenon. In the 1960s and 1970s, the marriage rate among northern women was either on the decrease or remained at a low level. This decline

TABLE 18.6 **Total Fertility Rate**[*]

	1958–59	1969–70	1978–79	1988–89
Russia: Total population[1]	2.6	2.0	1.9	2.1
Indigenous northern peoples[2]	4.7	4.4	3.4	3.6
Uzbekistan: Total population[1]	4.9	5.7	5.1	4.2

*Number of children each woman would have if current fertility rates applied throughout her childbearing years.

1. Demographic Yearbook (1991: 308, 310); Population (1990: 328–29).
2. My estimates from unpublished GOSKOMSTAT (State Statistical Department) data.

in nuptiality also caused some decline in the birth rate. However, as mentioned above, many northern children are born out of wedlock.

The differences in the educational background of indigenous women and men (women are better educated), in their occupations (men are usually engaged in traditional occupations and women more in service jobs like administrative, educational, and secretarial jobs), and quite often even in where they live (men in the tundra and taiga, women in villages) lead to different views on the institutions of matrimony and family. More and more often, indigenous women prefer to marry nonindigenous men, while marriages between indigenous men and nonindigenous women are very rare. As a rule, mixed marriages produce fewer children and are less stable.

The marriage rate among northern men is very low because of the late age at which they marry, because a rather large share (3 percent) never marry at all, and because there are many widowers as a result of the high death rate among women. At the same time, this large proportion of unmarried men contributes to their high death rate (i.e., married men have a longer life expectancy). Peoples of the North have distinctively more widows and widowers than do nonindigenous peoples (see Table 18.7). The numbers of widows—and especially widowers—are several times higher than the average figures for the country. That there are so many widowed people is due to the extraordinarily high death rates among indigenous people in their middle years. Because the high mortality occurs after the peak childbearing years, the birth rate is not heavily affected.

Ethnic Processes

Besides the natural growth processes, the dynamics of the northern indigenous population are also affected by the processes of assimilation (Kozlov 1969). The influence of assimilation may be evaluated by comparing the population growth of various peoples as recorded in census

TABLE 18.7 Widowhood (1988–89; per 1,000 same-age group)

Age Groups	Widowers Indigenous Northern Peoples of Russia[1]	Total Pop. of Russia[2]	Widows Indigenous Northern Peoples of Russia[1]	Total Pop. of Russia[2]
30–34	1	2	32	13
35–39	21	4	54	25
40–44	36	8	101	43
45–49	84	16	183	84

1. My computations from unpublished 1989 census data.
2. Vozrast' i sostoianie (1990: 62).

data with the natural growth recorded in current registrations. Such a comparison is technically not quite correct—because during a census, national or ethnic identity is self-reported, whereas in everyday registration, the information is taken from documents. Nevertheless, we can state that the peoples of the North are, in general, being assimilated by other ethnic groups and particularly by Russians. Despite the growing ethnic awareness among indigenous people in recent times, losses due to assimilation are in our estimation increasing (such losses have been calculated by comparing the difference in children born to indigenous women with the number of persons who report belonging to one of the indigenous groups). During 1959 to1969, such losses were at 2 percent of the total population of northern people; during 1969 to 1978 at about 4 percent, and during 1979 to 1988 at over 5 percent.

The probability of assimilation is increasing, if only because the proportion of children born to mixed marriages grows with every new generation. In 1990, half of the children born to northern women were of mixed ethnic parentage, whereas in the early 1960s they accounted for only 30 percent. The proportion of ethnically mixed families is also growing, and fewer and fewer northern families are completely indigenous. The impact of Russian culture is becoming stronger, which is apparent in the increasing number of people declaring Russian as their native language and the decreasing number of those speaking indigenous languages. In 1959, only 15 percent of the people of the North claimed Russian as their native language; in 1970, it was 23 percent; in 1979, 29 percent; and in 1989, a sizable 36 percent. Accordingly, there has been a decrease in the proportion of the peoples of the North who have command of their native languages (from 76 percent in 1959 to 52 percent in 1989). If we add those who have fluent second-language command of Russian to those people who consider Russian their native language, we arrive at a Russian-language proportion of 87 percent for the entire northern population in 1989. At the same time, 55 percent of all of the indigenous people of the North were fluent in their native language, used either as a first or second language.

Among northern ethnic groups, some—including the Khantys, Mansis, Sel'kups, and Kets—are assimilating more quickly than others; the assimilation losses among these ethnic groups are over 10 percent per decade. The Saamis, Oroches, Nivkhs, and Evenks (except the Evenks of Yakutia) suffer 5 to 10 percent losses per decade, while the Tofas, Nanais, and Evens experience less than 5 percent losses. The Chukchis, Koriaks, and Siberian Yupiks experience virtually no assimilation losses. And only a few of the ethnic groups—namely the Yukagirs, Aleuts, and Dolgans—have actually shown gains rather than assimilation losses in recent times. However, in our view, this increment is real only for the Dolgans. For the Aleuts and the Yukagirs, whose numbers are very small, the increase is more likely to be the result of statistical inaccuracies.

Conclusion

The demographic characteristic that stands out most when we look at the indigenous peoples of the North is their extremely high death rate, which up to the mid-1980s was decreasing exceptionally slowly (and in some periods, even increasing). Only during the last five years has there been a notable drop in the death rate. Birth rates among indigenous peoples tended to decline over the last thirty years due to widespread use of birth control, although wave-like fluctuations in the number of women of childbearing age may have created an impression of sharp, temporary increases in birth rates.

Concerning the issue of whether the northern peoples are becoming extinct, in our minds there can be no unequivocal answer. On the one hand, during the period under study (thirty years), a real increase in the annual number of deaths over the number of births occurred only a few times in small ethnic groups and was clearly atypical. Disastrously high death rates that significantly reduced the northern indigenous population did occur in the 1940s and early 1950s; hopefully, there will never be another similar period. During the last several years, a relatively high natural growth rate was observed. But to our minds, it would be wrong to extrapolate the tendencies of the late 1980s into the future, for an increase in the birth rate during an economic crisis is unlikely, and mortality among the indigenous peoples is still rather high. In the event of a decrease in the birth rate, such a high death rate might be enough to stop population growth.

If, on the other hand, we consider the ethnic processes at work, the way of life and the culture of the northern indigenous peoples may be at risk of extinction. This is due to the disruption of the northern fishing and hunting economy, damage to the environment, conversion of the indigenous northerners into a dispossessed minority on their own land, and loss of their national identity. Such extinction is made even more probable because of the very small numbers of these peoples. Therefore, stable population growth among the northern peoples, though not sufficient in itself, is an indispensable condition for their survival.

Notes

This chapter was originally edited for publication by Linda Leask and Matthew Berman, Institute of Social and Economic Research, University of Alaska Anchorage. The final edit was provided by Megan Biesele and Peter Schweitzer.

1. As of the last census (1989), the many ethnic groups that make up the northern indigenous peoples numbered only about 185,000—as compared with a population of Russia at 147 million (and more than 275 million in what was then the USSR). In spite of their small numbers, these peoples over the centuries settled and made themselves at home in the large region of northern Eurasia and, at present, are spread from the Arctic tundra of the Taimyr Peninsula to the north of the Saian foothills and the largely deciduous forests of Primor'ia to the south and from the Kola Peninsula in the west to Chukotka in the east. Their home regions—around seven million square kilometers—constitute two-fifths of the entire Russian territory.

References

Andreev, E.M., V. M. Dobrovolskaia, and K. Iu. Shaburov. 1992. "Etnicheskaia differentsiatsiia smertnosti." *Sotsiologicheskie issledovaniia* 7: 43–49.

Bogoiavlenskii, D. D. 1987. "Nekotorye aspekty zaniatosti narodov Severa i demograficheskie protsessy." In *Smena kul'tur i migratsii v Zapadnoi Sibiri*. 132–34. Tomsk: Izdatel'stvo Tomskogo universiteta.

Boiko, V. I. 1977. *Sotsial'noe razvitie narodov Nizhnego Amura*. Novosibirsk: Nauka.

Bondarskaia, G. A. 1977. *Rozhdaemost v SSSR (Etno-demograficheskii aspekt)*. Moscow: Statistika.

Chislennost'. 1985. *Chislennost' i sostav naseleniia SSSR. Po dannym Vsesoiuznoi perepisi naseleniia 1979 goda.* Moscow: Finansy i statistika.

Darskii, L. E., and E. M. Andreev. 1991. "Vosproizvodstvo naseleniia otdelnykh natsionalnostei v SSSR." *Vestnik Statistiki* 6: 3–9.

Demographic Yearbook. 1991. *Demographic Yearbook of the USSR, 1990.* Moscow: Finansy i statistika.

_____. 1994. *Demographic Yearbook of the Russian Federation, 1993.* Moscow: Izdanie Goskomstata RF.

Itogi. 1962. *Itogi Vsesoiuznoi perepisi naseleniia 1959.* Vol. RSFSR. Moscow: Gosstatizdat.

_____. 1973. *Itogi Vsesoiuznoi perepisi naseleniia 1970.* Vol. 4. Moscow: Statistika.

Kozlov, V. I. 1969. *Dinamika chislennosti narodov.* Moscow: Nauka.

Krasil'nikov, M. 1928. "K voprosu ob ugasanii severnykh narodnostei." *Statisticheskoe obozrenie* 3: 97–100.

Natsionalnii sostav. 1990. *Natsionalnii sostav naseleniia RSFSR.* Moscow: Respublikanskii informatsionno-vychislitel'nyi tsentr.

_____. 1991. *Natsionalnii sostav naseleniia SSSR. Po dannym Vsesoiuznoi perepisi naseleniia 1979 goda.* Moscow: Finansy i statistika.

Navasardov, S. M. 1985. "Sotsial'no-ekonomicheskie osobennosti razvitiia Severo-Vostoka. Chast' 2: Demograficheskoe razvitie korennogo naseleniia Chukotskogo avtonomnogo okruga." Magadan, unpublished manuscript.

Patkanov, S. K. 1911. *O priroste inorodcheskogo naseleniia Sibiri.* St. Petersburg: Izdatel'stvo Imperatorskoi Akademii nauk.

Pika, A. I., and D. D. Bogoiavlenskii. 1988. "Ogranichenie rozhdaemosti i kontratseptsiia v sem'iakh narodnostei Severa." In *Planirovanie sem'i i natsional'nye traditsii* (Materialy Vsesoiuznoi nauchno-prakticheskoi konferentsii). 170–74. Tbilisi.

Population. 1990. *Population of the USSR, 1988.* Moscow: Finansy i statistika.

Tomskii, I. E. 1980. "Tendentsii izmeneniia tsennostnykh orientatsii na razmer sem'i u zhenshchin Yakutii." In *Regional'nye voprosy naseleniia i trudovykh resursov.* 39–46. Iakutsk: Iakutskoe knizhnoe izdatel'stvo.

Vozrast' i sostoianie. 1990. *Vozrast' i sostoianie v brake naseleniia SSSR. Po dannym Vsesoiuznoi perepisi naseleniia 1989 goda.* Moscow: Finansy i statistika.

PART IV

GENDER AND REPRESENTATION

Chapter 19

GENDER ROLE TRANSFORMATION AMONG AUSTRALIAN ABORIGINES

———=≡«◎»≡=———

Robert Tonkinson

Introduction

Male-female relationships and issues of gender-based inequalities are a long-debated topic in anthropology, particularly in regard to hunter-gatherer societies. Australian Aboriginal women were depicted in early accounts as downtrodden chattels, totally under the control of male relatives. This extreme stance was later modified as some of the complexities of gender relations became recognized, rendering implausible any conclusions suggesting clear-cut male domination (cf. Hamilton 1981: 72). By the early 1980s, the corrective pendulum had swung to the opposite extreme, with the suggestion that women enjoyed complete equality and autonomy in traditional Aboriginal societies (Bell 1983; cf. Martin and Voorhies 1975). Since then, however, closer attention to the subtleties and complexities of power relations has led most Australianists to the view that there was a high degree of interdependence of the sexes, but that structural inequalities favored mature males (cf. Merlan 1988).

In this chapter, I first consider some general issues concerning the study of gender relations, and briefly outline the situation in Australia as reconstructed for the era prior to the advent of Europeans. Then follows a review of findings concerning post-European contact changes in gender relations, which leads to the conclusion that women's status relative to that of men appears to have improved. Finally, I draw on evidence from the Western Desert community in which I have worked to show how and why women's "autonomy" has increased since the time of European contact. The roots of women's increased independence are detectable in aspects of the frontier situation; although younger women's representation of themselves as "free agents" is highlighted, I note that elderly widows were the first to gain greater freedom from the control of men. This case study clearly indicates that satisfactory explanations for the growing prominence of Aboriginal women in contemporary social and political affairs require consideration of both endogenous and exogenous influences.

Gender Role Transformation: Some General Issues

First, it must be acknowledged that adequate understanding of social transformations depends on knowledge of the "traditional," pre-European situation as a baseline against which to assess the nature and degree of change. Secondly, although reconstructions of "precolonial" society inevitably rest on an unsteady empirical base, the recency of first contacts in Australia's interior deserts enables a relatively detailed depiction of the "traditional" situation. Thirdly, regional variations must be taken into account; factors such as the presence or absence of clan structures, for example, help explain important differences in the structuring of sociopolitical relations, which in turn affect gender relations (R. Tonkinson 1988b: 552–55).

There are also difficulties in assessing comparative status through the application of such inherently relative concepts as "independence" and "autonomy," which are often invoked without any clear specification of the social parameters within which they are held to obtain. Arguments for women's "autonomy" that separate economic pursuits from political realities tend to ignore or radically understate the force of kinship obligations and responsibilities (see Bell 1983). As Merlan (1988: 30) notes, "autonomy" has been used in a variety of ways in the Aboriginalist literature, in some cases clearly in reference to self-concepts and notions of self-direction, but also categorically to characterize women's structural independence from men. It is in the latter sense, and specifically in reference to postcontact changes in status, that I use "autonomy," though both meanings could legitimately be invoked to contrast the totality of "traditional" Aboriginal societies with their subsequent encapsulation.

A major problem with using the concept of "autonomy" in reference to either sex is that it deflects attention away from what was a defining feature of Aboriginal social life: high levels of male-female complementarity and interdependence. Catherine Berndt (1970) describes women's formal subordination to men in the religious arena, but stresses that this subordination is not universal. Berndt makes the important point that "the system rested as much on women's assent, or consent, as on men's more explicit and formalized control" (1970: 45). As Bern (1979) notes, rebellion on the part of either women or young men was unknown, and Stanner (1965) reminds us that the pervasive religious system successfully engendered a dominant attitude of assent to the terms of a life whose parameters were, in Aboriginal understanding, set for all time in the creative era.

The inseparability of the study of gender relations from that of power relations has been made explicit by Begler (1978: 374), who notes, "If the twin issues of equality and exploitation are to be confronted in our analyses of differential allocation of status among social groupings, we must address ourselves to the political aspects of group relations." However, the term "status" is problematic unless the researcher is context sensitive and conceives of the concept dynamically. As Merlan (1991: 265) notes, such conceptualizations evade "questions of male-female interrelation and power." Hamilton (1981: 74) captures the essence of what is required of the researcher in any ethnographic setting: we need to ask, "Which sex is the more powerful, in which contexts, and how is the pattern of those power relations maintained, reproduced and sometimes transcended?"

Adequate consideration of the status of women relative to men is possible only when the parameters of the comparison are those of the society taken as a whole. Rights exercisable by adult members of one sex must therefore be compared directly to those of the other across a wide range of structures and contexts. A suitably holistic approach necessitates close attention to conjunctive relations between the sexes—the structuring and content of male-female interaction. This approach also requires a focus on situations of conflict (cf. Begler 1978: 575–76), in which rights are loudly asserted, made explicit, and (especially in domestic conflict) often contested.

A frequently overlooked yet crucial factor explaining why so many Aboriginal societies seem to have exhibited an "egalitarian ethos" is the powerful controlling and leveling influence of kinship on social behavior (R. Tonkinson 1988b: 550–51). Discussions of egalitarianism in hunter-gatherer societies tend to either ignore kinship as a factor altogether or else to focus on interpersonal behavior between spouses to the detriment of other male-female relationships. Aboriginal Australia was perhaps unique in the extent to which kinship pervaded and ordered social relations most of the time. Life was lived in small, mobile bands of people either closely related, or at least very well known, to one another, so at this social level the need or occasion to give expression to hierarchical distinctions was minimal. Both within and between such groups, kinship-based behavioral norms dictated for every individual a balanced complex of symmetrical and asymmetrical relationships with all others of both sexes. Thus, respect and deference were owed to certain others, but were also owed to each person by different others. This egocentric web of relationships so thoroughly crosscut gender that "dominance" of one sex over the other in everyday interpersonal relations was rendered impossible. Apposite here is a key contrast made by Hamilton (1981: 74) between the power of *individual* women to exert influence and authority and the power of *men-as-a-group*, particularly in relation to religious concerns, to dominate *women-as-a-group*. However, Hamilton makes no reference to the constraints of kinship on the ability of individuals to exercise personal power. Attempts to assess status inequalities must begin by positioning people in terms of kinship statuses, and then proceed on the basis that power relations are normatively constrained by the force of kinship.

Gender Relations in Aboriginal Societies Prior to European Contact

Until relatively recently, there had been very little explicit focus on the status of Aboriginal women, and much of the early literature reveals widely discrepant views. Malinowski ([1913] 1963), in his pioneering study of the family among the Australian Aborigines, was mindful of the contradictions in the evidence he surveyed (and of the transformative impact of European influences) but unequivocal in his conclusion that "the husband had a well nigh complete authority over his wife" (p. 84). He concluded that, despite women's labor being "of much more vital importance to the maintenance of the household than man's work" (p. 283), in economic terms the relationship was "that of a master to his slave" (p. 288).

This view remained substantially unchallenged until Phyllis Kaberry (1939) presented the first female-centered study aimed at establishing the importance of women as significant social actors, neither "profane" nor lacking complexity in personality. Yet Kaberry was not successful in overturning the male-dominance view, mainly because, as Merlan (1988: 22) observes, she lacked "a theoretical perspective adequate to the task of exploring the constitution of gender relations." Nevertheless, the work of Kaberry highlighted ambiguities inherent in gender relations and laid the foundations for more considered approaches to this complex issue.

Hamilton (1981) has drawn attention to a puzzling contradiction: the existence of high levels of female "autonomy" along with high levels of sexual inequality favoring males. White (1970) had earlier offered a solution to this apparently paradoxical situation by designating Aboriginal women as "junior partners," whose economic and social importance is secure but whose status as a group is secondary to that of men. In a 1980 paper, Hamilton emphasized the separation of the sexes and women's autonomy in the eastern Western Desert, which led her to posit the existence of "dual social systems," though as Merlan (1988: 31) notes, her data nevertheless suggested "a measure of subordination of women." In subsequent writings, Hamilton (1981; 1986) placed greater emphasis on gender inequalities, but maintained the importance of "homosociality" as a powerful separative force—which did not, however, preclude men from dominating women in situations of conflict.

Since Kaberry, most scholars tackling the topic of gender relations in Aboriginal society have been women. The work of Goodale (1971; 1982), Munn (1973) and Cowlishaw (1979; 1982) points to structural inequalities favoring men, while that of a small minority (e.g., C. Berndt 1970; 1981; Rose 1992) appears to privilege interdependence over gender-based inequalities. Bell (1983) has been virtually alone in arguing a "separate and equal" thesis for gender relations in traditional contexts. She claims that, traditionally, women were economically independent and autonomous ritual and political actors whose responsibilities paralleled those of men and carried a similar social import. Bell's model was that of Leacock (1978: 247–48), a notable proponent of the view that egalitarianism and female autonomy characterized "pristine" hunter-gatherer societies. This argument is, however, unsustainable in the Australian context. Even among groups like the Tiwi, broadly characterized by Goodale (1971; 1982) as enjoying a "basic equality of the two sexes," she concludes that men nevertheless have greater opportunity for prestige and self-expression, rendering gender relations structurally unequal. Likewise, among the Yaraldi of southeastern Australia, where there was perhaps a higher degree of equality between the sexes than anywhere else in the continent (Berndt and Berndt 1993), clear evidence of inequalities nonetheless existed (R. Tonkinson 1993).

Dussart (1988), Merlan (1985; 1988), and Hamilton (1986) offer detailed critiques of Bell's work, and I have commented on it elsewhere (R. Tonkinson 1990), so I will not restate these arguments here. However, the gist of why Bell's contentions are ultimately unpersuasive is contained in Begler's (1978: 374) admonition: "The issue at hand when considering the relative statuses of the sexes ... is not what happens while the groups are separated, but rather, what happens when the groups come together." By downplaying the extent of social change in the postcontact milieu and avoiding any holistic view of the social system, Bell is able to ignore overwhelming evidence of both structural inequalities and the generally successful dominance of male interests over female whenever the two were in conflict.

To underline some of the complexities entailed in the assessment of precolonial gender relations, as well as the importance of both context and duration in situations where inequalities are manifest, I offer a brief summary of the situation among the Mardu, a Western Desert society (cf. R. Tonkinson 1988a; 1988b; 1990; 1991). In mundane life, there was a strong egalitarian ethos, crosscut but not undermined by the status differences inherent in the kinship system, and modified mainly by factors such as age; for example, children were exempt from these rules. Generally, it was only in times of conflict or when activities relating to the religious life were undertaken that gender-based differences in rights were asserted and thus disturbed the status quo. At such times, mature men were the initiators of action, and the inequalities that emerged favored men over women, and senior men over their not yet fully initiated juniors. Once invoked, these power differentials operated for the duration of the conflict or religious activities, but would then be again submerged when mundane life resumed.

In marriage, women clearly enjoyed far fewer rights than their spouses, for example, the right to divorce their husbands, or practice polyandry, or appropriate male sexuality to maintain or further relationships with other women (i.e., an equivalent to the practice of "wife-lending" by men), all of which rights men could exercise (cf. Merlan 1988: 28). Major decisions concerning their futures were made for them by older relatives, most often males. For example, infant betrothals associated with the major initiation ritual, circumcision, were decided by men via their choice of circumcisors, and the mother of the infant may not have had any involvement in the matter (R. Tonkinson 1991: 95). Widowhood was a temporary status, and the decision as to whom a widow would remarry was often, though not invariably, taken by male relatives (cf. Dussart 1993).

Women's greater contribution to the family's diet did not accord them more power than men; hunting received greater cultural emphasis and was accorded higher value. Mature men controlled access to the forces of production via secret rituals claimed by them to guarantee continued availability of food resources (cf. Bern 1979: 125). Aboriginal religion can thus be viewed as constituting the "economy," one that alienated women from the products of their labors (cf. Hamilton 1982: 90–92; R. Tonkinson 1991). Women were excluded from the secret-sacred core of major rituals, and during periodic "big meetings" in areas where there were exclusively female rituals, they had to schedule such activity to suit the demands of those organized by men. In these and many other aspects of the culture, gender-based differences in status invariably favored initiated males.

There were contexts and circumstances in which women operated separately (for example, in the case of exclusively female rituals, activities surrounding childbirth, certain subsistence activities, and so on), and "equally" in the arenas of male-female interaction (as, for example, in symmetrical cross-sex kin relationships between people related as grandparents and grandchildren). As in other Aboriginal societies, the face-to-face community of several families that composed the band was not predicated on any segregation of the sexes. Most food-getting activities entailed a gender-based division of labor, but the food quest occupied at most a few hours a day. For much of the time, then, families and bands were mixed sex groups, the tenor of whose interaction was dictated largely by the kin relationship involved. At times, initiated men segregated themselves for discussion and planning of secret-sacred business, but the hearth was home and the locus of much relaxed interaction among family and band members of both sexes. Even in the religious life, a great deal of ritual activity involved both men and women—and in fact all members of the society—in situations of intense sociality aimed at fostering the widest possible sense of belonging and community. In general, the social system was not dominated by gender-based segregation, though women's rights were not equal to those of men.

Postcontact Changes

The evidence with respect to gender role transformations in Aboriginal Australia in the wake of the European invasion is both sparse and conflicting (cf. Merlan 1988: 63). Departing mainly from conclusions reached via their reconstructions of the traditional situation, some writers have argued for a diminution in women's autonomy and greater oppression than was believed to be the case prior to European settlement, e.g., Bell; Bell and Ditton; others for an increase in women's status and power vis-à-vis men, e.g., Barwick, C. Berndt, Collmann, Gale, Grimshaw, and Tonkinson; and still others remain equivocal in their assessment of the situation, e.g., McGrath. All such conclusions could, of course, be right, since they pertain to different areas and points in time, but much depends on the view these scholars take of the precolonial situation.

Leacock (1982) blames powerful exogenous forces for bringing about the oppression of women and for their subsequent confinement to a devalued "familial" domain, allowing male dominance of the more politically important public domain. Significantly, Leacock entered a caveat in the case of Australian Aborigines, warning that it required detailed analysis. Bell (1983: 231) took up this challenge, arguing that in the postcontact era the once independent and autonomous women suffered disproportionately, from both "the settlement lifestyle" that prevented them from consolidating their former power, and the debilitative influence of the dominant society's alien patriarchal institutions. On the frontier, non-Aboriginal men regarded Aboriginal women merely as domestic workers and sex objects, and it was Aboriginal men who were able to take "real political advantage of certain aspects of frontier society." Once deprived of their land, Aboriginal women were no longer "negotiators with equal rights" and so lost their former bargaining power.

Bell provides no firm details as to which "aspects of frontier society" were available to Aboriginal men to exploit to their political advantage. Her frontier scenario contrasts markedly with that of R. and C. Berndt (1977: 511–12), who concluded: "Aboriginal women were regarded as ideal go-betweens for mediating between their menfolk and the settlers ... the men were often kept at arm's length, allowed much less latitude, treated less familiarly.... Aboriginal women, in this situation, had more avenues open to them than their menfolk did to enhance their status." As Merlan (1988: 29) observes, Bell treats as a given that the European intrusion resulted in a general direction of change from independence to dependence, "though it is hard to see how such a definitive and singular conclusion could emerge from complex, and also locally somewhat specific, situations of European-Aboriginal social interaction." Since the frontier lasted from 1788 to the 1960s in Australia, both regional and temporal variations are extremely important.

In her discussion of sexual politics on the pastoral frontier in the Northern Territory, McGrath (1987: 76) suggests that European men provided Aboriginal women with "an escape from tribal restrictions and rigors. White men thus provided the women with new choices which enabled them to evade due punishments, or avoid marrying a man they feared or disliked." (This was undoubtedly also the case on many Christian missions, where the missionaries' perception of Aboriginal women as enslaved was part of the reason why they attacked traditional marriage arrangements and practices; cf. Scanlon 1986.) Women who became the favored partners of station "bosses" learned to manipulate the situation to personal and family advantage, and obtain economic security and protection, against both Aboriginal and European pursuers. However, McGrath observes that for women the new options provided by the presence of European men on the frontier could yield disappointments as well as advantages, since the latter frequently hid and/or disavowed such relationships in the presence of other Europeans. As M. Tonkinson (1987: 30) notes, relationships between European men and Aboriginal women on the frontier were "complex and marked by hypocrisy." The frontier also had its violent side, devoid of negotiation, as Reynolds (1987: 73) suggests: "There is abundant evidence that [Aboriginal] women were forcibly abducted in all parts of Australia from the early years of settlement until the 1930s and 1940s."

In her account of Aboriginal women on missions and government stations in nineteenth-century Victoria, Barwick (1970: 31, 36) depicts a rapid and remarkable status transformation favoring Aboriginal women, from a "traditionally patriarchal social organization" that had allotted subordinate roles to women in community religious and political activities. Barwick suggests that official pressures on men to go in search of work undermined their social and economic roles, while at the same time women's domestic authority was strengthened. Aboriginal women were vital to settlement economic activities, and received better treatment from the missionary women than did their men. Also, women soon emerged as prominent political actors, whose better education and greater knowledge of the workings of European society were no doubt factors in men's acquiescence to this marked status change. As Gale (1972: 163) notes, "A rise in status of Aboriginal women in relation to the whole family group was a concomitant of the loss of male authority and leadership of the tribal kind."

C. Berndt (1970: 41) suggests that women appear to have "taken more readily to the new life of mission and government and pastoral stations—and possibly, in general, with fewer regrets," mainly because of the wider range of choices presented to them than their men. Located inside the "White" household, and sometimes involved in both sexual and domestic relations, women inevitably assumed roles as intermediaries between the Europeans and their men. Berndt (p. 43) concludes that, "On the whole, then, outside contact enhanced woman's already strong domestic and economic status and at the same time decreased the extent of her *formal* subordination *vis-à-vis* men."

Grimshaw (1981: 90, 92), while noting the hardships faced by Aboriginal women, suggests that the European invasion was less traumatic for them than their men because they had less autonomy to surrender and greater continuities in their family roles. Domestic employment offered a niche wherein skills valuable in the colonial context could be mastered; for example, women were more likely to gain literacy than men. Also, men's mobility increased women's responsibilities and enhanced their role as homemakers and providers.

Bell and Ditton (1980: 8), reporting on a three-month survey of Aboriginal women's opinions of their changing role in six communities in Central Australia, conclude: "Male political, economic and ritual roles have been given some status within the new social order, but the importance of the female role has been denied because of the negative perception of women's role and the limited opportunities for women with the new social order." Like Grimshaw, they note that both men and women have suffered loss, but not in equal measure. They assert that women are precluded from maintaining their former autonomy and independence by their exclusion from the new political structures. Undoubtedly, government agents would have presumed that Aboriginal men were politically dominant and so assigned roles, such as "camp boss" and, later, councilor, exclusively to them. However, Bell and Ditton's data also provide support for increased women's social and political activity and maneuver vis-à-vis men. Aboriginal women have made creative and effective use of representations of their "traditional" culture to increase their social visibility and power in modern contexts. For example, in relation specifically to a Northern Territory land claim, Lilley (1989: 94–95) argues persuasively that women articulated their transformed roles, as reproducers of both children and society rather than as sexual beings supporting male prestige, by "actively manipulating 'tradition' in their presentation of a fictitious indigenous Australian polity wherein men and women enjoyed complementary rights and responsibilities."

Collmann (1988) addresses the topic of welfare dependency, a major transformative force in Aboriginal societies, and the impact of the expansion of services targeting Aboriginal people. In an earlier paper (Collmann 1979: 381, 389, 395), he focused on transformations in the domestic group among Aborigines living on the fringes of Alice Springs, particularly the effects of state penetration of the family through ration distribution systems and family stabilization plans. This loss of autonomy affected the sexes differentially, for example, men were pressured to leave in search of work, and were refused rations if unemployed—a test that was not applied to women. With encouragement from government authorities, Collmann argues, matrifocal families emerged, and women's responsibility for their children gave them access to pensions and other welfare support. Collmann concludes that women are structurally positioned "... so as to construct a more satisfactory fringe-dwelling identity and existence than men," because "... few if any men can transform control of their domestic groups directly into the means to support them." In these circumstances, men need women's support if they are to survive in the town-fringe situation.

A major disruptive force in Aboriginal Australia is alcohol abuse and associated social traumas, of which violence is one of the most evident. Although in most communities drinkers are in a minority, and generally more men than women drink, alcohol abuse and violence often occur within both gender categories as well as between them (Brady 1991). In absolute numbers, more men than women die as a result of such violence, but in male-female conflict women tend to be more often the losers, much as in "traditional" situations. This aspect of gender relations cannot be ignored in any assessment of social transformations.

From the evidence discussed above, conclusions favoring increased status among Aboriginal women in the postcontact situation point to men's enforced detachment from their families as a result of European values regarding men and work. Women, in contrast, were more likely to benefit from their altered domestic situation on the frontier and from government policies facilitating their increased control over resources and family matters. Since my own fieldwork provides further confirmation of these regularities, in frontier and settlement contexts, I now present a brief case study (for a more detailed account, see R. Tonkinson 1990).

The Pastoral Frontier

The frontier along the western edge of the Western Desert early this century was largely peaceful and almost exclusively, on the European side, a male domain. The few non-Aboriginal bachelors who took up pastoral leases on the desert margins relied almost entirely on Aboriginal labor, which they recruited and trained, using as powerful attractions tea, tobacco, sugar, flour, and other rations. Pastoralists maintained strict spatial domains: Aboriginal men worked "outside," but some of their wives and daughters, usually the younger women, were recruited to the house, which was off-limits to their men. As domestic laborers and, very often, sexual partners, such women had free run of that domain, and could use the house as a safe haven in the event of domestic conflict in the camp. On pastoral leases northeast of Jigalong, the settlement in which I worked, some of the de facto relationships between Aboriginal women and European men were long term. When the traditional husband-wife dyad became a novel husband-wife-European man triad, this set in train an important transformation in women's status. Though more men than women learned some English in the course of their work, the women who frequented the homestead tended to become much better speakers of English, because they spent more time in relaxed and informal interaction with the pastoralist than did men. These women often became key intermediaries in relationships between house and camp.

Women as housegirls and rations providers supplied their men with valuable knowledge as well as greatly desired foodstuffs and tobacco (and sometimes alcohol). Men acting familiarly toward the boss risked rebuke as "cheeky" or "uppity" if they overstepped the mark (cf. Berndt and Berndt 1977: 510–11). So they, and other men not directly employed by the boss, were more likely to rely on their women to act as intermediaries because their better English and closer, less hierarchical relationship with the non-Aboriginal boss offered better prospects for a successful outcome.

Aboriginal women, relating their station experiences in "the early days," most often phrased their relationships with the pastoralists in terms of compassion and nurturance (both major cultural values): sorrow for the men's isolation from family and kin, and compassion for their ignorance about the land. The dominant situation on the stations was one of accommodation and mutual benefit: pastoralism was unsustainable without Aboriginal labor, and once the Aboriginal people became sedentary, their intensifying needs for certain goods tied them ever more irrevocably into the frontier economy. From my observations in the mid-1960s, I concluded that as a result of their work in the homestead domain most women had enhanced their importance to both of the males in the frontier triad, thus laying part of the groundwork for an increased assertiveness in their own society.

The Mission Era

The activities of fundamentalist Christian missionaries at Jigalong (from 1946 to 1969) failed to produce converts but had a considerable impact on social life, since the mission acted as an agency of the government, for example, in controlling ration distribution (R. Tonkinson 1974). The typical missionary view of their Aboriginal charges held all but the oldest men to be callous, violent, sexually depraved, and irredeemable, whereas Aboriginal women were downtrodden and ill-treated victims. The missionaries therefore assumed that women would be far less committed to traditional culture than men and thus less resistant to the Christian message. Because of these stereotypes, Aboriginal women generally fared better than their men in their dealings with the missionaries.

As on the pastoral properties, relationships between Aboriginal men and male missionaries in work situations were generally hierarchical and formal in tone. There was also an added dimension of mutual distrust, based on an awareness of deeply opposed interests on questions of religion and control. Between female missionaries and their "housegirls," particularly, there was a degree of intimacy and exchange of information that had parallels in the station milieu with European male-Aboriginal female relationships. If this observation is correct, it suggests that in both station and mission settings, Aboriginal women had greater access to, and control of, important new information and greater potential to act as mediators between the two groups.

The biggest contrast to the frontier was in European male-Aboriginal female interaction, which now assumed a restrained, paternalistic tone. The missionaries focused their evangelizing efforts strongly on the school-aged children and teenage girls in an effort to win them to Christianity and wean them from what the missionaries regarded as the evil and lustful life of the camp and the hegemony of old men. By supporting the teenage girls and actively attempting to turn them against their elders, the missionaries helped open, or enlarge, a line of cleavage that in any case would surely have widened under Westernizing pressures.

One interesting development concerned older Aboriginal women who became widowed on the mission. Since all of them received weekly rations, they were no longer dependent on the gathering activities of younger cowives or on the hunting prowess of their husbands. Some of them set up permanent widows' camps, ignoring men's frequent criticism, propositions, and attempts at securing their remarriage in accordance with tradition. This was an early and important manifestation of women's increasingly successful self-assertion in the settlement situation.

The Contemporary Situation

Only brief mention is possible here of some of the more notable changes in women's status, toward greater independence, that have occurred at Jigalong. For example, polygyny, though never universal, continued to be valued by men as an intrinsic part of "the old law," as were the related institutions of infant betrothal and arranged marriages (organized by pairs of men, usually in consultation with their wives). Yet the incidence of successful outcomes in all three institutions has declined steadily. The desire to marry girls and young women lost none of its appeal for most men. Polygyny's marked decline in the last two decades can be attributed largely to a combination of the assertiveness and persistence of many wives in opposing the addition of a junior wife to the family unit, and the reluctance of many young betrothed women to agree to marriage with a (usually) much older man. In such cases of conflict, attempts by senior men and women to bring community pressure to bear on the objecting wives have been increasingly unsuccessful. Some middle-aged men of strong personality and resolve have prevailed, and thus keep the practice of polygyny alive at Jigalong. Yet most men, especially the older ones, have been unable to realize or sustain polygynous marriages in the face of opposition from women. Increasingly, then, girls betrothed in infancy, or promised in marriage during childhood, have not eventually married their designated partner.

An important element in women's increased independence has been the payment of pensions and other welfare income directly to individuals. The rise of a traditionally unknown female category, the unmarried mother, and of young women representing themselves as "free agents" has been aided by their receipt of welfare benefits. Such regular income enables their financial independence; it also precludes the possibility of any successful withholding of reciprocity on the part of relatives angry at these women's refusal to conform to the dictates of tradition. In addition to the circulation of available cash via the kinship network, gambling at cards provides another very important locus for redistribution, involving women as both givers and receivers. It is thus impossible to posit a unilineal causal relationship between policies concerning welfare payments to unmarried mothers and the emergence of a successfully asserted "free agent" status among women in this category.

The strong desire of the senior men (and women) has been to marry off sexually active and recalcitrant young females, so that they are under the control and responsibility of their older spouses, who will "settle them down." The notion of young women "running around and causing trouble" is anathema to the older generation; they see such behavior as a major social problem and as a clear sign of breakdown in the old social order, in which females were daughters then wives then mothers, always under the authority of certain older male and female kin.

More recently, there has arisen a second and also unprecedented stage of female assertion of independence. This is the refusal of young women to marry *any* men, regardless of age difference, thus transforming the temporary status of "unmarried mother" to a more permanent one. Their frequent use of the term "free agent" suggests that these younger women see themselves as enjoying considerable independence of action. Yet their intention is not to segregate themselves from men; rather, they are seeking to distance themselves from the direct authority of particular males, as husbands. Their rebellion is not against society in general, which perhaps helps explain why they have been successful in their opposition to one part of it. Another reason is that older men and women continue to view the status of unmarried mother as a transitory one. They express the conviction that these young women will sooner or later "settle down" in a stable marriage, and in fact most such women do indeed eventually marry.

The scope for women's political activity has also broadened in an unprecedented way. In 1973, when the first community council was formed at the behest of government functionaries, eight men were subsequently elected from an all-male field of candidates. By 1976, four of twenty councilors were women, and later Jigalong became the first Western Australian Aboriginal community to elect a woman as its council chairperson. Initiatives involving women's issues have increasingly been introduced via agents of the dominant society, partly in response to a perception that women were disadvantaged in access to certain amenities. The provision of separate vehicles; participation by community members in a variety of regional training schemes; and representation on regional, state, and national women's organizations have redressed some of the inequalities manifest in the 1970s, following the establishment of many incorporated Aboriginal communities. Also very important are women-only "big meetings," held periodically at different locations around the desert. Women travel great distances to attend and perform rituals as well as to discuss issues of common concern, such as land claims and alcohol-related problems. Whatever their ultimate source, these initiatives have undoubtedly raised the political consciousness of Mardu women and increased their awareness of concerns shared with Aboriginal women within and beyond the desert.

At Jigalong, women remain in the minority on the council, but do not perceive themselves, or act, as a voting bloc. In reacting to certain pressing problems that affect the whole community, women and men have not as a rule expressed opposing interests, perhaps because community members see themselves as similarly affected, though it could reflect a degree of reluctance on the part of women to press their views publicly in opposition to men. Writing in 1980, Bell and Ditton suggested that Central Australian Aboriginal women were unrepresented in settlement political structures because they lacked a forum to make public their views. At Jigalong, however, the "camp meeting" has always performed this function for both men and women. It remains vital for the airing, debate, and possible resolution of major concerns, as well as the making of important decisions by the community at large. In this forum, women are always present and play an active, but rarely front-stage, role in the proceedings. At these public meetings, many of the issues raised in council are placed on the agenda of the community at large. So while some women councilors may feel reluctant to take the floor in the more alien structure of the council meeting, they and other women present make their opinions known to all in camp meetings, especially when the topic under discussion arouses their concern.

Conclusion

To understand the dynamics of women's status at Jigalong, a range of historical circumstances and changes stemming from frontier contacts with Europeans and the permanent abandonment of nomadism must be taken into account, as must the rapid increase in recent decades of powerful and intrusive influences flowing from the dominant society. Government policies favoring the individualization of welfare payments, and a range of other changes, have combined to increase the degree of independence being sought and won by women at Jigalong. Their status has shifted from one of structural inequality in a traditional society to one more equal in terms of women's capacity for independent action and their successful (but not uncontested) assertion of this degree of autonomy. The use of the English term "free agent" by many of the younger women aptly conveys a major self-perception that is verifiable independently through the observation of male-female interaction at Jigalong. When middle-aged and older women contrast their "traditional" past with the settlement present, their nostalgia for the desert and its food resources and tranquility is evident. In other respects, however, many seem to favor settlement life, and I suggest that one reason for this may be that the women are now less firmly under the control of men. That this gain appears to have bee· at the expense of "traditional" values and the structures of "the law," that it suggests a weakening in the control that mature men as a categ(can exert over women as a category, likewise cannot be attributed to single factor. Mardu women, however, do not see themselves as in r against "the law" that has been bequeathed to all Aboriginal people the creative era of the Dreaming. They continue to embrace it strongly as a major source of identity and security, but, recognizing that many accommodations have already been made in the wake of European impacts, they express no great desire to subscribe to aspects of gender relations that they have come to consider unduly restrictive.

References

Barwick, D. 1970. "And the Lubras Are Ladies Now." In *Women's Role in Aboriginal Society*. Fay Gale, ed. 31–38. Canberra, Australia: Australian Institute of Aboriginal Studies.

Begler, E. B. 1978. "Sex, Status and Authority in Egalitarian Society." *American Anthropologist* 80: 571–88.

Bell, D. 1983. *Daughters of the Dreaming*. Sydney: McPhee Gribble/George Allen and Unwin.

Bell, D., and P. Ditton. 1980. *Law: The Old and the New: Aboriginal Women in Central Australia Speak Out*. Report Prepared for the Central Australian Aboriginal Legal Aid Service.

Bern, J. 1979. "Ideology and Domination: Toward a Reconstruction of Australian Aboriginal Social Formation," *Oceania* 50: 118–32.

Berndt, C. H. 1970. "Digging Sticks and Spears, or the Two-Sex Model." In *Women's Role in Aboriginal Society*. Fay Gale, ed. 39–48. Canberra, Australia: Australian Institute of Aboriginal Studies.

_____. 1981. "Interpretation and 'Facts' in Aboriginal Australia." In *Woman the Gatherer*. Frances Dahlberg, ed. 153–203. New Haven, Conn.: Yale University Press.

Berndt, R. M., and C. H. Berndt. 1977. *The World of the First Australians*. Sydney: Ure Smith.

_____. 1993. *The Yaraldi: A World That Was*. Melbourne: Melbourne University Press.

Brady, M. 1991. "Drug and Alcohol Use among Aboriginal People." In *The Health of Aboriginal Australians*. J. Reid and P. Trompf, eds. Sydney: Harcourt Brace Jovanovich.

Collmann, J. 1979. "Women, Children and the Significance of the Domestic Group to Urban Aborigines in Central Australia." *Ethnology* 18: 379–95.

_____. 1988. *Fringe Dwellers and Welfare: The Aboriginal Response to Bureaucracy*. St. Lucia, Australia: University of Queensland Press.

Cowlishaw, G. 1979. "Women's Realm: A Study of Socialization, Sexuality and Reproduction among Australian Aboriginal People." Ph.D. diss. University of Sydney.

_____. 1982. "Socialisation and Subordination among Australian Aboriginal People." *Man* 17: 492–507.

Dussart, F. 1988. "Warlpiri Women's Yawulyu Ceremonies." Ph.D. diss. Australian National University.

_____. 1993. "The Politics of Female Identity: Warlpiri Widows at Yuendumu." *Ethnology* 31: 337–50.

Gale, F. 1972. *Urban Aborigines*. Canberra, Australia: Australian University Press.

Goodale, J. C. 1971. *Tiwi Wives: A Study of the Women of Melville Island, North Australia*. Seattle, Wash.: University of Washington Press.

_____. 1982. "Production and Reproduction of Key Resources among the Tiwi of North Australia." In *Resource Managers: North American and Australian Hunter-Gatherers*. N. M. Williams and E. S. Hunn, eds. 197–210. Boulder, Colo.: Westview Press.

Grimshaw, P. 1981. "Aboriginal Women: A Study of Culture Contact." In *Australian Women: Feminist Perspectives*. N. Grieve and P. Grimshaw, eds. 86–94. Melbourne, Australia: Oxford University Press.

Hamilton, A. 1980. "Dual Social Systems: Technology, Labour and Women's Secret Rites in the Eastern Western Desert." *Oceania* 51: 4–19.

_____. 1981. "A Complex Strategical Situation: Gender and Power in Aboriginal Australia." In *Australian Women: Feminist Perspectives*. N. Grieve and P. Grimshaw, eds. 69–85. Melbourne, Australia: Oxford University Press.

_____. 1982. "Descended from Father, Belonging to Country: Rights to Land in the Australian Western Desert." In *Politics and History in Band Societies*. E. Leacock and R. Lee, eds. 85–108. Cambridge: Cambridge University Press.

_____. 1986. "Daughters of the Imaginary." *Canberra Anthropology* 9 (2): 1–25.

Kaberry, P. 1939. *Aboriginal Woman, Sacred and Profane*. London: Routledge.

Leacock, E. 1978. "Women's Status in Egalitarian Society: Implications for Social Evolution." *Current Anthropology* 19: 247–75.

_____. 1982. "Relations of Production in Band Societies." In *Politics and Ritual Band Societies*. E. Leacock and R. Lee, eds. 159–70. Cambridge: Cambridge University Press.

Lilley, R. 1989. "Gungarakayn Women Speak: Reproduction and the Transformation of Tradition." *Oceania* 60(2): 81–98.

McGrath, A. 1987. *Born in the Cattle*. Sydney: Allen and Unwin.

Malinowski, B. [1913] 1963. *The Family among the Australian Aborigines*. New York: Schocken.

Martin, M. K., and B. Voorhies. 1975. *Female of the Species*. New York: Columbia University Press.

Merlan, F. 1985. "Review of D. Bell, Daughters of the Dreaming 1983." *Oceania* 55(3): 225–29.

_____. 1988. "Gender in Aboriginal Social Life: A Review." In *Social Anthropology and Australian Aboriginal Studies: A Contemporary Overview*. R. M. Berndt and R. Tonkinson, eds. 17–76. Canberra, Australia: Australian Institute of Aboriginal Studies.

_____. 1991. "Women, Productive Roles and Monetisation of the 'Service Mode' in Aboriginal Australia: Perspectives from Katherine, Northern Territory." *The Australian Journal of Anthropology (Formerly Mankind)* 2(3): 259–92.

Munn, N. 1973. *Walbiri Iconography*. Ithaca, N.Y.: Cornell University Press.

Reynolds, H. 1987. *Frontier*. Sydney: Allen and Unwin.

Rose, D. 1992. *Dingo Makes Us Human: Life and Land in an Australian Aboriginal Culture*. Cambridge: Cambridge University Press.

Scanlon, T. 1986. "'Pure and Clean and True to Christ': Black Women and White Missionaries in the North." *Hecate* 12(1/2): 83–104.

Stanner, W. E. H. 1965. "Religion, Totemism and Symbolism." In *Aboriginal Man in Australia*. R. M. and C. H. Berndt, eds. 207–37. Sydney: Angus and Robertson.

Tonkinson, M. 1987. "Sisterhood or Aboriginal Servitude? Black Women and White Women on the Australian Frontier." *Aboriginal History* 12(1): 27–39.

Tonkinson, R. 1974. *The Jigalong Mob: Victors of the Desert Crusade*. Menlo Park, Cal.: Benjamin/Cummings.

_____. 1988a. "'Ideology and Domination' in Aboriginal Australia: A Western Desert Test Case." In *Hunters and Gatherers (Vol 1): Property, Power and Ideology*. T. Ingold, D. Riches, and J. Woodburn, eds. 170–84. Oxford: Berg.

_____. 1988b. "Egalitarianism and Inequality in a Western Desert Culture." *Anthropological Forum* 5: 545–58.

_____. 1990. "The Changing Status of Aboriginal Women: 'Free Agents' at Jigalong." In *Going it Alone? Prospects for Aboriginal Autonomy: Essays in Honour of Ronald and Catherine Berndt*. R. Tonkinson and M. C. Howard, eds. 125–47. Canberra, Australia: Aboriginal Studies Press.

_____. 1991. *The Mardu Aborigines: Living the Dream in Australia's Desert*. Fort Worth, Tex.: Holt, Rinehart, and Winston.

_____. 1993. "Foreword." In *The Yaraldi: A World That Was*. R. M. and C. H. Berndt, eds. Melbourne, Australia: Melbourne University Press.

White, I. M. 1970. "Aboriginal Women's Status: A Paradox Resolved." In *Women's Role in Aboriginal Society*. F. Gale, ed. 21–29. Canberra, Australia: Australian Institute of Aboriginal Studies.

Chapter 20

NAMES THAT ESCAPE THE STATE

Hai//om Naming Practices versus
Domination and Isolation

========«(»)»========

Thomas Widlok

None of the Namibian Bushman groups escaped the national population census of 1991, the first census conducted in Namibia after its independence in 1990. A wave of enumerators, well equipped with four-wheel-drive transport, reached even the remotest settlements. The previous census of 1981, administered under the South African government, was far less comprehensive, especially in the so-called communal areas of the country. At that time, many Bushman settlements were either not visited or only superficially scanned (Marshall and Ritchie 1984: 24). Population figures were a highly political issue in 1991, as estimates of the United Nations and of the exiled SWAPO (South West African Peoples Organization, the independence movement and now the party in power) were far higher than those of the preindependence administration. Therefore, during the 1991 census, an effort was made to count as many people as possible. Radio news at the time reported that some areas in the rural north were visited twice to make sure that all remote places were reached. Hai//om settlements were no exception, and the validity of the 1991 census is not to be doubted on the grounds of people not being included. However, as with many national censuses, the people encountered were counted and made to fit preconceived categories that are based on biased views with regard to indigenous minorities such as hunter-gatherer groups.

This chapter analyzes the isolation and domination of Bushmen in southern Africa in terms of ascribed and expanded naming practices.

Taking the Namibian census as a point of departure, it shows how the nation-state strives to integrate Bushman groups. At the same time, new aspects of the relation between isolation, domination, and social identity emerge with a shift of emphasis from investigating ethnonyms toward investigating present-day Hai//om naming practices. Hunter-gatherers can be shown not only to respond but also to take initiatives in the social process that constitutes dependence and social rapprochement. Social action can no longer (and need no longer) be located exclusively on the side of the infringing state.

Isolating and Integrating Ethnic Identities

The first years of Namibian independence were the heyday of quantitative data gathering, which was regarded as the prerequisite for all state reforms—particularly those aimed at integrating previously marginalized populations. Procedures for the first national census were standardized throughout the country, but they exhibit a bias of the central administration toward the margins of the newly formed state. Any direct reference to ethnic identity was avoided, but the census questions inquiring about the "main language spoken at home" only thinly disguised—but obliquely skewed—the strategy of delimiting ethnic identities. Enumerators had to choose from census categories that were not so much based on linguistic grounds as on a categorization of Namibian groups according to the preindependence definition of ethnic groups. While Indo-European languages like English, German, and Afrikaans were granted separate categories, the Khoisan languages were lumped together under two categories: Nama/Damara and Bushman or Saan (*sic*). The Bushman languages were further split up into Kung, Heikum, and "other" Bushman languages, which follows the common ethnic division but which makes little sense linguistically since Heikum (Hai//om) and some of the "other" Bushman languages (such as Kxoé) should be grouped with the other Khoe languages Nama and Damara. Furthermore, notwithstanding the fact that there are only two standardized Owambo languages, seven Owambo languages (plus a residual category) were listed, corresponding to the so-called traditional tribal Owambo groups in the north of Namibia. By contrast, numerous Bushman groups, and languages, such as Nharo or Kxoé, were left out—a fate shared only by the Himba, themselves a marginal group.[1] Thus ethnopolitical structures rather than languages were the implicit base of this part of the census.

The published results of the census make it even worse. Kung, Heikum, and "others" were taken together as Bushman while again Afrikaans, German, and English continue to be neatly divided. One of the oddities that this practice has produced is that on the basis of the published census results, we still do not know the overall number of Hai//om-speakers in any of the districts, let alone nationwide.[2] By contrast, we do know, for instance, that one female and two male German-speakers with university degrees were residing in the Ondangwa district—easily identifiable as my wife, myself, and one of our expatriate friends (National Planning Commission 1993: 795–96). The system counts educated expatriates separately to the degree that they become identifiable as individuals while disregarding (and disguising) their expatriate status as they are incorporated into the overall population figure. At the same time, the census does not distinguish between linguistically and spatially distinct Bushmen groups that are part of the indigenous population of the country. This would probably not matter to the Hai//om if they lived in an environment in which ethnic identity was irrelevant. That, however, is not the case. By contrast, since the abolition of apartheid, several Namibian population groups have laid new emphasis on ethnic identities and boundaries. The San of Namibia are forced to engage in ethnic politicking and in forming a nationally and internationally recognized indigenous group in order to pursue their interests (Widlok 1996).

The labeling of census categories also indicates a reformulation in the state discourse as "Bushman" gave way to "San" which is now the official designation used in Namibian government publications including *New Era*, the government newspaper. Since there was no indigenous or academic call for this change of terminology at that time, it has probably resulted from an attempt of the new government to stand out against the preindependence discourse that had created an anti-SWAPO and pro-South African profile of Bushmen. The label "San"—although not regarded as any better, but sometimes even worse, by the people concerned—eliminates these connotations and reinforces new ones such as "marginalized," "handicapped," and "in need of government aid."[3] The census data "prove" the low status of San and their need to be developed in terms of literacy and schooling (the possibility of literate San was not even considered) and in terms of housing and employment.

Thus, the San were counted in, but they only count up in terms of their "undeveloped" status in the national context. San do not count for much in the national power politics of the country, but—at least at the time of independence—they were far removed from isolation. It is therefore not surprising that in the concurrent "Kalahari debate" the Hai//om were not brought in on the "isolationist" side of the argument. On the contrary, they were seen as prime examples of long-term integration and dependency (Gordon 1992). Isolation became the key criterion for judging whether San hunter-gatherer subsistence was primary and "genuine" and

for deciding whether their ethnic and cultural cohesion was autonomously generated or imposed onto them. As participants in the "Great
Kalahari debate" emphasized the explanatory power of archival and
archaeological sources, they tended to agree on the status of Hai//om
integration. Thereby, the "integrationist" critique was given some latitude
while the argument continued about the apparently more isolated and
more independent hunter-gatherer groups in western Botswana and its
bordering areas.

The Hai//om of the central north of Namibia not only have long-standing relations with neighboring groups and with the German colonists, but
dependency and integration have also long been regarded as their main
characteristics. Early travelers described Hai//om as heavily engaged in the
regional trade networks for copper and salt (Hahn 1859: 301), and an early
map has the words "Bushmen paying tribute to the Ndonga" ("Ondonga
tributzahlende Buschmänner") written across the area which was then
and still is today Hai//om country (Schinz 1891). Hai//om with intensive
interaction with neighboring groups were noted down as "bantuized" and
"dependent" (Lebzelter 1934: 10, 13). Since the early ethnographers (Cipriani 1931; Fourie 1928; Lebzelter 1934; Schoeman 1957[1951]; Vedder
1912) had focused on the Hai//om in and around Etosha, a tendency to
disregard Hai//om set in after the Hai//om were expelled from this game-
rich area in the 1950s. Hai//om "mixed" identity was part of the rationalization for expelling them from the park, and ethnographers like Gusinde
(1954) and Schoeman complied by testifying that the Hai//om were "im-
pure" (see Widlok 1994a).

While lack of isolation has long been identified with a decrease of
independent ethnic and cultural identity, it has more recently also been
regarded as tantamount to an increase of external control over identity
("ethnicization" and "creating an underclass" are the key terms). There
is, however, still little detailed documentation of social interaction
between Hai//om and their agropastoralist neighbors. This essay aims
to fill this gap by presenting field data collected in research with the
northern Hai//om, who also call themselves ≠Akhoe. Recent ethnography is brought in as a corrective for a debate that was dominated by reference to sources that rely on the dominant discourse (as in archival
records) and on the final outcome (as in archaeological remains) of
potentially open-ended processes. Relying on an ethnographic record of
social interaction opens up two new venues of investigation. Firstly, it
shifts attention from the ascription of ethnonyms and their qualifiers
(such as "bantuized" or "dependent") toward the practices of personal
naming. Secondly, it allows us to take full account of the multitude of
activities that constitute abstract processes such as integration and the
creation of dependency.

Dominating and Negotiating Personal Identities

Personal naming, like ethnic identification, reflects processes of integration and dependency. While "ethnicizing" groups has for a long time been part of the social style of Europeans and other hierarchical societies, it is less a part of the Hai//om sociality—or at least exists in a quite different manner (Widlok 1996). Personal naming, by contrast, is an important social strategy among both the Hai//om and their neighbors. Again, the 1991 national census provides a good example as it shows a clash between naming strategies.

Apart from noting the size and composition of "households," education and occupation, type of housing, etc., the recorders conducting the first national census in Namibia also had to write down personal names on each census form. While this was probably simply a matter of ensuring that individuals were not counted twice, the manner in which names were recorded reveals that many names and important forms of social relatedness escaped the enumerators. In the Ondangwa census district, where I witnessed the census being carried out by speakers of Oshiwambo, recorders took the first name of a man to be the second name of all children in the household, a common practice in former Owamboland. While it had no further implications in the context of the census, it reiterates a similar strategy commonly followed by administrators who made sure that everyone was issued an identity card.[4] These IDs or *kopkaarts*, as they are often called, provide a tool of control for a state that took little account of the realities of individual life histories but that had considerable impact on everyday reality. Ethnic identity was encoded on the card (setting limits to any attempts to shift one's ethnic identity), a date of birth was guessed (which up to this day causes problems, as many Hai//om need to wait a long time before receiving a state pension), and some bowdlerized version of a name became the official name of a person (still to be used today).

Ignorant of spelling click sounds or other features of non-European languages, civil servants turned names such as //Gam//gaeb into Kamkaib and established the correct surname of a person by following their own way of kinship classification. Officials who disregarded "unofficially" married couples tended to give the mother's surname to all children while others relied on their patrifocal bias and gave the surname of the father (or "male household head") to all children. For instance, in the course of the census a young Hai//om man was recorded as Willem Horetzo despite the fact that he was called Dādāb !Nabareb by his mother when he was born, that he was later baptized as Josef by the Owambo pastor, that he was usually called Jakkals by his employer, and that everyone in the ≠Akhoe settlement called him Teseb. Willem Horetzo—invoking his father's surname—was what his identity card said, an arbitrary token used for administering (and counting) the population in the district.

Identity cards serve their purpose by fixing a personal name over time and space for the purpose of nonambivalent, lasting identification by the state authorities. In local practices, by contrast, personal (first) names and identities are continually shifted as social roles are created and altered. Social bonds are created by following local rules of surname inheritance. In the administrative allocation of names, the power-holders disregard the indigenous and ingenious practices of those who have to accept whatever names (and types of work, payment, rules of conduct, etc.) are imposed on them. Workers are often given much less complimentary names by their employers than Jakkals (a name Teseb did not seem to mind). A German-speaking owner of a commercial farm in the Tsumeb district had the habit of adding a number to the Christian name of his (Hai//om) workers who share the same first name (e.g., Wilhelm 1, Wilhelm 2, Wilhelm 3). The first administrator of the Bushman settlement at Tsumkwe reportedly avoided confusion about names that were reproduced every second generation by calling the local !Xū by the number of their registration file (Budack 1981). The ≠Akhoe Hai//om of today voluntarily offer "appropriate" names to white or black power-holders. When Owambo-speaking nurses issue health cards, they are presented with the Owambo name because it is assumed that the clinic staff do not speak Hai//om anyway—and are unwilling to accept anything but Owambo first names.[5]

As a consequence, the name(s) adopted by a person give a good indication about that person's biography, whether that person has spent most of his or her life among Owambo or among white farmers, whether someone was baptized by Finnish missionaries in the north (with names such as Selma and Rauna) or by German missionaries in the south (as in the case of Rudolf and Gottlieb). In all of these cases, adopting new names does not necessarily interfere with the specific Hai//om naming system but only leads to a multiplicity of first names. This multiplicity of situationally shifting names is accepted by most Hai//om, probably because it suits their flexible way of kinship reckoning (see Widlok 1994a). By contrast, Western observers tend to interpret the imposition of names as the culmination of domination and as depriving people of their identity. One German-speaking farmer told me full of contempt about the "enslavement" of Bushmen by their Owambo masters "who even forced them to take on Owambo names." To be stripped of one's indigenous name, to be stripped of a social identity, and to be treated like an object is at the core of Western ideas of slavery (see Kopytoff 1989: 36). By implication, dependency and a separate, independent identity are assumed to be inversely correlated. The identity ascribed to dependents becomes the inverse image of an "autonomous" self-determined identity. Slavery is construed as the extreme endpoint of a continuum of states of dependency that also include "tribute paying," "serfdom," and "underclass." In a number of reports of Western commissions of inquiry into human rights abuses (London Missionary Society 1935; Tagart 1931), as well as among apologists of European colonization, relations of dependency between Bushmen and their Bantu-speaking neighbors have been discussed in terms of "slavery." In these arguments, the transferral of names is seen not only as an imposition by the master on his Bushman servant but also as identifying enslaved Bushmen.

There is no doubt that many Bushmen suffered harsh treatment at the hands of Bantu-speaking pastoralists—and of Europeans. However, the debate as to whether slavery is an adequate description of the various states of dependency reveals more about the relation between European missionaries or administrators and those who were accused of practicing slavery, usually the black pastoralists or agropastoralists, than about the actual nature of dependency. Hai//om themselves readily admit that they are often servants (!gãn) of the Owambo but maintain that they are nevertheless distinguished from slaves who were recruited from prisoners of war. In the Owambo kingdoms, as is common in Africa, prisoners of war were stripped of their old identity and integrated by being allocated a new identity, as a consequence of violent appropriation and domination (see Kopytoff 1989: 65; Loeb 1962: 124–25). When being asked whether they would leave a place and follow an Owambo who was moving elsewhere, the unanimous reply of ≠Akhoe living in close proximity with agropastoralists was that the Owambo would have to move on his or her own as they would not follow. This corresponds with the overall situation of Bushmen living among Owambo agropastoralists over the centuries. There is no evidence to suggest that genocide, capturing, or large-scale emigration has taken place. Instead, intermarriage, adoption, and other forms of social rapprochement seem to have led to a gradual disappearance of Hai//om-speaking groups from the area of Owambo settlement (also reported from Angola by Estermann 1976: 16). While Owambo oral traditions emphasize complementarity and peaceful coexistence with Bushmen, the accounts leave no doubt that economical, political, and technological (military) power increasingly shifted away from the Bushmen in favor of the Owambo (Widlok in press). These processes of change of identities and the creation of dependency are not, however, readily explained by violent domination as exemplified by the intrusion of Western colonial forces that threatened the more southerly Hai//om groups.

Names That Have Escaped the State

When decreasing isolation is interpreted in terms of increasing dependency of group identity upon external forces (Wilmsen 1989), naming practices appear to be primarily tools of these external forces. Integrating other names, or integrating other people into an existing system of names, is preconceived not only as fostering integration but also as marking the apex of domination. The ethnographic record of social interaction, by contrast, shows the range of activities that constitute integration and the creation or avoidance of dependency. It underlines that activities are also initiated by the Bushmen themselves. The remainder of this chapter provides a discussion of Hai//om strategies of managing interdependency by maintaining and expanding their naming practices.

Unlike in !Kung or Nharo society, first names do not matter structurally in the Hai//om kinship and naming system (see Barnard 1978: 616–20; Lee 1972: 356–57; Marshall 1976: 238–40). Namesakes (sharing first names) are considered /hon, friends and joking relations, but this has fairly limited implications given the Hai//om surname system. While employers and administrators are mostly concerned about first names, it is the *gai/ons* (surname, lit. "great name") that is of much greater importance to the ≠Akhoe Hai//om themselves. This is true with regard to internal social relations as well as with regard to dealings with outsiders. There is a much more direct link between the usage of *gai/ons* and other aspects of the kinship system than between the kinship system and first names.

The ≠Akhoe *gai/ons* is passed on in a cross-descent manner, that is from mother to son and from father to daughter. Figures 20.1 and 20.2 show how the *!narekhoen* (people of the same *gai/ons*) map onto the system of basic kinship categories for a male ego and a female ego respectively. The Hai//om *gai/ons* is an important part of their classificatory kinship system. There is no ambivalence or confusion about someone's *gai/ons*. Although German, Afrikaner, and recently also Owambo administrators have been imposing their own view of "proper name inheritance" as described above, ≠Akhoe Hai//om have no doubt about the "real" surname of the particular person. The cross-descent principle is recognized as valid and effective even in those cases in which the "errors" manifested on identity cards and in police records were then adopted by individuals. The young Hai//om man mentioned earlier (Teseb), despite having adopted his father's surname, is unlikely to marry anyone with his mother's surname since everyone knows that he truly belongs to his mother's exogamous surname group. Some informants maintained that in such a case he should not marry anyone with either his true or his given surname since persons with the same surname are not marriageable. The consistently cross-lateral pattern of the ≠Akhoe *gai/onte* (surname, pl.) disperses allegiance and prevents the creation of lasting unilinear coalitions, be they along the lines of gender, generation, or location. Furthermore, it allows rights in land and its resources to be spatially diversified, as will be shown in more detail below. In sum, the Hai//om *gai/ons* pattern supports flexibility in group structure and equal access to resources, both being hallmarks of many hunter-gatherer societies.

FIGURE 20.1 Cross Naming, Ego Male

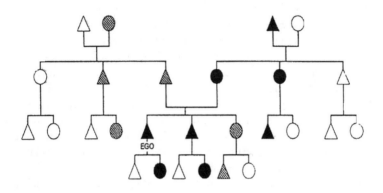

FIGURE 20.2 Cross Naming, Ego Female

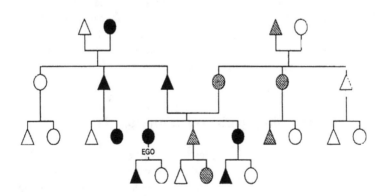

It is as important to know someone's *gai/ons* as it is to know the appropriate kinship term that one should apply. *Gai/onte* can serve as a shortcut in cases in which a kinship relation is distant in genealogical terms or in which there are several possibilities for working out a kinship relation. If a person with the same *gai/ons* is encountered who is not closely related in genealogical terms, then he or she may be simply subsumed under the same kinship term as a closely related person of the same surname and the same generation. Therefore, a boy a little younger than a male ego, with the same surname, would be ego's *!gāb* (younger brother). For a woman whose *omeb* (mother's brother) has the surname //Khube, all men of this name may be called *omeb* and all girls with that name */ais* (cross-cousin). Moreover, given the small overall ≠Akhoe population, there is a realistic chance that all people who are encountered with ego's surname (ego's *!narekhoen*) are indeed genealogically related kin anyway. Any person bearing the same surname as one's marriage partner may be seen as belonging to the */uin* (in-laws).

These "shortcuts" or "bridges" were usually distinguished for my better understanding from close genealogical relations by labeling them *vana tsu* (surname only, "van" being Afrikaans for "surname"). When comparing *gai/ons* relations with other kinship relations, there are intra- and interethnic features, to be discussed separately, that mark the *gai/ons* as particularly versatile in avoiding exclusiveness and in promoting social links across spatial and ethnic boundaries:

1. Intraethnically, the Hai//om system of "great names" provides basic rights, including rights to land, residence, and the use of resources along the lines of social networks that crosscut spatial boundaries.
2. The system is extended beyond the ethnic group, fostering interethnic relations and institutionalizing rights to residence and access to resources by crosscutting ethnic boundaries.

Escaping Spatial Isolation with Names

Surname relations are of particular relevance because properties of the spatial unit, the *//gāus* (band, house), are complemented with properties of an essentially nonspatial kin category: the *!narekhoen*, i.e., the people who share the same surname. Apart from a general fondness expressed in statements such as "*!narekhoen* should not fight with each other," "they should share their food," and "they should exchange presents," a more specific solidarity is also invoked. Most prominent are definitions according to which *!narekhoen* "drink the same water" and have a share in each other's land and its resources because it belongs to all *!narekhoen*.

!Narekhoen as a group do not assemble to form a group for corporate action, nor is it conceivable that a local group could be formed of people who all have the same *gai/ons*. However, in everyday life membership in a surname group is as omnipresent as kinship terminology. Bleek's *Bushman Dictionary* (1956) verifies *!narre* as a general term for "ancestor, relative" among Hai//om of the Etosha region. When Hai//om talk about an individual at a distant place and when they want to point out their relation with that individual, they may refer to *di !narekhoeb/s* (the man/ woman belonging to my surname group) rather than using the individual kinship term involved (or a first name, for that matter). People who meet each other for the first time can be observed elaborating on their *gai/onte* as part of the introduction and then proceeding to establish an adequate kinship term to be used. For instance, in one case an elderly man was introduced to some adolescents who had never visited the place where the encounter took place and whom the man had never met before. The first thing he demanded to know was their *gai/onte*. In another instance, I talked to some men about my impending departure to a place about 80 kilometers to the north. A man who had lost his job and was thinking of moving wanted to get a lift. When I pointed out to him that he had never been to any of the places we were going to visit and that the people up there are not his close family, he replied: "The mother of Abakub and Eliab [two men staying at the places to be visited] and my own mother were born of the same parents, and we are therefore all *!narekhoen*."

The *gai/ons* may also be invoked like kinship terms of address in order to ask for things from other people (and to explain sharing and gift-giving to the anthropologist) or to express fondness toward a person and to express grief at a person's death. Despite this range of subject matter, the way in which the *gai/ons* is invoked is very similar in all instances. However, it is misleading to think of it in terms of an abstract set of rules of behavior. Formally sharing a surname does not by itself lead to showing consideration for someone. It does not necessarily determine where people can visit or settle, nor can it be used to predict where someone might travel. All of these functions are only effective once the *gai/ons* relationship has been actively highlighted in a cooperative process of interaction. When a surname is invoked, a desired outcome cannot be predicted with certainty but can only be realized together with the interlocutors. The same holds true when a surname relationship is invoked across ethnic lines.

Escaping Ethnic Isolation with Names

When I inquired about the *gai/ons* identity of a Hai//om girl with an Owambo father, I was told that the baby girl had three first names: one

Hai//om, one Christian, and one Owambo. I was also told that her surname, which according to Hai//om practice should be that of her father,
was Horetsu, a common Hai//om name but neither that of the mother
nor of any close male relative of the mother. When I inquired further, I
was told that her name was Horetsu because her Owambo father is an
omukuamalanga, that is, a member of the elephant *ezimo* or *epata* (clan).
While the accumulation of the child's first names was an extension of
relations by addition, something more complex was involved with regard
to her surname.

According to the early ethnography, Owambo clans (*epata* in Kwanyama
and *ezimo* in Ndonga) were matrilineal in terms of inheritance, responsibility toward children, and solidarity in cases of material loss (Tuupainen
1970: 31). Despite the unilinear descent system, members of an *epata* are
dispersed over a larger area owing to the exogamous character of the
epata and its combination with patrilocality. There are, therefore, superficial similarities between the Hai//om and the Owambo pattern of social
organization because in the Owambo case, spatially dispersed clans go
together with a notion of mutual assistance and access to resources—
above all cattle. Important differences are the unilinearity of Owambo
kinship and the fact that Owambo clans are hierarchically ranked (Hahn
1966[1928]: 8; Tuupainen 1970: 31–33).[6] According to Owambo informants who live in the same part of Namibia as the ≠Akhoe Hai//om, the
acquisition of an *epata* identity now mostly follows the patrilineage. In
contrast to the Hai//om pattern, inheritance and allegiance follow one
line of descent, forming economically and politically strong lineages.
Reports of endogamous Kwankala clans, apparently of low reputation
similar to that of Bushmen today, have been interpreted as a tool for facilitating the incorporation of local San populations (Heintze 1972: 53).
But the Kwankala clan, glossed by Williams as the clan of the dwarf mongoose, not only involved San or other poor people (Williams 1991: 85).
Furthermore, San were reported to be members of other clans, too (Lebzelter 1934: 12; Tuupainen 1970: 27). More generally, the number and
naming of clans changed as clans amalgamated and split over time (see
Tuupainen 1970: 140–42; Williams 1991).

Owambo strategies of incorporating nontribesmen into the clan structure seem to have varied, but they all differ fundamentally from the prevalent universalistic or classificatory approach of the ≠Akhoe. According to
the ≠Akhoe view, all people, including Europeans, !Xũ, or Owambo, have
a Hai//om surname, but may not know about it. More precisely, what they
do not know is how their surname would translate into a Hai//om *gai/ons*.
It is simply a matter of whether one is interested in finding out about it.
Hai//om who spent most of their time on commercial farms said that
they did not know their Owambo surnames, but they were prepared to

TABLE 20.1 Hai//om "Great Names" and Corresponding Owambo Clan Names

gai/ons	epata
//Gam//gae (64)	ekuahepo "locust"
Gobose (25)	ekuanambwa "dog"
≠Nana (22)	ekualuwala "zebra"
//Khube (18)	a) ekuanaira "grain"
	b) ekualuwala "zebra"
	c) ekuanangombe "cattle"
Horetsu (17)	ekuamalanga "elephant"
!Nabari (15)	a) ekuanaifeta "crocodile"
	b) ekuanangombe "cattle"
	c) ekuanabuba "grain"
≠Gaose (14)	a) ekuanime "lion"
	b) ekuandimbe "grain"
Gonsõa (13)	ekuandimbe "grain"
!Nani (11)	ekuandimbe "grain"
//Khamamu (11)	a) ekuanaifeta "crocodile"
	b) ekuanegamba "hyena"
≠Aroa (8)	ekuanambwa "dog"
≠Nãse (7)	ekuanime "lion"
!Haribe (7)	ekwanyoka "snake"

Sources: See Widlok (1994a); Widlok (forthcoming) for more details.

recommend someone who has stayed with the Owambo for some time who would know. When asked about the origin of their knowledge, those people said that in the past they learned about their Owambo surnames from other Hai//om who were living close to the Owambo. Although it is generally accepted that there is one correct correspondence of names, the actual translations given show some degree of variance. A list of the thirteen most frequent ≠Akhoe surnames together with the matched Owambo clan name(s) shows that there is not a one-to-one correspondence between Hai//om surnames and Owambo clan names (Table 20.1). Note that some, but not all, Owambo clans invoked (such as dog or locust) are of low status. There is not a single incidence of membership claimed in the *ekuankala* (Bushman or dwarf mongoose) *epata*. Rather, the distribution of names is very much what one would expect to be also true for the Owambo population at large with high-status clans (such as lion and elephant) as well as clans of middle status (such as crocodile or zebra).

This conversion table is misleading insofar as it is not the way in which the conversion option presents itself to the parties involved. Knowledge about each other's surnames is locally shared (or, in other cases, not shared). There is no rule that makes surname relationship a necessary prerequisite for interethnic working relations. There are cases in which the Owambo may simply be called "friend" (/*ho*) when the relation is regarded as fair and advantageous by the ≠Akhoe. As the following cases demonstrate, *gai/ons-epata* correspondence is given by some ≠Akhoe and Owambo as a rationalization for their residing in one place and their economic cooperation.

A ≠Akhoe man who regularly works in the field of an Owambo pointed out that although there were difficulties between the two men about the terms of exchange, they were getting along with each other because they were *!narekhoen*. His wife, on the other hand, complained that the Owambo did not give her any tobacco: "He is my husband's *!narekhoeb* but still he does not give me any tobacco but asks me for money." In another instance, a ≠Akhoe widow had for some weeks moved into an Owambo household close by after her children had moved away from the local ≠Akhoe group and had left her without any *!narekhoen* in the camp. The Owambo who owned the homestead explained that since *omukuahepo* (the clan name of the Owambo woman) and //Gam//gaes (the surname of the ≠Akhoe visitor) were corresponding to each other, they were providing work opportunities, food, a hut to stay in, and a blanket for the ≠Akhoe woman.[7]

The conversion between *gai/ons* and *epata* is part of an overall cooperative effort. As such, it can be realized in different ways, depending on the underlying motivations. The outcome of this interactive process is indeterminate. Creating a social relationship with an Owambo with the help of this conversion is not idle play but rather the strategic construction and maintenance of desired modes of interaction. The adequate presentation of interethnic extensions of the *gai/ons* is therefore not a table but instead case studies in which the situational framework is retained. Past experiences with (other) Owambo as well as the availability of economic and social alternatives shape the overall process and create a considerable degree of variability.

Nevertheless, a pattern emerges from the diversity of cases. The *gai/ons-epata* correspondence is invoked to a high degree by Hai//om who live in the sparsely populated areas and who are in constant contact with a limited number of Owambo—who in turn benefit from their good relations with the hunter-gatherers. The conversion practice not only allows the social integration of Hai//om children with Owambo fathers but also has a more general function and significance: it allows any Hai//om who spends periods of his or her life within Owambo society to facilitate linking up socially with the new environment while maintaining a sense of belonging in the Hai//om kinship network, as well. By this means, Hai//om living among an Owambo majority may attempt to overcome their marginality as they extend their identity into the social organization of the Owambo.

Domination, Isolation, and Identity

The practices of naming and social reference discussed in this chapter suggest that the Hai//om practices of integrating "other" names are motivated by expected situational advantages in a potentially open process. Instead of allowing naming practices to compete and possibly to provoke conflict, these Namibian hunter-gatherers seem to count on the expected payoffs that may arise when links with other social actors are facilitated. *!Narekhoen* do not form unilinear or residential segments that compete in any way, but rather individuals are linked across genealogical and spatial distance. This sociality is also carried into the arena of interethnic rapprochement.

The Hai//om practice of accepting names introduced by outsiders is a strategy to decrease isolation and marginality since identities are extended without forfeiting social links with other Hai//om. Far-reaching effects are not brought about by the numerous changes of first names but instead by extending the surname naming practices. In the context of confrontation with the economic power and political dominance of Owambo in the region, the matching of "great names" and clan names facilitates Hai//om interdependence with their neighbors. While it does not prevent them from being allocated a subordinate social position under overall Owambo hegemony, it does not relegate them to the status of passive victims of violent domination or of an imposed social identity. The use of Hai//om *gai/onte* in interethnic relations shows an active involvement of Hai//om in the creation and translation of "great names." There is no indication in Hai//om oral history that these names were imposed on them, nor does anyone today resent this naming practice. The practice of converting surnames is taken as given—not as given by Owambo neighbors, but by virtue of universal rules that parallel the Hai//om classificatory kinship system. Hai//om claim *epata* identities that cover the whole spectrum, including some high-status clan names. It is therefore highly unlikely that this practice, as it is, was designed by Owambo as a tool for domination imposed on the Hai//om. Nevertheless, the preparedness of the Owambo to integrate non-Owambo into their society plays an important role and explains why the same strategy has not evolved in other contexts of interethnic relations.

In complete isolation, such a linkup of social identities could not have occurred. Ultimately, the immigration of Owambo groups into Hai//om country is a major factor because their mere presence would have exerted some economic and political pressure on the ≠Akhoe to establish links with their new neighbors. However, there is also much to suggest that the immigrants, too, felt a pressure to associate with the original inhabitants (Williams 1991), while on the Hai//om side, expanding their own naming practice has led to a decrease in isolation. It is illuminating that the Owambo who accept the Hai//om claim to an *epata* identity are those who themselves live some distance from their main settlement centers and who to some degree rely on Hai//om labor and cooperation. It therefore matched the Owambo interest to incorporate Bushmen both historically, in the course of migrating into the land they now occupy, and also currently, as part of their attempt to recruit cheap labor and to compensate for the effects of labor migration. The hunter-gatherers in turn try to link up with the agropastoralist economy in order to gain access to agricultural and other products. They use their own naming practices to create lasting social relations that are based on Owambo cooperation, not domination. Social links of the kind described above support the socioeconomic strategies of both Owambo and Hai//om. Today, the conversion from *gai/ons* into *epata* does not play (or no longer plays) an important role among those Hai//om who are fully dependent upon and fully integrated into Owambo society, as they permanently live in Owambo homesteads. This is to be expected because in a more densely settled Owambo area, farmers are no longer reliant on ≠Akhoe local knowledge or labor, and, with intensifying integration, individuals of Hai//om origin rely less on their links with the Hai//om kinship network and with Hai//om communal life.

The name conversion is also utilized to a much lesser degree among Hai//om living on commercial farms who have contact only with individual Owambo (mostly with migrant laborers). In these cases, Hai//om care less about the option to convert surnames. Instead, isolated Owambo individuals are often integrated into Hai//om society, or at least the children of mixed sexual relations are brought up as Hai//om, receiving the name of the mother. Similarly, adoption of Hai//om children by Owambo is a complete integration of the individual into Owambo life, including the *epata* of the Owambo man. Adoption and intermarriage may also proceed without out any of these considerations as the knowledge and relevance of clan membership has been declining sharply among urbanized Owambo. The *gai/ons-epata* conversion contrasts with both of these extremes, which suspend one system of social relatedness in favor of another. Isolation plays an important role in integration, but it seems to apply primarily to the increasing isolation of individuals from mainstream Hai//om society rather than to the decreasing isolation between groups.

Naming practices not only affect relative isolation but also touch upon the conditions of domination. Names play a role in domination, but the occurrence of other names may be neither the cause nor the effect of domination over people. More precisely, it seems that dominating an area—the political and economic conditions in it—makes a difference with regard to the development of ways in which naming practices are made to clash or to match in the process of interethnic contact. Today, the ≠Akhoe in the area investigated, who practice the name conversion as described above, still rely to a considerable degree on gathering, on some hunting, and on their mobility, which enables them to switch between different modes of subsistence including wage labor and clientship. In contrast to Hai//om on commercial farms and former Hai//om now living in Owambo homesteads, these people "in between" have retained a degree of autonomous choice with respect to the intensity with which they want to engage with neighboring peoples and with respect to the modalities of this engagement. Since they, like most Bushmen in Namibia, are not granted land rights, that choice is rapidly disappearing as farmers and pastoralists take complete control over the land and its resources.

Notes

An earlier version of this essay was presented at CHAGS 7 in Moscow, and a more elaborate discussion of the ethnography presented is found in Widlok (1994a) and Widlok (forthcoming). Field research in Namibia was carried out with the help of a University of London Studentship, the University of London Central Research Fund, the J. Swan Fund (Oxford) in 1990–92, and with funds of the Cognitive Anthropology Research Group at the Max-Planck Institut in Nijmegen (Netherlands) in 1993–94. This support is gratefully acknowledged.

1. In many ways the pastoralist Himba of the Kaokoland, much publicized as wearing traditional dress, took over most elements of the earlier image of the Bushmen as the nonintegrated, traditional people in Namibia. In independent Namibia, San were explicitly removed from the position of outsiders and became an integral if prototypical weak element of the nation. The population and housing census of 1991 underlines this shift. While the Himba do not appear at all but are "hidden" in the Herero category, the census ascribes an integral but low position to the San in terms of the standards of the new nation.
2. After I had made several unsuccessful inquiries over the years, the statistics office of the National Planning Commission kindly provided me with the following data: the total of 27,229 speakers of Bushman languages split into 7,506 Hai//om speakers, 6,849 !Kung speakers and 12,874 "others" (National Planning Commission personal communication, 2 September 1996).
3. While there are indications that the Hai//om and other (former) hunter-gatherers of southern Africa now prefer San to Bushman (Megan Biesele personal communication),

there was no such consensus on this matter in 1991. The problem of ethnonyms is discussed in more detail elsewhere (see Widlok 1996; Widlok 1997).

4. At the beginning of this century, the colonial administration was troubled by the fact that many Bushmen did not carry a pass or metal identity card for identification as was already enforced among black workers (Gordon 1992: 71, 90). Since then, the administration has made a considerable effort to control San within the white farming districts and beyond in communal areas. Hai//om told me that during the war (1975–88), army lorries took them more than 100 kilometers through the bush in order to have them photographed and issued with identity cards.

5. In the recent past, ≠Akhoe have been repeatedly asked to give their names and have been promised that they will receive something (medicine, food) in return; accordingly those names are offered that are expected to please whoever is in the role of the provider.

6. As for Owambo surnames (here only in the sense of second names), the father's name was used to name all of his children, which in recent times has led to fixed surnames derived from a forefather and handed down through the men of a family. This is paired with a general strengthening of the paternal line, which has been attributed to the intense Christianization of the Owambo during this century (Aarni 1982) but also to industrialization and urbanization (Tuupainen 1970: 33). Naming practices of the Evangelical-Lutheran Church in Namibia, which is evangelizing the ≠Akhoe, follows the Owambo pattern by which children are automatically given their father's first name as a surname. Hence, the Owambo naming practice is superimposed here, as is the naming practice of Europeans in other contexts.

7. Another element in this interethnic interaction is constituted by various strategies of cooperating in the keeping of livestock (see Widlok 1994b), which relies on forms of social grounding as they are outlined here.

References

Aarni, T. 1982. *The Kalunga Concept in Ovambo Religion from 1870 Onwards*. Stockholm: University of Stockholm.

Barnard, A. 1978. "The Kin Terminology System of the Nharo Bushmen." *Cahiers d'études africaines* 18(4): 607–29.

Bleek, D. 1956. *A Bushman Dictionary*. American Oriental Series Vol. 41. New Haven, Conn.: American Oriental Society.

Budack, K. 1981. "Die Völker Südwestafrikas (28)." *Allgemeine Zeitung*, 10 March 1981.

Cipriani, L. 1931. "Fra i Boschimani dell'Etoscia o del deserto di Kalahari." *L'Universo* 12: 550–82.

Estermann, C. 1976. *The Ethnography of Southwestern Angola. Vol. I*. New York: Holmes & Meier.

Fourie, L. 1928. "The Bushmen of South-West Africa." In *The Native Tribes of South-West Africa*. C. H. L Hahn, H. Vedder, and L. Fourie, eds. 79–105. Cape Town: South West Africa Administration.

Gordon, R. 1992. *The Bushman Myth: The Making of a Namibian Underclass*. Boulder, Colo.: Westview Press.

Gusinde, M. 1954. "Ergänzende Beobachtungen an den Buschmännern." *Journal of the SWA Scientific Society* 10: 55–60.

Hahn, C. H. 1859. "Reise der Herren Hugo Hahn und Rath im südwestlichen Afrika, Mai bis September 1857." *Petermanns Geographische Mitteilungen* 5: 295–303.

———. 1966 [1928]. "The Ovambo." In *The Native Tribes of South-West Africa*. C. H. L Hahn, H. Vedder, and L. Fourie, eds. 1–36. Cape Town: South West Africa Administration.

Heintze, B. 1972. "Buschmänner unter Ambo – Aspekte ihrer gegenseitigen Beziehungen." *Journal of the South West African Scientific Society* 26: 45–56.

Kopytoff, I. 1989. "The Internal African Frontier: The Making of African Political Culture." In *The African Frontier: The Reproduction of Traditional African Societies*. I. Kopytoff, ed. 3–84. Bloomington: Indiana University Press.

Lebzelter, V. 1934. *Rassen und Kulturen in Süd-Afrika. Bd. 2: Eingeborenenkultur in Südwest und Südafrika*. Leipzig: Hiersemann.

Lee, R. 1972. "The !Kung Bushmen of Botswana." In *Hunters and Gatherers Today: A Socioeconomic Study of Eleven Such Cultures in the Twentieth Century*. M. G. Bicchieri, ed. 326–68. New York: Holt, Rinehart and Winston.

Loeb, E. 1962. *In Feudal Africa*. Bloomington: Indiana University Press.

London Missionary Society. 1935. *The Masarwa (Bushmen): Report of an Inquiry by the South African District Committee of the London Missionary Society*. Lovedale: Lovedale Press.

Marshall, J., and C. Ritchie. 1984. *Where are the Ju/wasi of Nyae Nyae? Changes in a Bushman Society, 1958–1981*. Cape Town: Centre for African Studies, University of Cape Town.

Marshall, L. 1976. *The !Kung of Nyae Nyae*. Cambridge, Mass.: Harvard University Press.

National Planning Commission. 1993. *1991 Population and Housing Census*. Report A. Statistical Tables 5 vols. Vol. II. Windhoek: Central Statistics Office.

Schinz, H. 1891. *Deutsch-Südwest-Afrika: Forschungsreisen durch die deutschen Schutzgebiete Gross-Nama- und Hereroland nach dem Kunene, dem Ngami-See und der Kalahari 1884–1887*. Oldenburg: Schulze.

Schoeman, P. 1957[1951]. *Hunters of the Desert Land*. Cape Town: Howard Timmins. [First published in Afrikaans 1951].

Tagart, E. S. B. 1931. *Report on the Masarwa and on Corporal Punishment among Natives in the Bamangwato Reserve of the Bechuanaland Protectorate*. N.p.

Tuupainen, M. 1970. *Marriage in a Matrilieal African Tribe: A Social Anthropological Study of Marriage in the Ondonga Tribe in Ovamboland*. Helsinki: Academic Bookstore.

Vedder, H. 1912. "Die Buschmänner." *Allgemeine Missionszeitschrift* 39: 403–16.

Widlok, T. 1994a. "The Social Relationships of Changing Hai//om Hunter-gatherers in Northern Namibia, 1990–1994." Unpublished Ph.D. diss., University of London.

———. 1994b. "Space and the Other: Social Experience and Ethnography in the Kalahari Debate." In *Social Experience and Anthropological Knowledge*. K. Hastrup and P. Hervik, eds. 180–99. London: Routledge.

———. 1996. "Ethnicity in the Post-apartheid Era: A Namibian 'San' Case Study." In *Ethnicity in Africa: Roots, Meanings and Implications*. L. de la Gorgendière, K. King, and S. Vaughan, eds. 147–66. Edinburgh: Centre of African Studies, University of Edinburgh.

———. 1997. "≠Akhoe Pragmatics, Hai//om Identity and the Khoekhoe Language." In *Namibian Languages: Reports and Papers, Namibian African Studies*. Vol. 4. W. Haacke and E. Elderkin, eds. 117–24. Cologne: Köppe.

———. Forthcoming. "A Practice Approach to Hai//om Storytelling." In *Language, History and Identity: Papers from the Tutzing Conference on Khoisan Studies*, July 11–14, 1994. Ed. R. Ross, R. Vossen, and E. N. Wilmsen. Band 17, Quellen zur Khoisan-Forschung. Cologne: Köppe.

———. 1999. *Living on Mangetti: 'Bushman' Autonomy and Namibian Independence*. Oxford Studies in Social and Cultural Anthropology. Oxford: Oxford University Press.

Wilmsen, E. 1989. *Land Filled with Flies: A Political Economy of the Kalahari*. Chicago: University of Chicago Press.

Williams, F. 1991. *Precolonial Communities of Southwestern Africa: A History of Owambo Kingdoms 1600–1920*. Windhoek: National Archives of Namibia.

Chapter 21

CENTRAL AFRICAN GOVERNMENT'S AND INTERNATIONAL NGOS' PERCEPTIONS OF BAKA PYGMY DEVELOPMENT

—————=≡«◉»≡=—————

Barry S. Hewlett

In a recent paper, Hitchcock and Holm (1993) state that "external domination of hunter-gatherer societies is increasingly structured by the bureaucratic state rather than the market." The state establishes settlement schemes, social services, land-tenure policies, and political representation policies, all of which influence the lives of hunter-gatherers. While the market continues to dramatically impact African forest foragers ("pygmies"), especially international logging interests and local demands for game meat, the role of the bureaucratic state is rapidly increasing. This chapter examines perceptions of Baka foragers by government and nongovernment officials (of international NGOs and PVOs) who have responsibilities for establishing and implementing state policies and programs for the Baka.

The essay focuses on the Cameroonian government's project to sedentarize and socially and economically integrate the Baka into Cameroonian society. Most of the Cameroonian government officials who were interviewed are responsible for establishing and coordinating the sedentarization program, while the international NGOs (nongovernmental organizations) and PVOs (private voluntary organizations) are the primary agents responsible for implementing the Baka program. The aim of this chapter is to describe the nature and intensity of government and NGOs' perceptions of Baka with the hope of promoting greater understanding and respect for the different perspectives, which may in turn contribute to better services for Baka foragers. The essay is written with the assumption that how a particular problem is viewed, conceived, and defined patterns and limits the ways it can be solved. For instance, de Waal (1989) indicates that Europeans have a Malthusian view of famine, which emphasizes lack of available food. Consequently, Europeans' response to famine is usually to send food, when in fact many other factors may be contributing to the crisis (crowding at refugee camps, lack of medicines, lack of seasonal employment, etc.).

While several similarities exist between the government's and NGOs' views of tropical forest foragers, the differences are dramatic and often lead to conflicts in development programs. The nature of the conflicting views is illustrated in the following remarks from the annual report of an American NGO working with government officials in the Central African Republic to manage a tropical forest reserve, a project that is impacting the lives of Aka forest foragers. The author of the report indicates that "the success or failure of the conservation effort depends on the supportive attitude and active participation of the local population—and this includes all government functionaries assigned to work [on the project]. In-roads are being made with the local population. But, unfortunately, the same can not be said concerning the Central African government representatives. They have all been hostile, uncooperative, corrupt, greedy, jealous, and often-times vindictive. Local authorities continually hassle the [NGO] personnel with everything from unsubstantiated rumors to weekly summons to idiotic investigations into the 'lack of moral character' of the whites in the project sending letters full of outright lies to authorities in Nola and Bangui."

While NGO officials often have difficulty with government officials, the latter often question the motivations and interests of international NGOs working on state development projects. For instance, a Cameroonian official who establishes Baka policies has published a report that questions the motivations of French, American, and Dutch volunteers who have worked on development projects for the Baka in Cameroon. He entitles a section of his manuscript "Volunteers for Progress: Humanitarianism or Search for the Exotic." He suggests that many international volunteers may be serving because they cannot find work in their home country, or are searching for adventure and touristic curiosities or to conduct research for personal academic gain. He suggests that missionaries also have ulterior motives for working with Baka—to learn traditional Baka medicines in order to develop new Western drugs and to facilitate the exporting of ivory, cacao, and coffee.

The most illustrative example of these contrasting perceptions comes from the film made by Phil Agland on the Baka. In the U.S. it was a National Geographic Special entitled "Baka: People of the Forest," while in Britain it was a two-hour documentary shown on the BBC. This rather romantic portrayal of the Baka shows them collecting honey and highlights the important role of women in their society and the active role that fathers play in child-care. This film received excellent reviews in the U.S. and Europe and is often shown in U.S. universities to demonstrate the life of pygmies or foragers. However, the film was not shown on Cameroonian television because the government thought it gave a negative and primitive view of the country. Cameroonian television has broadcast several news stories about how the government, missionaries, and NGOs are assisting in the social development of the Baka by training them in farming techniques and providing formal education.

Such contrasting views are not limited to state projects for the Baka. The aforementioned Hitchcock and Holm article on the San is full of examples of conflicts between Tswana government officials and international NGO consultants, anthropologists, and officials. Ndagala presented a paper at the London CHAGS 4 meeting in which he described "doomed" versus "free" views of the Hadza, which were essentially government ("doomed," meaning a primitive stage of evolution that would either die out or needed the help of civilized peoples to survive) versus anthropologists' views ("free," meaning harmonious hunters, gleeful gatherers) of the Hadza (Ndagala 1988). He called for greater communication between government officials and anthropologists.

This essay is similar to Ndagala's in that it articulates contrasting views of those who are working toward the "development" of a hunting and gathering group, but is different in that it tries to point out some similarities as well as differences, and tries to explain why differences exist and why the different groups feel so intensely about their particular views.

Background

The Baka live in the tropical forests of southern Cameroon, northern Congo, and Gabon; are Oubanguian speakers; utilize spears and traps as their most important hunting technique; are relatively highly assimilated into village culture since they have small farms; and spend three to four months per year in the forest. The Baka population is estimated to be around forty thousand.

The Cameroonian sedentarization program for the Baka goes back to the early 1960s. The government wanted Baka foragers as well as farmers in the forested area to move onto permanent settlements along major and secondary roads in order to improve health conditions and increase the population's potential as a work force for cash crops. In 1968, Catholic missionaries started the East Cameroon Pygmy Project to get Baka to move to large sedentary villages, away from other villagers, where missionaries could provide health, education, agricultural, and evangelical services. In 1975, the Government of Cameroon (GOC) established the Ministry of Social Affairs, which was responsible for improving the living conditions of marginal groups. The Baka were the only marginal group identified and targeted for intervention (eventually the Bakola foragers of southwestern Cameroon were included). The Ministry established the policies and directions of the Baka sedentarization program and provided some financial support. Most of the government's money was utilized by Cameroonian anthropologists in the early 1980s to conduct preliminary studies of Bakola and Baka foragers (the Pygmy Research Unit of the Institute of Human Sciences was established to conduct the research) and to support field agents in towns with high concentrations of Baka. Some excellent research resulted from the government-sponsored studies (Loung and Godefroy 1986), and demonstrates the Cameroonian government's concern about the impact of their interventions for Baka. The Dutch NGO is starting to conduct research before intervention programs for Baka are implemented.

While the GOC has established the sedentarization program (also called social-economic integration program), the Baka have not been forced to sedentarize. The GOC agents encourage this when possible, but they have not actively tried to move Baka to the road, and in fact have done little to contribute to Baka sedentarization. For the most part, Baka have moved to the road on their own.

The GOC established the Baka sedentarization program, but the implementation of the program has been left primarily up to international NGOs (such as the Dutch Cooperation [SNV] and the French Association of Volunteers for Progress) and PVOs (Catholic missionaries). The French and Dutch groups became involved through contacts with French and Dutch Catholic missionaries. The Dutch volunteers officially began their technical assistance to the sedentarization program in 1979, and their involvement and participation has gradually increased over the years. Currently, SNV has six technical assistants who provide agricultural extension and health education services to the Baka. SNV does not feel it has been very successful and is trying to reorganize its efforts to make the Baka program more community based and bottom-up rather than the reverse. The French volunteers work directly with the Catholic missionaries to provide health services to Baka. They currently provide two nurses and one community development agent to work with Baka.

The Catholic missionaries have had the greatest impact as they have contributed the longest, most intensive, and most consistent program to large sedentary Baka communities that they have established. Their interventions include: health education (clothing, housing, hygiene), literacy training, agricultural education, leadership training to facilitate discussion of village issues, and evangelizing. As previously mentioned, the French volunteers work directly with missionaries in the Baka villages that they have established, while the Dutch work with Baka in different areas.

Thus, there are three groups involved with the Baka sedentarization program: the GOC, the SNV (Dutch Assistance), and Catholic missionaries with the assistance of French volunteers. GOC coordination of the Baka program is minimal, and each unit evaluates, sets priorities, and acts rather autonomously.

Methods

Government and international NGO staff that were responsible for the Baka sedentarization program were interviewed as part of a study of African tropical forest foragers being conducted by The World Bank (the result of that work is Bailey et al. 1992). Individuals from the Ministries of Social Affairs, Plan, Agriculture, and Higher Education and Scientific Research, Catholic missionaries, and SNV staff working with the Baka were interviewed. I was unable to meet with any of the French volunteers. Project reports (e.g., annual reports and project evaluations) and published papers of the various governmental and nongovernmental agencies were also examined.

There are two important limitations to this study: (1) it focuses only on those directly involved with implementation of the sedentarization program—it does not include the public's views of the Baka; and, (2) it does not discuss Baka views of the development process.

Finally, a cautionary note: the study discusses a generalized dichotomy. An inherent problem to this sort of discussion, it is that no particular individual clearly falls into one or the other perspective. There is a continuum of perspectives, and there are, of course, government officials who have perceptions similar to those of NGO officials and vice versa. But overall, the distinctive perceptions described provide a better understanding of some of the difficulties of government and international agencies working together on projects aimed at hunters and gatherers.

Underlying Differences in Perceptions

While talking to individuals responsible for Baka sedentarization, it became clear that the government officials' underlying perceptions about the nature of Baka and why they should help Baka were quite different from those of the NGO staff and missionaries.

Cameroonian government officials consistently mentioned the "evolution" of the Baka. Baka, while a nice people, were at an earlier and primitive stage of cultural evolution and needed assistance to move into the modern world. Ndagala calls this the "doomed" perspective of government officials—governments can either let these groups slowly die out or can help move them into the modern world. Cameroonian government officials were very proud of the fact that they were doing something to assist the Baka rather than just letting them slowly die out as was happening in some other central African countries. Some of the government officials' comments included the following:

1. The Baka are culturally evolving and moving *up*, and are currently in a difficult stage of evolution and therefore need government intervention.... Learning agriculture is the most important part of the sedentarization program, and other things will follow (e.g., better diet, health, money to attend school, money for taxes, identity card, etc.).
2. Their frequent residential mobility is an early stage of cultural evolution.
3. Sedentarization is a movement that is going on and is irreversible.
4. The Baka are evolving from a primitive to a modern stage where one *produces* and contributes to a national economy.

In the eyes of the Cameroon government officials, the Baka were at a low stage of evolution, had few redeeming characteristics, and had low social value. While there was a consistent theme of evolution and movement toward civilization, there was, of course, considerable variation in government officials' perceptions. The higher one went in the ministries, the more generalized and negative the comments about Baka. A secretary general, for instance, indicated that one sign of Baka's lower stage of evolution was their lowered mental capabilities. None of the junior-level government officials suggested this. Baka were noted as having extraordinary supernatural abilities and knowledge (e.g., their shamans are noted as especially good), but again these characteristics were perceived as an earlier stage of evolution.

The international NGO staff, missionaries, and consultant anthropologists, on the other hand, valued many aspects of Baka life. The Baka were at a higher rather than at a lower level of existence. Hunting-gathering Baka life was valued because it was close to nature, relatively egalitarian (special reports by SNV looked at the important role of women), and peaceful. The Baka had exceptional knowledge of the forest, were exceptionally good parents, and had emotionally and socially satisfying lives. The Baka needed to be protected from the assertive and exploitative farmers as well as from the national government. They did not believe that social-economic integration was necessarily advantageous to the Baka. Baka autonomy from the villagers was their primary concern. There was a general mistrust of the motives of the government integration program—they thought the government wanted them to sedentarize and integrate simply to control them more easily and so they could pay taxes. NGO staff and missionaries were interested in teaching Baka to farm and become sedentary so they could not be exploited by the villagers and government officials.

The Impact of Underlying Perceptions on Identifying the Problems

Government, NGO, and missionary reports and evaluations gave similar reasons for targeting the Baka for special services and intervention: exploitation by Bantu farmers, poor health and nutrition, lack of education, and lack of integration into the national social-economic system. There was also general agreement as to why things were particularly bad for the Baka: deforestation and population increases have caused a depletion of forest game animals and wild plant foods, and have resulted in the increased exploitation of peoples with fewer resources. While similarities existed in the reports and interviews, there were differences in the emphasis or intensity given to a particular problem and the way in which a problem was articulated. The differences in intensity and articulation of problems reflect the underlying differences in perception described above.

1. *Baka are exploited by Bantu.* This was the primary problem and driving force for NGOs' and missionaries' activities, while it was a secondary or tertiary point for government officials. Missionaries were especially strong on this point and used it to explain why it was important to have Baka settlements some distance from those of farmers.

2. *Baka are not part of the national social-economic system.* This was the greatest concern for government officials. It is seen in the current name of the government's Baka program—it is no longer called the Baka sedentarization program; it is now called social and economic integration of the Baka. Government officials frequently mentioned that Baka did not contribute to the national economy with cash crops nor did they pay taxes. NGOs and missionaries, on the other hand, emphasized the point that Baka do not use community services, such as primary health care and public schools, and are not

part of political decision-making. NGOs and missionaries want Baka to participate in the national social-economic system, but for different reasons: they do not want the Baka to be exploited and want them to have self-determination.

3. *Baka have poor health and nutrition.* Government officials emphasized the lack of food, reporting that Baka frequently had to steal from farmers, that they lived only on salt, and that malnutrition was common. Government officials tended to view Baka life as nasty and brutish. NGOs and missionaries, on the other hand, emphasized the poor sanitary conditions: Baka did not wear shoes; use latrines; or wash themselves, their children, or their eating utensils.

4. *Baka lack formal education.* Government officials, NGOs, and missionaries agreed that Baka needed formal education, but NGOs and missionaries emphasized the importance of formal education to understanding and utilizing the political and economic system so that the Baka might be more independent, while government officials emphasized the importance of learning how to read and write so that the Baka could get jobs, start to contribute to the national economy, and participate in the mainstream community.

The Impact of Underlying Perceptions on Solving the Problems

There are also similarities in the actions that the government, NGOs, and missionaries list to remedy the above-mentioned problems: develop agricultural abilities of Baka, identify and establish Baka leaders to represent them at community meetings, decrease child mortality and morbidity, and educate Baka children. But as described above, the underlying differences in perceptions influence how the solution is articulated and why these particular actions are important and necessary.

Developing the Baka's capabilities for agriculture is a central solution for both NGOs and the government, but for different reasons. Missionaries and NGOs emphasize the point that farming is the best way that the Baka can become financially and dietarily independent from Bantu, while the government is interested in how increased agricultural activity will help to integrate Baka socially and economically into Cameroonian society. If Baka have farms—cash crops, in particular—they can pay for the cost of formal schooling, medications, and taxes. It is worth noting that neither the government nor the NGOs or missionaries feel that hunting and gathering and nomadism are viable options.

The establishment of hierarchy (i.e., community leaders) and formally educating Baka are also desired goals of the government and NGOs, but again the emphases and articulation of these solutions are somewhat different. The government emphasizes integration into mainstream Cameroonian society, while the NGOs and missionaries emphasize independence from the exploitative Bantu.

Government documents seldom indicate an interest in maintaining or sustaining Baka culture. Missionaries' and NGOs' documents, on the other hand, list the importance of incorporating and maintaining Baka language, rituals, and traditional medicines.

It does seem somewhat ironic that with the adoption of agriculture, hierarchy, and formal education, few elements of Baka culture—e.g., egalitarian social relations, interactive styles, conflict resolution, sharing—would be left. What is maintained is what is perceived as culture (language, ritual, and medicines). Generally, both government officials and NGOs want the Baka to be more like them: sedentary, responsive to hierarchy, healthy, wealthy, and wise.

Resolving Conflicts

In many ways the government's and NGOs' agenda for Baka look very similar, but there are significant differences in their perceptions of Baka that can and do lead to conflicts. Understanding and resolving these conflicts can be difficult, but I think the recent work of Ross (1991) provides an insightful framework for analyzing ethnocentric and intergroup conflict. He identifies three different sources of conflict, which lead to three different proposals for effective conflict management. The three sources of intergroup conflict are intercultural miscommunication, psychocultural interpretation, and competition for scarce resources.

Intercultural miscommunication refers to conflict that arises or persists because different groups do not understand each other's styles of communication, belief systems, and behaviors. This study and Ndagala's have focused on this aspect of conflict between groups working with hunters and gatherers. In order to resolve this dimension of conflict, it is necessary to do what Ndagala advocated in his paper—create greater cooperation and communication between state officials and anthropologists. The parties involved (in this case, central African government officials and NGOs) need to meet regularly and articulate their philosophies and actions to each other.

The second source of conflict that needs to be considered is competition for scarce resources. How does an intervention program influence availability of jobs, land, access to medicines, education, etc.? It is necessary to understand and explore the nature of resources that are at stake with the Baka program. Resources are in very short supply in central

Africa at this time: government officials have not been paid for many months or years, Western medicines are hard to come by, formal education is more expensive than before and available to fewer people, and access to land is increasingly difficult. Central African farmers often do not want programs for Baka (or other forest forager populations) because it gives them greater access to land, medical supplies, education, and training. Government officials have to be responsive to the interests of the farmers as well as those of the Baka.

The third source of conflict, called psychocultural interpretation, draws attention to the mediating effects of shared and culturally reinforced mental representations of the world. It attempts to understand the *emotional intensity* and *ambiguity* of conflict by examining socialization patterns. This aspect of conflict is the least understood. It suggests that there are not only differences in behaviors and views, but that people have intense feelings about what they do. The intensity of these feelings may be ambiguous and difficult to articulate. These emotions develop as one grows up and learns particular social styles. Many government officials who are making policy decisions and implementing programs for Baka grew up in villages where formal education was difficult to come by, and infant and child mortality were high. Their parents or grandparents possibly lived a life in which illiteracy, high infant mortality, and inequality (e.g., forced labor by Europeans) were common. Government officials intimately know what village life is like, and many government officials have spent their adult life moving away from this lifestyle. While they often have positive memories of village life, they do not want to return to village conditions. European missionaries or international NGO staff, on the other hand, have little firsthand experience of what village life entails. NGOs and missionaries working on development projects for Baka grew up under much different conditions and are generally not living under village conditions while they are in central Africa. They certainly did not personally experience the negative consequences of village life, for example, high child mortality.

A better understanding of the various sources of conflict between government officials, NGOs, and missionaries on policies and programs for Baka or other forest forager populations can enhance the delivery of services to these populations. Whether or not these programs are appropriate is completely another issue, but there is a clear pattern of African governments and international NGOs working together more rather than less frequently to serve hunters and gatherers and other indigenous peoples. Therefore, the sorts of conflicts they encounter and the measures taken to resolve them might be useful and applicable to other parts of the world.

Conclusion

Seldom do anthropologists working with an international NGO on a development project for hunters and gatherers give much attention to views of government officials. Anthropologists have been trained to pay attention to the world-view, interests, and desires of the indigenous peoples. The government often becomes the villain because it has tremendous power and authority over indigenous peoples. In working and talking with Cameroonian government officials, I have come to better understand and respect their views (although I do not always agree with them). Cameroonian government officials work hard and are serious, highly motivated, well educated, and articulate. They feel strongly about their views, are trying to do what they can with the limited resources they have, and are trying to deal with missionaries and NGOs that they do not trust very much. This essay argues for greater understanding, communication, and empathy for the views and actions of government officials. Government officials are playing an increasingly important role in decisions about hunters and gatherers, yet anthropologists and international NGOs involved with development programs for indigenous peoples generally dismiss the abilities and qualifications of government officials. This neglect of the government role ironically often leads to more conflicts and fewer services for Baka.

References

Bailey, R. C., S. Bahuchet, and B. S. Hewlett. 1992. "Development in the Central African Rainforest: Concern for Forest Peoples." In *Conservation of West and Central African Rainforests*. Washington, D.C.: World Bank.

de Waal, A. 1989. *Famine That Kills: Darfur, Sudan, 1984–1985*. New York: Clarendon Press.

Hitchcock, R. K., and J. D. Holm. 1993. "Bureaucratic Domination of Hunter-Gatherer Societies: A Study of the San of Botswana." *Development and Change* 24: 305–38.

Loung, J.-F., and N. M. Godefroy. 1986. *Rapport d'activités pour l'exercice 1985/1986*. Yaoundé, Cameroun: Ministère de l'Enseignement Supérieur et de la Recherche Scientifique.

Ndagala, D. K. 1988. "Free or Doomed? Images of the Hadzabe Hunters and Gatherers of Tanzania." In *Hunters and Gatherers I: History Evolution and Social Change*. T. Ingold, D. Riches, and J. Woodburn, eds. Oxford: Berg.

Ross, M. H. 1991. "Managing Ethnocentric Conflict: Competing Theories and Alternative Steps Towards Peace." Paper presented at the Annual Meeting of the American Sociological Association.

Chapter 22

THE ROLE OF WOMEN IN
MANSI SOCIETY

───══◉══───

Elena G. Fedorova

In this work we will examine women's role and place in Mansi society. The Mansis, one of the numerically small peoples of northwestern Siberia, occupy the vast territory of the Ob region in small groups. This chapter is based on materials collected during expeditions, mostly to the Northern Mansis, between the second half of the 1970s and the beginning of the 1990s. The regions occupied by the Northern Mansis are the contemporary Berezovskii district of the Tiumen' region and the Ivdelskii district of the Sverdlov region. For comparative purposes, we will provide data collected during an expedition to the Iugansk Khantys in July 1993. This group of Iugansk Khantys has moved to the Salym River basin (between the Irtysh and the Ob).

Until recently, the ethnographic literature was dominated by the conventional view of the low status of women in Ob-Ugrian society in general, and among the Mansis in particular. It was thought that for women to live independently in these societies would be extremely difficult. Our examples will demonstrate that this view does not necessarily conform with reality.

Women's Role in Economic Activities

The role of women in traditional Mansi society can be looked at from different perspectives, one of which concerns their activities in production. Mansi subsistence has always been complex; the specifics of local conditions determined whether hunting or fishing would have the leading role in the Mansi economy. Hunting, however, was the predominant subsistence type in the majority of the territory occupied by the Mansis. Everywhere, fishing and hunting were complemented by gathering. Some Mansi groups also practiced reindeer-herding, mostly for transportation, and were sometimes involved in small-scale husbandry (cattle) and food production. Women took part in all of the main types of subsistence activities, to a lesser or larger degree. Their part in each instance was realized differently and depended on the specific type of activity and the physical abilities of a particular woman. The degree of a woman's involvement in specifically feminine activities was also important as it determined how much free time a woman had.

Gender division of labor among the Mansis is most noticeable in the activities that do not belong to the so-called main subsistence types, i.e., hunting and fishing. Gathering, taking care of the cattle, and gardening were women's work. Women also prepared soft materials and used them for making clothing and household utensils such as: fur coats, parkas, *malitsy* (special shirts made out of reindeer skin and fur), reindeer boots, fur bags, dishes (made out of tree bark), cradles, etc. Men prepared hard materials such as wood and bone. Wood was a popular material; it was used for houses and shacks, boats, skis, dog and horse sleds, and dishes. Wood was crafted almost exclusively by men. However, women helped make some wood-based items. For example, fur covers on skis used by hunters were made by women, but they were put on the wooden skis by men. Women also worked with tree bark. A special type of women's activity was the manufacture of cast-tin clothing decorations. It was exclusively women's work among the Mansis, the Khantys, and—as is shown by archaeological data—among a significant part of the prehistoric Ural-Volga population (Golubeva 1984: 86).

The most time-consuming women's activities were cooking, making clothes, and manufacturing decorations from local as well as traded materials. Every free minute was used for these activities. For example, patterns for clothes could be made while cutting grass (preparing hay) or in a hunting hut. To keep a house clean was always a woman's task as well. In addition, a woman had to take care of the children, further limiting her participation in subsistence activities. The amount of a living minimum was determined by the size of the family. Some part of procured resources was also used for trade and exchange. Therefore, if a family was large and had an extended trade network, subsistence activities had to be more and more productive.

Women's participation in hunting and fishing was also determined by the gender demographics of the family. For example, if there was no headman in the family (a husband or a son of the appropriate age), or if the husband was sick, a woman often had to provide for her family herself. In the past, if a man—the head of the household—died, his younger brother (if there was one) would take care of the widow and her children. The whole group was responsible for providing for those members of the society who could not do so themselves. For example, after a group hunt for moose, the meat was not only distributed among the hunters. Those who could not take part in the hunt (elders, widows with many children, etc.) also received a part of the procured meat.

During the twentieth century, especially during its second half, the number of unmarried women with children has increased. These women were forced to become more active in providing for their families. This was especially important since the institution of traditional sharing has been disappearing for a number of reasons. Therefore, for a woman to take part in hunting (which as a rule demanded a lot of time spent outside of her home and depended on the season and the type of animal hunted), one of the following two conditions had to apply: a lot of free time or loss of a providing man in the family. The first condition can explain the fact that it was usually grownup unmarried daughters in the family who took part in the hunting of fur animals and migratory birds. There are no data indicating that women ever took part in hunting large animals such as moose or caribou. Possibly the reason for this is the requirement of physical strength for this type of hunt. However, women were involved in transporting the procured meat from the hunting site to the dwelling, using hand sleds for this purpose. Sometimes they had to attach dogs to the sleds as well, since the cargo was rather heavy. It is important to note that women did not hunt bears.

As is well known, bear cults were present in many cultures of taiga hunters. The Mansis are not an exception in this respect. There were certain prohibitions for women related to the bear cult. The Ob-Ugrians believe that a bear does not touch women. It is held that a bear can tell a woman apart from a man by the scarf on her head. When informants were asked whether a woman can kill a bear if she accidentally sees it during the hunt and finds herself in a dangerous situation, they invariably answered: "Why would she kill the bear?" This illustrates that even today Mansi women have a special relationship with the bear.

Women's participation in fishing was more obligatory. In particular, it was generally a woman's task to check the nets and change net sites. In addition, women had to help with fishing operations, which required more complex gear or which demanded a large number of people when there were not enough men. During World War II, when almost all men were in the battlefields, fishing was done by women and children. Therefore, in traditional Mansi society women could be completely independent economically. Another issue is the question of which hunting grounds were available for a woman to use. These hunting grounds were not inherited through the female line. However, more research on this issue is needed.

During the twentieth century, Mansi culture has gone through substantial changes in subsistence activities and lifestyles. These changes have accelerated during the last decades. As a result, the traditional subsistence system has been practically destroyed. Today it is preserved only in remote villages where Mansis comprise 100 percent of the population. Usually, these villages are located in the deep taiga in the upper reaches of rivers and do not have more than three households. It is difficult to determine in each individual case what was the cause of preservation of these villages in the midst of relocation of small villages to larger settlements, a process that started at the beginning of the 1960s and played a large role in destroying traditional culture. It is important that young people today wish to move to the large settlements; however, this desire is expressed mostly by men. The connections of the level of education to professional orientation and changes in traditional culture are obvious.

We have analyzed economic documents from the second half of the 1970s through the 1980s. They demonstrate that women constitute the majority among the adult population in Mansi settlements of the Berezovskii district of the Tiumen' region. There is approximately an even number of men and women who have some kind of formal education. The larger a settlement is, the higher the level of education is. This is to be expected, since people with some qualification want to settle down in an area where they can use their skills and knowledge. Another reason for this phenomenon is that people who received education in the boarding schools in central villages did not want to return to their native settlements deep in the taiga region, considering life there humiliating. By the end of the 1980s, the number of people with secondary education had increased, due to the governmental policy requiring everybody to have secondary education. Practically in every settlement, there are more women with secondary vocational education than men. At the same time, everywhere in the Mansi territory there are more men than women with incomplete secondary (eight grades) and complete secondary (ten grades) education. These two types of education levels are the most common among the Mansis. In the cases when there are more women than men of the same age, the number of educated women is higher (Fedorova 1993). The majority of those students who continue their education in special vocational schools, technical secondary schools, and institutes are also women. At the same time, after graduation from these educational establishments, it is easier for men to find jobs in their native villages. The reason is the demand for so-called "male professions" in the modern economic setting. As a result, women who cannot find jobs and do not want to live in poor conditions leave first their small and then larger settlements; with them leave men who cannot find wives. Traditional subsistence suffers from these losses. Reindeer-herding is especially affected. Before the appearance of motorized sleds, the disruption of reindeer-herding was explained by the fact that women do not want to spend the majority of the year on the pastures and men do not want to become herders because they cannot find a wife. Another important factor is that herding requires a lot of physical strength on the part of women.

Some research was also done with the Iugansk Khantys, who have moved to the Salym River basin. These people live significantly far away from the Mansis and do not even know about their existence, although Khantys and Mansis are related linguistically and culturally (both groups traditionally depended on hunting, fishing, gathering, and reindeer-herding). The status of women in traditional Khanty society did not differ from Mansi women and depended first of all on women's roles in the economy. Khanty and Mansi women have a lot in common in modern times as well, proving yet again that the development and functioning of societies with similar subsistence types is governed by a certain regularity.

Women and Children

In traditional Mansi society, six- or seven-year-old children did not demand a lot of time; they needed only basic care. A child was kept in a cradle until it began walking. A cradle was usually placed in such a way as to create the most comfortable conditions for the child; for example, on a hot day it was suspended from a stick outside, away from sunny spots. At the same time, a cradle was placed so that it always would be within the mother's sight while she was working around the house. If a woman went to the forest to do some berry picking, she took the child in its cradle with her. A cradle could be of two types—for usage during the day and for night usage—and allowed carrying a baby over significant distances. In the forest, a cradle with a child was usually left at the site of berry picking under the supervision of older children. If there were older children in the family, especially girls, they were responsible for some part of child-care. It is important to mention that even today Mansis prefer to use traditional tree-bark cradles. Families that have store-bought furniture in their houses will also have tree-bark cradles. Parents especially strive to get one if a child is often ill or fidgety, since they believe that a child will grow healthy and serene if it sleeps in a tree-bark cradle.

Traditionally, women influenced mainly their daughters. A mother prepared her daughters for their future lives by teaching them how to take care of themselves, how to be a woman, etc., and a girl would learn by observing her mother. A mother would also explain to her daughters how to make things out of tree bark and fur, how to make clothes, and how to cook. Women skillful in sewing were highly valued. A girl sewed toys and clothes for her dolls under her mother's or older sister's guidance. These things were not to be thrown away, since later a suitor would determine by them whether his future wife would be a good and skillful sewer. In general, Mansi children matured very early (Fedorova 1988). Women taught not only girls; in cases when there was no father in the family, a mother was responsible for her sons' upbringing as much as her competence in male affairs allowed. Mansis have always had a tradition of adopting orphans. Even today it is not rare to see an adopted child in a Mansi family. Very often orphans are brought up by grandmothers and grandfathers. A Mansi family can adopt not only Mansi children but children with other ethnic affiliations as well.

When the government introduced a system of preschool child-care centers and boarding schools, the role of the family in child-rearing was tremendously decreased. In many families, children and parents could see each other only during school breaks. The result of this system is sad: People have lost a sense of personal responsibility. There has been a loss of traditional culture due to partial or complete destruction of the mechanisms of its transmission. There is psychological degradation of some persons who are torn out of the life they are used to but do not have the ability to easily get accustomed to the new ways.

Women's Participation in Rituals

In traditional rituals, men's and women's functions were strictly defined. The role of women was restricted in several ritual activities. For example, in sacrifices to the "guardians" of a settlement or of a region and to the higher "gods," women were merely observers. This restriction probably exists because women do not belong to their social group of residence by birth; rather, their ties are established only through marriage. I. N. Gemuev (1990: 193–94) has examined this hypothesis in the light of Mansi beliefs about *Mir-susne-khum* (the most important deity in the Ob-Ugrian pantheon). It is also supported by the analogous behavior of children and teenagers who are not yet full members of a society. However, this hypothesis needs further research. The role of Mansi women in relation to shaman activities has not been researched very well. Despite the fact that there were certain and sometimes very severe restrictions of women's behavior in the belief system and ritual practices of the Mansis, there were, nevertheless, strong female shamans who shamanized with a drum, which was not characteristic of all categories of Mansi shamans.

At the same time, women as participants/performers in ritual activities accompanied a person during her or his entire life. When a child was born, certain procedures were conducted that were held to have magical meaning. In the ritual that determined which of the deceased relatives became reincarnated in a newborn, elderly female relatives of the child's parents had a leading role (Chernetsov 1959: 140–41). Women also took part in the wedding ceremony. Finally, after a person's death, they performed a number of funeral rituals. They washed the deceased (if it was a woman), wept over her, prepared visual representations of the mourning, and dressed the relatives of the deceased or put signs of mourning on their clothes. A person's transfer from one world into another not only required the presence of a woman but made women the leading performers of the rituals that accompanied this passage.

Women were required to take part in the Mansi bear festival. They were not merely observers but rather performed dances at appropriate times during the festival. It is important to notice that Mansi women had their own holiday, Raven's Day, which was celebrated at the beginning of spring. This time of the year was associated with the resurrection and renewal of nature.[1] In a way, through this holiday women are perceived as being situated at the sources of life.

Mansi women had their own sacred places as well. These sacred sites, not far away from settlements, were marked by a cedar or a birch tree decorated with pieces of cloth that had coins tied in them. Suspended from neighboring trees were old things: clothes, footwear (including footwear of women who had just given birth), cradles, and a very important item—birch-bark boxes containing afterbirth. Ashes and grass insoles were placed under the trees. It was believed that all of these rituals had to be followed, with nothing left out in any place; otherwise, a horrifying monster would grow up and eat the people. Women came to these sacred places during church holidays, had a feast, and hung on the sacred tree new pieces of cloth—leftovers from sewing projects (Sokolova 1971: 222).

Conclusion

Due to a lack of data, certain aspects of women's roles in Mansi society were only touched upon in this article. More detailed research is needed in these areas. The fact that contemporary Mansi culture has preserved a number of traditional elements and the high level of expertise of many informants allow us to hope that the necessary data can be elicited during future field trips.

Notes

The original Russian text of the article was translated by Irina Dubinina and stylistically edited by Megan Biesele. The final edit was provided by Peter Schweitzer, in consultation with the author.

1. It is interesting that, according to some versions of the Ob-Ugrian calendar, spring was considered to mark the beginning of the year (Sokolova 1990: 78).

References

Chernetsov, V. N. 1959. "Predstavleniia o dushe u obskikh ugrov." In *Issledovaniia i materialy po voprosam pervobytnykh religioznykh verovanii*. 114–56. Moscow: Izdatel'stvo Akademii nauk SSSR.

Fedorova, E. G. 1988. "Rebenok v traditsionnoi mansiiskoi sem'e." In *Traditsionnoe vospitanie detei u narodov Sibiri*. 80–95. Leningrad: Nauka.

_____. 1993. "Mansi: sovremennaia situatsiia (po dannym pokhoziaistvennykh knig vtoroi poloviny 1970–1980-kh gg.)." In *Narody Sibiri. Kniga 1* (Sibirskii etnograficheskii sbornik; 6). 155–200. Moscow: Institut etnologii i antropologii RAN.

Gemuev, I. N. 1990. *Mirovozzrenie mansi: Dom i kosmos*. Novosibirsk: Nauka.

Golubeva, L. A. 1984. "Zhenschiny-liteishitsy (k istorii zhenskogo remeslennogo litia u finno-ugrov." *Sovetskaia arkheologiia* 4: 75–89.

Sokolova, Z. P. 1971. "Perezhitki religioznykh verovanii u obskikh ugrov." In *Religioznye predstavleniia i obriady narodov Sibiri v XIX–nachale XX veka*. 211–38. Leningrad: Nauka.

_____. 1990. "Traditsionnoe vremiaschislenie u obskikh ugrov." In *Traditsionnoe mirovozzrenie i kultura narodov Severa i Sibiri*. Moscow.

Chapter 23

PEACEMAKING IDEOLOGY IN A HEADHUNTING SOCIETY

Hudhud, Women's Epic of the Ifugao

————————

Maria V. Staniukovich

The study of hunter-gatherer societies has had a large impact on the discussion of the problems of aggression and violence. Ethologists and psychologists are more inclined to regard aggression as an innate characteristic of human nature, whereas many anthropologists—those studying foraging and post-foraging societies in particular—consider that to be a biased approach (cf. Howell and Willis 1989). Instead, this chapter brings us back to Konrad Lorenz (Lorenz 1966): love and hatred, aggression and peaceful ideology are two sides of the same coin. It was an aggressive headhunting Ifugao society that formed a unique peacemaking ideology, and, notably enough, this ideology was expressed in the form of a typically "aggressive" genre of heroic epic.

The Ifugao belong to a group of mountain-dwelling peoples of the Cordillera Central, Northern Luzon, the Philippines. Despite the differences in their ways of subsistence (hunters, horticulturists, dry- and wet-rice cultivators), all of the highlanders were regarded as a "similar grade of civilization" and opposed as such to the lowland population. This distinction, which is not based on either linguistic or cultural criteria, dates back at least to the end of the eighteenth century and results from Spanish colonial activities. Having conquered the coastal areas rather easily, the Spaniards tried in vain to subjugate the mountain peoples. As P. O. Afable puts it, "military assaults, in which men from lowland Christian missions marched against their pagan neighbors ... permanently set the social and political boundaries between lowlanders and highlanders in this Northern area" (Afable 1995: 13). In the opposition of "Christian" and "civilized" to "savage" and "wild," still noticeable today, headhunting is the most sensational point. Although the Spanish records of the sixteenth century are abundant in descriptions of headhunting in coastal areas (ibid.), in popular opinion this cultural trait is attributed exclusively to mountain-dwellers.

During my short stay in Manila, it struck me painfully that the image of "bloodthirsty Igorot" is exploited in modern Philippine mass media (movies, ballet performances, etc.). Needless to say, while with the Ifugao family that adopted me during my field research, as well as while hiking through different areas of Ifugao, I felt much safer than in Manila. Besides, having studied the epic as a genre, I can state that the Ifugaos so far are the only people in the world known to have developed peacemaking ideology in that typically aggressive genre of oral literature.[1]

The rich literature on epic traditions worldwide portrays a highly male-centered genre of songs glorifying heroic values and warlike acts. The Ifugao male epic represents aggressive ideology, which it shares with all of the corresponding genres from India to Iceland. But what is specific to Ifugao epic lore is that it contains two trends. The *hudhud*, the female epic tradition of the Ifugaos, is a unique specimen of peacemaking, even pacifist, ideology in epic form. It is important to bear in mind that this ideology developed during the nineteenth century (or even earlier) at the peak of the headhunting period. Thus, it is genuine and indigenous, not imposed by the influence of other cultures as were, for instance, the motives of regret that appeared in the Kalinga *Ullalim* under the influence of Christianization and American "order."

A comparative study of Philippine folk epics that I based on the criteria of the Russian school of folklore studies (Meletinskii 1968; Propp 1976; Putilov 1976; Zhirmunskii 1979) revealed that the female *hudhud* tradition of the Ifugao is a typical heroic epic with reminiscences of mythological traits. The male Ifugao tradition and the Kalinga *Ullalim* performed by male and female singers are mythological epics, the *Ullalim* being in transition to a heroic one (Staniukovich 1983).

Fr. Lambrecht, the major publisher of the *hudhud* texts (Lambrecht 1957; 1960; 1961; 1967) insists that the *hudhud* is sung only for entertainment and does not bear any connection to traditional belief and ritual (cf. Lambrecht 1965). This statement, however, seemed doubtful to me from the very beginning. Close ritual ties are generally characteristic of Philippine folk epics (Demetrio 1979; Jocano 1964; Manuel 1963). In my opinion, this was the main reason why the rich epic literature of the lowland population disappeared altogether in the course of Christianization:[2] being an inseparable part of the native religious system, it was wiped out just as the Ifugao epic forms that I studied in the field are being wiped out today.

In my earlier works (Staniukovich 1981; 1982b) and in the first version of this essay, I claimed that *hudhud* is a highly ritualized genre. At that time, this claim was based on close examination of Lambrecht's own materials, as well as of the data published by Amador Daguio (1983) and Roy Franklin Barton (1919; 1930; 1938; 1946; 1955), and was further supported by the study of unpublished field notes of R. F. Barton deposited in the archives of the Institute and Museum of Anthropology and Ethnology in St. Petersburg (Barton ms.).[3] Now I can prove this claim with field data.

During my field research, I found that the term *hudhud* extends beyond the heroic epic known in publications to a larger group of female ritual songs, including shamanistic narratives treating the journey of the soul of the deceased to the abode of the dead (cf. Staniukovich 1998a; 1998b). All of the *hudhud* texts published so far, including the three that are to be published in Dr. N. Revel's "Nusantara epics project" (Revel forthcoming), appeared to belong to one and the same genre known in northwestern areas of Ifugao as *hudhud di 'ani* (*hudhud* of the harvest), or *hudhud di page* (*hudhud* of rice). This genre conforms to the melody pattern, poetic system, and vocabulary of the two newly found *hudhud* traditions: *hudhud di kolot* (*hudhud* of the haircut) and *hudhud di nate* (*hudhud* of the dead). Although in my field research I particularly concentrated on the study of these additional *hudhud* types, which have never been researched before, I have also found a large variety of story plots of the main type (*hudhud* of rice). All of them appear to confirm the characteristics of female ideology, including peaceful solutions of hereditary feuds without bloodshed.

While reading the following, one must bear in mind that headhunting does not exist in Ifugao any more. Early in the twentieth century, "order" was imposed by the American colonial administration. This goal was achieved by General-Governor Gallman, a talented "white chief" (as the Ifugao used to call their American governors), who acted within the framework of traditional Ifugao culture and was loved and highly respected by them. He and his successors, Tomlinson and Dosser, succeeded in decreasing considerably the number of local killings and distant headhunting raids. A new outburst of murders was precipitated by World War II. The Ifugao Province was the area of most of the violent combats. Practically the whole Kiangan *poblacion* (municipal center) was destroyed by bombing; even the most distant areas of Asipulo became battlefields. It was in Ifugao that General Yamashito surrendered—the final point of World War II in the Philippines. It is only natural that in such a situation headhunting was resumed, as for instance, the custom of vendetta was revived recently in Chechenia. Later on, military tension was characteristic of the Ifugao of the 1970s, during the martial law period. President Marcos endowed the military and Philippine Constabulary with such uncontrolled power that they aroused hatred in the native population. The NPA (National People's Army) became very active in Cordillera; though it was rather popular among the local people, it surely meant additional military pressure. By the late 1960s and early 1970s, headhunting in the mountainous areas of Northern Luzon had ceased altogether (cf. R. Rosaldo 1980). Although I was lucky enough to witness headhunting rituals on Good Friday of 1995 in Ifugao, including a war dance and *him-ung* (a ritual defining the avenger for the killing), they were performed for a person killed by *armelite* (machine gun) as a result of a land dispute that could occur in any peasant society anywhere in the world. Therefore, for the purposes of this chapter I shall use the materials on headhunting that date back to the beginning of the twentieth century.

Having said this, I shall return to the issue of how women's epics transform violence, while male epics glorify it, i.e., to the aspects that characterize the relevant male and female ideologies. The separate inner worlds of male and female epic traditions can be compared to each other and to the "objective" world of epic singers. Let me give a brief sketch of these three realities by concentrating on the following points: division of space into friendly and hostile zones; reasons for headhunting; the way warfare was performed; desirable male traits; final aims and perspectives of headhunting.

According to the classic definition of R. F. Barton, the "objective" world of the Ifugao was divided into three main zones: home region, neutral zone, and zone of warfare. Even within the home zone, it was only one's immediate relatives who were considered to be real allies. The affines, not to mention neighbors, might be sources of danger, as representatives of a different kinship group. In the neutral zone, relatives were outnumbered by nonrelatives. In the hostile zone, all of the inhabitants were regarded as potential killers and victims. In addition, every kinship group also had hereditary enemies of their own. The reasons for headhunting, apart from vendetta, were "evening the score" after funerals, getting access to higher grades in the rank system, and curing childlessness.

Most of the killings were initiated by the surprise attack of a headhunting group on another Ifugao group in hostile territory. A boy who went to the forest to get firewood or a woman gathering food plants might be ambushed, killed, and beheaded. After the attack, headhunters would flee at full speed to the home region. As R. F. Barton puts it, "the Ifugao has no pride against admitting fear and running away when there is danger—provided he does not abandon a kinsman" (Barton 1955: 21). In a way, it can be said that headhunters were seen as ordinary hunters, not as warriors. The victim was regarded more as game than as an adversary. Bravery was not so much appreciated but rather regarded as foolish. The key words in the native discourse regarding headhunting were "deceit" or "fraud." The Ilongot, neighboring headhunting people discussed in the classic works of Michelle and Renato Rosaldo, designate the internal killings by the term *ka'abung*—"by deception" (M. Rosaldo 1980: 6). The name of *Manahaut*, the supreme war deity of the Ifugao, means "Deceiver." Often the whole class of gods of war and sorcery is called "the Deceivers" (Barton 1946: 38). Headhunting in actuality, as opposed to mythology, thus gave no hint of the ethics of the warrior (Staniukovich 1997b).

Ifugao history of the period of headhunting could not be divided into intervals of war and peace. Headhunting was a constant part of everyday life. According to the dominant ideology, the whole kinship group, men and women alike, benefited from a headhunting raid. The general aim of headhunting could be defined as keeping the world in harmony and order, and this provided no ideological perspective for cutting short the cycle of reciprocal revenge killings.

How is the reality of reciprocal killings reflected in epic songs? In male epic traditions—the Ifugao *Galidu* (Barton 1955: 46–79)[4] and the Kalinga *Ullalim* (Billiet and Lambrecht 1970)—the friendly and hostile zones overlap. There are no strict boundaries between them, or, rather, they are very flexible, ranging from inside the home village to the boundaries of the human-inhabited world. Enemies might vary from playmates of a young hero to giants whose residence is in the Upstream or Downstream cosmological areas, beyond the boundaries of cosmological earth. The reasons for killing are either vengeance (vendetta or just a reaction to an insult) or the struggle with an adversary in order to win a girl's hand.

The fight often takes the form of a duel in which the opponents demonstrate their valor, fighting skill, and magic power. The song ends usually with a scene of a massacre during which all of the enemy's kin or even the whole population of the hostile region is killed. As already mentioned, some versions of the *Ullalim*, performed in the post-American period of "peacetime," present scenes of the hero's regret for being so bloodthirsty.

Highly appreciated male characteristics, demonstrated by heroes in male epics, are ferocity, valor, fighting skills, and magic powers. The criterion of bravery is introduced and cowardliness is depreciated. Just like male mythological texts, male oral epics define the result of a hero's warlike activities with an internally contradictory formula: "He slaughtered them all, including the infants, and made a peace pact with the rest of them." In the *Galidu* it goes like this:

Balitok,
He sees the sons of Ambalitayon
Tumbled heels over head.
Their sleeping place is their weapons,
There is left of them no remainder,
They're as if to skeletons crumpled ...
The new-made widows
And the mourning-band wearers and fasters ...,
Becoming some like kindred to them,
Becoming like uncles the others
                                        (Barton 1955: 76–77)

That is to say, the enemies are weakened by massacre and pacified by magic and peace pact, but as vengeance is always to be retaliated, the perspective of the conflict is preserved. The *hudhud*, the women's epic, differs greatly in its ideology and in the way it depicts warfare, both from reality and from the world of the male epics. There is no hostile territory in "*hudhud* of rice." Its topography presents a doubled home region, centered in a home village with outskirts surrounded by *Kadaklan* (the Big River), which serves as a *hudhud* analogy of a mythological river in the waters of which human Earth floats (Staniukovich 1997a). In other words, the whole universe is reduced to the limits of the female home space. No danger awaits the hero while he travels through the "empty space" that is outside his home region. Having crossed it, the hero comes to a duplicate of his home region, which is also surrounded by *Kadaklan*. It is the marginal place *pantalan* (the river bed), either near the home region or its duplicate, that is the only place of danger. Here the character might be ambushed from the river reeds. But even at *pantalan* no death or injury ever occurs.

Actually, there is no category of enemy in *hudhud*, despite the fact that the words *ngayaw* (headhunting) and *buhol* (enemy) are widely used. The personages are organized into family groups, each consisting of a hero, his sister, and their parents. The plot is based on the interaction of two families, initially depicted as being in hereditary feud. In moral characteristics and behavior, as well as in appearance and conduct, the members of these families duplicate each other absolutely. That is to say, the main hero is an absolute copy of a young man from the other family, his sister is a copy of the corresponding man's sister, etc. Members of both families are endowed with highly positive traits.

In more complicated versions of *hudhud*, a third family group appears. Members of this additional family are characterized negatively and treated with contempt. They do not pose any danger for the heroes. Being inferior from every point of view, they are no rivals to real heroes and therefore no enemies. They are always losers. A youngster from an unworthy family tries to win one of the girls (sisters of positive heroes). He never succeeds. His own sister is sometimes depicted as an unworthy wife of one of the positive heroes. She is usually sent back to her parents as soon as a better bride appears on the scene.[5] The home region of the third group, which is a second copy of the hero's home region, is not really a hostile territory. Besides, the positive hero never visits it. The negative personages are eliminated without being killed or wounded. Therefore, no feud or conflict results in the future.

The main intrigue revolves around the relationships of two positive heroes. The initial episodes introduce the hero as an aggressive youth. He plays dangerous games with his playmates, and nearly destroys through carelessness the precious jewels that are the hereditary sacred fortune of his family. He disobeys his parents: they want him to marry, but he instead declares that he will start a headhunting raid. When asked about the name of their hereditary enemy, the old father gives it with the following noteworthy words: "Exceedingly great is our feud with the Old man, Old man of old, Pangaiwan ... I tell you, bring only joy and happiness into their house ... in Bilibil" (Lambrecht 1957: 48). Or as it goes in the other version of the same text, published by A. Daguio:

> Why not find a girl to bring to Iken
>   [Old man, i.e., "to me, your father"]
> A beautiful daughter of Pangaiwan ...
> That the tribal feud be forgotten
> Between your father and Pangaiwan?
>   (Daguio 1983: 21)

The two sides of the story are thus given from the very beginning. The hero pretends to go headhunting while his actual aim is to marry the daughter of his father's enemy, and so to put an end to the old feud. In other words, the hero's aggressiveness is only pretense. Having reached the village of his "enemy," the hero once again shows his aggressive inclinations. He destroys all the rice in the fields of his "enemy." But as soon as the battle begins, all the signs of aggression disappear. Adversaries are depicted as valiant knights. Their battles (always three in number) are epically long. Needless to say, they have nothing to do with real headhunting practices. Much more important is the fact that *hudhud* battles have no analogies in epic literature. Using the *hudhud* vocabulary, we can call them "war dances," the typical formula being "as if dancing they are, two youths in the battlefield." During the many-year-long battles, the heroes show their skills, bravery, valor, but also politeness and good manners. They address each other exclusively with the appellation *biyawku* (my friend). Local girls who watch the battle from the village slope nudge their hero and induce him to cut off the adversary's head "that it may have fresh air at the door of our house." But the hero defends the dignity of his battle companion:

> Soften your cries, lovely ladies,
> For worthy as an opponent is Aliguyun,
> He is as good as I.
>
> (Daguio 1983: 29)

It is worth pointing out that in *hudhud* it is a male warrior who is idealized, whereas women are depicted as the violent sex. They induce killings and are pacified by men. From that point of view, *hudhud* contrasts with European medieval romances, which created idealized images of ladies fair (cf. Staniukovich 1999). Both heroes fight with all their strength. They sweat and breathe hard. They clench their teeth with effort, but one can not help feeling that they are only pretenders—good actors, not warriors.

Another important trait characteristic of all the positive personages is that both heroes and their sisters are ready to feel ashamed. The formula "very much ashamed I am" is sometimes used as a label quite out of context. It may be used when a new character is introduced and it is important to point out that he or she is a positive actor. Unworthy rivals and unworthy wives never feel ashamed. *Hudhud* heroes, like all epic heroes, are endowed with magic power. After a series of three battles in which no one is killed or wounded, the positive characters trade sisters and celebrate a double marriage. Thus, the aim and result of the heroes' activities is total elimination of enmity. The next generation will have no enemies.

Conclusion

To sum up, we can easily see the difference between male and female Ifugao ideologies as expressed in their epic lore. It emerges that while the male epic concentrates on violence expressed through the system of headhunting based on rage, enmity, and vengeance, the female epic represents a tradition of heroic exploit in which no blood is spilled whatsoever. The treatment of space in *hudhud* also undergoes radical changes from the male pattern. The picture of a tiny home region surrounded by the big hostile world is replaced by the universe reduced to the small "female" space of the home village. It can be doubled or tripled, but it never loses its dominant characteristic of safety.

Hudhud transforms the image of the headhunter, that is, of a hunter whose game is a human being, into a valiant knight. The women's epic introduces a new character. He is brave but pitiful, generous, polite, and modest. His aggressive intentions are dangerous only to inanimate objects like jewels, tops, food baskets, etc. With the introduction of this new image comes the idea of peacetime as a desirable perspective. As an expression of female ideology, the *hudhud* has much in common with women's literature of much later periods. It demonstrates both strong and weak points, the latter including simplification, varnishing of reality, and substitution of false conflicts for real ones. *Hudhud* can also be regarded as a kind of unconsciously dissident literature that keeps to the formal rules of a dominant male ideology, but stealthily fills the canonical form with inappropriate content.

Acknowledgments

I am most grateful to the Wenner-Gren Anthropological Foundation for the Small Grant that enabled me to update this study during my fieldwork in Ifugao (January–August 1995). I am deeply indebted to Dr. Harold Conklin, who generously shared with me his encyclopedic knowledge of Ifugao culture since 1978, long before the possibilities of fieldwork opened for Russian anthropologists. I also owe a great deal to Dr. Piers Vitebsky of Cambridge University and to John Gillow of Cambridge, U.K. I am grateful for help and advice to Dr. Bion Griffin of the University of Hawaii and Dr. Tom Headland of SIL, both of whom I first met at CHAGS 7, and to Dr. Nicol Revel of Centre de Recherche sur L'Oralité. During my stay in the Philippines, I enjoyed friendly cooperation with Dr. Jesus Peralta and Artemio Barbosa from the National Museum and the valuable help and hospitality of Mrs. Rosario Guinid from the Ifugao Museum.

Notes

The original Russian text was translated by the author; the translation was edited by Megan Biesele and Peter Schweitzer.

1. The only other sample of peacemaking solution of conflicts can be found in *tuitak* Ainu female epics (Philippi 1979). This tradition shows similarities to *hudhud* in some other aspects, including plot formation and ritual use (cf. Staniukovich 1982a).
2. There are examples when conversion into Christianity (e.g., of the Russians) did not result in the abandonment of the traditional epic songs, as they were not evidently and directly linked to pre-Christian pagan practices.
3. R. F. Barton worked in the Institute of Anthropology and Ethnology, Leningrad, from 1930 to 1940. Before leaving Russia, he donated his library, a number of unpublished manuscripts and field notes (cf. Staniukovich 1979). Barton's manuscripts and notes are deposited in the archives of the Institute and Museum of Anthropology and Ethnology in St. Petersburg (Barton ms.).
4. This text, called "Galidu, or Virgin birth" by Barton, appeared to be well known in the Ifugao village of my fieldwork. It was used some thirty years ago in *hagoho* sorcery rituals designated to settle a land dispute between two families. Both families in question

performed rituals using this text, and a family from my village was defeated. A number of small children from this family died, and the rice field became the property of their adversaries.

5. There is, however, an exception to the rule. In the *hudhud* "Dinulawan and Bugan at Gonhadan" (Lambrecht 1967), a negative heroine remains the wife of the hero, Aliguyun. This happens because of the unusual characteristics of Bugan, Aliguyun's usual bride, in this particular version: here she is depicted as a female warrior.

References

Afable, P. O. 1995. "The Peoples of Eduardo Masferre's Photographs." *Discovery* 25(2): 11–19.

Barton, R. F. 1919. "Ifugao Law." *University of California Publications in American Archaeology and Ethnology* 15(1): 1–186.

_____. 1930. *The Half-Way Sun: Life among the Headhunters of the Philippines*. New York: Brewer and Warren.

_____. 1938. *Philippine Pagans: Autobiographies of Three Ifugaos*. London: Routledge.

_____. 1946. "The Religion of the Ifugaos." *Memoirs of the American Anthropological Association* 65: 1–219.

_____. 1955. "The Mythology of the Ifugaos." *Memoirs of the American Folklore Society* 46: 1–244.

_____. ms. R. F. Barton's Manuscripts, Field Notes and Materials. Archives of the Institute and Museum of Anthropology and Ethnology (Kunstkamera), St. Petersburg, Russia. Fond K-I.

Billiet, F., and F. Lambrecht. 1970. *The Kalinga Ullalim*. Baguio City: Catholic School Press.

Daguio, A. T. 1983. "Hudhud hi Aliguyun." In *Epics of the Philippines: Anthology of ASEAN Literatures, vol I*. J. V. Castro and A. T. Antonio, eds. 17–66. Quezon City: EDSA.

Demetrio, F. R. 1979. "An Overview of Philippine Epics." *Kinaadman (Wisdom): A Journal of the Southern Philippines* 1: 9–28.

Howell, S., and R. Willis, eds. 1989. *Societies at Peace: Anthropological Perspectives*. London and New York: Routledge.

Jocano, L. 1964. "The Epic of Labaw Donggon." *Philippine Social Sciences and Humanities Review* 29: 1–103.

Lambrecht, F. 1957. "Ifugao Epic Story: Hudhud of Aliguyun at Hananga." *University of Manila Journal of East Asiatic Studies* 6(3–4): 1–203.

_____. 1960. "Ifugaw hu'dhud. *Hudhud* of Aliguyun Who Was Bored by the Rustle of the Palm Tree at Aladugen." *Asian Folklore Studies (Tokyo)* 19: 1–174.

_____. 1961. "Ifugaw hu'dhud. *Hudhud* of Bugan with Whom the Ravens Flew Away, at Gonhadan." *Asian Folklore Studies (Tokyo)* 20: 136–273.

_____. 1965. "Ifugao *Hudhud* Literature." *Saint Louis Quarterly* 3(2): 191–214.

_____. 1967. "The *Hudhud* of Dinulawan and Bugan at Gonhadan." *Saint Louis Quarterly* 5(3–4): 267–713.

Lorenz, K. 1966. *On Aggression*. London: Methuen.

Manuel, E. A. 1963. "A Survey of Philippine Folk Epics." *Asian Folklore Studies (Tokyo)* 22: 1–76.

Meletinskii, E. M. 1968. *Proiskhozhdenie geroicheskogo eposa*. Moscow: Izdatel'stvo Vostochnoi literaturi.

Philippi, D. L. 1979. *Songs of Gods, Songs of Humans: The Epic Tradition of the Ainu.* Tokyo: University of Tokyo Press.

Propp, V. Ia. 1976. *Fol'klor i deistvitel'nost.* Moscow: Nauka.

Putilov, B. N. 1976. *Metodologiia sravnitel'no-istoricheskogo izucheniia fol'klora.* Leningrad: Nauka.

Revel, N., ed. Forthcoming. *Nusantara Epic Traditions.* UNESCO Project.

Rosaldo, M. 1980. *Knowledge and Passion: Ilongot Notions of Self and Social Life.* Cambridge: Cambridge University Press.

Rosaldo, R. 1980. *Ilongot Headhunting 1883–1974: A Study in Society and History.* Stanford, Cal.: Stanford University Press.

Staniukovich, M. 1979. "Neobichnaia biografiia: Roy Franklin Barton, 1883–1947" (An Extraordinary Biography: Roy Franklin Barton, 1883–1947). *Sovetskaia etnografiia* 1: 76–83.

_____. 1981. "Epos i obriad u gornikh narodov Filippin" (Epic and Ritual among the Mountain Tribes of the Philippines). *Sovetskaia etnografiia* 5: 72–83.

_____. 1982a. "Ifugao i ainy: nekotorie dannye fol'klora" (The Ifugaos and the Ainu: Some Folklore Data). Summary of the communications to the annual research meeting of the USSR, Academy of Sciences Institute of Ethnography. Leningrad: Nauka.

_____. 1982b. "Izmenenie obriadovikh sviazei eposa Ifugao v khode etnicheskogo razvitiia" (Change of the Ifugao Epics' Ritual Ties in the Process of Ethnic Development). Summary of communications to the all-Soviet conference of anthropological fieldwork, dedicated to the 60th anniversary of the USSR. 251–52. Nalchik: Nauka.

_____. 1983. "Istoricheskaia tipologiia i etnokul'turnie sviazi geroicheskogo eposa ifugao, Filippini" (Historic Typology and Ethnocultural Links of the Heroic Epics of the Ifugao, Philippines). Ph.D. diss., St. Petersburg Institute of Anthropology and Ethnography.

_____. 1997a. "Kadaklan – bol'shaia reka v epose i mifologii Ifugal (Filippini)" (Kadaklan—the Big River in Ifugao Epics and Mythology [the Philippines]). In *Priroda i tsivilizatsiia. Reki i kul'tury.* L. R. Pavlinskaia, ed. 45–49. St. Petersburg: Evropeiskii dom.

_____. 1997b. "Okhota za golovami u Ifugao: praktika i ritual (po materialam nachala XX veka)" (Headhunting among the Ifugao: Practice and Ritual [Based on the Sources of the Early Twentieth Century]). In *Etnografiia, istoriia, kul'tura stran iuzhnikh morei. Maklaievskie chteniia 1995–1997 gg.* E. V. Revunenkova and N. A. Butinov, eds. 141–50. St. Petersburg: MAE Publications.

_____. 1998a. "Calendar of Fieldwork in the Philippines." In *Field Studies Materials in Anthropology, Issue 4.* E. G. Fedorova, ed. 66–72. St. Petersburg: MAE Publications.

_____. 1998b. "Paths of the Soul among the Ifugaos, the Philippines." In *Conference Book, International Conference "Concepts of Humans and Behavior Patterns in the Cultures of the East and West: Interdisciplinary Approach."* 53–54. Moscow: State Russian University for Humanities Publications.

_____. 1999. "Zhenskii vzgliad na voinskii etiket: *Hudhudi* Ifugao" (Female Ideas of the Etiquette of a Warrior: Ifugao *Hudhud*). In *Etiket narodov Iugovostochnoi Azii.* E. V. Ivanova and A. M. Reshetov, eds. 180–88. St. Petersburg: Peterburgskoe vostokovedenie.

Zhirmunskii, V. M. 1979. *Izbrannye trudy.* Leningrad: Nauka.

PART V

WORLD-VIEW AND
RELIGIOUS DETERMINATION

Chapter 24

PAINTING AS POLITICS

Exposing Historical Processes in
Hunter-Gatherer Rock Art

========∎◎∎========

Thomas A. Dowson

Hunter-gatherers are increasingly being empowered to speak for them-selves. Their voices are being heard all over the world in a variety of con-texts ranging from local media to high-profile meetings at the United Nations, talking about the diversity of social and political concerns cur-rently affecting their communities. The image of scantily clad Natives leading a primitive existence is not only insensitive to a different way of life, it ignores a more accurate role that hunter-gatherers play in interna-tional politics today. Besides the obvious and much discussed problems with "man the hunter," we can no longer escape or ignore the idea of "hunter-gatherer people as politicians."

But hunter-gatherer people have not just recently entered world poli-tics to survive the twentieth century and the impact of European colo-nialism. They have always been politicians. Their exclusion from the histories of their regions is a reflection of Western historiography, not because they have lived a simple, carefree utopian existence devoid of political change. To get at the politics of the past, it is necessary, then, to escape the hegemony of Western intellectual traditions that sanction cer-tain ways of thinking about the past in favor of others.

The generally accepted path to constructing the past is through the academic disciplines of history and archaeology. The written text and the excavated artifact provide us with the tangible evidence for events in his-tory. Or so we are led to believe. The way in which hunter-gatherers are summarily dismissed in history requires social historians to think very carefully about their work. I argue that exploring another line of evidence, namely rock art—hitherto ignored as a source of historical information—not only brings hunter-gatherer people back into history, but shows that these people have always been negotiating complex power relations, both among themselves and with outsiders. In this chapter I look at the way in which history and archaeology have essentially failed to right San people's role in southern African history. By examining two themes in the rock art of the mountainous area in and around Lesotho (an area I call the southeastern mountains), I then demonstrate how images can be used to uncover social dynamics of the past.

Southern African History and Archaeology

There is a widespread misconception about the writing of South Africa's past. The past has been divided in two, with archaeologists assigned to writing precolonial history and historians, colonial history. Although some archaeologists have out of necessity ventured into the colonial period, their work centers on excavation as a means of gaining access to the past, making it quite distinct from history. The distinction between archaeology and history is simply technical. Both archaeologists and historians employ the same methods and theories to construct the past. But because of the technical differences used to retrieve information about the past, the subject matter necessarily differs considerably. Hence, archaeologists and historians vary in the ways in which they have dealt with San people.

In many earlier studies the San were not mentioned at all. South Africa's "history" unashamedly began with the arrival of European colonists and the written text. In Thompson's edited volume, *African Societies in Southern Africa* (1969), there is, despite the title, no chapter dealing with the San and their "society" in southern Africa. In one of the essays in Thompson's volume, Harink (1969) discusses the interaction between the Xhosa and Khoi pastoralists, but he ignores interaction between these groups and San groups. Again, in *Religion and Social Change in Southern Africa* (Whisson and West 1975), the San are ignored. When they are included, they are used as no more than an introductory device. Interestingly, Saunders, in his historiography dealing with "major historians on race and class," criticizes Theal for giving the blacks of South Africa a subordinate role to the European colonists (Saunders 1988: 44), but nowhere does he mention the nonexistent role historians have afforded San people of southern Africa.

In a South Africa that has recently undergone radical political changes, there is a growing interest in history, particularly in a revised history that

challenges myths propagated by earlier political and ideological domina-
tions. To satisfy this interest, a number of "histories" have recently been
produced. This is not in itself significant because histories are constantly
being produced the world over. What is interesting is that with these
political changes there are aspects of southern Africa's past that can now
be presented to the public without fear of recrimination. These more
recent histories take on a "new" identity.

These recent histories, such as Davenport's (1991) *South Africa: A
Modern History*, are advertised as "modern." The *Illustrated History of
South Africa*, produced by the Reader's Digest (1988), with Christopher
Saunders as the consulting editor, is subtitled "The Real Story." The preface, in fact, ends in the following manner: "Here, then, is the real story of
South Africa's past...." Not only does this book lay claim to novelty, it also
claims finality based on some empirical "reality." With new adjectives to
describe them and new photographs to illustrate their covers (Nelson
Mandela and F. W. de Klerk standing side by side; Davenport 1991), these
histories create the impression that they represent a decisive break with
historiographic tradition.

Unfortunately, for some people there is nothing new, modern, or real
about these histories. The San are one such group: they have been, and
still are today, significantly misrepresented in southern African history. In
these "new" histories San people are still used as introductory devices.
This attitude toward the San is deeply rooted in South Africa's written
past; they have long been hidden from southern Africa's history. One or
two historians have already confronted this issue (Marks 1972), but historians in general have not been able to develop a viable approach that
incorporates the San fully and meaningfully into southern African history
as active rather than passive participants. This failure is the result of many
"historians" relying heavily on written documents and ignoring archaeological evidence and discourse, as well as relying almost exclusively on
cultural stereotypes.

Archaeologists, on the other hand, could not ignore the San, and their
work in southern Africa has provided a basis from which many stereotypes about these people have been effectively challenged. For instance,
during the last decade a number of studies have demonstrated that contact between San and Bantu-speaking farmers was much more complex
than previously thought (see for example, Denbow 1986; Hall 1990; Kinahan 1991; Mazel 1989; Parkington 1984; Smith 1986). In the Thukela
Basin, for example, excavations have provided empirical evidence for
interaction between Stone Age and Iron Age groups (for a recent synthesis and discussion, see Mazel 1989). Pieces of talc schist and soapstone,
often used to make bowls and other vessels, have been found at hunter-
gatherer sites in deposits postdating 2000 B.P.; this material has not been

recovered from deposits prior to this date, that is, before contact with Iron Age farmers (Mazel 1989: 141). These sites are in the upper reaches of the Thukela River and some distance from the sources of these rock types. Similar stone was recovered from sites occupied by farming communities, one of which also produced an assemblage of Stone Age or hunter-gatherer tools that Maggs (1980) believes are contemporary with the farming occupation of the site.

Maggs and Mazel argue that the patterning of material culture in the Natal area shows that interaction between hunter-gatherers and farmers, which must have started as soon as the farmers came into contact with the San, was initially extensive and amicable. Mazel has demonstrated that these relationships, certainly at the outset, were on a relatively equal footing, unlike the kind of clientship the hunter-gatherers entered into with the farmers as reported in the nineteenth-century records (Mazel 1989: 142). The possibility that clientship became more substantial as a result of decimation of the San people by European colonists should be investigated; I touch on it again below. Further, there is every indication that new complex social relations accompanied and formed the basis of the new economic relations. San reactions to Bantu-speaking farmers and European colonists can no longer be seen in terms of weaker people meekly submitting to more sophisticated people with more advanced modes of subsistence.

But, like the historians who accord prominence to textual sources over visual material (see Haskell 1993), archaeologists in southern Africa promote excavation and the analysis of lithic material as the most important means of accessing the past—at the expense of rock art research (Dowson 1993; Lewis-Williams 1993). Until the 1960s, archaeologists regarded rock art as no more than a source of evidence for two rather straightforward areas of interest. First, they believed that the art was a record of the ways in which the San used certain artifacts, such as bows and arrows, and bags. Second, they sought evidence for the migrations of communities through the subcontinent. Today, archaeologists (see, for example, Mazel 1993; 1996) maintain that rock art lacks a "firm chronological context" and therefore cannot be used to construct the more complex historical processes that they uncover. But as Lewis-Williams (1993: 49) has pointed out, "The linear, pinpointing concept of chronology privileges colonial history at the expense of pre-colonial history." In a similar vein, Yates (1993: 35) suggests, "Archaeological data is not limited, only the minds that interpret it." He also proposes that "the way forward for rock art analysis is not to address issues of chronology but to theorize the art—a theorization which must extend way beyond the stale discussions of terminology—and study its appearance and meaning in local and regional terms" (Yates 1993: 35). I now turn to a theorization of southern African rock art.

Rock Art and the Study of Art

Perhaps one of the most glaring omissions in the study of rock art is its exclusion from art history—a discipline that one would expect to be discussing all forms of art in southern Africa. In one of the most recent histories of art in South Africa, Berman (1993) acknowledges the temporal primacy of southern Africa's rock paintings, but she dismisses them as only being able to "tantalize archaeologists and to fascinate students of aesthetic form." Berman's justification for this omission is that the paintings are related to a past that "waits to be conclusively unraveled" (p. 3). There are a number of problems with such a dismissal, but I briefly touch on four.

First, Berman gives the reader the impression that her story, which begins only in the second half of the nineteenth century, is conclusive. The epistemological problems with such a claim are so blatant that this position must itself be dismissed. A second and more pressing concern is her belief that the paintings today can only tantalize archaeologists. This position ignores the vast amount of research that earlier archaeologists and a handful of more recent archaeologists—not anthropologists, not art historians, not historians—have conducted. While other researchers—art historians, for example—may feel this work is lacking in certain regards, that is a point itself worthy of discussion. However, such interdisciplinary disagreement is simply not sufficient to dismiss archaeologists' research. It is more than interesting, and certainly relevant, to note in a history of southern African painting that certain archaeologists have done more for rock art than art historians or artists. It is *because of* research by these archaeologists that interest in rock art *can* go beyond a fascination with aesthetic form.

Thirdly, because rock paintings are relegated to a past as yet waiting to be unraveled, and because Berman's history begins in the second half of the 1800s, this work serves to reinforce a segregationalist view of South African history, particularly where the San people are concerned. This view actively reinforces and confirms the widely held belief that the San played no role in South Africa's history.

Finally, and because of the three points I have already discussed, I wonder about Berman's idea that the aesthetic qualities of rock paintings serve to "fascinate" us. There appears to be no doubt that from an aesthetic point of view southern African rock paintings are extremely well executed. But why should this *fascinate* us? Such a notion recalls early colonists' amazement at the rock paintings. Sir John Barrow, for instance, wrote: "[T]he force and spirit of drawings, given to them by bold touches judiciously applied, and by the effect of light and shadow, could not be expected from savages" (Barrow 1810: 239). Preconceived European notions of art, particularly from the Renaissance, hold that complex art goes hand in hand with complex, highly intellectual societies. Berman's fascination simply reinforces colonial stereotypes about so-called primitive people and their artistic abilities.

Berman's book demonstrates that Eurocentric attitudes toward Bushman art are still commonplace today. However, a much deeper appreciation of the art is possible; by carefully examining the appearance and meaning of the imagery in local terms, as Yates suggests, one can find in rock art the sociopolitical context within which these images were produced and consumed.

The current trend began by recognizing that much of the rock art in southern Africa reflected shamans' experiences during a curing ritual and their beliefs about it (see Dowson and Lewis-Williams 1994). I argue that rock art is not just a reflection or depiction of beliefs and experiences associated with the trance ritual. Rather, the art is a material item that was always actively implicated in the reproduction and transformation of social relations, specifically those relations involving shamans.[1] Most panels, if not all, have some depictions that can be unequivocally associated with trance belief and experience. Because of the detailed and abundant trance imagery in the paintings, it is highly likely that shamans were the principal, but perhaps not the only, producers of the art. San art and historical documents are thus strikingly similar. Both create, transform, and reinforce dominant ideologies: the historical documents continue to negotiate European settler ideologies, whereas rock art negotiated shaman ideologies.

To be able to discern exactly how the art played this role, we need to understand, first, how the depictions were produced. The cognitive structure of the art was socially produced in that meanings attached to specific combinations of formal attributes, such as color or size, come out of day-to-day social practice. The art was thus intimately implicated in developing social relations and the reproduction and transformation of social forms. This approach builds on such theoretical approaches as Bourdieu's theory of practice (1977) and Giddens's structuration theory (1979; 1984), as well as related theoretical approaches to the social production and consumption of art (for example, Wolff 1981). Generally, and very briefly, I will demonstrate how these processes came together and how the art negotiated San ideology, particularly shaman ideology. For the purposes of this essay, I concentrate on the mountainous region in the southeast of the southern African subcontinent.

The proximity of Bantu-speaking farmers generated a new set of social relations in which the San in general and the shaman in particular were implicated. Farmers recognized the San as the original inhabitants and custodians of the land, and it was natural for the farmers to turn to them. The relationship, posited essentially on land-ownership, came to center on rain-making. The farmers, more than the hunter-gatherers themselves, were dependent on rain; even minor droughts and, perhaps more importantly, delayed rains affected their crops and herds far more than they did the hunter-gatherers' antelope and plant foods. The mediator thus turned out to be the shaman, part of whose symbolic work was rain-making (Lewis-Williams 1981: 103–16; 1982; Campbell 1987). Even though the farmers had occupied the land, they were unable to farm successfully without rain. The farmers requested Bushman rain-makers to perform rituals and gave them cattle in return. It was the shaman who had (ideological) control over the farmers' economy.

Because the shamans were paid for their rain-making services with cattle, presumably among other things, they acquired a new status as procurers of meat, and no doubt they achieved power through a newly developed right to distribute the meat (see Campbell 1987). With the depletion of antelope herds by European hunters and the extermination of the San by European commandos, San shamans were forced to become more dependent on the farmers: the shamans had to tighten their grip on the farmers. This resulted in San shamans' families going to live with Bantu-speaking farmers (Peires 1981: 24). It could be that these people were acknowledging the farmers' control of the land, but at the same time, trying to retain some power and status.

Within San communities, diminishing traditional resources and, at the same time, new sources of wealth resulting from social and economic relations with the farmers engendered competition between shamans. People looked to them as their go-betweens with the farmers and, increasingly, as the most reliable procurers of food. Shamans thus began to compete with one another and with important nonshamans of the group for positions of influence. These power struggles, as well as the stresses of cultural contact between farmers and hunter-gatherers, were manifested in the art. The art, produced by shamans, became active and instrumental in forging new social relations that developed out of these power struggles.

People negotiate personal and social identities by means of stylistic statements (Wiessner 1984; 1989; 1990). Social identities become important during situations of intergroup competition and when there is the need for cooperation to attain social, political, or economic goals. Competition among individuals and an increase in options for individual enterprise result in strong personal identities. Contact between Bantu-speaking farmers and San hunter-gatherers created situations in which both social and personal identities were implicated in social relations, and both of these are negotiated in the art, according to the social regime of a given time and place. I give two examples of how this happened.

First, the rock art in the southeastern mountains contains the most variation in "styles," but at the same time, it is in this region that the diversity of animal depictions is not as marked as elsewhere in southern

Africa. Eland and rhebuck are by far the most frequently painted animals. The limiting of animal diversity in the paintings of this region was one result of a new interest in projecting a social identity and a social unity during changing social conditions. At least one San community of that area spoke of themselves as being "of the eland" (Vinnicombe 1976; Lewis-Williams 1988). The paintings of eland found throughout the southeastern mountains suggest that using the art to negotiate a social identity was in fact a regionwide response to changing social relations. But the careful attention to a second theme, that of trance dances and the way in which shamans are painted, shows that there were also differences within this region.

The kind of rock painting illustrated in Figure 24.1 is found throughout the southeastern mountains. Here all of the human figures are uniformly painted: the figures are all more or less the same size, and none depicts a person who is more elaborately decorated or dressed than any of the others, shamans or nonshamans. I suggest that these paintings point to social circumstances in which a number of people in the community were shamans and no one was preeminent; even though shamans could contact the spirit world, heal, and make rain, they were no "better" than anyone else. Service to their community was a privilege not a power base. This situation is like that described by Marshall (1969), Lee (1968; 1979), Biesele (1978), and others for parts of the Kalahari in the 1950s and 1960s. At that time, about half of the men and a third of the women in any camp were shamans. Communal healing dances to which everyone came were held frequently when there were enough people present. Although some shamans earned reputations for being especially effective healers, they did not assume positions of more general leadership or political influence.

It is arguable that these uniformly painted trance dances were implicated in social processes that limited the development of personal power. The art did not simply reflect social conditions, any more than it merely pictured the use of artifacts and the presence of certain animals. It was part of active material culture that negotiated social relations and statuses. Imbued with potency, these images of "equality" helped to reproduce specific kinds of social relations. As "potent" statements of what happened in the ultimately real, spirit world, they were coercive in the sense that they presented a supernaturally sanctioned social, indeed cosmological, order in which shamans were numerous and no one was more powerful than the other.

Paintings pointing to a development of power roles are, apart from a few outliers, found in a comparatively small area of the southeastern mountains. Part of this area, known to the colonists as "nomansland," was the last southern refuge of comparatively independent Bushman

FIGURE 24.1 Rock Painting of a Trance Dance from the Eastern Free State Province, South Africa

Note: The human figures lack facial features and are all painted in much the same way.

FIGURE 24.2 Rock Painting of a Trance Dance from the Area in the Southeastern Mountains Colonists Called "Nomansland"

Note: Unlike the human figures in Figure 24.1, here there is a marked differentiation in the way human figures are painted.

communities. Given the acknowledged San occupancy of the area, the name "nomansland" is grimly ironic. Here there are paintings of trance dances in which there is one prominent shaman figure, often larger, often highly elaborately decorated, and with facial features.

The example reproduced in Figure 24.2 shows a large, central figure with facial features, "decorated" body, two long "streamers" issuing from his head, and lines on his face, some of which probably depict the nasal hemorrhage associated with Bushman trance performance (Bleek 1935; 1936). On either side of him are seated figures; those on the right are clearly women, and they are in clapping postures, their fingers being individually drawn. To the left of the central figure and facing him are three grotesque figures with claws that probably suggest feline affinities; one also has enigmatic "tusks." These figures may depict the frightening spirits of the dead that often take on the form of lions. There are also numerous bags painted around the central figure; nineteenth-century southern San myths suggest that these bags are probably symbols of trance experience (Lewis-Williams and Dowson 1989: 116–17). The political centrality of one striking, preeminent shaman figure, supported in his spiritual tasks by other members of the community, is, I argue, suggested by this painted group.

A comparable, but not identical, trajectory has been observed in the Ghanzi area of the Kalahari. Here the land was appropriated by European farmers, and the San were forced to accept employment with them. When wage labor restricted San movements in this way, the shamans (who did not make rock art in this area as there are no suitable rock surfaces available) became fewer and itinerant, moving from farm to farm to perform their healing rituals. Today, their enhanced social status is underwritten by their possession of potency, their prestige as well-known healers, and the political implications of the small herds of cattle they keep at a home base (Guenther 1975; 1975–76; 1986). They are emerging as political, not just spiritual, leaders.

Figure 24.2 and other similar rock paintings that depict preeminent shamans show that painters were not ineluctably governed by conventions and structures. Rather, we should, as Giddens (1984) has suggested, think of structure as resources on which individuals can draw: design elements such as size, color, and detail, can be manipulated to suit an artist's political purpose (see also Dowson 1994; 1995; in press). In the production of preeminent shaman paintings, artists manipulated design elements to negotiate a prominent political position in their community. As I have argued, the association of at least some of the images with supernatural elements and the spirit world (clearly suggested in Figure 24.2 by the clawed figures) imparted an incontrovertible factuality to the images and to the kind of cosmos they depicted. Manipulating the art was therefore not far from manipulating the universe itself. The potent essence of the rock art images imparted a factuality to, or naturalized, the social relations and cosmology that they depicted.

The Sociopolitical Context of Hunter-Gatherer Rock Art

The categories of "San" or "hunter-gatherers" were not a pure, ethnic entity, but rather a political entity by which a community defined itself to maintain an existence in daily social practices. Rock art was a material means for San politicians to negotiate, on behalf of their community, a place on a dramatically changing landscape. This conceptualization represents a different way of thinking about San rock art. Rock art does not simply depict the complex experiences and beliefs of shamans. It played a more active role than this. The images negotiated social relations—those associated with shamans and their symbolic work—in the communities within which they were produced and consumed.

Three decades of increasingly detailed ethnographic interpretation have laid a firm foundation for change in the evidential status of southern African rock art. Here I have argued that the images need no longer be seen as simply pictures from and of the past. More importantly, they are items of evidence in their own right for historical processes.

Some archaeologists have already experimented with rock art as a historical document (Kinahan 1991; Yates et al. 1994). But other archaeologists still remain skeptical. This skepticism derives from what Barrett (1987: 14) identifies as a "methodological obsession to give an archaeological record meaning." In the case of archaeologists and rock art, the obsession is with chronology. For example, Mazel and Watchman contend, "A problem confronting archaeologists … has been their inability effectively to integrate the information derived from excavations with that from rock art. This has been largely due to the inability to date the majority of paintings, and thereby to place them into a chronological context derived from dating charcoal from layers of deposit" (1997: 445; see also Mazel 1996). Searching for chronology in this manner merely ensures "history appears as a by-product" (Barrett 1987: 14). As Barrett continues, "We should instead set out to make history. By that labor we will necessarily encounter our evidence, and by working with it we will discover something of its significance within the context of social practice."

Like researchers in the Western Cape Province (see Yates et al. 1994 for a recent synthesis) and Namibia (Kinahan 1991), I have not encountered insurmountable problems of integrating excavated remains and imagery found in rock shelters of the southeastern mountains (Dowson 1994; 1995; in press). This is primarily because we have set out to make history, but more importantly because we have managed to theorize the art in regional terms as well as to conceptualize the archaeological context as something other than a positivist's entity awaiting excavation. By questioning current disciplinary practice, archaeologists will be able to challenge the apparent irrelevancy of archaeology in the social sciences (Barret 1987: 5).

Consequently, these exquisite images need no longer simply tantalize or fascinate archaeologists as they do art historians. By exploring these images and analyzing their meaning and appearance on a localized level, we are able to think our way beyond what others have come to view as limitations. After many years of comparative invisibility in southern African cultural studies (Barnard 1989; Dowson and Lewis-Williams 1993; Smith 1985; Voss 1987), the San, together with their art, can be recognized as significant players in the transformation of southern African history and politics.

Note

1. There is considerable debate about the use of the term "shaman." Various contributors to this debate offer valid and sensible thoughts. I am not able to do justice to these discussions here, but I deal with them elsewhere (Dowson in preparation).

References

Barnard, A. 1989. "The Lost World of Laurens Van der Post?" *Current Anthropology* 30: 104–14.

Barrett, J. C. 1987. "Fields of Discourse: Reconstituting a Social Archaeology." *Critique of Anthropology* 7(3): 5–16.

Barrow, J. 1810. *Travels into the Interior of Southern Africa, 1797–1798.* London: Cadell and Davies.

Berman, E. 1993. *Painting in South Africa.* Johannesburg: Southern Book Publishers.

Biesele, M. 1978. "Sapience and Scarce Resources: Communication Systems of the !Kung and Other Foragers." *Social Science Information* 17: 921–47.

Bleek, D. F. 1935. "Beliefs and Customs of the /Xam Bushmen. Part VII: Sorcerers." *Bantu Studies* 9: 1–47.

_____. 1936. "Beliefs and Customs of the /Xam Bushmen. Part VIII: More about Sorcerers and Charms." *Bantu Studies* 10: 131–62.

Bourdieu, P. 1977. *Outline of a Theory of Practice.* Cambridge: Cambridge University Press.

Campbell, C. 1987. "Art in Crisis: Contact Period Rock Art in the South-eastern Mountains." Master's thesis, University of the Witwatersrand, Johannesburg.

Davenport, T. R. H. 1991. *South Africa: A Modern History.* London: Macmillan.

Denbow, J. 1986. "A New Look at the Later Pre-history of the Kalahari." *Journal of African History* 27: 3–28.

Dowson, T. A. 1993. "Changing Fortunes of Southern African Archaeology: Comment on A.D. Mazel's History." *Antiquity* 67: 641–44.

_____. 1994. "Reading Art Writing History: Rock Art and Social Change in Southern Africa." *World Archaeology* 25(3): 332–45.

_____. 1995. "Hunter-Gatherers, Traders and Slaves: The 'Mfecane' Impact on Bushmen, Their Ritual and Their Art." In *The Mfecane Aftermath: Reconstructive Debates in Southern African History.* C. Hamilton, ed. 51–70. Johannesburg and Pietermaritzburg: Witwatersrand University Press and University of Natal Press.

_____. 1998. "Rain in Bushman Belief, Politics and History: The Rock Art of Rain-Making in the South Eastern Mountains, Southern Africa." In *The Archaeology of Rock Art*. C. Chippindale and P, Tacon, eds. Cambridge: Cambridge University Press.

_____. In prep. *Shamanism and Diversity of Interpretation in Rock Art Studies*. Cambridge: Cambridge University Press.

Dowson, T. A., and J. D. Lewis-Williams. 1993. "Myths, Museums and Southern African Rock Art." *South African Historical Journal* 29: 44–60.

Dowson, T. A., and J. D. Lewis-Williams, eds. 1994. *Contested Images: Diversity in Southern African Rock Art Research*. Johannesburg: Witwatersrand University Press.

Giddens, A. 1979. *Central Problems in Social Theory: Action, Structure and Contradiction in Social Analysis*. Berkeley: University of California Press.

_____. 1984. *The Constitution of Society*. Cambridge: Polity Press.

Guenther, M. 1975. "The Trance Dancer as an Agent of Social Change among the Farm Bushmen of the Ghanzi District." *Botswana Notes and Records* 7: 167–70.

_____. 1975–76. "The San Trance Dance: Ritual and Revitalization among the Farm Bushmen of the Ghanzi District, Republic of Botswana." *Journal of the South West African Scientific Society* 30: 45–53.

_____. 1986. *The Nharo Bushmen of Botswana: Tradition and Change*. Hamburg: Helmut Buske Verlag.

Hall, S. L. 1990. *Hunter-Gatherer-Fishers of the Fish River Basin: A Contribution to the Holocene Prehistory of the Eastern Cape*. Ph.D. diss., University of Stellenbosch.

Harinck G. 1969. "Interaction between Xhosa and Khoi: Emphasis on the Period 1620–1750." In *African Societies in Southern Africa*. L. M. Thompson, ed. 145–69. London: Heinemann.

Haskell, F. 1993. *History and Its Images*. New Haven, Conn.: Yale University Press.

Kinahan, J. 1991. *Pastoral Nomads of the Central Namib Desert*. Windhoek: New Namibia Books.

Lee, R. B. 1968. "The Sociology of !Kung Bushman Trance Performance." In *Trance and Possession States*. R. Prince, ed. 35–54. Montreal: R. M. Bucke Memorial Society.

_____. 1979. *The !Kung San: Men, Women and Work in a Foraging Society*. Cambridge: Cambridge University Press.

Lewis-Williams, J. D. 1981. *Believing and Seeing: Symbolic Meanings in Southern San Rock Paintings*. London: Academic Press.

_____. 1982. "The Economic and Social Context of Southern San Rock Art." *Current Anthropology* 23: 429–49.

_____. 1988. "'People of the Eland': An Archaeo-linguistic Crux." In *Hunters and Gatherers: Property, Power and Ideology*. T. Ingold, D. Riches, and J. Woodburn, eds. 203–12. New York: Berg.

_____. 1993. "Southern African Archaeology in the 1990s." *South African Archaeological Bulletin* 48: 45–50.

Lewis-Williams, J. D., and T. A. Dowson. 1989. *Images of Power: Understanding Bushman Rock Art*. Johannesburg: Southern Book Publishers.

Maggs, T. M. O'C. 1980. "Msuluzi Confluence: A Seventh-Century Early Iron Age Site on the Tugela River." *Annals of the Natal Museum* 24: 111–45.

Marks, S. 1972. "Khoisan Resistance to the Dutch in the Seventeenth and Eighteenth Centuries." *Journal of African History* 13: 55–80.

Marshall, L. 1969. "The Medicine Dance of the !Kung Bushmen." *Africa* 39: 347–81.

Mazel, A. D. 1989. "People Making History: The Last Ten Thousand Years of Hunter-Gatherer Communities in the Thukela Basin." *Natal Museum Journal of Humanities* 1: 1–168.

_____. 1993. "Rock Art and Natal Drakensberg Hunter-Gatherer History: A Reply to Dowson." *Antiquity* 67: 889–92.

_____. 1996. "In Pursuit of San Pre-colonial History in the Natal Drakensberg: A Historical Overview." In *Miscast: Negotiating the Presence of the Bushmen*. P. Skotnes, ed. 191–95. Cape Town: UCT Press.

Mazel, A., and A. L. Watchman. 1997. "Accelerator Radiocarbon Dating of Natal Drakensberg Paintings: Results and Implications." *Antiquity* 71: 445–49.

Parkington, J. E. 1984. "Changing Views of the Late Stone Age of South Africa." In *Advances in World Archaeology 3*. F. Wendorf and A. E. Close, eds. 89–142. New York: Academic Press.

Peires, J. B. 1981. *The House of Phalo: A History of the Xhosa People in the Days of Their Independence*. Johannesburg: Ravan Press.

Reader's Digest. 1988. *Illustrated History of South Africa: The Real Story*. Cape Town: Reader's Digest Association.

Saunders, C. 1988. *The Making of the South African Past: Major Historians on Race and Class*. Cape Town: David Philip.

Smith, A. B. 1985. "Concepts of Khoi and San in South African History." *Khoisan Special Interest Group Newsletter* 3: 10–12.

_____. 1986. "Competition, Conflict and Clientship: Khoi and San Relationships in the Western Cape." *South African Archaeological Society, Goodwin Series* 5: 36–41.

Thompson, L. 1969. *African Societies in Southern Africa*. London: Heinemann.

Vinnicombe, P. 1976. *People of the Eland: Rock Paintings of the Drakensberg Bushmen as a Reflection of Their Life and Thought*. Pietermaritzburg: Natal University Press.

Voss, A. E. 1987. "The Image of the Bushman in South African English Writing of the Nineteenth and Twentieth Centuries." *English in Africa* 14(1): 21–40.

Whisson, M., and M. West. 1975. *Religion and Social Change in Southern Africa*. Cape Town: Balkema.

Wiessner, P. 1984. "Reconsidering the Behavioural Basis for Style: A Case among the !Kung San." *Journal of Anthropological Archaeology* 3: 190–234.

_____. 1989. "Style and Changing Relations between the Individual and Society." In *The Meaning of Things: Material Culture and Symbolic Expression*. I. Hodder, ed. 56–63. London: Allen and Unwin.

_____. 1990. "Is There a Unity to Style?" In *The Use of Style in Archaeology*. M. W. Conkey and C. A. Hastorf, eds. 105–12. Cambridge: Cambridge University Press.

Wolff, J. 1981. *The Social Production of Art*. London: Macmillan.

Yates, R., A. Manhire, and J. Parkington. 1994. "Rock Paintings and History in the South-Western Cape." In *Contested Images: Diversity in Southern African Rock Art Research*. T. A. Dowson and J. D. Lewis-Williams, eds. 29–60. Johannesburg: Witwatersrand University Press.

Yates, T. 1993. "Frameworks for an Archaeology of the Body." In *Interpretative Archaeology*. C. Tilley, ed. 31–72. Oxford: Berg.

Chapter 25

GIFTS FROM THE IMMORTAL ANCESTORS
Cosmology and Ideology of Jahai Sharing

==≈·《❲》·≈==

Cornelia M. I. van der Sluys

How are we to explain the continuity of the way of life of present-day "immediate return system" (Woodburn 1980; 1982) or "non-complex society" (Price and Brown 1985) hunter-gatherers?[1] Is the reproduction of their cultures determined predominantly by ecological-economic circumstances or mainly by cultural factors, with the latter being dependent on a favorable ecological environment (Bird-David 1990; 1992; Minnegal 1996)?

The aim of this chapter is to discuss evidence supporting the latter hypothesis through an analysis of the ideas about sharing in the world-view of the Jahai, who are "non-complex society" hunters-gatherers-traders and occasional swidden cultivators, located in the rain forest of northern Peninsular Malaysia. Most of the approximately 875 Jahai have been settled or semisettled since the late 1970s, mainly due to an increase in the logging activities in the area and to the construction of the Temeng-gor Reservoir in Upper Perak, which drowned more than 150 square kilo-meters of land. However, about 150 of the Jahai were still nomadic in 1993. Research was conducted mainly with the nomadic groups in north-ern Perak, who dwell in the forests around Temenggor Reservoir, inter-mittently from 1990 to 1993, amounting to a total of two years.

During the last decades of hunter-gatherer studies, we witnessed the so-called "forager controversy debates," which center mainly on the gen-esis of the Bushman cultures. Both groups of protagonists focus almost exclusively on ecological-economic issues and pay little attention to the forces inside these cultures that tend to perpetuate their reproduction from generation to generation. The "traditionalists" explain Bushman cultures as adaptations to the physical environment, while the "revisionists" see them as responses to political and economic domination by outside peoples and ultimately to the power structures of the wider economic system (for overviews, see Barnard 1992; Burch and Ellanna 1994; Denbow and Wilmsen 1986; Kent 1992; Lee 1992; Lee and Guenther 1991; Schrire 1984; Silberbauer 1991; Solway and Lee 1990; Yellen 1990).

Similar debates about the status of present-day hunter-gatherers in tropical rain forests were dominated from the 1980s onwards by the hypothesis, put forward by several anthropologists, that these forests have always lacked sufficient foodstuffs to support such populations independently of agricultural production or trade relations with outsiders. A lack of carbohydrates was thought to characterize the Southeast Asian primal rain forests and a lack of proteins to be a feature of the primal rain forests in South America (Bailey et al. 1989; Headland 1986; Headland and Bailey 1991; Headland and Reid 1989; Hoffman 1984).

However, evidence fails to support this view, especially with regard to the Malay Peninsula (Bailey et al. 1989; Bellwood 1985; Dunn 1975; Gorman 1971; Hall 1968; Zuraina 1988–89; Zuraina and Tjia 1988; and articles by Bailey and Headland, Brosius, Dwyer and Minnegal, and Endicott and Bellwood in the special 1991 issue of *Human Ecology* devoted to this subject). Bailey et al. (1989), for example, point to at least five sites in central Peninsular Malaysia, dating from 10,000 to 3000 B.C., with faunal remains that are consistent with exclusive rain forest exploitation.

In view of these findings, we have to consider the possibility that the present-day hunter-gatherers in Peninsular Malaysia, and probably also several of the hunter-gatherer populations in other parts of Southeast Asia, are not "degenerated" agriculturists (Brosius 1991; Endicott and Bellwood 1991; Sellato 1989), but have continued to reproduce the fundamentals of their cultures from prehistoric times up to the present. The flexibility of their mixed subsistence economy of hunting, fishing, gathering, trading, and occasional small-scale swiddening, which Dentan has called a "broad spectrum opportunistic foraging strategy" (Dentan 1991: 425), has enabled them to adapt to changing circumstances—such as by obtaining goods from a widening economic system through the trading of forest products—without feeling the need to change their cultures profoundly.

An instance demonstrating that long-time contacts with "outsiders" do not necessarily imply a profound change in a hunter-gatherer culture's core premises and embedded values can be found in Turnbull's (1965) description of the Mbutis, hunter-gatherers in Zaire. Despite relationships with their agriculturist Bantu neighbors, the Mbutis safeguard the reproduction of the core of their own culture by adopting certain Bantu customs and taking part in Bantu rituals. Similar strategies are also used by other hunter-gatherers (Bicchieri 1990: 123; Bird-David 1988: 29–30; Kent 1992: 56; Patterson 1990: 133).

Below I shall show how a configuration of core premises and embedded values regarding the way in which their society effectuates well-being reinforces the continuity of the Jahai forest-based hunting-gathering-collecting way of life, most likely from prehistoric times onwards and despite long-time contacts with representatives of cultures with a more complex social organization (Price and Brown 1985). By stating this I do not mean that I rule out possible influences from these latter cultures with regard to the more peripheral ideas in the Jahai world-view.

Several ecologically oriented anthropologists have put forward the "risk reduction" theory to explain generalized food sharing that features in "non-complex" hunter-gatherer societies. They postulate that the risk of individual families going hungry, especially in times of scarcity, is diminished through the sharing system (Cashdan 1985; Gould 1982; Ingold 1980: 144; Lee 1968; Smith 1988; Wiessner 1977; 1982; Woodburn 1982). Although this is obviously one of the effects of communal sharing, other implications, such as its reinforcing effect on affective well-being have been overlooked by most of them.[2]

In this study I will show that the Jahai's specific configuration of core cultural premises and embedded values with regard to well-being not only motivates their nonreciprocal way of sharing as "a passing-on of free gifts," but also serves as a logically consistent explanation for the prevalence of several other features in the Jahai culture. Observed also to be prevalent in other "non-complex society" hunter-gatherer cultures, these features include generalized sharing, trust in the environment, egalitarianism, individual autonomy, and dynamics that preserve peacefulness, such as the prevention of conflict escalation through processes of fission and fusion (Gardner 1991; Sahlins 1972; Woodburn 1980). This makes it probable that variations of the configuration feature, as a cultural substratum, also in those other cultures, as may be the case for several "non-complex society" swiddener cultures. However, this must be a subject of future research.

Theoretical Assumptions

Before proceeding further to an analysis of the Jahai configuration of cultural core premises and values that motivates their way of sharing, I shall first discuss a few general theoretical issues regarding world-view research.[3] Above I have argued that a culture's predominant premises are about the way the society should be organized for the optimal realization of well-being and that core values are embedded in these premises. The latter guide the behavior of the society members more directly.

Well-being is culturally defined: whereas the Ilongot swiddeners in the Philippines, who are former headhunters (Rosaldo 1980), do, in certain contexts, value "hot," aroused emotional states positively, the Jahai do not. Therefore, as guidelines for our research, we can only use vague, neutral indications such as "what people consider as a 'good life'" or "what makes them feel 'good'" (Colby 1987). Because they are about well-being, cultural core premises and embedded values contain a valuation of affect-states, a factor to which anthropologists from the 1980s onwards have begun to give more attention (Heelas 1986; Howell 1989; Karim 1990; Lutz 1986; Rosaldo 1980).

Because the construction of a world-view is essentially comparative as it involves transposing another culture's concepts into those of the researcher, there is a danger of ethnocentrism and subjectivism. In my opinion, we can do no better than show respect for the cultures we study by grounding our theories in detailed ethnographic data from various sources: observed daily behavior and recorded conversations, as well as myths, rituals, and artifacts. By adopting this Grounded Theory Approach (Glaser and Strauss 1967; Spradley 1980), we obtain an intimate understanding of the informal logic of the individual culture through what Geertz (1973; 1983) has called a "thick description," which provides a solid basis for a verifiable metalevel analysis.

More than fifty years ago, Sol Tax (1941) and Robert Redfield (1941) defined a world-view as "The *sum of ideas* which an individual within a group or that group has of the universe in and around them" (quoted by Mendelson in the *International Encyclopedia of the Social Sciences* 1968: 576, italics by the author). Consequently, their research resulted merely in compilations of separate cultural ideas that held little promise for comparative research (Tax 1990: 280).

In my opinion, Dumont (1980; 1987) has made a valuable contribution to the theory of cultural anthropology by developing the concept of idea-value hierarchies in what he calls "holistic" cultures. He maintains that the highest value encompasses its contrary on a lower level, which becomes apparent in other contexts. While keeping Dumont's observations on hierarchy in mind, I think it necessary, for the purpose of making a proper analysis of a culture's world-view, to make a distinction between value-laden cultural premises and values proper. As I described above, by the first I mean the configuration of cultural ideas that form the "background theory" of a culture, and by the latter I mean the emotionally loaded ideas that, while arising from these premises, guide more directly the actions and attitudes of its participants. Therefore, I propose to redefine the concept of "world-view" as *the hierarchical configuration of value-laden premises and values proper, through which the participants of that culture, in a continuous dialogue with their environment and themselves, give meaning to the cosmos in which their lives are embedded.* I argue that only by focusing on the relationships, often multiple, between the different aspects of the whole world-view can we discover the dynamics that reinforce the continuity of a culture.

The Jahai's Ideas about the Life Soul (*Rəway*) in Relation to Well-Being

In the course of my research, I gradually became aware of the importance that the Jahai attach to caring for each other's well-being, which they define as the emotionally quiet, nonaroused, "cool" (but not cold) state of one's *rəway* (life-soul), expressed with the word *bud'ed,* which is also used to express "good" in general. Although well-being is thought to be present in the whole body, its main concentration is supposed to be in the heart area, the center of emotions and thought; feelings of well-being are often expressed as "a contented heart" (*jəgʉg kəlaŋis*).[4] Thermic codes, such as "cold" and "hot," actually gradable antonyms (Lyons 1977), are widely used over the whole of Southeast Asia to refer to general states of health and emotional well-being (Karim 1990; Laderman 1991). A balanced *rəway*—neither too hot nor too cold—is associated with a sense of satisfaction in several interrelated contexts, mainly with feelings of attachment to others, which includes relatedness to the primordial immortal ancestors (*cənɔy*), and also bears upon being respected as an autonomous person. In addition, it is associated with basic physical comforts, such as satisfaction of hunger and thirst, and with health.

The Jahai see the *rəway*'s periphery as expandable and permeable, properties that enable it to mix with and incorporate another being's soul-substance, visualized as a fine, invisible vapor, similar to the scent that emanates from a flower's nectar or from the fragrant sap of crushed leaves. They view the mixing of soul-substances as a mixing of smells. This concept of soul-substance is reminiscent of a similar concept (Dutch: *zielestof*) that the Dutch anthropologist Kruyt (1906) has postulated to be prevalent in the world-view of many Indonesian societies.

During dreams *rəway* is supposed to leave the body through the fontanel and associate with other beings, such as with other human *rəway* or with primordial immortal ancestors or their emanations. In the latter case, the dreamers are prone to become spirit-mediums, who are believed to have the ability to generate emanations from their souls, which can travel to different places at the same time.

The Jahai take great care to avoid arousing "hot" emotions (*mamuɲ*) in others, as these are thought to push the cool, healthy soul-substance out of the body, similar to the fire that pushes out the smoke from burning logs.

"Hot" emotions, often expressed as a "hot heart," are thought to prevent relatedness to others, which depends on the mixing of "cool" soul-substances. Whenever there is a likelihood of "hot" emotions occurring, the Jahai will utter the warning, "*mamuɲ!*" This word refers to different states of aroused emotion that, in Western languages, are rendered by different terms, depending on the context: anger, resentment, jealousy, mourning, rejection, and, especially, the frustration of strong desires.

If "hot" emotions happen to occur, the afflicted person is believed to become weak and prone to sickness or even death, unless a spirit-medium (*hala'*) restores the *rəway*'s coolness by blowing a healing liquid (*cəboh*) into the patient. The *hala'* receives this liquid, which is only visible to him (most *hala'* are males), from his spirit guides (*cənɔy*), who are primordial immortal ancestors or their emanations.

This concern for the emotional quietness of each other's *rəway* can be encountered in different domains of the Jahai social life. Especially with regard to sharing, great care must be taken not to leave someone out as this would put the injured party in a state of accident-proneness (*pəhunɛn*), which will be described below. Such concern is also encountered in the idea that to coerce a person into doing something that he or she does not want to do is considered to arouse *mamuɲ* and thus to be bad for the *rəway*. If someone says: "*Yɛ' yi'*" (I don't want to), others will usually respect his or her wish and say: "*'o'-sərik*" (he is not in the mood). In the Jahai society individuals enjoy a high degree of autonomy in decision-making regarding their own daily activities, as long as these do not endanger other peoples' soul-balance This focus on avoiding hot emotions is also prevalent in the idea that ego should fulfill other people's wishes to the extent possible, since strong, unfulfilled desires are thought to arouse *mamuɲ* and result in an imbalance of the *rəway*. In the context of this chapter I cannot pay further attention to the myths that depict the dilemma between these contradictory demands—to fulfill another person's strong wishes and at the same time to preserve one's autonomy to decide about one's actions. These myths invariably contain the message to show care for others by not expressing one's desires too forcibly.

The Jahai ascribe different properties to the *rəway* of living persons and to the souls of the dead, called *yəl*. While the former are thought to seek affective attachment to other society members, the latter are believed to have malevolent attitudes toward their former life companions. Especially soon after death, a *yəl* is thought to be in a kind of somnambulant state, full of *mamuɲ* over the loss of its body and unable to remember even its loved ones clearly. If a *yəl* were to encounter a living person, it would try to force him or her to accompany it to the land of the dead in the "west," far away from the Jahai's territory, where they subsist only on fruits. Here the *yəl* are believed to return to the care of their primordial immortal ancestors, who regenerate a huge fruit forest for them in a perpetual cycle. Another type of soul-substance, which is believed to evaporate from a decomposing corpse, is thought to finally dissolve in the air. It is important to note here that the Jahai make a very sharp distinction between two kinds of ancestors, namely, the primordial immortal ancestors, including their emanations, and the deceased mortal humans. While the former category plays a very important role in the Jahai world-view as regenerators of the forest and donators of a healing liquid to the spirit-mediums, the latter category plays no significant role in the life of the Jahai, who do not trace descent lines further than two or three generations.

In the Jahai world-view, the souls of the deceased mortals occupy a similar position of relationship toward the immortal ancestors as the living, as both are believed to be nurtured by them. Only the souls of deceased *hala'* are thought to occasionally join the mythical ancestral spirits, but their names are usually forgotten after a few generations have passed.

Although the Jahai assume that all living humans are descendants of primordial immortal ancestors, they claim precedence by declaring to be their ancestors' first-born. They make a distinction between *mənra'* (real people), a category which comprises, besides the members of their own society, also neighboring Orang Asli groups and *gob* (outsiders). The latter are considered "hotter" than *mənra'*, who should be careful to keep them at a distance to prevent their soul-substances from mixing. In the context of dealings with "outsiders," the Jahai value separation. The right attitude toward outsiders is thought to be timidity and fearfulness, unless they are well known to individual Jahai as being trustworthy. This attitude reinforces, to a great extent, the preservation of the Jahai cultural identity.

Do the Jahai Form a Band Society?

From superficial observation it may appear that the Jahai, like other "non-complex" hunter-gatherer societies, are organized in small, kin-related groups, often called "bands" (Bird-David 1994; Damas 1969; Service 1962; Steward 1936; 1955) or "family-level foragers" (Johnson and Earle 1987). I argue that the Jahai themselves view their society primarily as a whole, of which the category of the primordial immortal ancestors forms an essential part, and that this view of their society is closely connected to their way of sharing food as a "passing-on of received gifts."

The Jahai conceptualize the whole of their society, while being embedded in a wider universe, as hierarchically organized in two layers: a "higher layer," consisting of primordial immortal ancestors, and a "lower layer," comprising primarily all living present-day Jahai, but, depending on the context, being extendible to include other Malaysian indigenous populations and ultimately all of humankind. All are believed to be largely dependent on the "higher layer" for their well-being. Although in the context of the face-to-face interactions between members of camp communities close relations are important and highly valued, and the nuclear family can be regarded as their basic unit, individual camp members perceive the composition of their camp groups basically as incidental, and identify themselves primarily with the "two-layered whole" of their society. It follows, as I shall elaborate further below, that all present-day Jahai consider themselves as equal kin, because all of them stand in an equal position of distant kinship-relatedness to the category of "higher beings," the primordial immortal ancestors. The dead, as I have pointed out above, are seen as forming a separate society from that of the living, but with similar relationships to the primordial immortal ancestors. The latter are supposed to regenerate fruit forests in their abode.

The Jahai perceive the hierarchically "lower layer," which comprises primarily all present-day Jahai, as being dispersed over the whole of their primordial ancestors' territory *(sakah)* in mobile "people patches" or camp communities. These usually consist of a core of adult married female and/or male siblings and their families, who are joined by others, such as relatives, affines, and potential marriage partners, as camp members. These camp communities are characterized by fuzzy boundaries and fluctuations in composition, the latter seemingly forming a strategy to prevent the escalation of conflicts, as is known to be the case among other "non-complex society" hunter-gatherers (Gardner 1991; Leacock and Lee 1982; Lee and DeVore 1968: 8; Woodburn 1980). Among the Jahai, however, regular visits to other camps are also a means to reinforce social ties. In these camp communities, incidental sharing groups are formed, each consisting of five partners, families or individuals. The number of five is based on the number of parts into which most hunted animals are divided. In the case that an animal is shared out by a hunter, these partners, in turn, share out parts of the meat to others.

As I shall describe below, the Jahai way of sharing as "a passing-on of received gifts" is primarily to be understood from their cultural premise regarding the existence of affective bonds between the two layers of their society, that is, between the primordial immortal ancestors and the present-day Jahai, and vice versa. In order to gain a better understanding of this idea, we have to examine the Jahai perception of their history.

The Jahai Concepts about Their Mythical History

The Jahai distinguish roughly four periods in their cosmogenic "history," but have no idea of approximate time lapses. They believe that during the first, relatively short period the earth with its landscape and most of its present-day flora was created, but there is no unanimity among them over how many mythical ancestors were involved.

During the subsequent period, which was stable and long-lasting, the first mythical ancestors and their descendants—who were immortal, possessed a nonfirm body, and were of much smaller stature than the present-day Jahai—came into being. They are believed to have subsisted mainly on a nonseasonal supply of nectar, seedless fruits, and plant food, which sustained their creative powers to regenerate the forest in a perpetual cycle. Their immortality is ascribed to cool *cəboh* (a transparent liquid, similar to nectar), which flowed through their bodies, unlike the hot blood of present-day humans. They are therefore thought not to have felt any cravings for meat or for sexual acts, but to have been extremely vulnerable to heat. The Jahai believe that during this period, couples formed their children from the juice (*cəboh*) of *canluŋ* leaves (*Zingiber* sp.), by sucking up air through the opening at the top of their fists, in which crushed ginger leaves were clutched. The small being thus formed was placed on its father's chest, face down, a bonding practice that is common among the present-day Jahai.

The third period was marked by transitions, the most important being the onset of human mortality and the subsequent splitting off of mortal humans from the immortals. Other important events marked the coming into existence of animals, who originated from humans.

The Jahai tell how at some point in time, the so-called "Pig-tailed Macaque People" began to indulge in "hot" sexual acts and subsequently transformed permanently into pig-tailed macaques (*Macaca nemestrina*). When other couples imitated them, the women became pregnant and delivered babies as women do today. Instead of *cəboh*, "hot" blood now flowed in the veins of their offspring, causing sickness and mortality, a craving for meat and for sexual intercourse, and proneness to "hot" emotions— such as anger, jealousy, and greed (all denoted by the word *mamuɲ*)—and resulting in humans growing to their present stature. Shortly after these events, several of the mortal humans split off from their society members by transforming into various animal species, tubers, bamboo plants, dart poison, and other entities. These ideas show how the present-day Jahai consider themselves to be the distant "progeny" of the primordial immortal ancestors as well as distant relatives of animals and other entities.

The Jahai suppose that the acquired "hotness" of these first humans caused their ancestors, who had preserved their immortality by abstaining from copulation, to distance themselves by moving up into the seven-layered firmament, where they now live in huge nonseasonal fruit forests that grow on the three lower layers (the upper layers are uninhabited). They are thought to still show their care for their "progeny" by regenerating the forest for them in a perpetual yearly cycle with their supernatural powers.

While during the first three periods many transformations took place, the Jahai think that the present fourth period is characterized by relative stability. However, they foresee an apocalypse caused by earthquakes due to the dissatisfaction of the immortal ancestors, if the rain forest were to be destroyed.

Why the Jahai View Sharing as "Passing-On of Received Gifts"

The argument of this section of my essay is that the Jahai way of sharing is primarily to be understood from the presumed affective relatedness between the primordial immortal ancestors[5] and the present-day Jahai. The former are believed to display affectionate nurturant care that flows down to their classificatory "great-grandchildren," and is manifested in two ways.

On the holistic level of the "two-layered" society this premise is prevalent in the idea that the primordial immortal ancestors nurture all of their human "progeny" by regenerating the forest for them in a perpetual yearly cycle, marked by the flower and the fruit seasons. The Jahai therefore refer to fruits (*bɔh*) and vegetables (*tə'a'*) as their "original food." This idea generates a trust in the general affluence of the forest environment (Sahlins 1972), even in times of scarcity.

On the level of individual relationships between representatives of the two "layers," this premise is manifest in the belief that a *cənɔy* (a primordial ancestral spirit or its emanation) may select a Jahai *hala'* (spirit-medium and healer) by appearing to him in a dream and teaching him a song. A *cənɔy* is believed to solicit being adopted by the future *hala'* as his child or spouse and, after establishing a close bond, to donate to him a "cool" healing spiritual liquid, the *cəboh*, only visible to the *hala'*, which he passes on to his patients during curing rituals to balance their *rəway*.

The Jahai idea of the existence of generalized kinship relations between all present-day society members, on the basis of their belief that they all are the distant "progeny" of the primordial immortal ancestors, is reinforced by their bilateral kinship system with a generational terminology: siblings of both parents are referred to as "father" ('*ɛy*) or "mother" (*bə'*) by ego. The Jahai only occasionally use the terms that differentiate them from ego's real parents: '*ɛy bɛh* (uncle) and *bə' mo'* (aunt). Bilateral first cousins are addressed as "siblings" (*bɛr*). It follows that individuals have many classificatory "grandparents," "parents," and "siblings." Kinship relationships are generalized through many lines. The more distant the relationships, the more generalized they become.

In the Jahai language, distant ancestors and their progeny are respectively called *dɔn* (great-grandparents) and *gǝdaw* (distant grandchildren). Because, according to the Jahai mythical history, during the third period their mortal mythical ancestors were the "siblings-turned-human" of the primordial immortal ancestors, all present-day Jahai classify themselves as the immortals' "great-grandchildren" who are all in an equal position of kinship-relatedness to them and are therefore equally entitled to their "nurturing gifts," which the ancestors donate as an expression of their love and care. Through this premise of their equal relatedness to the primordial immortal ancestors, all Jahai feel that they are kin among themselves. To the contrary, they do not attach much importance to the tracing of descent lines from mortal ancestors.

According to the classic theory of Mauss (1925), gifts establish attachment between the giver and the recipients because part of the giver is contained in the gift. The Jahai concept of unbounded, contagious soul-substance generates a similar view, namely, that the gifts from the mythical immortal ancestors' spirits, that is, fruits and plant food, contain some of the latter's soul-substance, the *cǝboh*. Through consumption of these foodstuffs, the Jahai believe that they incorporate some of the soul-substance, which reinforces their bonding with the primordial immortal ancestors as well as among themselves.

Forest fruits and vegetables are considered to be "cooler" than meat, wild tubers, or honey, which are believed to have a different origin. The way of sharing of this "original food" as a "passing-on of ancestral gifts" to others serves as a model for the sharing of these other foodstuffs.

From the analysis of the Jahai ideas so far, it is clear that sharing, viewed as "a passing-on of received gifts," is to be distinguished from sharing viewed as generalized reciprocity—i.e., exchange without calculation of amounts or frequency—(Mauss 1925; Sahlins 1972: 193–94), because the latter is based on the premise of ownership, however temporary it may be. Instead, the Jahai "original gifts" are believed to be donated by the primordial immortal ancestors as nurturance, equally destined for all of their "progeny," which engenders nonreciprocal sharing.

I argue that because the Jahai perceive the existence of affectionate, nurturing immortal ancestors as a reality and explain the growth of the forest through being imbued with their ancestors' generative powers during a perpetual yearly cycle, it would be inaccurate to interpret their cultural premises about a nurturant, caring environment merely as a "metaphor they live by" (Lakoff and Johnson 1980), similar to the concept "the forest is as a parent," which Bird-David (1990; 1992) postulates to be a core metaphor for the Nayakas in central India, the Mbuti in Zaire (based on Mosko 1987), and the Batek in Malaysia (based on Endicott 1979a; 1979b). The Jahai do not regard the forest as an independent entity, acting like a parent, but as an expression of the care shown by their nurturing primordial immortal ancestors.

To reinforce their bonding with the immortal ancestors, the Jahai make use of two important sensory modes, namely, sound, mainly of songs and bamboo repercussion, and scent, especially of gingers and other fragrant flowers and leaves with which they often decorate themselves. Especially on the fine, cool evenings that mark the beginning of the flower season, the Jahai, often gathered in larger groups than usual, may hold *sewaŋ*, communal singing and dancing sessions, to celebrate "communitas" (Turner 1969: 66), an experience of communal existence and shared affection with the *cənɔy*. The latter are believed to glide down along fluorescent threads, which they release from their hands, to dwell on earth and cause the flowers, especially those of the fruit trees, to bloom. The Jahai take care to extinguish all fires on such occasions, as these beings are believed to be extremely vulnerable to heat.

The Jahai Core Values

Above I have analyzed how the Jahai ideas about sharing of the "received gifts" of the primordial immortal ancestors, which serve as a model for sharing in general, is interrelated with their cultural core premises. Especially, their well-being is thought to depend on the continuation of their "two-layered society." It is clear that as a prerequisite for the cultural reproduction of the premises that bear upon this idea, the Jahai have to value the promotion and maintenance of affective relatedness, which pertains on the two morphological levels of their society: between the "higher layer," the immortal ancestors' spirits, and the "lower layer," the present-day Jahai, as well as among the members of the latter category.

To maintain good relations with the primordial immortal ancestors, Jahai spirit-mediums have to take initiatives to organize communal singing and dancing sessions, which are thought to please these beings and entice them to regenerate the forest for their human "progeny." Individual immortal ancestors, on their part, are believed to display altruistic behavior by taking the initiative to select a future spirit-medium to whom he or she will donate a healing liquid, to be passed on to patients during curing rituals.

In order to maintain good relations among the members of the society, the displaying of altruistic behavior is valued. The Jahai daily life requires that individuals make autonomous decisions and take initiatives. They have to construct traps, fashion blowpipes, go hunting or gathering, build huts, and do many other daily chores. They must, in particular, take initiatives to share food and goods with other community members.

With regard to the "lower level" of their society, the core value can be phrased as "maintaining of affective relatedness, through displaying altruistic individual autonomy." Because of their presumed equal kinship relations between all present-day Jahai and their primordial immortal ancestors, none of them is in a position of power privileging him or her to coerce others. Instead, Jahai value the promotion of well-being in others, which is phrased by them as taking care to preserve the "coolness" of each other's *rǝway*, especially by trying to prevent the occurrence of "hot" emotions such as anger and jealousy. The latter would cause separation instead of relatedness.

The mode of autonomy that the Jahai value is reminiscent of what Benedict et al. (1970) have called "pro-social individual autonomy," a concept recently brought to the fore by Colby (1987). It can be defined as "implying respect for the autonomy of others and care for their well-being" (p. 881), and is to be distinguished from "antisocial" or "selfish autonomy" (in fact, the two concepts are poles on a continuum), which can be defined as "aiming to increase autonomy for the self at the expense of the well-being of others" (ibid.). It is obvious that if individualism in the form of "selfish autonomy" were to emerge as a value in the "non-complex" society of the Jahai, it would interfere with their premise that all social members share equal kinship-relatedness to the primordial immortal ancestors.

The tendency to display altruistic behavior by the Jahai is reinforced by the model of the supposed display of "altruistic," or "prosocial" autonomy by the primordial immortal ancestors, who are believed to regenerate the forest in a perpetual cycle for their "progeny." This is considered to be a real display of altruism, as the Jahai believe that their immortal ancestors' modest needs are already completely fulfilled by the fruit forests that are supposed to grow on the three lower layers of the firmament. Moreover, individual *cǝnɔy* are also thought to act in an altruistic way by engaging in face-to-face relationships with spirit-mediums (*hala'*), during which they donate to them an invisible healing liquid, *cǝboh*, which is meant to be passed on to their patients during curing rituals.

Dumont has theorized that the highest value encompasses its contrary on a lower level (Dumont 1980; 1987). In several contexts of the Jahai world-view, the contrary of their core value, namely, "displaying nonaltruistic or antisocial behavior" and thereby creating separation, is valued. Several of the Jahai myths show how an extremely selfish autonomous person, thought to be "hot," is avoided by other members of the community or even ostracized by them. Also, in the context of relationships with "outsiders," keeping one's distance or even displaying forms of antisocial autonomy are valued, for example, when dealing with untrustworthy traders (*tawkeh*), who may in turn be tricked and cheated by the Jahai.

My research has not revealed any context in which compassion regarding personal status or possessions is valued. Obviously, the Jahai ideas with regard to their equality of kinship-relatedness with the primordial ancestors do not entail competition as a value. Potential competition between persons who aspire to become a spirit-medium is diminished through the Jahai view that this is not a matter of such a person's own choice, but rather that he is being selected by the spirits.

Why Meat Is Also Shared as a "Passing-On of Gifts"

The Jahai rationale for sharing meat as "received gifts" is different from that for sharing the "original gifts" of forest fruits and vegetables, as animals are not believed to have been given to them by their primordial immortal ancestors, but to originate from humans.

The Jahai believe that before the third period of their mythical history, real animals did not exist, but that their immortal (primordial) mythical ancestors were able to assume the appearance of an animal at will. Especially antisocial humans are believed to have performed lycanthropy by taking the shape of an animal into which they would later change permanently. Two genres of myths (*canɛl*) explain this exegesis of animals. The first genre describes the transformation of humans into specific animal species as a consequence of displaying antisocial autonomous behavior favoring the autonomous individual at the cost of others in the group (Colby 1987: 881), such as coercing others or selfishly consuming food in excessive quantities. These humans changed, for example, into stinging insects, leeches, the flying lemur (*Cynosephalus variegatus*), and rhinoceros hornbills (*Buceros rhinoceros*). I postulate that these myths evoke the association in the Jahai mind that displaying antisocial autonomy causes a separation from other humans in an "individualistic" way—by species-specific transformation. This cultural idea seems to be reflected in the fact that the Jahai language has no general term for the category "animals," but instead refers to them by their species names.

Of the second genre, which explains how various animal species originated from a single being, I know of only one example. This myth explains the origin of animals—in particular, of the hunted species—from an ogre, the "Giant Spectacled Leaf Monkey Man." He was so overcome by craving for meat that he devoured whole Jahai camp populations until two *hala'* finally killed him and scattered the pieces of his cut-up body. These then turned into the various animal species, among them the present-day spectacled leaf monkey (*Presbytis hosei hosei*). The mythical situation has since been reversed: whereas the ogre was a cannibal in the past, the monkey species that now bears his name is vegetarian. It feeds mainly on tough leaves, has a complex stomach to process the large amount of plant food it eats, and consequently sports a bulging belly. Because of its vegetarian, "cool" diet, it is one of the most favored prey animals of the Jahai.

The myth depicts how craving for meat led to cannibalism, which, because it involves the incorporation of another person's body into one's own, is the most extreme form of "antisocial autonomy" (in the form of coercion) that is imaginable. However, while cannibalism would be considered destructive in present-day society, in the context of the myth this extremely "hot" act turns out to be generative.

Hunting is believed to be a necessity for the present-day Jahai, due to their having hot blood in their veins, which is thought to cause a craving for meat. They think that meat consumption is necessary to sustain them and to prevent the occurrence of cannibalism among them. The Jahai use the myth of the Spectacled Leaf Monkey Man as a legitimization for hunting and consuming animal meat, saying: "The ogre ate our people long ago; so now it is our turn to eat the meat of animals that grew from the pieces of his body."

If we consider that according to the Jahai world-view animals have a human origin, it follows that hunting and consuming animal meat does, in a way, make the Jahai "cannibals" themselves. However, the Jahai often emphasize that animals are no longer part of the human society. "They don't dream about us," Jahai explain, because to them dreaming about someone means being related to that person. While the primordial immortal ancestors, their emanations (cɛnɔy), and humans preserved their affective bonds—although separated by a distance in space—here we encounter a reversal: the transformation of some humans into animals resulted in a proximity in space (the forest) but a separation with regard to their mutual affective relatedness. Nevertheless, Jahai often raise the orphaned young of the animals they have killed, such as gibbons, spectacled leaf monkeys, short-tailed macaques, long-tailed macaques, slow lorises, giant squirrels, and others. The very young are even breast-fed and undergo rituals during which cɛboh is blown into their bodies by a *hala'* to improve their health and quieten their emotions. Those pets, because they share soul-substance with their owners, are never eaten by the Jahai.

As pointed out above, for the Jahai the killing of animals is mainly problematic because it involves coercing an animal's life-soul out of its body. Considered the epitome of "antisocial autonomy," this action requires aroused, "hot" emotions and behavior. If, in this context, the Jahai were to value such aggression positively, it would cause cognitive dissonance (Festinger 1957) with their positive valuation of emotional quietness of people's rɛway. Expectedly, the Jahai do not express aroused emotions while killing animals, even when they kill them through direct contact, such as by strangling. When hunting with the blowpipe, their most frequently used hunting technique, they do not conceive of the meat as being appropriated by the hunter, but rather as being "given" to him by his bamboo blowpipe (*bəlaw*). "*Bəlaw ʾoʾ ʾɛg ʾay*" (the blowpipe gives meat), Jahai hunters say. Although the actual killing is effected by the dart poison, it is the *bəlaw* that guides the dart in the right direction. In the past, they probably had similar concepts about the bow and arrow, which they used until the 1950s to hunt big game, before shotguns were introduced by the British (Rambo 1978).

Both the bamboo from which the blowpipe is fashioned and the dart poison (*dɔk*) are believed to be transformed humans and, therefore, living entities who possess a soul, but of a nature different from that of humans. Bamboo is thought to have transformed from excessive, noisy, easily excitable—and hence not very alert—humans, whose "hot" character is still seen in its abundant and fast growth; the noise produced by the friction of the stems; and the flammability of dry stands, which occasionally starts a forest fire.

The poison (*dɔk*), made from the latex of the Ipoh tree (*Antiaris toxicaria*), is cooked and sometimes mixed with *Strychnos* sap to increase its lethal effect. One of the Jahai myths describes how a human being, a man named *Dɔk*, transformed into the poison because of his antisocial behavior: he alone knew the art of making fire and of roasting wild tubers, but refused to share this knowledge with his society members. The other Jahai, after first stealing his secret, beat him to death, upon which he transformed into the poison. *Dɔk*'s extreme "hot" character, as shown in his antisocial behavior and aggravated by his violent death, is now manifest in the poison's eagerness to penetrate and kill living beings. The mythical situation has thus been reversed: whereas in the myth *Dɔk* showed a form of antisocial autonomous behavior, now, as dart poison, he is coerced to supply the meat of prey animals to the present-day Jahai.

Although game is considered to be a "gift" from the blowpipe primarily to a single Jahai hunter, he does not claim ownership. Based on the model of the sharing of the primordial immortal ancestors' gifts of forest fruits and vegetables, game (*ʾay*) is also shared as a "received gift," to be passed on to others.

Ideas about the Origin and Sharing of Wild Tubers

Wild tubers (*Dioscorea* spp.) are also believed to have a human origin and to possess a soul. A myth tells how a Jahai father felt such craving for meat that he lured his three sons to follow him into the forest where he killed and devoured them one by one and hid the bones, tied up in bundles, under a tree. His wife escaped a similar fate by climbing up a rattan and hiding in a treetop. Failing to find more meat and overcome by a craving for it, the man finally devoured the flesh of his own arms and legs. Only then did his wife dare to climb down and call her relatives who beat him to death, upon which he transformed into a *takob* (*Dioscorea* sp.), a tuber with many offshoots. The bones of the three sons were scattered around and transformed into all of the other wild tuber species (*Dioscorea* spp.), of which the Jahai know at least sixteen varieties.

Unlike forest fruits and plant foods, which are easy to harvest, most wild tubers grow as deep as two meters or more below the ground and have to be dug out with a digging stick, a strenuous task which is often done by the men.

The supposed human origin of wild tubers places them in the same position of relationship to humans as that of animals. The difference in acquiring them is that wild tubers are not totally destroyed, as Jahai harvesters take good care to leave a small part of the tuber in the ground for regrowth.

Apparently, the collection of these tubers is viewed by the Jahai as merely taking away the excess offshoots that these tubers produce, owing to their "hot" emotional state (*mamuɲ*) caused by their violent death that occurred before their transformation. Based on the "model" of the sharing of the original ancestors' "gifts" of forest fruits and vegetables, wild tubers are divided up in the same way.

Ideas about the Origin and Sharing of Honey

The Jahai know of two kinds of stingless bees (*Trigona* spp.) and one species of stinging bees (*Apis dorsata*). They are all believed to be transformations of human beings who were coercive and overdemanding. During mythical times, the stinging bees are thought to have lived for some time with an antisocial human named Karey, who later transformed into the thunder spirit that now dwells on the dark clouds in the sky. Bees suck the nectar from the flowers, considered as the "cool" food of the *cənɔy* and their source of *cəboh*, which, however, turns "hot" when it changes into honey in the bees' "hot" body. Honey from *Apis dorsata* is collected only on dark moonless nights, when the collectors camp in simple leaf-shelters near a *Tualang* tree (*Koompassia excelsa*), which is the tallest tree in the forest and is also where these bees usually build their honeycombs, suspending them from its highest branches. In the middle of the night, one or two men carrying torches climb up lianas into the tree to smoke the bees out and collect the honeycomb. The honey, which rightfully belongs to the *cənɔy*, has now become too "hot" for them to consume. The Jahai therefore consider themselves entitled to this "indirect gift" from the primordial immortal ancestors, apportioning it out as they do with other "gifts."

Sharing and the Reinforcement of Affective Relatedness

So far I have argued that despite the presumed different origin of the various categories of food, all are treated as "received gifts," of which shares have to be passed on to other society members.

The Jahai practice two ways of sharing: spontaneous passing-on and sharing on demand (see also Barnard and Woodburn 1988: 12; Bird-David 1990). The first mode, passing-on, is initiated by a person who has obtained an item of food and seems to feel an urge to immediately apportion some of it to others, even if these persons already have a sufficient supply. The second mode, sharing on demand, is initiated by a person who is in need of something. Asking is done bluntly, for example, by saying: "*ʔɛg də-yɛʔ gulaʔ, wa-ʔɛm teh*" (Give me sugar to drink tea). If an item is visible, a request for it cannot be denied without causing *pəhunɛn*, a concept that will be discussed below.

The Jahai language contains no polite terms equivalent to the English "please" and "thank you." The recipient of a share will take it in silence and just walk away. This, I argue, reflects the aforementioned Jahai idea of relatedness as equal kin.

The analysis of the Jahai world-view thus far, has shown that sharing reinforces the affective relatedness between the category of the primordial immortal ancestors and their mortal "progeny" as well as among the mortal Jahai.

The Jahai core symbol of affective relatedness is *cəboh*, which has a "multivocality of meaning" (Turner 1974). It refers to nourishment in the form of nectar, fruit juice, and plant juice, and evokes associations with vitality and immortality, because the primordial ancestors are thought not to have been susceptible to diseases or death, and also with creation and regeneration, because these ancestors are supposed to have created the forest flora and fruits and to have caused the creation of their babies from plant sap. Its other connotations are quietness and nonviolence as *cəboh* is thought to cool down "hot" emotions, such as *mamuɲ*, and to balance the soul.

Cəboh is believed to flow in the bodies of all Jahai, not only through their consumption of fruits and plant food, but also through having undergone rituals during which a *halaʔ* blows *cəboh* into a patient to balance his or her *rəway*. The first occasion for this to be done is shortly after birth, since all Jahai are supposed to have some *cəboh* in their bodies from early childhood onwards. *Cəboh* symbolizes affective relatedness on the two morphological hierarchical "layers" of Jahai society: between the primordial immortal ancestors and the present-day Jahai, and, motivated by these, among the members of the latter category. Moreover, the use of this symbol reinforces the Jahai feelings of connectedness to the forest.

As described above, the contradiction of relatedness—namely, separation from other society members—is negatively valued by the Jahai in the context of their social life (although in the context of relations with "outsiders" it is valued). Such separation is thought to be caused mainly by the arousal of "hot" emotions, symbolized by the concept of "hot blood." In the context of sharing, the danger of this occurring is always present, and the Jahai are very much aware of this. For example, they think that to leave someone out of sharing is considered to be very dangerous for that person, as will be discussed further below. Bickering over unequal parts of shares is largely prevented by a taboo on mentioning the name of an animal or a wild tuber until a day or so after its consumption. In contrast, talking about the "original foods" of forest fruits and vegetables is freely allowed.

The Preservation of Peacefulness and the Concept of *Pəhunɛn*

As would be expected, the world-view of the Jahai contains dynamics that preserve peacefulness, as this is interlinked with their configuration of cultural core premises and values. Above I have described their cultural idea that due to their equal relatedness to the primordial immortal ancestors, none of the present-day Jahai is in a position of power that would allow him or her to coerce others, which is reinforced by the premise that this would be bad for the other person's *rəway*. Also, I briefly referred to the taboo on talking about shares of meat and tubers, which prevents bickering. These ideas promote peacefulness and form an important factor for inhibiting the emergence of stratification. Below I shall discuss another cultural dynamic that helps to preserve peacefulness, namely, the concept of *pəhunɛn* in relation to sharing. A further important dynamic, the concepts regarding a violent thunder spirit named Karey, will be dealt with in a separate publication.

The Jahai believe that it is dangerous to leave someone out of sharing, because this would arouse "hot" emotions (*mamuɲ*), which would endanger that person's soul balance. This, in turn, would make him or her prone to accidents, such as being crushed by a falling tree, devoured by a tiger, bitten by a snake or centipede, or stung by a scorpion. This accident-proneness is called *pəhunɛn* (probably adapted from Malay *keempunan*, which, according to Dentan [1968: 138], has the same root as the Polynesian "taboo").

The victim of *pəhunɛn* has to undergo a curing ritual, performed by a *hala²*, to restore the emotional quietness of his or her soul. After this the victim has to stay in the settlement for about a week, as all of the accidents referred to above are expected to occur in the forest. Through the concept of *pəhunɛn*, the idea of the Jahai social environment as safe and nurturing is reinforced, even in a rare case of the sharing rules having been violated.

It is interesting to note that not the offending party but rather the victim is believed to become accident-prone, which to the Western mind would seem unfair. However, if we understand *pəhunɛn* in relation to the Jahai conceptualization of social attachment as a mixing of soul-substances, it makes sense. Losing a community member is considered as the loss of a "part of themselves," and thus the concept of *pəhunɛn* can be seen to reinforce their mutual care, especially in their everyday face-to-face contacts.

At this point I shall briefly discuss the Jahai concept of *pəhunɛn* in relation to psychological theories about human aggression because of their relevance in understanding the Jahai value of peacefulness, which is to be understood as interrelated with the core value of "maintaining affective relatedness as equal kin." According to the "frustration-aggression hypothesis," put forward by Dollard et al. (1939), frustration in receiving one's entitled share would give rise to feelings of anger in the victim, which might be expressed by aggressive acts against the offending party. However, because in the Jahai world-view accident-proneness or *pəhunɛn* is a consequence of such anger, a victim will feel fear of possible calamities instead of anger. Berkowitz (1982) in his revision of the "frustration-aggression hypothesis," postulates that feelings of anger and fear cannot arise simultaneously. Thus, for the Jahai, fear instead of anger is the culturally determined emotion that a frustrated individual experiences. This "cultural choice" for fear instead of for anger inhibits the emergence of anger and aggression, both of which would interfere with the Jahai core value of "maintaining affective relatedness as equal kin by displaying prosocial autonomy," and might ultimately lead to a disruption of the present social organization.

Due to space limitations, I cannot elaborate on other contexts in the Jahai world-view in which this dynamic is also prevalent. Nonviolence features in all hunter-gatherer-swiddener and swiddener-hunter-gatherer cultures of Peninsular Malaysia (see for the Semai: Dentan 1968; 1978; 1988a; 1988b; Robarchek and Dentan 1987; Robarchek 1977; 1980; 1988; 1989; for the Batek: Endicott 1979a; 1979b; and for the Che Wong: Howell 1984; 1989). However, their cultural focus on maintaining peacefulness does not imply that the Jahai cannot be provoked into anger (Leary 1995; Robarchek and Dentan 1987).

Would Sedentarization Engender Changes in the Jahai Configuration of Core Premises and Values?

I have argued above that the Jahai view of sharing as "a passing-on of received free gifts" is interrelated with a specific configuration of core premises and values in the Jahai world-view that goes together with their cultural definition of well-being, which is associated with the maintenance of an emotionally nonaroused, "cool" state of their life-souls (*rǝway*). Their core value is "maintaining affective relatedness by displaying prosocial autonomy," which prevails on two levels of their society: between the immortal ancestors' spirits and their mortal "progeny," as well as among the members of the latter category.

I postulate that the Jahai will tend to reproduce their culture for as long as their ecological circumstances allow. A transformation into a "more complex" or stratified society (Price and Brown 1985; Woodburn 1980) would involve a rise in the number of stressors (Selye 1936; 1956; Davison and Neale 1996) or moments of emotional tension, owing to an increase in conflicting behavior choices for the society members as a consequence of the emergence of conflicting values.

I do not think that sedentarization alone can be considered as the critical factor or "prime mover" that would inevitably cause profound changes in the Jahai world-view and, more precisely, in the configuration of their core cultural premises and values, but rather that the way they perceive the source of their subsistence and their concept of equality are crucial. This configuration bears upon their idea that all society members are equally entitled access to the forest, which is viewed as their primordial immortal ancestors' territory (*sakah*), being regenerated by them during a perpetual yearly cycle. It is expected that fundamental changes in the Jahai world-view will occur only after these ideas change, when free and equal access to the forest is no longer possible.

During a short comparative study among those Jahai who have been sedentarized since the late 1970s due to the expansion of logging activities in the area and the construction of Temenggor Reservoir, I could not find profound differences in their world-view compared to that of the nomadic Jahai. An example of emerging differences is, perhaps, that they consider the small plot of land that is allotted to each sedentary community for cultivation (mainly of tapioca and maize), and which still falls under the jurisdiction of the Malaysian government, primarily as community property and not as accessible to all, like their *sakah*. A few individuals, who had access to school education and had started a business, seemed to behave in a rather selfish way. But although the youngsters increasingly engage in wage labor (logging) and claim ownership of their earnings, the majority of them would exchange these for items from the shops and would share these items with others in the traditional way.

Most of these settled Jahai still retreat to the forest for lengthy periods, where they stay in makeshift camps, not only to collect forest products such as rattan and gaharu wood (*Aquillaria* spp.) for trade, but also to enjoy their stay in the forest while subsisting on its products. An in-depth follow-up study is necessary to reveal the further developments and eventual changes in the Jahai world-view.

Here I can only hypothesize about the changes that may occur over time if sedentarization goes together with a further diminishing of access to the forest, for example, due to still further expansion of the logging activities in the area. I expect that in such a case, over time, individual Jahai will begin to fluctuate between identifying themselves with their own community and with the whole of their society, the latter now becoming viewed as a conglomerate of more or less separate communities. This may enhance group competition over the scarcer resources and result in an increase in the chances of conflict (cf. Kent 1989). Within the communities, stratification in the form of stronger leadership will develop as a necessity for negotiations with representatives of other communities. These leaders will often have to choose between the conflicting options of keeping good relations with other communities on the one hand and of pursuing the interests of their own group, on the other hand. One would expect competition for status to become valued within the communities, which will result in a way of sharing that is based on reciprocity and is no longer viewed as "a passing-on of gifts." The tracing of descent lines will probably gain importance, while spirits of the mortal ancestors may begin to play a role as mediators between the living and the dead, which will engender an ideological change of Jahai society from two-layered into three-layered. Such a view of society can be seen in more complex societies in the Indonesian archipelago (Carsten and Hugh-Jones 1994; Howell 1996). Such follow-up and comparative research is a project for future study.

Conclusion

Through the above analysis of their ideas I have shown that the Jahai way of sharing is to be understood from the prevalence, in their world-view, of a specific configuration of cultural core premises and embedded values. It is essential that the Jahai believe that their well-being is safeguarded by their hierarchically structured "two-layered" society, of which the "higher layer" comprises primordial immortal ancestors who take care of the "lower layer," the present-day Jahai. These, as classificatory "progeny," all stand in a position of equal kinship-relatedness to the former category, and therefore nobody can claim a privilege that would allow him or her to coerce others. The latter idea promotes peacefulness. The affective relatedness, based on nurturance, between the primordial immortal ancestors and the present-day Jahai is thought to be prevalent on two levels in their society. On a holistic level, which comprises relationships between all society members, these immortal ancestors and their emanations are believed to regenerate the forest for their "progeny" in a perpetual yearly cycle. On the level of individual relationships, this relatedness is present in the idea that representatives of the immortal ancestors occasionally engage in an individual relationship with a spirit-medium, during the course of which the medium is given a healing liquid which he passes on to his patients during curing rituals.

The Jahai behavior is largely guided by the configuration of core values that is embedded in these premises. The core value can be phrased as "maintaining the affective relatedness between all society members, on two morphological levels of their society." With regard to the relationships between the nurturant primordial immortal ancestors and the present-day Jahai, the core value can be phrased as "promoting and preserving affective relatedness." With regard to the "lower" level of their society, the relationships among the living Jahai, the core value can be phrased as "promoting and preserving relatedness through displaying altruistic, prosocial, individual autonomy." The latter is defined as behavior aimed at promoting the well-being and the autonomy of others. It prevents, to a large extent, the emergence of stratification in the Jahai society. This core value encourages individuals to take initiatives to share and explains why sharing is viewed as a "passing-on of received free gifts" that does not generate ideas of obligatory reciprocation. Although only forest fruits and plant foods are seen as direct gifts from the primordial immortal ancestors, other foodstuffs are shared in a similar way based on this model. The Jahai belief in the existence of immortal nurturing ancestors generates a trust in the affluence of their environment (Sahlins 1972), which includes their fellow society members. An important related dynamic in the Jahai world-view is the concept of *pǝhunɛn*, the accident-proneness of someone who is left out of sharing.

I have argued that the Jahai way of sharing plays a pivotal role in the process of their culture's reproduction, especially with regard to the reproduction of the configuration of core premises and embedded values in their world-view, which bear upon the Jahai cultural ideas about well-being. Provided that favorable ecological conditions remain, the Jahai will continue to reproduce the core features of their culture as this engenders a lower number of stressors—instances of emotional tension—than would ensue from a configuration of cultural premises and values that goes together with a "more complex" social organization. Although it may be going too far to call a "non-complex society" like that of the Jahai an "original affluent society" (Sahlins 1972) in the modern economic sense, it is obviously affluent in the affective sense.

Notes

The author extends thanks to the Socio-economic Research Unit of the Prime Minister's Department of Malaysia, the Jabatan Hal Ehwal Orang Asli (Malaysian Welfare Department for Aborigines), both located in Kuala Lumpur, and to Prof. Dr. Hood Mohammed Salleh of the Institute for the Study of Environment and Development (Lestari) at Universiti Kebangsaan Malaysia in Bangi for giving all the assistance needed for the present research. I am also grateful to Prof. Geoffrey Benjamin of the University of Singapore, who gave useful comments on an earlier draft of this chapter and helped with the phonetic transcription of the Jahai terms.

1. The latter term is used in this essay.
2. See, for example, Marshall (1976) who argues that food sharing among the !Kung Bushmen reinforces the social bonds among group members, thus promoting beneficial cooperation in daily life.
3. It is the intention of the author to present a more holistic in-depth analysis of the Jahai world-view at a later date.
4. The Jahai do not center emotions in the liver as do the Malays (Laderman 1991) and the Chewong (Howell 1989).
5. These ancestral spirits are probably the Orang Hidup (Mal.: immortals), referred to by Schebesta (1957; [1928] 1973), called *cəmrɔy* or *cənɔy* (the latter word is used in this chapter).

References

Bailey, R. C., G. Head, M. Jenike, B. Owen, R. Rechtman, and E. Zechenter. 1989. "Hunting and Gathering in the Tropical Rainforest: Is it Possible?" *American Anthropologist* 91: 59–82.
Bailey, R. C., and T. Headland. 1991. "The Tropical Rainforest: Is it a Productive Environment for Human Foragers?" *Human Ecology* 19 (2): 261–285.
Barnard, A. 1992. *The Kalahari Debate: A Bibliographical Essay*. Edinburgh: Centre for African Studies, Edinburgh University.
Barnard, A., and J. Woodburn. 1988. "Introduction". In *Hunters and Gatherers, Vol. 2. Property, Power and Ideology*. T. Ingold, D. Riches, and J. Woodburn, eds. Oxford: Berg.
Bellwood, P. 1985. *Prehistory of the Indo-Malayan Archipelago*. London: Academic Press.
Benedict, R., A. Maslow, M. Mead, and J. J. Honigman. 1970. "Synergy: Some Notes of Ruth Benedict." *American Anthropologist* 72(2): 320–33.

Berkowitz, L., ed. 1982. "Aversive Conditions as Stimuli to Aggression." In *Advances in Experimental Social Psychology* 15.

Bicchieri, M. G. 1990. "Comment On: Foragers, Genuine or Spurious?" *Current Anthropology* 31(2): 123.

Bird-David, N. 1988. "Hunter-Gatherers and Other Peoples: A Re-Examination." In *Hunters and Gatherers, Vol. 1, History, Evolution and Social Change*. T. Ingold, D. Riches, and J. Woodburn, eds. Oxford: Berg.

_____. 1990. "The Giving Environment: Another Perspective on the Economic System of Gatherer-Hunters." *Current Anthropology* 31: 189–96.

_____. 1992. "Beyond 'The Original Affluent Society.'" *Current Anthropology* 33(1): 25–47.

_____. 1994. "Sociality and Immediacy, Or: Past and Present Conversations on Bands." *Man* 29: 538–603.

Brosius, J. P. 1991. "Foraging in Tropical Rain Forests: The Case of the Penan of Sarawak, East Malaysia." *Human Ecology* 19(2): 123–50.

Burch, E. S., and L. E. Ellanna, eds. 1994. *Key Issues in Hunter-Gatherer Research*. Oxford: Berg.

Carsten, J., and S. Hugh-Jones, eds. 1994. *About the House: Lévi-Strauss and Beyond*. Cambridge: Cambridge University Press.

Cashdan, E. 1985. "Coping with Risk: Reciprocity among the Basarwa of Northern Botswana." *Man* 20: 454–74.

Colby, B. 1987. "Well-Being: A Theoretical Program." *American Anthropologist* 89: 879–95.

Damas, D. 1969. *Band Societies. Proceedings of the Conference on Band Organization*. Ottawa: National Museums of Canada.

Davison, G. C., and J. M. Neale. 1996. *Abnormal Psychology*. New York: John Wiley and Sons.

Denbow, J., and E. Wilmsen. 1986. "Advent and Course of Pastoralism in the Kalahari." *Science* 234: 1509–15.

Dentan, R. K. 1968. *The Semai: A Nonviolent People of Malaysia*. New York: Holt, Rinehart and Winston.

_____. 1978. "Notes on Childhood in a Nonviolent Context." In *Learning Non-Aggression*. A. Montagu, ed. Oxford: Oxford University Press.

_____. 1988a. "Band-Level Eden: A Mystifying Chimera." *Cultural Anthropology* 3: 276–84.

_____. 1988b. "On Reconsidering Violence in Simple Human Societies." *Current Anthropology* 29: 625–29.

_____. 1991. "Potential Food Sources for Foragers in the Malaysian Rainforest: Sago, Yams and Lots of Little Things." *Bijdragen tot de Taal-, Land- en Volkenkunde* 147(4): 561.

Dollard, J., N. E. Doob, O. H. Miller, R. R. Mowrer, C. S. Sears, C. I. Ford, C. I. Hovland, and R. T. Sollenberger. 1939. *Frustration and Aggression*. New Haven, Conn.: Yale University Press.

Dumont, L. 1980. "On Value." *Proceedings of the British Academy, LXVI*. London: Oxford University Press.

_____. 1987. "Individualism and Equality." *Current Anthropology* 28(5): 669–672.

Dunn, F. L. 1975. *Rain Forest Collectors and Traders: A Study of Resource Utilization in Modern and Ancient Malaya*. Monograph of the Malaysian Branch of the Royal Asiatic Society, No. 5.

Dwyer, P. D., and M. Minnegal. 1991. "Hunting in Lowland Tropical Rain Forest: Toward a Model of Non-Agricultural Subsistence." *Human Ecology* 19(2): 187–213.

Endicott, K. 1979a. *Batek Negrito Religion*. Oxford: Clarendon Press.

_____. 1979b. "The Batek Negrito Thundergod: The Personification of a Natural Force." In *The Imagination of Reality*. A. L. Becker and A. Yengoyan, eds. Norwood, N.J.: Ablex.

Endicott, K., and P. Bellwood. 1991. "The Possibility of Independent Foraging in the Rain Forest of Peninsular Malaysia." *Human Ecology* 19(2): 151–85.

Festinger, L. A. 1957. *When Prophecy Fails: A Theory of Cognitive Dissonance*. Evanston, Ill.: Row Peterson.

Gardner, P. M. 1991. "Forager's Pursuit of Individual Autonomy." *Current Anthropology* 32(5): 543–72.

Geertz, C. 1973. "Thick Description: Toward an Interpretative Theory of Culture." In *The Interpretation of Cultures*. New York: Basic Books.

_____. 1983. *Local Knowledge*. New York: Basic Books.

Glaser, B. C., and A. Strauss. 1967. *The Discovery of Grounded Theory*. Chicago: Aldine.

Gorman, C. 1971. "The Hoabinhian and After: Subsistence Patterns in Southeast Asia During the Pleistocene and Early Recent Periods." *World Archeology* 2: 300–320.

Gould, R. 1982. "To Have and Have Not: The Ecology of Sharing among Hunter-Gatherers." In *Resource Managers: North American and Australian Hunter-Gatherers*. Boulder, Colo.: Westview Press.

Hall, G. E. 1968. *A History of South-East Asia*. Third edition. London, Melbourne, and Toronto: MacMillan.

Headland, T. N. 1986. *Why Foragers Do Not Become Farmers: A Historical Study of a Changing Ecosystem and Its Effect on a Negrito Hunter-Gatherer Group*. Ann Arbor: University of Michigan Press.

Headland, T. N., and R. C. Bailey. 1991. "Have Hunter-Gatherers Ever Lived in Tropical Rainforests Independently of Agriculture?" *Human Ecology* 19(2): 115–19.

Headland, T. N., and L. A. Reid. 1989. "Hunter-Gatherers and Their Neighbors from Prehistory to the Present." *Current Anthropology* 30(1): 43–66.

Heelas, P. 1986. "Talk Across Cultures." In *The Social Construction of Emotions*. T. Harré, ed. Oxford: Basil and Blackwell.

Hoffman, C. L. 1984. "Punan Foragers." In *Past and Present in Hunter-Gatherer Studies*. C. Schrire, ed. New York: Academic Press.

Howell, S. 1984. *Society and Cosmos: The Chewong of Peninsular Malaya*. Singapore and New York: Oxford University Press.

_____. 1989. "To Be Angry Is Not to Be Human, but to Be Fearful Is." In *Societies at Peace: Anthropological Perspectives*. S. Howell and R. Willis, eds. London: Routledge.

Howell, S., ed. 1996. *For the Sake of Our Future: Sacrificing in Eastern Indonesia*. Leiden: Research School CNWS.

Ingold, T. 1980. *Hunters, Pastoralists and Ranchers*. Cambridge: Cambridge University Press.

Johnson, A. W., and T. Earle. 1987. *The Evolution of Human Societies*. Stanford, Cal.: Stanford University Press.

Karim, W. J., ed. 1990. *Emotions of Culture: A Malay Perspective*. Singapore: Oxford University Press.

Kent, S. 1989. "And Justice for All: The Development of Political Centralization among Newly Sedentary Foragers." *American Anthropologist* 91:703–71.

_____. 1992. "The Current Forager Controversy: Real Versus Ideal Views of Hunter-Gatherers." *Man* 27: 45–70.

Kruyt, A. C. 1906. *Het Animisme*. 's-Gravenhage: Martinus Nijhoff.

Laderman, C. 1991. *Taming the Wind of Desire: Psychology, Medicine and Aesthetics in Malay Shamanistic Performances*. Berkeley, Cal.: University of California Press.

Lakoff, G., and M. Johnson. 1980. *Metaphors We Live By*. Chicago: University of Chicago Press.

Leacock, E., and R. B. Lee, eds. 1982. *Politics and History in Band Societies*. Cambridge: Cambridge University Press.

Leary, J. D. 1995. *Violence and the Dream People*. Monograph No. 95, Southeast Asia Series. Ohio University Center for International Studies.

Lee, R. B. 1968. "What Hunters Do for a Living and How to Make out on Scarce Resources." In *Man the Hunter*. R. B. Lee and I. DeVore, eds. Chicago: Aldine Press.

_____. 1992. "Science or Politics? The Crisis in Hunter-Gatherer Studies." *American Anthropologist* 94: 31–54.

Lee, R. B., and I. DeVore, eds. 1968. *Man the Hunter*. Chicago: Aldine Press.

Lee, R. B., and M. Guenther 1991. "Oxen and Onions: The Search for Trade (and Truth) in the Kalahari." *Current Anthropology* 32: 592–601.

Lutz, C. 1986. "The Domain of Emotion Words on Ifaluk." In *The Social Construction of Emotions*. Tom Harré, ed. Oxford: Basil and Blackwell.

Lyons, J. 1977. *Semantics*. Cambridge: Cambridge University Press.

Marshall, L. 1976. *The !Kung of Nyae Nyae*. Cambridge, Mass.: Harvard University Press.

Mauss, M. 1925. "Essai sur le don. Formes et raisons de l'échange sans les sociétés archaïques." *Année Sociologique* 1: 30–186.

Mendelson, E. M. [1956] 1968. "Worldview." In *The International Encyclopedia of the Social Sciences*. London: Crowell, Collier and Macmillan.

Minnegal, M. 1996. "A Necessary Unity of the Articulation of Ecological and Social Exploration of Behaviour." *Journal of the Royal Anthropological Institute* 2: 141–58.

Mosko, M. S. 1987. "The Symbols of 'Forest': A Structural Analysis of Mbuti Culture and Social Organization." *American Anthropologist* 89: 896–913.

Patterson, T. 1990. "Comment On: Foragers, Genuine or Spurious." *Current Anthropology* 31: 133–35.

Price, T. D., and J. Brown. 1985. "Aspects of Hunter-Gatherer Complexity." In *Prehistoric Hunter-Gatherers: The Emergence of Cultural Complexity*. T. D. Price and J. Brown, eds. New York: Academic Press.

Rambo, T. 1978. "Bows, Blowpipes and Blunderbusses: Ecological Implications of Weapon Change among the Malaysian Negritos." *Malayan Nature Journal* 32(2): 209–16.

Redfield, R. 1941. *The Folk Culture of Yucatan*. Chicago: Chicago University Press.

Robarchek, C. A. 1977. "Semai Nonviolence: A Systems Approach to Understanding." Unpublished Ph.D. diss., Berkeley, Cal.: University of California.

_____. 1988a. "Ghost and Witches: The Psychocultural Dynamics of Semai Peacefulness." Unpublished paper, presented at the 87th Annual Meeting of the American Anthropological Association.

_____. 1988b. "Helplessness, Fearfulness and Peacefulness: The Emotional and Motivational Context of Semai Social Relations." *Anthropological Quarterly* 59: 177–83.

_____. 1989. "Primitive Warfare and the Ratomorphic Image of Mankind." *American Anthropologist* 91(4): 903–20.

Robarchek, C. A., and R. K. Dentan. 1987. "Blood Drunkenness and the Bloodthirsty Semai: Unmaking Another Anthropological Myth." *American Anthropologist* 89: 356–64.

Rosaldo, M. Zimbalist. 1980. *Knowledge and Passion: Ilongot Notions of Self and Social Life*. Cambridge: Cambridge University Press.

Sahlins, M. D. 1972. *Stone Age Economics*. London: Tavistock.

Schebesta, P. [1928] 1973. *Among the Forest Dwarfs of Malaya*. Oxford: Oxford University Press.

_____. 1957. *Die Negrito Asiens: Wirtschaft und Soziologie*. Vienna: St.-Gabriel Verlag.

Schrire, C. 1984. "Wild Surmises on Savage Thoughts." In *Past and Present in Hunter-Gatherer Studies. Selections from the Proceedings of the Third International Conference on Hunter-Gatherers*. C. Schrire, ed. New York: Academic Press.

Sellato, B. 1989. *Nomades et sedentarisation à Borneo*. Paris: Éditions de l'École des Hautes Études en Sciences Sociales.

Selye, H. 1936. *The Physiology and Psychology of Exposure to Stress*. Montreal: Acta.

_____. 1956. *The Stress of Life*. New York: McGraw Hill.

Service, E. 1962. *Primitive Social Organization: An Evolutionary Perspective*. New York: Random House.

Silberbauer, G. B. 1991. "Morbid Reflexivity and Overgeneralization in Mosarwa Studies." *Current Anthropology* 32(1): 96–99.

Smith, E. A. 1988. "Risk and Uncertainty in the 'Original Affluent Society': Evolutionary Ecology of Resource-Sharing and Land Tenure." In *Hunters and Gatherers, Vol. 1: History, Evolution and Social Change*. T. Ingold, D. Riches, and J. Woodburn, eds. Oxford: Berg Publishers.

Solway, J. S., and R. B. Lee. 1990. "Foragers, Genuine or Spurious? Situating the Kalahari San in History." *Current Anthropology* 31(2): 109–28.

Spradley, J. P. 1980. *Participant Observation*. New York: Holt, Rinehart and Winston.

Steward, J. H. 1936. "The Economic and Social Base of Primitive Bands." In *Essays Presented to A. L. Kroeber*. R. H. Lowie, ed. Berkeley, Cal.: University of California Press.

_____. 1955. *Theory of Culture Change: The Methodology of Multilinear Evolution*. Urbana, Ill.: University of Illinois Press.

Tax, S. 1941. "World View and Social Relations in Guatemala." *American Anthropologist* 43: 27–42.

_____. 1990. "Can World Views Mix?" *Human Organization* 49(3): 280–86.

Turnbull, C. M. 1965. *Wayward Servants: The Two Worlds of the African Pygmies*. Garden City, N.J.: Natural History Press.

Turner, V. W. 1969. *The Ritual Process*. Ithaca, N.Y.: Cornell University Press.

_____. 1974. *Dramas, Fields and Metaphors*. Ithaca, N.Y.: Cornell University Press.

Wiessner, P. 1977. *Hxaro: A Regional System of Reciprocity for Reducing Risk among the !Kung San*. Ph.D. diss., Dept. of Anthropology, University of Michigan, Ann Arbor.

_____. 1982. "Risk, Reciprocity and Social Influence on !Kung San Economics." In *Politics and History in Band Societies*. E. Leacock and R. Lee, eds. Cambridge: Cambridge University Press.

Woodburn, J. 1980. "Hunters and Gatherers Today and a Reconstruction of the Past." In *Soviet and Western Anthropology*. E. Gellne, ed. London: Duckworth.

_____. 1982. "Egalitarian Societies." *Man* 17: 431–51.

Yellen, J. 1990. "Comment On: Foragers, Genuine or Spurious?" *Current Anthropology* 31: 137–38.

Zuraina Majid. 1988–89. "The Tampanian Problem Resolved: Archeological Evidence of a Late Pleistocene Lithic Workshop." *Modern Quaternary Research in Southeast Asia* 11: 71–96.

Zuraina Majid, and Tjia. 1988. "Kota Tampan Perak. The Geological and Archeological Evidence for a Late Pleistocene Site." *Journal of the Malaysian Branch of the Royal Anthropological Society* 61(2): 123–24.

Chapter 26

TIME IN THE TRADITIONAL WORLD-VIEW OF THE KETS

Materials on the Bear Cult

⇒◅◉▻⇐

Evgeniia A. Alekseenko

The bear cult in general and the bear festival in particular (i.e., a ritual that accompanies the hunting of this respected animal) are widely known among the indigenous peoples of the taiga regions in both the New and the Old World. It must undoubtedly be recognized as one of the most colorful aspects of Ket traditional culture. Among various Siberian peoples, both the nearest neighbors of the Kets (such as the Khantys, Sel'kups, Evenks, and others) and those who lived far away from them, the brown bear was distinguished in the animal world as a special creature that was close to humans, or was even perceived as a transformed human being. It was believed that the bear possessed the ability to think and the capacity to understand and react appropriately to human language and behavior. At the same time, bears were seen as the masters and rulers of furbearing animals and could therefore influence the outcome of a hunting enterprise.

The above-mentioned beliefs are also held by the Kets. However, their spiritual ties to this animal seem to be particularly deep and intimate. Perhaps this is why traditional beliefs about the bear have been alive for such a long time among the Kets, why there is such a wide range of folklore about the bear, and why there is a special emotional and very personal attitude toward ritualized behavior while hunting a bear.

Practically every field season I spent among the Kets—covering a span of more than thirty years (1956–89)—provided me with information on new aspects of this phenomenon. Especially memorable in this respect is my 1989 field trip, during which the ties between the killed (or sighted) bear and a real person who had already left the world of the living came into clear perspective (Alekseenko 1960; 1985; 1992).

According to the beliefs of the Kets, a human continues to live a different kind of existence after death; the tie between the deceased and the living is not interrupted once and forever. This bond was expressed in various forms, such as the institution of living substitutes for the deceased, special shamanistic seances, etc. Another of these forms was the bear festival. A bear was seen as a postmortem living representation of the deceased who willfully continued to have relationships with the living, especially with his or her relatives.

Situations in which people met a close and unforgotten deceased person were colored by a special emotional state. Who exactly had come was determined by omens and through oracles performed with a chopped-off bear paw. The guest could have died a long time ago, and only memories of his or her name could be preserved. Nevertheless, even in cases when among the participants of the ritual there were no people who had known the deceased, he or she received all of the attention ascribed to his or her status by the rules of etiquette.

The total number of possible visits by a deceased person seems to be indeterminate; however, the number should not exceed seven visits. The first visit must not take place earlier than seven years after the death of the person. Earlier visits would be considered a violation of the rules and a bad omen. Children who died before they reached the age of seven were considered an exception. Such a deceased child could show up for a visit as early as two or three years after its death. This is perhaps connected with Ket beliefs about a special life substance, which results in complete individualization of a person only at a particular age.

Deceased people can visit their relatives seven times. At any one time they can appear at the same age as during a previous visit, or at a different age, whether as a teenager, a mature adult, or an older person. However, at each appearance the person's age must be within the actual life span of the individual in question. A person who left this world at a young age could not appear to his or her relatives as an old bear. An old man could appear as an old man, a boy, a young man, or a mature adult, as if (in Western terms) he had reversed his life course. The bear that was found or killed had to be of the appropriate age. Moreover, sometimes deceased people could visit their relatives with their children or nephews/nieces (in such a case, bear cubs would be found in the den). In reality, these people could have died as adults and later than their parent (or uncle or aunt). However, their appearance as children or adolescents looked illogical only to me, the outsider, who was recording the information. The recorded information includes many examples of similar ritual visits that the Kets had with their relatives who appeared before them in the form of a bear.

In these images, complex from a European point of view but natural from the point of view of the Kets, one can find a specific understanding of time flow, in particular, an understanding of time periods that correspond to Western notions of "past," "present," and "future." Such a reconstruction is possible in the context of the beliefs about the life cycle present in the bear cult. All individuals at some point in time of their "real" existence have a past, a present, and, perhaps, a future within the frame of that existence. They also have a future in a different and special kind of existence (after death). Such a different kind of existence is the past, the present, and the future of their "real" existence, all at the same time. It is a complete repetition of the person's "real" existence. During this different kind of existence, a person has a past as well as a present and a future that have the same meaning as the "real" existence. In this view, categories of the past and the future for people who saw the real and the special kind of existence as one uninterrupted continuum of existence appeared more prolonged in time than the present or real, but illusionary reality. Perhaps it is here that one should look for the origins of the special value assigned to the past and the future.

The mythological, ritual, and social spheres give us enough examples of this special value. Mythological heroes (Great Al'ba, Ul'git, and others) lived among the people in the past and will return in the future. In the present, they exist in a transformed appearance (state); they are believed to have turned into a mountain range, river rapids, islands, and other forms (Alekseenko 1976: 74–75; Dul'zon 1972: 121–22; Ivanov and Toporov 1969: 151). Older Ket women could obtain high "male" social status. Their long past substantially influenced the norms of their everyday and ritual behavior.

If the data presented above were to be represented graphically, it would look something like the following:

"real" existence	different existence

0—1————————————2————————————3

time of one's existence

0 = point of "real" birth;
0–1 = a time period included in the life span of one's mother;
1–2 = existence of an individual (life as we understand it);
2–3 = different kind of existence.

Any reconstruction is an outsider's view and, therefore, may be an inadequate representation of reality. The notions of past, present, and future are given here only as possible Western counterparts of the Ket notions. The reconstructed time line is correct only if it is understood as one of the periods ("real" existence + a different kind of existence) in the general cycle of possible reincarnations of the individual. To what extent does the model representing a human time of existence refer to other temporal characteristics? In the Ket language, the notions of "future" or "next year" are rendered with the word *onte* or *ontel'*. It means "something that is behind, coming from the back, after this year." In graphic representation, the "future" should, therefore, take a place behind the "present" (as part of the "past"). This is possible only when time is viewed as a closed cycle. One can give many examples from Ket mythology that demonstrate the existence of the notion of cyclical time with natural and historical processes taking place within that cycle (temporal categorization of the world, general idea of reincarnation, and others). One can draw many such typological parallels between other cultures and the culture of the Kets in this respect.

The bear cult among the Kets shows another characteristic feature of a mythological perception of the world: the original divisionlessness of the space-time domain. An example of this feature is a metaphor in the myth about Kaigus, which gives sense to the whole bear ceremony: a bear reaches marriage age (temporal category), and this is seen as the ability "to overcome" seven stairs—seven steps of the father (spatial category).

Connections established with the deceased relative are the content of the second stage of the bear festival among the Kets. The other semantic stage (in the ceremony it was the first part) simulated the magical hunting practices of the people in order to revive the animals that had been killed, and to ensure future hunting luck. The two stages of the festival were independent in terms of their contents and time, and were marked by special dividing symbols. These symbols expressed the notion of changes in time as the result of cyclical renewal, a notion that is characteristic of Ket traditions in general. An example of renewal symbolism is the ritual washing of the head, which took place during the ceremony. The washing marked the independence of the second part and showed that people who were receiving the guest/deceased relative did not have anything to do with hunting the bear. O. V. Tyganova, a Ket knowledgeable in her language and traditions, put it this way: "They washed their heads and became new people" (Kreinovich 1969: 20). Living places were also to be renewed: "During the period of time when people were in their *chum*s [Ket dwellings] (i.e., after the men finished eating the boiled head of the bear), I put conifer needles around the fireplace and made a new *chum*" (Kreinovich 1969: 20). When the present author took part in a bear festival in 1971 on the Elogui River, the same goal was reached by washing the floor of the room where the ceremony took place.

Renewal in the mythological tradition of the Kets is always connected to temporal semantics (cf. the belief about the world's cyclical disappearances and appearances in a renewed state; by the way, this happens after the earth is "washed" by water [Anuchin 1914: 14]). Cyclical floods that divide the world's existence into temporal stages are characteristic of Ket cosmological myths (Alekseenko 1976: 69–70). The old name for the universe is related to the word "water": *ul's* (*ul'* is water). This word also means "a big water reservoir" (Yenisei, "sea").

The characteristic features of the traditional Ket world-view, as seen in their bear cult, can be looked at from various perspectives. One of them can be a general typological perspective, which shows, once again, that human consciousness develops along similar lines, no matter whether we are talking about an industrialized society or a society of taiga hunters. Another, not less important, aspect of this study is that it permits us to more adequately understand another culture and to avoid superficial approximations.

Note

The original Russian text of the article was translated by Irina Dubinina and stylistically edited by Megan Biesele. The final edit was provided by Peter Schweitzer, in consultation with the author.

References

Alekseenko, E. A. 1960. "Kul't medvedia u ketov." *Sovetskaia etnografiia* 4: 90–104.
_____. 1976. "Predstavleniia ketov o mire." In *Priroda i chelovek v religioznykh predstavleniiakh narodov Sibiri i Severa.* 67–105. Leningrad: Nauka.
_____. 1985. "Na medvezh'em prazdnike u ketov." *Sovetskaia etnografiia* 5: 92–97.
_____. 1992. "Materialy k izucheniiu kul'ta medvedia u ketov." Field materials, 1988–89.
Anuchin, V. I. 1914. "Ocherk shamanstva u eniseiskikh ostiakov." *Sbornik muzeia antropologii i etnografii* 2(2): 1–89.
Dul'zon, A. P. 1972. *Skazki narodov Sibirskogo Severa.* Tomsk: Izdatel'stvo Tomskogo gosudarstvennogo universiteta.
Ivanov, V. V., and V. N. Toporov. 1969. "Kommentarii k opisaniiu ketskoi mifologii." In *Ketskii sbornik: Mifologiia. Etnografiia. Teksty.* 148–66. Moscow: Nauka.
Kreinovich, E. A. 1969. "Medvezhii prazdnik u ketov." In *Ketskii sbornik: Mifologiia. Etnografiia. Teksty.* 6–112. Moscow: Nauka.

Chapter 27

LEXICON AS A SOURCE FOR UNDERSTANDING SEL'KUP KNOWLEDGE OF RELIGION

———————≫«◎»≪———————

Alexandra A. Kim

Religion is one of the most ancient, universal, and prominent spheres of social life. Naturally, it is reflected in language symbols, because, as Sapir established (1993: 272), in the lexicon one can find the reflection of the physical and social environment in which humans exist. In connection with this idea, the investigation of the linguistic aspects of religious beliefs may add new knowledge about the spiritual culture of hunters', fishermen's, and gatherers' societies that do not have written traditions. This chapter analyzes the linguistic aspects of the perception of the soul that have not been thoroughly investigated in the religion of the Sel'kups (one of the Siberian ethnic groups of the Samoyedic linguistic branch).

The life cycle of humans is closely connected with the notion of the soul. In Prokof'eva's opinion, each culture expresses its world-view through the soul, so that world-view is clearly expressed in humans' knowledge about themselves. It is of no use to try to isolate the specific notion of "soul" from the other aspects of religious beliefs, signs, elementary knowledge, culture, etc. (Prokof'eva 1961: 120).

It is taken for granted that "soul" constitutes a religious and mythological domain, and that the soul appears based on personifications of life processes in the human organism (Mify 1980: 414). But prior to the appearance of the concept of "soul" (which is linked to general animation), there existed a period when different features of human life activity (breath, blood, parts of organs of the body, consciousness, senses, motions, health, etc.) were personified. This is still true of the Samoyedic peoples. They long ago formed the picture in their minds of the plurality of souls living in a human being: breath-soul, shadow-soul, life-soul, blood-soul, etc.

The Sel'kup understanding of "soul" is rather complicated. It is not fully described in the anthropological literature; there are some partial data in papers and monographs, concerning, as a rule, no more than one of the aspects of this understanding. But the key to the definition of the stages of the development of the concepts of natural phenomena and their laws lies in a many-sided approach to the problem (Prokof'eva 1976: 7). In the Samoyedic lexicon, the word for "soul" (in the Christian understanding) is absent. In order to express the concept of "soul," a special lexical field is used that includes a number of elements, each of which has broad conceptual meanings. When translated, they will acquire different meanings, depending on the context of the utterance. Samoyedic people use a rather wide range of words that are generally translated into Russian as "soul" (Gracheva 1983: 52). For example, the Nganasans may translate all of the followings words as "soul" when talking in Russian: eyes (*seimy'*), brain (*die*), heart (*se*), blood (*kam*), breath (*bačü*), and in some other ways as the context requires (Gracheva 1983: 57). The Sel'kups usually include in this grouping the concepts of "soul" breath (*kɜjty*) and shadow (*tika*) (Prokof'eva 1976: 120). There is no generic word for the concept of "soul" in Nenets as well. The Nenetses, like other Samoyedic peoples, link life with the presence of breathing (*ind'*) (Khomich 1976: 23).

Sel'kup linguistic tradition shows a whole complex of soul concepts, consisting of soul components. I will provide an analysis of these concepts below. The choice of these soul terms was made according to the following criteria: (a) the existence of the term in the ethnographic literature and in folklore; (b) the presence of the term in dictionaries of any period; and (c) the usage of the term in linguistic literature.

Soul *qwej*

The term *qwej* was rather widespread among the Sel'kups from time immemorial. It is found in many different sources (mentioned above, see a, b, c). This term is likely to be a proto-Uralic remnant, because the lexeme *wajŋe/*wajm3 is seen in all Uralic languages; it meant "soul-breath" (Ajkhenwald 1989: 158). Janhunen proposes a very close reconstruction of the term for proto-Samoyedic, as close meanings are still preserved in different Samoyedic languages (Janhunen 1977: 173).

The Sel'kup word is given in the following variants in Castrén's dictionary: *kuei/kuai/kuaji*, and means "soul" (Castrén 1855: 279). According to to Grigorovskii's research, in the Ket group of the Sel'kups the word *qwai/qwoi* has more meanings: spirit, breath, soul, air (Helimski 1983: 81). Contemporary Sel'kup texts of a religious character use the word *kwej* in the meaning of "soul, spirit," e.g., *qup qwej nomne waz'ec'kun* "the man's spirit flies to god"; *qwə̄jə̄w čandʒin* "my spirit (or soul) has departed."

The word *qwaj* is fixed in the language of the Sel'kups of the Middle Ob River as a place name. They used it to refer to the river Ob or any other river in general. The etymology of this term leads to the meaning of "soul." Evidently, it is linked with a respectful attitude of Sel'kups to the major waterways of the region (Maloletko 1992: 12). The most interesting material is found in the Tym area. Besides the usual meanings for this base, it has entered a number of words connected with religious beliefs: (1) *wargy kuwei*—literally "great soul," e.g., the basic human's soul dwelling in his or her body and namely somewhere in the heart or forehead; (2) *kop podʒegyl tärgu kuwei* (or it can be met in abbreviated form as *kuwtärge*)—literally "the soul that has left man," which dwells in a family or tribal storehouse; (3) *kuwaloz* (*kuwej*— "soul" + *loz*—"spirit"), which was materialized in the form of *kuwtärge*; (4) *kuwtärge/qwudargu/kodargu/qudargu*—spirit, head of family spirits in the family cult storehouse; (5) *qudargu*—a shaman, "who has all the magic power," which permits him to perform religious duties (Kim 1992: 61; Uraev 1994: 78).

Northern Samoyedic data help us to understand the whole system of the functioning of soul-breath and its dynamics. The Nganasan *bačǔ, bait'u'* was translated by Castrén as "soul" (Castrén 1855: 279). Now the meaning "breath" is more widely accepted (Kosterkina and Khelimskii 1994). The Nganasans imagine that the soul-breath is living in the heart and is modeled in the form of strings, the sunbeam, and vapor. Enets *b'éddu'* has the meaning of "soul, breath" (Katzschmann and Pusztay 1978: 32). The Enetses have placed the soul-breath in the chest and in the abdomen. This soul departs to the upper world after a person's death, having left the body through the mouth or abdomen (in case of injury or autopsy) (Prokof'eva 1953: 206). Nenets *jind'* is met in the same meanings as "soul, air, vapor" (Castrén 1855). These meanings are given in detail in Tereshchenko's dictionary (1965). We must admit that this word in all Samoyedic languages possesses nearly the same meanings: breath → vapor/air → soul. This order is not counter to the thesis expressed by Borodina and Gack (1979: 9) that the meanings of concepts related to people's spiritual life are historically secondary, all of them being derived from designations for the objective reality, existing apart from humans.

The Samoyedic specific location of the soul-breath testifies to relics of the period when humans personified different parts of the body or its functions. With different localizations of the soul-breath, Samoyedic peoples left us different ways of conceiving of it. All of this permits us to

make a supposition that each Samoyedic group of people made an independent development of the notion "soul-breath." Thus, the proto-Uralic
people knew something concrete, connected with the living organism—
breath. The proto-Samoyedic people animated it; they began to transform it into soul. This conclusion is supported by the fact that in the
lexicon of proto-Uralic, no traces of shamanism, spiritual life, or ancestor
cult have been discovered (Osnovy 1974: 411). All meanings are likely to
have been developed from "breath" as an important component of vital
activity of human beings.

Soul *ella/ilsat*[1]

The terms *ella/ilsat* are used in the Sel'kup linguistic-cultural tradition
for designating "soul" and related concepts. The term *ella* was found in
the Vasiugan dialect, e.g., *qut larymbadyt tabyn ella pone igi čanǯeja*
"people feared lest his soul should get out"; *kedyl qunnan elladi t'aha* "the
shaman hasn't got his own soul"; *kubyl kunnan elladi idetko edekuk* "the
soul of the dead man turns into a spider." The Sel'kups from this region
thought that the souls of dead people (drowned, lost in the forest, or
frozen)—*elladyt*—turned into *mad'et qut* (wood-goblins) and lived in
the forest in *porelika* (small barns or storehouses).

In the Tym dialect, the word *ilsat* is used with the meaning "soul."
This term is also met in the Taz dialect and was investigated by Prokof'eva. In her morpheme analysis, the stem *il-*, which is common to
many languages, is singled out; the other component, *sat-*, is an ancient
Samoyedic suffix of the verbal noun of instrument of action. Literally,
the word *ilsat* signifies "the thing by means of which one lives" (Prokof'eva 1976: 120).

As Prokof'eva's materials show, the Sel'kups on the Taz River have a
concept of the soul that somewhat differs from the above mentioned.
This soul is "humanlike": he (or she) takes after a man in every aspect.
Ilsat leaves a human for a period of time while he or she is sleeping, but
the person remains safe. If it leaves someone for a long period of time,
that person becomes seriously ill. If the soul is away for a very considerable period, the person dies. Every living being has its own *ilsat*, which can
eat and drink. It can turn into different things. Thus, the shaman can free
the *ilsat* from evil spirits and insert it in the form of a fish egg back into a
human (Prokof'eva 1976: 123–124).

Ivar Paulson calls *ilsat* "free soul" (*Freiseele*), which after a person's
death goes into the lower world, where it lives the same life as before
(Paulson et al. 1962: 117). In A. V. Golovnev's interpretation, the *ilsat* of
an ordinary person never crosses the line separating the earth from the

sky and the earth from the underground world. After a person's death, it settles into a bear, assuming the bear's appearance, and continues its existence. The exceptions are the shamans' souls, which are capable of breaking the border between the earth and the sky and entering the solar circle. The borderline between the earth and the underground world can be broken by the soul that appears as a bear, because the bear is the representative of "the lower world" (Golovnev 1992: 48).

The Sel'kup stem *il-* is met in the mythological term *ilyntyl kota imyl'a* "a living old granny," "the old woman of vitality." This mythological image is found only in northern Sel'kup (Taz River) material. In Prokof'eva's opinion, the Sel'kup interpret *ilyntyl* as "containing life," "having (possessing) life," etc. The earliest image of *ilyntyl' kota* is connected with the horizontal concept of the world. Its (the soul's) dwelling in the upper course of the river was associated with the "upper world." *Ilyntil kota* is the creator of life (Prokof'eva 1961: 57). The Sel'kup stem *il-* can be also found in a number of words connected with the conception of life: "to live"; "life, existence"; "to come to life"; "living," etc. (Kim 1995a: 136). The verb *ilyqo* has some additional meanings, e.g., "to graze, to feed on growing grass," etc. The meanings "youth" and "young" are found in the words *il'mat, il'matyl*.

The component analysis, combined with the data of cultural anthropology, permits us to interpret the term *ilsat* as a certain life subsistence (life source, meal, sun) existing in space. The data on Sel'kup correspond to those of other Samoyedic languages. The life cycle of the Nganasans is also linked with the lexical field whose words have developed from the proto-Uralic stem **elä-*. Everything that is connected with the existence of living organisms (humans, animals, plants) can be combined by the word *nilu/nily* or *nilimti/nilymny* "life" (Gracheva 1983: 53).

The Nganasan lexeme *nilu/nily* is present in mythological material as well; the demiurge *n'əlⱥta ŋuo* (lit., life spirit) gives each person a thread of life—*nilu byny*, which links him or her with the creator and which exists during his or her entire lifetime. It is likely that in this mythology a more ancient solar cult is reflected, which was substituted later on by a syncretistic figure or demiurge (in the period when Christianity was introduced) (Lamber 1994: 173). The soul is responsible for the psychological functions of humans and is often personified in the image of a bird—the representative of the "upper world," where the soul travels after a person's death (Popov 1976: 31–32). In the Nenets language, the stem *il'/iler'* has entered a number of words linked with the concept "life." A considerable part of this lexical field is connected with the secular sphere. Tereshchenko's dictionary (1965) gives the words with the same stem that can express rather abstract notions (such as *il'/iler* "life," *iles'* "to live," *ilen'z* "the source of existence"), as well as words signifying quite concrete referents (e.g., *ilebts'* "wild reindeer," *ilebej* "fresh, green plants," etc.).

The same stem is used in the sacred sphere: *il'ca* signifies two objects that are put together and are used by the shaman to foretell the future or during a talk with the dead. The verb with this stem means "to fortune tell or to talk to the soul of the dead by means of two objects leaned against each other." In mythology, this stem has entered a word combination that signifies "God who is the patron of deer-breeding and who is often identified with Num," e.g., *jilembert*, lit., "owning the herd" (Mifologicheskii slovar' 1990: 397). In Enets ethnology, the lexeme *jire* "to live," as it is seen from the synchronic layer, seems not to enter any complexes linked with the notion of the soul, and it does not show any cult meaning. However, in Enets mythology this stem is preserved in the name of their supreme deity—demiurge *djireponde* (cf. Nenets *jelembert*)—"the owner of the deer's life" (Katzschmann and Pusztay 1978). This correlation allows us to propose the development of abstract notions from the secular sphere, such as deer > meal > source of existence > life.

Thus, the analysis of the lexical field of the proto-Uralic stem *elä-, restricted only to Samoyedic materials, has allowed us to single out a semantic dominant, "life," which has various contextual tints of meaning: life-meal, life-growing/blooming, life-sun/ray/thread, life-soul.

In all Samoyedic languages, the stem under analysis has many derivatives often used with ancient proto-Samoyedic/Uralic exponents. Many Samoyedic derivatives refer to the vocabulary of psychic phenomena and the notion of the soul. The statistical method of Büky (which he applied to the Hungarian language) allows us to consider such words to be very important for signifying human psychic phenomena in the language of an ancient period (Büky 1989: 130). The Samoyedic and Hungarian materials show that even in proto-Uralic times the stem *elä- started to be used to signify the human psychic state. Peripheral meanings of the Uralic stem, preserved in Samoyedic languages, as well as separate mythologemes have led to the hypothesis that mental meanings of the stem *elä- have developed from the secular sphere: the concrete source of life (sun, meal, umbilical cord) > life > soul.

The identification of life with one of its sources—meals, warmth (sun)—probably refers to the most ancient time. This is supported by other ancient cultures: cf. *Ila, Ida* in Vedic and Indic mythology is the goddess of sacrifice and prayer. *Ilamatekutli* (old owner) in Aztec myths is the goddess tied with the cult of the earth and maize (Indian corn), which is one of the aspects of the goddess of the earth and childbearing (Mifologicheskii slovar' 1990). The Uralic stem *elä- correlates with the Altaic *el* "population; peaceful life"; Dravidian *il/?el* "dwelling"; Afroasiatic *(j)l* "existence, being, population." Illich-Svitych traces this stem to Nostratic *ʔeLA* "to live" (Illich-Svitych 1971: 267).

Soul *kaga*

In order to single out the word *kaga*, anthropological materials connected with Sel'kup shamanism were used. These were collected by G. I. Pelikh during her expeditions to the Sel'kups on the Taz River, and are used along with cultural and linguistic data from other Samoyedic groups as well. According to Pelikh, *kaga* meant only a person's soul, and it was closely linked with a finger, e.g., *kagal' mun* "a thumb" (Pelikh 1980: 32). Sometimes this term served to indicate not only a thumb but the soul itself. Respectively, the combination *kagal' mun* literally means "a grave thumb" or "a grave soul." Only a human can possess such a soul. It was believed that a human who had lost a thumb turned into an animal. After death, the soul, *kaga*, together with the body, descends into the grave. It lingers longer on the surface of the ground only as an exception. It happened in this way with the shaman Gordeika, whose thumb was cut off. His soul *kaga* became a soul-assistant of somebody who held his "bone" (Pelikh 1980: 22–31).

The word *kaga* has the other meaning "grave," which is even more widespread and more archaic. The Sel'kup name for the mole is *kaglal'*, which is sometimes translated as "the grave spirit" (from *kaga*—"the grave") and thus is linked with the term *kaga*. It is the spirit in the image of "the ground mole." Spoken about indirectly, it is usually called *medvedka* (the ground bear). During his ceremonies, the shaman called the grave spirit *kala* (Pelikh 1980: 28–30). We find this word in the expedition materials, e.g., *qalat; qall'i* "the ground mole." The relationship of this word to the lexeme *kålmɜ(-)* "dead body (corpse)," "spirit" (Janhunen 1977: 59) and further to *kåə̂-* "to die" is evident (Janhunen 1977: 56). In G. M. Vasilevich's opinion, words containing *kɜl/hɜl* are rooted in ancient Asiatic languages, and these words are connected with the world of the dead (Vasilevich 1949: 156).

The Sel'kup word *kaga* goes back to proto-Samoyedic *kə̂jkə̂-* "spirit" (Janhunen 1977: 51). Its cult meanings are found in the languages of the northern Samoyedic group. In Enets, the relic of this proto-Samoyedic stem is the lexeme *kaga/haha/kiho*. This term means a mediator between people or, to be more precise, between a shaman *budtodɜ* and the upper (sky) spirits, who will convey the request to *ngo*. The spirit *kiho* had its personal contacts with the supreme deity/sky/sun. Besides, *kiho* had the meaning of "the spirit of a sacred place" (Prokof'eva 1953: 223). In Nenets, the lexeme *hɜ-hɜ* is also a true relic of a proto-Samoyedic stem.

According to Nenets cult tradition, *hз-hз* is the host of a sacred place (defined by the shaman). The word *hз-hз* (*hз* in the western tundra, *hзg*, *hзgi* in old literature) possessed many meanings. It signified sacred rocks and stones of average size, the cut-off parts of rocks of quaint shape, and anthropomorphic figures of wood or metal, which were usually kept in a *chum* (tent-shaped dwelling) or a special sledge (*hзhз han*). In combination with other substantives, the word *hз-hз* can be translated as "holy," "sacred" (Khomich 1971: 24). The word *hз-hз* could mean not only objects of surrounding reality but also figures made by humans. It can be easily supposed that this term was common for cult objects among the Nenetses (Khomich 1971: 240–41; Prokof'eva 1953: 224). It is notable that A. S. Schrenk in 1854 paid attention to the word *haj*, which primarily signified an idol and which entered a number of word combinations of religious character. Later these combinations migrated from pagans to the Christian religion (Donner 1932: 160).

Soul *kedo*

One more term is met in the anthropological literature to signify the grave spirit—*kedo* (Pelikh 1972: 116). In Pelikh's materials, the spirit *kedo* is very similar to the spirit *kaga*. The Narym Sel'kups (except shamans) know the spirit *kedo*, which after a person's death descends together with the corpse into the grave. *Kedo* remains in the head of the dead body until the body becomes rotten. After having turned into a spider, *kedo* remains in the soil (Pelikh 1972: 116). The word combination *qзtysymyl' tзtty*, seen in other Sel'kup religious sources, literally meant "mysterious, quaint ground," and the word *qзtysymyl'* is derived from *kety* "wisdom, mystery, quaintness." The term *qзtysymyl'* is used to define places that have become notable through certain events. The example given by Prokof'eva refers to a territory that is known because of the death of a shaman during his ceremony (Prokof'eva 1977: 67).

The term *kedo*, to signify soul, evidently has its origins in the proto-Samoyedic stem **ket-*: "cunning (slyness)" (Janhunen 1977: 66). The Sel'kup language stock presents the following examples: *qзty* "the shaman's slyness, which is demonstrated in performing miracles"; *qзttyqo* "to foretell"; *qзtypōqy* "dangerously (astonishingly)"; *pengyrhe kedyča* "playing the *pengyr* (a national instrument) during the shaman's action"; *kedhul qup* "shaman," etc. The stem **ket-* is found in Donner's materials to signify the shaman's magic clapper (stick), which is covered with a bearskin and has a picture of a serpent or any other animal inside (Joki 1978: 376).

It is necessary to mention as a typological parallel the lexeme *kot/ kut/hat*, which is used with similar meanings by the Tatars, Bashkirs,

Chuvashes, Udmurts, and Maris. This lexeme has a wide range of meanings: "soul," "spirit," "happiness," "wealth," "coziness," "prosperity," "good appearance" (Akhmet'ianov 1981: 34), and is widely spread in other Turkic and Altaic languages as well. In Teleut and Yakut it has the meaning of "soul," "the soul of living beings" (Räsänen 1969: 241). It is possible to compare this material with the Sel'kup stem *ket-, because one of its derivatives has the meaning of "luck" (cf. *kyne* "luck in hunting") (Irikov 1995: 46).

We can make a supposition about the development of the abstract and cult meanings from the Samoyedic lexeme *ketə̑. In my opinion, it has diverged from the lexeme *ket- "to say, to tell" (Janhunen 1977: 66; Kim 1995b: 164–65). This is not surprising because the act of uttering was accepted by ancient peoples as something sacred and magic. The person who possessed the power of foretelling was considered to have supernatural abilities, wisdom, and slyness. Later on, the words expressing these qualities started to express abstract notions, but they did not lose their ties with the inner form of the word.

Soul *kor*

The Sel'kups use the word *kor* to signify the abstract notion "male source (basis)." At the same time, it is the name of one of the men's souls (Pelikh 1992: 79). G. I. Pelikh writes that all males had an additional soul, *kor*. Having lost this soul, they turned into defective creatures (*mombel* "fool," *kurugatijn'a* "mad, rabid") and probably into women. The latter change is connected with transvestism that is widely spread among shamans; the shaman is supposed to turn into a woman after the devil has eaten one of his souls (Pelikh 1980: 29–32). Evidently, the soul *kor* is tied to the "third finger" (Castrén 1855: 119), which defines somehow its location, *kor-mun*. The Sel'kup lexeme *kor* is often used to signify male animals: "ox, stallion," "white salmon," "ermine (or stoat)," "male," "wild stag." The supposition that the lexeme *kor* probably was used in rather an abstract sense (cf. male soul) is based on indirect evidence, for it served as a name of a storehouse for men (cf. *sessan* "the storehouse for women") (Pelikh 1980: 30). This term was also used in the word combination *qorkumyl' qagly* "male sledge" (Prokof'eva 1977: 71).

The Sel'kup lexeme goes back to proto-Samoyedic *korå "male, stag" (Janhunen 1977: 74), and even further to proto-Uralic *koj(e)-ra "male" (Rédei 1986–88: 168). It is possible to draw the conclusion that the meaning of the proto-Uralic reconstruction was more concrete (evidently close to the proto-Samoyedic reconstruction of the meaning "stag"). In other words, the names for concrete male animals existed prior to the name signifying "man's source (basis)." This very meaning allows us to analyze the word *kor* alongside all of the other names for soul.

Soul *sang*

There are also reasons to consider the lexeme *sang*, as the name for a partial soul, if we take into consideration the works in Sel'kup anthropology. Of course, the lexeme *sang* is conventionally translated as "soul." A more precise translation, however, is "power/life vitality/shaman's power." This soul (or a life-vital element) is found in all living beings. In space, this soul is connected with the sun; in the human body, it is evidently tied to the little finger (*sengai muna*) and with the umbilical cord (*šon'*, *son'*, *san'*—"umbilicus"). The life vitality *sang* remains in the body of a newborn only after the umbilicus has been healed (or skinned over). The appearance of the first teeth testifies to the fact that the life vitality *sang* has strengthened in the baby's body (Pelikh 1980: 27, 33).

Anthropological and linguistic analysis allows us to link *sang* "soul/vitality" with the following elements, all of which have sacred meanings. *Sytky/sit* means a divine place in the *chum* (tent-shaped dwelling), which was situated opposite the entrance, behind the hearth (fireplace). The back part of the *chum* was also considered sacred and called *sytky*. It was strictly forbidden to go through this place or outside near it. A dead person was usually placed on this very spot if he or she was from the people's kin (Prokof'eva 1977: 69–70). These words have originated from the proto-Samoyedic root *sɨŋ (Janhunen 1977: 141).

Sä means "coffin." The burial ceremony from the village of Makovskoe (Krasnoiarsk region) is described as follows: the coffin *sä* was made of planks and was placed directly into the grave and covered with chesses (boards) above. The same term was used in the region of the Middle Ob, e.g., *säm od'ingu as k'er'eg'eŋ* "the coffin (acc. case) needn't be covered." The verb *sangergu* "to bury" is denominative. In the settlement Ust'-Ozernoe on the river Ket, the coffin was called *syj mat* "the house of the dead." Maybe this lexeme has a common origin with Finno-Ugric *s'ure "to die" (see Rédei 1986–88: 489); compare also Nenets *s'urtva* "funeral" (Tereshchenko 1965: 591).

Sesan means "a sacred family *lozil* (storehouse)." According to Prokof'eva's data, there was *sesan* "a sacred storehouse of spirits" on the family territory deep in the taiga (Prokof'eva 1952: 99). In the village of Makovskoe, we find the word in the following form: *så sanykka* "the storehouse for deities."

Se/sy/š'ö means "umbilicus, umbilical cord": *syl' myty* "(man's) stomach," *söl'/süja* "umbilicus"; *söl' čermə* "umbilical cord." These terms are likely to take their origin from proto-Samoyedic *suj₃ "kidney" (cf. Jan-hunen 1977: 143). The folklore tradition links ideas of death and immortality with the umbilicus. In G. I. Pelikh's opinion, the Sel'kup notion of umbilicus is rather complicated. Sel'kups use the word *se* to signify only that part of the umbilical cord that is linked with the placenta, which is under the influence of evil forces of the underground world. Therefore, the umbilical cord and the placenta are buried in the ground. Apart from *se*, there are some derivatives that signify different parts of the umbilicus. *Šenilaka* means a part of a tied umbilicus, which is left on the baby's body to dry and fall off. This section of umbilicus was sewn into a rag and was kept all through the person's life. The Sel'kups thought that one could influence *šenilaka* and in this way change the person's fortune. The other word *šön'* means the umbilicus on the man's abdomen (belly). It is also connected with a special mystic power. This shamanic power differs from usual physical strength (named *or*). A man gets this power through the umbilicus and in the same way returns it. As the legend goes, the mytho-logic Sel'kup hero *Itt'e* used his umbilicus in addressing God: he asked an old woman to cut his abdomen and threw his umbilicus up toward God. The umbilicus was the medium between him and God. Having performed its function, the umbilicus returned to its place (Donner 1913: 9; Pelikh 1980: 27).

Šütty has the meaning of "shaman's little iron spade." It is known from Pelikh's work that one Sel'kup shaman (Ivan Kalin) was addressed like that. This "little spade" evidently possessed the shaman's power. It displayed an enormous invisible power, which appeared on the spade in the form of a mask and was ready to act under the shaman's orders. The speakers say that the shaman Kalin wanted to rub this mask away, because he could not get rid of it by his magic power. The Sel'kups believed that if the mask remained and did not disappear, the spirit would become independent and would not submit to the shaman any longer (Pelikh 1980: 83).

It is easy to proceed to correlating these terms and notions with others, if we take the words for heart (Nganasan *sa*, Sel'kup *sicy*), scabbard (sheath) (Nganasan *sieŋ*, Sel'kup *sen*), eye (Nganasan *sejmy*, Sel'kup *sej*), serpent (Sel'kup *sü*), and others. E. P. Boldt, who worked with the Nganasans, tes-tifies that a number of words can be easily explained, even by middle-aged people who refer to such objects as cult things (Boldt 1989: 58). Boldt considers that such examples are not a mere phonetic coincidence but rather that they have sprung from a common Ob-Ugric/Samoyedic source (stock). Their persistence is explained by the fact that the pecu-liar world-view to which they refer is still maintained by these peoples (Boldt 1989: 56).

Soul *tika*

Ti/tika means "soul-shadow, shadow." Although we find some information in one of Prokof'eva's articles, the concept of this soul is not quite clear to us as yet. Evidently, every human possesses *ilintil' tika*, literally, "living shadow." The dead do not have such a soul. Sel'kups explain that a person's shadow disappears after death and turns into a spirit, which is called *kogynčitil ilyl' tika*, literally, "the shadow which is ceasing to exist." Perhaps this is an idea about the dead and about one of the most complicated souls, namely soul-shadow (*tika*). Maybe after a person's death, this soul continues to live underground, bearing the name of one component—*tika* (Prokof'eva 1976: 120, 125).

In the Sel'kup language, the term *tika* is found in the meaning of "shadow," "reflection." The Sel'kup word *tika* consists of two components. The second component is the nonproductive suffix (at present, the diminutive suffix) -*ka*, which goes back to the ancient proto-Samoyedic suffix *-k. The latter is supposed to have been developed from a full word (morpheme) of spatial meaning (Boldt 1989: 39–40; Kuznetsova et al. 1980: 336). Evidently, the following words were formed from the first component *ti-*: *tity* "cloud"; *tinoly* "cloud, black cloud"; *timpyqo* "to fly" (of birds and planes); *til'ciqo* "to fly for a while." It is possible that this stem is found in some words of sacred, cult character, e.g., *tinaliqo* "to be delirious (rave)"; *tissa* "an arrow with an arrowhead in the form of two-toothed fork" (shamans used such a fork during the ceremony dedicated to the dead, cf. Prokof'eva 1976: 124); *ti* "the distance between the tips of the third fingers of outstretched arms" (the arm and fingers often had some cult meanings, because they were used in rituals, cf. Bykonia 1995: 36); *tityk* "the shaman's cap" (this component of the shaman's dress is not yet deciphered; cf. Prokof'eva 1949: 341; 1971: 22).

The Sel'kup lexemes with the base *ti-* originated from proto-Samoyedic *tiə̂ and its derivative *tiə̂tə̂, which both mean "cloud," "shadow" (Janhunen 1977: 162). The meaning of soul-shadow is marked in Nenets, e.g., *t'i* and other phonetic variants (Lehtisalo 1956: 130). In Tereshchenko's Nenets-Russian dictionary, the lexeme *tid* (except in the meaning of "shadow") can have such abstract meanings as "envy" or "offense" (Tereshchenko 1965: 657).

The absence of a word with the meaning "soul-shadow" from Samoyedic materials may be explained by the fact that these peoples have already lost their animistic religious beliefs. It is, however, evident that other abstract notions, characterizing emotional and psychological states, have appeared on the basis of a previous abstraction, namely "shadow-soul."

Conclusion

From the Sel'kup ethnolinguistic data on spiritual culture, we single out seven partial soul concepts that constitute the complex of vital elements necessary for life. The concept of "soul" has developed in Sel'kup spiritual culture from signifying concrete things (breath, vapor, air, etc.) through models extracted from these material things into the direction of abstractness. Not all partial soul concepts represent highly developed abstract notions. In many cases, one can trace their development from the signification of concrete things into abstract concepts. The cultural abstractness appears to be based on objective reality; in a similar way, the lexical symbol is borne on the basis of already existing symbols signifying concrete things. This correlation may result from a general tendency of cultural and linguistic development—from the simple to the complex, and from the concrete to the abstract. The Sel'kup material shows that there is only one term for "soul," *ilsat*, in which the abstractness is linguistically marked by means of a word-building suffix. This word-building element evidently favored the transformation into abstract meaning. As the result of its constant usage, this lexeme started to express the general notion of "soul." Other words for "soul" were used without such special suffixes and therefore have preserved their plurality. Here, their central meaning is defined by the inner form of the word, which is linked with concrete things, and their abstract meanings shifted to the periphery.

Notes

The original Russian text was translated by the author and stylistically edited by Megan Biesele. The final edit was provided by Peter Schweitzer, in consultation with the author.

1. Data about the proto-Uralic stem *elä- were reported at the Eighth Congress of Finno-Ugrists in Finland, August 1995 (Kim 1995a).

References

Ajkhenwald, A., E. Helimski, and V. Petrukhin. 1989. "On Earliest Finno-Ugrian Mytho-logic Beliefs: Comparative and Historical Considerations for Reconstruction." In *Uralic Mythology and Folklore*. Ethnologica Uralica 1. M. Hoppál and J. Pentikäinen, eds. 155–59. Budapest: Ethnographic Institute of the Hungarian Academy of Sciences. Helsinki: Finnish Literature Society.

Akhmet'ianov, R. G. 1981. *Obshchaia leksika dukhovnoi kul'tury narodov Srednego Povol'zh'ia*. Moscow: Nauka.

Boldt, E. P. 1989. *Imennoe slovoobrazovanie nganasanskogo iazyka*. Novosibirsk: Nauka.

Borodina, M. A., and V. G. Gack. 1979. *K tipologii i metodike istoriko- semanticheskikh issledovanii*. Leningrad: Nauka.

Büky, B. 1989. "Hungarian Terminology for Soul and Related Concepts." In *Uralic Mythology and Folklore*. Ethnologica Uralica 1. M. Hoppál and J. Pentikäinen, eds. 129–34. Budapest: Ethnographic Institute of the Hungarian Academy of Sciences. Helsinki: Finnish Literature Society.

Bykonia, V. V. 1995. "Istoki novoobrazovanii v sisteme chislitel'nykh sel'kupskogo iazyka." In *Metodika kompleksnykh issledovanii kul'tur u narodov Zapadnoi Sibiri*. 35–37. Tomsk: Izdatel'stvo Tomskogo gosudarstvennogo universiteta.

Castrén, M. A. 1855. *Wörterverzeichnisse aus den samojedischen Sprachen*. St. Petersburg.

Donner, K. 1913. "A Samoyed Epic." *Journal de la Société Finno-Ougrienne* 30: 1–12.

Donner, K., ed. 1932. *Samojedische Wörterverzeichnisse*. Helsinki: Suomalais- ugrilainen Seura.

Golovnev, A. V. 1992. "Space View of the Sel'kup." In *Ural'skaia mifologiia*. 50–52. Syktyvkar.

Gracheva, G. N. 1983. *Traditsionnoe mirovozzrenie okhotnikov Taimyra*. Leningrad: Nauka.

Helimski, E. 1983. *The Language of the First Selkup Books*. Studia uralo-altaica 22. Szeged.

Illich-Svitych, V. M. 1971. *Opyt sravneniia nostraticheskikh iazykov*. Moscow: Nauka.

Irikov, S. I. 1995. "Traditsii i obychai sel'kupov." In *Materialy nauchnoi konferentsii 'Istoriia i sovremennost' narodov Iamala'*. 43–46. Salekhard: Okruzhnaia nauchnaia laboratoriia etnografii i etnolinguistiki: Iamala.

Janhunen, J. 1977. *Samojedischer Wortschatz. Gemeinsamojedische Etymologien*. Castrenianumin toimitteita 17. Helsinki: Suomalais-ugrilainen Seura.

Joki, A. J. 1978. "Notes on Selkup Shamanism." In *Shamanism in Siberia*. V. Diószegi and M. Hoppál, eds. 373–86. Budapest: Akadémiai Kiadó.

Katzschmann, M., and J. Pusztay. 1978. *Jenissej-Samojedisches (enzisches) Wörter-verzeichnis*. Hamburg: Buske.

Khomich, L. V. 1971. "O nekotorykh predmetakh kul'ta nadymskikh nentsev." In *Religioznye predstavleniia i obriady narodov Sibiri v XIX–nachale XX veka*. 239–47. Leningrad: Nauka.

———. 1976. "Predstavleniia nentsev o prirode i cheloveke." In *Priroda i chelovek v religioznykh predstavleniiakh narodov Sibiri i Severa*. 16–30. Leningrad: Nauka.

Kim, A. A. 1992. "Tomskii etnograf R. A. Uraev o funktsionirovanii sistemy dush u tymskikh sel'kupov." In *Sibirskie chteniia. Tezisy dokladov*. 60–62. St. Petersburg: Rossiiskaia Akademiia nauk.

———. 1995a. "Preuralic *elä- in Samoyedic Ethnos." In *Congressus Octavus Internationalis Fenno-Ugristarum, pars VI*. 135–38. Juväskylä: Gummerus kirjapaino Oy.

———. 1995b. "Shamanit' po-sel'kupski." In *Iazyki narodov Sibiri*. 161–66. Tomsk: Izdatel'stvo Tomskogo gosudarstvennogo universiteta.

Kosterkina, N., and E. A. Khelimskii. 1994. "Malye kamlaniia bol'shogo shamana." In *Taimyrskii etnolingvisticheskii sbornik*. 17–146. Moscow: Rossiiskii gosudarstvennyi gumanitarnyi universitet.

Kuznetsova A. I., E. A. Khelimskii, and E. V. Grushkina. 1980. *Ocherki po sel'kupskomu iazyku*. Moscow: Moskovskii gosudarstvennii universitet.

Lamber, J.-L. 1994. "Doch' solntsa dlia nganasanskogo shamana." In *Taimyrskii etnolingvisticheskii sbornik*. 172–89. Moscow: Rossiiskii gosudarstvennyi gumanitarnyi universitet.

Lehtisalo, T. 1956. *Juraksamojedisches Wörterbuch*. Helsinki: Suomalais-ugrilainen Seura.

Maloletko, A. M. 1992. *Paleotoponimika*. Tomsk: Izdatel'stvo Tomskogo gosudarstvennogo universiteta.

Mifologicheskii slovar'. 1990. *Mifologicheskii slovar'*. Moscow: Sovetskaia entsiklopediia.

Mify. 1980. *Mify narodov mira: entsiklopediia. Tom 1, A-K*. Moscow: Sovetskaia entsiklopediia.

Osnovy. 1974. *Osnovy finno-ugorskogo iazykoznaniia (voprosy proiskhozhdeniia i razvitiia finno-ugorskikh iazykov)*. Moscow: Nauka.

Paulson, I., Å Hultkrantz, and K. Jettmar. 1962. *Die Religionen Nordeurasiens und der amerikanischen Arktis*. Stuttgart: W. Kohlhammer.

Pelikh, G. I. 1972. *Proiskhozhdenie sel'kupov*. Tomsk: Izdatel'stvo Tomskogo gosudarstvennogo universiteta.

———. 1980. "Materialy po sel'kupskomy shamanstvu." In *Etnografiia Severnoi Azii*. 1–64. Novosibirsk: Nauka.

Popov, A. A. 1976. "Dusha i smert' po vozzreniiam nganasan." In *Priroda i chelovek v religioznykh predstavleniiakh narodov Sibiri i Severa*. 31–42. Leningrad: Nauka.

Prokof'eva, E. D. 1949. "Kostium sel'kupskogo (ostiako-samoedskogo shamana)." In *Sbornik muzeia antropologii i etnografii 11*. 335–75. Moscow-Leningrad: Izdatel'stvo Akademii nauk SSSR.

———. 1952. "K voprosu o sotsial'noi organizatsii sel'kupov (rod i fratriia)." In *Sibirskii etnograficheskii sbornik I*. 88–107. Moscow-Leningrad: Izdatel'stvo Akademii nauk SSSR.

———. 1953. "Materialy po religioznym predstavleniiam entsev." In *Sbornik muzeia antropologii i etnografii 14*. 195–230. Moscow-Leningrad: Izdatel'stvo Akademii nauk SSSR.

———. 1961. "Predstavleniia sel'kupskikh shamanov o mire (po risunkam i akvareliam sel'kupov)." In *Sbornik muzeia antropologii i etnografii 20*. 54–74. Moscow-Leningrad: Izdatel'stvo Akademii nauk SSSR.

———. 1971. "Shamanskie kostiumy narodov Sibiri v XIX–nachale XX veka." In *Sbornik muzeia antropologii i etnografii 27*. 5–100. Leningrad: Izdatel'stvo Akademii nauk SSSR.

———. 1976. "Starye predstavleniia sel'kupov o mire." In *Priroda i chelovek v religioznykh predstavleniiakh narodov Sibiri i Severa*. 106–28. Leningrad: Nauka.

———. 1977. "Nekotorye religioznye kul'ty tazovskikh sel'kupov." In *Pamiatniki kultury narodov Sibiri i Severa (vtoraia polovina XIX–nachalo XX v.) (Sbornik muzeia antropologii i etnografii 33)*. 66–79. Leningrad: Nauka.

Räsänen, M. 1969. *Versuch eines etymologischen Wörterbuchs der Turksprachen*. Helsinki: Suomalais-ugrilainen Seura.

Rédei, K. 1986–88. *Uralisches etymologisches Wörterbuch, Band 1*. Wiesbaden: Otto Harrassowitz.

Sapir, E. 1993. *Izbrannye trudy po iazykoznaniiu i kul'turologii*. Moscow: Progress.

Tereshchenko, N. M. 1965. *Nenetsko-russkii slovar'*. Moscow: Sovetskaia entsiklopediia.

Uraev, R. A. 1994. "Materialy k shamanizmu tymskikh sel'kupov." *Trudy Tomskogo gosudarstvennogo ob"edinennogo istoriko-arkhitekturnogo muzeia 7*: 73–85. Tomsk: Izdatel'stvo Tomskogo gosudarstvennogo universiteta.

Vasilevich, G. M. 1949. "Iazykovye dannye po terminu khel ~ kel." In *Sbornik muzeia antropologii i etnografii 11*. 154–56. Moscow: Izdatel'stvo Akademii nauk SSSR.

NOTES ON CONTRIBUTORS

Evgeniia A. Alekseenko graduated from Moscow State University in 1953 with an M.A. thesis in ethnography entitled "The Ethnographic Materials of I. Lepekhin" (in Russian). Her book *The Kets: Historical-Ethnographic Sketches* (in Russian; Leningrad: Nauka) was published in 1967, and was based on her Ph.D. thesis. Altogether, she has published approximately 150 publications, most of them on the ethnography of the Kets. Between 1956 and 1991 she conducted numerous field studies in various districts of the Krasnoyarsk region. She is currently a senior scientific staff member of the Department of the Ethnology of Siberia at the Museum of Anthropology and Ethnography in St. Petersburg, Russia. Her research interests include ethnogenesis, the ethnic history of the peoples of the Yenisei North, and the traditional world-view of the peoples of Siberia.

David G. Anderson (Ph.D., Cambridge, 1996) is Assistant Professor of Anthropology at the University of Alberta and Adjunct Professor at the Canadian Circumpolar Institute. Dr. Anderson lectures on ecological anthropology, aboriginal rights, national identity, and on the ethnology of the circumpolar North. His continuing research is on the ecology and epistemology of caribou hunters and reindeer herders in both the Siberian and Canadian Arctic. His forthcoming book, *Identity and Ecology in Arctic Siberia: The Number One Reindeer Brigade*, will be published by Oxford University Press (scheduled for 2000).

Elena P. Batianova received her Ph.D. from the Department of Ethnography at Moscow State University and is currently a senior scientific staff member at the Institute of Ethnology and Anthropology of the Russian Academy of Sciences. She has conducted many field research studies in southern and northeastern Siberia. She is the author of more than fifty articles about the peoples of those areas. Her research interests include social organization, world-view, and spiritual culture.

Megan Biesele currently teaches as a self-employed academic at Texas A&M University, College Station, Texas. She has adjunctships at A&M, Rice University in Houston, and the University of Nebraska/Lincoln, and is a Research Associate at the Texas Archaeological Research Laboratory of the University of Texas/Austin. She helped found the Kalahari Peoples Fund in 1973 and currently serves as its coordinator. For periods in the 1970s, 1980s and 1990s, Biesele worked with Ju/'hoan San communities in Botswana and Namibia as an advocate and documentarian, and served as director of a nongovernment organization (NGO), the Nyae Nyae Development Foundation of Namibia, during the years spanning Namibia's transition to independence (1987–92). She is an elected member of the Committee for Human Rights (CfHR) of the American Anthropological Association.

Dr. Biesele received her Ph.D. in social anthropology from Harvard University in 1975. Her research interests include religion, belief systems, and verbal and visual art of hunting-gathering societies; cognitive systems and environmental resource use; and contemporary political, economic, and human rights of indigenous peoples. Biesele's publications include *Shaken Roots: Bushmen of Namibia Today* (Johannesburg: Environmental Development Agency, 1990), *"Women Like Meat": The Folklore and Foraging Ideology of the Kalahari Ju/'hoan* (Johannesburg: Witwatersrand University Press and Bloomington: Indiana University Press, 1993) and *"Healing Makes Our Hearts Happy": Spirituality and Cultural Transformation among the Kalahari Ju/'hoansi* with Richard Katz and Verna St. Denis (Rochester, Vt.: Inner Traditions International, 1997).

Dmitrii D. Bogoiavlenskii is a Senior Research Associate with the Laboratory of Regional Forecasting of the Population Health Center for Demography and Human Ecology, Institute for Economic Forecasting, Russian Academy of Sciences, Moscow. His research interests include ethnic demography, the demography of Russian/Soviet ethnic groups, historical and regional aspects of the demography of Northern indigenous peoples, and methods and techniques in population studies. His publications include numerous articles in Russian and a recent English-language article, "Native Peoples of Kamchatka: Epidemiological Transition and Violent Death" (*Arctic Anthropology*; 1997, 34(1): 55–67).

Volker von Bremen received his Ph.D. from the Free University of Berlin, Germany. Since 1979 he has been working with indigenous peoples of the Gran Chaco (Argentina, Bolivia, Paraguay). His research is focused on topics of international development cooperation and indigenous peoples (land rights, organizational development, indigenous strategies within acculturation processes, etc.). He is a consultant for European development agencies and indigenous organizations in the Gran Chaco, and teaches at the Institute of Ethnology at the University of Berne, Switzerland.

Jean L. Briggs is Professor Emeritus in Anthropology at the Memorial University of Newfoundland. She has been a student of Inuit life since 1960 and has spent six years in the North, mostly in the Canadian Arctic. Her book *Never in Anger: Portrait of an Eskimo Family* (Harvard University Press, 1970) was one of the first reflexive ethnographies written by an anthropologist and also one of the first studies of emotion in a non-Western culture. A second book, *Inuit Morality Play: The Emotional Education of a Three-Year-Old* (Yale University Press and ISER Books, Memorial University of Newfoundland, 1998), is an ethnography of the "playful" and emotionally powerful, character-creating dramas that Inuit adults enact, primarily with small children. Dr. Briggs was educated at Vassar, Boston University, and Harvard, and holds an honorary doctorate from the University of Bergen. She has been Visiting Professor at the University of Tromsø (Norway) and the Hebrew University of Jerusalem; Visiting Scholar at the Scott Polar Research Institute (University of Cambridge) and the University of Bergen; Simon Professor at the University of Manchester; Munro Lecturer at the University of Edinburgh; and MillerComm Lecturer at the University of Illinois, Urbana-Champaign.

Liudmila A. Chindina is an archaeologist, Doctor of Historical Sciences, Professor at the Tomsk State University, and President of the Union of Archaeologists and Ethnologists of Siberia. Her research interests include the archaeology and ethnology of the Ural region and Siberia, the culture and ethnogenesis of Siberian peoples, and the community organization of hunters and fishermen. Dr. Chindina's publications include *Mogilnik Relka na Srednei Obi* (Tomsk: Izdatel'stvo Tomskogo universiteta, 1977), *Drevniaia istoriia Srednego Priob'ia v epokhu zheleza. Kulaiskaia kultura* (Tomsk: Izdatel'stvo Tomskogo universiteta, 1984), *Istoriia Srednego Priob'ia v epokhu rannego srednevekov'ia* (Tomsk: Izdatel'stvo Tomskogo universiteta, 1991), and *O voine i mire u okhotnikov i ribolovov iuzhnoi taigi Zapadnoi Sibiri* (Tomsk: Izdatel'stvo Tomskogo universiteta, 1996).

Leland Donald is a Professor in the Department of Anthropology at the University of Victoria, British Columbia, where he has taught since 1969. He received his Ph.D. in anthropology from the University of Oregon in 1968. He has conducted ethnographic field research among the Navajo of northern Arizona and the Yalunka of Sierra Leone. He has been engaged in ethnohistoric research on the aboriginal peoples of the North Pacific coast of North America since the early 1970s. He has been particularly interested in the aboriginal Northwest Coast resource base and its use, and in the social inequality (especially slavery) and intergroup relations (especially warfare and trade) in this region. He is the author of *Aboriginal Slavery on* *the Northwest Coast of North America* (Berkeley, Cal.: University of California Press, 1997).

Thomas A. Dowson is a Lecturer in the Department of Archaeology, University of Southampton. Here he teaches undergraduate and postgraduate courses on archaeological approaches to art. Prior to this he spent ten years in the Rock Art Research Unit, University of the Witwatersrand, South Africa, as a Research Officer and Deputy Director. He has carried out research on rock art in southern Africa, North America, and Europe. Over the last fifteen years Thomas Dowson has been principally researching the rock art of southern Africa, both paintings and engravings. With the rock paintings of the southeastern mountains of Lesotho and South Africa, he has shown that rock art does not simply "reflect" historical developments. Rather, rock art constitutes a source of evidence for historical processes. The results of his research have been published in numerous academic and popular articles. He is the author of the first interpretative book on southern African engravings (*Rock Engravings of Southern Africa*, Johannesburg, 1992), and coauthor, with David Lewis-Williams, of two books on the rock paintings of southern Africa. He is also the editor of a major collection of papers that attest to the diversity of southern African rock art research (*Contested Images*, Johannesburg, 1994).

Elena G. Fedorova graduated with a degree in history from Leningrad State University in 1975. Her M.A. thesis was entitled "Anthropomorphous and Zoomorphous Wooden Sculptures of the Peoples of Northwestern Siberia" (in Russian). In 1987 she defended her Ph.D. dissertation entitled "Contemporary Material Culture of the Sos'va-Liapin Mansis" (in Russian). Fedorova has published approximately 90 publications, including the monograph *Historical-Ethnographic Sketches of Mansi Material Culture* (in Russian; St. Petersburg, 1994). She has conducted numerous field trips since 1971; most of them were to visit various Mansi groups, but she also worked with Khantys, Maris, and Russians of the Arkhangelsk region. She is currently a senior scientific staff member of the Department of the Ethnology of Siberia at the Museum of Anthropology and Ethnography in St. Petersburg, Russia. Her research interests include ethnogenesis, the ethnic history of the Ob-Ugrians, clothing of the peoples of Siberia, and the contemporary situation of the Khantys and Mansis.

Andrei V. Golovnev (Doctor of Historic Sciences, in Russian terms) is the head of the Ethnological Section of the Institute of History and Archaeology of the Russian Academy of Sciences (Ural Division, Ekaterinburg). Dr. Golovnev is an anthropologist and filmmaker who has worked for more than twenty years on issues of Russia's indigenous peoples, mostly among Samoyedic and Ugrian groups of Siberia. He is the author of two Russian monographs, *Historical Typology of Northwest Siberian Peoples* (Novosibirsk, 1993) and *Talking Cultures* (Ekaterinburg, 1995), and has published several English articles in the journal *Arctic Anthropology*. Among his films are *The Yamal Gods* (1992), *Devil's Lake* (1993), and *Way to the Sacred Place* (1997). He lives in the Ural city of Ekaterinburg.

Jean-Guy A. Goulet is the director of the Research Centre at Saint Paul University, Ottawa, Ontario, where he also teaches anthropology. He is coeditor of *Being Changed by Cross-Cultural Encounters* (Broadview Press; second printing 1998) and author of *Ways of Knowing: Experience, Knowledge and Power Among the Dene Tha* (University of Nebraska Press, 1998).

Marcus B. Griffin (Ph.D., University of Illinois, 1996), the founder of Griffin Social Technologies, works on cultural resources and heritage management in Southeast Asia and North America. He has published articles in *Pilipinas, Anthropos, The Australian Journal of Anthropology*, as well as essays in popular magazines. His current writing project is a young adult novel that explores adolescence among the Agta.

Barry S. Hewlett (Ph.D., University of California-Santa Barbara, 1987) is an Associate Professor of Anthropology at Washington State University and has worked with tropical forest foragers of central Africa (also known as "pygmies") for over twenty years. He has conducted basic research, primarily on forager family life, and has worked as a consultant for U.S. (WWF) and European Community (ECOFAC) conservation groups. Recent publications include: *Intimate Fathers: The Nature and Context of Aka Pygmy Paternal Infant Care* (1991, Michigan University Press); "Cultural Diversity among African Pygmies" (1996, in *Cultural Diversity Among Twentieth-Century Foragers: An African Perspective*, S. Kent, ed., Cambridge University Press); "Die Reziprozität der Ehepartner und die Vater-Kind-Beziehung bei den Aka-Pygmäen" (1997, in *Familien in verschiedenen Kulturen*, Bernhard Nauck und Ute Schönpflug, eds, Ferdinand Enke Verlag); "Culture and Early Infancy Among Central African Foragers and Farmers" (*Developmental Psychology*, in press).

Robert K. Hitchcock is an Associate Professor of Anthropology and Chair of the Anthropology Department, as well as the Coordinator of African Studies, at the University of Nebraska-Lincoln. In addition to his administrative and teaching duties, he has worked for the past twenty-three years in applied research and development project monitoring, evaluation, and implementation, primarily in southern and eastern Africa and in North America. His research interests include human rights, indigenous peoples, international social and economic development, hunter-gatherers, Africa, the Middle East, and native North America. From 1979 to 1997 Hitchcock served as Co-President of the Kalahari Peoples Fund (KPF), a nonprofit organization aimed at helping the peoples of southern Africa. He is a founding member of the Committee for Human Rights (CfHR) of the American Anthropological Association.

Hitchcock's publications include *Organizing to Survive: The Politics of Indigenous Peoples' Human Rights Struggles* (New York: Routledge, 2000); an edited volume with C. Patrick Morris, *International Human Rights, Indigenous Peoples, and the Environment* (Tucson: University of Arizona Press, 2000); *Kalahari Communities: Bushmen and the Politics of the Environment in Southern Africa* (Copenhagen, Denmark: International Work Group for Indigenous Affairs, 1996); and "Centralization, Resource Depletion, and Coercive Conservation among the Tyua of the Northeastern Kalahari" (*Human Ecology* 23(2): 169–98; 1995).

Mitsuo Ichikawa (D. Sc., Kyoto University) is currently a professor of anthropology at the Graduate School of Asian and African Area Studies, Kyoto University, Japan. Since 1974, he has conducted fieldwork among the Mbuti, Efe, and other hunter-gatherers in central African forests; Dorobo in Kenya; and the fishermen in the Bangweulu Swamps in Zambia. His major interest is in cultural and historical ecology and its implications for sustainable use of the forest environment. He has published *Hunters in the Forest* (1982) and *The Co-existence of Man and Nature in Central African Rain Forest* (1996), and has edited *Man and Nature in Central African Forests* (1998).

Takashi Irimoto (Ph.D.) is Professor at the Faculty of Letters, Hokkaido University, and Visiting Professor at the National Museum of Ethnology. His major research interests encompass cultural and ecological anthropology of North and Central Asia, Japan, and northern North America. His book publications include *Chipewyan Ecology* (National Museum of Ethnology, 1981), *From the World of Canadian Indians* (in Japanese, Tokyo, 1983), *Ainu Bibliography* (Hokkaido University, 1992), *An Anthropology of Nature and Culture* (in Japanese, University of Tokyo Press, 1996), as well as two coedited volumes (with T. Yamada), *Circumpolar Religion and Ecology: An Anthropology of the North* (University of Tokyo Press, 1994) and *Circumpolar Animism and Shamanism* (Hokkaido University Press, 1997).

Alexandra A. Kim is the Head of the Linguistic Department at Tomsk State Pedagogical University in Tomsk, Russia. She received her Ph.D.

from the University of Tartu, Estonia, in 1988, with a thesis on "The Expression of the Category of Possessivity in Selkup Dialects." In March 1999, she defended her "doctoral dissertation" (in Russian terminology) on "Sel'kup Cult Lexicon as an Ethnolinguistic Source: The Problem of Reconstructing the World Picture." Her research interests focus on the indigenous languages and cultures of Siberia. She has conducted nine seasons of fieldwork among the Selkups, Khantys, and Evenkis of Siberia, and has made two trips to Canada to work with the Cree. Dr. Kim has participated in several international conferences in Russia, Hungary, Finland, France, and Germany. She has published over sixty-five articles, abstracts, and books. Her most recent book publication is "Ocherki po sel'kupskoi kul'tovoi leksike" (Essays on the Selkup Cult Lexicon), which was published by the "Izdatel'stvo nauchno-tekhnicheskoi literatury" in Tomsk in 1997.

Olga Murashko graduated from the Department of Ethnography at Moscow State University. Currently, she is a scientific staff member of the Institute of (Physical) Anthropology at the same university. She has published extensively on the history and ethnology of the native peoples of Kamchatka, including several English-language articles in the journal *Arctic Anthropology*. In recent years she has participated in several international research projects, such as creating a database for genealogies of the Kamchadals (funded by the Soros Foundation), "Social Transition in the North" (funded by the National Science Foundation), and in establishing procedures for the defense of rights of native communities in Kamchatka over traditional resources (funded by the MacArthur Foundation). In addition, her research interests include indigenous rights, ethnic identity, and the construction of "neotraditional" ideologies.

Laura Rival is currently Lecturer in the Department of Anthropology at the University of Kent at Canterbury. Her main research interests are the theories of learning and knowledge acquisition; Amerindian conceptualizations of nature and society; historical ecology; Latin American nationalisms and politics of culture and identity; and the impact of national development policies on indigenous peoples. Her doctoral research was among the Huaorani of the Ecuadorian Amazon (1989–90, 1991, 1994, 1996), on whom she has written a number of ethnographic articles and papers. She is currently preparing a monograph entitled *Trekking Through History: The Huaorani of Amazonian Ecuador*.

Peter P. Schweitzer is Associate Professor of Anthropology at the University of Alaska Fairbanks and Lecturer at the Institute of Ethnology, Cultural, and Social Anthropology, University of Vienna. Dr. Schweitzer received his Ph.D. from the University of Vienna in 1990. He has been actively involved in the field of Siberian anthropology since the mid-1980s, and—since 1990—has conducted several seasons of fieldwork in northeastern Siberia and western Alaska. His areas of interest include politics, kinship, and history. He is the editor of *Dividends of Kinship: Meanings and Uses of Social Relatedness* (London: Routledge, 2000) and is preparing (jointly with Evgenii Golovko) the monograph *Travelers' Tales: Remembering and Narrating Contacts Across Bering Strait.*

Matthew Spriggs is Professor of Archaeology and Head of the Department of Archaeology and Anthropology, Faculty of Arts, Australian National University in Canberra. He has carried out extensive fieldwork in Island Southeast Asia and the Pacific, most recently in the Aru Islands of Eastern Indonesia, Vanuatu and Manus in the Bismarck Archipelago. He has published articles on the origins of agriculture, the Pleistocene settlement of Melanesia, the Austronesian settlement of Southeast Asia and the Pacific, human impacts on island environments, and politics and archaeology. His most recent book is *The Island Melanesians* (Blackwell, Oxford, 1997).

Maria V. Staniukovich studied Philippine and Indonesian languages and anthropology at the Department of Oriental Studies and the Department of Anthropology at Leningrad State University, Russia. She graduated in 1977 with the M.A. thesis "The Creative Heritage of R. F. Barton" about the famous American anthropologist who lived and worked in Leningrad between 1930 and 1940. In 1982, she defended her Ph.D. dissertation "Historical Typology and Ethnocultural Links of Ifugao Epics" at the Institute of Anthropology and Ethnology, Academy of Sciences of the USSR. Since 1980, she has been working at this institute (which is now called Museum of Anthropology and Ethnography) in St. Petersburg, where she is currently a senior researcher. In addition, she teaches Philippine anthropology and oral literature at the St. Petersburg State University. She has conducted fieldwork in Tadzhikistan, Kazakhstan, Uzbekistan, the Caucasus, and Cuba, focusing on the anthropology of religion and gender. In 1994, she finally received the opportunity to conduct fieldwork in the Philippines through a grant by the Wenner-Gren Foundation. She is the author of numerous articles on Philippine oral literature and anthropology, and of a book-length manuscript about Ifugao oral literature.

Robert Tonkinson is Professor of Anthropology at The University of Western Australia, where he began his training in anthropology under Ronald and Catherine Berndt in 1957, and took his Honours and Masters degrees. Prior to his return to Perth in 1984, he taught at the University of Oregon (1968–80) and the Australian National University (1980–84). He took his doctorate at the University of British Columbia (1972). He has done extensive fieldwork in the Western Desert region of Western Australia (since 1963) and in Melanesia (Vanuatu, since 1966). In addition to four coedited volumes and a monograph, he has published two books, *The Jigalong Mob* (1974) and *The Mardu Aborigines* (1978/1991), and numerous articles. His interests include social organization, religion, change, gender, migration, identity, and the politics of tradition. Since returning to Western Australia, he has also undertaken numerous consultancies connected with land and native title issues.

David S. Trigger is Associate Professor in the Department of Anthropology at The University of Western Australia. He has a wide range of research interests, including the study of Aboriginal relations with the wider Australian society, and the nature of cultural assumptions underlying contesting visions of land use. Dr. Trigger has conducted research for twenty years in Australia's Gulf Country. In 1992, he published *Whitefella Comin': Aboriginal Responses to Colonialism in Northern Australia* (Cambridge University Press), a book focused on the nature of social relations and political life in an Aboriginal town. He has conducted much applied research, having been the principal anthropologist involved in a number of land claims and native title applications, as well as heritage surveys and mining negotiations in Queensland, the Northern Territory, and Western Australia. Recently, Dr. Trigger's publications have included analyses of pro-development perspectives on the importance of natural resource extraction industries, environmentalism as a social movement challenging such pro-development sentiments, and the ways in which indigenous views about land both differ from and overlap these perspectives.

Thomas Widlok received his M.Sc. and his Ph.D. in anthropology from the London School of Economics and Political Science (University of London). Between 1990 and 1994 he carried out 23 months of field research with the Hai//om of northern Namibia. Since then he has also worked with ≠Aoni in the central Namib desert as well as with Aborigines in southern Kimberley (Western Australia). He has published on anthropological and linguistic topics in Aboriginal and Khoisan Studies and his monograph on the ≠Akhoe Hai//om of the Mangetti area is forthcoming. He has taught anthropology at the universities of London and Cologne and is currently associate researcher at the Department of Anthropology at the University of Cologne. His comparative research on Khoisan southern Africa and Aboriginal Australia is funded by the German Research Council (Deutsche Forschungsgemeinschaft).

Cornelia M. I. van der Sluys has studied psychology, education, and cultural anthropology at Leyden University, the Netherlands. She has conducted two years of fieldwork among the Jahais of Malaysia. Her research interests include the anthropology of hunter-gatherers, cognitive anthropology, human ecology, land rights, and issues regarding intellectual property. She has contributed an article to the *Cambridge Encyclopedia of Hunters and Gatherers* (Cambridge University Press, 1999). Until recently, she was attached to the Institute of Environmental Studies at the National University of Malaysia.

APPENDIX: A NOTE ON THE SPELLING OF SIBERIAN ETHNONYMS

The spelling of Siberian ethnic groups in English-language publications is notoriously ambiguous. For example, the group of people we refer to as "Evenks" in this publication are known as "Evenk," "Evenki," and "Evenkis," in addition to the nowadays rarely used old designation "Tungus." The basic problem is that all of the currently used ethnonyms are Russianized, even when originating from native labels. Thus, in Russian the singular form "Evenk" is pluralized to "Evenki." In English, three questions arise: whether to pluralize at all, and, if yes, whether to do so on the basis of the Russian singular or plural, and whether to use Russian or English endings. We have decided to use plurals where appropriate and to add the English plural ending "s" to the Russian singular form. Exceptions to this rule were made in cases in which in Russian the prevalent form is plural (e.g., "Chukchi," "Khanty"). In these cases we added the English plural to the Russian plural form. The "Siberian Yupiks" fall outside this rule, since their Russian labels ("Eskimos/Eskimosy") would be too ambiguous (and unspecific) outside the Russian context. Finally, David Anderson provides arguments in his chapter as to why he uses an alternative terminology, which we gladly accept. The following list contains our usage of singular/plural forms in referring to Siberian ethnic groups.

- Ainu/Ainus
- Aleut/Aleuts
- Buriat/Buriats
- Chukchi/Chukchis
- Chuvan/Chuvans
- Dolgan/Dolgans
- Enets/Enetses
- Even/Evens
- Evenk/Evenks
     (except in Anderson's chapter: Evenki/Evenkis)
- Itel'men/Itel'mens
- Kamchadal/Kamchadals

- Ket/Kets
- Khanty/Khantys
- Koriak/Koriaks
- Mansi/Mansis
- Nanai/Nanais
- Negidal/Negidals
- Nenets/Nenetses
- Nganasan/Nganasans
  (except in Anderson's chapter: Nia/Nias/Ngos)
- Nivkh/Nivkhs
- Orok/Oroks
- Oroch/Oroches
- Saami/Saamis
- Sel'kup/Sel'kups
- Siberian Yupik/Siberian Yupiks
- Tofa/Tofas
- Udege/Udeges
- Ulchi/Ulchis
- Yakut/Yakuts and Sakha/Sakhas
- Yukagir/Yukagirs

INDEX

Aboriginal and Torres Strait Islanders Commission (ATSIC), 8
Aboriginal Land Rights (Northern Territory) Act, 1976, 18
Aborigines. *See* Australian Aborigines
Absolute Poverty Level (APL), 8
accidents, 98, 105, 445
accountability, 59, 67
acculturation; degree of, 33–35; Soviet policies, 33–35
Ache, 5
Adivasis (Scheduled Tribes), 2, 4, 5
adoption, 396
affiliation; ethnic, 13, 186, 396; socioeconomic, 186
Africa, 1, 5, 6, 11, 12, 14, 16, 38, 39, 44, 45
African National Congress, 305
Agenda 21, 9
aggression, 3, 20, 83, 98–102, 446; covert, 58, 68–69; overt, 55, 58, 67, 70, 72, 78–93; suppression of, 55–56, 161, 399–409
Agrarian Reform Act (Japan), 208–11
agricultural societies, 36, 289
agriculture, 207, 265, 300–302, 333, 387, 428; threshold of, 36, 289
agropastoralists, 364, 367
Agta, 20, 94–109
Ainus, 5, 9, 14, 34, 206–22
Alaskan Indians, 2, 5
alcohol, 57, 65, 67–68, 105–6, 155, 198, 224; and homicide, 98;

abuse, 333, 352; and violence, 95, 99, 102, 352. *See also* intoxication
Aleuts, 2, 5, 329, 330, 338
Allen, J., 291
alliances, 15, 111
allies, 128
altruism, 438–39
ambiguity, 112, 113, 116, 120, 121
American Anthropological Association, 10, 11
ancestors, 34; distant, 277, 431–54
Andaman Islanders, 5
/'Angn!ao /'Un, 314
Angola, 314
animals, 7, 10, 19, 20, 33, 38, 44, 91; human relations with, 225, 234, 455. *See also* hunting
anthropologists (archaeologists; ethnographers; physical anthropologists), 6, 10, 23, 32, 39, 100, 382, 383, 390; Austrian economic, 36; German, 36; North American, 30, 36, 44; Russian, 29–47; Soviet, 30, 35–39; Western, 29–47, 32, 35, 41, 42, 43, 46n.5
anthropology, 2, 10, 20, 80, 165, 414; English-language, 31–32, 225; French-language, 46n.2; German-language, 46n.2; Russian, 22–24, 35–39; Soviet, 22–24, 35–39; Western, 22–24, 31–44
Apache, 34
apartheid, 14, 305
apocalypse, 436

applied research, 41
Argentov, A., 154
arms. *See* weapons
Artemova, O., 40
assimilation, 208, 215, 337
Athapaskans, 34
attitudes; Cold War 32; Soviet post-war 32, 46n.5; toward aliens, 145; toward death, 152–62
audience, 111, 112, 120, 121
Australia, 2, 5, 8, 9, 13, 14, 16, 17, 18, 21, 38, 192–205
Australian Aborigines, 2, 5, 7, 8–9, 12, 18, 19, 40; post-European contact, 192–205, 343–60
autonomy, 257, 322, 377, 446, 449; as value, 57, 60–61, 253; respect for, 55, 61, 62–64, 343–60, 438–39, 441
Ayoréode, 12, 275–86

Bailey, R., 288, 294, 301, 384, 428
Baka Pygmies, 12, 380–90
Balof, 294, 295, 296, 298, 299, 300
Balzer, M. M., 32
band societies, 40
Banks Islands, 298
Baraka, 315
Barton, R. F., 401, 402, 407n.3,4
Basarwa, 306
Basic Education Reform Program, 317
Batek, 437
battle, 125, 129, 133, 134, 137, 143, 144; forest, 132; tundra, 132
Batwa, 5
bear, 393, 464; cult, 24, 393, 455–59; festival, 397, 455–59; brown, 455
Bell, D., 347, 350
Berman, E., 417
biogeographic boundaries, 287–88
Bird-David, N., 224
birth, 397
birth control, 338
birth rate, 334–35; crude, 334; "real," 457

Bismarck Archipelago, 287–88, 290, 292, 293, 294, 297, 300. *See also* New Ireland, New Britain, Manus
Bjorkland, I., 234
blowpipe, 442
boarding schools, 333, 396
Boas, F., 31, 35, 177n.10
Bogoraz, V. G., 32, 151, 153, 158–60
Bolivia, 5, 21, 275–76
Borzunov, V. A., 81
Botelle, A., 310
Botswana, 7, 8, 12, 13, 14, 15, 17, 364
Bougainville, 292
"bride capture," 161
Brody, H., 56
Buang Merabak, 290–97; Cave, 291–92, 293, 294, 296, 297, 298, 299, 300
Buka, 292, 294
Buriats, 152
Bushman Advisory Council, 313
Bushmanland, 313
Bushmen, 361, 427–28
Bushmen Battalion, 6

California Indians, 20, 34
Cameroons, 380–90
Canada, 5, 6, 14, 17, 18, 20, 21
cancer, 156, 311, 332
canoes, Northwest Coast, 168
cannibalism, 441
Caprivi Strip, 314
Castrén, M. A., 125, 461
casualties in Northwest Coast war-fare, 171
census, 6, 327, 339, 361–65
Central African Republic (CAR), 12
Century Mine, 192, 194–98, 201–4
charanke, 217
Cheyenne, 17
chiefdoms, "democratic," 146
childcare, 395–96; pre-school, 395
children, 107, 185, 387, 395–96, 456

Christianity, 252, 354, 407, 464
Christianization, 400
Chukchi Autonomous Okrug, 162n.1, 189
Chukchis, 33, 150, 189, 329, 330, 338
Chukotka, 32, 150
Chuvans, 329
class relations, 36, 37
clientship, 416
clinic, 11; staff, 366
clothes, 7; making, 392
Colombia, 21
colonialism, 275–76; European, 42
colonization, 399–400, 413
communal land, 15, 16
community, 40
Community Development Employment Projects (CDED) Scheme, 8
Companie Général de Géophysique (CGG), 249–50, 259n.10
component analysis, 464
Conferences on Hunting and Gathering Societies (CHAGS), 1, 2, 3, 10, 20, 22; Seventh, 223–24, 239n.1, 382
conflict, 16, 18–22, 85, 94, 110–13, 115–17, 119, 121, 125–49, 164–79, 192–205, 345, 353, 388–90; external, 130; resolution, 101, 159, 164–79; traditional management of, 97, 111–13, 434; modern management of, 117–22; with local government, 381
confrontation, 111–12, 116, 117, 119–21
consciousness, human, 460
conservancy, 320
contractual relationships, 116
Convention on Protection of World Cultural and Natural Heritage, 188
Coon, C., 33
cooperation, 9, 94

Corporación Estatal Petrolera Ecuatoriana (CEPE), 247–48, 258n.7, 8
Corporation, Hokkaido Utari Association, 211–14, 216
corruption, 199–200
cosmology, 2, 225, 403, 434–36
cradle, 395
Crees, 239n.4
crime, 333
criticism, 19, 111, 120, 121
cross-descent naming, 368
cuenta (credit account), 282–84
cultivators. *See* agriculture
cultural ecology, 35
cultural revitalization, 9, 206, 207, 214, 216–20
cultural survival, 196, 207
cyclical time, 157, 458

Damara, 362
death, 19, 456; causes of, 332; violent, 13, 85, 334; visits by the deceased, 456; living substitutes, 456
death rate, 331, 334, 335; crude, 331; standardized, 331
deception, 403
decorations, 392; manufacture of, 84
defense. *See* warfare
Delimitation Commission, 322
demographics, 42, 77–78, 83, 245, 310, 330–31, 338
Dene Tha Women's Society, 56
Department of Veterinary Services, 310
dependence, 6
development programs, 381–90
Directorate of Nature Conservation, 308
discriminatory policies, 306
"diseases of development," 311
diseases of the circulatory and respiratory system, 332
dispossession, 16, 17, 198
disputes, 19, 94

djireponde, 465
Dolgans, 228, 231, 232, 233, 238, 329, 330, 338
domination, 24
Drimiopsis, 307
drunkeness, 56, 68, 70. *See also* alcohol

Eastern Bushmanland, 306
Eastern Otjozondjupa, 7, 321
economy, 194, 199, 268–74; political, 245
ecological crisis, 78, 87, 191
ecological problems, 188, 207, 275
Ecuador, 5, 12, 17, 21, 244–48, 258n.7, 8
education, 210, 215, 394, 447; level of, 387; secondary, 394
egalitarian society, 19, 345, 347, 385
emotions, 24, 97, 431–33, 441, 446, 455
employment, 8, 12, 18, 199
empowerment, 314
enemy, 35, 128–33, 166, 167, 171, 403; category of, 404
Enetses, 126, 132, 329, 330, 462
Engels, F., 37
environment, 77–78, 280, 449; protection of, 245, 306, 318
environmental damage, 195–98, 339
epics, 129, 400–09; Ainu female; heroic, 399–409; male, 400; women's, 400–09
ethnic identity, 185, 215–18, 279, 306, 339, 358, 362–79; processes, 336–38; history, 43; rights, 185–87, 189
ethnicity, 186, 306
ethnoecological refuge, 12, 183–91
ethnogenesis, 10, 43, 224
ethnography, 91n.1, 364; Soviet history of, 22–24, 223–24; Western history of, 22–24, 223–24
ethnonyms. *See* Appendix
ethnopolitics, 42

Etosha, 9
European contact, 165, 173, 199, 343, 349–52, 414
Evens, 338
Evenks, 31, 91n.1, 152, 328–30, 338, 455. *See also* Evenkis and Tunguses
Evenkis, 10, 79; ethnonyms, 225, 226; herding practice, 225–26, 229–30, 235–36, 240n.16; hunting practice, 224, 233–35, 236; industrial impacts, 230, 237, 240n.11, 241n.20; self-identity, 231; shamanism, 225; State National Policy, 226–27, 231, 233, 235, 237, 240n.17
exchange, 2, 6, 7, 8, 11, 16, 17
existence, "real," 457; different, 457
extinction ("dying out"), 297, 339

family, 352; nuclear, 88
farmers, 40; interaction with hunter-gatherers, 382, 385–86, 418–19
Feit, H., 224, 225, 234
Fergusson Islands, 298
fertility, 12; rate, 310, 331, 336
festivals, 254
fieldwork, Siberian (in Siberia), 42–43; stationary, 47n.13; Western, 43; Western model of, 43
Fienup-Riordan, A., 175, 225, 234
fishermen, 34, 45, 81; sedentary, 34, 45
fishing, 82, 185, 189, 339, 392, 393
floods (cyclical), 459
folklore, 22, 23, 24, 125, 147n.1
food, 4, 6, 7, 8, 17, 97, 152, 380, 428, 435–54; appropriation, 4, 250, 419; honey, 443–44; meat, 437; "original food," 436–37, 445; sharing, 436–54; wild tubers, 442–43
foragers, 1, 2, 8, 9, 11–15, 20, 25, 97, 294

foraging, 4, 6, 7, 12, 15, 17, 19, 22, 99, 253; space, 96; quality, 96
Forde, D., 31
forest, 381, 428, 437, 448; primary, 96; secondary, 96
Fort Laramie Treaty of 1868, 17
fortifications, 80, 88; on Northwest Coast, 165, 168–69
fortresses, 135
Fourth World, 327
friendship, 6, 19, 97, 256
functional approach, 95, 151
funeral rituals, 84, 162n.4, 397,
fur trade; impact on Northwest Coast warfare, 174
"future," 457

gai/ons, 368–77
Garoeb, M., 315
//gaus, 370. *See also* household
Gellner, E., 22, 23, 38
Gemuev, I. N., 42, 396
gender, 2, 11, 18; male/female relationships, 161, 249, 318, 343; equality, 129, 310, 382, 390–98; division of labor, 94, 346, 349, 392–95
geosource, 249, 250, 259n.10
Germany, 2
gift-giving, 19, 371, 437
gifts, 437
glasnost, 47n.9
Gobabis, 307–8
Gosden, C., 293, 299
government; intervention, 382–90; officials, 381, 385
Government of the Republic of Namibia, 317–24
Gow, P., 233
Gran Chaco, 275–76, 279, 284
"Great Kalahari Debate," 34, 47n.14, 363–64
Greenland, 5, 14, 17, 18, 151
Grootfontein, 307–8
Grosse, E., 36

group mediation, 95
Guadalcanal, 292

Hadza, 5, 7, 19, 382
Hai//om, 9, 12, 361; San, 363
Haida, 164
Harris, D., 389
hatred, 399
Hausiko, M., 315, 316
headhunting, 400, 401–9, 430
health, 383, 387
Hearne, S., 176
Helm, J., 55, 74
Herero, 313–16
Hereroland, 314, 316
heritage, 192–204; cultural, 186; natural, 186
hero, 90, 128–30, 457
Himba, 362, 377n.1
history, 43, 276, 413–16; art, 417; oral, 147n.1
HIV/AIDS, 24, 311–12
Hiwi, 5
Hobbes, T., 125
Hokkaido Association Ainu (HAA), 208–11, 215
homelands, 313
homicide, 94–109, 152, 334
Honigmann, J.J., 55, 56, 57, 73
horticulturalists, 165, 399
hostility, 19, 20, 111, 112, 121
household, 333, 351
Huaorani, 5, 12, 21, 23, 244–60
hudhud, 400–409
human rights, 307, 367
Human Rights Commission of the United Nations, 13
hunter gatherer debate, modern Western, 33; "new," 34; in Siberia, 36
hunter-gatherer, category of; 33, 34, 36, 44, 45, 47n.7, 47n.11; complex, 45, 289; egalitarian, 34; nomadic, 34; non-complex, 427–54; "real," 35; sample of, 34,

hunter-gatherer, category of (*cont.*)
45; Siberian, 33, 34, 38, 39, 40,
41, 45; "simple," 34, 175
hunter-gatherer society, 387; ethnogenesis, 224; ideal-type, 224–25,
238; interpretive model, 225,
237; study of, 381–82
hunters, 77, 224; "lower"and
"higher," 45; mounted, 33
Hunters, Gatherers, Fishermen, 39
hunting, 33, 82, 189, 339, 348, 392,
441; practices, 458

identity, 207, 215–18, 364, 419;
cards, 264, 365–66, 378n.4,
433
ideology, 84, 85, 419; dominant
male, 84; female; peacemaking,
400–409
Ifugao, 399–409
il'sat, 463–66
immigrants, 96; farmers, 98, 103
immortality, 470
incarceration, 59, 65
incipient tillers, 33
income, 4, 6, 8, 12, 18
India, 2, 4, 5, 12, 17
Indians (North America), 2, 5, 11
indigenism, 2, 3, 4, 5, 197, 200, 20
indirection, 111, 120
Indonesia, 14
industrialization, 333
infant mortality, 310
infanticide, 150
Ingold, T., 2, 11, 32
injuries, 333
insults, 99–103,
integration, 11, 24
interdependency, 368
interethnic relations, 95, 186, 245,
346, 370, 374–75, 377n.8
intermarriage, 367, 376
International Congress of Anthropological and Ethnological Sciences (1963), 46n.5

International Convention of Inde-
pendent Countries on Indige-
nous Peoples (Convention 169),
183–88
International Ethnoecological
Refuges Fund, 188, 190
International Work Group for
Indigenous Affairs, 184
intoxication. *See* alcohol
Inuit, 2, 5, 11, 18, 21
Inuit Circumpolar Conference, 21
invasion, 88, 126, 138, 249, 275, 333,
349, 351
Irtysh River, 77
Island Melanesia, 287–301
isolation, 207, 363, 376–77
Itel'mens, 33, 45, 150, 329, 330
Itt'e (Selkup hero), 470
Ituri Forest, 263, 267–68
Ivanov, V. N., 154

Jahai, 11, 427–54
Janhunen, J., 461
jealousy, 95, 103
Jenkins, T., 311
jnanibajade, 277–78
joking, 99, 101, 111, 112, 113, 120,
123n.8, 124n.17
Jomon, 206–7
Ju/'hoan women, 310
Ju/'hoansi San, 7, 9, 15–16, 305–24
Ju/'hoansi, 15, 310–26
Ju/Wa Farmers Union (JFU), 314
Ju/Wasi, 307
justice, 21; Dene cencept, 60
justice system, 59, 65

Kabo, V. R., 39–40, 47n.11
kaga (grave soul), 466–67
Kalinnikov, N., 157
Kamchatka, 45, 150, 157
Kane, P., 170
Kastren, M. A. *See* Castrén, M. A.
kapita (Mbuti government liaison),
263–64

Kaudum Game Reserve, 314
Kavango, 313
Kennan, G., 153
Kenya, 7
Kets, 24, 33, 152, 329, 330, 338, 455–59
Khantaiskaii state farm, 229
Khantaiskoe Ozero, village of, 224, 232, 230n.17
Khantys, 32, 79, 91n.1, 126–49, 329, 330, 338, 391–98, 455
Khoe, 308, 362
Khoisan languages, 362
Khwe, 314
Kilu, 292–93, 294, 296–97, 298
kinship, 6, 15, 19, 44–45, 78, 79, 97–102, 170–71, 193, 253, 255, 266, 344, 365, 403, 433–34
kinship organization, 86; matrilineal, 39, 372; patrilineal, 37
kinship systems, 436; bilateral, 37
Koriaks, 33, 150–63, 158, 162n.1, 329, 330, 338
Kosarev, M. F., 91n.4
kpara (patron client relationship), 266
Krasheninnikov, S., 157
Krasil'nikov, M., 327
Kunene, 308,
!Kung, 102, 307, 368
kuwaloz, 462

labor, 108, 223, 252, 272, 276, 280–84, 333, 346, 352, 353, 380, 447
Lakota, 17
Lambrecht, Fr., 400–401
land; rights, 349, 356; tenure, 15–16, 308, 380
Land Boards, 194
language, 460–74
Lapita pottery, 300, 301
laughter; for breaking tension, 101
law, 183–91
Law Concerning Promotion of Ainu Culture and Dissemination and

Enlightenment of Knowledge about Ainu Traditions 1997, 214, 219
Leach, E., 233
Leacock, E., 2, 11, 46n.6, 349
leaders, 129–30, 155
leadership, 11
legends, 128–49
Lesotho, 413–26
life expectancy, 331; average, 331
life substance, 456
lifestyles, 12; diversity of, 114, 119
lineage, 15, 40
linguistics, 460–74; self-determination, 13
literacy, 12; program, 317, 383
literature, 328, 400; unconsciously dissident, 407
lithics, 203, 292–93, 295, 298–99, 416
livestock raising, 7, 8
Living in a Finite Environment Project (LIFE), 317
logging, 9, 96, 107, 108, 380, 427, 447
Lorenz, K., 399
love, 95, 103, 130, 399
Luxemburg, R., 36
lycanthropy, 152, 440

M'kata, 307
Mabo Decision (Australia), 18
MacAndrew, C., and R. B. Edgerton, 57
McArthur River Mine, 194–95
magic, 134, 458; hostile, 144–45, 403
Makuri, 321
Malaysia, 2, 5, 9, 11, 14, 427–54
Man the Hunter, 29, 33, 34
Man the Hunter Conference, 1
Mangetti Block, 307
Mansis, 126, 329, 330, 338, 391–98
Manus, 287–88, 290, 295, 297, 300
Mardu, 347–60
Mariental, 316

marriage, 244, 253, 345, 348, 355–
56; ceremony, 397; problems,
130; mixed, 335–36; rate, 335
Marshall, J., 312–13,
Marshall, L., 420, 450n.2
Marx, K., 252, 259n.14
Marxism, 23; Western, 37
Marxist-Leninist, 36
Matenbek, 294, 296, 298, 299, 300
Matenkupkum, 292, 293, 294, 296,
298, 300
matriarchy, 39, 172
Mauss, M., 437
Maxus, 21, 245–47, 256–58, 258n.5
Mbuende, K., 306
Mbuti, 12, 263–74, 428, 437
mediation, 94
medicine fight, 69, 73
mediums, 438, 440, 466
Mennonites, 279, 283, 285n.3
Mexico, 17
migration, 88–89, 126, 189, 190,
207, 268, 416
militarization, 88
military, 98, 103; expansion, 127;
norms, 128; customs, 128;
actions, 84
Minister of Lands, Resettlement and
Rehabilitation (MLRR), 315
Ministry of Environment and
Tourism, (MET), 310, 319
Ministry of Health, 311
Ministry of Wildlife, Conservation
and Tourism, (MWCT), 310, 318
minority (status), 207, 306–7,
Misisil, 288, 295–96
missionaries, 63, 244, 256, 258n.2,
276, 350, 354, 366, 383–90
mobility, 17
modernization, 183, 190
mogau (*Dichapetalum cymosum*), 313
Moore, P., and A. Wheelock, 68
Morgan, L. H., 44
Morning Sunlight Society (MSS),
208–9, 215

Moscow Institute of Ethnography,
38, 39
motivation, 10; of volunteers, 381
Mount Witori, 290
movements; indigenous political, 41
multiculturalism, 306
multinational corporations, 306
murder, 20, 97–109, 157. *See also*
homicide
Murdock, G. P., 33, 34
Myers, F., 3, 224
mythology, 42, 277–79, 440–41, 457;
Enets, 465; Sel'kup, 464

n!ore kxaosi, 322–23
n!oresi, 16, 310, 315
Nama, 462
Namibia, 7, 8, 9, 12, 15, 16, 17, 18,
305–26, 361–79
Namibian Ministry of Basic Educa-
tion and Culture, 317
naming, 361–79
Nanais, 329, 330, 338
Nande, 267–68
National Conference on Land
Reform and the Land Question,
308, 315
national sovereignty, 20
Native Title Act of 1993, 205n.1
natural resource management, 317
nature conservation. *See* environ-
ment, protection of
Nature Conservation Amendment
Act of 1986, 320
Navasardov, S. M., 332
Nayakas, 437
Negidals, 329, 330
Nenetses, 79, 91n.1, 126–40, 329,
330, 461; forest, 138
neoevolutionism, 3, 5
neolithic, 77, 80, 91n.2; of Eurasia,
39; revolution, 37
New Britain, 287–88, 290–91, 298,
300, 301
New Caledonia, 287–88, 298, 294

New Guinea, 17, 175, 287–88, 297, 298, 299, 300, 301
New Ireland, 287–88, 289–90, 291, 292, 293, 297, 298, 300
Nganasans., 126, 228, 329, 330, 461, 462. *See also* Nias
Nharo, 7, 368
Nias (Nganasan), 228
Nivkhs, 40, 329, 330, 338
nomads, 130, 137, 146, 387
non-governmental organization (NGO), 12, 15, 245–60, 306, 314, 380–90
noninterference. *See* autonomy
Northern Territory Land Council, 194
Northwest Coast (North America), 16, 20, 164–78
Northwest Coast societies, 34
Nujoma, President Sam, 307
"Numerically Small Peoples of the North," 22, 183–86
Nyae Nyae, 306–26
Nyae Nyae Development Foundation of Namibia (NNDFN), 310, 314, 317
Nyae Nyae Farmers Cooperative (NNFC), 306, 317, 319, 322–23

Ob region, 91n.1, 136, 391–98
Ob River, 77, 462
obshchina, 40
obsidian, 295–300
Ob-Ugrian society, 140, 391–98
Oceania, near, 288; remote, 288
ocean crossings, 289, 296
Odendaal Commission, 312
Okongo, 307
Omaheke, 308
Omatako, 307
Ondangwa, 365
opponents; in Northwest Coast warfare, 171–79
Orang Asli, 5, 433
Organización de la Nacionalidad Huaorani de la Amazonia

Ecuatoriana (the Organization of the Huaorani Nationality of the Ecuadorian Amazon) (ONHAE), 245–50
Oriente, 21, 246–47
"original affluent society," 37, 450
Oroches, 329, 330, 338
Oroks, 328, 329, 330
Oshikati, 308
Ostiaks, 126
Oswalt, W., 33
Otjozondjupa, 7, 306, 321
outstation, 199, 317
Owambo, 362

Pam Islands, 298–99
Pamwak, 294, 297, 298–99
Panakiwuk, 294–95, 298, 300
Papua New Guinea, 17
para juru (day-based labor), 268
Paraguay, 5, 12, 275–76
parenting, 62, 385. *See also* autonomy
"past," 457
pastoralism, 33, 45, 77, 83, 90
pastoralists, 353, 367
Patkanov, S. K., 79, 328
patriarch, 79
"patrilocal band hypothesis," 33
peace, 85, 128, 446; oaths, 145
peacemaking, 3, 399–409; on Northwest Coast, 172–73
Pelikh, G. I., 79, 466
People's Land Conference, 316
perestroika, 42, 47n.9, 233
pervobytnoe obshchestvo, 36, 38, 47n.7
PetroCanada, 251
PetroEcuador, 248, 258n.7, 8
Philippines, 94–109, 399–409
"Piebald Horde," 126, 135
Pleistocene, 287, 288; climate, 288; fauna, 288
police, 64, 66, 69
political anthropology, 44

politics, 197–204, 351, 356, 380, 422–23
polygyny, 355
Popov, A. A., 46n.4, 228
Poverty Datum Line (PDL), 8
power (*echint'e*), covert, 44, 45, 68–70, 345. *See also* aggression
"present," 457
princes, 135
Private Voluntary Organization (PVO), 380–84
Proclamation 208 of South West Africa, 313
production; forces of, 29, 38; modes of, 36, 37
Protection Law for Former Natives, 1899, 207–11, 212–14, 219
Pugachev, N., 153

Quinchuas, 250, 258n.3, 259n.12

radio; local, 117–22, 123n.11–14, 123–24n.16, 124n.17; compared with song duels, 120–22, 123–24n.16,
raiding, 79, 80, 95, 103, 131, 137–38; for slaves on Northwest Coast, 164–79
reciprocity, 224, 234, 238
reindeer herders, 33, 45, 130, 146
reindeer herding, 126, 136, 146, 185, 327, 392, 395; Evenkis (Tungus), 225–26, 229–30, 235–36, 240n.16; religion, 460–74
residue analysis, 292, 298
resources, 108, 388
retaliation, fear of, 56, 57
revenge, 78, 126, 128, 403; blood, 130, 150, 159; as motive, 169
revolts, 212
Ridington, R., 60, 69
ritual, 32, 42, 142, 144, 150–63, 171, 348, 388, 396–97, 407n.4, 438, 458
rock art, 413–26; analysis, 416

rod, 37
Rosaldo, M., 403
Rosaldo, R., 402, 403
Rousseau, J-.J., 125
Rushforth, S., 60
Russia, 22–24, 42, 43, 328
Russian administration, 155–56
Russian-language, 337; competence, 32; data, 32
Russians, 126, 224
Rwanda, 13

Saamis, 329, 330, 338
sacred places, 198, 397
sacrifice, 152
Saint, R., 256, 259n.15
Samoyeds, 91n.1, 125–49, 460–74; "stony," 126
San, 5, 7, 11, 13, 15, 16, 18, 19, 306, 382, 413–26
sang (shaman's power), 469–70
Santa Cruz, 288
Saunders, C., 414
Schweitzer, P., 223–24
Scollon, R., and S. B. K. Scollon, 60
Scott, C., 225, 234
scouts, 131
sea mammal hunters, 33; sedentary, 45
sea mammal hunting, 185
sedentarization, 244, 263, 353, 380, 382–83, 447–48
Sel'kups, 24–25, 78–81, 91n.1, 126, 135–40, 329, 330, 338, 455, 460–74
Semushkin, T., 153
senilicide, 152
senior "law" experts, 200–203
Service, E., 33
shamans, 126, 140, 152–53, 159–60, 165, 225, 396, 418–22, 424n.1, 462, 464; shamanistic narratives, 401; shamanistic attacks, 137, 146, 167; Evenkis (Tungus), 225; trance dances, 418–22

sharing, 217, 245, 252–53, 257, 371, 393, 434, 444–45, 448

shell artifacts, 299

Shnirel'man, V. A. (also Shnirelman, V. A.), 40, 43

Shternberg, L. Ia., 47n.13

Shuar, 250, 259n.12

Siberia 5, 6, 7, 10, 22, 186, 189; eastern, 78; northeastern, 31, 150–63; western, 77

Siberian; peoples, 29–51, 45; Yupiks, 189, 329, 330, 338

slavery, 165, 170, 366

Slobodin, R., 55, 175

"Small Peoples of the North" (former USSR), 5, 12, 22

sobriety, 62–63, 68

social; control 57, 355; evolution, 35; planning, 42; relations, 32n.2; status, 126; stratification, 347

socialism, 38

society, 450

sociopolitical processes, 41

Solomon Islands, 287–88, 290, 292, 293, 294, 297, 300

Somalia, 6

song duels, 111, 112, 120–22, 122n.4, 123–4n.16; compared with radio, 120–22, 123–24n.16

songs, 438; epic, 400–409, 407n.2; female ritual, 400–09

soul, 446, 460–74; breath, 461–63; shadow, 461, 471; life 431–33, 461

South Africa, 413–26

South African Defense Force (SADF), 314

South West African Administration, 311, 324

South West African Peoples Organization (SWAPO), 306, 314, 361, 363

Southeast Asia, 39, 288

Soviet Union, 32, 41, 43, 46n.5, 125, 328

Speranskii, M. N., 190

spirit, 156, 159, 422, 445

spirituality, 193, 271

status, 345, 351

Stebnitskii, S. N., 154

Steward, J., 31

stone artifacts. *See* lithics

strategies, 80; offensive, 142

stress, 94, 106, 447, 449

subsistence, 77, 189, 394; mode of, 36

suicide, 162n.5, 334

Summer Institute of Linguistics (SIL), 244–45, 256, 258n.2

Supreme Soviet of the Russian Federation, 183

"survivals," 47n.10

Swaziland, 322

syncretism, 216, 219–20

tactics, 80, 89, 126, 128, 136, 173; raiding, 131; survival, 135. *See also* warfare

Taimyr (Dolgano-Nenets) Autonomous District, Russian Federation, 10, 224, 227, 228, 239n.5, 239n.6

Tanzania, 5, 7

Tasmania, 38

Taz River, 91, 126, 135

tensions between generations, 18

Third World, 191

Tjum!kui, 313, 322

Tlingit, 164–79

Tofas, 329, 330, 338

trabajo (wage labor), 282–84

trade, 207, 266–67, 298, 392, 448

tradition, 79; oral, 147, 176

traditional, forms of self-government, 185; lifestyle, 188; subsistence lifestyle, 189; subsistence techniques, 184–85; sharing, 185

transformation, 11

Tridacna (clamshell adze), 299

Tsamkxao= Oma, 314

Tsimshian, 164–79

Tsumeb, 366

Tsumkwe, 366

Tunguses, 226, 228, 231, 232, 239n.3. *See also* Evenkis and Evenks
Turuchedo Lake, 132–34
"twin cult," 151
Tym, 79, 462, 463

Udeges, 329, 330
Ugrians, 125–49
Ulchis, 329, 330
Union for Ainu Liberation (UAL), 212
Union of Soviet Socialist Republics (USSR), 2, 16, 22, 23
United Nations, 9, 413
United Nations Conference on Environment and Development (UNCED), 9
United Nations Transition Assistance Group (UNTAG), 314
U.S. Agency for International Development (USAID), 317
United States of America, 17, 18
Utari, 212

Vanuatu, 287
Vayda, A., 165, 175
Vietnam, 12
violence, 13, 20, 94–109, 164, 306 ; against women, 150, 161; ritual, 22, 150–63
"voluntary death," 152–58
volunteers, 381

war; leader, 128; morale, 143; rituals, 126; rules, 133; "spirit of," 147; tactics, 128

warfare, 78–93, 107, 125–49; "prestate," 125; Northwest Coast, 164–79
warriors, 78–80, 128, 406, 408n.5
Watson, G. and J.-G. A. Goulet, 60, 69
weapons, 7, 78–93, 102, 106; long distance, 83–84, 167–68
welfare, 12; dependency, 352
Widlok, T., 10, 12
widowers, 336
widowhood, 336, 337, 348, 354
widows, 336, 344
witchcraft, 167; Chukchi, 156, 159–60
Working Group of Indigenous Minorities in Southern Africa (WIMSA), 321
World War I, 314
World War II, 31, 103, 208, 393, 401
world-view, 32, 42, 430–33, 446, 455–59, 460
Wrangell, F. (Vrangel', F.), 150, 152, 154

Yakuts (Sakhas), 228–29, 240n.10
Yasuni National Park, 246, 249
Yen, D., 297
Yenisei River, 77, 126, 132, 147, 228
Yomban, 290, 296, 301
Yombom, 290, 296
Yukagirs, 31, 33, 329, 330, 338

Zaire, 263–74, 269–70, 272, 273n.1
Zelenin, D. K., 153, 158